EDUCATIONAL FACILITIES PLANNING

EDUCATIONAL FACILITIES PLANNING

Leadership, Architecture, and Management

C. KENNETH TANNER

University of Georgia

JEFFERY A. LACKNEY

University of Wisconsin, Madison

PEARSON

Boston ■ New York ■ San Francisco
Mexico City ■ Montreal ■ Toronto ■ London ■ Madrid ■ Munich ■ Paris
Hong Kong ■ Singapore ■ Tokyo ■ Cape Town ■ Sydney

Senior Editor: *Arnis K. Burvikovs*
Series Editorial Assistant: *Kelly Hopkins*
Marketing Manager: *Tara Kelly*
Editorial Production Service: *Nesbitt Graphics, Inc.*
Composition Buyer: *Linda Cox*
Manufacturing Buyer: *Andrew Turso*
Electronic Composition: *Nesbitt Graphics, Inc.*
Cover Administrator: *Joel Gendron*

Between the time website information is gathered and then published, it is not unusual for some sites to have closed. Also, the transcription of URLs can result in typographical errors. The publisher would appreciate notification where these errors occur so that they may be corrected in subsequent editions.

Library of Congress Cataloging-in-Publication Data

Tanner, C. Kenneth.
  Educational facilities planning : leadership, architecture, and management / C. Kenneth Tanner, Jeffrey A. Lackney.
    p. cm.
  Includes bibliographical references and index.
  ISBN 0-205-34246-9 (casebound)
    1. School facilities—United States—Planning. I. Lackney, Jeffrey A. II. Title.

LB3218.A1T36 2006
371.6'21—dc22

                                                              2005051313

Printed in the United States of America

10 9 8 7 6 5 4 3 2 1   10 09 08 07 06 05

CONTENTS

CHAPTER ELEVEN

Financing School Infrastructure Projects   250

Catherine C. Sielke

PART VII   RESEARCH ON THE PHYSICAL ENVIRONMENT   263

CHAPTER TWELVE

The Physical Environment and Student Achievement in Elementary Schools   266

CHAPTER THIRTEEN

Classifications of Middle School Design: Toward a Pattern Language 307

C. Kenneth Tanner and Scott A. Andersen

CHAPTER FOURTEEN

Research Priorities: How Facilities Affect Educational Outcomes   323

Sheila J. Bosch

What visions of educational learning environments might be created if we could magically diminish the gaps of misunderstanding among perspectives on the school environment held by architects, planners, teachers, school administrators, the community, parents, and students? What if all these groups better understood the complexities involved in planning and designing educational facilities? With these questions serving as a guide, this book was developed to improve the knowledge base, skills levels, and communications practices among the various groups involved in planning, designing, constructing, using, and managing educational facilities. One of the objectives of this book is to introduce concepts that encourage people who plan and design physical learning environments to become more responsive to students' needs and community cultures. Another objective is to provide a reference work for educational leaders and architects. Finally, this book is developed as a textbook for students of educational leadership, school architecture, and educational planning.

We have organized the book's contents to include conceptual, descriptive, and applied aspects of developing educational facilities. Conceptualization includes school architecture, planning, programming, and design, while the descriptive segments contain information on capital outlay activities, school construction management, maintenance, and operations of school buildings. Legal and financial issues in developing educational facilities are described. One applications segment includes an example of planning a capital project and research on the places where students learn. Finally, the applications "tool kit" includes a detailed procedure for forecasting student populations, with accompanying Web content containing student population forecasting programs, and an extensive exercise in strategic planning for school facilities. The research chapters incorporate statistical analysis relating design principles and characteristics to student outcomes, a case study on environmental quality in schools, and a Delphi study identifying plausible relationships among physical factors and measures of student, school, and school district success.

This work is offered as a guided step toward planning for improved educational learning environments around the world. Rich historical perspectives of school architecture and educational planning in the United States are provided from the perspectives of an architect and a planner. The rich heritage of school architecture and educational planning is explored in detail, with specific examples of architecture matched with its era, along with the names of planners and architects and examples of their work. The book emphasizes how evolving information technologies can be deployed to support more innovative school design. Not only are there how-to examples and step-by-step procedures, every chapter invites the reader to think both "inside and outside the box." Practitioners and students are given a set of learning activities in each chapter to sharpen their perspectives on educational leadership, planning, programming, design, and architecture.

Educational leaders are invited to integrate the steps on planning a capital project with their own experiences. Architects are challenged to lead clients to researched-based school designs, to avoid complete replication of existing schools, and to create innovative designs for learning. School leaders and architects are encouraged to authentically involve students, educators, and the community in planning, programming, and designing the school facility. Increased knowledge about creating innovative educational learning environments will lay the foundation for improved communications and ensure developmentally appropriate twenty-first-century learning environments.

C. Kenneth Tanner
Jeffery A. Lackney

PART I

EDUCATIONAL ARCHITECTURE
History and Principles of Design

This section presents a history of educational architecture that follows three general periods of American social, economic, and political history: the agrarian colonial period, the Industrial Revolution, and the so-called information age. A detailed exposé of the various trends in educational architecture that continue to influence the design of learning environments is presented. Thirty-one design principles are categorized according to site and building organization, principles for primary educational space, principles for shared school and community facilities, community spaces, principles related to the character of all spaces, and principles related to site design and outdoor learning spaces. The purpose of this section is to set the stage for linking educational planning to school architecture. There appears to be a widening gap between sound educational programs, the concept design phase of school facilities planning, and the resulting architecture. Far too often, function follows form in schools that are being constructed today. This entire work is aimed at reversing this trend to allow form to follow function.

CHAPTER ONE

HISTORY OF EDUCATIONAL ARCHITECTURE

The history of the American schoolhouse reflects the history of education that, in turn, mirrors a plethora of contextual societal forces including social, economic, and political. Architectural form, aesthetics, and the symbolism and layout of the school building should be directly influenced by the evolution of educational philosophy and goals, curricular objectives, instructional methods, and the cultural background and value systems of the schools' governing boards. The architecture of the small one-room country school building was an appropriate design response that served the basic educational and social needs of small rural communities for well over two hundred years starting in the colonial period of the United States. As the social problems associated with the Industrial Revolution grew in the mid and late nineteenth century, the need for educating larger groups of immigrants in urban centers became a necessity. The common school movement and large multi-storied classroom buildings provided the necessary educational and architectural response at that time. After World War II, societal changes created by the baby boom created a need for school construction never before seen. The rate of building demanded new methods of school building construction that allowed for further experimentation in flexible and adaptable space for education. Along with innovations in educational delivery suggested by the progressive movement led principally by John Dewey, school architecture soon responded with more child-scaled, flexible, and open environmental settings.

Studying the relationship between architecture and education over time provides an instructive lesson in the theory of change in social institutions. The general acceptance of various innovations and paradigms in educational design usually occurs many years following a specific innovation, and not without some social and political resistance. Many colonialists did not see the need for a separate schoolhouse when they could teach their own children at home, since the objective was to learn how to read the Bible or be apprenticed in the family trade. The progressive movement in education beginning in the late nineteenth century did not significantly influence education or school architecture until the middle of the twentieth century. A relevant comparison in the receptiveness of new ideas may be seen in the acceptance level of distance education and computer-assisted instruction. Today, the social resistance to distance education and asynchronous Web-based learning will more than likely subside once children who have been raised using the computer as a form of communication take over the leadership of the educational system.

This chapter presents a history of educational architecture that follows three general periods of American social, economic, and political history: the agrarian colonial period (1650–1849), the Industrial Revolution (1850–1949), and the so-called information age (1950–present). The focus is on general trends in education as they relate to educational architecture. Similarly, looking at the architectural design of schools over time can provide us with an opportunity to infer what may have actually happened in the classroom and reveal the essence of the pedagogy that influenced educational practice in the past (McClintock & McClintock, 1970).

EDUCATIONAL ARCHITECTURE IN THE COLONIAL PERIOD

Societal Influences on Education in the Colonial Period

Early American society consisted of village settlements where land was cultivated for agricultural purposes. Land was also the primary basis for the economy, life, culture, family structure, and politics. In the United States, until 1750, the first settlers out of necessity adopted an agrarian, egalitarian agricultural culture idealized through the concept of Jeffersonian democracy. Settlers quickly pushed westward, building subsistence farms and agricultural villages and dispossessing the indigenous populations further into the interior of the continent and eventually to the Pacific Ocean.

The economy was decentralized and locally based. Politically, the village was typically under the control of a single authority or a small group of social elite. Community life was organized around the social support of the village settlement pattern of semi-isolated communities. Houses were typically grouped around a central public meeting space containing public structures such as the church that acted as a meeting hall and sometimes a school.

Agricultural life required the family structure to be multigenerational and extended. Work life and home life were intermingled. Work was performed in fields or the home with the entire household toiling together as an economic unit. The imperative of group survival required an individual's personal needs to come second to those of the group. People rarely left the confines of their own village. When they did, they were limited to walking or traveling by horse and wagon, or sometimes by boat.

Illiteracy was high, with the spoken word relied on for day-to-day communication, and oral traditions kept the collective memory of the community alive. Even as the written word was available at this time, many people relied on others to read aloud the material that might benefit the whole community.

Education during this period could be characterized by two words—"survival" and "informal." The most informal process occurred in farm families where children needed to contribute labor in order for the family to survive. The necessary skills and knowledge were learned from parents and older siblings as the child participated in the work of the family. Before the Industrial Revolution, there were very few Americans who viewed schooling as relevant to occupational success or economic development (DeYoung, 1989). Through apprenticeships, craftsmen and tradesmen would pass on their skills and knowledge of their trade to the next generation. While the young person's learning occurred in an informal setting, there was a formal structure through which the young person progressed from novice to apprentice to skilled craftsman.

When English settlers arrived in New England, they took little time to establish Latin grammar schools and colleges (Herbst, 1996). The most formal structure involved the academy and university. Harvard College was established in 1636, while William and Mary followed in 1688. These opportunities were reserved for the elite and, to some degree, perpetuated the survival of the elite in the classicist society. State-mandated public education did not exist prior to the nineteenth century, but rather was run by parents and trustees (DeYoung, 1989).

The need for literacy in the village focused almost entirely on exposure of Christian morality and the teaching of the Bible. This was evidenced by the passage of the Old Deluder Satan Act of

1635, a Massachusetts law, the first educational legislation in the United States, requiring parents to teach their children how to read the Bible. The Sunday school movement in the early nineteenth century was one of several precursors to the common school movement (DeYoung, 1989).

In the New England colonies, the first schools were set up in either private homes or churches (Graves, 1993). Home schooling and informal education was very common in colonial America. One form of informal school was the originally English institution known as the "dame school" (Johnson, 1963). Unmarried or widowed older women often held classes in their own homes, while wealthy parents hired tutors to come into the home to instruct their sons in the classics. As the population increased in the colonies, subscription schools evolved, with support for these schools coming from subscriptions, tuition, land rental fees, and taxes (Gulliford, 1984). In 1647, the government of Massachusetts Bay enacted the first statue in America providing for the establishment of a school system requiring the construction of school buildings (Gulliford, 1984).

The One-Room Country Schoolhouse

The one-room schoolhouse best characterizes the typical educational facility of the colonial period (Figure 1.1). This school was multiaged by necessity due to the relatively small size of the village community. One teacher would preside over instruction, emphasizing recitation, and direct supervision. Learning was by rote but self-paced depending on the developmental level of the student. One-room schools often had very simple furnishings, poor ventilation, and relied on oil lamps for light and wood-burning stoves for heat. Schoolhouses in urban areas were variations on the theme of the country schoolhouse often containing two, four, or six self-contained rooms, frequently with their own entrances.

Along with the church, the school was the social center of the community where town meetings,

FIGURE 1.1   Bear Creek School (c. 1870), Iowa (Iowa State Historical Society).

Source: Courtesy and permission of Andrew Guildford (1984), *America's Country Schools*, National Trust for Historic Preservation.

voting, fund-raisers, and celebrations of all kinds took place. In essence, the entire community, not only school-age children, was served by the school building. The school housed the activities that integrated people into their community and provided an identity that to this day is linked with the school (Gulliford, 1984). For example, in 1991, a New Hampshire school superintendent proposing to close a one-room schoolhouse dating back to 1840s was criticized by parents who opposed children being moved to a more "impersonal school setting" (Graves, 1993; 22).

At the beginning of the twentieth century, the process of school consolidation, itself a response to urbanization and population growth, created much resistance in rural communities where the symbol of the one-room schoolhouse was the focus of rural life and of community spirit. As late as 1913, one-half of the schoolchildren in the United States were enrolled in the country's 212,000 one-room schools (Gulliford, 1984). Although only 729 of these one-teacher, one-room schools existed near the end of the twentieth century, less than one-half of 1 percent of all public school buildings in operation. The country school continues to be a powerful cultural symbol for Americans (Gulliford, 1996).

Lancasterian Schools

Not all nineteenth-century school buildings were one-room schoolhouses in rural settings; there were many schools planned for growing cities that responded to completely different societal forces and educational philosophies (Brubaker, 1998). Many of these early urban school buildings evolved from the paradigm of the one-room schoolhouse to accommodate much larger groupings of students.

One short-lived school was the Lancasterian monitorial system developed by Joseph Lancaster, an English educator in the early 1800s. Lancaster's objective was to lower the cost of educating poor children who were forced into labor under harsh conditions in England. His method consisted of employing older, more advanced students as assistants to allow one educator to teach several hundred students simultaneously in a large hall. Monitors were used to control the crowd of students assembled, thus creating the term "monitorial schools." In 1806, the Free School Society of New York City brought the Lancasterian method to the United States, with the first school established in Baltimore. Although the school was a failure economically, Lancaster's monitorial system emphasizing group instruction over costly, time-consuming individualized instruction was successful in convincing some people that the cost of universal education did not have to be prohibitive. This system encouraged the development of free, public, tax-supported schools (Graves, 1993).

EDUCATIONAL ARCHITECTURE OF THE INDUSTRIAL REVOLUTION

Societal Influences on Education during the Industrial Revolution

The Civil War marked the end of the dominance of agricultural society and the beginning of industrial society. On the heels of the farmer were the industrialists, the agents of the Industrial Revolu-tion who brought with them railroads, factories, and cities. By 1850, industry in the northeastern United States was producing firearms, watches, farm implements, textiles, and sewing machines, while the rest of the country was still living a rural agricultural life.

Although present-day descriptions of the industrial society personify oppression, dreariness, and psychological repression, at the time this period was seen as a fantastic extension of human hope. Many believed that poverty, hunger, disease, and tyranny might be overthrown and replaced by peace, harmony, equality, and opportunity.

Integration of the market economy, the technology of mechanization, and the rise of the corporation, the legal entity sometimes referred to as the "immortal being," were the drivers that fueled the Industrial Revolution. Production shifted from the farm to the factory and accelerated. Higher levels of interdependency required collective efforts, highly specialized division of labor, coordination, and the integration of many different skills, from the unskilled to an industrial caste system of technicians, secretaries, and clerks. Correspondingly, in the public sector, an abrupt shift occurred from autocracies and monarchies to highly centralized, hierarchical bureaucracies based outwardly on representative democracy but influenced by powerfully organized special interest groups.

Populations shifted from rural to urban, from village to city. Urban life provided a forum for balancing private interests against public good, was a powerful school for social learning, and created a common ground for meeting strangers while at the same time engendering alienation, anonymity, and a lack of consensus on values experienced in the village. The smaller family structures began to replace the extended family based on economic and social pressures. Procreation needs decreased as a result of raised health standards and the lack of need for extra farm hands. Work was now taking place in other settings, creating a work/home split. The rise of social institutions to standardize and centralize the care of the population segregated the entire society: the young in schools, the elderly in nursing homes, the sick in hospitals, social deviants in prisons, and workers in offices and factories.

The Common School

Factories created to produce things led to factories to produce learning. Rapid urbanization and economic development in the mid-nineteenth century created numerous social problems for urban leaders. The chief problem for industrialists was that of instilling in children of all social classes the values and character traits, such as working hard and obeying authority, necessary for employment in industrial settings (DeYoung, 1989).

The common school movement took hold in America's cities between 1840 and 1880. Educational reformers argued that rural community education was not sufficient in America's industrial and urban areas where poor rural and immigrant children were grouped together. Horace Mann, Henry Barnard, and other educational reformers argued that public schooling would be essential for the economic possibilities of both the individual and the nation. No longer would apprenticeship systems or family members provide the education necessary for success (DeYoung, 1989).

The common school movement gave rise to the public education system as a result of popularizing the principle of free schooling supported by the local property tax (Herbst, 1996). This school was a highly formalized, hierarchical structure designed to sort students who were eligible for promotion to a higher level in the system from those who were not. Agrarian immigration from Ireland and Southern Europe created a demand for Catholic schools and the formation of a private Catholic school system as an alternative to the Protestant public school system.

An overt curriculum of reading, writing, arithmetic, and history was overlaid on a covert curriculum of punctuality, obedience, rote, and repetitive work. As the formal compulsory education system grew, younger children were required to attend and for longer lengths of time. The goal of

the educational system was an overt attempt to prepare students for the workplace.

Standardization in educational programs closely followed the principles of the industrial society. Based on work done in France for the purpose of military use, psychological testing (IQ tests) was adapted for use in school placement during this period. A new universal purpose of education was formulated that focused on the enhancement of the individual. Carnegie units were developed as a way to count credits and to give access to college entrance to more people.

Many of the early urban school buildings simply replicated the one-room schoolhouse model in what is commonly referred to as the factory model school building: a double-loaded corridor of self-contained classrooms leading to a centralized administrative center. The factory model school layout was a direct response to the needs of the common school educational system that required repetition and uniformity.

It is customary to class Henry Barnard (the first U.S. Commissioner of Education), along with Horace Mann, as one of the great practical reformers of antebellum public schooling. Barnard's influence in advancing the cause of the common school in Connecticut and Rhode Island from 1838–1854 was almost as great as that of Mann in Massachusetts from 1837–1848 (McClintock & McClintock, 1970). With the publication of his book entitled, *School Architecture, or Contributions to the Improvement of School-Houses in the United States* in 1838, Barnard is credited with raising the standards of school buildings serving the common school movement. Barnard noted the inferior quality of school environments attended by the poor while simultaneously providing models of what constituted good educational architecture. The book became a manual on the art of building schools, offering suggestions for ventilation and heating systems, furniture, floors, schoolyards, and Greek revival facade designs. Barnard is credited with defining the character of school architecture in the United States by integrating the concerns of architecture with pedagogy. He emphasized school "architecture" over school "building" by suggesting that the architect is ultimately concerned with the cultural, spiritual, and humane value of his work, while the builder is primarily concerned with its physical structure, reasonable cost, and the service of function (McClintock & McClintock, 1970).

Starting in the mid-nineteenth century, urban schools could be found on tight sites of less than a quarter acre with no landscaping. Students were segregated by age into a graded organization. One hundred students might be housed in a single classroom. The classroom, other than corridor spaces, was often the only type of space in the school. Multiple levels consisted of stacking one-room schoolhouses on top of each other. Most schools were constructed of masonry and wood frames with brick walls and pitched roofs and towers. The average class size may have been fifty or more students, with desks often bolted to floors in row and column arrangements.

Toward the end of the nineteenth century, school buildings began to be designed and constructed with other functional considerations. Golda Meir School in Milwaukee, designed in the Romanesque Revival style by architect H.C. Koch & Company, provides a classic example of these school designs (Figure 1.2). Hallways were widened to accommodate increased traffic flows, auditoriums were built to support whole-school events, administrative offices were included, and cloakrooms were added to classroom layouts. Expanded offerings in art and science begin to dictate the development of specialty classrooms. These characteristics of the schoolhouse remained the most common into the first half of the twentieth century.

Boston's Quincy Grammar School is a good example of the early factory model design principles. Built in 1848, Quincy Grammar School was the first graded public school in the United States (Graves, 1993). The design response consisted of a four-story building with a basement and an attic. Designed to house 660 students, the first three floors had a series of four classrooms opening onto

FIGURE 1.2   The Golda Meir School (c. 1889).
Source: Milwaukee Public School System.

a common corridor. Each classroom housed 55 students in rooms measuring 31 × 26 feet. Each classroom had an attached closet. Individual desks, at the time an innovation in school design, were bolted to the floor, seven rows of them, eight to a row. The top floor was a large assembly hall with benches to seat the entire student body, while the administrative office was located on the first floor (Graves, 1993). This general school design was replicated in dozens of cities across the United States from the late nineteenth through early twentieth century.

Immigration, Urbanization, and Urban Schools of the 1920s

At the turn of the twentieth century, an unprecedented number of immigrants from Europe arrived on the shores of the United States. The case of New York City provides a good example of the effect immigration had on educational architecture.

During the 1920s, over 200 public schools were constructed in New York City, many of them built with modified repetition of similar plan types and architectural styles both to reduce costs and shorten design and construction schedules. This large-scale school building program with its standardized building plans paralleled efforts to further standardize the school curriculum and continuing efforts to "Americanize" the diverse student population (Rieselbach, 1992).

During the first quarter of the twentieth century, sites were set aside for school facilities as student populations increased in size and crowding emerged as a problem. Buildings designed to specialize in the housing of junior high school and high school educational programs were constructed, and many more types of auxiliary spaces were added. Auditoriums, laboratories, art studios, gymnasiums for physical education, and home arts spaces were routinely added to the educational building program.

The growth of high schools in the United States was helped by the Kalamazoo Decision of 1874, in which the Supreme Court of the United States ruled that free schools maintained by locally imposed taxes were legal. The high school had become an extension of the elementary school. The Boston Massachusetts English Classical School, later named the English High School, was the first public high school in the United States, opened in 1821 (Ringers & Decker, 1995). By 1851, eighty cities had public schools, at the time known as "people's colleges" (Herbst, 1996). The number of high schools in the United States went from 300 in the 1860s, before the decision, to over 6,000 by 1900 (Graves, 1993).

In the 1890s, the National Council of Education of the National Education Association commissioned the Committee of Ten to define the nature and purpose of American secondary education (Herbst, 1996). The committee argued that the academic program that had its roots in Europe served well for preparation in college as well as in life. Its report did not address the growing demand for nonacademic, manual, or vocational education and instead believed that secondary institutions could extend the common school as well as provide for college admission.

Advocates of vocational education quickly challenged the Committee of Ten recommendations, and with it the course of American second-

ary education in the United States. By the end of the 1920s, vocational education with its training for particular trades and apprenticeships and subsequent on-the-job training took the place of the old manual training. In large cities, vocationalists introduced public technical and industrial high schools and established new forms of schoolwork relationships through cooperation with industry such as textiles and machine trades as early as the 1880s (Herbst, 1996). By the turn of the twentieth century, secondary education had become part of common schooling, with Americans holding the belief that all youth should benefit from high school attendance and giving rise to the development of the comprehensive high school (Herbst, 1996).

From the experience of grouping younger adolescents with older adolescents in high school, yet another school organization was invented in the early part of the twentieth century—the junior high school. Its purposes were to ease the transition from elementary school settings to the departmentalized high school settings, and solve the problem of general overcrowding in both elementary and high schools (Rieselbach, 1992).

THE PROGRESSIVE MOVEMENT

During the late nineteenth century, a progressive movement emerged in Europe as well as the United States as a general critique of the public educational system. One of the main principles of the progressive movement was the notion of child-centered education. The beginnings of the progressive movement can be traced to a number of scholars and educators, from Friedrich Froebel in Germany, Maria Montessori in Italy, and John Dewey in the United States. The roots of progressive education can be traced back to the early-nineteenth-century work of Johann Heinrich Pestalozzi who was one of the founders of modern pedagogy. He developed educational concepts such as teacher training and curriculum innovations such as group work, field trips, grade levels, and ability grouping allowing for individual differences. Influenced by the ideas of Rousseau, Pestalozzi contended that the traditional means of teaching moral character through discipline and learning by rote produced tyrants and slaves. As an alternative, he proposed a method of teaching that involved exposing a child to appropriate stimuli that would generate positive life experiences.

Common to these educators was the argument that that the needs of the state, the church, or the economy should not take precedence in shaping child development (Saint, 1987). Friedrich Froebel was a German educator who developed the kindergarten and espoused free play, creative self-activity, and motor expression. Froebel was one of the first to recognize the value of social participation as a valid teaching method. His contribution to the Progressive movement was making his generation aware that children's play is essential to their growth (Tanner, 1997).

John Dewey's experimental school, called the Laboratory School at the University of Chicago, operated from 1896–1904. The school opened in January 1896 as a small school of 16 students ranging in age from 6 to 9 years, with 1 teacher and an assistant. The school grew to 140 students with 23 staff members and 10 assistants by 1904 (Tanner, 1997).

The Laboratory School was based on the theory that the school is a small cooperative society in which children gain social experience and insight as well as intellectual and manual skills. The school was, as suggested by its name, experimental in that Dewey saw his school as a laboratory for testing and verifying new educational theories and principles. The objective of the Laboratory School was not simply to perpetuate the traditional curriculum by making it developmentally appropriate. The objective was rather to create a new curriculum in which developmental, intellectual, and social goals were integrated. The practices of Dewey and his teachers are still being attempted today in areas such as relating the curriculum to children's experiences, integrating the curriculum, teaching critical thinking and problem-solving skills, stimulating creative thinking, supporting cooperative learning, providing hands-on activities, and supporting collaborative decision making by the teaching staff. Dewey developed the idea of the schoolhouse as a true home in which the activities of social and community life were expressed in the curriculum. The child's interest in the home was used as a vehicle for social activities and learning at school (Tanner, 1997).

The physical setting of the Laboratory School was a means through which the developmental curriculum was supported. For instance, children would work in their garden in the school yard, apply principles learned in their classes as they cooperated in building and furnishing a clubhouse (Figure 1.3), make articles in a shop for use in connection with their other work, eat a gourmet lunch they planned and prepared in their French class (Figure 1.4, page 10), study industrial history by working out the entire process of making cloth, study the nature of community life with the help of model houses brought into the classroom (Figure 1.5, page 10), and use technologies of early peoples to turn grain into food. All these activities took place in more or less traditional classrooms, but the arrangement of the classroom was completely revised depending on the type of activity they were engaged in (Tanner, 1997; 91–94).

FIGURE 1.3 Children apply principles learned in their classes as they cooperate in building and furnishing a clubhouse.

Source: Used with permission, L. N. Tanner (1997), *Dewey's Laboratory School*, Teachers College Press, p. 91.

FIGURE 1.4 Students eat a gourmet lunch they planned and prepared in their French class.

Source: Used with permission, L. N. Tanner (1997), *Dewey's Laboratory School,* Teachers College Press, p. 92.

The work of progressive educational reformers such as Francis Parker and John Dewey had a strong impact on schools in New York City. Parker's methods were tested first in Massachusetts and later at the practice school of Cook County Normal School in Chicago, where daily morning assemblies and informal classrooms reinforced the idea that each member of the school community

FIGURE 1.5 Students study the nature of community life with the help of model houses.

Source: Used with permission, L. N. Tanner (1997), *Dewey's Laboratory School,* Teachers College Press, p. 94.

was a participant in shaping his or her own education. In some cases, children participated in the development of their curriculum by using readers made up of their own stories (Rieselbach, 1992).

Schools linked to the progressive movement beyond the experimental schools of Dewey and Parker included the experiments in public schools in New York. The Lincoln School of Teacher's College, founded in 1917, was one of the first schools created specifically to explore the possibilities of progressive education. The Dalton School, opened in 1919 and founded by Helen Parkhurst, synthesized her teaching experience and study with Maria Montessori by creating a new teaching system she called the "laboratory plan" whereby students worked independently on long-term assignments with teachers' guidance. The Dalton School building was co-ed through the eighth grade, with the high school limited to girls until the mid-1960s. Originally, the lower floors of the building housed staff offices on three sides of a double-height auditorium. A lunchroom with indoor and outdoor seating occupied the space above the auditorium. The remainder of the building contained laboratory or classroom spaces, as well as art, craft, and music rooms. Secondary stairs connected pairs of floors by age group, creating smaller schools within the school. A glassed-in "open-air" gymnasium occupied the roof of the building (Rieselbach, 1992).

THE BIRTH OF EDUCATIONAL FACILITY PLANNING

It was not until the first quarter of the twentieth century that educators began investigating the possibility that there might be a relationship between learning and the design of instructional spaces within a school building. A few early studies suggested that there was a potential relationship between buildings and learning. Based on these studies, the profession of educational facility planning had its roots just prior to World War II. One of the pioneers in the field was Nicholaus Engelhardt, Sr., a professor at Teachers College, Columbia University, in the 1920s. He did not hesitate to use innovative approaches to solving problems confronting school planners. He developed basic techniques for conducting school facility surveys and he devised methods for making both long- and short-range enrollment projections. After the war, Engelhardt was joined by his son Nicholaus Engelhardt Jr. and Stanton Leggett. During this period, the list of educational planners increased significantly in relation to the increased demand for school buildings following the war.

In 1921, three concerned educators, Samuel Challman of Minnesota, Charles McDermott of New Jersey, and Frank H. Wood of New York, met to discuss the formation of an organization to deal with problems of "school plant" planning. The original intent of the proposed organization was "to promote the establishment of reasonable standards for school buildings and equipment with due regard for economy of expenditure, dignity of design, utility of space, healthful conditions, and safety of human life (NCSC, 1953). In 1922, a larger group met to officially form the National Council of Schoolhouse Construction (its name was later changed to the Council of Educational Facility Planners, International). In 1930, the council began its work by publishing documents that provided information focused on the dissemination of specific minimum standards for the planning and construction of school buildings. Then in 1946, fearing that minimum standards would become maximum practice, the council deemphasized minimum standards and promoted basic principles of sound educational facility planning with the intent of encouraging innovation and creativity in planning.

EDUCATIONAL ARCHITECTURE IN THE INFORMATION AGE

Societal Influences on Education in the Information Age

Many names have been given to the historical period following World War II: information age, postindustrial, postmodern, and third wave. What most social critics agree on is that this period in

American history represents a period of great cultural transformation from the industrial factory model to a new cultural paradigm that is in the process of unfolding as we move forward in the twenty-first century.

The information age requires a global economy with unpredictable, accelerated, differentiated, diverse, and miniaturized markets based on industries such as electronics, molecular biology, space sciences, computer science, and telecommunications. Corporations are more fluid; transnational; team-oriented; downsized and flatter; customer-, quality-, and service-oriented; knowledge-driven; and entrepreneurial. The manufacturing process is based on customization and quality principles. The industrial caste system is breaking down to include employees on a part-time and flextime basis (Toffler, 1980).

Community is getting smaller and larger at the same time. People want to spend more time in their home communities while at the same time be able to travel globally and virtually. Travel and telecommunications have created a desire on the part of many people to accommodate diverse cultures, locally as well as globally—accepting and celebrating diversity. The definition of the family has changed rapidly, with the nuclear family of the mid-twentieth century now a minority outnumbered by nearly a quarter of the population living alone, and dozens of different combinations of adult cohabitation. Family life and work life are reintegrating as more people telecommute.

Educational approaches to accommodate the information age have created much experimentation and controversy. It could be argued that the 1960s witnessed the most dramatic educational reform in America's history in both educational research and the practice of curriculum and instruction. Open education, community education and the community school concept, the middle school concept, and alternative and magnet schools were all explored during this period. A second wave of educational reform in the 1980s focused on restructuring school governance through site-based management, choice and voucher systems, and standardized testing. Toward the end of the 1980s and into the 1990s, new emphasis was placed on methods of curriculum and instruction begun in the 1960s that included the exploration of multiaged and nongraded classrooms, cooperative learning strategies, integrated curriculum, and interdisciplinary instruction. Attempts have been made by schools to recast the school as a "community of learners" where everyone in the community, including adults, parents, and the community as a whole, are learners. Partnerships with surrounding community organizations and other public agencies have become more prevalent, but are still not widespread. Schools are increasingly being seen as places in the community amenable to one-stop shopping for social services, such as before- and after-school day care, adult literacy, parenting academies, and health and employment services.

The Emergence of the Modern School Building

After World War II, the baby boom created the demand for thousands of new school buildings nationwide. The student population increase exceeded 2.3 million children and $40 billion was required for school and university construction from 1958–1968 (Marks, June 2000). Similar to the rapid urbanization that fueled a school construction boom at the turn of the twentieth century, the construction industry looked for less expensive, efficient, and timely methods of construction to meet the new demand for school buildings.

New school buildings were no longer classical or colonial, Georgian or Gothic in architectural style but were truly modern in that they were one-story, flat-roofed structures enclosed in either glass and metal window wall systems or brick and concrete wall systems. In addition, the 1950s schools were for the first time air-conditioned (Brubaker, 1998).

This period was the beginning of a new age of innovation in educational architecture, although many school boards missed the opportunity to create better school facilities as they struggled to cope with ever-increasing enrollments. Many schools

were built too inexpensively, creating poorly insulated roofs and walls and poor-quality building systems (Brubaker, 1998). The design of the school during this period in the United States did not necessarily evolve from the educational program, but often reflected lack of knowledge of the relationships between the physical and learning environments. Like the building boom earlier in the century, the 1950s saw a proliferation of standardized plans and façades that has characterized educational architecture of that period.

The school building that more than any other defined modern educational architecture in the United States was Crow Island School in Winnetka, Illinois, which opened in 1940 (see Figures 1.6 through 1.8 on pages 12–14). It demonstrated a new kind of architecture for education. In terms of architecture, it was in stark contrast to the traditional, multistory, masonry buildings at the turn of the twentieth century. Crow Island instead was an informal one-story brick with an asymmetrically placed clock tower that also served as a chimney that identified the main entrance. As unique and dramatic as the architecture was, it could be argued that the most significant contribution of the Crow Island School was the progressive and innovative educational program that it contained and supported (Brubaker, 1998).

FIGURE 1.6   Crow Island School building entrance emphasized by a large vertical clock tower.
Source: Courtesy of Perkins & Will, Architects.

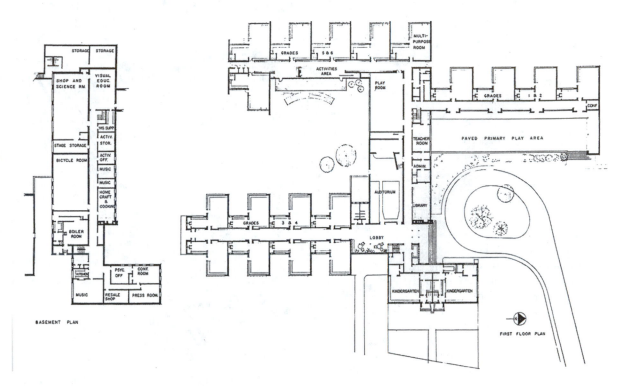

FIGURE 1.7   Crow Island School floor plan illustrating the classroom "finger plan" concept.
Source: Courtesy of Perkins & Will, Architects.

The district had previously established a continuous progress curriculum to ensure mastery of basic skills, along with attention to social development, activity-based and experientially based learning. In fact, it was the explicit objective of the superintendent of schools of Winnetka to create a significant example of modern architecture that was simultaneously supportive of the learning process intended for the school (Meek, 1995).

Designed by Eliel Saarinen and Larry Perkins, the school emphasized child-scaled environments throughout the building, with classrooms designed to support a variety of learning activities and provide a sense of belonging. The classroom was designed in an L-shape that provided for an entrance foyer with storage and an adjacent bathroom, a separate kitchen project area, and a main classroom space with exterior glass wall on two sides of the classroom and a door to a semienclosed outdoor classroom. Crow Island served as a national model for many schools after World War II when the baby boom began and thousands of new schools were needed.

THE EDUCATIONAL FACILITIES LABORATORIES

Responding to the demographic increase following World War II, the American Institute of Architects (AIA) formed a Committee on School Buildings in 1953 that included a number of national organizations, including the U.S. Office of Education. It along with the Teachers College of Columbia University requested funds from the Ford Foundation to conduct school facilities research (Marks, June 2000). Out of this request, the Ford Foundation created a separate nonprofit

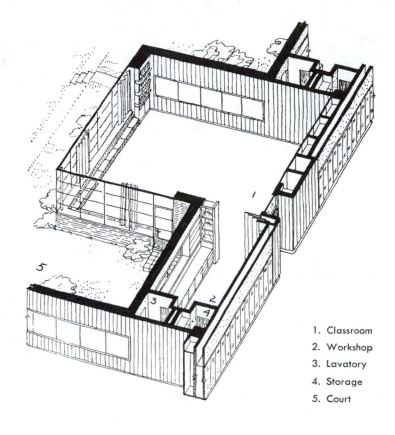

FIGURE 1.8 Crow Island School axonometric drawing illustrating a typical classroom pod that separates wet from dry spaces (2), windows on two sides of the classroom that provide high-quality natural daylight (1), and an exterior door to an outdoor court that serves as an outdoor classroom (5).

Source: Courtesy of Perkins & Will, Architects.

1. Classroom
2. Workshop
3. Lavatory
4. Storage
5. Court

corporation, the Educational Facilities Laboratories (EFL), in 1958 for the purpose of "helping schools and colleges with their physical problems, stimulate research, and disseminate information useful to those who select sites, plan, design, construct, modernize, equip, and finance educational structures and the tools therein" (Marks, June 2000; 1).

EFL working with educators, architects, and suppliers studied and promoted the use of folding wall partitions to create flexible space, investigated and funded examples of system building components to build schools that were of higher quality and less expensive, explored the use of new technologies, and encouraged schools to implement new curriculum and instructional methods (Brubaker, 1998). In addition, EFL supported the introduction of middle schools, joint-use occupancy of buildings, advances in acoustics, air-conditioning, improved school furniture design, energy conservation, conversion of school buildings, developing community schools, and increasing community participation in the planning of new schools (Marks, June 2000).

One program EFL funded was the School Construction Systems Development (SCSD) program (1961–1967) under the direction of Erza Ehrenkrantz to build schools in California. Based on his experience with industrialized building in England, Ehrenkrantz developed a standardized method for the construction of school buildings and established a program for component manufacturers that consisted of a coordinated series of components for structural, heating/ventilating/cooling, lighting, interior partitions, and door and window systems (Marks, June 2000).

The EFL program lasted for 28 years, from 1958–1986, and had an enormous influence on the direction of educational architecture in the later half of the twentieth century. During this time two educational training programs also flourished—the School Planning Laboratory of Stanford University and the School Planning Laboratory of the University of Tennessee. James D. McConnell directed the Stanford program, and the director of the Tennessee program was John Gilliland, followed by Charles Trotter. Each of these programs served as a fertile training ground for students interested in educational facilities planning. The gap left in formal school facilities planning training as a result of the termination of these programs was evidenced in the 1990s as graduates of these programs retired from service. EFL's greatest single contribution, under the leadership of well-known people such as Harold B. Gores and Ben Graves, was to institutionalize progressive thought in school planning, design, and construction in the building industry as well as in the educational community.

OPEN EDUCATION AND OPEN PLAN SCHOOLS

The origins of open education began in the mid-1960s with American educators' interest in the English "infant" (elementary) schools and their use of what the English called "informal education." Informal education, along with what was called the "integrated day," had evolved in England since the 1920s. It was in the small private schools of the 1930s that progressive ideas emerged on the care and teaching of younger children through the use of methods espoused by Froebel and Dewey of group work, or child-sized, movable furniture advocated by the Montessori (Saint, 1987). The movement for nursery education recognized the child as autonomous, as an object for attention and care. The nursery movement believed that buildings must serve the child, and must not inhibit or distract for the sake of some ideal architecture (Saint, 1987). During the war, many children had been evacuated to the countryside to protect them from bombing raids. Schooling continued during

this period, with students of all ages living with their teachers. After the war, the London schools found themselves faced with children of different ages and with different levels of academic achievement due to differences in educational opportunities during the war. The educators developed an organization of teaching students of diverse achievement levels within one classroom. Teachers were convinced that education was strengthened when different aspects of the curriculum were integrated and related to ongoing daily activities (Rothenberg, 1989).

During the 1960s in the United States, challenges to traditional education forced a radical change in educational philosophy. Educational reform movements favored the teaching model adopted from the British informal education model. Open education, it was argued, provided more educational opportunities for children, provided freedom and autonomy for self-directed study, required less guidance by the teacher, and helped foster self-responsibility. As a result, open education and its complementary physical counterpart, the open classroom, were soon espoused (Barth, 1972).

The EFL's most influential innovation was the development of the "open plan" school design, a concept that influenced the design of thousands of schools from the late 1950s through the early 1970s (Marks, 2000). Schools were planned with large, open, flexible spaces adaptable to team teaching and small group and individualized instruction that characterized open education. The Disney School in Chicago (c. 1960) designed by Perkins & Will, Architects provides an example of the types of environments envisioned for open plan schools (see Figures 1.9 through 1.11 on pages 16–17).

Almost immediately, teachers complained of noise and visual distractions in these open plan schools. Hundreds of educational research studies were performed to determine the validity of open plan schools with inconclusive and highly controversial results. Soon permanent wall partitions went up in once open plan school buildings across the country and traditional teaching methods were reasserted.

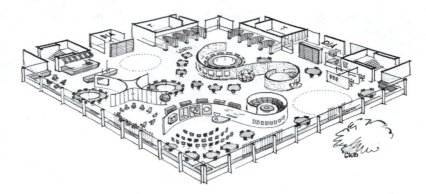

FIGURE 1.9   Disney School, an early idealized open plan concept diagram by C. William Brubaker.
Source: Courtesy of Perkins & Will, Architects.

Many reasons for the failure of the open plan school and open education movement have been asserted. Noise and visual distraction were the most prevalent and transparent. But, there were much deeper reasons for the failure. There was no systematic teacher training in open education that accompanied the change in building concept. Teachers rejected or did not bother to implement the open education program. Even if teachers desired to change the program, there was neither the time nor the space to plan "team lessons" together. The problem of what constituted open education and open classrooms because a stumbling block in the very early days of the movement. The most serious problem has been one of definition for the word "open" and the degree of "openness"

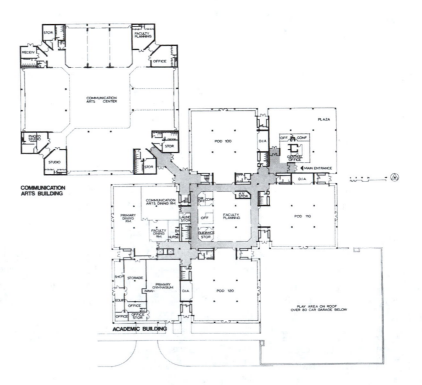

FIGURE 1.10   Disney School floor plan.
Source: Courtesy of Perkins & Will, Architects.

FIGURE 1.11   Disney School, open classroom space.
Source: Courtesy of Perkins & Will, Architects.

(Marshall, 1981). The ambiguity of "openness" was never resolved: Many educators felt that an open education program could be accommodated in traditional self-contained classroom settings, that is, there was no correlation between an open space and open education (Lackney, 1994). Finally, the root of the failure of open classroom design solution may have simply been the lack of proper funding support for open education (Ehrenkrantz, September 1999).

ALTERNATIVE SCHOOLS MOVEMENT

During the 1960s social unrest, various critics of the educational establishment (John Holt, Paul Goodman, Jonathan Kozol, Herbert Kohl, Ivan Illich, George Leonard, and others) raised questions regarding the efficacy of public education and expressed disenchantment with the current system of education. Criticism was especially centered on urban cities where large neighborhood comprehensive schools were not providing adequate education in meeting the needs of minority, disadvantaged, and low-income youths, and were per-

petuating racial segregation. Criticism also focused on the perception that public schools were stifling to creativity and destroying children's natural love of learning and self-expression across the social classes (Campbell et al., 1980).

Out of these criticisms, the alternative schools movement formed; it saw the creation of a variety of alternative school organizations such as freedom schools, storefront schools, black power schools, free schools, and street academies. By 1974, the New Schools Directory Project listed 467 schools in 39 states, most located in urban centers. The teachers and administrators of many alternative schools showed great interest in open education, schools without walls, schools within schools, house plans, mini-schools, work-study programs, and systems of alternative schools working in cooperation (Campbell et al., 1980).

As the social activism of the 1960s slowed, public schools adopted the spirit of the alternative schools movement in encouraging innovation within to provide a diversity of choice for students and to decrease the size of the comprehensive high schools to be more responsive to student needs, both social and intellectual. The rise in magnet high schools in the 1970s, school choice and voucher programs in the 1980s, and charter school, school-to-work business initiatives, and the return of home schooling in the 1990s can be seen as having its roots in the alternative schools movement.

NEIGHBORHOOD SCHOOL MOVEMENT

The concept of the neighborhood school has a long and complex history, having been deeply engrained in the American culture over the past 200 years, from the country school to the community school of the twenty-first century. The most general definition of a neighborhood school is a school that is physically located in the surrounding community and is within walking distance of the households it serves. The advantage of the neighborhood school is that it is accessible to use by all community members before, during, and after hours for a variety of community activities.

The neighborhood school concept has been used as a means of blocking various social reforms from the consolidation movement of the late nineteenth century to the desegregation movement of the middle to late twentieth century (Hennessey, 1976). The issue of racial segregation in American schools in the 1950s set the stage for a series of historical events that for the first time challenged the long-held assumptions of the value of neighborhood schools. Blacks were for the most part segregated in schools that could only be considered as neighborhood schools, yet it was argued these schools did not provide equal educational opportunities afforded in white segregated schools. The 1955 U.S. Supreme Court decision in *Brown vs. the Board of Education* directed lower federal courts to permit local school boards to solve the problems of desegregation. It was not until the early 1970s that court-ordered busing began to create an avenue for providing African Americans with equal opportunities in education. Students in urban school districts were assigned and bused to schools outside their neighborhoods to achieve a racial balance. White families responded by moving to suburban school districts, a phenomenon known as "white flight," as the first arguments for the failure of court-ordered busing emerged (Harris & Fields, 1979).

In the 1980s, federal courts began reversing forced busing laws as urban school districts began to return to neighborhood schools as a means of improving the quality of public education. Neighborhood school plans in most cases have abandoned forced busing as a means of desegregation, relying rather on a combination of neighborhood and community schools, voluntary busing to other alternative, magnet, and specialty schools. Some school districts such as the Milwaukee public schools have gone further by developing plans that form joint-use partnerships with community, business, and faith-based organizations. Urban school districts make the argument that the close proximity of a school to the home and neighborhood of the child

creates strong social ties between school and community that will ultimately support and improve education. Some critics see the return to neighborhood schools and the subsequent elimination of busing as a step back for integration and diversity in public education.

COMMUNITY EDUCATION, COMMUNITY SCHOOLS, AND SCHOOLS IN THE COMMUNITY

Along with the church and the courthouse, the school has been one of the major physical structures that can define a community's identity. Schools have been used for more than educating youth; they serve the broad interests of children, their families, and other members of the community. Since the beginning of schooling in America, they have been used for community meetings, community theater, polling places, adult and continuing education (Ringers & Decker, 1995). Early influences on the development of the community school were inspired by John Dewey's book *Schools of Tomorrow* that advocated community schools that center the curriculum around the lives of students while involving members of the community as educational resources.

In 1911, Wisconsin became the first state in the nation to pass legislation providing open access to school facilities for all citizens paid for by the state's first community education tax levy. The community education program, under Dorothy Enderis's direction, expanded the notion of community education by promoting the concept of linked education, community, and recreation. She became known as the "Lady of the Lighted Schoolhouse," a reference to the after-school activities found in many Milwaukee schools, such as efforts to teach immigrants basic English skills (Wilson, 1988).

The foundations of community education and the community school can be traced back to 1934 in Flint, Michigan, when educator Frank Manley and industrialist Charles Stewart Mott developed the concept of the "lighted school-house," opening the first community education program in the Flint public schools for community activities after school hours (Boo & Decker, 1985). These centers spread throughout Michigan, and later throughout the efforts of the Mott Foundation, community education centers were established in universities and state education departments throughout the United States. Sloan Foundation grants in the 1940s allowed several universities to establish experimental community schools, but only a few remain in operation (Pulliam & Van Patten, 1999).

With the advocacy of the EFL in the 1960s, the concept of the community school became more widespread. There were several factors that influenced the development of the community school in the 1960s and 1970s. New schools constructed after World War II were built away from populated areas in order to find larger and less expensive sites. School buildings became physically separated from the communities they were intended to serve. This development made access more difficult for communities desiring the multiple use of school buildings. Schools began to establish their own library, transportation, and health service systems, further separating them from the community (Ringers & Decker, 1995). Another factor encouraging the development of community schools was that of taxpayer resistance to school bond issues. Schools who entered into partnerships with other agencies in occupying new buildings found that taxpayers would support increases in school taxes. As a result, schools began offering the community adult-sized gyms; auditoriums; expanded adult education opportunities; branch libraries; and after-school child care, preschool, and day care programs (Ringers & Decker, 1995).

To respond to various community concerns in the late 1960s, several federal laws were passed in 1974. The Community Development Act encouraged the establishment of a program for community development block grants in deteriorating neighborhoods, and the Community Schools Act encouraged interagency planning, operation, and programming (Ringers & Decker, 1995). Formal joint-use agreements between school districts and the community, government and business organizations have furthered the stability of long-term relationships between schools and their surrounding community. A federal grant program called the Twenty-First Century Community Learning Centers accelerated the formation of community learning centers (CLCs) across the country. According to the U.S. Department of Education, as of 2000, over 3,600 rural and inner-city public schools in 903 communities—in collaboration with other public and nonprofit agencies, organizations, local businesses, postsecondary institutions, scientific/cultural and other community entities—were participating as CLCs.

An early twenty-first century trend in educational facility planning (refer to Chapter 6 for current trends and exemplary twenty-first century educational architecture) was to view whole communities as a learning laboratory for students. The assumption was that learning takes place everywhere. Schools and school district administrators across the country realized that working to improve schools included the larger collaborative effort of working to improve their community's overall learning ecology. Second, in order to provide students with project-based, authentic, real-world learning experiences, educators were increasingly pursuing opportunities for learning outside the structured classroom that would otherwise not be possible inside the classroom. Another assumption was that learning happened in many settings and each setting needed to be strengthened. Schools operating under this plan were decentralized into a network of partnerships and smaller structures (Lackney, March 1999).

MIDDLE SCHOOL PHILOSOPHY AND THE HOUSE PLAN

The junior high school was the first form of schooling that responded to the unique needs of early adolescents. It was the dominant school between elementary and high school between the 1920s and the 1960s. Growing dissatisfaction with both the K8–4 and 6–3–3 school organizations and a lack of consensus on what constituted the junior high school led, in the 1960s, to the alternative organization now commonly known as the middle school—the school "in the middle." The main criticism of the junior high program was that the needs and interests of young adolescents were not being met due to adjustment problems caused by the abrupt change from a self-contained classroom environment to a departmentalized organization characterizing high schools (George & Alexander, 1993). Since 1960, over 15,000 middle schools have been instituted in the United States alone (George & Alexander, 1993), coexisting with junior high schools (7–9) and other forms of intermediate schools.

The middle school was originally characterized by several grade structures (6–8, 5–8, or 7–8). The intent of the middle school movement was to advocate the concept of "a school in the middle" that would bridge between the childhood level of elementary education and the older adolescent level of secondary education. The middle school was conceived as balancing the child-centered, supportive interpersonal structure of instruction in the elementary school with the subject-oriented teacher specialization of the high school. The most distinctive feature of the middle school is that it is organized to provide instruction and learning through an interdisciplinary team of teachers (Carnegie Foundation, 1988).

Unlike elementary self-contained classrooms or subject-oriented high schools, teachers in the middle school setting form a small team that shares the same group of students (100–120), block schedule, areas of the school building ("house" or "pod" plan), and the responsibility for planning the basic academic subjects. The goal of an interdisciplinary team is to manage a "planned gradualism" from K–12, going beyond the notion of team teaching (George & Alexander, 1993).

The school facility has an equally important role in supporting the efforts of the interdisciplinary team, as does block time scheduling that cre-ates blocks of time necessary for interdisciplinary teams of teachers to creatively and flexibly plan their instruction. The supportive nature of the school building is most evident when middle school organizations are implemented within existing school buildings originally designed for elementary or high school programs. Neither facility design is adequate for the unique programs and activities that are anticipated with the middle school concept. During the 1960s, open space planning was associated with middle schools, but complete open space, while allowing the maximum flexibility, is not necessary to accommodate the middle school concept (George & Alexander, 1993).

The most common strategies have included modifying existing structures through adaptive reuse, the construction of new schools with an emphasis on flexible space design, and the construction of new facilities as small schools within a larger building often known as the schools-within-schools concept.

Two types of middle school designs have dominated new construction, however: pod-style and house-type layouts. Pod plans were first developed in the 1960s, while the house plan has a more recent history, being most fully developed in the 1980s. Oak Point Middle School in Eden Prairie, Minnesota, exemplifies the house plan concept for middle schools in the late 1980s (Figure 1.12). Both layouts allow for the creation of families of students. Presumably, these foster a sense of community—thus, the notion of a "house" for a "family"—while providing larger more common spaces to which the entire school has access, including libraries, media centers, administrative offices, gymnasiums, and special art, music, computer instruction, and language arts rooms or laboratories. A family can consist of as few as 100 students and 4 teachers and as many as 200 students and 8 teachers. The house can include anywhere from four to eight self-contained classrooms oriented toward a centralized resource center and supported with a specialized classroom, teacher offices, small seminar rooms, and other support spaces.

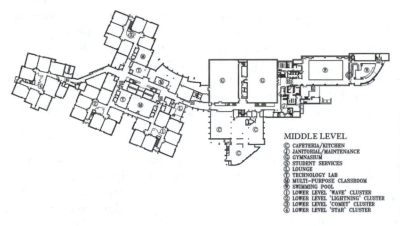

MIDDLE LEVEL
ⓒ CAFETERIA/KITCHEN
ⓙ JANITORIAL/MAINTENANCE
ⓖ GYMNASIUM
ⓢ STUDENT SERVICES
ⓛ LOUNGE
ⓣ TECHNOLOGY LAB
ⓜ MULTI-PURPOSE CLASSROOM
ⓦ SWIMMING POOL
① LOWER LEVEL 'WAVE' CLUSTER
② LOWER LEVEL 'LIGHTNING' CLUSTER
③ LOWER LEVEL 'COMET' CLUSTER
④ LOWER LEVEL 'STAR' CLUSTER

FIGURE 1.12   Oak Point Middle School in Eden Prairie, Minnesota, illustrating the main classroom areas organized in four "clusters" on each level.

Source: Courtesy of Cuningham Architects, Minneapolis, Minnesota.

The house plan concept is currently being applied in high school environments as an appropriate response to advances in self-directed learning and interdisciplinary instruction. The goal of keeping groupings of learners small enough to support individualized attention and cooperative learning is now seen as having developmental value throughout the K–12 learning experience. More recently, the metaphor of the house has been extended to the "neighborhoods" and "main streets" in middle school and high schools carrying further the notion of a community of learners (Lackney, March 1999). Celebration School, a K–12 school in Celebration, Florida, that opened in 1997, is an example of a school that uses the neighborhood concept consisting of 100 students, 4 teachers, and their assistants.

TECHNOLOGY, THE VIRTUAL SCHOOL, AND THE INTERNET

The rapid growth in digital technologies has created the need to rethink what we mean by "school" and "schooling." Some of the earliest anomalies in the old paradigm of the school building appeared in the early 1960s, with the reconceptualization of the library as an "instructional media center" containing stations for listening to tape recorders, and areas for viewing and storing television and video-tape machines. The computer room was added to the school building program in the early 1980s to accommodate the growing addition of computer technologies. As computers became more available, schools began to place technology in existing self-contained classrooms, and plan for additional space in new classrooms. The advent of laptop computers and voice/data communications, Internet, and wireless technologies only further moved technology resources closer to the classroom and the student and teacher. Resource centers have increasingly been located near classrooms, with technology dispersed throughout the school where it is needed rather than housed in a main computer room.

Distance learning began as a series of correspondence courses broadcast over the television in the 1960s. In the past decade, distance learning classroom space with real-time, two-way conferencing capabilities has appeared in many new and existing school buildings, especially in rural schools that require access to additional educational resources such as foreign language instruction.

The ability to gain access to the Internet has increased the ability of schools to become "virtual," offering a wide range of educational programs via the Internet. As of the year 2000, at least six states have launched virtual high schools that offer complete online courses to students in school or at home (Trotter, October 25, 2000). The school as an organization is becoming more virtual. Learning environments may be physically spaced across the entire community in libraries, businesses, community centers, and homes in addition to the traditional schoolhouse and temporally scheduled, both synchronous and asynchronous through the Internet. With the rapid increase in the use of wireless Internet connections, the school of the near future may take on a design completely different from anything we have seen to date. This school may become smaller as functions are relegated to other parts of the community. Media centers, for instance, may become smaller as the majority of knowledge is contained on virtual networks instead of in hardcopy. Computers have gone from being stand-alone desktop machines, to being networked laptops and handheld technologies. Learning activities can be liberated from the self-contained classroom that may become more of a home base to collectively plan learning activities that will take place all over the school site and community. The next chapter will explore in more detail the principles from which many new school designs are emerging.

SUMMARY

An overview of three periods of educational architecture, the colonial period, the Industrial Revolution, and the information age, demonstrates how educational facilities have evolved over time in response to societal and political influences. The colonial period (1650 – 1849) was characterized by an agrarian society in which many did not value formal education. Education primarily occurred in informal settings, such as the home or church, and the main focus was to teach children a trade or skill. The country one-room schoolhouse in small villages typifies educational buildings of the colonial period. Similar structures were utilized in urban areas, but to accommodate more students, they often included two or more self-contained rooms. As cities grew, there was a need to educate larger groupings of students. In response, the Lancas-

terian monitorial system, which utilized older students serving as monitors to teach younger children, allowed one educator to provide instruction for hundreds of students.

The Industrial Revolution (1850–1949) occurred as factories proliferated in the United States to produce products such as firearms, textiles, and sewing machines. The common school movement arose between 1840 and 1880 in response to a belief that education provided mainly by family members or through apprenticeships was insufficient to prepare children to work in factories and offices. Educational reformers, including Henry Barnard and Horace Mann, argued that public education was essential to our nation's economic success. Beginning in the middle of the nineteenth century, schools typically were made up of classrooms and corridors, but by the end of the century schools often incorporated specialized spaces such as auditoriums and administrative offices. Specialized facilities for junior high and high schools emerged during the Industrial Revolution. The progressive movement of the late nineteenth century, led principally by John Dewey, focused on child-centered education and flexible spaces.

The information age (1950–present), following World War II, is characterized by a society in which people appreciate travel, celebrate diversity, and seek to reintegrate their work and family lives. The baby boom fueled the need for many new schools that were often built as quickly and cheaply as possible, resulting in buildings with poor insulation and low-quality building systems. The open classroom became popular during the 1950s through the early 1970s to encourage group work and team teaching, but changes in teaching styles often did not accompany the changes in classroom design and teachers complained of distractions. During the 1960s, criticism that public schools were not adequately addressing the needs of minority and low-income students gave rise to the alternative schools (e.g., freedom schools and street academies) movement. This movement is believed to have influenced many other educational reforms, including magnet and charter schools, school-to-work initiatives, and the more recent reemergence of home schooling. The concept of the community school has reemerged as city and county agencies seek to leverage tax dollars to create joint-use facilities that involve the local community in student education. During the information age, computers have become an absolute necessity for students. Once housed in media centers, computers may now be found anywhere on campus through the use of wireless and palmtop technologies.

Throughout the history of American education, educational reformers have often met strong opposition to their theories about how children should be taught what they need to know to succeed in society. Even as new ideas are adopted, it often takes many years for the physical school setting to respond to changes in pedagogy.

ACTIVITIES

1. Identify an old school in your region (preferably 100 or more years old). Document additions and major renovations and describe how these modifications reflect social trends of the time.

2. Describe how you believe new school designs will differ in twenty years as a direct result of the use of computers in schools, assuming that wireless and palmtop technologies will proliferate.

3. Identify two nontraditional schools (e.g., an environmentally focused charter school, a Montessori school) in your local area. Arrange a visit to each school. Document aspects of the physical design and furnishings that support the school's unique educational program. Also, describe how the physical environment could have been modified to provide better spaces to support the program.

REFERENCES AND BIBLIOGRAPHY

Armsey, J. W. (1976). *A Commentary on a Series of Grants by the Ford Foundation to the Educational Facilities Laboratories, Inc. 1958–1975*. New York: Ford Foundation.

Barth, R. (1972). *Open Education and the American School*. New York: Agathon.

Boo, M. R., & Decker, L. E. (1985). *The Learning Community*. Alexandria, VA: National Community Education Association.

Brubaker, C. W. (1998). *Planning and Designing Schools*. New York: McGraw-Hill.

Campbell, R. F., Cunningham, L. L., Nystrand, R. O., & Usdan, M. D. (1980). *The Organization and Control of American Schools*, 4th ed. Columbus, OH: Charles E. Merrill Publishing.

Carnegie Foundation (1988). *An Imperiled Generation: Saving Urban Schools*. Princeton, NJ: The Carnegie Foundation for the Advancement of Teaching.

DeYoung, A. J. (1989). *Economics and American Education: A Historical and Critical Overview of the Impact of Economic Theories on Schooling in the United States*. New York: Longman.

Ehrenkrantz, E. (September 1999). "Planning for Flexibility, Not Obsolescence." http:// www.designshare.com/Research/EEK/Enrenkrantz1.htm.

George, P. S., & Alexander, W. M. (1993). *The Exemplary Middle School*. Fort Worth, TX: Holt, Rinehart and Winston.

Graves, B. (1993). *School Ways: The Planning and Design of America's Schools*. New York: McGraw-Hill.

Gulliford, A. (1984). *America's Country Schools*. Washington, DC: Preservation Press.

Gulliford, A. (1996). *America's Country Schools*, 3rd ed. Washington, DC: Preservation Press.

Harris, J. J., & Fields, R. E. (1979). Busing and the Evolving Socio-Legal Concept of the Neighborhood School. *NOLPE School Law Journal*, 8(2), pp. 154–165.

Hennessey, G. J. (1976). *The Neighborhood School Concept as a Deterrent to Desegregation in the 1960s and 1970s*. ERIC Document #ED134661.

Herbst, J. (1996). *The Once and Future School: Three Hundred and Fifty Years of American Secondary Education*. New York: Routledge.

Johnson, C. (1963). *Old-Time Schools and School-books*. New York: Dover. (First published in 1904 by Macmillan.)

Lackney, J. A. (1994). *Educational Facilities: The Impact and Role of the Physical Environment of the School on Teaching, Learning and Educational Outcomes*. Milwaukee, WI: Center for Architecture and Urban Planning Research, University of Wisconsin-Milwaukee.

Lackney, J. A. (March 1999). "Changing Patterns in Educational Facilities." http://www.designshare.com/Research/ChangingPatterns/ChangingPatterns1.htm.

Marks, J. (June 2000). *The Educational Facilities Laboratories (EFL): A History*. Washington, DC: National Clearinghouse for Educational Facilities.

Marshall, H. H. (1981). Open Classrooms: Has the Term Outlived Its Usefulness? *Review of Educational Research*, 51(2), pp. 181–192.

McClintock, J., & McClintock, R. (1970). *Henry Barnard's School Architecture*. New York: Teachers College Press.

Meek, A. (ed.) (1995). *Designing Places for Learning*. Alexandria, VA: Association for Supervision and Curriculum Development.

National Council on Schoolhouse Construction (NCSC) (1953). *Guide for Planning School Plants*. Nashville, TN: Peabody College. (National Council on Schoolhouse Construction now Council of Educational Facility Planners, International.)

Pulliam, J. D., & Van Patten, J. J. (1999). *History of Education in America*. Upper Saddle River, NJ: Prentice Hall.

Rieselbach, A. (1992). Building and Learning. In The Architectural League (eds.), *New Schools for New York: Plans and Precedents for Small Schools*. New York: Princeton Architectural Press.

Ringers, J., Jr., & Decker, L. E. (1995). *School Community Centers: Guidelines for Interagency Planners*. Charlottesville, VA: Mid-Atlantic Center for Community Education.

Rothenberg, J. (1989). The Open Classroom Reconsidered. *Elementary School Journal*, 90(1), pp. 69–86.

Saint, A. (1987). *Towards a Social Architecture: The Role of School Building in Post-War England*. New Haven: Yale University Press.

Tanner, L. N. (1997). *Dewey's Laboratory School: Lessons for Today*. New York: Teachers College Press.

Toffler, A. (1980). *Third Wave*. New York: Bantam Books.

Trotter, A. (October 25, 2000). States Virtually Carried Away Over Online High Schools. *Education Week*, 20(8), p. 22.

Wilson, G. T. (July 1988). Dorothy Enderis: Milwaukee's "Lady of the Lighted Schoolhouse." *Community Education Journal*, pp. 16–17.

CHAPTER TWO

TRENDS IN EDUCATIONAL ARCHITECTURE THAT INFLUENCE THE DESIGN OF LEARNING ENVIRONMENTS

The first chapter outlined a history of educational architecture in North America from the precedents of eighteenth-century Europe to the modern concepts of community schools and schools in the community. In Chapter 2 we explore the various trends in educational architecture that continue to influence the design of learning environments.[1]

The body of knowledge concerning well-designed learning environments is contained in the following thirty-one global school design principles that appear to have currency in today's school planning and design. These principles are derived from a variety of sources: from the reflective practice of educators and design professionals to the empirical research of environmental psychologists and educational researchers. Each school design principle takes as an underlying premise that all learning environments should be learner-centered, developmentally and age-appropriate, safe, comfortable, accessible, flexible, and equitable in addition to being cost-effective. These premises run through all the principles and should be understood to moderate the appropriateness of each principle

in practice. The school design principles are presented here as an extended checklist format that can be used as a guide for a school design visioning process.

No single school building process will be able to address and implement all these principles; some may not apply to the situation, others might not be appropriate because of budgetary limitations. Certainly, if school size research suggests learner groupings of one hundred, building a school this small may not be cost-effective—other principles may need to be employed in combination to meet this principle, such as the principle of creating schools within schools, although we do not recommend this as a solution to poor planning and designs of the past.

The chapter is divided into principles for site and building organization, principles for primary educational space, principles for shared school and community facilities, community spaces, principles related to the character of all spaces, and principles related to site design and outdoor learning spaces.

---

[1]Material for this chapter was sponsored by the National Clearinghouse for Educational Facilities (NCEF) under the original title *Thirty-three Educational Design Principles for Schools and Community Learning Centers*. Go to http://www.edfacilities.org.

PRINCIPLES FOR SITE AND BUILDING ORGANIZATION

Many of the principles for site and building organization have evolved from earlier forms but have taken on new significance in twenty-first-century school design. For instance, the neighborhood school, a cornerstone of early-nineteenth-century schools, has taken on new significance with controversies to end "forced" busing in urban school districts as well as create smaller learning communities. There is a new emphasis on formalizing the learning that can take place within the surrounding community of the school. In addition, the size and scale of school buildings are being seriously challenged. Schools are becoming smaller and more intimate in many urban school centers. Finally, buildings are being organized in ways that help transition from smaller home environments that are safe, secure, and inviting.

1. Plan Schools as Neighborhood-Scaled Community Learning Centers

The potential exists to transform the traditional school building into a community learning center that serves the educational needs of the entire population in the community. Typically, a community learning center can be created by interlacing residential neighborhoods, various existing community and school organizations, functions, and facilities (Bingler et al., 2003; Decker & Romney, 1994; U.S. Department of Education, 1999; OECD, 1996a). The community school most often functions as a cohesive facility or network of closely adjacent facilities (Hodgin, 1998; Fanning/Howey Associates, 1995). Locating the community learning center in neighborhoods will provide a symbolic identity for that community. Facilities that are close to the neighborhoods of the children they serve provide opportunities for children to walk and bike to school, with the added public health benefit of increasing their physical activity, rather than relying on more costly modes of transportation. Community schools often will provide a variety of services, at flexible

schedules, accessible by people of different backgrounds. By providing facilities accessible for the entire community, the center will create increased involvement and awareness of the value of education (Warner & Curry, 1997). School facilities that act as true community centers serve the broader societal goals of providing the setting for meaningful civic participation and engagement at the local level.

2. Plan for Learning to Take Place Directly in the Community

A variety of social and economic factors have created an environment in which many educators recognize that learning happens all the time and in many different places (Duke, 1999). The school building is just one place learning occurs. While the school building is often perceived as a community center, the idea of embracing the whole community as a learning environment has evolved in a complementary fashion. Educational programs can take, and are taking, advantage of educational resources in urban, suburban, and rural settings alike. Formal educational program partnerships have been established with museums, zoos, libraries, other public institutions, as well as local business workplace settings (Bingler et al., 2003; Fielding, 1999).

In addition, increasing costs of public spending for education have encouraged the sharing of school and community facilities, which in turn prevents cost duplication of similar facilities such as gymnasiums, auditoriums, performance spaces, and conferencing facilities (Fanning/Howey Associates, 1995; OECD, 1995a, 1996a). Sharing facilities can also realize long-term maintenance and operating cost savings over the life of the building. Sharing school facilities with a variety of community organizations may foster meaningful interorganizational partnerships that can strengthen educational opportunities for learners.

3. Create Smaller Schools

Barker and Gump (1964) in their classic *Big School, Small School* demonstrated through their research that small schools (100–150), in comparison with large schools (over 2,000), offer students greater opportunities to participate in extracurricular activities and to exercise leadership roles. In particular, they found that participation in school activities, student satisfaction, number of classes taken, community employment, and participation in social organizations have all been greater in small schools relative to large schools. Garbarino (1980) later found that, small schools, on the order of 500 students or less, have lower incidence of crime levels and less serious student misconduct. Subsequent research by others suggests a negative relationship between mathematics and verbal ability tests and elementary school size controlling for socioeconomic differences (Fowler, 1992; Howley, 1994). Additionally, the same research indicates that smaller elementary schools particularly benefit African American students' achievement.

For educational planners and architects, the research on small schools suggests that the size of learner groupings should be roughly between 60–75 students in preschool, 200–400 students in elementary school, 400–600 in middle school, and not more than 600–800 students in secondary school (Raywid, 1996, 1999; Lashway, 1998–1999; Irmsher, 1997). If a community learning center must house more than 75 preschoolers, 400 elementary or middle school students, or more than 800 high school students, it is often recommended that the facility be decentralized not just in the size of student body, but also curriculum, administration, and architecture. Architectural forms of these smaller units may include a village, campus, or multifaceted building made up of a series of interconnected schools within a school for a maximum of 400 students. Another strategy for reducing the scale of educational facilities is to distribute and network various school and community functions throughout the neighborhood in both new and existing sites.

4. Respect Contextual Compatibility While Providing Design Diversity

As real estate development sprawl has expanded, the principle of creating well-defined neighborhoods has been ignored in urban planning. While a strong neighborhood may not directly influence educational performance, the sense of cohesion experienced by community members may help increase parental involvement in neighborhood schools. Research has shown that parental involvement in the school is critical to a learner's success. By creating a contextually compatible school, people may feel that the school is part of the neighborhood and, in turn, part of them. While maintaining a sense of continuity through contextual design, creating diversely designed environments that have their own identity is equally important in enabling community members to recognize the school as a symbol of their community (Moore & Lackney, 1994).

Well-defined neighborhoods blend schools into the pattern and character of the local, surrounding community. In a complementary fashion, one might create differently styled schools with, for example, variations on the overall design theme, to respond to the need for community identity and as a response to active parental, children, teacher, administration, and community participation (OECD, 1996a).

5. Consider Home as a Template for School

The transition from the home setting to institutional settings such as the school environment can be stressful, especially for younger children in child care settings. Experience tells us that building in physical and social homelike characteristics may reduce anxiety on the part of both parent and child, help children feel more comfortable, and enable them to concentrate on learning (Moore et al., 1979).

Use friendly, "homelike" elements and materials in the design of the school at all scales when appropriate and possible (Crumpacker, 1995). Homelike characteristics might include: creating smaller groupings of students often called "families" according to the middle school philosophy, designing appropriately scaled elements, locating restrooms near instructional areas, providing friendly and welcoming entry sequences, creating residentially sloping roofs, and creating enclosed "backyards" (Moore et al., 1979). Use familiar and meaningful elements from the surrounding residential neighborhood as the "template" for the imagery of the new school.

6. Meander Circulation While Ensuring Supervision

Providing for meaningful social interaction in schools is important in encouraging a positive school climate. Unfortunately, in many large school buildings not all learners and faculty share a common room or floor where they can come into regular contact with each other. Often, social anonymity can result. Many times the only meeting these occupants have is in areas of circulation. It is important to take advantage of these impromptu meetings by designing the circulation space within the school as a place to converse and share information and ideas.

Simultaneously, public circulation space is known to be one of the most difficult places in a school to keep safe from illicit activity. The goals of encouraging positive social behaviors and reducing violence do not have to be mutually exclusive. In fact, if appropriately addressed through design, encouraging positive behaviors can have a mediating effect on the reduction of unwanted social behaviors (Moore & Lackney, 1994).

Circulation pathways such as hallways and corridors are a costly percentage of a school building construction. However, circulation can double as an active learning space for the school. Whenever possible, design meandering pathways to increase opportunities for social interaction. Use circulation to create gentle transitions from different spaces, taking advantage of turns and bends to create unique areas of learning. Conversely, for issues of safety, circulation paths should be designed to ensure adequate supervision not only by administrators, but also by students, teachers, and parents to create a condition of natural surveillance that has been found to reduce disruptive behaviors (Crowe, 2000). Creating central activity nodes that connect short paths is one strategy for maintaining

visual supervision without creating long institutional-style corridors (Moore et al., 1979).

7. Design for Safe Schools

Safe school building designs must be seen as being one important component of a larger system of crime prevention in schools that include administrative procedures, student, staff, and community training programs, and the implementation of security programs and systems (Crowe, 2000; Schneider, Walker, & Sprague, 2000; Cornell, 1999). Design and use of the environment directly affect human behavior that, in turn, influences opportunities for crime and fear of crime, and impacts quality of life (Department of Education & Department of Justice, 1998). These opportunities for crime can be reduced through appropriate planning and design decisions.

Crowe (2000) in his highly influential, *Crime Prevention Through Environmental Design* identifies three critical safe school design principles, including access control, natural surveillance, and definition of territory. Natural access control denies access to a crime target and creates a perception of risk in offenders. Access control uses doors, shrubs, fences, gates, and other physical design elements to discourage access to an area by all but its intended users. Surveillance is commonly solved through the use of surveillance camera technologies, which may or may not be monitored. As an important adjunct to these systems, providing for natural surveillance assures that offenders and intruders will know they are being observed. It increases the likelihood that individuals who care but are not officially responsible for regulating the use of space will observe these individuals and either challenge their behavior or report it to someone who is officially responsible. Natural surveillance is achieved by placing windows in locations that allow intended users to see or be seen, while ensuring that intruders will be observed as well. Opportunities for surveillance are enhanced through the provision of adequate lighting and glass and landscaping that allow for unobstructed views. Locate administrative areas directly adjacent to the main entrance to the school. Territorial reinforcement suggests that physical design can contribute to a sphere of influence so users develop a sense of "ownership" that is perceived by offenders. Territory can be defined by the use of sidewalks, landscaping, porches, and other elements that establish the boundaries between public and private areas.

PRINCIPLES FOR PRIMARY EDUCATIONAL SPACE

Based in large part on changes in curriculum and instruction, primary educational spaces are changing as well. Although many of these innovations in primary learning and instructional space began over forty years ago, they are beginning to become standard practice in new school designs. Instructional spaces are being clustered to form smaller learning communities of either same grade or multigrade configurations. Additional space is often being provided that is shared by these clusters of learning areas. The recognition that there are a variety of learning styles precipitates the provision of a variety of learning groupings and spaces beyond the traditional self-contained classroom. Class sizes have become smaller to increase contact time with teachers. The need to provide enough space within the primary learning area for resource-rich activity areas is now seen as critical to development. The desirability of integrating early childhood education into the traditional school grade configuration has become more pronounced with the advent of the implications of brain-based research for learning in the early years.

8. Cluster Learning Areas

A central concept of clustering learning spaces around central cores of shared instructional support and resource spaces emerged in the early 1960s and remains a sound strategy for school design today (Brubaker, 1998; OECD, 1996). When clustered around larger resource spaces, learning spaces act as learning alcoves rather than the isolated self-contained classrooms of the past. The

core shoul include informal meeting space, seminar and shared conference rooms, a small computer hub, and teacher offices.

Open plan designs of the 1960s and 1970s may have been partially successful at broadening the educational experience of learners, but both teachers and learners found that too many physical distractions were experienced for these open physical settings to become the norm (Weinstein, 1979). The key to new clustering arrangements then is to provide spaces that are open yet have areas of enclosure for more task-specific activities. These spaces will then be diverse in use but not have the sight and sound distractions experienced with open plan schools (Moore & Lackney, 1994).

The concept of the cluster of instructional spaces is adaptable to a number of pedagogical goals and curriculum and instructional philosophies and strategies (Taylor & Vlastos, 1983; Sanoff & Sanoff, 1988). For instance, each cluster may support either traditional disciplinary teaching such as history, mathematics, and the arts, or interdisciplinary teaching that supports thematic learning units. Each cluster may contain either grade-level groupings, or multiage groupings of learners. To maximize the agility of instructional clusters, one may use any appropriate combination of stand-alone movable partitions, movable modular furnishings, or large door openings to shared core spaces.

9. Provide Space for Sharing Instructional Resources

For educators to be successful, the availability of resources by students and faculty is important. Students that do not have access to learning spaces, resources, and teachers will be at a disadvantage. The reality of limited physical and economic resources in school settings demands the sharing of all available instructional resources. One way to address this concern is to provide a well-defined area directly adjacent to instructional alcoves and core spaces that provide technology-rich resources which can be shared by all learners in an instructional cluster (OECD, 1996). Resources can take a wide variety of forms from small, specialized libraries, information technology, and other instructional media to special equipment and general workspace (Chupela, 1994; Feinberg, Kuchner, & Feldman, 1998). By creating instructional areas that have direct accessibility to these resources, the learning process will be supported.

10. Design for a Variety of Learning Groups and Spaces

Learning naturally takes place in many different kinds and qualities of space. Although the self-contained classroom continues to have a role in facilitating instruction in schools, it can no longer provide the variety of learning settings necessary to successfully facilitate innovations in curriculum and instruction (Crumpacker, 1995; Meek, 1995). Space needs to accommodate, for instance, a wide variety of group learning sizes from an entire "family" of 100 learners, to five groups of twenty learners, to groups of twelve, four to six, and one to two learners. One approach to this problem is to create a variety of adjoining learning spaces and arrangements inside and outside the main instructional space or area. Another approach might be to create partially open space with appropriate visual and acoustical barriers, with adjacent, smaller, enclosed spaces (Taylor & Vlastos, 1983; Sanoff & Sanoff, 1988). In this manner, smaller learning spaces are separated yet connected. Articulate each cluster of instructional areas by gathering several small-group learning areas around the main instructional space for large-group instruction. Each of the small-group areas can be further divided into individual activity areas to allow for quiet, individualized self-directed learning (Weinstein & Mignano, 1997; Weinstein, 1996; McMillan, 1997).

11. Keep Class Sizes Small

The size of the primary learning group in which the child spends the most time makes a significant difference in the quality of education and development (Crumpacker, 1995; NAEYC, 1999). Create instructional areas that allow for twelve to sixteen learners in early childhood and elementary grade levels, sixteen to twenty learners in middle school grade levels, and twenty to twenty-four learners in secondary school grade levels. Class size research points directly to a social and physical link to achievement (Department of Education, 1998–1999). In one of the largest longitudinal studies of class size to be conducted, the Tennessee Student Teacher Area Ratio (STAR) Project (Achilles, 1992; Finn & Achilles, 1990) found that children in smaller classes (thirteen to seventeen per room) outperform those in regular-sized classes (twenty-two to twenty-five per room). In the early grades, children in smaller classes were found to outperform children from regular class sizes in all subjects, but especially in reading and mathematics test scores with average improvements of up to 15 percent. Smaller classes were especially helpful for children in inner-city schools. A follow-up study by Achilles and his associates, called the Lasting Benefits Study (Nye et al., 1992) indicated that students previously in small classes demonstrated statistically significant advantages two years later over students previously in regular-sized classes. Performance gains ranged from 11–34 percent. Reasons for these gains may be that more and higher-quality student–teacher interactions are possible in a smaller class (Bourke, 1986), and that spatial density and crowding are also reduced, thereby decreasing distractions in the classroom (Loo, 1976).

12. Provide Resource-Rich Well-Defined Activity Pockets

Small activity spaces have been found to be important to the development of young learners. Moore (1986) found that small well-defined spaces tend to encourage greater learner engagement in a learning task, greater teacher involvement with individual learners, fewer teacher interruptions, and greater exploratory behavior, social interaction, and cooperative behaviors among learners. Smaller clusters lead to the increased use of learning materials, more substantive content questions, less non-task-oriented movement, quieter conversations, longer attention spans, and overall greater satisfaction. Moore also determined that secluded study space within an instructional area is important for students' development and found to be empirically related to students' performance. For instance, structured reading areas have shown to significantly increase students' literature use (Meek, 1995).

Providing the raw space for learning activities to take place is only the first step in providing a successful place for learning. Ensure that each large-group, small-group, and individual learning space is an architecturally well-defined "activity pocket" for two to five learners with all the surfaces, display, storage, and resources necessary for that learning activity contained within (Taylor & Vlastos, 1983; Sanoff & Sanoff, 1988; Moore & Lackney, 1994). Activity pockets can take on a variety of architectural forms from simple learning centers, to lofts, small alcoves, and lecture pits. Another strategy might be to provide a variety of furniture layouts for learner activities—some centripetal for group work, some facing outward for individual work in the same activity pocket.

13. Integrate Early Childhood Education into the School

Reasons for including early childhood programs within the school go well beyond the more reactive reasons such as teenage pregnancy and unavailability of affordable day care for working mothers and even teachers (OECD, 1996b; U.S. GSA, 1998). Research indicates that windows of opportunity for learning start at a very early age, and providing some structured learning experiences for children can be beneficial in their later years (Harms, 1994). Cooperation between the school and the early childhood education/child care facility can ease the transition for the student. Many schools find that providing child care encourages parents to keep their child at that school site, further easing the transition from home to school (Jones & Nimmo, 1994). In addition, child care can also ease the return to school for teenage parents to complete their secondary education

(Coburn, 1999). When possible, include a developmentally oriented childcare center and early childhood development education center that are both integrated programmatically with the larger school organization. Site the center in the same neighborhood, close to the school, or on the same site if possible (see Olds, 2001, for a excellent primer on child care design).

14. Provide a Home Base for Every Learner

Research indicates that personalization of space is an important factor in the formation of an individual's identity and sense of self-worth (Bredekamp & Copple, 1997). Learners in schools are a lot like workers in the workplace in that it is important for most people to have some space that is their own. A desk or locker for possessions and personal belongings are the basic elements of any work setting. By providing similar forms of personal space within the school for each learner, those learners will gain a more positive sense of self and take pride and ownership in their school.

However, a locker along a corridor does not make a home base. Moore and coworkers (1979) outline a variety of strategies for creating a meaningful home base for learners. Within the physical boundaries of each instructional area, create a home base for the learner for whom that learning group becomes his or her personal space (Taylor & Vlastos, 1983; Sanoff & Sanoff, 1988). Include cubbies and lockers for personal belongings arranged in small groups to provide space for informal social interaction. Allow learners to personalize their space as much as possible. For younger children (infant through 3 or 4 years old), provide space for naps. When possible, locate washrooms and lunchtime eating areas near the home bases at the primary grades.

15. Regard Teachers as Professionals

Providing shared facilities for school faculty will create opportunities for teachers to reflect on, form, and communicate ideas central to their development as professionals (Johnson, 1990). In the factory-model school, teachers are more like laborers than professionals, and students are the products of their labors. The teacher's workspace in the factory-model school consists of a desk in the front of the self-contained classroom, which is neither private from students, nor connected to other faculty.

By providing shared offices for the faculty adjacent to learning areas, teachers would still be accessible to learners, but would have privacy from the formal instructional area and a space in which to adequately plan learning activities. Teachers need home bases as well as students. Many new school designs provide teachers with private or semiprivate office space, including space for personal belongings, a phone/fax, a personal computer, information technologies, a desk, and personal library. Due to limited resources, teacher offices can be clustered together to form a grouping of no more than four teachers, thus encouraging collaboration. The location of teacher offices should be adjacent but not central to instructional areas—teachers are not the center of education, learners are. In place of the old "teachers' lounge," provide conferencing rooms where larger groups of teachers can meet formally to exchange information and teaching experiences among themselves and with school visitors. Include a balance formal and informal/break-out meeting space, with support spaces such as kitchenettes, storage, and private restrooms.

16. Provide Studios to Support Project-Based Learning

One of the most natural ways of learning is that of learning by doing. Research indicates that participating in a learning exercise, activity, or experiment in addition to attending a lecture engages a broader array of "multiple intelligences" than relying on a lecture alone (Costa & Liebmann, 1997). Project-based learning and studio-based instruction emphasize learning as a team and foster cooperation and the sharing of ideas that will enable students to

process material better (Bridges, 1992). Rather than struggle as individuals, learners can use the strengths of a group to decrease the time it takes to learn a lesson and increase the amount of information absorbed.

New instructional methods based on real-world authentic learning and authentic assessment methods will require a new form of instructional space suggested by studio-based learning settings common in art education (Schon, 1983; Lackney, 1999). Provide locations for the generation and storage of semester-long projects as well as student portfolios. Include space for individual, small-group, and larger-group productions, including but not limited to audio/visual/digital studios, dance and performance studios, workshops for various visual arts, photocopy machines, and large open project tables. Adjacent to the portfolio process studio, provide flexible experimental lab stations for groups or individuals to explore and demonstrate discoveries in the physical and biological sciences. Include movable laboratory furnishings, storage space for equipment, and visibility and ease of movement throughout the space (Meek, 1995; Moore & Lackney, 1994).

17. Encourage Educational Leadership by Decentralizing Administrative Space

Research indicates that schools which have an effective leader in the role of the principal are often the most successful socially and academically (English, 2005). Effective leaders do not hide in back offices. However, in many schools, administrative functions and decisions take place in locations remote from teachers, students, and classrooms. School leaders find ways to involve the staff and students in decisions that will affect their lives at the school.

Decentralizing administrative functions throughout the school building, such as assistant principals and student advisors and counselors, provides not only supervision in more remote areas of the school, but also ensures the presence of leadership throughout the school. A common strategy for decentralizing the administration function when a school is subdivided into more than one school-within-a-school is to disperse administrative staff into each wing, pod, or cluster (Moore & Lackney, 1994). An organizational strategy that can complement the physical placement of administrative staff is to consider alternative approaches to developing leadership in the school, such as having decentralized student government offices and implementing site-based management.

PRINCIPLES FOR SHARED SCHOOL AND COMMUNITY FACILITIES

There are a number of spaces within schools, in addition to shared gymnasiums, auditoriums, and performing arts spaces, that are in effect shared and require joint-use agreements between school institutions and community entities. Some of these spaces are considered below: community forum and shared conferencing space, distance education facilities as well as virtual space.

18. Establish a Community Forum

Common gathering areas respond to the recognized need to provide an identity for the learning community. Schools traditionally have not provided space that was completely open in use, with the exception of the gymnasium and possibly auditorium, performing arts, and assembly spaces (Fanning/Howey Associates, 1995), thus reducing opportunities for developing this cultural identity within the school. In addition, with the added needs of the community, areas that provide for a variety of uses can assist in connecting the school to the surrounding community (OECD, 1996a).

A now widespread school design strategy is to provide a public assembly space to act as a community forum connecting the school and the community that is accessible, open, free-flowing, and flexible (Graves, 1993; Brubaker, 1998). A community forum is more than a big, open, undifferentiated space. The forum should have a "town

square" quality with small areas of the space for more specific activities. Provide for medium to large numbers of people for dance, music, drama, community meetings, exhibitions, and displays of student and community work (Fanning/Howey Associates, 1995). Auditoriums, as well as physical education facilities such as gymnasiums and natatoriums, should be directly adjacent to this public space. The forum also acts as a break-out space for these large-assembly community activities. To meet students' behavior patterns in free time, allow some space off the public space for informal multipurpose recreation and social gathering area with, when possible, direct access to informal outdoor gathering spaces. The social gathering space should have a living room feel. Include semiprivate areas for individuals or groups to meet. Integrate the common gathering area with the formal entry sequence of the school.

19. Allow for Community Conferencing Space

Communication is essential for the success of any organization. Like the workplace, the school needs meeting and conference rooms distinct from the more specialized instructional space for staff, students, parents, and community members to meet. These spaces can be used for community meetings and special events. Adjacent to the commons area, provide a medium-sized multipurpose conference rooms to serve up to twelve community members for private interviews, group meetings, or counseling. Place a large round table, movable seating within the largest space, along with storage, kitchen area, and display space.

20. Create Privacy Niches

Often, visitors to the school have no identifiable place to inhabit when visiting. School partners who visit the school frequently have more sophisticated needs and require space to set up shop or facilitate special events within the school in order to be effective. In addition, the relationship between a student and teacher is extremely important to the success of the educational process. To help foster this relationship, a school needs places of privacy for small, occasional meetings between its users.

One design strategy would be to include a series of publicly facing niches off main public spaces for visitors, parents, and adjuncts to conduct special activities or performances in the school. To further define the privacy niche, provide an area for informational displays and murals that communicate school activities and events. The niches are best located so as to attract attention when in use, but be unobtrusive when empty. When possible, develop several privacy niches or intimate counseling spaces for one-on-one or small group meetings for two to four persons that are relaxing, nonthreatening, comfortable, and private. Include comfortable fire-resistant living-room-type furniture. Connect these privacy niches to multipurpose conferencing spaces, instructional areas, and administrative areas.

21. Weave Together Virtual and Physical Learning Spaces

Information technology is rapidly becoming ubiquitous in our society and has become an essential tool for business and industry. It is precipitating a variety of changes in the organizational and physical form of schools (DeJong, 1997; OECD, 1995b; Stuebing et al., 1995). In the goal of integrating information technology into present school curricula, a variety of changes are being experienced. With respect to curriculum content and structure, technology is driving the curriculum in many schools to become more integrated between disciplines. With respect to instructional processes, technology is driving the movement toward self-directed learning and individualized instruction.

Although learning becomes increasingly virtual and Web-based, information technologies must still be physically located for access by the end-user. At present, information technology is unevenly distributed in many schools, creating a so-called digi-

tal divide (Kennedy & Argon, 1999; Butterfield, 1999). Technology may be isolated in computer labs in schools with a few computers scattered around the school building in classrooms, while in other schools almost every instructional space contains some form of information technology. As information technology becomes more available, it will become further decentralized within the school. The rise of laptop computers, personal data assistants (PDAs), and wireless local-area networks indicates clearly that technology is quickly becoming a highly fluid tool in the hands of learners, and all are challenging traditional instructional methods in the classroom (Nair, 2000).

Planning for technology and telecommunications calls for highly agile, integrated, virtual, and distance-learning spaces that support and complement the physical "bricks and mortar" school. The challenge for school designers and administrators will be to provide adequate digital, audio, and video connectivity, both wired and wireless, to all parts of the school as well as to home and community environments through the Internet. Schools have connected to, and will continue to connect to, a broad array of tertiary learning environments such as business and community organizations, community colleges, and institutions of higher learning to supplement the curriculum and instruction taking place within their walls (OECD, 1996a).

COMMUNITY SPACES

The twenty-first-century school design takes seriously community use space. Some community spaces being designed into schools include job training facilities, parent information centers, and school-based health centers.

22. Provide Opportunities for Job Training

In many smaller rural communities, the school is the largest public institution in the area, and as such these schools begin to take on social service functions often provided by local government. In larger urban districts, tech-prep and traditional vocational educational programs are being integrated into school-to-work and school-to-career programs offering students opportunities to explore career choices while still in school (OECD, 1996a). In addition, many school districts are forming programmatic linkages between secondary and community college to ease the transition from school to career (OECD, 1995a).

A vital part of overall community learning is that of job preparation and training. When possible, weave program space into the school for job training for the surrounding community and for students. Provide several small interview and assessment spaces, a setting for small-group training activities and projects, and a large general space for support material. Ideally, these job preparation/training spaces should be managed in partnership with local business and industry. Conversely, business and industry sites can be used as extensions of the school for students and community members. When resources are limited, job-training activities could take place in community conferencing space.

23. Provide a Parents Information Center

Research has shown clearly that parental involvement in the school is associated with student success (Berner, 1993; Becher, 1984). Parents who are engaged in their child's school take an active interest in his or her progress. Offering a home base for parents within the walls of the school may create a sense of ownership in the school and encourage parents to stay involved in their child's educational experience. An ideal strategy for supporting parental involvement is to provide a parents information center within the school that is managed and operated directly by parents. The parent information center can serve to help interested parents learn more about the school, to

exchange and share their diverse knowledge and information on any number of topics, to act as a public relations office, and, most important, to act as a home base for parents within the school. Provide a separate entry for the public, a direct link to the school, an informal seating area with information about the school displayed so that visiting parents and the community can get an idea of school activities, and one or more private meeting rooms.

24. Provide Health Care Service Centers

Many schools have realized that they must take on some social service functions to better serve the immediate needs of their learners. Communities throughout the United States have shown an interest in their states establishing school-based health centers (SBHCs). According to a recent survey, SBHCs have grown rapidly over the past decade, from 200 in 1990 to 1,380 in 2000, an increase of almost 600 percent (Center for Health and Health Care in Schools, 2000).

Expanding the old nurse's office into a more comprehensive partnership with local health care providers on the school grounds is one strategy by which schools can respond to the health needs of their learners without taking on the added administrative responsibility of operating the center (OECD, 1995a, 1996a). Consider forming partnerships with local health agencies in providing an on-site health care center for students, parents, and members of the surrounding community. Provide space for a waiting area, separate from the school, and several private individual exam rooms, and a private office for the care provider.

CHARACTER OF ALL SPACES

There are a number of principles that can be applied to any number of spaces within and around the school that have become standard concerns for educators, planners, and designers. Design should take into consideration the scale of the environment as it relates to the developmental needs and capabilities of the learner. School design should consider building systems that promote health by maintaining good indoor air quality, thermal conditions, natural lighting, and acoustical quality.

25. Design Places with Respect for Scale and Developmental Need

No one would doubt that child-scaled and familiar user-friendly spaces are more pleasant and comforting for children and the young (Taylor & Vlastos, 1983; Greenman, 1988). In addition, there is some evidence that "soft" classrooms are related to higher levels of voluntary participation and that overall aesthetic quality in educational facilities is related to students' persistence in task performance.

The size and scale the building, its exterior elements and its interior spaces, make it possible for children to use spaces independently in a manner consistent with their evolving developmental capacities (Harms, Clifford, & Cryer, 1998; Frost, Shin, & Jacobs, 1998). For child-centered spaces, elements and spaces can be smaller and their heights lower to accommodate children. Minimize the institutional character of buildings by creating more intimate spaces. Use natural materials and colors, a variety of forms and textures, vernacular elements, and extensive landscaping to create interesting and engaging spaces (Tanner, 1997; Moore et al., 1979). Comfort for both children and teachers will require some compromises between child, youth, and adult scales.

26. Maximize Natural and Full-Spectrum Lighting

Natural light and artificial full-spectrum lighting has been found to minimize mental fatigue as well as reduce hyperactivity in children (Dunn et al., 1985), while fluorescent lighting is suspected of causing hyperactivity in some children (Ott, 1976). Studies have shown that students tend to react more positively to classrooms that have windows (Grocoff, 1995; Kleiber et al., 1973). By installing full-spectrum lighting and maximizing controlled natural daylighting, schools may not only improve student performance but also achieve more responsible economic and energy-conscious buildings (Tiller, 2000; Dunn et al., 1985; Mayron et al., 1974; Heschong Mahone Group, 1999).

In both new and existing school buildings, maximize task-appropriate lighting, eliminate standard cold-white fluorescent lighting, and emphasize natural and full-spectrum lighting whenever economically possible. When siting the building, face indoor learning spaces toward the most favorable microclimatic directions, for example, south-facing activity spaces leading to outdoor learning areas (Moore & Lackney, 1994).

27. Design Healthy Buildings

Achieving good indoor air quality is as essential as providing comfortable, healthy thermal conditions. Thermal comfort has been shown to influence task performance, attention spans, and levels of discomfort (McGuffey, 1982). Thermal conditions below optimal levels affect dexterity, while higher than optimal temperatures decrease general alertness and increase physiological stress (Cohen et al., 1986). Two types of energy conservation measures (often blamed for so-called sick-building syndrome) have been shown to directly increase indoor air pollutant concentrations: inappropriately reducing ventilation and using sealants and caulks that emit pollutants (Berglund & Lindvall, 1986). These factors may be affecting not only performance but also the overall physical health of children. Children in "sick buildings" have been found to exhibit clear signs of sensory irritation, skin rashes, and mental fatigue—all factors with the potential of decreasing the ability of students to perform (Miller, 1995).

Design environmental control systems to maintain temperatures well within the thermal comfort zone and maximize individual control as much as possible at the site of learning. Strategies for improving indoor air quality include increasing levels of fresh-air intake and increased ventilation rates in buildings. These preventive design measures cost very little and save energy, as well as provide a healthier environment for learners (U.S. Green Building Council, 2003).

28. Design for Appropriate Acoustics

It is well accepted in the scientific community that prolonged exposure to high-intensity noise in community or work settings is often harmful to the health and behavior of large segments of the exposed populations (Nelson, 1997; Cohen et al., 1986). Noise in the learning environment can originate from within as well as from outside the school building and can be both short- and long-term (Evans & Lepore, 1993). Both forms of noise can have major effects on student behavior and, in some cases, achievement. Studies have concluded there are significant increases in blood pressure associated with schools being near noisy urban streets (Evans, Kliewer, & Martin, 1991). Exposure to traffic noise at elementary schools also has been associated with deficits in mental concentration, making more errors on difficult tasks, and the greater likelihood of students' giving up on tasks before the time allocated has expired (Maxwell & Evans, 1998). Noise may, for example, decrease teaching time for forcing teachers to continuously pause or by making it difficult for the student and teacher to hear one another (Picard & Bradley, 1997).

Whenever possible, provide sound-absorbing materials on floors, walls, and ceilings, locate schools away from noisy and congested urban streets, separate active noisy areas in the school from quiet study areas. Within instructional areas provide acoustical barriers that diminish the effects of different sounds, noises, and speech patterns that distract learners from focusing (Maxwell & Evans, 1998). Provide acoustically controlled, well-defined areas within a single instructional area that respond to the special learning activities requiring concentration such as self-directed study and individual reading areas.

SITE DESIGN AND OUTDOOR LEARNING SPACES

A long neglected aspect of the learning environment has been the opportunities presented by the outdoor surroundings of the school building. More than a place to burn off steam, the natural environment has an untapped potential for direct hands-on and project-based learning. Well-designed transitional spaces between the indoor and outdoor environments provide opportunities for learning even in poor weather. Outdoor environments provide opportunities for a variety of learning settings that should be explored by both educators and designers. Finally, providing for safety in playgrounds as well as parking lots should also be planned for.

29. Allow for Transitional Spaces between Indoor and Outdoor Spaces

Learning space within the building should connect to outdoor learning spaces while creating additional transition spaces for school and community activities (Greenman, 1988). Create weather-protected transition spaces between the inside and outside, including porches and decks a minimum of 6 feet in depth that can serve as learning activity spaces in their own right (Moore & Lackney, 1994). Maximize views in and out of the building. Transitional spaces such as overhangs and porches will encourage various levels of learning activities in the outdoors that might not otherwise occur since they offer more opportunities to engage with the natural environment visually, aurally, and kinesthetically (OECD, 1996b).

30. Establish a Variety of Outdoor Learning Environments

Outdoor space can be used for more than simply "burning off energy" before the real studying begins inside. Outdoor settings are often a missed opportunity for learning and can be a valuable resource and laboratory for exploratory learning not possible in built environments. Create spaces outside and adjacent to the building on site or on neighboring sites that mirror learning space within the building.

Locate outdoor play and activity areas on the south of the building to catch as much sun and light as possible, especially in the winter, spring, and fall months (Moore & Lackney, 1994). To maximize the chance of year-round use of parts of the outdoors, create favorable microclimates by protecting outdoor activity areas from prevailing winter winds and from the extreme summer sun while allowing winter sun to penetrate.

As much as possible, learning environments should allow for a variety of learning activities and experiences not available indoors, such as nature trails, gardens, exploratoriums, fields, forested areas, ponds, and other natural outdoor learning settings (Tanner, 2001, Stine, 1997; Brett, Moore, & Provenzo, 1993; Moore, 1990; Moore, Goltsman, & Iacofano, 1992; Kritchevsky, Prescott, & Walling, 1977). In school settings where land is not available, or funds do not allow the creation of outdoor learning environments, the school might take advantage of the local community's existing neighborhood resources, such as parks, public space, walking tours, and community and business establishments. Outdoor activity areas for younger learners, such as in child care facilities, can be modeled after a series of interconnected developmentally appropriate backyards, with resource-rich activity pockets zoned appropriately and linked by "clear circulation that overlooks" (Moore et al., 1979). Provide for a diversity of activities (i.e., not only gross-motor play, but also reading/listening, gardening, and fantasy play) (Olds, 2001).

31. Separate Children and Pedestrians from Vehicles and Service

For purposes of safety, buffer all children and pedestrian areas away from all vehicular and service areas (Olds, 2001; Moore et al., 1979). The building may be the buffer between these zones, with children's activity areas and pedestrian access from the south, vehicular access from the east or west, and service and parking on the north, or the buffer may be created by a combination of landscaping and fencing.

SUMMARY

Thirty-one design principles (categorized into five groupings) for school facilities have been developed to aid school districts and their designers in creating facilities that enhance desired educational outcomes. *Principles for site and building organization* suggest considering how the school will be integrated into the local community. Integration may be achieved by (1) creating schools that serve as community learning centers to educate community members and provide space for community activities; (2) embracing the entire community as a learning environment by developing partnerships with zoos, museums, and similar local resources and by sharing facilities (e.g., auditoriums and gymnasiums); and (3) providing design diversity while respecting the contextual compatibility of the school with the surrounding neighborhoods. Other design principles include (4) creating smaller schools (or schools within schools) to potentially increase student participation in extracurricular activities, reduce crime, and improve academic achievement; (5) using the home as a template for school designs to create more homelike environments (e.g., enclosed "backyards"), to ease the transition from home to school; (6) meandering circulation spaces to provide areas conducive to informal meetings and other types of unique learning activities; and (7) designing safe schools, perhaps utilizing access control, natural surveillance by students and teachers, and territory definition by using strategies to distinguish public and private areas.

Principles for primary education suggest that consideration be given to (1) clustering learning areas around a core of shared spaces and resources, such as teacher offices, a computer hub, and conference space; (2) providing additional spaces where instructional resources are shared (e.g., specialized libraries, special equipment); and (3) providing a variety of types of learning spaces. Also, (4) class sizes should be kept small (approximately twelve to sixteen in early childhood and elementary grades, sixteen to twenty in middle school, and twenty to twenty-four in high school) to improve academic performance, particularly among disadvantaged populations; (5) activity pockets that are well defined and rich in resources may increase student performance, social interaction, and satisfaction; and (6) a home base (more than just a locker in a corridor) where students feel that a sense of ownership is important to students' individuality and sense of self-worth. School districts should also consider (7) programmatic and physical integration with a child care center and early development center to ease transitions for young students and to assist teenage mothers with completing their education; (8) providing teachers with spaces, such as private or semiprivate offices as appropriate, to indicate that they are valued as professionals; and (9) providing studio areas and laboratories for project-based learning activities where students can develop semester-long projects and student portfolios, work in groups, and demonstrate scientific discoveries. Finally, to encourage administrative leadership, a school system may consider (10) decentralizing administrative functions, both physically and organizationally (e.g., through the use of student advisors).

Principles of shared school and community resources suggest that the school may (1) establish a community forum by providing public assembly spaces with a "town-square" quality and/or (2) provide community conference space for community meetings and special events. Schools may also include (3) privacy niches that are relaxing, nonthreatening, and comfortable for visitors, teachers, and students to use and they must consider how they will (4) incorporate information technology contained in virtual learning environments into the physical school facility.

To better integrate the school facility with the surrounding community, *community spaces* may be provided, including (1) spaces for job training and job preparation areas, ideally managed in partnership with local business and industry, (2) a parents' information center to increase parental involvement, and (3) health care service centers, in partnership with local health care providers, to provide on-site health care for students, teachers, parents, and community members.

Design *principles of the character of all spaces* target strategies designed to ensure that learning environments promote age-appropriate development and good health. These include (1) ensuring that the size and scale of the facility, both exterior and interior, are appropriate and comfortable; (2) maximizing the use of natural and full-spectrum lighting through building orientation, daylighting controls, and fixture/bulb selection; (3) designing healthy buildings with good indoor air quality and comfortable temperatures; and (4) designing buildings with good acoustics to minimize unwanted distraction and to improve communication among occupants.

Principles of site design and outdoor learning spaces highlight the importance of (1) transitional spaces, such as porches and decks, between the indoors and outdoors in which learning activities may occur; (2) varied outdoor spaces, such as fields, ponds, nature trails, and play areas to provide learning activities and experiences that are unavailable indoors; and (3) separating children and pedestrians from vehicular traffic for safety.

ACTIVITIES

1. Think about your own experiences as a student or teacher, particularly with respect to the design principles discussed in this chapter (e.g., healthy buildings, studio spaces). Write a description of the best physical learning environment you experienced and what physical factors contributed to making that learning environment successful. Also, describe the worst learning environment you experienced, as well as the physical conditions that seemed to stifle the learning process.

2. There are several principles throughout the five categories described in this chapter that address school integration with the local community. Describe physical and organizational strategies that may encourage greater interaction among local businesses and students.

3. Describe an ideal outdoor learning environment for either the elementary, middle, or high school level. How might you, as a participant on a design team, convince a school system to allocate money to create such an environment?

REFERENCES AND BIBLIOGRAPHY

Print Sources

Achilles, C. M. (September 1992). The effect of school size on student achievement and the interaction of small classes and school size on student achievement. Unpublished manuscript, Department of Educational Administration, University of North Carolina-Greensboro, Greensboro, NC.

The Architectural League of New York & Public Education Association (1992). *New schools for New York: Plans and precedents for small schools*. The Architectural League of New York, The Public Education Association. New York: Princeton Architectural Press.

Barker, R., & Gump, P. V. (1964). *Big school, small school*. Palo Alto, CA: Stanford University Press.

Becher, R. M. *Parent involvement: A review of research and principles of successful practice*. Urbana, IL: ERIC Clearinghouse on Elementary and Early Childhood Education, 1984 (ED 247 032).

Berglund, B., & Lindvall, T. (1986). Sensory reactions to sick buildings. *Environment International*, 12, pp. 147–159.

Berner, M. M. (April 1993). Building conditions, parental involvement, and student achievement in the District of Columbia Public School System. *Urban Education*, 28(1), pp. 6–29.

Bingler, S., Quinn, L., and Sullivan, K. (December 2003). *Schools as centers of community: A citizen's guide for planning and design*, 2nd ed. Washington, DC: U.S. Department of Education.

Bourke, S. (1986). How smaller is better: Some relationships between class size, teaching practices, and student achievement. *American Educational Research Journal*, 23(4), pp. 558–571.

Bredekamp, S., & Copple, C. (1997). *Developmentally appropriate practice in early childhood programs*. New York: National Association for the Education of Young Children (NAEYC).

Brett, A., Moore, R. C., & Provenzo, E. F., Jr. (1993). *The complete playground book*. New York: Syracuse University Press.

Bridges, E. M. (1992). *Problem-based learning for administrators*. Eugene: ERIC Clearinghouse on Educational Management, University of Oregon.

Brubaker, W. C. (1998). *Planning and designing schools*. New York: McGraw-Hill.

Chupela, D. (1994). Ready, set, go!: Children's programming for bookmobiles and other small spaces. Atkinson, WI: Alleyside Press.

Cohen, S., Evans, G. W., Stokols, D., & Krantz, D. S. (1986). *Behavior, health, and environmental stress*. New York: Plenum.

Costa, A. L., & Liebmann, R. M. (1997). *Supporting the spirit of learning: When process is content*. New York: Corwin.

Cornell, D. G. (1999). *Designing safer schools for Virginia: A guide to keeping students safe from violence*. Charlottesville, VA: Thomas Jefferson Center for Educational Design.

Crowe, T. D. (2000). *Crime prevention through environmental design: Applications of architectural design and space management concepts*. National Crime Prevention Institute. Boston: Butterworth-Heinemann.

Crumpacker, S. S. (1995). *Using cultural information to create schools that work*. In Meek, A. (ed.), *Designing places for learning*. Alexandria, VA: Association for Supervision and Curriculum Development, pp. 31–42.

Decker, L. E., & Romney, V. A. (August 1994). *Educational restructuring and the community education process*. A special report of the National Coalition for Community Education. Fairfax, VA: National Community Education Association.

DeJong, W. S. (June 1997). Building change into new buildings. *The School Administrator*, pp. 10–12.

Dempsey, J. D., & Frost, J. L. (1993). Play environments in early childhood education. In Spodek, B. (ed.), *Handbook of research on the education of young children*. New York: Macmillan, pp. 306–321.

Dunn, R., Krimsky, J. S., Murray, J. B., & Quinn, P. J. (May 1985). Light up their lives: A review of research on the effects of lighting on children's achievement and behavior. *The Reading Teacher*, (39)19, pp. 863–869.

English, F. W. (ed.) (2005). *Handbook of educational leadership: New dimensions and realities*. Thousand Oaks, CA: Sage.

Evans, G. W., & Lepore, S. J. (1993). Nonauditory effects of noise on children: A critical review. *Children's Environments*, 10(1), pp. 31–51.

Evans, G. W., & Maxwell, L. (1997). Chronic noise exposure and reading deficits: The mediating effects of language acquisition. *Environment and Behavior*, 29(5), pp. 638–656.

Evans, G. W., Kliewer, W., & Martin, J. (1991). The role of the physical environment in the health and well-being of children. In Schroeder, H. E. (ed.), *New directions in health psychology assessment*. New York: Hemisphere, pp. 127–157.

Fanning/Howey Associates (1995). *Community use of schools: Facility design perspectives*. Celina, OH: Fanning/Howey Associates.

Feinberg, S., Kuchner, J. F., & Feldman, S. (1998). *Learning environments for young children: Rethinking library spaces and services*. Chicago: American Library Association.

Finn, J. D., & Achilles, C. M. (1990). Answers and questions about class size: A statewide experiment. *American Educational Research Journal*, 27(3), pp. 557–577.

Fowler, W. J., Jr. (1992). What do we know about school size? What should we know? Paper presented to the American Educational Research Association Annual Meeting, San Francisco, CA. Available from the Office of Educational Research and Improvement, National Center for Educational Statistics, U.S. Department of Education, Washington, DC.

Frost, J. L., Shin, D., & Jacobs, P. (1998). Physical environments and children's play. In Saracho, O. N. & Spodek, B. (eds.), *Multiple perspectives on play in early childhood education*. New York: State University of New York Press, pp. 225–294.

Garbarino, J. (1980). Some thoughts on school size and its effects on adolescent development. *Journal of Youth and Adolescence*, 9, pp. 19–31.

Gardner, H. (1993). *Multiple intelligences: The theory in practice*. New York: Basic Books.

Graves, B. E. (1993). *School ways: The planning and design of America's schools*. New York: McGraw-Hill.

Greenman, J. (1988). *Caring spaces, learning places: Childrens' environments that work*. Redmond, WA: Exchange Press.

Harms, T. (1994). Humanizing infant environments for group care. *Children's Environments*, 2, pp. 155–167.

Harms, T., Clifford, R. M., & Cryer, D. (1998). *The early childhood environment rating scale*, rev. ed. New York: Teachers College Press.

Hill, A. B., Cohen, U., & McGinty, T. (1979). *Recommendations for child care centers*. Report No. R79-2, Center for Architecture & Urban Planning Research, University of Wisconsin-Milwaukee.

Johnson, S. M. (1990). *Teachers, power, and school change*. Cambridge, MA: Harvard University Press.

Jones, E., & Nimmo, J. (1994). *Emergent curriculum*. New York: National Association for the Education of Young Children (NAEYC).

Kennedy, M., & Argon, J. (October 1999). Bridging the digital divide. *American School and University*, 72(2), pp. 16–18, 20, 22.

Kleiber, D., et al. (1973). *Environmental illumination and human behavior: The effects of spectrum light sources on human performance in a university setting*. Ithaca, NY: Cornell University Press.

Kritchevsky, S., Prescott, E., & Walling, L. (1977). *Planning environments for young children: Physical space*. Washington, DC: National Association for the Education of Young Children (NAEYC).

Loo, C. (1976). *The effects of spatial density on behavior types of children*. Bethesda, MD: ERIC, National Institute of Mental Health.

Mayron, L. W., Ott, J., Nations, R., Mayron, E. (1974). Light, radiation and academic behavior. *Academic Therapy*, 40, pp. 33–47.

McGuffey, C. W. (1982). Facilities. In Walberg, H. J. (ed.), *Improving educational standards and productivity: The research basis for policy*. Berkeley, CA: McCutchan Publishing, pp. 237–288.

McMillan, D. (1997). *Classroom spaces and learning places: How to arrange your room for maximum learning*. Charthage, IL: Teaching & Learning Company.

Meek, A. (ed.) (1995). *Designing places for learning*. Alexandria, VA: Association for Supervision and Curriculum Development.

Miller, N. L. (1995). *The healthy school handbook: Conquering the sick building syndrome and other environmental hazards in and around your school*. Washington, DC: National Education Association Professional Library Publication.

Moore, G. T. (1986). Effects of the spatial definition of behavior settings on children's behavior: A quasi-experimental field study. *Journal of Environmental Psychology*, 6, pp. 205–231.

Moore, G. T., & Lackney, J. A. (1994). *Educational facilities for the twenty-first century: Research analysis and design patterns*. Report No. R94-1, School of Architecture and Urban Planning, Center for Architecture and Urban Planning Research, University of Wisconsin-Milwaukee.

Moore, G. T., Lane, C. G., Hill, A. B., Cohen, U., & McGinty, T. (1979). *Recommendations for child care centers.* Report No. R79-2, Center for Architecture & Urban Planning Research, University of Wisconsin-Milwaukee.

Moore, R. C. (1990). *Childhood's domain: Play and place in child development.* Berkeley, CA: MIG Communications.

Moore, R. C., Goltsman, S. M., & Iacofano, D. S. (1992). *Play for all guidelines: Planning, design and management of outdoor play settings for all children.* Berkeley, CA: MIG Communications.

Nye, B. A., Achilles, C. M., Zacharias, J. B., Fulton, B. D., & Wallenhorst, M. P. (November 1992). Smaller is far better: A report on three class-size imitative, Paper No. 5, Center of Excellence for Research in Basic Skills, Tennessee State University. Paper presented to the Mid-South Educational Research Association, Knoxville, TN.

OECD (1995a). *Schools for cities.* PEB Papers. Paris: Programme on Educational Building, Organization for Economic Co-operation and Development.

OECD (1995b). *Redefining the place to learn.* PEB Papers. Paris: Programme on Educational Building, Organization for Economic Co-operation and Development.

OECD (1996a). *Making better use of school buildings.* PEB Papers. Paris: Programme on Educational Building, Organization for Economic Co-operation and Development.

OECD (1996b). *Schools for today and tomorrow.* PEB Papers. Paris: Programme on Educational Building, Organization for Economic Co-operation and Development.

Olds, A. R. (2001). *Child care design guide.* Washington, DC: McGraw-Hill.

Ott, J. N. (August/September 1976). Influence of fluorescent lights on hyperactivity and learning disabilities. *Journal of Learning Disabilities*, 9(7), pp. 22–27.

Raywid, M. A. (1999). *Current literature on small schools.* ERIC Digest. Charleston, WV. (ED425049 99). ERIC Clearinghouse on Rural Education and Small Schools.

Sanoff, H., & Sanoff, J. (1988). *Learning environments for children. A developmental approach to shaping activity areas.* Humanics Learning.

Schneider, T., Walker, H., & Sprague, J. (2000). *Safe school design: A handbook for educational leaders.* University of Oregon, Eugene: ERIC Clearinghouse on Educational Management.

Schon, D. A. (1983). *The reflective practitioner: How professionals think in action.* London: Temple Smith.

Stine, S. (1997). *Landscapes for learning: Creating outdoor environments for children and youth.* New York: John Wiley & Sons.

Stuebing, S., Wolfshorndl, A., Cousineau, L. K., DiPetrillo, S. E. (1995). *Redefining the place to learn.* Paris: Programme on Educational Building, Organization for Economic Cooperation and Development.

Tanner, C. K. (2001). Into the woods, wetlands, and prairies. *Educational Leadership*, 58(7), pp. 64–66.

Taylor, A., & Vlastos, G. (1983). *School zone: Learning environments for children.* Corrales, NM: School Zone, Inc.

Tiller, D. K. (2000). Lighting recommendations. In Spengler, J. D., Samet, J. M., & McCarthy, J. F. (eds.), *Indoor air quality handbook.* New York: McGraw-Hill, pp. 18.1–18.22.

U.S. Green Building Council (February 2003). *Building momentum: National trends and prospects for high-performance green buildings.* Washington, DC: USGBC.

Warner, C., & Curry, M. (1997). *Everybody's house: The schoolhouse, best techniques for connecting home, school and community.* Thousand Oaks, CA: Corwin Press.

Weinstein, C. S. (1996). *Secondary classroom management: Lessons from research and practice.* New York: McGraw-Hill.

Weinstein, C. S., & Mignano, A. J., Jr. (1997). *Elementary classroom management: Lessons from research and practice.* New York: McGraw-Hill.

Internet Sources

Butterfield, E. (May 1999). Planning today for tomorrow's technology. DesignShare. http://www.designshare.com/Research/Meeks/MeeksTech1.htm.

The Center for Health and Health Care in Schools (2000). School-based health centers: Results from a 50-state survey, school year 1999–2000. http://www.healthinschools.org/sbhcs/survey2000.htm.

Coburn, J. (January 1999). Childcare in high school. School planning and management. http://www.spmmag.com/articles/1999_01Jan/ChildCare.html.

Department of Education & Department of Justice (August 1998). Early warning, timely response: A guide to safe schools. http://www.ed.gov/offices/OSERS/OSEP/earlywrn.html.

Department of Education (April 1998). Class size and students at risk: What is known? What is next? http://www.ed.gov/pubs/ClassSize/.

Department of Education (March 1999). Reducing class size: What do we know? http://www.ed.gov/pubs/ReducingClass/.

Duke, D. L. (February 1999). The future of high schools: What will secondary education look like in the next century? Texas A&M University, CRS Center. http://archone.tamu.edu/~crscenter/programs/Rowlett99/FutureOfHighSchools.html.

Fielding, R. (August 1999). Planning the learning community: An interview with Concordia's Steven Bingler. http://www.designshare.com/Research/Bingler/LearningCommunity1.htm.

Grocoff, P. N. (December 1995). Electric lighting and daylighting in schools. Council of Educational Facility Planners International (CEFPI) Issue Track. http://www.cefpi.com.

Heschong Mahone Group (August 1999). Daylighting in schools: An investigation into the relationship between daylighting and human performance. Daylighting Initiative, the Pacific Gas and Electric Company on behalf of the California Board for Energy Efficiency Third Party Program. http://www.pge.com/pec/daylight/schoolc.pdf.

Hodgin, P. A. (January 1998). District wide planning: Schools as community resources. AIArchitect. http://www.e-architect.com/pia/cae/distwide.asp.

Howley, C. (June 1994). The academic effectiveness of small-scale schooling (an update). ERIC Digest ED372897. http://7-12educators.about.com/education/primseced/7-12educators/msub10.htm?COB= home&terms=downsizing.

Irmsher, K. (1997). School size. ERIC Digest, ED414615 97. http://www.ed.gov/databases/ERIC_Digests/ed414615.html.

Lackney, J. A. (August 1999). A history of the studio-based learning model. Educational Design Institute. http://schoolstudio.engr.wisc.edu/studiobasedlearning.html.

Lashway, L. (Winter 1998–99). School size: Is smaller better? Research Roundup 15, 2, ERIC Clearinghouse on Educational Management. http://eric.uoregon.edu/publications/roundup/W98-99.html.

Maxwell, L., & Evans, G. W. (1998). Design of child care centers and effects of noise on young children. http://www.designshare.com/Research/LMaxwell/NoiseChildren.htm.

NAEYC (1999). Reducing class size: A goal for children's champions. National Association for the Education of Young Children. http://www.naeyc.org/public_affairs/pubaff_index.htm.

Nair, P. (July 2000). Schools for the 21st century: Are you ready? DesignShare. http://www.designshare.com/Research/nair/15%20rules.htm.

Nelson, P. B. (June 7, 1997). Impact of hearing loss on children in typical school environments. Lay paper presented at Acoustical Society of America 133rd Meeting, State College, PA. http://www.acoustics.org/133rd/2paaa2.html.

NSBN (January 2000). The development of educational facilities through joint use mechanisms. New Schools/Better Neighborhoods Joint Use Working Group. http://www.nsbn.org/symposium/01_21_00/report.html.

Picard, M., & Bradley, J. B. (June 7, 1997). Revisiting speech interference by noise in classrooms and considering some possible solutions. Lay paper presented at Acoustical Society of America 133rd Meeting, State College, PA. http://www.acoustics.org/133rd/2paaa3.html.

Safer places: The crime prevention through environmental design resource site. http://www.arch.vt.edu/crimeprev/pages/home.html.

Sanborn, F. (1997). How to choose learning stations & seating for your technology-based classroom. NCSA/NCREL & ITEG, LLC. http://www.ncsa.uiuc.edu/idt/html/learnstat.html.

Tanner, C. K. (1997). Chart of architectural/natural support systems for school design and construction. University of Georgia. http://www.coe.uga.edu/sdpl/archives.html#anchor1107537.

U.S. Department of Education. (April 1999). Design principles for planning schools as centers of community. http://www.edfacilities.org/ir/edprinciples.html.

U.S. GSA. (June 1998). Child care center design guide. U.S. General Services Administration, Public Buildings Service, Child Care Center of Expertise. http://www.gsa.gov/pbs/centers/child/childcare.pdf.

PART II

EDUCATIONAL FACILITIES PLANNING

This volume is designed for architects that build schools, educational leaders, and all other individuals involved and interested in educational facilities planning, design, construction, and management. We began the work with an introduction to educational architecture (Part I); and have postulated that there is a gap in conceptualization of educational learning environments between educational leaders and architects. It is our intention to minimize this gap by presenting trends in architecture, first, followed by an integration of principles of planning and architecture. There is more literature addressing educational planning than educational architecture available to the clients of educational architecture. Furthermore, because the clients of educational architecture outnumber the architects, we describe and explain the lesser-known topic first, followed by the more widely known methods of educational facilities planning. Finally, these two areas of thought are integrated in this text as a means to diminish the gap between planning and architecture.

We suggest that by knowing about the history of educational architecture found in Chapter 1, all people involved in the exciting process of developing educational learning environments will have a better foundation for the context of activities necessary to complete the process of developing educational facilities. Once the context is explored, we suggest that people involved in educational fa-

cilities planning will benefit from our review of general design principles in Chapter 2 that guide the early stages of planning and programming.

Providing good school architecture is one of the most significant contributions we make to our children and community. The architecture of educational facilities is, in effect, a community policy statement on the importance of education and students, and the quality of school architecture reveals the culture of the people who plan, design, and build the school. School facilities should reflect sound teaching and learning philosophies, but this may not always be the case in some school districts. Although some people may argue that the physical quality and educational compatibility of school facilities in communities are tied directly to the monetary wealth of each district, it is not difficult to find poor physical quality and design in affluent school districts, while good schools may also be found in districts having less wealth.

Ideally, planning and designing educational facilities require the involvement of people representing the school and community, with state representatives playing the role of regulators according to published minimum standards. With a team planning effort, a new school facility or a renovated structure can be a relevant place for learning, housing spaces that actually "facilitate" the school curriculum. Without a team effort, the resulting school architecture may represent the wishes of only a few individuals. Such spaces will often represent the values and beliefs of public officials elected or appointed for short, incremental periods of time. Yet, the school facility is expected to serve the community for fifty or more years. Often, there are stakeholders in key decision-making roles that may be led to the building of schools having low-quality construction, in the shortest time possible, and at the lowest bid. Occasionally, these stakeholders do not envision the critical importance of value engineering, the curriculum compatibility of the school, the design, or construction quality—all strategies that would provide the very outcome they seek. Decision makers need to understand that the schools they build now speak to the community long after the individuals who planned, designed, and built them are gone from public office. Schools are monuments to the culture.

To take advantage of scarce community resources, governing boards of schools, when making deliberate moves to provide constructed and natural spaces for learning, should work according to a comprehensive school and community plan—a plan that has been fully integrated into all other aspects of local and regional planning efforts. Such regional plans include, for example, the location, magnitude, and impact of airports, power plants, farms, forests, shopping malls, highways, parks, commercial and industrial developments, residential sections of the community, and other aspects of local and regional growth or decline. Places for the school curriculum and learning environments should, whenever possible, be planned, designed, and constructed with knowledge of formalized local and regional plans, a sound philosophy of teaching and student learning practices, plus knowledge of environmental psychology.

One purpose of this section is to outline a framework for planning and design that is validated through research, the literature, and the experiences of successful practitioners in the field. Another purpose is to review highlights of the educational facility planning and design process as it has evolved over the past fifty years. Our goal is to describe and explain a conceptual framework that integrates the multiple perspectives of educational planners, designers, architects, and the public. The model presented in Chapter 3 is expected to serve as a conceptual guide for connecting the complex aspects of educational facilities planning.

A PROCEDURAL MODEL FOR DEVELOPING EDUCATIONAL FACILITIES

A model involving major aspects of developing, providing, and maintaining school learning environments in the public education sector of the United States is introduced in this chapter. It is derived partially from the literature, while giving special consideration to our personal experiences in the planning, conceptual and architectural design, construction, and management phases of school buildings and outdoor learning environments. We contend that such a model is needed because the school and community must see school facilities as environments having specific influence on learning experiences and student–teacher behavior. This is especially true if we are to grow beyond what Bingler (1995) called conventional wisdom. "The conventional wisdom . . . is that educational facilities simply provide the containers in which learning occurs, but that the form of the containers, and even the process of making them, has little to contribute to the real purpose of education, which centers around the curriculum and instruction delivered by the educator and received by the student" (p. 23). Perhaps we can somehow flavor conventional wisdom with research-based wisdom.

We envision a comprehensive model having a wide application to various school systems—large, small, rural, urban, or suburban. As in all situations pertaining to the complex process of developing and providing school facilities, finding resources and relevant information is the main concern. Therefore, *one assumption for a comprehensive model is availability of relevant information and resources for planning and decision making*. Relevant information is not enough, however. The interpretation of the relevant information, in light of political and shared decision-making reality, becomes cumbersome, requiring a structure that encompasses social design theory—working with people rather than for them and involving them in critical, relevant aspects of the process.

With the available textual materials, including this book, and Internet search engines, information on almost any planning topic may be easily retrieved. However, sometimes Internet information is incomplete and too condensed to be of real value, but as in condensed hard copy publications, most websites offer some useful information. The conceptual planning model that we propose here will be effective if the correct data and information are collected, analyzed, interpreted, and properly utilized in the process. Proper utilization of information encompasses the perceptual, political, and leadership aspects applied to the process as well as the technical skills of the people involved. For example, will the governing board, the state, the architect, the planner, and the community understand the importance of learning activities involving various philosophies? Or, will only one philosophy dominate? Consider essentialism, for example. Historically, some school leaders may have been educated under the "blank tablet" method—teachers lectured and students listened and responded through pencil-and-paper tests as measures of learning and accountability. If decision makers favoring the essentialism philosophy or any other single philosophy dominate the decision process, then the community could be left with a school facility accommodating only one way of thinking for fifty years or more. Therefore, one important aspect of developing facilities is educating decision makers regarding teaching and learning. The process of providing decision-making bodies with a balanced perspective requires strong leadership from the planning team and school leaders.

PREMISES

Since a primary concern for any model is its basis, we offer eight foundational premises for developing school facilities. These are appropriately integrated throughout the book to provide connections and clarify relationships among the various functions of the planning model.

Premise 1: *Strong Leadership Is Essential*

Furthermore, the importance of leaders knowing about the impact of school facilities on student behavior and learning is vital. It is significant that the leader should create an atmosphere where people within the organization can assist in the complex job of developing school facilities. Individuals in charge of developing, providing, and managing school facilities should be knowledgeable in the basic aspects of school facilities and also be able to communicate the goals of education and the nature of the relationship between the community and the school. They must have the ability to lead the school system toward its ideals. Those in leader-

ship have inherent responsibilities to the public they serve. Exactly who takes the lead depends on precisely where the process is within the context of all activities necessary to design and build a school. For example, the curriculum planner might not be the best person to lead a group on school funding. Leadership may be situational as the various tasks are addressed in the development process. However, it is usually the chief school officer who makes recommendations to the governing board, the final decision-making body.

Premise 2: *The School System Has a Defined Direction—a Mission and a Vision*

We assume that the people in leadership have developed strategies to actualize this direction. The mission and vision must be clearly defined and understood by the school and community, especially when school development is on the agenda. Above all, direction must include basic concerns for school facilities planning and design—a vision for learning and teaching. Somehow, within the mission statement and master plan for school leadership we must see that educational facilities exist to contribute to the accomplishment of the mission. We must work to ensure the connections among student behavior and learning and the natural and constructed learning environments. Lack of this connection may represent a 'black hole' in our educational system.

Premise 3: *Long-Range Goals and Objectives Are Established*

Because schools may last for fifty years or more, they should be seen as community resources and architecture. Therefore, long-range planning means searching for various possibilities in terms of program and economics—cost-benefit analysis of all phases of a capital project need to be specified as a requirement in the long-range plan. Expected student enrollment and value engineering are examples of two important aspects in the decision-making process for future school building projects, helping to circumvent errors that reduce benefits to learning, and that minimize overall costs. But, long-range planning may be difficult to maintain in an atmosphere where school boards serve short terms, and chief school officers have high turnover rates. It becomes the responsibility of the community to guarantee that long-range goals and objectives are monitored and revised as leadership changes occur.

We all know of sudden changes in direction of goals and possible reorganization when leadership at the top changes. These changes certainly influence the development of school facilities. When a new school superintendent is employed, we often hear about "reorganization and redirection." According to Townsend (1971), reorganizing should be undergone about as often as major surgery. He exhorts the wisdom of Petronius Arbiter who stated, "I was to learn in life that we tend to meet each new situation by reorganizing; and a wonderful method it can be for creating the illusion of progress while producing confusion, inefficiency, and demoralization" (p. 146).

Premise 4: *Goals and Objectives Are Translated into Physical Places and Spaces for Teaching and Learning*

Planners and architects should clearly understand what the implications for the curriculum and instructional program are with respect to school learning environments. The physical environment does influence student behavior; therefore, learning is also influenced. The places where students learn are important elements of curriculum and instruction, and should be addressed in research and professional conferences on leadership, curriculum, and supervision of instruction.

Activities pertaining to premise 4 have been called the "educational programming" phase and extend all the way into design development and construction documents. The curriculum will certainly change and the way teachers are expected to teach will also change over the life of a school. Therefore, a review of the present and expected curriculum and instructional program is important to prevent obsolescence of the school in relationship to course content, student learning, and teaching methods. Such concerns bring up the need to plan for flexible and developmentally appropriate learning spaces, school furniture, and technology.

Premise 5: *Planning and Design Activities Are Integrated*

While the majority of planning methods found in the historical literature are linear, the model suggested here is comprehensive, allowing for interaction across leadership and stakeholder lines. We concur with McGuffey (1973), who suggested that "careful management of the planning, design, and construction processes will provide for a comprehensive, overlapping, non-linear approach to the delivery of a facilities project" (p. 24). The management of time for planning, designing, bidding, and constructing the project is vital. Hence, we suggest a modified version of Kowalski's (1989) idea of an integrated planning model. This modification includes the leadership component; a data, resources, and information base; and the specified involvement of the community and educators. Moor and Lackney (1994) proposed a similar procedure entitled an "integrated educational facility development model" (p. 84).

Integration means more than compressing the time between steps. It also means shared decision making and collaboration in both the educational planning, programming, and concept design phases. The distance between planning and concept design represents perhaps the largest gap in the entire school facilities planning and building process. Often, people in the school and community have complained that they participated in planning and concept design, but when the school buildings were completed, they were shocked to see nothing of their work. This should never occur, given proper leadership and information in the world of school facilities today. Our model encourages and requires involvement in planning, programming, and concept design and continues through the design and construction phases.

Premise 6: *Management Is Systematic: Data- and Goal-Driven*

The minimization of crisis occurrence through effective crisis management is greatly needed in the information age. The management system should include accountability, the comparison of stated goals to outcomes. This is the glue that holds together the organization. Sometimes the manager is a leader, and sometimes the leader is a manager. Managers and leaders must know what is to be done, have a strategy ready to do what is planned, and recognize how the final outcomes compare with the expected outcomes. They also must recognize that the landscape for developing and providing schools is often confusing and messy.

The development model we introduce here should help produce schools that meet the goals of learning and teaching. The performance of even the constructed environment can be measured in terms of stated goals and objectives. Although measurements of effectiveness may be taken in postoccupancy evaluations, this activity may be too late if a design is then shown not to facilitate learning and teaching. The political reality is that unless all parties share the stated goals for learning and teaching students in the beginning of the process, the end results may not be built environments that facilitate the educational goals and objectives. We all know stories of a project in which architectural plans were not completely followed because the contractor did not want to build in a certain way—leaving out a window here and there, failing to put a vent in a certain space, and skimping on acoustical and insulation treatments, for example. General management goes beyond the planning, design, and construction phases in providing school facilities. It encompasses the messy political environment of these activities. Under the general umbrella of management, we find operations and maintenance of the structures and land that supports the buildings, playgrounds, nature trails, and other outdoor learning environments. Management of operations and maintenance starts with planning and design.

Premise 7: *The Demand for Resources Is Greater Than Those Available*

Hence, the goal is to maximize the returns to the community with the available resources. To maximize returns we must know, among other things, just how the physical environment influences teaching, students, learning, and behavior; and employ value engineering strategies during planning and design. It does not require any new knowledge to build a set of rectangular one-room schoolhouses without windows, divided by a not too wide hallway, and call the result a new school. With some variations in color and roof pitch, we all have seen such structures even called "schools of the future." Yes, they are schools of the future, if the community does not expect much from its students.

Acquisition of fiscal resources is vital, since this function dominates all planning, design, and construction activities. Recently, state and federal education policies have given much attention to financing school construction. Even with more focus on the financing of school building projects, educational administrators are often more interested in securing funds than in ensuring that the needs of educational program are met in building design and the management of operations and maintenance. Efficient and effective use of capital is expected, including the investment of time, personnel, and labor that goes into the whole process of planning, building, and maintaining a school and its surrounding property. The goal is to produce a structurally sound and educationally efficient, accountable, reasonable, and thrifty product, including outdoor learning areas. The educationally efficient aspect of school buildings can only be met if the built design accommodates the educational program and caters to learning and teaching. The words "thrifty" and "reasonable" do not necessarily mean cheap, and "efficient" does not mean cutting out necessary spaces and places for learning. After all, the building must be accountable to the educational program, while reflecting fiscal responsibility.

Premise 8: *Collaboration and Cooperation Between the School and Community Are Essential*

The school and community should work in a collaborative manner to ensure that schools are designed and built to enhance teaching and learning and serve as centers of the community. Essentials such as a safe context and the safety and security of the teachers and students are the expected natural by-products of this process. Community involvement allows for ease of "buying into" the project and its outcomes. Sanoff (2000) has provided one of the most comprehensive descriptions of community participation in print today. Under the topic "scope of social architecture," he notes that participation is necessary for transforming the environment and people that live in it. It is highly important in school facilities planning that the community not be treated as passive clients, but as involved consumers.

Myers and Robertson (2004) offer several suggestions for community connections involving stakeholders, emphasizing the benefits of community involvement. Their models run parallel to strategic planning methods that may be employed in most stages of school facilities planning, but exactly how aspects of strategic planning can become an integral part of the process can take many paths. Regardless of the path or model selected for involvement, an ultimate goal is to influence change in school design that matches and facilitates the changing curriculum.

CONNECTIONS IN THE DEVELOPMENT MODEL

While many of the planning models that we found in the review of literature suggested various collaborative procedures, they were actually linear or circular presentations of required activities with

steps delineated to drive them sequentially. Some were integrated. For example, McGuffey (1973), Kowalski (1989), and Moor and Lackney (1994) presented models suggesting integration of process and information and interaction among all the players and systems involved in building a school. Earthman (2000a) outlined the positive and negative aspects of collaborative planning for school facilities, noting that "cooperation between agencies and levels of government has long been viewed as advantageous to the community and at the same time a good use of limited resources" (p. 2). Taylor (2000) emphasized the involvement of communities, and stated "communities seeking to design schools for the future must think in an integrated manner to join the goals of education to those of architectural design" (p. 3).

Our model draws heavily from these writers, while adding emphasis to the use of expertise, information, resources, and data and to the whole spectrum of participation of the school and community, especially in the planning, programming, and concept design process. McGuffey (1973) saw planning educational facilities as an input, process, and output system, with significant interrelationships and data sharing among the school facility planners, the school district, and all the other schools within the district. We contend that these relationships also extend to the state where the school is located and even to the federal level in the United States through laws, codes, and restrictions, especially in the field of special education. There are six broad assumptions supporting the structure of the development model:

1. The total facilities program in a school district is planned and managed to advance the mission of the school, with emphasis on student learning and teaching.
2. All students can learn in a developmentally appropriate environment.
3. The development of schools always occurs in the context of local, state, and federal regulatory policies, including funding methods and all legal aspects of providing school learning environments.

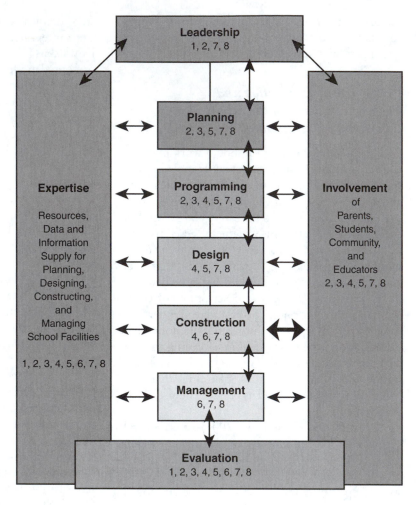

FIGURE 3.1 A procedural model for developing educational facilities.

4. The development of educational facilities is a continuous process; therefore, the school system is always accruing data and information relevant to all aspects of this complex process.
5. The outcomes of the model are safe, comfortable, and developmentally appropriate learning environments for teaching and learning in a multicultural society.
6. An ample supply of relevant information and resources for planning and decision making is available.

Figure 3.1 is a representation of a procedural model for planning and designing educational facilities, with evaluation as a continuous process throughout. Horizontal oval designs show the process of planning in a linear and interactive mode, while the vertical ovals represent sources of information, expertise, and involvement. The shadowed, dark arrows depict the responsibility and involvement of people and groups in the designated process, while the larger light-shadowed arrows depict interaction and involvement. For example, there may be involvement of parents, students, community members, and educators in the construction process (citizens' oversight committee), but often experts having resources, skills, and data will be involved in the construction phase without much input from the community. Construction is a direct responsibility of people in leadership positions, while resulting from the planning, programming, and design phases.

Data and information are crucial to developing and maintaining schools that facilitate teaching and learning. Quality and flow of information and how it is shared among the many individuals involved in providing school facilities are essential for people in leadership positions, as well as for those that participate in the process. Leadership, the major premise, also performs a significant function in the model, indicating the importance of direction, vision, mission, decision making, and allocation of resources. Leadership is found at all levels, indicating shared vision and responsibility as various jobs emerge in this complex process. Notwithstanding, the final decision always rests with the governing board and the chief school officer. The chief school officer is directly responsible for the outcomes of any construction project. Note that the numbers below each of the descriptors in the model represent combinations of the eight premises outlined earlier in this chapter that most appropriately complement that specific function.

Since this is an interactive model, involvement of the community and educators is significant, especially in the areas of planning, programming, concept design, and management. Individuals in these positions make valuable contributions through collecting and analyzing data and information and in sharing various leadership positions—for example, heading a committee and influencing plans and concept design.

Planning by its very nature includes the utilization of leadership, expertise, resources, volumes of data and information, and the involvement of the community and educators. Like planning, programming (translating data and information from ideas to spaces for learning) utilizes expertise, the community, and educators in defining learning areas in the school. Note that there is also interaction between the leadership and all five phases. The design phase includes the traditional architectural building delivery process and utilizes a scaled back number of participants from the design phase. However, in this conceptual framework, design depends on information from the planning and programming team and also relies heavily on expertise and the data and information supply. Here goals and objectives are translated into physical spaces for teaching and learning, and the planning and design activities are then integrated into the construction documents.

Construction of the school, notwithstanding the sets of plans and all the contractors, architects, and engineers, depends on the involvement of people in the design phase and interaction with the people who provide the data and information supply. The outcomes of construction are heavily monitored by people in leadership positions and by construction managers. Facilities management, also a function and a premise (premise 6), includes the occupancy and postoccupancy evaluations— operations and maintenance. We contend that managing the facility starts with the planning and design process; hence, management as used here entails planning, design, and the management of the facility after construction. Here the model helps decision makers to determine if the educational objectives were met in the construction phase. Management further includes reliance on the community, educators, and the expertise of people working in operations and maintenance for support and involvement.

Direct involvement of people in leadership is necessary throughout the entire process of developing school facilities (see the thread running from leadership to evaluation in Figure 3.1). This is depicted through the interaction and involvement of experts, the community, and educators. For example, the community and educators have the responsibility for providing certain data and information (e.g., historical information and development and interpretation of philosophy). They

TABLE 3.1   Premises for Developing School Facilities

PREMISE	DESCRIPTOR
Premise 1	Strong leadership is essential.
Premise 2	The school system has a defined direction—a mission and a vision.
Premise 3	Long-range goals and objectives are established.
Premise 4	Goals and objectives are translated into physical places and spaces for teaching and learning.
Premise 5	Planning and design activities are integrated.
Premise 6	Management is systematic: data- and goal-driven.
Premise 7	The demand for resources is greater than those available.
Premise 8	Collaboration and cooperation between the school and community are essential.

interact in the planning, programming, design, and evaluation phases, but do not take an active role in the construction and management phases. Note that the community and educators interact directly with the people who have expertise in the various aspects of developing school facilities by providing data and information and drawing on this resource to assist in work in planning, programming, concept design, and management. Premise 7, the demand for resources is greater than those available, permeates all phases of the model.

Table 3.1 provides a summary of the premises for developing school facilities. These premises connect the model's components through relationships as suggested by the numbers under each function in Figure 3.1.

Experienced planners and architects will quickly recognize that the model outlined in Figure 3.1 is only a single slice of exceedingly multifaceted activities involved in the development of educational learning environments. In the following section we address leadership, expertise, involvement, and evaluation, while the remainder of the text focuses on primary aspects of planning, programming, design, construction, and management.

Leadership

Planning and building a school requires the combined efforts of the board of education, representatives of community groups, the superintendent

of schools and his or her staff, and a large group of specialists retained specifically for any aspect of the project. In large school districts, the specialists may already be employees, while in smaller districts the specialists are hired from outside the district. However, regardless of school size, the responsibility for coordinating the work of these individuals and groups rests largely in the chief school officer's agency (Engelhardt, Engelhardt, & Leggett, 1956). This complex job may be described as leadership. The person performing the leadership function has the responsibility for setting direction and establishing objectives and performance measures. He or she also emphasizes the development and implementation of long-range goals and objectives, integrated planning and design activities, and acknowledgment that the demand for resources is greater than those available. One necessary aspect of leadership in developing school facilities is the recognition of the importance of translating goals and objectives into physical learning environments for teaching and learning. Many leaders and governing boards have not grasped this concept, as evidenced by the lack of harmony in various schools between the physical environment and teaching and learning strategies of the adopted curriculum.

Things go wrong, and "Leadership is often invoked as the solution to any and all problems" according to Johnson (1996, p. xi). At least, people expect school leaders to attack the problem of developing good schools in the face of scarce resources. Even with restricted budgets and school construction as major problems, school superintendents must devise ways to lead professionals who work in public bureaucracies that are entrenched in local and state political systems. Johnson (1996) crafted three particular classifications of leadership relevant to this process after work by Cuban (1988). First, she presented the notion of *educational leadership* entailing the creation of a vision, leading reform movements, and engaging school leaders in change. But, Johnson conceded a vision is not necessarily a word from a prophet. Instead, it might be as simple as a plan for the future, the importance of learning, certain pedagogical approaches, or a belief that "all children can learn" (p. 62).

Next, Johnson described *political leadership*. She stated that "curiously, those intent on educating the public's children often hope to do so without touching or being touched by politics. Though they realize that interest groups influence programs, loyalties bias resource allocation, and coalitions gain consensus that individuals cannot, many educators persist in believing that politics is beneath them" (p. 153). In school development, as well as other aspects of political leadership, the leader "must ascertain the character of local politics, identifying the competing interests, sizing up the players, and making connections" (p. 186). Politics can be good for school facilities development if building a new school means getting a community on the map, for example. "It is the comprehensive high school that garners the most attention: This high school has to be the jewel in the crown. People move into the community and pay exorbitant taxes because the high school is perceived as providing an excellent education" (p. 189). We have known for a long time that a good school, and especially a new school, will draw people into a school district. Thus, the politics of building or even renovating a historical school pay off in terms of school and community pride.

Finally, Johnson focused on *managerial leadership*, arguing that leaders can manage and managers can lead. For example, "School boards delegate their authority for providing educational services to the superintendent, who is expected to appoint staff, allocate resources, and oversee teaching and learning. The superintendent may foster creative teaching and nurture innovative programs, but if the busses don't run or children are unaccounted for, he or she is judged to have failed as a manager, not to have succeeded as a leader" (pp. 219–220). Furthermore, if schools are falling down, maintenance is poor, and roofs are leaking, the school is perceived as a failure. Sound managerial leadership is imperative.

Mauer and Davidson (1998) presented a paradigm for building a *community of leadership*. This approach has overtones of the school survey movement, especially in the phase of involving people, and is extremely relevant to the model shown in Figure 3.1. It is relevant because leaders, the community, and educators are involved in planning, programming, and design—a vital element in the construction documents. "The formal leader facilitates the community of leadership but is joined and supported by teachers, parents, students, school staff, and interested community and business leaders. Membership in the community of leadership demands that each participant contribute her expertise to the organization" (p. 3). These writers compare the difference between constructivist models and knowledge-transmission or skill-based models (or in philosophical terms: progressivism versus essentialism, e.g.). This is an especially important aspect of leadership when school and community groups design spaces for learning and teaching. For example, Mauer and Davidson compared the two ways of teaching and learning under the title "Getting Better and Better at Doing the Wrong Thing."

Effective development of learning environments demands that teaching and learning styles be discussed and understood by the community of leadership prior to programming.

> Principals and teachers recognize that the constructivist perspective is not the instructional model used in most schools. Many of us were taught to use a knowledge-transmission or a

skill-based model in which the teacher is active and the student is passive, with lecture or lecture-demonstration being the preferred instructional strategy. Surely this model dominates in today's schools. Much of the challenge in educational leadership is to encourage teachers to understand both models. (Mauer & Davidson, 1998, p. 6)

Using descriptions presented by Au (1993), these authors specified the difference between constructivist and knowledge-transmission (the student is a blank tablet) models:

CONSTRUCTIVIST METHODS

1. The child is an active participant in her own learning.
2. Learning is based on wholes and is reduced to parts.
3. Learning is a social element—children can learn by cooperation.
4. The child is asked to explore the purpose of literacy or of knowledge.
5. Teaching and learning are student-centered, and learning respects individual differences.
6. Learning supports observation, hypothesis generation and testing, and reflection.
7. Teaching and learning profit from individual group differences. (Mauer & Davidson, 1998, pp. 6–7)

SKILL-BASED (KNOWLEDGE-TRANSMISSION) METHODS

1. The teacher actively transfers her knowledge to the child, who accepts learning passively.
2. Learning is based upon decontextualized parts, and the child is expected to grasp the wholes.
3. Teaching and learning are abstract and do not rely on any social context, not even on authentic teaching materials.
4. Skills and knowledge are taught for their own inherent value, not for any special purpose or function.
5. Teaching and learning are skill and knowledge based, and children are assumed to be more alike than different.

6. Teaching and learning are product-centered, that is, based upon completion of assignments without regard for the child's prior knowledge or schema elaboration.
7. The values associated with teaching and learning are those of the mainstream, usually of the principals and teachers, and the values deny contribution of diversity and difference to teaching and learning. (Mauer & Davidson, 1998, p. 7)

Ensuring the above discussion is part of the involvement and interactive process in the process model for developing school facilities is a very significant job for *leadership*. A discussion of these helps to extract from the community and educators exactly what type of physical learning environment they believe to be necessary for teaching and learning. People in leadership positions should not say which method is right or wrong, or what combinations of the various perspectives (philosophies) are best.

One interesting school of thought to add to the traditional arguments of constructivist versus. skill bases was given by Fielding (1999) in an interview with Roger Shank, Director of the Institute for Learning Sciences, Northwestern University. Shank stated, "Classrooms are out! No more classrooms! Don't build them" (p. 1). Perhaps Shank was referring to learning environments as neighborhoods, for example, those initially introduced at Celebration School located in Celebration, Florida. He advocated getting people to think about the environmental implications if learners were to spend one-third of their day at the computer, one-third of their day talking with others, and one-third making something. Shank described student behavior that parallels these three activities as active, interactive, and focused, respectively. An extension of Shank's concept to a review of how students learn has been addressed by Hall and Handley (2004). These authors focus on "the new curriculum," recognizing multiple intelligences and learning how to learn. The challenge is straightforward: Educational leaders should have a large supply of information and resources and/or employ people with expertise in the various fields represented in the complex arena of building educational learning environments.

What leadership styles work best with the model for developing school facilities? The answer may best be presented through the work of Carter and Cunningham (1997) who indicated that leaders must be adroit at identifying and solving specific functional problems as well as analyzing broad issues. The leader's job is to orchestrate the relationships among system functions, such as governance, finance, and management. With respect to the discussion here, the superintendent and other leaders should harmonize the interactions among activities pertaining to planning, educational programming, design, construction, and management. It is the job of people in leadership positions to provide direction for developing facilities for the future, encourage *participatory leadership* among the various groups involved in the process, foster continuity, and encourage innovative solutions to problems. When appropriate, people in leadership positions should provide training opportunities for participants in the facilities development process. Incentives such as extra pay or released time for the long hours spent in planning are important. Furthermore, showing respect and support for new ideas and ways to provide positive places for students to learn and for teachers to teach is significant in actualizing the goals of education.

Expertise, Resources, Data, and Information

These four items may have similar meanings to some readers. For example, expertise as intended for use in this model refers to people having special knowledge and experience in a specific area (a demographer, e.g.). Resources are linked to the availability of funding for planning, design, and construction, technology for planning and communications, people, and materials and supplies, and so on. Data in this text refer to "hard data" such as student population forecasts, demographics,

budget, school capacity, and needed spaces expressed in specific measurements. Information involves the expression of facts, curriculum preferences, codes, and policies through various channels of communications.

No one person should attempt to plan and design a school in today's complex society, with its array of information and teaching and learning styles. The only approach that is appropriate in our heterogeneous educational and political environment is "team participation." Furthermore, the adage that "the person serving as his or her own lawyer has a fool for a client" may be applicable to the development of school facilities by one person in a given district. For example, a school district that is involved in the development of educational facilities without assistance from experts from outside the system may be practicing educational and architectural incest—producing some very strange-looking, educationally challenged, and malfunctioning school facilities over the long run. It is easy for large school districts to become complacent and "design and build their own" because they have been doing the same thing the same way for such a long time. Their argument is usually that they are saving the taxpayer money through efficiency. However, the effectiveness of this practice is questionable because of the lack of new ideas from outside sources and forward thinking, or "thinking out of the box."

The arguments that Castaldi (1994) gave for involving various teams in the school survey apply to the expertise and involvement functions as delineated in Figure 3.1. The question is "how and by whom" will the development of school facilities be performed. The expert approach to development of school facilities includes people in education, planning, and architecture who are usually from outside the school district. Organized teams made up of people from universities, state departments of education, and private firms are suggested. Representatives from each of these sectors may be the ideal combination. Castaldi noted that the products provided by experts were more consistently sound educationally than those resulting from locally conducted projects. He further noted that the degree to which recommendations are implemented is directly related to the public acceptance of the results. Likewise, the acceptance levels are most likely determined by the degree of confidence that the public places in those who plan, design, and build a school. Credibility is a key issue, including confidence in people working in leadership positions in the school district.

Regarding credibility and acceptance, it is interesting to consider the large number of groups that are involved in making recommendations that may have long-lasting effects on the quality of school facilities in the district. Governing boards are faced with questions concerning the people who should be involved in developing and providing educational facilities. For example, we have heard people ask these questions: Are professionals from outside the school district the only persons that will be involved? Can the local citizens provide most of the data and information for the school development project? Are not local educators best qualified to make programming and design decisions? Will we have a better school if we contract the job to outside firms and let them build the school? Can we design and build our own school without outside help? The answer to all these questions is "No." We find advantages in cooperative planning and design (outside consultants and local citizens and educators) because local people have a voice in the school they are paying for with their tax money, and they also have the added dimension of employing expert guidance in the process to lead them to the best decisions. One disadvantage of cooperative planning is that interactive and cooperative planning and design may require more time than a packaged program or a "one size fits all approach." But, an extended timeline is a small price to pay if the end product is better and especially if local people see their ideas implemented. That is, the community will be more likely to support a bond issue to finance their schools if they know they will be completely involved in the process.

There are areas of the United States where the same group of planners and architects work exclusively and build questionable and perhaps unsound schools. Usually, these groups are selling the same plans and designs over and over again in the name of efficiency, with little regard for short- or long-term educational effectiveness. The schools they erect may be accountable as far as low cost is concerned, but are they educationally responsible? Does the claim "best practice" dictate the same school building that was constructed in an adjacent school district? When this practice occurs, we may find weak school leadership at the state and local levels, with little to no community involvement in planning, programming, and design. So, does employing the same school design "over and over" mean that those involved in this practice are getting better and better at doing the wrong thing? Are state and school system policies permitting this practice responsible to the public? Could the result of the practice of replication become a downward spiral toward slum architecture, and educational mediocrity?

Assuming collaboration in the development of school facilities, the resources needed to plan, program, design, and build a school facility may be classified as community resources, school resources, state and regional resources, and federal and national resources. Since the school facility serves community needs, we expect a large number of resources to be provided by the school and community. The following list may serve as a guide in determining the resources, data, expertise, and information needed in the process:

Teachers
Students
Parents
Community representatives
School administrators
School service personnel
Local planning commission

County agent and/or commerce representative

Land use plan

Alternative school sites

Accumulation of relevant research and literature

Educational planners

Regional or urban planners

Technical consultants

Legal counsel

Financial counsel

Building contractors

School equipment specialists

Architectural firms

Engineering firms

Special interest groups

Those resource teams marked by an asterisk (*) may also be selected from the state and regional or federal levels. It is also likely that in our global society, we might find international representatives working at some levels.

The human resources from the *state and regional* levels include:

Educational curriculum consultants

Educational data analysts

Educational finance experts

Concept designers

Representatives from the State Department of Education

Educational planners

Regional or urban planners

Technical consultants

Legal counsel

Financial counsel

Building contractors

School equipment specialists

Architectural firms

Engineering firms

Special interest groups

Resources from the federal and national levels may include the following:

National organizations

Federal agencies

Special interest groups

Technical consultants

Legal counsel

Financial counsel

Building contractors

School equipment specialists

Architectural firms

Engineering firms

Planning and developing educational learning environments has the goal of producing safe, comfortable, and developmentally appropriate learning environments for students of all ages in a multicultural society. To achieve this goal, full involvement of school personnel and the community is necessary. Only when this process is thought out in the context of a model such as the one we pre-sent here can this goal be reached. The danger of involving only a few people is that the resulting learning environment may meet the needs of the few people who participated, but it may be unfit for the community as a whole. We suggest widespread involvement of educators and citizens, with the assistance of experts. This approach to developing schools has the potential for convincing the populace that the school facility is not for a small group of people.

Involvement of Students, the Community, and Educators

There are several ways to ensure community involvement. Much of the organization for this important component dates back to the survey movement, but there are other participation methods such as strategic planning, the charrette process, community action planning, participatory action planning, participatory action research, participation games, and workshops (Sanoff, 2000). These activities clarify school and community needs and lead to what Sanoff called a responsive school, instead of a warehouse for students and teachers.

Historically, in the comprehensive school survey, we found a review of the background of the community to be helpful in defining a context and a perspective for school development. An economic analysis of the community, inventory of social services, review of transportation capabilities and needs, description and analysis of the population and student enrollment, and a study of the financial ability of the school district were expected. Further, a complete evaluation of current school facilities and sites was necessary. Finally, before a school was built, emphasis was placed on collecting data regarding the education program the people want. This included development of the philosophy of the schools, depth of the desired educational program, breadth of the desired educational program, provisions for special education, student services, organization of the total program (K–12), and the administration of the educational program. From this factual information, plans were drawn up on ways to house the educational program, including site requirements, space requirements, size of attendance units, grade-level organization, special services, and general design of the building. Given this information, an elaborate set of documents was drawn up and recommendations were made regarding the school building program (Sumption, 1952). This process placed emphasis on community involvement. Several activities in this process are still valuable to our school development process today.

There are some changes that should be noted, however, for planning. First, in the era of the survey movement, there was no mention of programming and design. This was considered the job of the architect. We recommend the involvement of the community and educators in this critical stage of developing schools. Other changes include the utilization of resources such as the regional planning commission, land use plans, spreadsheet technology for budget planning and student population analysis, and geospatial technologies. Most of these resources and technologies were not available in the 1950s.

Slagle (2000) discussed geographic information systems (GIS) in community-based school planning. He described how GIS has increased cooperative planning activities among the school district residents, the planning and facilities committee, and school district administration. From a school planning perspective, "GIS can best be described as a system that allows for the capture, storage, retrieval, analysis, and display of spatial data for the purpose of advancing school planning activities" (p. 3). Spatial data deal with location and space.

> For example, it is not uncommon for school districts to develop a student records data base. This data base consists of such things as student name, address, grade level, report card, health records, test scores, and the like. Users of this database could perform such aspatial queries as "find all of the ninth-grade students who scored 95% or above on a standardized test." If however, it were possible to map where these students are located, a spatial query could ask "Find all of the ninth-grade students who scored 95% or above on a standardized test and who live in the northeast part of the school district." (p. 4)

This system might contribute to the process of developing school facilities by locating schools serving a certain geographic area that have a common positive design feature. As Slagle explained, "By spatially enabling the data base, new ways to look at old problems can be found, and often hidden trends can be discovered" (p. 3). One word of caution: Privacy issues will emerge in this area of personal data usage. Therefore, we must guard against misuse and the wholesale distribution of confidential information. This may be a limitation to a fantastic futuristic idea.

GIS has the capability of providing data on housing development trends, allowing planners to identify where student population changes are occurring. It also maps student location and projects future locations. This technology can replace the traditional "spot map" used for locating students. GIS generates data on topography, hydrology, proximity to transportation links, student enrollment potential, and land use to help decision makers locate sites for new schools and set attendance boundaries.

Various school and community needs are identified as committees are formed and activated. To identify data and resources within the larger community, participants can consult a wide variety of sources, "everything from the Yellow Pages to real estate listings, from calendars of cultural activities to directories of local businesses. When teachers, students, parents, and business representatives all work together in this process of discovering and mapping assets, they will not only enlarge their own individual understandings but also help develop a public knowledge base about the diverse interests and interrelationships that make up the community. The results are likely to be broad-based and extremely valuable" (U.S. Department of Education, 2000, p. 43).

Sanoff (2000) stated that "although the idea of participation in building and planning can be traced to pre-literate societies, community participation is of more recent origin. It is commonly associated with the idea of involving local people in social development" (p. 1). The process of developing and producing school facilities should involve the people of the community and the school because all stakeholders need to decide the kinds of learning environments that will best support the direction of the school. "By encouraging respectful and productive communication among diverse constituencies, a broad-based planning process can result in a much superior end result than one developed by educators or architects or any other single group. Many heads and multiple perspectives really are better than just a few" (U.S. Department of Education, 2000, p. 32).

An inclusive planning and design process can forge renewed commitment to the schools of a community. People tend to support what they help to create. The amassed synergy of shared decision making, problem solving, and goal setting can build a strong foundation for collective responsibility and enduring support for schools. Often, the people most directly affected by the learning environment, the students, are the ones who may frequently be excluded from planning and design decisions. Why should students be involved?

> First they have much to offer to the process. They represent a wealthy pool of creativity, and enthusiasm. Young people definitely know about schools—how they feel, how they work, how people feel and work when they are in school. Yet they are often free of entrenched assumptions about why things are as they are or why they cannot be changed. Thus, they can be a source of refreshing ideas and innovative suggestions. With enough students to provide peer support, and with proper facilitation, they can, in fact, be a tremendously productive force in the planning process. (U.S. Department of Education, 2000, p. 33)

Another significant point, according to the U.S. Department of Education (USDE), is that students have much to learn from the process; the chance to interact with adult colleagues can provide them with a rich learning context that no formal class can. The rich experiences students can gain in working on committees include the application of research skills, data analysis, communication, problem-solving activities, and teamwork. These, according to the USDE, are all necessary for workplace survival in our complex multicultural society and global community.

The facilities development process can serve as a model for the very type of education experiences that we are trying to deliver to students in the school that is being planned and designed. Together, students and adults may take regional field trips to ideal schools to gain ideas for design, and may also make virtual field trips to schools around the world by way of the Internet. Learning is integrated and applied, teaming and collaborative problem solving are the norms, and the work that is being done is important and worth doing. The interactive process allows students and educators to design, draw, and create some of the conceptual models that will be used to communicate with the architects who take over in the design phase. As the USDE sees it, the community has much to gain by involving students in the planning process. "By collaborating with adults in advocacy efforts, students may develop an ethic of community service and the practice of caring for a greater society. Asking them to join in such a collaborative action is a critical strategy for fostering the spirit of community for the future" (U.S. Department of Education, 2000, p. 33).

Parents have also traditionally been underrepresented in the school planning and design process. As the USDE points out, parents have been the most underutilized resource in American education. Although we know that parent involvement with students has a positive influence on academic achievement and behavior at school, planning and design projects often exclude them as essential partners. Parents have valid ideas and opinions about where their children should be educated. They know their children better than anyone else. This special parent knowledge and love make their perspectives uniquely valuable. It qualifies them as authorities when it comes to determining what supports they and their families need to provide to develop educationally sound learning environments.

> Parent participation in the facilities planning process can lead to greater shared understandings about current educational theory and practice. For some parents, there have been too few opportunities to interact with schools in meaningful roles as adults. Therefore, their perspectives on education have been formulated primarily from their own school experiences. (U.S. Department of Education, 2000, p. 34).

In cooperative planning, programming, and design, parents and teachers can become fellow researchers and discover better ways to teach students. Close contact with parents is likely to result in good ideas about design. Involvement will empower parents to become staunch allies of schools. After all the educational planning, designing, and building activities are completed, it is much of the

parents' tax dollar that goes toward paying for the schools.

Parent participation in the facilities planning and design process can increase the likelihood of parents' ongoing involvement in schools. Traditionally, parents' needs have not been reflected in the design of school buildings. We really need to incorporate places for them to park their cars and hang their coats. We should also provide small group areas for tutoring, and develop workspaces for using computers or making phone calls. Some recent school designs have incorporated actual parent centers within the building complex, thereby signaling to parents in a very concrete way that the schoolhouse is their house. Through involvement we can show them that they are welcome and encouraged to take an active role in the work of educating students (U.S. Department of Education, 2000).

The need to include educators in the planning and design process is critical to the success of school design.

> Although the need for such participation may seem obvious, it has not always been the case. In the 1950s and 1960s an entire generation of "open plan" schools was designed and constructed with limited input from the affected educators. While there may have been significant educational benefits from these open designs, their potential was never realized because they were developed totally apart from their users. (U.S. Department of Education, 2000, pp. 34–35)

We all know that the results of excluding the users proved to be expensive when significant structural modifications were made to align the school and the curriculum. The problem was that the "configuration of the learning environment was changed without changing the practices of teachers and learners and educating parents on the modifications. Based on observation, the original Celebration School, in Celebration, Florida, has experienced some of the same symptoms.

Recently, architects who assumed that the teaching methods of the past thirty years would continue designed some high schools in the historical departmental style. The assumption of self-contained classrooms and double-loaded corridors placed restrictions on team teaching, interdisciplinary learning, and block scheduling, for example. Furthermore, high school teachers have begun to explore ways in which the evolving technologies can enhance learning. They tend to minimize the traditional lecture method as the instructional method of choice in favor of more active and effective learning strategies. High school teachers are involving students in cooperative group work, collaborative problem solving, and projects requiring application of computer technology and multimedia presentations. This leaves the departmentalization and double-loaded corridor concept behind. New and innovative approaches to teaching have influenced the kinds of learning spaces and school furniture and equipment that are required for schools.

What we see in the above example is a mismatch between design and use—between form and function. One way to avoid this problem is to allow educators to play a key role in planning, programming, and design. "In these times of complexity and change, when educational practice involves a wider range of teaching and learning strategies than ever before, providing a place at the table for teachers in particular is more critical than ever before. As practitioner experts and primary users, teachers—not just school administrators—must take a leading role in the process of developing facilities master plans that support the best they know about learning" (U.S. Department of Education, 2000, p. 35).

Local business and industry, like students, parents, and educators, can enhance and legitimize the development of educational facilities. Because business and industry are the primary customers for the products schools produce, they have particular needs and unique perspectives to add to the process of planning and design. People in business and industry have effective practices and successful models to share since they are constantly going through the process of remodeling their own thinking about facilities design, the use of work spaces, and how these variables affect productivity. It is wise to include representatives of business and industry in the school facilities development process because they see supporting schools as "good business" in the long run. Recently, many businesses have made substantial investments in restructuring their work environments. Reflecting the new ways people need to work in the information age, new designs for physical space discovered by business and industry can be instructive for schools. For example, Alco Aluminum eliminated private offices and cubicles and emphasized equality and ease of communication, reflecting the design philosophy that the physical nature of the workplace does affect business and operations. Alcoa reduced the amount of space for individuals and reallocated it to a wider variety of places where people may interact—break areas, meeting rooms, and team areas, for example. What this reallocation of space did was to make the individual workstations only places for people to "hang their hats." As individuals' work tasks change during the course of the workday, they may move from place to place, gravitating to areas where they can most comfortably perform their jobs, according to the U.S. Department of Education (2000).

One benefit of including representatives of various companies is that they can be instrumental in developing the kind of educational programs and environments that will better prepare students to enter the workforce. The quality of local schools has been shown to be a key factor in recruiting employees for business and industry. Therefore, the involvement of corporations in school facilities planning is good business for the community, business and industry, and the schools.

Partnering with community organizations and governmental agencies in developing schools is recommended. As the U.S. Department of Education (2000) noted, "When museums, libraries, zoos, parks, and/or hospitals join forces with schools, a community can extend the use of the resources such institutions represent by applying them directly to enhance student learning. At the same time, such partnerships can help to create the kinds of connections which build broader based support for the institutions themselves, ultimately resulting in a stronger sense of community" (p. 37).

The Henry Ford Academy (see Chapter 6) is an example of such a partnership (To view this outstanding program, you may go to your favorite search engine on the Internet and type in "Henry Ford Academy"). This is the nation's first charter school developed jointly by a global corporation, public education, and a major non-profit cultural institution. This model partnership focuses some of the best thinking from the business, nonprofit, and public education worlds toward the common goal of building a school that will prepare students for life in the twenty-first century. The academy's long-term goals include creating new models for education reform, demonstrating the power of community partnership in education, and developing innovative curricula. The academy has generated significant savings in capital costs realized through the joint use of existing school facilities.

The School of Environmental Studies is an optional high school for about 420 students located on the grounds of the Minnesota Zoo in Apple Valley, Minnesota (see Chapter 6). It is a collaborative project between the State of Minnesota, the city of Apple Valley, and Independent School District 196. The School of Environmental Studies is centered around a curriculum that enables students to "enhance the relationship between humans and their environment." To this end, the school offers studies in a select number of courses, rather than surveys of content as presented in thick course catalogs at more traditional high schools. Each student has a computer station, works as part of a ten-person team, and conducts projects using the zoo as a living laboratory. In other communities across the country, school-to-work programs have extended the use of school facilities by providing students with opportunities to apply their learning in government, recreational, health care, and other community settings. "By shifting appropriate programs off-site, the school districts in these communities have been

able to increase their capacity by as much as 15 percent" (U.S. Department of Education, 2000, p. 37).

Joint ventures can lead to better uses of tax dollars, space, and expertise. Finding more space within the school is not necessarily the only goal for partnering with the community. Support for school programs is equally important as evidenced by the partnership between the town of Celebration, Florida, and Celebration School. The town library is located inside the media center at Celebration School. This enlarges the school's library, adds library staff paid for by the community, and brings the school and community closer together. This has often been a question school planners have asked: Why can the school and public library not be one and the same? The partnership in Celebration, Florida, is worth exploring as communities search for scarce resources.

Other governmental agencies that should be included in the design of school facilities are fire departments and law enforcement (U.S. Department of Education, 2000). The reason for this is to address issues of safety and security. At Columbine High School in Littleton, Colorado, mazes of corridors, obstructed lines of sight, and fire alarms without appropriate shut-off mechanisms made it difficult for law enforcement and health officials to provide aid and protection to students during the school shootings there on April 20, 1999. We need professionals on the design team who have been specifically trained to notice safety and security features in schools. "It makes sense to engage representatives of local [fire and safety] agencies since they will be the ones charged with maintaining the safety of school facilities—and the welfare of their users—long after the planners and architects have finished their work" (U.S. Department of Education, 2000, p. 38).

Two segments of the community having considerable influence among people are civic clubs and religious organizations. These organizations have the good of the community at heart and frequently serve as opinion leaders for various community projects. They often have a progressive philosophy about teaching and learning that becomes especially important in the planning, programming, and concept design phases of school development. It is wise to seek out members of these organizations when developing a new school because of their expertise in outreach programs.

Finally, the sanction of the local school board is important to the success of the development of school facilities as outlined in Figure 3.1. The governing board has the power to influence decisions and the leverage necessary to gain support for the process. School board involvement in school facilities development may vary from community to community. School board members know that buildings do not arrive in kit form. "Each school building, whether a new facility or a renovation, must be responsive to the needs of the education program and community. While a few school designs can be 'cookie cut' for repeated use within a community, most cannot be transported successfully to other communities" (National School Boards Association, 1998, p. 5). Boards know that time is money. As a result, it appears that most buildings are planned in the emergency mode. Money is available and the school was needed yesterday. Consequently, a breakneck effort gets underway to plan, design, and build the school in the shortest amount of time possible.

> Breakneck planning rarely creates the most cost-effective design. Planners need significant time to develop plans and suggestions that provide options for the client. Many times it is a second solution that provides the best, most cost-effective design. Unrealistic time constraints should be avoided. (National School Boards Association, 1998, p. 5)

More school board participation is expected in smaller school systems that have experienced only a few building projects as compared to larger systems where building is an everyday occurrence. In the interactive model that we have been describing and explaining throughout this chapter, information flow and two-way communication are vital. The board, the chief school officer, and school district officials must be kept informed of major activities that influence a school construction project.

> An inclusive, broad approach to planning based upon participatory decision-making and shard governance...does not free district officials from their leadership roles. Rather, it makes strong leadership more complicated, more complex, and even more necessary. Leaders for this new paradigm must be skilled listeners as well as articulate communicators. They must be facilitators of understanding as well as disseminators of information. They must be effective consensus builders as well as good decision-makers. (U.S. Department of Education, 2000, p. 38)

Above all situations and problems that arise in this complex process of developing school facilities in the context of state, local, and federal regulatory policies, school board members must be able to empower others, use their powers wisely, serve as stewards of the collaborative vision, and have the ability to see the future in the face of their own biases. This attitude will help ensure educationally sound and developmentally appropriate school facilities.

Evaluation

Several dimensions of evaluation are necessary in the complex process of planning and designing educational architecture. One straightforward approach is to assess the inputs, the process, and the outcomes of the procedure. Overlay a method of formative and summative evaluations on this traditional systems model and an evaluation procedure unfolds. For example, consider the following inputs: leadership, expertise, resources, and involvement. Is it certain that top-quality leadership, reliable and valid resources and information, and sincere involvement of the community will ensure an outstanding evaluation for the inputs? Not necessarily, but that is an excellent beginning. Next, review the process and determine if the basic five components of planning, programming, design, construction, and management are performed according to the principles offered in this text and other related literature. Finally, review the outcomes of each of the five areas according to the comprehensiveness of planning and programming, responsiveness of design as related to student learning, quality of construction, and thoroughness of management.

Although the literature provides examples of postoccupancy evaluations (see, e.g., Earthman, 2000b), there is a dearth of information on any formative evaluation of planning and designing educational architecture as presented in Figure 3.1. The postoccupancy evaluation (a limited summative evaluation for a school that has just been completed), however, is performed too late to make a difference in major aspects of design. Therefore, the minor change in a new school that may result from postoccupancy evaluation (summative evaluation) is minimal compared to those changes that could occur in a formative evaluation process.

A PRACTICAL APPLICATION OF THE MODEL

Now that the macro view has been presented, translating this model into a procedure amenable to application is not difficult when broken down into phases. Understanding the dynamics of the connections becomes vital for implementation of this model. Thus, in Chapter 17 (strategic planning), we outline the basic connective steps that complement the procedural model for planning and programming educational architecture as depicted in Figure 3.1. The remainder of the book is devoted to a discussion of the processes of planning, programming, design, construction, research, and management of educational facilities. The evolution of school facilities planning is presented in the following chapter.

SUMMARY

Chapter 3 presents an interactive model for developing educational facilities that can be applied to a wide variety of school systems. The model rests on eight foundational premises. *Strong leadership* is

essential and the leader must have knowledge of school facilities, be a strong communicator, and create an atmosphere that is conducive to active participation by those involved in the design and construction processes. The school system must have a *defined direction* (i.e., mission and vision), including a vision for teaching and learning that is understood by the school and community. The direction must be supported by *long-range goals and objectives* regarding the school program, since the school will serve the community fifty years or more, even though those in leadership serve for a relatively short time. And, those goals and objectives must be *linked to physical places for teaching and learning* to ensure that the school facility supports pedagogical strategies, even as they evolve over the life of the building. Integrating the planning and design activities, rather than relying on the traditional linear approach, encourages interaction among leaders and other stakeholders to ensure that their needs are met in the resulting educational facility. The *management of a school building project must be systematic* and utilize data to ensure that the resulting facility supports teaching and learning goals. Since the *demand for resources is always greater than those available*, strategies such as value engineering must be appropriately applied so that fiscal responsibility can be achieved without compromising important facility features that support educational goals.

The development model (see Figure 3.1) relies heavily on integrated collaboration of a variety of stakeholders to ensure that educational facilities meet or exceed stakeholder expectations. The role of the leader (or leaders) in providing direction, encouraging participation among represented groups, fostering continuity, and igniting innovation cannot be overstated. The leader (or a small group of leaders) must not work in a vacuum, but rather rely on team participation to navigate the complexities of current educational and political environments. There are many resources to tap into at the community, state/regional, and national levels, including people, data (e.g., economic analyses, demographic analysis, and land use plans), and technologies (e.g., GIS). It is important to include experts from outside the school, as well as stakeholders more closely affected by the school facility. Students involved in the process may provide innovative and creative suggestions, while their parents (perhaps the most underutilized resource) provide a unique perspective that is valuable as well. Their involvement during planning and the design process may increase their on-going involvement with the school. It is also important to include educators who will be utilizing a variety of pedagogical strategies in and around the facility, local businesses (the primary customer of the products that schools produce), other governmental agencies (e.g., parks, libraries, and fire departments), civic clubs, religious organizations, and school boards. Although it will likely add time to the planning and design process, the inclusion of a variety of stakeholders will increase the likelihood that the resulting educational facility provides the type of learning environment which will, in turn, provide maximal benefits to students, teachers, and community members. The entire process should undergo a formative and summative evaluation— something much more effective than the postoccupancy evaluation.

ACTIVITIES

1. Although the chief school administrator will be the primary leader throughout the planning, design, construction, and operation of educational facilities, other leaders emerge during specific phases to ensure that necessary activities occur. Given your current position (or anticipated future position), describe where in the building process you will likely take a leadership role. How will your management or leadership style strengthen the process?

2. Assuming that you are on the design team to build a new high school that promotes constructivist teaching methods, describe several of the learning spaces that you will recommend to be included in the design. How might this be different (or similar to) the types of schools you personally attended?

3. Develop a checklist of items needed in a formative and summative evaluation of the planning and development of a new school (see Figure 3.1). This activity might be undertaken as a brainstorming exercise and evolve to an individual or group research project. In a class of several individuals, small groups might complete one or more of the eight areas and share information in an open forum.

4. Suppose that you are responsible for the formation of a team involved with the design of a new elementary school. List the positions (e.g., lead architect, school superintendent) of those you will invite to participate. Describe how you will include them in the planning and design process. For example, will you hold facilitated meetings, charrettes, or some other form of information exchange? How many of these will you host? Where might they be held? *Hint:* You may review Chapter 16 to get some ideas for this activity.

REFERENCES

Au, K. H. (1993). *Literacy instruction in multicultural settings.* Fort Worth, TX: Harcourt Brace Jovanovich.

Bingler, S. (1995). Place as a form of knowledge. In Meek, A. (ed.), *Designing places for learning.* Alexandra, VA: Association of Supervision and Curriculum Development, pp. 23–30.

Carter, G. R., & Cunningham, W. G. (1997). *The American school superintendent: Leading in an age of pressure.* San Francisco, CA: Jossey-Bass.

Castaldi, B. (1994). *Educational facilities: planning, modernizing, and management,* 4th ed. Boston: Allyn and Bacon.

Cuban, L. (1988). *The managerial imperative and the practice of leadership in schools.* Albany, NY: State University of New York Press.

Earthman, G. I. (2000a). *Collaborative planning for school facilities and comprehensive land use.* Paper presented to the Stein & Schools Lecture Series: Policy, Planning, and Design for a 21st Century Public Education System, Cornell University, Ithaca, NY.

Earthman, G. I. (2000b). *Planning educational facilities for the next century.* Reston, VA: Association of School Business Officials.

Engelhardt, N. L., Engelhardt, N. L., Jr., & Leggett, S. (1956). *School planning and building handbook.* New York: F.W. Dodge Corporation.

Fielding, R. (1999). The death of the classroom: Learning cycles and Roger Shank. http://www.designshare.com/Research/Schank/Schank1.html.

Guide for planning educational facilities (1969). Columbus, OH: Council of Educational Facility Planners.

Hall, E., & Handley, R. (2004). *High schools in crisis.* Westport, CN: Praeger.

Johnson, S. M. (1996). *Leading to change.* San Francisco, CA: Jossey-Bass.

Kowalski, T. J. (1989). *Planning and managing school facilities.* New York: Praeger.

Mauer, M. M., & Davidson, G. S. (1998). *Leadership in instructional technology.* Columbus, OH: Merrill.

McGuffey, C. W. (1973). *Systematic planning for educational facilities.* Chicago, IL: Chicago Board of Education.

Moore, G. T., & Lackney, J. A. (1994). *Educational facilities for the twenty-first century: Research analysis and design patterns.* Report R94-1, Center for Architecture and Urban Planning Research, School of Architecture and Urban Planning, University of Wisconsin-Milwaukee.

Myers, N., & Robertson, S. (2004). *Creating connections: The CEFPI guide for educational facility planning.* Scottsdale, AZ: Council of Educational Facility Planners, International.

National School Boards Association (1998). *Technology & school design: Creating spaces for learning.* Alexandria, VA: National School Boards Association.

Sanoff, H. (2000). *Community participation methods in design and planning.* New York: John Wiley & Sons.

Slagle, M. (2000). *GIS in community-based school planning: A tool to enhance decision making, cooperation, and democratization in the planning process.* Paper presented to the Stein & Schools Lecture Series: Policy, Planning, and Design for a 21st Century Public Education System, Cornell University, Ithaca, NY.

Sumption, M. R. (1952). *How to conduct a citizens school survey.* New York: Prentice-Hall.

Taylor, A. (2000). *Programming and designing public schools within the context of community.* Paper presented to the Stein & Schools Lecture Series: Policy, Planning, and Design for a 21st Century Public Education System, Cornell University, Ithaca, NY.

Townsend, R. (1971). *Up the organization.* New York: Fawcett World Library.

U.S. Department of Education (2000). *Schools as centers of community: A citizens' guide for planning and design.* Report No. 20794-1398, Jessup, MD.

CHAPTER FOUR

A REVIEW OF EDUCATIONAL FACILITIES PLANNING PROCEDURES

A DEFINITION OF PLANNING

Planning is defined in many ways. Definitions vary from planner to planner and from architect to architect. To illustrate one dimension of these multiple variations, comparisons of rational and interactive models for planning are necessary. For example, Adams (1991) concluded there is no one planning model that fits all situations. This is also true when we seek models to plan for schools and outdoor learning environments. A rational model assumes an analytical process administered by specialists, while an *interactive model requires frequent exchanges of information, negotiation, the cooperation of stakeholding groups, dialogue, and consensus building* (see Figure 3.1). Implementation of a plan under a rational model is achieved through clear lines of authority with huge amounts of data to use as a basis for decision making. In comparison to the rational model, *an interactive model assumes decentralized authority and decision making with diffuse means of articulation and aggregation of interests.* The interactive model usually draws from both rational and collaborative philosophies. A consensus model may best be explained by saying that "we agree on the essentials and our differences are not worth fighting about." Educational facilities planning may include various portions of these three distinct paths. Regardless of the combination of paths, planning leads to a course of action whereby a set of organized activities permits decision makers to select choices from a set of feasible alternative solutions (Tanner, 1991). Strong leadership is required to make planning effective. Leadership is the key to developing educational facilities, as noted in Chapter 3.

Many of the planning activities referenced in this chapter relate directly to effective leadership. The "school survey movement" depended on strong leadership from the educational community. Today, it is required from both the educational and architectural communities.

THE OBJECTIVE FOR PLANNING AND PEOPLE WHO PLAN

The literature confirms the good intentions of people over the years whose aims, collectively, were to make physical learning environments educationally sound, student and teacher friendly, and responsive to the total community. Most writers in the field of educational facility planning have tied planning to professional positions or people who should be involved in the process. They have described the resources and steps necessary to accomplish this complicated task, but have made limited contributions to a theoretical framework for the planning and design of physical environments.

Historically, educational facilities planning was frequently accomplished by teams led by consultants from outside the school district and favored the school survey process—a labor-intensive, detailed, and somewhat collaborative approach involving working with many people from the school and community. The school survey is not necessarily the administration of questionnaires, but includes a curriculum review, a needs assessment, and a plan for financing school construction. It may also be completed with a comprehensive set of educational specifications. There are many aspects of the survey process that have survived the tests of time as we note in various sections of this book. Among many other important activities, the planning process involves educating people about how the school's physical environment influences student behavior, attitudes, and cognitive performance. Planners need to know how to translate the community's philosophies of teaching and learning into school design. This has not been achieved consistently in the literature; neither has it been accomplished in practice consistently throughout time as evidenced by some of the schools that have been built. There are far too many schoolhouses across the United States that are in no better physical condition and do not facilitate learning any better than schools found in developing countries throughout the world. Unfortunately, this is the rule rather than the exception in some school systems, albeit there are some excellent school facilities scattered throughout the United States.

Planning educational facilities is complicated, and not as simplistic as a few publications may imply. Unlike the field of architecture, the process of educational facilities planning has not reached a clear distinction in the arts and sciences of the academic world; neither has it achieved the high place that it deserves in practice. According to Brooks, Conrad, and Griffith (1980), "Educational facility planning has evolved through a series of processes developed and refined over the past half century and is best viewed from this vantage point. . . . Its evolution has been sporadic and helter skelter. . . ." (p. 1). Planning for physical learn-

ing environments in schools has often been only a collection of loosely tied together tools, tricks, and methods. This slack approach may be because when done properly, school facilities planning requires an extensive amount of hard labor—plus superior knowledge and skills of people representing many disciplines.

Ideally, school facilities planning and the design of spaces for learning environments require special contributions from a multitude of professional people. For example, planning activities should be guided by leaders working with groups of individuals who have technical knowledge and skills in the following areas: curriculum planning, environmental psychology, philosophy of teaching and learning, the design of spaces and spatial relationships, implementation of plans, demographic analysis, economic analysis, architecture, engineering, and other aspects of management, strategic planning, and leadership. In addition to these highly important characteristics, those who lead successful planning and design teams must possess good group dynamics skills. Historically, the specialty and function of the individuals involved in this complex process may have varied because of the sometimes sporadic flow of new information. Yet, whether or not we agree that a consistent planning objective was achieved in the past, *the objective today should be to advance the design and planning of safe, comfortable, and developmentally appropriate learning environments for students of all ages in a multicultural society.*

A BROAD CONTEXT FOR PLANNING

Henry Barnard (1848), the first U.S. Commissioner of Education, began his classic work *School Architecture* by discussing the common errors in school architecture. He noted that public schools are almost universally badly located, exposed to noise, dust and danger of the highway, unattractive, if not positively repulsive in their external and internal appearance. He further elaborated on the fact that schools were built at the least possible expense of material and labor and also charged that schools are too small, badly lighted, not properly ventilated, imperfectly warmed, not properly furnished, lack appropriate apparatus and fixtures, and deficient in outdoor and indoor arrangements. Barnard's concern for trees, shrubbery, and flowers for the eye were also noted. Given the current state of school architecture in the United States, many of Barnard's concerns are still valid. In fact, with overcrowding in schools in the United States today, we are experiencing a new culture of "slum architecture" in public schools—trailers (schools on wheels). This slum architecture is a result of only one thing—the lack of sound planning principles. Could this planning fault be based squarely on state funding policy and the difficulty of finding construction funding at the local level?

An expeditious review of the broader international scene in school planning and design has revealed similar concerns in other countries. Seaborne (1971b) conducted a study of English schools. The purpose of his research was to open up questions relating to primary school design for more general discussion, by showing the relevance of past experience to present problems and by sampling views of teachers and architects. In line with the notion of planning spaces for learning, Seaborne (1971b) found that schools in use at the time of his study were all designed with certain educational and architectural aims in mind. "At some periods the architectural aspect has overwhelmed the educational—as, for example, where a school built in the 1840s (and still in use today) was given lancet windows of perfect Gothic design without apparently taking account of the lack of natural light inside the building which resulted" (p. 5).

Vickery and Kayser (1972) compiled a comprehensive book on school buildings in Asia. Their work was aimed at improving quality—a feature of Asian educational endeavor in the 1970s. The purpose of their work was to stimulate discussion on the main factors affecting the design, costs, and use of primary and secondary general schools in the special context of the Asian region. As compared to

the 1970s, by the end of the twentieth century their study called for larger schools, more years in school, more subjects, and a reduction from fifty to thirty students per class in primary schools. This goal paralleled the trend in the United States at the beginning of the twenty-first century.

Seaborne (1971a) and Seaborne and Lowe (1977) published a comprehensive historical investigation of school planning and architecture (1370–1870 and 1870–1970). These works examined English school buildings from the educational as well as the architectural point of view. "Even those schools with little or no architectural merit are often important from the educational and sociological points of view" (Seaborne, 1971b, p. xxi). As school curriculum changes and educational reform creeps incrementally through our schools, school organization, administration, and physical structure also change, albeit at a seemingly slower pace. "Similarly, the ideas of educational reformers, if they are really to take effect, must sooner or later be expressed in organizational and architectural terms. Changes in the curriculum and methods of teaching are also likely to be reflected in the layout of buildings and the arrangement of classes" (Seaborne & Lowe, 1977, pp. 277–278).

Worldwide, as the school curriculum changes and educational reform eventually moves through schools, including school management, school architecture also changes. The key in keeping up with change is information, and with the rapid transmission of information through the Internet, people from around the world may view literature and images of new schools, quickly gaining insights about change in school design from many cultural perspectives. Until recently, this could not be done quickly. Virtual tours are readily available for viewing on numerous Internet websites around the world. When information such as this is shared, people want what they see happening in other parts of the globe. Viewing images of ideal schools in person and via the Internet is perhaps a motivator. Furthermore, shared information helps formulate the questions of what to plan, when to plan, and how to plan and design school environments.

Unfortunately, answers to these questions can be illusive. This limitation provides a sound reason for planners and designers to integrate virtual reality with the literature and personal cite visits for the purpose of gaining in-depth information about process and products, about why and when to plan, and how to plan and design school buildings. This book, acknowledging constant change in information technology and political realities, was written with these significant issues in the foreground.

Early Planning Movements (the 1940s, 1950s, and 1960s)

Historically, the comprehensive school survey was the main tool used to protect a community's educational interest when planning for educational facilities. In the early 1950s, the local school facilities survey was deemed to be the process that would best ensure the interests of the community served. In fact, in his comprehensive work on conducting a school survey, Sumption (1952) regarded it as a tool to give the board of education a long-range plan for meeting the educational needs of the community.

Writing after economic recovery from World War II was well on its way, Sumption viewed community involvement as a way to gain support and also provide the needed labor force to collect and analyze the huge amount of data necessary to complete a survey. As we reflect on his suggestions for planning, we must consider that there were no electronic databases such as spreadsheets. Neither was the Internet available to planners in the 1950s. Sumption's book, entitled *How to Conduct a Citizens School Survey*, offered planning strategies that involved selecting and organizing the central survey committee and providing the planning team with readings from timely sources. Here is an example of readings he suggested: Caudill (1941), Commission on American School Buildings (1949), Mort & Vincent (1946), National Council on Schoolhouse Construction (1949), Engelhardt, Engelhardt, & Leggett (1947), Perkins and Cocking (1949), Strayer (1948). The composition of this citizens school survey committee was similar to

that of a strategic planning committee (see, e.g., Kaufman, Herman, & Watters, 1996).

Following the section on committee selection, Sumption's work addressed issues concerning organizing a central or leadership committee and how to work with subcommittees comprised of local citizens and school personnel. Its function was to coordinate activities dealing with the study of school finance, the community and its people, public relations, educational program, and the present school plant, each of which contained smaller subgroups of people to help collect and analyze the enormous amount of information pertaining to the school and community. This historic work also included a comprehensive outline for a school survey and made suggestions for analyzing factual data collected by each committee. There were hints on how to study the community, school transportation, financial ability of the school district, take a student census, and analyze the results. Information was provided on how to appraise school housing. Each section offered useful materials relevant to the 1950s, with ample "how to" sections. Educational program planning involved determining the school's philosophy, depth and breadth of the program, provisions for "exceptional" children, special services for students, how to organize the educational program (K–3, 4–6, etc.), and administrative structure of the program.

Sumption's version of the school survey depended heavily on the program analysis (curriculum needs assessment in current terminology) as the basis to develop a master plan. In the end, the school facilities plan was based on program need: "Those studying the educational program have not only informed us of its present suitability, adequacy, and overall quality, but have pointed out how it should be improved. They have drawn meanings from the facts and opinions they have collected from pupils, teachers, graduates, parents, and others" (pp. 156–157). After completing activities from all areas of the school and community, the central survey committee was charged with coming together: "Henceforth, each area has been considered separately. The time has now come to look at each one [section of the survey] in relation to the others" (p. 157).

After considering all reports, the survey process focused on facts and opinion in completing two major tasks: (1) outlining a coordinated, flexible educational program adequate for the needs of the community and within the financial means available, and (2) developing a long-range, flexible building plan to adequately and efficiently house the desired educational program for years to come. The design of spaces for learning was not addressed. At this point in the survey process, an outside educational consultant was employed to assist with the step-by-step development of a master plan (remember that the whole process proposed by Sumption was a "local citizens school survey"). Finally, with the assistance of outside consultants, the school survey team drafted an educational program, with emphasis on future needs and a building program to facilitate the proposed educational program. Careful investigation of this work leads us to the conclusion that the comprehensive school survey was a labor-intensive activity that could involve up to 300 people and take up to 15 months for completion in a school district having large student populations (10,000 or more students).

Overall, the citizens school survey can still be a positive planning adventure for the school and community (especially in smaller schools and communities) if it is well organized and guided by a competent planning staff of consultants. In current terminology the traditional school survey may be called "strategic planning for educational facilities." It is a vehicle for focusing on community attitudes, values, and visions for education. The citizens school survey can be a feasible, yet labor-intensive, process to follow in school districts needing support for funding building programs when tax dollars are requested. It allows people who pay taxes to get involved in planning. Plans drawn up by involving local citizens have a high probability of being accepted, especially if referenda are involved. The greatest disadvantage of the citizens school survey is the amount of time and number of people required to bring a school facilities plan to the implementation phase. The model for planning and designing learning environments that we propose in this book includes some aspects of the school survey.

In 1953 Engelhart, Engelhardt, and Leggett wrote, "The study of a community and its school facilities, as a basis for determining future plans, has proven its value beyond all doubt" (p. 186). According to these authors, the foundation for long-range school planning had two elements: the direction of community change and the status of school facilities. Their procedures for planning included involvement. For example, various individuals in the community evaluated the schools and participated in the development of a long-range plan for educational and community needs. The process included a comprehensive school survey and a community analysis that were usually led by consultants from outside the school and community. Whereas the citizens school survey as presented by Sumption (1952) used the school census as a means to estimate student enrollments, Engelhardt, Engelhardt, and Leggett (1953) employed early modifications of the "survival ratio technique." This method depended on the rate of flow of students from grade level to grade level as a means of establishing "survival ratios." In turn, these ratios were multiplied by resident live births and subsequent current and projected enrollments to forecast student population. Early versions of the technique used only two years of historical data and made linear extrapolations for the forecast that were usually tied to birthrates.

Engelhardt and coworkers (1953) utilized many activities similar to those found in the citizens survey. However, their comprehensive analysis of birthrate trends, mapping of housing (student location maps) by school organization (K–6, 7–9, 10–12, etc.), and estimated enrollments by grade-level cluster were more technical. Perhaps, their work was intended for larger and rapidly growing school districts, as compared to the methods utilized during the citizens school survey movement (perhaps for smaller districts). Both works were significant and made outstanding contributions to the growing field of school facilities planning with Sumption giving many lessons on "how to," and Engelhardt and coworkers providing detailed emphasis on scientific demographic analysis and contributing a comprehensive scorecard for use in evaluating school buildings. During this time period, Church and colleagues (1953) provided suggestions for school mapping, a checklist to evaluate school facilities, a method to give a rough estimate of student population, and a procedure for obtaining capital revenues for construction.

Planning guides were issued by the National Council on Schoolhouse Construction prior to and during the school survey movement. In 1930 the Council began publishing the results of its early planning efforts (Council of Educational Facility Planners, 1969). This organization later became the Council of Educational Facility Planners, International (CEFPI) and continues to offer revised and modernized versions of the earlier guides. The 1969 CEFPI work stated that "a serious shortage of educational facilities continues to exist. Add to this the expanding and changing educational programs that can make existing facilities obsolete and inadequate and you have multiplied the problems and increased demands for more effective planning. The number, size, type, location, and cost of educational facilities is astounding" (p. 17). These statements may be made about school issues in many areas of the United States and countries around the world today.

Of those involved in school facility planning—the governing board, the planner, the school staff, the architect, the consultants, and state officials—it is the school superintendent or a designated facility planner who plays a major role in producing educationally sound school buildings (Council of Educational Facility Planners, 1969). Regarding involvement of other people who have special interests in planning and decision making, McClurkin (1964) noted that "countless decisions must be made by many people before school facilities are ready for use. Important to wise decisions is the accumulation of all available information and knowledge related to the issues. Planning, an essential prelude to decision making, is the process by which essential elements are assembled and arranged to indicate optimum choices involved in a decision" (p. 10).

The theme of tight resources, the need to construct school facilities, and necessity to involve various stakeholders has existed for many years. For example, James D. McConnell wrote in the booklet entitled *Planning Tomorrow's Secondary Schools:*

> Secondary schools everywhere are faced with expansion problems. In many cases facilities will have to be doubled within a few years. Evolving concepts of secondary education, inflated building costs and continuing difficulty in obtaining adequate financial support confounds the problem. In order to obtain needed facilities, educators will have to know what is needed and must be able to justify these needs to the public. Adequate planning in which there is wide participation by educators, architects, engineers, consultants, and lay groups will determine these needs and will aid materially in providing a satisfactory end product for the community. (Stanford University School Planning Laboratory, 1954, p. iv)

McConnell (1957) also made a special contribution as director of Stanford's School Planning Laboratory. From his work we note that the involvement of lay groups was very important in the late 1950s.

Educational Facilities Planning Procedures (the 1970s and 1980s)

Models for planning involving somewhat more than the traditional school survey were emerging in the literature in the early 1970s. For example, McGuffey (1973) developed a process called the Facilities Resource Allocation Management Evaluation System (FRAMES). The first stage of the FRAMES method consisted of the development of goals, objectives, and needs assessment. He referred to this as the GONA model (GOals, Needs Assessment). It included a thorough community analysis, student enrollment forecasts, a study of key curriculum and instruction factors, an appraisal of existing buildings, and an analysis of the fiscal requirements and available resources needed to support the long-range capital improvement program. This system was primarily a rational model although it allowed for the plan to be drawn up by several major players. The variations of players included expert planners, local district employees, a combination of state and local government personnel, or groups of citizens working with committees of school personnel. While the traditional school survey depended heavily on outside consultants for leadership and local school and community participants to collect and analyze data, the FRAMES system allowed more local school, state, and community involvement and minimized involvement of a large number of outside consulting teams. The writers of this book have drawn from many of McGuffey's planning procedures, thanks to his generosity.

Banghart and Trull (1973) advocated the rational systems approach to educational planning, a process conceptually different from the McGuffey model. Although their work was more theoretical than the processes discussed above, it focused heavily on the importance of clearly defining the problem. Much of their extensive work was aimed at developing "long-range goals" in education. The basic theme of their volume was comprehensiveness in planning.

> The failure to attack problems and utilize opportunities has sharply exposed the theoretical foundations of educational planning. Most school districts make good plans only partially, if at all. Most of the planning systems are limited to relatively short-range objectives (i.e., data gathering, curriculum planning, the developing of educational specifications, and annual budgeting). Only in rare instances has planning been used for comprehensive purposes to extend to long-range goals. (p. v)

They offered a setting defining educational planning in broad quantitative terms. One aspect of their conceptualization included educational planning in physical terms—layout of school buildings and their proper settings for intervals of five, ten, fifteen, and twenty years. Another component looked at educational planning in social terms. This depended on surveys reflecting people's wants, curriculum planning, instructional strategies, and physical designs that enhanced personal and social interaction. Finally, they presented educational planning in administrative terms involving control of development, decision making, management and operations, inventory control, transportation planning, and school plant surveys.

In comparison to Banghart and Trull, the work of Brooks, Conrad, and Griffith (1980) took the perspective of planning from program to educational facilities in a more specific, less global setting. This book was heavily process-oriented. Its objective was to allow the reader to personally determine solutions to problems within the context of his or her school district and state. Table 4.1 on page 76 reveals an interpretation of the Brooks and coworkers' (1980) comprehensive planning model (p. 3).

Evaluation was not presented as a specific component of the model (Brooks, Conrad, & Griffith, 1980) because it was assumed to be continuous throughout the process. One important feature of this method of planning was the development of a plan for planning. This phase identified personnel, their responsibilities, time estimates for completion of tasks, and the estimated cost of the planning project. Determining the type of information needed to plan and the broad goals necessary for direction dictated the amount and types of data for decision making. Other key elements in the process were the products entitled "Start" and "Start Over," emphasizing the continuous nature of planning. If after implementation and adjustments in the plan, it was assumed that the process could again start over.

Tanner and Holmes (1985) presented a planning and management method for the educational program and school facilities that was more aligned with Banghart and Trull's rational approach than

TABLE 4.1   A Process-Product Comprehensive Planning Model

PROCESSES	PRODUCTS
	Start
Development of the planning strategy	Plan for Planning
Establishment of goals for the system	Goals
Development of the data information system	Initial Data
Suboptimization of the means of goal achievement	Alternative Plans
Synthesis of plan alternatives	Plan to Be Implemented
Implementation and possible plan adjustment	Adjusted Plan
Goal reassessment and possible complete replanning	Start Over

some of the other procedures reviewed in this section. Their technical model allowed the comparison of the present program and school philosophy with a desired or futuristic program philosophy, including goals, objectives, policies, and delivery system. Various combinations of alternatives were generated by this model, which included a set of possible outcomes that could range from limited need to the significant need for a new educational program and new school facilities. Their work offered a computerized approach to calculating school facilities and space requirements, an example of educational specifications, and an overview regarding evaluation of school facilities.

The literature shows no single model has been developed that is best for all tasks or situations in planning. Kowalski (1989) revealed why this contention was true. For example, he noted that one of the primary considerations for planning with the guidance of a model is the attribute of integrating planning components and tasks. "Leaders in public organizations experience a constant friction between two conflicting public demands— low costs and better services. This mentality often pressures school administrators to minimize planning costs" (p. 22). What often results is cutting corners of quality, ignoring key issues such as the relationship between school design and learning, and labeling the input of professional planners and designers as unnecessary.

Contributions by Kowalski (1989), in comparison to the models outlined here, included a more integrated set of models for planning. His volume, written from a rational systems standpoint, offered a five-step approach for structuring visions of the future (monitoring, filtering information, inputting data, analyzing the effects, and structuring visions). Like Banghart and Trull's (1973) work, Kowalski's focused on developing long-range plans (twenty years). By restricting input, according to Kowalski, the needs of a community and school district are never really identified. Isolated input eliminates conflicting ideas and the need for compromise in planning. It is time-efficient, but usually overlooks vital information such as cost of energy and the relationship between the learner and the physical environment.

Planning for schools with limited input was called the closed-planning process (nonintegrated approach). Closed planning results from two conditions: "(1) the administration not consciously selecting a planning model, and as a result, using a nonintegrated approach by default; (2) the superintendent and board deciding that only a select number of individuals should have input in order to control efficiency" (Kowalski, 1989, p. 24). On the other hand, integrated planning models are more complicated and difficult to use, but they are more precise and usually produce higher quality of information for decision making.

In identifying an integrated systems model for facility planning, Kowalski (1989) indicated that the primary factors to give rise to the process were philosophy and needs. The Kowalski model focused on philosophy, values, and beliefs of the school and community as guiding tenets. It generated ideas and thoughts influencing educational specifications, and the outcomes of planning. Similarly, needs (the difference between the ideal and what exists) served to influence educational specifications and the outcomes of the planning model. As a result, the model provided a physical environment with aesthetics, identity, economy, flexibility, adaptability, expandability, functionality, efficiency, health and safety, adequacy, and sustainability. A notable strength of this work was that it then tied the integrated model for planning to linear planning, which is a process very similar to the school survey discussed earlier.

According to Kowalski (1989), planning and managing school facilities are two of the most neglected areas of school administration. He argued that in many preparatory programs for school administrators no course of study is available for this critical area, yet school buildings are multimillion dollar investments and school superintendents and other educational leaders are expected to help shape them and keep them operational. This work addressed planning from the perspective of individual facility projects and district-wide planning. Special emphasis was also given to the management of school facilities. The book addressed the responsibilities associated with administering school buildings from the district and the individual school perspective. It contained materials relevant to administrative procedures associated with planning and managing schools. The examination of contemporary issues, presentation of planning models, and treatment of school facilities as a change process were major strengths of this text. Regarding school design, this work allowed the architect to translate a program into learning spaces.

Hertz and Day (1987) edited a volume for practitioners on pertinent topics for planning and construction of educational facilities. The objective of this summary booklet was to present guidelines in the planning, design, remodeling, and construction of educational facilities. Although concise, the focus was on practice rather than

theory: conducting a feasibility study, developing a master plan, writing educational specifications, selecting an architect, school site location, spaces for learning, building interiors, visual environment, fiscal planning, construction management, construction observation and administration, remodeling, and classrooms that may be relocated. As an example regarding practicality, Christopher (1987) stated that "the master planning starts with a facility survey to determine the enrollment capacity of existing schools" (p. 15). However, he was discussing the school site survey that investigates parameters affecting the functional capacity of a facility: building capacities, the size of the site, configuration and topography, and space utilization. Here we note the difference in terminology of educational planners and architects—survey and site survey. Terminology among educators and architects may present some problems, but it is the intent of this book to present a context and content to help minimize this gap.

Planning Procedures (the 1990s and Beyond)

In 1994 Ortiz conducted a study about how, when, and why public school districts build new schools in California. She provided eight parameters as the context for building schools:

> the reorganization of the school district structure to embark on a building project; the search for expert and special knowledge and skills outside the organization in order to complete the project; the solicitation of community support for the facility; the solicitation of funds in order to complete the facility; the development of working relationships with a variety of regulatory agencies; the coordination of all parties throughout the process; the management of the project from inception to completions; and the solicitation of continuing support and ownership of the facility after completion. (p. 4)

Ortiz looked at school facility planning as an opportunity for school districts to examine how they manage projects and reorganize themselves. She noted the need for specialized technical help from outside the school district and focused on how organizations integrate outside specialists in conducting a planning project. The relationship between the school and state regulatory agencies was viewed as ongoing throughout the construction process. The theoretical framework of the study evolved from two basic questions: What tensions tend to develop among key actors at various steps during the process of design, construction, and school building occupancy; and what are the typical conflicts of interest in orientation among executive leaders, professional experts, and political representatives participating in these processes? These questions and related literature gave rise to a theoretical basis for school construction and organizational functions. The framework included the comparison of nine linear steps in planning with three basic governmental functions: executive leadership (usually the school superintendent), professional expertise (the various experts involved in the planning process), and representative legitimacy (community representatives such as school board members and special interest groups). This theoretical base provided a view of responsibility among the various levels of the organization and community. A special comparison was also made of the relationship between the linear steps in planning and actual construction and linkage to state agencies, whose functions were primarily regulatory and distributive. This conceptual model is extremely valuable in understanding why certain actors in the planning process do infallible things.

According to Ortiz (1994), the importance of viewing the planning process through some theoretical perspective is of value. A theoretical context should not be minimized because tension and conflict will surely arise among key players in a process as complex as school facilities planning, design, and construction. Ortiz gave a perspective to possible discord by emphasizing conceivable conflicts among the three broad functions (executive, representative, and professional) represented in the theoretical framework. She stated,

Smooth and efficient completion of tasks and transition from one step to the next in the planning and building process requires that the three competing functions become integrated and maintain an appropriate balance in their respective domains. To ensure stability and consistency, the executive function will permeate the entire planning, construction, and opening process. The representative and neutral competence functions operate when called upon by the executive. (pp. 18–19)

Ortiz's scholastic publication certainly helps to clarify the context and perspective for many of the rigorous planning activities found in this book and in the classic works such as Kowalski (1989) and Castaldi (1994).

From 1982 until 1994 Castaldi provided timeless and comprehensive updated works on school facilities planning. He paid special attention to principles of planning, but not necessarily the executive, representative, and professional functions as Ortiz suggested. This balance between planning principles and activities also included subjects on remodeling and maintenance of educational facilities. Castaldi (1994) explored various teaching and curriculum methods and suggested their implications for school facilities planning. Formulae for determining instructional spaces, school modernization, and custodial staffing reflect the comprehensiveness of his work. He struck a neutral ground when confronting arguments such as school size, thus providing the reader with information to adjust a local problem to norms of size and space relationships. He provided a plan of action for the identification of school plant needs, exploring alternative solutions, and developing suitable options. This classic text offered specific steps for school facilities planning, drawing many ideas from the survey movement. It also integrated some aspects of school design into the process.

While Castaldi focused on the broad and comprehensive view of school planning, Holcomb (1995) provided a primer based on his experience as a school planner and administrator, his insights being from a practitioner's perspective. For example, he contributed an outline for educational specifications and made suggestions for avoiding planning errors. The book supplemented Castaldi's text by showing the reader some of the basic nuts and bolts of how a school board might view and react to the planning process.

Here is an example of some of his expert advice: Once the planning process reaches the construction phase, decisions are usually irrevocable. At first glance, this might seem trite to the inexperienced planner. As Holcomb (1995) saw the procedure, such difficulty arises because many school boards and administrators are reluctant to enter a building program as each new decision is based on previous decisions. He described something akin to a "snowball effect."

> Future planning, construction and curricular programs are based on prior decisions made regarding the physical aspects of the building. The trauma of making these final-type decisions has prompted many boards of education and their school administrators into delaying building commitments until the district is forced into a hastily-conceived and ill-planned program of construction expedience. The results of this kind of a building program are seldom satisfactory, but are often justified by stating, "We had to have the schools in a hurry." (p. v)

He attributed this result to delaying decisions until a real emergency develops.

Like Castaldi and Holcomb, Earthman (2000) brought the planning of schools into focus from the perspective of practical experience. In addition, he provided academic quality, significant references, and many thorough discussions of complicated problems, emphasizing the need for addressing the planning process forthrightly and showing the administrator how to plan a building. Specifically, "Planning for new school buildings or for major renovations to existing facilities requires considerable effort on the part of many highly skilled professional and technical personnel both inside and outside of the school system. In some instances, the working efforts of these individuals

comprise separate and distinguishable steps" (p. 25). That is, he emphasized a series of activities that come together to successfully implement a school facilities plan. Earthman's procedures included eleven steps:

- Organize the school staff.
- Determine the size of the student population.
- Select and acquire a site for a new school building.
- Select and employ an architect.
- Develop a funding package.
- Develop a set of educational specifications.
- Monitor the design.
- Advertise and bid the project.
- Monitor the construction phase to completion.
- Orient the staff to the building.
- Evaluate the building and planning process. (p. 26)

While these steps are not necessarily linear, they follow a normal progression of phases. According to Earthman, someone must be responsible for all planning efforts on an organizational level. For example, in a small school system, the responsibility to coordinate these eleven activities might be an administrative assistant. In larger school systems, there may be an office of planning and architecture that assumes the planning responsibility. Furthermore, Earthman, as well as Ortiz (1994), warned about the possibilities for discord resulting from planning efforts. The objective of planners in small or large school districts is to involve school staff and community representatives. *The ideal situation is to plan with people, not plan for them.* Earthman's approach to planning drew from components of the comprehensive survey movement, which included such critical activities as the community analysis, a review of the educational program, an estimate of the student population, an assessment of the facility needs based on the number of students expected, and a capital improvement plan (how will the facilities be funded). Most important, Earthman addressed the planning process forthrightly, from "planning to plan" to "postoccupancy evaluation."

Classic Planning Approaches

One of the early publications on planning (Engelhardt, Engelhardt, & Leggett, 1953) offered impressive floor plans (to illustrate space relationships) for the entire school, sketches of school sites, plans for classrooms and specialized spaces, suggestions for furniture and furnishings, and an important section on vision, light, and color. Their work brought together school architecture and educational planning and was state of the art in the 1950s; hence, it was a premier book that emphasized aspects of school architecture and planning simultaneously. It exceeded insight beyond the traditional school survey and brought implementation (the design of spaces) into the literature. Regarding school design, Engelhardt and coworkers (1953) noted that after receiving the work of the citizens committee, the educational specifications, and hiring a professional school building consultant,

> the architect is directed to prepare preliminary plans and cost estimates for the building. It is understood that he must have extensive conferences with the Board, consultant, and Citizens' Committee and school staff before he draws a line. With the help of the consultant, the architect translates the educational functions, which constitute the Board's program, into space requirements. Cost estimates are prepared from preliminary plans and specifications. (p. 204)

More important aspects of school design appeared in 1975 through the challenging ideas presented by Taylor and Vlastos. Many of their ideas paralleled the suggestions of Engelhardt and colleagues, especially those suggesting the involvement of many people in the planning and design process. Taylor and Vlastos (1975) wrote,

> In the past, educators have tried to improve the quality of education by recommending the purchase of newly designed textbooks and teaching materials, by sending teachers back to summer school, or by holding in-service workshops to "tool-up" for better teaching. . . . But all these changes have not addressed themselves to the crucial issue of the physical learning environment as a support system for education. Despite new training, new textbooks, and greater teacher sensitivity, our classrooms remain approximately the same everywhere—colorless, textureless, and sometimes even windowless. (p. 8)

Their work offered a process for designing alternatives to existing learning environments. Emphasis was placed on the learners who they contended are constantly learning, in an integrated way.

The importance of the work of Taylor and Vlastos (1975) was found in such topics as "curriculum as a design determinant," "new ways to use space," "the need for variety and scale," and the increasingly popular idea today of adding the outdoor environment as part of the learning experience. Perhaps, one of the most stimulating sections of the book focused on an alternative design process—from concept to reality. Here the authors made suggestions of how to get people without a design background involved in the design process. The reason for this was stated as follows:

> When people want a new building or wish to modify an old one, they usually approach the architect who, after several consultations, begins to design a structure for them. Traditionally, a construction firm is hired, and the plans, once fixed, become the designer's contract to actualize what he has drawn. The plan is fixed or static and the people who will be using the space sit back and wait for the structure to be completed. This process, efficient though it is, may be neglecting the use of valuable design information and energy. (p. 132)

Instead of this role, Taylor and Vlastos suggested that the architect step down from the classical role and open up the design process to the group—teachers, children, and parents. They insisted that the architect should use expertise and experience to expand the awareness of people involved in the design of the school so they may make better aesthetic decisions. The challenge was for the architect to work with people, rather than for them.

Another valuable aspect of this work was the involvement of children in the design process. It was suggested that children might be asked to draw a picture of their favorite place in the classroom. Subsequently, they would be questioned regarding where the place was and how they would place themselves and others in the picture. Taylor and Vlastos's *School Zone* made a significant and unique contribution to thinking about planning and design in the mid-1970s. The work is still important for today's planners and designers.

Planning flexible learning places, the theme and title of a pragmatic book written by Leggett and coworkers (1977), offered many valuable illustrations of school design. It expanded on ways to refine educational specifications as provided by writers such as Engelhardt, Engelhardt, and Leggett (1956). The challenge of small versus large schools did not go unnoticed.

> What happens if you plan a high school for a maximum of 250 students? Ask most educators, and they'll frown, especially if they were weaned on the Conant dictum that high schools of fewer than 750 students don't count. A lot of first-rate schools across the country are big, but a lot of big schools are not first-rate. "There is something about largeness that attracts more problems," said a principal who was quoted in *Education USA*, "but we continue to build larger and larger schools." It makes sense to consider a small secondary school for a variety of reasons, including these: Because a small school is small, each student is really needed. This need creates an important counterbalance to our impersonal culture. New curriculum developments, which take into account reorganized programs and human talent, can help make a small school workable and desirable. (Leggett et al., 1977, p. 41)

Not only did Leggett and coworkers (1977) advocate the smaller school, they offered suggestions for a teaching model, organizational patterns, and curriculum diversity in a small school. In addition, faculty and student scheduling were discussed, and illustrations for a high school design

for students of 200–240 students (this was called the "Smallway School"), twin Smallway Schools (400–480 students), cluster schools (800–960 students), and larger complexes including several Smallway Schools were provided.

How to create territory for learning in the secondary school was also given serious attention by Leggett and colleagues (1977). The concept of a multischool was developed and presented as a method to give attention to the increasing masses of students. "One approach to the problem of impersonal size is the development of multi-schools, in which the sophisticated task of providing an environment in which young people can grow toward adulthood is linked with the specialization potential of the large institution. An enormous monolithic school has little reason for existence" (p. 59). This advanced thinking about school design provided an example of taking students into a group setting and allowing them to "create their own turf." Designs were shown that accommodated a curriculum for students grouped in clusters of five. Alternative space designs included arts, science, planning, micro learning, individual study, technical emphasis, and group learning emphases.

Emphasizing the whole and the interdependence of its parts in school design was the main theme found in the volume by Leggett and colleagues (1977). This "cutting edge" work also addressed practical issues such as the quality of living in a school setting. It raised questions students have regarding the physical learning environment. For example, "Are [gymnasium] lobbies for basketball games only? Why not use them for students? Where are outdoor milling places that can accept students and not bother others? Where are indoor milling places?" (p. 148).

A trend away from conventional thinking best describes Greenman's 1988 work entitled *Caring Spaces, Learning Places: Children's Environments That Work*. Greenman contended that an environment is a living, changing system. More than physical space, the environment includes the way time may be structured and the roles we are expected to play.

It conditions how we feel, think, and how we behave; and it dramatically affects the quality of our lives. The environment either works for us or against us as we conduct our lives.

Greenman stated that his book was written for teachers, directors, parents, and children—all those who have a stake in having settings work for them. While the majority of the book focused on all-day child care settings, these settings encompass nearly all the environmental issues and needs for other early childhood settings. The book's central tenet was that planners should view these settings as places where children and adults live together.

First, Greenman (1988) established a context, understanding children's settings by asking these questions: Are the environments oriented toward children or adults? Do the settings bring feelings of personal power or significance, security, or fear?

> Space speaks to each of us. Long corridors whisper "run" to a child; picket fences invite us to trail our hands along the slats. Hot colors like reds and oranges stimulate; they are used in restaurants because they stimulate our appetites and speed up our eating. (p. 16) . . . Our experience of space and time is individual, but it occurs in a cultural context. (p. 19)

Next, he discussed the nature of schooling, and the factory model was called into question. He contended that many schools are mindless, joyless, rigid, and petty. They destroy the hearts and minds of children in them. "Back to the basics" was regarded as back to old methods and old materials—back to the factory emphasis on worker productivity (teachers' accountability) and quality control (student testing).

Other topics covered in Greenman (1988) included:

- Children need an environment rich in experience.
- Children need a childhood rich in play.
- Children need a childhood rich in teaching.
- Children need a childhood rich with people.
- Children need a childhood where they are significant.
- Children need a childhood with places to call their own.

Open- and closed-program structures were discussed. Closed centers were proposed as the hardest setting with the fewest opportunities for sensory play, exploration, discovery, and experiences with ranges of materials and people. Open structure centers were regarded as significantly higher in these dimensions, but family day care homes were rated the highest. That is, Greenman advocated making the school into a homelike atmosphere.

The play environment, according to Greenman (1988), should be developed as a wonderful, interesting place that continually captures a child's attention and is laid out to ensure individual and small-group experiences, without the continual presence of many watchful adults. The learning environment should include built-in opportunities for motor and sensory experiences and ranges of places to be with different visual and auditory stimulation. "Lying on the floor you should see pathways and small divided spaces—opportunities to go in and out, up and over, and so on; to be alone, to be enclosed on three sides, and to peer over thirty inch walls" (p. 55).

Greenman (1988) further noted that space characteristics are important to the child's physical environment. Size and scale give a space its feel and sense of workability.

> Scale is the proportion of an object relative to its surroundings. The most significant objects to consider as reference points are people. Scale is an aspect of size, numbers, and even time. It is an important dimension to children's programs where inhabitants may range from 18 inches tall and 10 pounds to 6 feet, and let's just say very large. (p. 61) . . . Children, who operate most of the time in outsized surroundings, gravitate to the tiny in spaces, objects, and living things. But

children grow big before they grow well coordinated, and their need to move and exercise makes larger spaces desirable as well. (pp. 61–62)

Many other aspects of school design were presented in this work, including social density, the sense of crowding, and ethnic groups and how they function. Greenman (1988) made a sound case for aesthetics and the aspects of aesthetic appeal. Under the "aesthetic" heading, he reviewed lighting, art and its display, and texture. Other significant design patterns included entries and pathways and spatial variety. He demonstrated that he knew something about children and how they learn by calling attention to how best to plan for young children. "The path of learning is more like a butterfly than that of a bullet" (p. 82).

Graves (1993), with many insights analogous to Greenman's, contributed numerous points regarding the process of planning and designing schools. Much of his writing was grounded in his experiences at the Educational Facilities Laboratories (EFL) funded by the Ford Foundation. The EFL theme is evident in his work: (1) "Facilities should be more sensitively designed to the new needs of education in a period of rapid, indeed revolutionary, change in instruction and social conditions." (2) Economy is critical in an inflationary period, so intelligent economy should be encouraged wherever, whenever, and however it can be" (p. v). Emphasis was given to trends in school design, with Chapter 1, written by Brubaker, noting that school architecture is a pendulum swinging back and forth

> from individual classrooms cells to the open plan, from national priority to national disgrace. Certainly such swings of fortune and changes in attitude are not limited to planning and design of educational buildings. We are a nation of great resources but limited attention spans. When we set our minds to a task, we usually do it well. After proving that we can do something well, we often stop doing it. Eventually a crisis develops and we rediscover the importance of whatever we stopped doing. (p. 3)

Graves (1993) further outlined several of his concerns when designing a school. The identity of the school was at the top of the list. He noted that the architect and client should be able to put down on paper not only the physical requirements of the building, but also some of the less tangible characteristics that will give the school its own personality. To make his point, Graves repeated the concerns of architect Lawrence Perkins who believed that seeing, approaching, and entering a school building are not separate steps. "Going toward and going into a school are one. You see the building from a distance, then you see into the building, then you are in the building without being conscious of a defined entry" (p. 70). That is, "going to school" should be a gradual and natural action. "When we say that the school is part of the world around it, the phrase is more than figurative" (p. 70).

> The integration of public places into school design was important, according to Graves (1993). In the well designed facility, the office is readily identifiable and easy to reach. . . . In recent years there has been a trend to locating the main office off a "great space" that serves as the main interior crossroad of the school. . . . The library, especially when it is also a community resource, is another element that can be designed as a memorable public space. (p. 70)

Graves provided rationale for various plans that have been used over the years: The compact plan was suggested as a way to minimize the amount of land, perimeter wall area, and interior circulation space needed (these are two- or three-story complexes usually built in high-density areas). The loft plan was noted because it provides flexibility as open spaces at great economy. A straightforward arrangement for classrooms spread out from a central corridor, the finger plan, was presented as a design whereby all classrooms may have direct access to the outside, allowing natural ventilation. The campus and cluster plans were also noted as designs to break down the massing and scale of large monolithic structures.

Graves (1993) then asserted, The question that educational consultants most often hear concern size of educational spaces. . . . Good consultants usually explain that a particular project's program should determine the size of various facilities, [but] administrators and architects always want justification for the dimensions of their proposed rooms or a benchmark they can use in comparing their facilities with those of some national "average." "Average" or "minimum," however, all too often become the standard. (p. 72)

Regarding indoor–outdoor relationships, Graves (1993) contended that

Most architects today understand the importance of bringing, natural light and views into schools interiors and relating appropriate rooms to outdoor spaces. . . . While athletics is perhaps the most obvious program requiring access to outdoor facilities, it is not the only one. Classrooms, especially those designed for younger students as well as art and science programs, can all benefit from outdoor areas. . . . A school's site itself can also be a teaching tool. (p. 73)

The character of the school was deemed important, with the suggestion of incorporating ethnic or community-based design elements to make the students feel at ease. Furthermore, Graves suggested that architects should be more sensitive to regionalism when designing schools. He offered comments on community uses of schools, school size, human scale, energy concerns, design for technology, and expansion. This work placed design in the forefront of educational planning activities.

"Shaping the learning environment to support educational objectives," the theme of Sanoff's 1994 collection of school building projects, complements ideas by other writers reviewed in this section. Sanoff placed heavy emphasis on the participatory design process that recognized the student, the teacher, the parent, the administrator, and the architect as vital ingredients in the process of educational change. In discussing planning and design, he included a wide range of school types, including children's centers, university structures,

and public and private settings. In essence, he wrote about planning and design "wherever formal learning occurs" (p. vii). A variety of experiences and resources were used to produce appropriate case studies.

Sanoff (1994) contended that many school buildings do not properly serve the functions for which they were designed.

School buildings are said to be made for people, yet ironically those who actually occupy or otherwise use school buildings are seldom able to influence the way in which they are designed. In fact, nearly all the important decisions are based on factors that have very little to do with the way people use the buildings or the way school buildings affect their uses. Administrators, public officials, builders, architects, and others, who in most instances, do not occupy the buildings ultimately constructed make those decisions. This lack of user participation has been cited as a major reason for dissatisfaction. Yet these same users can serve as valuable sources of information in the building development process. (p. 1)

According to Sanoff (1994), there is a need for greater variety in physical facilities to accommodate various teaching and learning styles. There is also a need to recognize that schools should be hospitable places for teaching and learning. "The social and learning problems experienced in middle schools and high schools, combined with the variations in learning and teaching styles, provide overwhelming evidence for the need to alter present approaches to school building design" (p. 1).

Following several excellent case studies on planning and school design that included child care centers (with a description of the Reggio Emilia project, e.g.), elementary, middle, and high school projects, alternative schools, and higher education environments, Sanoff (1994) offered some important principles of participatory design. He concluded that "there is no 'best solution' to design problems, 'expert' decisions are not necessarily better than 'lay' decisions, a design or planning task can be made transparent, all individuals and interest groups should come together in an open forum, and the process is continuous and ever changing" (p. 179).

A most significantly tangible tie between school curriculum and school planning and design was made in 1995 when two national organizations joined forces to produce a book entitled *Designing Places for Learning*. The Association for Supervision and Curriculum Development (ASCD) and the Council of Educational Facility Planners, International (CEFPI) supported this effort edited by Meek (1995). This work centered on school as a place—a place to be coached, a place to learn, and a place to play. In Chapter 1, Fiske noted the implications for architecture, after expounding on the school reform movement. He advocated the move away from the factory model and suggested that smaller and more personal learning environments are best for learning. Next, Moor and Lackney reviewed the evidence that architectural characteristics affect the attitudes, behaviors, and academic achievement of students. They also advocated smaller schools, smaller classes, and the school as a community hub. Design patterns were rated according to their status in the research literature. These patterns were classified as planning issues, building organizing principles, character of individual spaces, portfolio process studios, cluster of teacher offices, and critical technical details.

In Chapter 3 Bingler discussed the notion of place as a form of knowledge. For example, he noted that "architecture is a repository for mathematical equations, scientific principles, historical references, geographical design determinants, and literary content. It is also a lot of fun" (p. 23). He challenged the conventional wisdom of people who think of schools as containers to hold children while they learn. In Chapter 4 Crumpacker recommended using cultural information to create schools that work. The ideas that the home should be the template for the school and that animals may play a significant role in children's lives were discussed. She concluded with a recommended floor plan for an elementary school that

might incorporate her vision of the ideal school with respect to culture. Hawkins wrote about revitalizing an older school. He described an improvement project through the eyes of a school principal and noted specific improvements and their estimated costs. Another important result of this project was a set of guidelines for flexible room arrangements. Meek, in Chapter 6, described some of the important design features of Crow Island School. For example, on the issue of scale, she wrote "Then you are at the front door, and what you notice is that the door handle is too low. Too low for you, just right for children" (p. 53). With the mixture of excellent color photography by Steven Landfried and a brief account of the collaborative architectural planning that went into Crow Island (led by Larry Perkins and Carleton Washburne), Meek showed there is a sense of place at this outstanding school.

Planning your school's technology future was the theme of the next chapter by Bob Vallant. He suggested that your ultimate goal should be to design a flexible system that will allow growth as resources become available and as technology continues its rapid, inexorable transmutations. The redesign of spaces was the theme of Chapter 8 written by Taylor. "The current revolution in education demands that we rethink the architecture that houses our children. To accommodate new teaching styles such as interdisciplinary and team teaching, schools need updated classrooms" (p. 68). Taylor discussed architectural programming and recommended that this may best be achieved through collaborative efforts. In designing for cultural diversity, she noted that different cultures have different spatial needs. For example, Navajo children prefer round rooms as compared to the rectangular space. Furthermore, Navajos prefer that buildings should not be connected because they want their children to experience nature, hot and cold, snow and sun. In keeping with most of her previous works, Taylor concluded the chapter with an informative section on a curriculum for architecture.

A timely photo essay entitled "Opening Doors for Students with Disabilities" was presented by Barton and Smith in Chapter 9. The themes were achieving independence, feeling safe and comfortable, and gaining access to learning. Next, Brener discussed the connections between school building conditions and student achievement. Brener noted that poor school facilities convey the message that what is going on inside the school is not important, the school system is uncaring, and neglect is tolerated. Furthermore, she stated "older buildings are often in better condition than those built to accommodate the baby boom" (p. 86). The final chapter exposed the cost of neglecting the nation's infrastructure. Lemer noted, "The use of school facilities as a means for cutting government costs is unfortunately common and widespread" (p. 90). He contended that deferred maintenance is widespread and in many schools, "Despite custodial efforts, students, who desire and deserve order, beauty, and decent, safe surroundings, point out bathrooms filthy because of water-damaged floors and fixtures" (p. 92). Issues pertaining to this important area may be addressed in the design phase of the school. For example, proper drainage, the location and equipping of custodial closets, and selection of materials are direct examples.

The concept of school design was addressed by Brubacker, Bordwell, and Christopher (1998), when they tied together planning and school design by exploring the architectural heritage of schools from the 1850s through 1980s. Countless illustrations make this excellent work an exciting reference for the educational planner, designer, and architect. Principles of school architecture were presented in sections on flexibility, form and size, space for individualized learning, large and small schools, and regionalism. Regarding the principle of form, they wrote:

> The plan and shape of a school building—its form—are determined by the program of space requirements (the educational specifications) and by the site (the size, shape, and characteristics of the land and neighboring properties). This simple and straightforward fact is recognized by architects, engineers, and planners, but is not widely appreciated by lay people, who may believe that the designer or design team more or less arbitrarily selects a form for a school building. Of course, the form of some schools is unrelated to the program and site, but such structures are seldom deemed appropriate. (pp. 34–35)

Brubacker and colleagues (1998) further elaborated on the planning and building process and provided examples of design.

> When the demographic pressure is on—when the schools in a community are overcrowded and the enrollment projections call for steadily increasing numbers of students—it's time to study the demographic changes and determine where and how changes in the various schools are needed, whether some structures should be removed, and how and when new schools should be built. A district wide inventory of existing facilities should be made. Good planning requires an accurate analysis of the existing schools, including their size, location, condition, and suitability. The size of each site is important in determining whether the expansion of schools is practical. Are new sites available? What are the financial facts of the district? What are the goals of the community? Good schools, of course, attract high-quality development and families that want high-quality schools are willing to pay the taxes. . . . The board and the administration may wish to create a number of committees to focus on different topics, such as the program committee (to work with the educational consultant), the technology committee, the site committee, the architect selection committee, and the finance committee. (p. 169)

These activities were also part of the traditional school survey outlined earlier in this chapter.

It is the job of the program committee to develop educational specifications, according to Brubacker, Bordwell, and Christopher (1998).

> It is highly desirable to assign the responsibility for preparing the program to one individual: An educator who knows the goals and values of

the community, the rules and regulations of the state and city, and what is happening in education nationwide. That individual can be related to other members of the planning and design team in a number of different ways: 1. He or she can be an administrator, such as the assistant superintendent for curriculum development, working with and reporting to the board of education. 2. In a small district the superintendent of schools can serve as the head of the program committee. (p. 170)

These writers also elaborated on selecting the site and preparing a master plan, since site and program dictate form. They contended that the design of the school is influenced heavily by the site (its shape, size, orientation, access, views, neighbors, geology, and drainage). In fact, they insisted that the educational specifications should be prepared and the site should be selected with these interrelationships in mind. They went on to discuss preschematic design. An example of this important task involved citizens in the review of a large map of the school site and community. Citizens and educators were asked to record their comments (opportunities and problems) on the map concerning problems they saw pertaining to traffic flow patterns, location of playing fields, and access for pedestrians, cars, and buses. The result of this activity was an improved design because the large group could see more opportunities and problems than the planner and architect.

After identifying and studying the site, Brubacker and colleagues (1998) presented other ideas for establishing the schematic of the concept design. This provided the basic idea for the school plan—the plan of the proposed building and space requirements set forth in the educational specifications. They continued with specifics regarding design development, construction documents, bidding, the construction phase, occupancy, and evaluation of the product. For example, they were concerned with the achievement of the goals set out early in the planning process, and functionality of the school building.

A VIEW OF THE PHILOSOPHY OF TEACHING AND LEARNING

Complementary to the various resources and procedures mentioned here, the information provided by MacKenzie (1989) revealed another perspective vital to the complex tasks of planning for educational facilities—the discussion of function rather than form. He explored this topic from the viewpoint of the educational planner or educational leader, focusing on concerns regarding how educational planners transition from the planning process to a school design that matches student needs, community needs, and program needs.

> Many people know how to build a public school. Using a combination of local and state funds, land is purchased, an architect is hired to draw the plans and a general contractor is engaged to build the desired facility. Those steps plus a hundred others will result in a school building. Unfortunately, although many people think they know how to build a school, they may get halfway through the project before they discover that something was left out of the plans, or that at this late date, a better procedure could have been used to accomplish the task. If people ask the right questions before they get too far into a building project, they could avoid unnecessary frustration, expense, and wasted time. (p. 15)

MacKenzie further maintained that questions derived from philosophy of living and education must be asked during the planning process. As the activity unfolds and the process becomes more vivid, we may ask exactly where is the proper place for this important phase? The remainder of this section provides some initial answers to this question.

According to MacKenzie (1989), a facility will have a better chance of meeting community needs when questions about philosophy and learning are asked and answered. These answers may then be used in almost all other steps of the planning process, especially in the design phase. MacKenzie recommended the thorough investigation of teaching and learning, teaching styles or preferences, educational philosophy, personality types, and characteristics of the learners. For example, teaching styles are based on one's educational philosophy and personality and vary from teaching large groups to small groups, and from individualized instruction to computer and Internet-based learning. Teaching style is a direct function of the educational program. If large-group instruction with the use of minimal to no technology is the goal, then a traditional lecture "room" for 125 students or more is suitable. Of course, there might be places for television and computer monitors along with the required electrical outlets and connections.

However, if individualized instruction and computer-based instruction is the goal, spaces for learners may be smaller and designed and "wired or unwired" for technology, depending on the advances in technology and curriculum within a particular school system or school. Computer-assisted instruction might be in a laboratory setting, it might include carrels for individualized learning, clusters of computer stations, or it might assume that each student has a laptop computer without the need for connections through wires—a local area network delivered by laser technology where students might connect anywhere within the school, for example.

Regarding learning styles, MacKenzie (1989) presented the argument that many learners benefit from studying concrete examples of the world around them and having the opportunity to see and touch the actual "thing" they are studying. What does this mean for school design? It could mean that the school design should involve the integration of outdoor and indoor learning activities—rooms with exits to natural habitat and views of life, for example. It might also mean the need for a laboratory, a zoo, a technical shop, or a production studio. Consequently, the program might require spaces for learners to study abstract ideas (traditional classrooms as places for abstract learners),

and spaces for learners who learn best by touching things (tactile learning). This modest illustration should help planners to open doors for discussion of what philosophy and learning theory have to do with school design and the design of places and spaces for learning. Obviously at the planning stage, it is not known exactly which teachers or learners will actually use the school that is being planned: Hence, the concept of flexibility might enter the discussion.

Not only did MacKenzie (1989) encourage the exploration of educational philosophy and learning theory in the context of the school, but he encouraged planners to extend the philosophical boundaries to include the community—governmental agencies, parks, business, and libraries. In a global and multicultural society, we may extend this parameter to information and experiences available through media, especially the Internet. His main point was to encourage a learning environment designed to accommodate a variety of teaching and learning experiences.

MacKenzie (1989) suggested that a brief discussion of educational philosophy and learning theory early in the planning process could prevent an embarrassing situation later when the question might be asked whether or not the school design will facilitate a certain teaching/learning opportunity. Acknowledging the existence of numerous educational philosophies and learning theories, MacKenzie offered four educational philosophies as examples for discussion: perennialism, essentialism, progressivism, and existentialism. These were tied to the philosophies of life—idealism to pernnialism, realism to essentialism, pragmatism to progressivism, and existentialism. He viewed these philosophies on a continuum—idealism to realism to pragmatism to existentialism. Furthermore, he asserted that public school teaching fell within the essentialism and progressive areas while defending the exclusion of the other two as follows:

> Perennialism, with its reliance on the Great Books series and church dogma, is seldom found

TABLE 4.2   Table of Architectural/Natural Support Systems for School Design (Progressive Philosophy)

CATEGORY	AGE LEVEL	DEVELOPMENTAL CHARACTERISTICS	LEARNING GOALS	LEARNING ACTIVITIES	SUPPORT SYSTEM
Cognitive development	7+	Concept	Problem formation, problem solving, writing, spelling, research, technical skills	Discover the influence of beavers on biology, ecology	Beaver pond, lecture/activity room, camera, boat, computer terminals, internet, printer, library

in public school organizations today. The same can be said for existentialism. Existentialism is relatively new, and its emphasis on individual judgment would make it difficult to implement in public school organizations where emphasis is also placed on group conformity. (p. 18)

The procedure for putting function before form as discussed by MacKenzie (1989) may be illustrated by asking: How are each of the following translated into spaces for learning?

1. Philosophies of Life Related to Philosophies of Teaching and Learning
2. Goals for Learning
3. Teaching and Learning Strategies
4. Characteristics of the Learner
   a. Babies (Ages 1–4)
   b. Pre-Kindergarten (Ages 4–5)
   c. Kindergarten (Ages 5–6)
   d. Primary Grades (Ages 6–9)
   e. Upper Elementary (Ages 9–12)
   f. Middle School (Ages 12–15)
   g. Senior High School (Ages 15–18)
   h. Adult (Ages 18+)

Although we may have heard of these ideas in a context other than planning for educational facilities, it is significant that we think about how they fit into the equation of school design and planning. For ex-

ample, we might categorize the developmental characteristics and goals for learning as shown in Table 4.2. Under the progressive philosophy, we assume that learners do not come to school with a blank tablet, but rather they come to experience the world. In this example, students will learn by producing their own account of a beaver pond and its ecology system. Perhaps the students would be led to develop a photo essay about a beaver pond. In this context, the teacher serves as a facilitator, mentor, and guide to learning—not a lecturer. Students, therefore, would need a place to write, a place to develop pictures or transpose digital images, and a place to conduct research. They would learn subjects such as spelling, biology, ecology, grammar, publication techniques, and research skills. This set of activities might require a support system that includes a small lecture room, a library, computer stations with digital equipment, a scanner, and printer, a photo laboratory, and dark room (and, of course, visits to view a beaver pond). While this illustration includes only cognitive development, we would certainly expand it to include the behavioral and affective dimensions of learning as well as what we know about brain-based learning. For this one illustration, we have identified six space needs. This process should continue until the general set of learning goals and learning activities have been matched with an architectural or natural learning support system.

ENVIRONMENTAL PSYCHOLOGY AND SOCIAL DESIGN

The field of environmental psychology provides a vital body of knowledge in which school planners, designers, and architects must become immersed. McAndrew (1993), in writing on environmental psychology, regarded it as "the discipline that is concerned with the interactions and relationships between people and their environments" (p. 2). He made the point that environmental psychology may be identified as the built, the natural, and the social environment, emphasizing how it is concerned with the reactions of individuals to the environment. One of the major beliefs of the field is that people have the innate tendency to organize their cognitive world as simply as possible. People take an active role in structuring their perceptions of the environment because they rely heavily on past experiences with the environment in an attempt to make sense out of the places and spaces they are currently experiencing.

Likewise, the liaison between design and the behavioral sciences must be considered as we move to humanize schools. Sommer (1983) noted that many of the concepts supporting social design may be traced to Lewis Mumford, Richard Neutra, Jane Jacobs, and Paul and Percival Goodman in architecture and urban planning and Roger Baker, James J. Gibson, and Kurt Lewin in psychology.

> The movement was not associated with a particular style or aesthetic. The emphasis was more on the process (that is, identifying user values and bringing them into the planning process) than on a specific form or architectural product. The approach was guided by recognition of the designer's responsibility to the people affected by their work. Obviously, the client, as the person who signed the contract and paid the bills, was crucial from the standpoint of economic survival. Without clients, an architect will quickly become a nonarchitect. However, the satisfaction of the occupants is critical also for the moral justification of the profession. (p. 6)

Instead of defining social design, Sommer (1983) chose to characterize it.

> Social design is working with people rather than for them; involving people in planning and management of the spaces around them; educating them to use the environment wisely and creatively to achieve a harmonious balance between the social, physical and natural environment; to develop an awareness of beauty, a sense of responsibility to the earth's environment and to other living creatures; to generate, compile, and make available information about the effects of the built environment, including the effects of the built environment upon human beings. Social designers cannot achieve these objectives working by themselves. The goals can be realized only within the structures of larger organizations, which include the people for whom a given project is planned. (p. 7)

Relating closely to this body of knowledge, the issues of school density, school size, and classroom size, to name a few, appear on the horizon as the questions of student comfort and safety, satisfaction, and academic achievement (productivity). Is there a harmonious balance between the social and physical environment in a crowed classroom and an overcrowded school? We know that the physical environment has an influence on learning, behavior, and productivity. But, the extent has not been made absolutely clear to decision makers. McAfee (1987) in studying classroom density and aggressive behavior of handicapped children, suggested that although many other factors such as classroom management and location of adults can influence behaviors, it is believed that overcrowding in a learning environment yields a higher rate of aggressive behaviors in moderately/severely retarded students. This finding also implies safety and security issues.

Clients in a crowded school become dissatisfied with the results of the planning project—the school building. Burgess and Fordyce (1989) examined the effects of environmental design on toddlers. From their study it was learned that density has an effect on the social distances of toddlers. As the total amount of spaces was increased, toddlers staked out more personal space for themselves in play and interaction with other children and adults. These authors concluded that the classrooms used in their study were too small for the number of students that occupied them.

Such findings not only consider harmony in the physical environment, but also suggest a concern for architectural standards as they relate to student behavior and productivity. For example, all our current sets of measurements (used in planning and architecture) must be challenged in light of the fact that most standards for space needs were established as minimums. Notwithstanding, this does not even address the broader issues in a multicultural society, which was not a main concern when the existing minimum standards for school architecture and planning were written.

Personal space is a topic that has been studied for many years and will probably continue to be the focus of many studies. Personal space is the area around a person's body into which others may not intrude without arousing discomfort. It is a factor in any environment and causes people to react when this space is invaded. Depending on the surrounding environment and individuals, this area of personal space may be larger or smaller. "Personal distance extends from 18 inches to about 4 feet" (McAndrew, 1993, p. 102). If schools are social institutions, then we may consider social distance as a factor in design. "Social distance includes a zone ranging from 4 feet to 12 feet. The closer distances (4 to 7 feet) tend to be used by people who work together and those conducting informal business. The longer social distances (7 to 12 feet) require raising the voice level and are reserved for more formal business and social interaction" (pp. 102–103). Personal space is not only situational, but changes with age, sex, and racial background of the individual. While females use a smaller space when relating to known individuals, males are more sensitive to invasions of personal space. Personal space requirements of children have been shown to increase with age and even out as the child reaches puberty.

Swift (2000) conducted a study to determine if density was related to the academic achievement of elementary school students. She selected a sample of twenty-nine schools, where density was classified as high, medium, or low. Density was determined as the ratio of architectural square feet per school to the number of students attending the school. Strict and controlled statistical analysis led to the conclusion that elementary schools having an architectural square footage of less than 100 square feet per student had significantly lower science, social studies, and composite academic achievement scores than schools having more than 100 architectural square feet per student. Schools ranging from 100.27 to 134.1 architectural square feet per student had significantly higher achievement scores in science, social studies, and composite scores at the third grade level. This study opened the discussion of just how many square feet are necessary for classrooms. Tanner (2000a) conducted research on density with social distance theory (territoriality) as a guide and determined that the optimal space for each person in an elementary classroom setting was 49 square feet (this study assumed the upper limit of 7 feet, where "close social distance" is measured in the range of 4–7 feet). This calculation assumed that the 49 square feet were "usable" square feet per student. Therefore, a classroom having twenty students and one teacher should have 1,029 usable square feet, excluding storage and toilets.

Crowding and density have been used to describe conditions of congestion. "Density is an objective measure of the number of people per unit space, and it can be specified precisely" (McAndrew, 1993, p. 143). Crowding is a physiological feeling that is a result of density. Both crowding and density have a direct impact on humans emotionally and behaviorally. According to McAndrew, many studies have been conducted on the effects of crowding on a short- and long-term basis. Individuals in a crowded, dense environment for a short period of time demonstrate behaviors such as aggression, lower task performance, poor memory, and anxious feelings. Although it has been shown that people in higher-density environments show an increased amount of aggression, it has also been shown that during competition this was not the case. During competition in a high-density environment, individuals were withdrawn rather than aggressive. Long-term crowding research is in the beginning stages. The effects of long-term crowding on prison inmates were high blood pressure, higher death rates, and higher psychiatric needs. In addition to prisons, college dormitories have been studied. Crowded conditions in dormitories are linked to social withdrawal. There is still much more to learn about the effects of long-term crowding, according to McAndrew. He introduced several models that present theories of crowding. The ecological model focuses on having the ideal number of people for an environment to function well. The overload model highlights the negative effects of crowding. The density-intensity model theorizes that the present reaction is merely intensified by crowded conditions. The arousal model theorizes that the feelings of crowding are caused by the arousal of the situation. Finally, the control models link crowded feelings to individuals' need for control in a situation. Each theory attempts to explain a specific physiological state.

McAndrew (1993) discussed the effects of the ambient environment (sound, temperature, lighting, color, and odor), noting that these aspects tend to influence the mood, emotions, behavior, and learning capabilities of individuals. He documented that these human senses cause physical effects. The affective qualities of an environment determine mood and memories an individual obtains from that environment. Moods are caused by physical, neuro-chemical activity. In addition, mood has been linked to cognitive performance, memory, and creativity. Therefore, the ambient environment has a great deal of influence on individuals.

Regarding color and sound, McAndrew (1993) stated that they have distinctive influences on individuals. A bright room with light colors is preferred over a room with dark colors. Such

physiological reactions as respiration rate and blood pressure have been linked to room color. The effects of noise tend to be more controversial. Some believe distraction noise interferes with learning. Other researchers contribute the interference to feelings of control that individuals desire. The effects of noise on learning can also be linked to gender, age, and academic ability. Temperature and light are also influential factors of the ambient environment. Temperature tends to influence social behaviors such as aggression, while light, especially natural light, has been shown to enhance the performance of elementary-aged students. "Cool-fluorescent lamps may cause [an] increase in the activity levels of children" (p. 62). The ambient environment includes many facets of the physical surroundings. These have each been linked to behaviors in humans, with many focusing on learning environments. Color is complicated in that it means different things to different people. Color has three dimensions: brightness, hue, and saturation. Brightness refers to the intensity of light coming from a source. Hue refers to the color, which is the wavelength of the light reflected from the source, while saturation refers to the amount of white light in the hue—the less white light there is, the more highly saturated the color. "Most studies indicate that people prefer light to dark colors, saturated colors to unsaturated colors, and colors from the 'cool' end of the spectrum (green, blue) to 'warm' colors such as orange or red" (p. 64). Color influences the arousal levels in people. For example, "People walk faster in hallways painted in warm colors (red or orange) than in hallways painted in cooler colors" (p. 65). Pink reduces anxiety, causes relaxation, and may be used to reduce aggression. What we learn from research on color is straightforward: The amount of natural light in a given setting influences the way we see various colors. However, all older studies and current beliefs that planners and designers have pertaining to color should be reevaluated in terms of the cultures represented by the subjects that were studied. What we know about white middle-class students (the subjects in many of the older studies—studies that influenced standards) may not be true for students in a global and multicultural society.

The structure of the learning environment is vital. In addition to the ambient environment, the arrangement and materials used in the environment contribute to the amount of learning taking place in that environment. The design of the classroom allows for many of these changes, while others are teacher-specific. As discussed earlier in this section, the size of the classroom is probably one of the leading problems in schools today. All too often classrooms that were already too small for unique arrangements are pressed with more students as enrollments increase. With limited space and density issues, teachers are often limited to a traditional classroom arrangement. Given the traditional arrangement, discipline problems occur as a result of the density of the classroom. Along with the disruption of discipline, resources in the classroom are in high demand, which in turn yields further disruption as students compete and disagree over materials.

Today's classrooms require an arrangement of a special style. In order to function in our workforce, many individuals must work alongside others to achieve a common goal. A classroom designed with group work in mind is a must. Small, overcrowded classrooms do not allow for such arrangements. McAndrew (1993) identified the open classroom as an arrangement that is conducive to student needs, but clearly pointed out that research indicates traditional classroom students outperform open classroom students in academics. However, the research he cited may not have taken into consideration any ethnicity and cultural issues since the bulk of his research was conducted in the 1970s. The benefits of the open classroom, as McAndrew saw it, included student motivation, attendance, and satisfaction. Until we find research for current cultural situations, a mix of traditional large-group instruction areas should be mixed with small-group and individual areas. Students need to interact with others at times.

The learning environment is a special place and what exactly should it be? The planning and design research show specific trends, and it is apparent that we are in need of change in the way we view the physical environment, especially in multicultural societies. Unfortunately, there are administrators, planners, designers, architects, and construction managers who do not consider research when designing our classrooms and schools. If they used the concepts of social design and environmental psychology, then environments would improve. Until then, teachers and students are limited to the type of environment they inherit.

SUMMARY

Planning may be defined as a course of action wherein a set of organized activities permits decision makers to select choices from a set of feasible alternative solutions. School facility planning models may be described as rational (involving specialists, requiring a large amount of data, and implemented through clear lines of authority), integrated (involving many stakeholders and frequent exchange of information, implemented through decentralized authority), or consensus models (involving aspects of the other two models). Effective school facility planning requires the input of a wide variety of professionals and future building occupants, as well as leadership by individuals with effective group dynamics skills. The objective of the school planning process should be to advance the design of safe, comfortable, and developmentally appropriate learning environments for students of all ages in a multicultural society. Throughout time and across the globe, critics have argued that school facilities are inadequate and inappropriate, but the architecture does eventually respond to educational reforms. A sound planning process may ensure that a facility is capable of meeting (or adapting to) the needs of a community over the life of the building.

The 1940s, 1950s, and 1960s were dominated by integrated approaches to school facility planning that required large amounts of data which were difficult to assemble, often a large number of people (the survey movement), and consequently a relatively long period of time. The school survey process relied on a leadership committee working with many subcommittees to collect and analyze data regarding the educational program, school finance, public relations, the community and its people, and the present school plant. Outcomes of this process included an educational program to meet community needs and long-range, flexible building plans. Other approaches introduced during this period utilized methods for quantifying additional data, such as birthrate trends, estimated enrollment by grade-level clusters, and capital revenues for construction in school facility planning.

Planning models introduced during the 1970s and 1980s were primarily rational models and ranged from the more theoretical to the highly practical. Although common practice of this period often limited input from outside specialists and consultants to reduce planning time and associated costs, some of the planning models called for a more integrated approach. It was recognized that no one planning model would work best in all situations, and a variety of models were presented.

Since the 1990s writers have carefully addressed the conflicts that often arise when a variety of stakeholders engage in the school planning and delivery process. This era has also seen scholarly work in developing theoretical underpinnings for educational facility planning, as well as very practical recommendations for collecting and analyzing relevant data and working through the school delivery process, from planning to postoccupancy evaluation.

Over the years, scholars and practitioners have offered recommendations for improving school designs. When designing environments for students, careful consideration must be given to the size and scale of the building and its components, outdoor environments, technology integration, comfort, places that encourage social interaction, aesthetics, variety, school identity, public spaces, and accommodating a variety of teaching styles. It is vitally important to gain an understanding of the educational philosophies supported within a school in order to ensure that learning environments are appropriately designed. The field of environmental psychology (in which the relationships between people and their surrounding environment are studied) offers important information to school planners, designers, and other stakeholders. Research data on topics such as crowding, density, ambient conditions (e.g., color, temperature), and classroom arrangement may be used to improve school designs, and therefore are relevant to school planning and design activities.

ACTIVITIES

1. Conduct an interview with a facilities director in a local school district to learn about the process(es) used in that district to plan, design, and construct a new school. What stakeholders are involved in the process and how do they interact?

2. In small groups, brainstorm a design solution to a school to be constructed that recognizes at least three teaching and learning philosophies. Bring together participants after the brainstorming activity and compare and contrast the results.

3. Prepare a bibliography of literature that addresses how one of the following physical conditions affects educational outcomes: *indoor air quality*, *thermal conditions*, *lighting*, *acoustics*, *furniture arrangement*, or *school size*.

REFERENCES

Adams, D. (1991). Planning models and paradigms. In Carlson, R. V., & Awkerman, G. (eds.), *Educational planning*. New York: Longman, pp. 5–20.

Banghart, F. W., & Trull, A., Jr. (1973). *Educational planning*. New York: Macmillan.

Barnard, H. (1848). *School architecture*. Cincinnati, OH: H.W. Derby & Co.

Brooks, K. W., Conrad, M. C., & Griffith, W. (1980). *From program to educational facilities*. Lexington, KY: Center for Professional Development, College of Education, University of Kentucky.

Brubaker, C. W. (1993). Emerging trends in school design. In Graves, B. E. (ed.) *School ways: the planning and design of America's schools*. New York: McGraw-Hill, pp. 3–11.

Brubaker, C. W., Bordwell, R., & Christopher, G. (1998). *Planning and designing schools*. New York: McGraw-Hill.

Burgess, J. W., & Fordyce, W. K. (1989). Effects of preschool environments on nonverbal social behavior: Toddlers' interpersonal distances to teachers and classmates change with environmental density, classroom design, and parent-child interactions. *The Journal of Child Psychology and Psychiatry*, 30(1), 23–34.

Castaldi, B. (1994). *Educational facilities: Planning, modernizing, and management*. Boston: Allyn and Bacon.

Caudill, W. W. (1941). *Space for teaching*. College Station, TX: Bulletin of the Texas Agricultural and Mechanical Art College.

Christopher, G. (1987). Developing the master plan. In Hertz, K. V., & Day, C. W. (eds.), *Schoolhouse planning*. Reston, VA: Association of School Business Officials International, pp. 15–20.

Church, H. H., Seagers, P. W., Barr, M. W., Fox, W. H., & Stapley, M. E. (1953). *The local school facilities survey*. Bloomington, IN: Division of Research and Field Services, Indiana University.

Commission on American School Buildings (1949). *American school buildings*. Washington, DC: American Association of School Administrators, NEA.

Council of Educational Facility Planners (1969). *Guide for planning educational facilities*. Columbus, OH: Council of Educational Facility Planners.

Earthman, G. I. (2000). *Planning educational facilities for the next century*. Reston, VA: Association of School Business Officials International.

Engelhardt, N. L., Engelhardt, N. L., Jr., & Leggett, S. (1947). *Planning secondary school buildings*. New York: Reinhold Publishing Company.

Engelhardt, N. L., Engelhardt, N. L., Jr., & Leggett, S. (1953). *Planning elementary school buildings*. New York: F.W. Dodge Corporation.

Engelhardt, N. L., Engelhardt, N. L., Jr., & Leggett, S. (1956). *School planning and building handbook*. New York: F.W. Dodge Corporation.

Graves, B. E. (ed.) (1993). *School ways: the planning and design of America's schools*. New York: McGraw-Hill.

Greenman, J. (1988). *Caring spaces, learning places: Children's environments that work*. Redmond, WA: Exchange Press, Inc.

Hertz, K. V., & Day, C. W. (eds.) (1987). *Schoolhouse planning*. Reston, VA: Association of School Business Officials International.

Holcomb, J. H. (1995). *A guide to the planning of educational facilities*. New York: University Press of America.

Kaufman, R., Herman, J., & Watters, K. (1996). *Educational planning: Strategic, tactical, and operational*. Lancaster, PA: Technomic Publishing Company.

Kowalski, T. J. (1989). *Planning and managing school facilities*. New York: Praeger.

Leggett, S., Brubaker, C. W., Cohodes, A., & Shapiro, A. S. (1977). *Planning flexible learning places*. New York: McGraw-Hill.

MacKenzie, D. C. (1989). *Planning educational facilities*. New York: University Press of America.

McAfee, J. K. (1987). Classroom density and the aggressive behavior of handicapped children. *Education and Treatment of Children*, 10(2), 9–17.

McAndrew, F. T. (1993). *Environmental psychology*. Pacific Grove, CA: Brooks/Cole.

McClurkin, W. D. (1964). *School building planning*. London: The Macmillan Company.

McConnell, J. D. (1957). *Planning for school buildings*. Englewood Cliffs, NJ: Prentice-Hall.

McGuffey, C. W. (1973). *Systematic planning for educational facilities*. Chicago, IL: Chicago Board of Education.

Meek, A. (ed.) (1995). *Designing places for learning*. Alexandria, VA: Association for Supervision and Curriculum Development.

Mort, P. R., & Vincent, W. S. (1946). *A look at our schools*. New York: Cattel and Company.

Myers, N., & Robertson, S. (2004). *Creating Connections: The CEFPI Guide for Educational Facility Planning*. Scottsdale, AZ: Council of Educational Facility Planners, International.

National Council on Schoolhouse Construction (1949). *The 1948 guide for planning school plants*, rev. ed. Nashville, TN: Peabody College.

Ortiz, F. I. (1994). *Schoolhousing: Planning and designing educational facilities*. Albany, NY: State University of New York Press.

Perkins, L. B., & Cocking, W. D. (1949). *Schools*. New York: Reinhold Publishing Corporation.

Sanoff, H. (1994). *School design.* New York: Van Nostrand Reinhold.

Seaborne, M. V. J. (1971a). *The English school: Its architecture and organization, 1370–1870.* London: Routledge & Kegan Paul.

Seaborne, M. V. J. (1971b). *Primary school design.* London: Routledge & Kegan Paul.

Seaborne, M. V. J., & Lowe, R. (1977). *The English school: Its architecture and organization, Vol. II, 1870–1970.* London: Routledge & Kegan Paul.

Sommer, R. (1983). *Social design.* Englewood Cliffs, NJ: Prentice-Hall.

Stanford University School Planning Laboratory (1954). *Planning tomorrow's secondary schools.* Stanford, CA: Stanford University Press.

Strayer, G. D., Jr. (1948). *Planning for school surveys.* Bulletin of the School of Education, Vol. 24, No. 2, Division of Research and Field Services, Indiana University, Bloomington.

Sumption, M. R. (1952). *How to conduct a citizens school survey.* New York: Prentice-Hall.

Swift, D. O. (2000). *Effects of student population density on academic achievement in Georgia elementary schools.* Unpublished doctoral dissertation, University of Georgia, Athens.

Tanner, C. K. (1991). Planning in the context of state policy making. In Carlson, R. V., & Awkerman, G. (eds.), *Educational planning* New York: Longman, pp. 87–107.

Tanner, C. K. (2000a). The classroom: Size versus density. *School Business Affairs,* 66, pp. 1–23.

Tanner, C. K. (2000b). The influence of school architecture on academic achievement. *Journal of Educational Administration,* 38(4), pp. 309–330.

Tanner, C. K., & Holmes, C. T. (1985). *Microcomputer applications in educational planning and decision making.* New York: Teachers College Press.

Taylor, A. P., & Vlastos, G. (1975). *School zone: Learning environments for children.* York: Van Nostrand Reinhold.

Vickery, D. J., & Kayser, R. A. (1972). *School building design Asia.* Colombo, Sri Lanka: Kularatne and Co., Ltd.

PLANNING, PROGRAMMING, AND DESIGN OF EDUCATIONAL LEARNING ENVIRONMENTS

Part III focuses on a conceptualization of planning, programming, and design activities supported primarily by premises 1, 5, 7, and 8 introduced in Chapter 3. Two complementary methods of developing educational facilities are described and explained. First, the phases of planning necessary to conceptualize the learning environment are addressed. This facet of planning entails a very broad perspective, including the contextual climate and environmental scanning (see Chapter 16), and parallels specific milestones that are outlined to plan and implement a capital project.

Chapter 5 provides a discussion of planning and programming procedures, leading the school system up to the point of making an agreement with an architectural firm to complete the design and construction documents, while identifying the remainder of activities needed to ensure the development of a physical learning environment. The planning and programming phases are highly interactive involving many stakeholders (including selected builders and subcontractors): and it is imperative that these activities be *integrated* through communications and sharing among team members to achieve the optimal school facility, based on the desired educational programs. Some individuals may use planning and programming interchangeably, but we view these activities to be separate, yet complementary. For example, programming is a verbal and symbolic description, complemented by an explanation of all activities the learning environment is expected to facilitate. Planning integrates community and educational needs and programming to influence design through a thorough study of the school system or educational organization, communications, and sharing among stakeholders. Collaboration between the educational organization and community, then, is vitally important, and the premise that the *demand for resources is always greater than those available* becomes the "reality check." Below are four of the eight key premises introduced in Chapter 3 and assumed vital for an effective planning, programming, and design process.

Premises for Developing School Facilities

PREMISE	DESCRIPTOR
Premise 1	Strong leadership is essential.
Premise 5	Planning and design activities are integrated.
Premise 7	The demand for resources is greater than those available.
Premise 8	Collaboration and cooperation between the school and community are essential.

A conceptual procedure assuming a "grass-roots" stakeholder approach to planning for educational facilities is presented. It assumes the selection of the architectural firm following completion of the educational planning and programming activities. This procedure assumes qualified planners as the primary leaders, involvement of the stakeholders, and may include architects, landscape architects, and contractors as team members. *Architects are not the main leaders of the planning and programming under this procedure.* One advantage of qualified educational planners developing the educational facilities plan is that specific teaching and learning philosophies can be discussed and presented to the stakeholders for decision making. A "from the bottom up" approach is followed in this process, where everyone is allowed to make input and influence decisions based on findings from educational and environmental research activities (survey research/environmental scanning). Thus, it is absolutely necessary that educational planners be well informed about research as it relates to affective, behavioral, and cognitive learning activities. Furthermore, it is a requirement that the educational planners be highly knowledgeable about the various methods of teaching that fosters positive student outcomes, and the spaces needed to facilitate various educational philosophies and programs. Traditionally, one main outcome from the educational programming process has been the completion of educational specifications, but the process advocated here goes a milestone further, requiring the educational facilities plan to include conceptual diagrams (possibly preliminary conceptual designs and drawings) of the desired educational facility. This procedure has the advantage of better communications with the contracting architectural firm charged with the job of developing the school's design and managing the construction phases of the project. Usually, a construction management team, perhaps external to the architectural firm, is employed by the owner to contribute to the planning process and monitor day-to-day management of the construction process.

Unlike the procedures described in this chapter, Chapter 6 describes a procedure based on the assumption that the architectural firm will be in charge of planning, programming, and design activities. Regardless of the method (Chapter 5 or 6), the chief planner and top educational officials should exhibit *strong leadership* in completing the facilities project, since there are numerous players having special interests in the outcomes. Either the architect is selected to lead the entire process, or the architect assists the facility planning process by teaming with an educational planning group and local facility staff. The governing board, as the owner, enters into a contract for services with the chosen architectural firm after the educational plan is completed. Under this process, the architect, in turn, may enter into subcontracts with a variety of consultants such as engineers and other professionals.

If the architectural firm develops the educational facilities plan and provides the design services, the process may be less time-consuming, but under this approach there is a danger that stakeholders, especially students and teachers, will have minimal input into the school's design. Thoroughly involving ***all stakeholders*** can be an extremely time-consuming process, which may require as much as an entire year for the development of the educational facilities plan, program, and design. The decision makers representing the stakeholders must carefully weigh the cost/benefit of devoting an entire year or more for planning against such factors as economics, urgency or political expediency, community acceptance of the finished product, and the need for a "buy-in."

CHAPTER FIVE

PLANNING AND PROGRAMMING FOR A CAPITAL PROJECT

NEED FOR PLANNING ACTIVITIES

Billions of dollars are being spent each year to retrofit, renovate, and build schools in America, and yet these "new" designs are often based on outmoded concepts, ignore special ecological principles, and fail to include substantive client input. All stakeholders, from students to community members, must be involved in the planning and design of learning environments according to Taylor (2000). Planners and architects should be aware that school maintenance begins while the school is in the planning and design phases. Hence, personnel representing theses vital areas should be involved in the planning and design of the school. In the design phase, it may be the maintenance personnel who can have the greatest impact on future maintenance costs in a school.

This point of view serves as a basis for the driving force behind what we shall identify as "educational facilities planning" in this chapter. Programming, a necessary aspect of the process, has too frequently depended on planning based on predetermined square footage needs built into the most frequently government-sanctioned educational specifications or even the "cookie cutter school," also known as prototype schools.

We advocate the process of "planning to programming" of educational facilities including significant contributions from students, the community, educational professionals, and professionals in the field of planning and design. Furthermore, it is strongly recommended that these community and school representatives be involved throughout the entire process, not just in the beginning as noted in Figure 3.1. Given a sound collaborative process, the results will have a better chance of serving the community's educational and social needs, whether the final product is intended to be a grade school, community library, vocational center, or college. Participatory planning involves collectively identifying values about learning environments, developing a mission corresponding to the community's values for learning environments, the construction of surprise-free scenario statements about the school environment founded on the values and beliefs, mission, and environmental scans; and the formulation of a vision of the ideal school environment (see Chapter 16 for a practical exercise employing these concepts).

Educational programming yields specifications for the desired program or activities, space relationships, and design sketches founded on outgrowths of the community's philosophy of teaching and learning, not on prepackaged government specifications and plans. Hence, when such participatory planning and programming happen, exciting new issues emerge concerning colocation of school activity settings for child care, health care, museums, art galleries, science labs, community cultural centers, vocational schools, colleges, studios instead of classrooms, and outdoor "learning landscapes" instead of barren playgrounds (Taylor, 2000).

Regarding participation in the planning and programming that lead to the design process, Sanoff (2000) has stated that "the activity of community design is based on the principle that the environment works better if people affected by its changes are actively involved in its creation and management instead of being treated as passive consumers" (p. x). He warned that community participation is neither a panacea nor a total solution for social change and noted further that participation means the collaboration of people pursuing objectives they themselves have defined. A vital component of the participatory process is individual learning through increased awareness of a problem. Both the planner and the participants learn from each other. Participation can lead to the ultimate agreement about what the future should look like and includes awareness, perception, decision making, and implementation. Awareness involves persuading participants to speak the same language, perception takes awareness a milestone forward—it facilitates an understanding of the physical, social, cultural, and economic ramifications for the project outcomes. Decision making allows participants to actually craft physical designs based on their priorities, which, in turn, the professional architect synthesizes for final plans. Implementation should include the participants to ensure that they and the professional architect catch sight of the expected results (Sanoff, 1994). This type of participation allows people to be involved up to the opening of a school and even during postoccupancy evaluation. In fact, since the school is community-owned, it is forever a community concern that the educational environment be held to high standards. Chapter 6 provides detailed information on collaborative design.

What triggers the *need for school facilities planning*? Any one of the following items can awaken the need for capital planning for a new school or remodeling an existing structure: student population increases (increased density), old or dilapidated buildings, fire, population shifts (the current school is located in a blighted area or no longer has a sustainable enrollment), educational program changes, and natural disasters. *The most likely occurrence to activate the need for any new school building is increased student population.*

It is unlikely that a capital project happens overnight, unless there is a fire or natural disaster. Large-scale planning is usually an ongoing process in larger school systems and more periodic in smaller school systems. Regardless of school system size, school facilities planning entails regularly scheduled feasibility studies of the school environments. Thorough checks should take place to ensure that the school program is being facilitated, not constrained, by the physical environment. If the program and school facilities are not in harmony, modifications to existing structures need to be made or new physical environments should be created to accommodate program changes. There are several ways to assess structures to determine adequacy.

A new approach to the investigation of facilities for educational adequacy is through the design assessment scales found in the research section of this book (Part VI). Complementing these assessment instruments is the *Guide for School Facility Appraisal* published by the Council of Educational Facility Planners, International (http://www.cefpi.com). The guide helps to evaluate the physical condition of the school, while the design appraisal scales (Part VI) measure the likelihood that the school facilitates student learning and behavior. The resulting scores on these instruments provide valid information for decision making. Both are useful tools to help plan a new school or remodel an existing school facility. Studies conducted by the authors reveal there is a strong correlation between the scores on the *Guide for School Facility Appraisal* and the design assessment scales. While neither the guide nor the scales are perfect for all aspects of design and structure, they provide approximate measures of the school environment. They also contain principles of design and planning that are subsets of the design principles found in Chapter 2 of this book.

PHASES IN PLANNING FOR EDUCATIONAL LEARNING ENVIRONMENTS

The phases we propose as a gateway leading to concept design for schools are largely interactive. In Chapter 3 we posited six assumptions, one of which was "all students can learn in a developmentally appropriate environment." Key aspects of the procedural model discussed in Chapter 3 are planning and programming—the two major activities leading to concept design.

The phases of facilities planning addressed in Figure 3.1 assume learning is a lifelong process, and citizens, students, and educators know what they want or can envision the ideal school with leadership from a qualified school planner. The chief guiding principle is that the *learning environment should result from an interactive process involving all stakeholders.* Design is always evolving as new research findings reveal flaws in various former designs and flaws in former assumptions and beliefs about the very processes of learning (see, e.g., the ideas in Chapter 13). To link planning programming and design, we must first specify some basic principles of developing learning environments.

In 2000 the U.S. Department of Education released a document entitled *Schools as Centers of Community: A Citizens' Guide for Planning and Design.* A revision of this document was published in 2003 (Bingler, Quinn, & Sullivan, 2003). According to these documents, effective learning environments are designed to

- Enhance teaching and learning and accommodate the needs of all learners.
- Serve as centers of the community.
- Result from a planning/design process involving all stakeholders.
- Provide for health, safety, and security.
- Make effective use of all resources.
- Allow for flexibility and adaptability to changing needs.

These six nationally recognized design principles produced by the U.S. Department of Education should be presented to the planning team early in the process. They also serve as guides to programming. Above all, throughout the process the six design principles should be applied with knowledge of Sanoff's (1994, p. 179) five participatory design principles:

1. There is no best solution to design problems.
2. "Expert" decisions are not necessarily better than "lay" decisions.
3. Milestones achieved and alternatives considered by the architect-planners (traditionally in their own minds in the privacy of an office) can be brought to the surface for the users to discuss.
4. All individuals and interest groups should come together in an open forum.
5. The process is continuous and everchanging.

Planning, programming, and design are not necessarily a set of linear procedures, implying that in some instances, parts of two or more phases may be parallel. For example, in the six phases of planning discussed below, phase III might parallel phase II and part of phase I. The total process is guided by the basic principle that the health, safety, and security of the learning environment are the top priorities.

The following subsections contain a description of the procedures that lead to school design. There are six planning phases preceding the formal programming activity.

Phase I: Determine the Principles and Values of the Community

Early in the process of developing the educational facilities plan we must come face to face with two central questions: What is to be learned? How does learning occur? Included in this line of reasoning is the question of how do stakeholders view learning; and equally important, are their theories of learning complementary to teaching methods currently in existence or amenable to those theories likely to evolve later on in the schools?

Exactly what is to be learned by the students is a curriculum problem requiring knowledge of learning theories, program development, and the principles of teaching. The operant conditioning (behaviorist) theory attributed to Skinner (1957), Thorndike (1923), and Watson (1958) contends that learning is the result of the application of consequences. Learners begin to connect certain responses with certain stimuli. This connection influences the probability of the response to change, and learning occurs. Operant conditioning is based on the concept that learning is a function of change in observable behavior. Changes in behavior are the result of an individual's response to events (stimuli) occurring in the environment. A response produces a consequence such as defining a word, hitting a ball, or solving a mathematics problem. When a particular stimulus–response (S–R) pattern is reinforced (a reward given), the individual is then conditioned to respond. The distinctive characteristic of operant conditioning relative to previous forms of behaviorism is when the organism can emit responses instead of only eliciting response due to an external stimulus. These theories support the notion of practicing a task until the performance is perfected or memorizing facts for a test. Many components of behaviorism are still used in schools around the world; hence, it must be considered when schools are planned.

Beyond behaviorist theory, constructivist theory views the student as one who acts on objects and events within his or her environment and thereby gains some understanding of the features held by the objects and events. Constructivism, during the 1930s and 1940s, was the leading perspective among public school educators in the United States, although in its purist form was not widely implemented in the schools. In this theory, the emphasis is placed on the student rather than the teacher. One popular movement introduced by Montessori (1967) did have limited success worldwide. This constructivist approach viewed the natural aptitude of children and their potential for development, focusing on how they learn and build themselves from what they find in their immediate environment. Montessori had the intuition and insight to recognize that a growing child has keen sensitivities and a highly absorbent mind, and children take in impressions and learn patterns of behavior, knowledge, and skills through a series of personal experiences offered in the environment around them, and these are the first milestones of learning in their lives.

In the constructivist theory, teachers are seen as facilitators or coaches who assist students in constructing their own conceptualizations and solutions to problems. Two schools of thought, social constructivism and cognitive constructivism, fall within this larger classification. Although these theories differ, they both contend that the child's individual development is at the center of instruction. Social constructivist theory, most frequently attributed to psychologist Lev S. Vygotsky, emphasizes the influences of cultural and social contexts in learning and supports a discovery model of learning. This type of model places the teacher in an active role, while the students' mental abilities develop naturally through various paths of discovery. Cognitive constructivism, attributed to Jean Piaget (1924, 1936), a Swiss psychologist, stressed the holistic approach. A child constructs understanding through many channels: reading, listening, exploring, and experiencing his or her environment. Piaget's stages of cognitive development include sensorimotor (infants use sensory and motor skills to explore and gain understanding of their environments); preoperational (children ages 2–7 years begin to use symbols and respond to objects and events according to how they appear to be); concrete operations (at ages 7–11 years children begin to think logically); and formal operations (from age 11 years on, children begin to think systematic and abstract thoughts).

These theories of learning, with some of their branches of divergent thought, must be considered in planning a physical environment. Emerging brain research is expanding the concept of how people learn. It, however, tends to lead to strategies making use of the physical environment for teaching, much like the Montessori approach. For example, consider this case in point for mathematics taken from a brain-based curriculum": Estimate how many Gummy Bears are in the teacher's jar. How can you make a good estimate? Explain your thinking. Other illustrations from social studies include viewing televised newscasts, listening to radio newscasts, tapes, watching videos, and recording notes from these activities for class discussion and debate. These activities strongly suggest constructivism theory. So, the physical environment needed to accommodate various learning theories is definitely different from the one-room schoolhouse with straight rows where students focused on the teacher. Nevertheless, it is the job of the planner to find out what is expected by the stakeholders in order to decide the purpose of the physical learning environment.

The behaviorist theory, when linked to the physical environment, implies a teacher-centered approach to teaching. The teacher lectures and the student listens, studies, memorizes, practices, and passes a test. The behaviorist theory assumes a space where the teacher does most of the work and the student absorbs the knowledge. While this is an abbreviated explanation of what is needed in the physical environment to facilitate the behaviorist theories, there is a need to have some of the physical structure of the school set aside for lecturing, listening, and testing. The problem we have experienced too often in the past is that the whole school was designed with operant conditioning as the basic theory. What type of a structure do you need for a mathematics class where the teacher explains that $(x)(x) = x^2$, followed by twenty-five problems of similar nature ($2 \times 2 = 4$; $3 \times 3 = 9$, $4 \times 4 = 16$. . .)? This is a simplistic illustration of rote learning tied to operant conditioning. The ideal facility for operant conditioning, then, is a series of one-room schoolhouses on either side of a corridor. This structure does well when the teacher is the worker and students sit and absorb the message that is repeated over and over again until the

student, at best, memorizes that x times x is x squared, or that 2 to the second power is 4. But most stakeholders know that there is more to learning than operant conditioning, albeit an important aspect of learning.

Some of the cognitive constructivism theories that apply directly to the planning of physical environments are as follows: The important role for the school planner and teacher is to provide an environment where the child can experience spur-of-the-moment research; the classroom should be filled with genuine opportunities to challenge the students; the students should be given the freedom to understand and construct meaning at their own pace through personal experiences as they develop through individual developmental processes; learning is a very active process where mistakes will be made and solutions may or may not eventually be found; and learning is a social process that should take place among collaborative groups where there may be peer interaction in a setting that is as close to "natural" as possible. "The learning environment should enhance teaching and learning and accommodate the needs of all learners" (U.S. Department of Education, 2000, p. 5). Mixing all these theories together to form an educational learning environment implies large- and small-group instruction areas, some lecturing, small-group work, and large-group work. In some cases, the community becomes a classroom—one example of the Montessori method.

The basic assumptions as we progress from learning theory to curriculum to the plan of the learning environment include provisions for health, safety, security, flexibility, and adaptability to changing needs. Flexibility has had frequent skirmishes with simplistic thinking over the years. Perhaps the most misused aspect of flexibility has been to continue to add on rooms to an already overcrowded school. When planners and designers talk about flexibility, what do they really mean?

A curriculum example requiring flexibility for structures is offered in Canady and Rettig (1995). It assumes parallel block scheduling as a means to ensure several small classes (ten to fourteen students) in a setting where there may be as many as twenty-eight students assigned to each teacher. Assuming this concept of delivering a curriculum, we might arrive at some principles of learning environments under "mixed learning theories" that will reduce the student–teacher ratio for mathematics, English, and science or exposure to higher-level curricular content. Part of the day a student would attend "pull-out" programs in large heterogeneous groups (twenty-eight students in classes such as art, music, and social studies), while at least half the school day in small, homogeneous groups (fourteen students in English, science, and mathematics).

A design to accommodate parallel block scheduling might have interconnecting classrooms with shared teacher workrooms, provide several windows for natural light in every classroom as a necessity, include flexible learning spaces to meet changing curriculum and student needs, employ low density in major subject areas, assume small schools as a way to overcome discipline problems and enhance student safety and security, and maximize large- and small-group activities. Such programming for educational facilities might also include well-planned and well-designed outdoor learning environments.

Phase II: Develop a Purpose for the Physical Learning Environment

Does the quality of the learning environment influence student achievement, attitudes, and behavior? We affirm the answer to this question is "yes" and later on give some examples of research findings in Part VII of this book. But, when engaging in the planning and programming process, what is really perceived by the stakeholders about how the physical environment influences learning? Perception is the reality of the stakeholder. How can the physical environment facilitate the educational program? Should the perceptions be based on the research findings?

Planners and designers must not overlook the needs of the community going beyond the traditional school we frequently see being built in the name of "new." The school of the future in many districts will include community centers, food services for the students and others, health centers, recreational areas and buildings, studios instead of classrooms, museums, art galleries, shared school and community media centers, and outdoor learning centers. Our goal should be to provide the community with a structure and grounds to be used more than just part-time students. Hence, we should aim for a multipurpose, educational environment to provide spaces for the students and community on a 24-7, 365 days per year basis.

National design principle number 2 states: "The learning environment should serve as a center of the community" (U.S. Department of Education, 2000, p. 6). The plausible argument for this line of reasoning is that the school provides strength for the community because it serves as a name tag or identity. The idea of the school as the "hub" of the community goes back to pioneer days in the United States, where the school often served as a social gathering place for activities ranging from religious services to pie-eating contests. There are many examples of the hub approach across the United States, but one outstanding example is found at Oconee County High School in Watkinsville, Georgia. Here sports fields, a civic center, a high school, an agricultural and a horticultural center provide specialized areas for learning and community activities. The foresight in planning, designing, and constructing such an outstanding community-based learning environment is to be commended, since this project was planned in the 1980s, long before the movement for national design principles had materialized.

A physical environment serving the community strengthens the relationship between school and community. Such a partnership promotes a broad spectrum of civic and learning activities, a concept surely supporting constructivist learning theories. The learning hub minimizes abstract and irrelevant learning, allowing parents and community leaders to become active participants in the school's activities.

One primary design concept to be gleaned from the purpose of the school as a hub is that the school environment should be an inviting place. Less institutionalization and a user-friendly atmosphere is the goal. Thus, the site should be accessible all year. Fewer fences and locks and more people who are constantly involved, working in the school after hours and on weekends, and a sequence of continuous community activities may be safety and security features that are often overlooked. One example of an open campus plan school in an inner-city context is Glynn Academy, Brunswick, Georgia. There are no fences, the school's units are in open areas. Because of community involvement and constant activities in the school, there is a minimal amount of vandalism. The community takes pride in the school because it is not only historic, but also a hub.

The "community use concept" extends the schools' programs to include other resources such as zoos, parks, pools, wildlife management areas, agricultural centers, manufacturing firms, technical operations, governmental services, and commercial areas. Students may actually perform community service in these organizations and learn about the relationships between the school and the community. A week of shadowing an executive, a forest ranger, a zoo manager, and other professions will add depth to the student's program of learning. Activities of this nature may be facilitated by a school having a "community display" area, and a place where teachers, students, and community members meet. This space might include traditional displays, Internet and computer access, and a place to discuss ideas and make presentations. This space might be called a community studio. Notwithstanding, this activity space should be aesthetically pleasing, inside and out, not a back room in a building having no amenities.

Phase III: Examine the Context

Social and cultural components of the community and state influence the thinking of the leaders and planners of schools, which in turn is reflected in the final outcome—a school. Obviously, the political influence of the community and state and national policies affecting facilities come into play as well. It is difficult to determine where politics stop and the economics of the area begin, and the converse is also true. Finally, the demographics of the area link closely with the multicultural, social, political, and economic workings of the context of schools.

To make an attempt to view all the variables that might influence the school building and its outdoor learning environments, a comprehensive survey or "environmental scan" can be useful in establishing what the community wants, what it can afford financially, and what is can accept culturally. The results of a contextual study will influence educational specifications by describing and explaining goals, objectives, and their relationships to the educational environment. Early in the process, perhaps at the beginning of the programming process, expect to launch a student population forecast, a demographic analysis slanted toward how trends might influence the school population and the school program, a study of space needs based on program needs, a program review, and a review of research and literature on school design as it relates to teaching and learning. Also, in this process it is recommended that the financial arrangements necessary to support school planning, design, and construction be solidified. Once the school's program, student population forecast, demographic analysis, and financial information are completed, the total context will take shape in terms of facts and possible scenarios, especially the specification of space needs and capacity.

No organization exists in a vacuum. Outside events and organizations always influence schools. In looking outside the school district, the impacts that may not be obvious to people inside the school system can sometimes be discovered, thereby preventing possible conflicts. For example, if economic growth in a neighboring city or county is expected to increase, it is likely to spill over into the school area under study. Knowledge of the context of the school setting should reveal the possibility of new types of students and new demands on program and facilities. For example, a new industry paying a minimum wage to 400 employees will have a different impact on a community than a white-collar industry employing 400 employees. The numbers will be the same, but the expectations of the parents and the number and type of student will certainly differ.

The following categories reveal some examples of what one might expect to find as the outcomes of the internal scan: The possible internal trouble spots in the school organization, politicians' agendas for education, and local politics concerning the schools may appear as issues. For example, there may be political pressure to develop a school without many windows as a ploy for saving energy and taxpayer money. Such suggestions need to be challenged with research on the influence of natural light on learning to ensure efficient and effective use of money to improve learning, aesthetics, and behavior. While student achievement is always on the mind of school boards, we as planners and designers should try to broaden their thinking to include issues of how the physical environment influences student attitudes and behavior. The argument can be made that a student with a good attitude has a better chance to achieve a high test score than a student with a bad attitude. Designers already know this, but many school board members may not have given this important idea very much thought.

Whom do we serve? Knowledge of the context places light on the average age of the population, changing family structures, immigration, at-risk students, and the impact of the local housing/job market on types and numbers of families within the school district. The student population may increase sharply, or it may decline. Space needs may rise or fall. Economically, local job positions in the service/information economy may change. For example, the environmental scanning activity may uncover plans to close an industry employing a workforce of 750 people within two years. Trends such as these imply certain lifestyle changes that may impact other community members. The children of these workers and the people themselves are clients of the school.

Cultural and societal values are in constant change; therefore, we must consider aspects of school design that will complement these changes. With school violence as a key concern, do we put up fences and install metal detectors at the expense of providing a community meeting place in the school? Issues of this nature bring up trade-offs that should be considered. Chapter 16 explains a process to help implement the model for educational planning that facilitates concept design.

Phase IV: Specify What Is Realistic, Given the Context, Mission, Values, and Beliefs

In this phase of the model, we make the assumption that data about the context are available and perhaps have been interpreted by a group of professionals and shared with the stakeholders. The job of the planner is now to interpret the information collected so far in light of what is possible politically and economically within the community. This does not mean the programming and design have to be compromised to the point where they resemble a 1960s school. This phase requires a planner with excellent leadership skills, a special characteristic that will help the client get past roadblocks. If complete community participation has taken place up to this point, this phase can be straightforward. Decisions are not (should not be) made in a vacuum. A possible approach to answering the question regarding reality with respect to context, purpose, principles, and beliefs might include some acceptable findings for educational specifications as revealed in the examples of surprise-free scenarios below (scenarios having bases in facts and the consensus of stakeholders):

- We plan to build a small school for no more than 600 students.
- The theories of learning adopted by the planning and design team will need spaces approximated as follows: 30 percent for teachers working under the behavioral model, 30 percent for delivering the program according to the constructivist theory, and 40 percent

needing spaces to accommodate the brain-based theories.

- The teaching strategies will approximate the learning theories: 30 percent essentialism, 30 percent progressivism, and 40 percent with a compromise of theories such as progressivism, pernnialism, and existentialism (see MacKenzie, 1989, pp. 15–28).
- The curriculum will be delivered through parallel block scheduling to maximize the number of small classes in mathematics, English, science, and technology.
- A comprehensive educational program will be offered through the school, including performing and graphic arts, and community service.
- The school's physical environment will have an abundance of views overlooking life. There will be places for outdoor learning near the school building as well as nature trails and wetlands nearby.
- The school's design will foster a sense of safety and security without giving the impression of a prison to students and parents.
- Natural light will be plentiful in every classroom.
- The school will integrate technology throughout its classrooms and also provide some technology laboratories.
- The school will be aesthetically pleasing.
- The school will include well-planned and maintained outdoor learning environments.
- Each student will be provided with ample space for learning. The student will not feel like the learning spaces are crowded.
- Ethnicity will be a major social factor in the community, and the school will be designed to accommodate a multicultural student population.
- The school population five years from now will be more diverse than it is today, with an expected increase in the Latino population of 10 percent.
- Religious or spiritual values of the community will be more visible as various cultures move into the school district.

- Racialism will continue to decrease among students and parents as the community becomes more multicultural.

If the planning teams and school leaders can accept some basic outcomes such as those above, which should be in context and given the results of the first three phases, then the work of the planning and design teams can turn to expanding these outcomes to generate feasible alternatives for a design solution. This activity may begin with envisioning the school of the future.

Phase V: Envision Alternative School Environments That Capture the Surprise-Free Scenarios

A vision of the ideal learning environment may begin by having stakeholders brainstorm what the curriculum and physical attributes of the ideal school will be like in the future. Hopefully, this will be an extension of the outcomes of phase IV. Emphasis must be placed on the roles of students, parents, teachers, principals, and community members. It becomes vital to know what learning theories and teaching philosophies the teachers will be involved with in the future. The outcome of this phase should be a vision for a learning environment accommodating the results of phase I through phase IV. Such expectations provide the foundation for programming a flexible learning environment, allowing for adaptability.

It is important to work with stakeholders in helping them to create a vision of what they want their school environments to become. Once the school and community have a shared vision, they are more likely to support it. The following alternative based on surprise-free scenarios is a possible outcome for phase V.

Within ten to fifteen years, the schools in this district will have a balance between preparing students academically for the future and preparing them to be productive and ethical members of the community. There will be stronger programs to reach these goals. The schools will be smaller, aesthetically pleasing, and well designed; the curriculum will be delivered through block scheduling, employing the constructivist philosophy of teaching and learning. As few as 3 percent of the high school freshmen will not graduate. There will be a significant change in education in terms of governance, since educational partners will have more voice in what the schools are doing. The schools will have an abundance of appropriate physical designs to help teach values, including spaces for life (plants and animals) and a community service unit. Natural light will be plentiful in every classroom to enhance student and teacher attitudes. School design patterns will change and there will also be a special emphasis on student safety and security. Outdoor learning activities and technology-based learning will increase as the curriculum becomes integrated. Community service and a school-to-work program will be a reality. Computer technology *will be available to every student and it will enhance, rather than dominate, the school programs.*

Complementing the above outcome, the basics for learning will still be the foundation of the curriculum; hence, theories of learning and philosophies of teaching will play a major role in determining the physical learning environment. There will be far greater emphasis on how to learn. "Just in time" learning and problem-based learning will replace the traditional methodology where lecturing and testing were the guiding principles. For example, an integrated curriculum will replace the traditional English, science, and mathematics classes. The curriculum will be delivered through parallel block scheduling. School days will include community service activities and the school year will be extended. The Internet and other multimedia will play a vital role in the lives of students and their families. Activities in this phase are aimed at generating a realistic, yet visionary pool of alternatives. A vision should be realistic.

Phase VI: Select the Best Alternative

Selecting the "best" alternative includes the investigation of alternatives that includes cost-benefit analyses, since premise 7, "the demand for resources

is greater than those available," supports the implementation of feasible solutions. The planning team may have been intensely creative in generating solutions to the problem of developing the best school environment. However, this solution may not be within the scope of the available financial resources. Hence, cost-benefit analysis will help in deciding whether to implement a specific alternative scenario. The benefits of a selected scenario are added and costs associated with it are subtracted. Costs may be "one-time" or ongoing, while benefits are most often received over time (Campbell & Brown, 2003). The effect of time is calculated according to a payback period. This is the time it takes for the benefits of a change to repay its costs. Many school systems look for payback over a specified period of time, usually ten years. In its basic form, using only financial costs and financial benefits completes a cost-benefit analysis. For example, a simple cost-benefit analysis of a two-story school would be the measure of the cost of building the school, and then subtracting this from the economic benefit of building another design. It would not measure either the cost of damage to the environment by leveling a large field or the benefit of the learning environments created.

Given all the program information, especially that tied to a compilation of all the previous planning phases, including some acceptable decision model such as cost-benefit analysis, it is time to come to agreement regarding the best alternative program. Therefore, it is time to select from the visionary environments created in phase V. Here we are setting the stage to go from words to spaces and places. All stakeholders are expected to participate in this activity to generate creative translations of the school's program. As the many ideas are debated, it is time to complete very rough visual images of what ought to be. The stakeholders will be able to view and critique the concept sketches of "the program translated to a drawing." Many creative solutions usually emerge at this stage. Sometimes, visits to existing schools will aid this activity. It is recommended that people be encouraged to visit innovative schools. The

Council of Educational Facility Planners, International (ww.cefpi.org) can provide a list of award-winning schools.

The goal of phase VI is to select a program based on the alternatives generated by the plan developed by the design team and stakeholders. If the stakeholders have been involved, then a good chance exists that there will be agreement both philosophically and financially. Beyond program selection, the larger picture here would include a decision on style of building (one-story, multistory, campus plan, etc.).

Phase VII: Program the Best Alternative

A straightforward definition of programming is "specify the physical environment." Therefore, at this point, it is suggested that "general" educational specifications reflecting the program and concept sketches selected in phase VI be completed to help define and refine the physical learning environment. More detail on educational specifications is given in Chapter 16.

First, it may be appropriate to use only bubble diagrams to lay out some space relationships. The traditional bubble diagrams, however, may be replaced directly by scaled drawings done in cooperation with an architect or completed by a team member having skills in working with simple computer-aided design (CAD) programs. With the new technology in use today, laypeople can actually create good concept drawings to express what they view as the best school design. It is important not to allow any one to dominate this creative activity, especially someone having a "plan in the hand."

The concept drawings may include:

- Space needs per indoor and outdoor areas
- Equipment needs per space
- Furniture needs per space

- Storage needs per space
- Technology requirements
- Other special considerations

This activity may be identified as the "pre-design phase" to some readers. The charge is to be creative and design spaces for program needs. Consider the following classroom floor plans (Figures 5.1 through 5.3, pages 110–111) created by a layperson.[1]

In Figures 5.1 through 5.3 there are several concepts that could have possibly emerged from the activities which have taken place in the six preceding phases. First, note there is ample natural light. This is a learning neighborhood, modeled after those found at Celebration School, Florida. The constructivist learning philosophy drives this design. There are large- and small-group areas, a library area, integrated computer technology, and circulation patterns are ample, including a hearth area. Two exits lead to the outdoor classroom areas, and there is an open teacher workstation within the learning area. As safety and security measures, there are toilets inside the learning areas.

The learning environment should make use of all available resources. This design principle has been illustrated in the descriptions of the three figures above, since the diagrams reveal integrated technological resources, and also the inclusion of natural resources. This plan provides for the best use of materials and books, while storage is provided throughout the learning space.

Phase VIII: Complete Final Design and Preconstruction Activities

Assuming the planning and design team has identified the space relationships, it is time for a professional architect to translate the planning, programming, and sketches into a specific design of the desired physical environment. Hence, we assume educational specifications have been generated as a

---

[1]We wish to thank Dr. Christopher McMichael, a former student in school design and planning at the University of Georgia, for granting us permission to use these drawings.

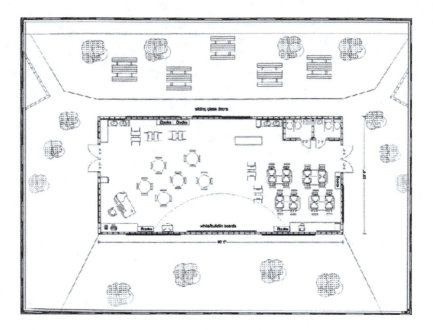

FIGURE 5.1   Learning Area Floor Plans.

Source: Used by permission of Dr. Christopher McMichael (http://www.geocities.com/cmcmichael1/2dfloorplans.html).

result of phases VI and VII (see Chapter 16 for more detail on educational specifications). And, there is attention given to class size, scheduling, and the type of program. For example, in parallel block scheduling smaller classes for academic subjects are possible. Assuming a thorough educational facilities plan, this phase should be made uncomplicated for the architectural firm to move the project into the final design and construction stages. The underlying assumption here is that "form should follow function." Therefore, if the functions are clearly conceptualized and described through program and specifications and the concept drawings (phase VII), a capable architect may easily specify

FIGURE 5.2   The Learning Area Shown in Figure 5.1 as a Three-Dimensional Drawing.

Source: Used by permission of Dr. Christopher McMichael.

FIGURE 5.3   Another View of the Learning Area.

Source: Used by permission of Dr. Christopher McMichael.

and diagram the learning environments and provide accurate cost estimates for decision making.

The architect will need to know if the program goals match the educational specifications. Given the process we have described, this guarantee is met. The program goals and educational specifications should correlate with the philosophy and values of the community. Hence, they are direct outgrowths of the overall values, philosophy, vision, and the environmental scan generated in phases III and IV.

Some goals for the architect include the following:

- Build a safe, comfortable, and aesthetically pleasing school.
- Provide a design that will accommodate more than one teaching and learning philosophy.
- Select furniture that is comfortable, flexible, and amenable to the teaching and learning philosophies.
- Provide ample usable space (at least 49 square feet) for each student and teacher within each classroom.
- Allow for the use of technology in instruction and research.
- Ensure space for student services.

- Guarantee spaces for community use and service.
- Set forth specifications to ensure safety and security for students, teachers, and administrators.
- Allow for flexibility and versatility.
- Accommodate a multicultural student body and diversity.

This is a straightforward, yet truncated, list to make the reader and student of planning and design aware of the complexity surrounding school design. Many more of these concepts will be discussed in the following chapter.

Phases IX and X: Construct and Occupy the Facility

Chapter 7 provides a review and discussion of the construction process. As experienced planners, designers, architects, and builders will agree, there is not necessarily a straightforward milestone-by-milestone process for arriving at a completed project. The milestones outlined in the following section may be used as guidelines—some may be parallel, while others may be linear and dependent. Whether they are parallel or linear will depend on the context, legal, and environmental issues that extend well beyond the scope of this text.

BASIC MILESTONES IN PLANNING CAPITAL PROJECTS

Using the global perspectives of planning phases as outlined above, we can be more specific regarding the possible organizational constraints and milestones that facilitate educational planning. Early in the process, it is imperative that the principles and values surrounding the learning environments be established. Furthermore knowing the educational purposes for the physical environment is of importance. Thus, as noted in Table 5.1 on page 113, phases I through V will most likely complement milestones A through E. At this time it is important to examine the context as suggested in milestones B and C, while specifying reality, context, mission, values, and beliefs (phase IV). Phase V, envisioning alternative school environments, also correlates with milestones C and D. While there is no precise set of linear milestones (or dependent milestones) that fit all planning problems, those presented here should provide sound direction for realistic involvement in the important job of developing educational learning environments.

The overall context for educational planning in the United States, given local, state, and federal policy constraints, was depicted in Figure 3.1. You may review it to gain a perspective of the total process discussed here. To make the process more realistic, we must consider that planning takes place in the context of state and local policy constraints, and the phases and stages may overlap from one project to another and among school systems. The major and most frequently followed generic *activities* or milestones (not necessarily listed chronologically) of planning a capital project in the United States are outlined below.

A. Begin the Planning Process. This initial activity has been termed "planning to plan." It represents the organizational phase in the long-range planning process, including a timeline and assignment of responsibility and authority.

B. Forecast Student Enrollment. Forecast the school district's student population to determine trends in growth, decline, and location within the district. This vital activity may be reviewed in Chapter 15. Enrollment forecasting requires a thorough demographic analysis. This phase includes a comparison of square footage needs per student with existing square footage of spaces for learning. Milestone B certainly helps to document the "need" for educational learning environments.

C. Determine Educational Feasibility. Study existing educational program and space needs in view of the philosophy of teaching and learning, the school size, and organizational structure (K–5, 6–8, 9–12, etc.). Compare the expected program needs to present program offerings. Is the current educational program relevant? Has it kept pace with technology? Given answers to these and similar questions, the next job is to determine the number and types of educational spaces the expected new programs and enrollments will require five to fifteen years into the future. The scores on the appropriate design assessment scale (see research section of this text) will assist in determining educational feasibility.

D. Establish Architectural Feasibility. Study existing school spaces in light of the educational program and compare current space needs to program space needs five to fifteen years into the future. This entails an educational facilities survey, an overlay of the various types of student scheduling on current spaces, determining if the teaching and learning styles can be accommodated, and an appraisal of the current conditions of the schools. Activities C and D will be expedited by determining the school capacity needs and by comparing space needs in view of school schedules. A rule-of-thumb approach may be used to approximate the capacity of a secondary school. For example, consider estimating school capacity by multiplying the

TABLE 5.1   Phases and Milestones in Planning a Capital Project

BROAD PHASES	BASIC GENERIC MILESTONES*
Phase I. Determine the principles and values of the community.	A. Begin the planning process.
	B. Forecast student enrollment.
Phase II. Develop a purpose for the physical learning environment.	C. Determine educational feasibility.
	D. Establish architectural feasibility.
Phase III. Examine the context.	E. Prioritize needs.
Phase IV. Specify what is Realistic given the context, mission, values, and beliefs.	
Phase V. Envision alternative school environments that capture the surprise-free scenarios.	
Phase VI. Select the best alternative.	F. Adopt findings of the needs assessment.
Phase VII. Program the best alternative.	G. Choose to build a new school or renovate existing structures.
	H. Develop capital budget estimates.
	I. Acquire financing for the project.
	J. Appoint the school's principal.
Phase VIII. Complete final design and preconstruction activities.	K. Select an architectural firm.
	L. Design the school.
	M. Stipulate the needed school furniture.
	N. Select the construction manager.
	O. Schedule the project.
	P. Obtain 35 percent cost estimates.
	Q. Prepare final construction documents.
	R. Secure final cost estimates.
	S. Advertise bids for construction.
	T. Receive bids for construction.
Phase IX. Construct the facility.	U. Award construction contract.
	V. Obtain permits to begin construction.
	W. Advertise bids for school furniture.
	X. Receive bids for furniture.
	Y. Construct the school.
	Z. Monitor construction program.
	AA. Install school furniture.
	BB. Complete punch list/verify performance.
Phase X. Occupy the facility.	CC. Accept the school.
	DD. Orient school staff and community to building.
	EE. Evaluate the school planning, design, and construction.
	FF. Complete warranty inspection.

*Milestones are not necessarily linear.

number of teaching stations needed by the desired class size ($TS \times N$ = capacity) or apply the gross square footage formulae developed by Hawkins and Lilley (1998, p. 5). A teaching station (TS) is any space where one teacher (conventional school) instructs a group of students. The number of students (N) represents the desired average class size. Libraries, meeting rooms, cafeterias, and auditoriums are excluded from the determination of teaching stations; however, a gymnasium designed so that four classes might be taught in it simultaneously could be counted as four teaching stations. Immediate needs (within five years) are translated into cost estimates.

E. Prioritize Needs.   Based on the educational and architectural needs (translated into cost estimates), a team of qualified individuals develops a list of priorities for schools in the district. Determining educational and architectural feasibility is a needs assessment based on the following premise: "The school system has a defined direction—what do we have as compared to what do we need?" From this activity, the school board obtains information regarding the various needs for capital expenditures.

F. Adopt Findings of the Needs Assessment. The local school board reviews the findings of the facilities study outlined in previous milestones. This set of findings should include educational specifications. Allowing for possible modifications, these findings are adopted by the school board. In some states, the results of these activities are filed with the facilities section of the state education agency.

G. Choose to Build a New School or Renovate Existing Structures. Information regarding the ratio of the number of students to the student capacity of the physical environment and the percentage of space utilization is important in the decision process. If crowding is prevalent and if priorities have been established, the governing board may decide to build a new school or renovate existing structures. If a new school is the best option, it is highly important to determine its size

at this time. If remodeling or renovation is an option, school capacity also becomes a factor. Capacity is difficult to determine because of the subjectivity involved in determining it (see activity D). A reduction in capacity and density usually indicates an improved educational program. The basis for renovating a school is presented later in this chapter under the heading "Planning a Capital Project for Remodeling a School."

H. Develop Capital Budget Estimates.   At this point, assume that the need has been established and the decision has been made to build a new school or renovate an existing structure. The decision to build a new school is accompanied by *site acquisition* (if property has not been purchased at an earlier date). The proposed site must pass environmental and seismic requirements and is usually *approved by the state education agency*. The site should be safe and also located out of any flood plain. Local and regional zoning boards may get involved in the site approval process. After the site is acquired and approved, estimates for the cost of planning and design; architectural services; site preparation; furniture and furnishings; administrative, legal, and construction management services; insurance; contingencies for change orders and reserves (approximately 10 percent), and debt retirement are arrived at. One of the better approaches to this problem is to seek information from school districts in the region that have recently completed a similar activity. The state education agency may also provide information. Cost estimates should be guided by making comparisons with similar projects in the region where the school is to be constructed. One immediate source is to seek comparative information through the Internet; for example, go to http://www.schoolclearinghouse.org/ or http://www.edfacilities.org/index.html.

I. Acquire Financing for the Project.   There are several generally recognized methods for financing the construction of a new school. The capital expansion or *sinking fund* (defined as entitlement earnings in some states) is established by the state. Under this plan, schools accumulate funds annually to be used for future capital projects. In addition to capital expansion funds, *long-term bonds* may be used to pay for costs associated with school construction. *School tax revenue*, based on property tax, is also a source of funding. A plan that is gaining in popularity, and especially aimed at the reduction of the property tax burden, is special *local option sales taxes* designated for capital improvements. Chapter 11 provides a more comprehensive guide for financing school infrastructure projects.

J. Appoint the School's Principal.   When the decision is made to build a new school, educational leaders should immediately designate the school's principal to assist in the planning and design of the learning environments. Since the planning activities may require at least one year and construction may continue for approximately two years thereafter, the new school principal may be assigned other duties during the duration of the project. The appointed school principal should be involved in leading school and community participants in the planning and designing of places for learning. It is very important for the school principal and the superintendent (or the director of planning) to have special training in school design and educational facilities planning in order to lead the school and community through the concept design stages of the project. Even if an outside consultant is hired to assist in the planning and development of educational specifications, the leadership inside the school system must be knowledgeable of the important aspects of this complex process. To improve the planning situation in schools across the United States, certification in school design and planning is offered by some schools and universities. In addition to training at the university level, the Council of Educational Facility Planners, International offers a training program for school planners (the Recognized Educational Facility Planner program).

K. Select an Architectural Firm.   The selection of the architectural firm is a vitally important activity to be completed with caution. This act, however, should not be viewed as more important than ensuring school and community involvement

in the planning and design of the school. Once the firm is hired, it should not ignore the school and community in favor of personal design solutions or perhaps prototype school designs that are not wanted by the educators or the community. Initial planning and design activities should originate through leadership from the school superintendent and school principal. Allowing the architectural firm complete control over educational learning spaces should never happen because the educational function must be emphasized over all architectural design. The school district should invite proposals from architectural firms located close enough to the community and construction site to ensure adequate interaction with the community in designing the educational spaces and monitoring progress during construction.

The standard American Institute of Architects (AIA) contract may serve as a beginning point. It should be negotiable since fees vary from new structures to renovation jobs. Important aspects of employing an architectural firm include its record of experience in designing and constructing schools and the number of engineers and other specialists that work with the firm. A question often overlooked is "What are your current project commitments?" In addition to the firm's experience and current commitments, it is important to find out how change orders are dealt with and how architectural mistakes are addressed. How well will the architectural firm receive advice on design solutions that are made by the concept design team (school leadership, educators, community, and school principal, e.g.)? Former legal actions with other schools and contractors should be disclosed before a firm is employed to build a school.

The base architectural fee may not cover close architectural supervision of the school project. In partnership with the construction manager, the architectural firm must be willing to provide adequate supervision of the project. Additional fees may be required beyond the standard architectural fee, if close supervision of the project is requested.

L. Design the School.   The architect and members of the architectural firm work closely with the school leadership, the school principal, the educators, and the community in developing the school's concept design (preliminary design). Educational specifications are used as a basis to ensure appropriate spaces and their interrelationships (Myers & Robertson, 2004). The basic floor plans and three-dimensional renderings are completed in this phase. This preliminary design should represent at least 35 percent of the completed design, excluding engineering details, for example. During this phase, the proposed design is weighed against the school's teaching and learning philosophies. The overriding question is, "Are the suggested spaces capable of facilitating all aspects of the curriculum?" A clear understanding of the number, size, location, and function of the educational spaces to be included in the structure is addressed in this phase. Also, power requirements, computer and Internet linkages, equipment, outdoor learning areas (including outdoor classrooms), and ADA requirements.

M. Stipulate the Needed School Furniture.

Parallel to completing the school design, furniture and equipment should be specified that match the goals and philosophy of teaching and learning in the school. In essence, there are two types of school furniture: fixed or built-in and movable. It is important that the school furniture be flexible to meet the curriculum needs. Perhaps more portable tables and fewer traditional desks are needed. It has been suggested that the furniture should have wheels to make it flexible and easier to rearrange to accommodate various class activities. Value engineering techniques should be applied in the costing of furniture prior to the bidding process.

N. Select the Construction Manager.

Some large school systems have construction managers as part of their administrative team, and it is recommended that the construction manager be included early in the design process. It is essential, however, to involve a construction manager before the project is scheduled in order to minimize any unforeseen difficulties. The construction manager should represent the owner, not the architect or contractor.

O. Schedule the Project.

Once the architectural firm and the school principal have been selected, it is important that they, along with the school leaders and construction manager, come to an understanding of exactly when the school will be completed. This schedule must conform to the school's calendar. It is especially important that the school principal and the school superintendent assist the architectural firm in the development of the schedule. It is also advisable to acquire assistance from a potential general contractor when developing the schedule.

P. Obtain 35 Percent Cost Estimates.

Given the preliminary design, and excluding some details (at least 35 percent of the design is complete), this phase provides probable construction costs, with specific reference to the time of construction and the area where the construction is to be completed. This estimate assumes a competitive bid situation, and is an opinion of probable costs based on fair market value. At this time it is important to optimize the project's potential to give the taxpayer the best value for the dollar by completing a value analysis of the supplies and materials to be used in the project. Value analysis eliminates the need for expensive redesigning later in the process. It is especially important to include a life-cycle analysis of sustainable design features incorporated into the design, since they can sometimes increase first costs but save large sums of dollars over the life of the building. Value engineering can be an important process for keeping down school facility costs, but care must be taken to ensure that important components are not cut out or swapped with inferior products that will reduce building performance. Value engineering also focuses on the cost/risk aspects of environmental remediation, if applicable. Since preliminary costing and value analysis is not at the forefront in educational architecture, specialists such as U.S. Cost, Inc. may be consulted (http://www.uscost.com). There are other sources that may be found through Internet search engines.

Q. Prepare Final Construction Documents. This phase includes the completion of a comprehensive set of architectural and engineering drawings, including a project manual, technical specifications, addenda, process for change orders, bidding, and construction. The project manual is a document containing the invitation to bid, instructions to bidders, conditions of contract, and necessary forms for submitting bids. The proper authorities must approve these documents before bids are advertised.

R. Secure Final Cost Estimates. This activity assumes that all the architectural and engineering drawings are complete. The discussion outlined in activity P also applies here. This is the final milestone before construction documents are prepared.

S. Advertise Bids for Construction. Assuming a design-bid-build approach, it is time to advertise for bids. Local and state laws vary on the process of advertising for bids. It is vital to the project that proper bidding procedures be followed to minimize problems and save time. This process may require from one to two months depending on local and state laws.

T. Receive Bids for Construction. Bids are received by the school board and opened promptly following the required time for advertising.

U. Award Construction Contract. Given that value engineering has been applied in the costs of construction and all the legal obligations are met, the contract is most often awarded to the lowest bidder who is also bonded and licensed. It is important to emphasize that value engineering should become a necessary part of school construction for reasons of safety of the students, and ensuring the best use of tax dollars.

V. Obtain Permits to Begin Construction. It is usually the responsibility of the local board of education to have all final drawings and the project manual approved by the local fire marshal,

Department of Human Resources, and local agencies prior to construction.

W. Advertise Bids for School Furniture. Along with the school design team, the architect, an interior designer, and furniture and equipment consultants specify the appropriate furniture and equipment for the educational environments. Appropriate bidding documents are prepared and advertised according to legal guidelines.

X. Receive Bids for Furniture. Bids are opened in accordance with local policy and state laws. Bids received should be evaluated for compliance with educational specifications and quality. Value engineering for school furniture is important and is encouraged. As with school construction, legal issues such as bonding, liability, and safety must be addressed when selecting ergonomically appropriate furniture.

Y. Construct the School. It is understood that the construction contractors will be bonded, licensed, and insured to protect the local school district. Construction, depending on the size of the project, may require from eighteen to thirty-six months. Timing of construction to ensure compliance with the school schedule is vital. There are situations where penalty clauses may be written into the contract if construction is not finished by a specified date. Likewise, the contractor has the right to request a bonus for finishing a project before the scheduled date of completion. It is vital, therefore, for the owner (school board) to employ a general contractor who has an outstanding record of quality work and promptness.

Z. Monitor Construction Program. It is not only the job of the construction manager and architect to monitor the project, but also the responsibility of the school principal to continuously review the progress of the school construction project. We traditionally think of this job being left to the architect or the construction manager. However, the school principal designate should follow the process to check design specifications for learning spaces as well as to gain knowledge of where various drains, switches, and other mechanical devices are located. One simple example is for the principal to know where the filters on the air exchange systems are located, since he or she is responsible for the safety, security, and well-being of the students.

AA. Install School Furniture. Furniture installation requires close attention and a checklist is a good tool to use for ensuring that this activity is completed properly. The architect, interior designer, and perhaps an equipment consultant can be invaluable during this important phase. Furthermore, the school principal must be present during furniture installation to ensure that the school furniture is located and installed in its intended spaces. There is nothing more frustrating at the end of a construction project than to discover that improper furniture has been installed or that the wrong order was delivered, especially if school is soon to open for students and teachers. Above all, it is important to verify that all furniture and equipment purchased are delivered and installed as specified. Checks should be made on electrical items, doors, cabinets, and mounted objects. Here is the overriding question: "Is everything working properly and located in the correct place?"

BB. Complete Punch List/Verify Performance. A common activity that may be performed as construction progresses is the completion of a detailed checklist regarding mechanical devices and other items. This is a verification process to ensure that the school is working as planned. To ensure that systems (e.g., lighting, mechanical, plumbing) and components are working as intended, a commissioning agent, preferably brought on board earlier in the project, can begin to test all commissioned systems to ensure that they are properly installed and performing as intended. This process goes beyond the traditional "test and balance" of the mechanical systems. A detailed discussion on commissioning is outside the scope of this textbook, but school

officials and their representatives should become more knowledgeable about this important tool.

CC. Accept the School. This activity involves the formal notification by the builder that the school is ready for occupancy. Usually, a formal meeting is arranged and the school board completes a guided tour of the facility along with the architect, the school principal, the builder, and other interested parties. If the school is substantially complete, the school board votes to receive the school, and clearance is made for the "move in."

DD. Orient School Staff and Community to Building. This important phase of the process includes the introduction of the school staff and the community to the new building, grounds, and outdoor learning areas (including outdoor classrooms). This activity may be classified as a "grand opening." It is important for the staff to learn how to use the school building and other areas, and for the students to learn about the various patterns of traffic flow within the building and how the school facilitates learning. People need to view the school as a community resource. This is one of the most important public relations activities the school board can produce.

EE. Evaluate the School Planning, Design, and Construction Process. This activity involves the postoccupancy evaluation of the school and the evaluation of the process used to complete the school. Consultants or university researchers are sometimes hired to conduct these studies. The architect, the planners, the school principal, representatives of the school board and community, and other interested parties are involved. Usually, the best question to ask is: "If we had this project to do over again, what would we do differently?" Some school systems have developed surveys that help in the postoccupancy evaluation. These may deal with design issues as well as process. Overall, the concern is for effectiveness of the process and the educational adequacy of the building. The appropriate design assessment scale (see Chapters 12 and 13) and the CEFPI's *Appraisal Guide* may be beneficial in this process.

FF. Complete Warranty Inspection.   Prior to the expiration of the contractor's warranty, the owner is expected to inspect the facilities to determine deficiencies to be corrected by the contractor. This activity is conducted under the terms of the general guaranty provisions of the contract. Since the school principal has been involved from the beginning of the project, the activity is greatly enhanced by his or her knowledge of any faults in the facility. The commissioning agent, if hired, is typically responsible for ensuring that components and systems are properly functioning before manufacturers' warranties expire.

Scheduling Activities with CPM.   There are at least three major schedules that must be developed to ensure the proper management of the capital project. The school superintendent's office should have a master schedule entailing all the major activities (not detailed subnetworks); there should be a detailed schedule of the construction project, and a project management schedule corresponding to the school schedule (a subnetwork of the construction project that deals with major construction milestones and opening school on time). Earthman (2000) has developed flowcharts similar to those outlined below to select a school site and develop educational specifications. His work illustrates the complexity of the overall scheduling process when compared to the major milestones outlined in the above section.

Scheduling involves the collection of time estimates for all activities. A schedule takes into consideration the school organization, constraints as a result of required approval, the school site, climate, and workforce. The *master schedule* for the school superintendent is a consolidation of the construction and project management schedule. The director of facilities and the school principal should monitor this schedule to keep track of progress and

inform the school board of the completion of major milestones. The main objective is for project completion to correspond with the opening of school (a just in time schedule (JITS)). *Construction scheduling* usually involves critical path method (CPM) scheduling, a technique displaying the relationships between activities for the purpose of project control. The person or team involved in construction scheduling monitors the construction progress relative to the original schedule to determine if activities are being completed on time. If a certain activity is taking too much time (slippage), then the allocation of resources is immediately influenced. Although time is the main concern, cost can also be a variable involved in scheduling. For example, interior construction materials arriving on the site before the roof is completed can prove to be a costly mistake, since there may not be any available storage facilities. *Project management scheduling*, a process similar to that of the master schedule, but more detailed, helps the project manager process work and cash flow, while staying current on time management.

There are computerized systems and consulting teams available to assist in scheduling beyond the outline presented here. One of the most popular basic project management tools is the Microsoft Project software. This begins as a computerized version of the traditional Gantt chart and helps to create a work schedule with information provided on tasks, resources, and costs (work breakdown structure). To enhance project management, U.S. Cost, Inc. (http://www.uscost.com) has produced a complementary software package for complex construction projects that deal with cost loading and critical paths for project performance.

The first milestone in developing a schedule for a capital project is to define the activities such as we have done in Table 5.2 on page 120. This planning task includes the creation of time expected for completion of each activity, and persons or organizational components responsible for the activity's completion. Estimating time is critical; therefore, people having experienced the various

TABLE 5.2   Work Breakdown Schedule, Time, and Responsibility Chart

MILESTONE/ACTIVITY	ESTIMATED TIME (MONTHS)	RESPONSIBILITY
A. Begin the planning process.	1	School superintendent
B. Forecast student enrollment.	2	Research unit
C. Determine educational feasibility.	2	Facilities director
D. Establish architectural feasibility.	2	Facilities director
E. Prioritize needs.	1	School board and superintendent
F. Adopt findings of the needs assessment.	1	School board
G. Choose to build a new school or renovate existing structures.	1	School board
H. Develop capital budget estimates.	2	Director of finance
I. Acquire financing for the project.	4	School board and superintendent
J. Appoint the school's principal.	1	School board
K. Select an architectural firm.	2	School board upon recommendation by superintendent
L. Design the school.	6	School principal, educators, community, and architect
M. Stipulate the needed school furniture.	2	School principal, educators, community, and architect
N. Select the construction manager.	1	Superintendent, facilities director
O. Schedule the project.	1	School officials and architect
P. Obtain 35 percent cost estimates.	2	Architect and facilities director
Q. Prepare final construction documents.	2	Architect and facilities director
R. Secure final cost estimates.	3	Architect
S. Advertise bids for construction.	3	School board and superintendent
T. Receive bids for construction.	1	School board and superintendent
U. Award construction contract.	1	School board and superintendent
V. Obtain permits to begin construction.	1	Superintendent and facilities director
W. Advertise bids for school furniture.	1	School board and superintendent
X. Receive bids for furniture.	1	School board and Superintendent
Y. Construct the school.	18	General contractor
Z. Monitor construction program.	18	Construction manager, school principal, and facilities director
AA. Install school furniture	1	Vendors, school principal, and facilities director
BB. Complete punch list/verify performance.	1	Principal, construction manager, and general contractor
CC. Accept the school.	1	School board
DD. Orient school staff and community to building.	1	School principal
EE. Evaluate the school planning, design, and construction process.	1	School principal, community, facilities director, superintendent, and school board
FF. Complete warranty inspection.	1	Construction manager

activities are the best sources for good time estimates. Even if the time estimates are reliable, changes may occur because of "good or bad" weather, for example. When variations occur, the scheduling technique is designed to provide information to the project manager for minimizing the problems through a printout indicating there is a slippage in some area. Information may necessitate a needed work slowdown in one area, the addition of more resources to certain activities because the project is getting behind schedule, or just staying in the ongoing milestone with the current pace of activities.

We cannot overemphasize the importance of valid time estimates. Early research on program evaluation and review technique provided a formula having six parameters that may be used to develop PERT or CPM activity time estimates. The three classifications of the six parameters include the weight of *one* for the "optimistic time" estimate, *four* for the "most likely" time estimate, and *one* for the "most pessimistic" estimate. An activity receiving one month for the optimistic estimate, three months for the most likely time estimate, and five months for the most pessimistic time estimate, when subjected to the weighted formula, would yield three months as the time expected to complete the activity $[1(1) + 4(3) + 1(5)]/6 = 3$ months.

Charting the MASTER Schedule of Activities

The master schedule presented in Table 5.1 reveals only the major milestones of the project. To shorten the illustration, and hopefully to clarify this rather comprehensive procedure, details of activities such as purchasing the furniture that would logically be placed in the sequence between activities X and AA have been left out. Note that this activity parallels the construction of the school (activity Y). Other needed additions of subnetworks will be discovered in reviewing Table 5.1 and Figures 5.4 and 5.5 on pages 122 and 123. These illustrations are truncated here to serve as a guide to scheduling. Participating in a small-scale scheduling activity such as the one outlined in Table 5.4 should make the reader keenly

aware of the need to move to a computerized program to obtain actual time and completion updates on a regularly scheduled basis during the project. The purpose of moving to electronic data processing is to minimize calculation time and ensure that the project is completed on time. One important reason for leaders to participate in the scheduling of activities is to think "inside and outside" the complex box of developing school facilities.

Activities that are most likely to be critical on the first analysis (tracing all the various paths from the beginning to end and comparing the amounts of time required for completion along each path) will usually include budgeting, design, and construction. The activities critical to completing the project "on time" are always located on the critical path (the complete path from the beginning to end requiring the most time). Envision every arrow in the figures as paths (the rule is that movement only occurs from left to right as the arrows indicate). The most likely critical path in Figures 5.4 and 5.5 include A, D, d3, E, F, G, H, I, J, K, d6, L, M, N, O, P, Q, R, S, T, U, Y, AA, BB, CC, EE, and FF.

Planning a Capital PROJECT for Remodeling a School

Remodeling, rehabilitation, and modernization are common activities among schools, and they can mean different things to various people. Rehabilitation refers to the restoration of the building and grounds to something close to their original appearance and function. Modernization refers to remodeling an area for technology, for example, or completely changing the facility. Castaldi (1994) indicated that remodeling goes beyond rehabilitation by changing sizes, shapes, and colors. Therefore, a remodeled school could improve its educational functions. In the discussion here modernization and remodeling will be used synonymously.

It is common knowledge that remodeling a school to accommodate a changing program can be more complex and time-consuming than planning for a new facility. It is much easier to change drawings than move walls and partitions, and reroute

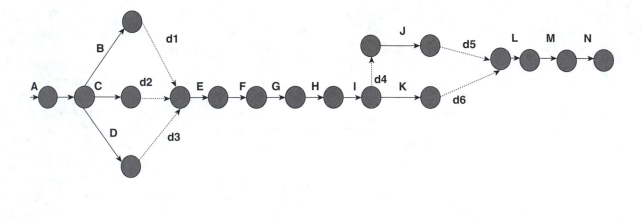

di   Indicates an activity that does not require time—a connector activity.

———▶   The solid arrow indicates an activity requiring time.

·········▶   The dotted arrow indicates an activity having no time requirements. It is a connector activity.

●   The beginning and/or end of an activity.

FIGURE 5.4   Network of Planning Activities (A to N).

wires and pipes. However, given a school's historical and political value to a community, the restoration and/or modernization of a town icon can be a rewarding activity for the school and community. Furthermore, keeping the building materials out of a local landfill is also a positive action. Many of the activities in remodeling parallel those of constructing a new school (conducting a feasibility study, developing a master plan, transforming concepts and educational specifications into designs that match the educational philosophy of teaching and learning, redesigning spaces, fiscal planning, construction, evaluation, and occupancy).

The feasibility study for remodeling a school entails a comprehensive study of what the people want and what they are willing to pay for. In essence, a strategic plan could be drawn up where

the expected outcome is a remodeled school. This involves both rational planning and interactive planning and may follow milestones such as those outlined in Table 5.3 on page 124.

Essential to remodeling is the question of feasibility. If the school has no overwhelming historic salvage value for the people in the community, then we may use some "rule-of-thumb" guidelines regarding whether or not to start such a project. Castaldi (1994) suggested that *if the estimated cost of remodeling was within 40 to 50 percent of the cost of a new facility, then the feasibility of remodeling should be questioned.* This percentage holds true for schools that have been in service for no more than forty years. Because older buildings always bring unexpected problems during remodeling, it is almost impossible to determine the cost until the

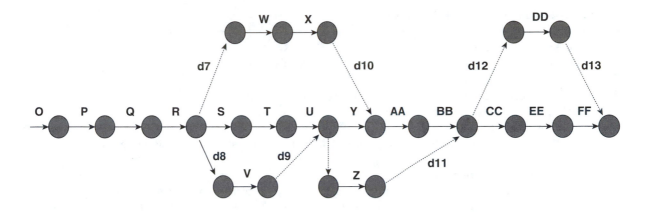

di Indicates an activity that does not require time—a connector activity.

———▶ The solid arrow indicates an activity requiring time.

┄┄┄▶ The dotted arrow indicates a dummy activity, requiring no time.

⬤ The beginning and/or end of an activity.

FIGURE 5.5   Schedule of Financial and Construction Activities.

project is completed. If a detailed formula is needed for justifying remodeling, then the reader may refer to pages 385–389 in Castaldi (1994). These pages may be summarized as follows: For the new building, if the average capital cost per year (twenty to thirty years, e.g.) *is less than* the average capital cost of the remodeled building per year, then the old building should be replaced. This formula assumes that maintenance and operations are the same over the number of years in question. Maintenance and operations are held constant.

While this rule of thumb is used by many planners and architects, the age of computerized costing systems has provided programs for the comprehensive analysis of renovation (see http://www.uscost.com). A detailed discussion of

school renovation, including how to operate the school during renovation, is provided by Earthman and LeMasters (2004).

In addition to determining feasibility in terms of cost (which is usually the number one consideration), other factors must also be well thought out. These questions (after Castaldi, 1994) must be answered in the affirmative if remodeling is to be completed:

1. Should public capital be invested in a remodeling project when the school is expected to be phased out of service within twenty years?
2. Is it impractical to reassign students attending the school?

TABLE 5.3 Planning Phases for Remodeling

1. Agreement to Conduct a Feasibility Study
   (Can remodeling be justified? See section below to answer this question.)
2. Identify Program Objectives
3. Collect the Data Needed to Support Program Objectives
   (Complete internal and external scanning and estimate program needs.)
4. Develop Preferred Design Solutions
   (Translate program needs into spaces and determine if the remodeled structure will accommodate the new design.)
5. Formulation of Architectural Solutions
   (Translate concept design into architectural drawings. Estimate costs from 35 percent drawings.)
6. Develop Capital Plan and Acquire Public Support
7. Implementation of Architectural Solutions
   (Construct and remodel spaces.)
8. Evaluation of Outcomes
   (Compare objectives to outcomes.)

3. Are the current school and site amenable to improvement and expansion?
4. Will the remodeled school fit into the short- and long-range plan for all facilities in the district?
5. Will the site of the remodeled facility accommodate expansion?
6. Can the educational obsolescence of the remodeled building be eliminated as effectively as in a new structure?

The most practical consideration in remodeling is whether the modernized structure and grounds will facilitate the educational program as well as a new structure. Beyond this, there are some positive aspects of remodeling that outweigh the aspects of a new structure. For example, capturing the aesthetics of a Romanesque Revival school structure built in the late 1800s may be more important to a community than erecting a new school.

Constraints on design and construction imposed by an older structure may be difficult for the architect to overcome. Renovation is a challenging problem for planners and architects, and compromise among several least harmful alternative solutions is always expected. One goal for the re-

modeled facility is that it should be equivalent to a new structure when program demands are compared. The assumption underlying the decision to remodel a facility is that it is always equivalent to a new school, which would be constructed to replace it. The available spaces in the old structure that need no change should be identified early in the planning process, and every effort should be made to match certain program needs with these spaces before alterations to the structure are made to facilitate other program needs. Above all, safety and supervisable circulation patterns should be considered when converting existing larger spaces into places for small groups. This procedure is especially challenging because it is easy to perceive that many small spaces can accommodate the same number of students as the original larger space. The overall objective of renovation is to improve the building educationally while improving it physically.

SUMMARY

Chapter 5 provides a model and specific strategies for developing educational facility plans to guide concept design and ensure that stakeholder goals for a facility are met. This approach assumes that many stakeholders will be involved in the planning and programming phases. Prior to the development of concept designs, planning teams must *first determine the principles and values surrounding learning environments* by answering the questions: What needs to be learned? How will learning occur?

Teachers utilize a variety of teaching methods based on their perceptions about how students learn. Operant conditioning (behaviorist) theory supports repetitious practice and memorization as techniques that lead to learning. Learning is a function of observable behavioral changes based on an individual's response to stimuli. When operant conditioning occurs in the classroom, the teacher is the one who provides knowledge and the students learn it. Constructivist theory, popular in the 1930s and 1940s and again today, focuses on individual students, with the teacher acting as a "coach" or "facilitator" as students construct their own understanding of and solutions to problems. The theories to which educators subscribe affect the type of physical learning environments they will need. Implementation of the behaviorist theory requires spaces where lecturing, listening, and testing can occur, while the constructivist theory requires that spaces provide an environment that stimulates students to collaborate with one another, as well as work individually to discover answers and solutions.

Second in the planning process, the planning team will *develop a purpose for the physical learning environment*. For example, if the school is to become a center for the broader community, the concept of shared spaces (e.g., auditorium or health center), as well as partnerships with other places (e.g., a local museum or zoo), must be considered. To support the purpose of a community "hub," an inviting atmosphere with appropriate security measures would be essential. *Third, examine the context* (political, social, economic, and cultural) in which the school will be built. A comprehensive survey (i.e., environmental scan) may include a demographic analysis, student population forecasting, space needs identification, and an analysis of financial considerations. The result of the contextual study will be a description of goals and objectives and how they relate to the educational facility plan. *Fourth,*

a planner with excellent leadership skills must lead the planning team to *specify what is realistic given the context, mission, values, and beliefs*. By examining all the information collected during the first three phases, specific findings may be articulated (e.g., natural light will be plentiful in every classroom). *Fifth, envision alternative school environments that capture the surprise-free scenarios* by articulating an agreed upon vision (based on the previous four phases) of what stakeholders expect their school to become (e.g., what learning theories will prevail, what the graduation rate goal is, etc.). *Sixth*, participants in the planning process will *select the best alternative* by conceptualizing spaces that support their vision, perhaps even deciding on the style of the school building (e.g., multistory, campus plan). Visits, either in person or virtually, to other schools can assist them with this activity. Next, participants can begin to actually "draw" the spaces they have envisioned to support the educational program, first by using bubble diagrams and then scaled drawings. This is the phase in which the planning team *will program and specify the physical environment*. The results from this phase, as well as previous phases, can be given to the professional architect who will translate the planning, programming, and sketches into a specific school design.

The design assessment scales presented in the research section in this text and the *Guide for School Facility Appraisal* available from the Council of Educational Facility Planners, International may be used to evaluate a school facility to determine if there is a need to provide new or different learning environments, either through remodeling or new construction. If the decision has been made to construct a new school, the model described in this chapter may be applied to facilitate the planning process. This model includes the following milestones, although they are not necessarily implemented in the linear manner in which they are presented. First, the school decision makers must plan to engage in the planning process and then forecast student enrollment. Determining educational feasibility involves studying existing educational program needs with respect to the school's philosophy of teaching and learning, the school size, and organization (K–5, 6–8, 9–12, etc.) and then determining the number and types of educational spaces the expected enrollments will require five to fifteen years into the future. To establish architectural feasibility, existing school spaces must be studied in light of the educational program, and current space needs must be compared to program space needs five to fifteen years into the future. Cost estimates for needs in the next five-year period are developed during this milestone.

District needs are prioritized and the school board may elect to adopt the findings of the needs assessment developed during the preceding milestones. Once the decision has been made as to whether to renovate or build a new facility(ies), capital budget estimates must be developed and financing acquired. If a new school is to be built, it is important to select the school principal early in the process to oversee design and construction activities. The architectural firm is selected and the school is designed (with input from a number of stakeholders). The selection of the type of school furniture (fixed or movable) must occur in conjunction with the design. A qualified and experienced construction manager should be selected early in the process to ensure that the owner (school district) is well represented throughout. The project must be scheduled to ensure that construction activities will work in harmony with the school calendar. Once the preliminary design is completed, a 35 percent cost estimate is obtained. Final cost estimates are secured on completion of the final architectural and engineering drawings. Then, construction documents are prepared. If the school system is using a design-bid-build method, bids for construction will be advertised, bids received, and contracts awarded.

Permits to begin construction are obtained. Bids for school furniture must be advertised and received. Once construction begins, it may take as many as eighteen to thirty-six months to complete. Monitoring of the construction program is the responsibility of not only the construction manager and architect, but also the school principal. The next milestones prior to moving into the new school include furniture installation, the development of the final "punch list," accepting the school (once formal notification from the builder is received stating that it is ready for occupancy), and orienting the school staff and community members to the building. Once the school is in use, a postoccupancy evaluation may be used to answer the key question, "If we had this project to do over again, what would we do differently?" Finally, prior to the expiration of the contractor's warranty, the owner is expected to inspect the facilities to determine deficiencies to be corrected by the contractor. To keep the construction process on track, it is critical that realistic activity schedules be developed and routinely updated. Computer programs can streamline this task.

Although restoration or remodeling of an existing school is typically much more complicated than constructing a new facility, the advantages of doing so must be carefully weighed against the disadvantages. If existing facilities will be modernized, the following milestones are involved: Agree to conduct a feasibility study, identify program objectives, collect the data needed to support program objectives, develop preferred design solutions, formulate architectural solutions, develop a capital plan and acquire public support, implement architectural solutions, and evaluate outcomes.

ACTIVITIES

1. Working in teams of three or four persons (as if you are part of the planning team for a new middle school), identify the specific types of data you would include in your "environmental scan" and describe from where or from whom you would obtain that data.

You may wish to create a table such as the one below:

TYPE OF DATA TO OBTAIN	SOURCE OF DATA

Also, describe how would you organize the information for analysis once it was obtained?

2. Based on the sample vision statement (see phases V and VI), write a brief set of educational specifications to support that vision (milestone 8, Chapter 16). Ideas for brief educational specifications may be found in Myers and Robertson (2004, Chapt. 5, pp. 2–41).

3. Identify one specific example of a school design that supports behavioral theories and one example that supports constructivist theories, and explain how each design supports teaching strategies that are in line with those theories.

4. Identify one exemplary school with a published mission statement or goals. Describe how the physical facility supports the mission or goals.

5. For a local school district, describe and explain the process for advertising bids for construction. Locate an advertisement (either past or current) and include it in your analysis.

6. Identify and describe at least one specific, credible tool that may be used for postoccupancy evaluation of a school setting. Discuss advantages of using this tool, and also challenges you might anticipate.

7. Building commissioning is a process to ensure that building elements and systems are designed, installed, and functioning as intended. Describe the process of fundamental building commissioning and why it is advantageous for school systems to include commissioning in the design and construction process.

8. Review Table 5.1, "Phases and Milestones in Planning a Capital Project." Should these phases and milestones be rearranged or modified? Defend your decision based on experience or research findings. Develop a new CPM chart to show your reasoning.

REFERENCES

Bingler, S., Quinn, L., & Sullivan, K. (December 2003). *Schools as centers of community: A citizen's guide for planning and design*, 2nd ed. Washington, DC: U.S. Department of Education.

Campbell, H. F., & Brown, R. P. C. (2003). *Benefit-cost analysis*. New York: Cambridge University Press.

Canady, R. L., & Rettig, M. D. (1995). *Block scheduling: A catalyst for change in high schools*. Princeton, NJ: Eye on Education.

Castaldi, B. (1994). *Educational facilities: Planning, modernizing, and management*. Boston: Allyn and Bacon.

Earthman, G. (2000). *Planning educational facilities for the next century*. Reston, VA: Association of School Business Officials, International.

Earthman, G., & LeMasters, L. (2004). *School maintenance and renovation: Administrator policies, practices, and economics*. Lancaster, PA: ProActive Publications.

Hawkins, H. L., & Lilley, H. E. (1998). *Guide for school facility appraisal*. Scottsdale, AZ: Council of Educational Facility Planners, International.

MacKenzie, D. G. (1989). *Planning educational facilities*. New York: University Press of America.

Montessori, M. (1967). *The discovery of the child*. Mattituck, NY: American House.

Myers, N. & Robertson, S. (2004). *Creating connections: The CEFPI guide for educational facility planning.*

Scottsdale, AZ: Council of Educational Facility Planners, International.

Piaget, J. (1924). *Judgment and reasoning in the child*. London: Routledge & Kegan Paul.

Piaget, J. (1936). *Origins of intelligence in the child*. London: Routledge & Kegan Paul.

Sanoff, H. (2000). *Community participation methods in design and planning*. New York: John Wiley & Sons.

Sanoff, H. (1994). *School design*. New York: Van Nostrand Reinhold.

Skinner, B. F. (1957). *Verbal learning*. New York: Appleton-Century-Crofts.

Taylor, A. (2000). *Programming and designing public schools within the context of community*. Paper Presented to the Stein and Schools Lecture Series, Policy, Planning and Design for a 21st Century Public Education System, Cornell University, Ithaca, NY.

Thorndike, E. L. (1923). *Education: A first book*. New York: Macmillan Co.

U.S. Department of Education (2000). *Schools as centers of community: A citizens' guide for planning and design*. Washington, DC: U.S. Department of Education.

Watson, J. B. (1958). *Behaviorism*. Chicago: University of Chicago Press.

CHAPTER SIX

ARCHITECTURAL DESIGN

This chapter outlines the design process that follows educational planning and provides exemplary case studies that illustrate the various phases of the design process and the final outcomes of that process: educational architecture. Following the model presented in Chapter 3, this chapter begins with the premise that planning and design activities are integrated (premise 5), and provides a more detailed description of the nature of this integration and overlap between planning and design. Once the final design phase commences with the hiring of the architect, there are a series of well-defined phases to the facility development process that have been established by design professionals and the building industry. Both the professional knowledge base concerning the architectural design of schools, as well as the nature of community involvement, have an impact on the final form of the school facility.

THE RELATIONSHIP BETWEEN PLANNING AND DESIGN ACTIVITIES

The conceptual design process at its best involves an assessment of functional needs in light of the educational program developed during educational planning. There are several names for this process: Educators refer to the development of *educational specifications* (Holcomb, 1995), while architects refer to it more generally as *facility programming* (Sanoff, 1994). Facility planning, as

presented in the previous chapter, includes any or all of the following activities: feasibility studies, district master planning, site selection, client and user needs assessment and project cost analysis. Spatial requirements and relationships between various program elements will be established during this process. The outcome of the facility planning process is a publicly available facility program document, or educational specifications document designating physical space requirements and adjacencies and special design criteria the school facility must meet.

THE ARCHITECTURAL DESIGN PROCESS

There are a series of well-defined phases to the design process, which have been established by the design professions and building industry and which the school district may typically follow. Ideally, upon having completed the educational specifications, the *architect is hired. This section provides a brief outline of the process followed in the architectural design and construction process.*

Selecting an Architect

An architect may be selected to assist in facility planning in cooperation with the educational planning team and in-house facility staff. The school board, as the owner, enters into a contract for services with the chosen architect. In this top-down process, the architect, in turn, enters into subcontracts with a variety of consultants including interior designers, landscape architects, mechanical, electrical and civil engineers, and land surveyors.

When selecting an architect, the public school board's primary concern is to retain the highest-quality professional services for the taxpayers' money, while simultaneously conducting a fair and equitable public selection process. The Qualification Based Selection (QBS) process developed by the American Institute of Architects (AIA) is one method that arguably provides owners with "a fair, rational and efficient method of selecting an architect based on an evaluation of the architect's qualifications and competence as they relate to the demands and needs of a specific project" (Wisconsin AIA, 1999). The selection of professional design services through QBS over the traditional bidding process can have several major advantages:

1. Clarification of project scope by both parties in a nonadversarial environment is essential to project success. QBS procedures foster a healthy and desirable dialogue between the client and the architectural/engineering firm before a final fee is determined and contract completed.
2. Low architecture and engineering fees often translate into less design and higher project costs. Design and construction value comes with mutual scope definition, not by less expensive professional fees. Price bidding on professional design fees may reduce valuable resources available to the design firm, thereby limiting the time it will be able to spend on the project and decreasing the quality of the overall project.
3. QBS avoids conflicts. In an architect/engineer negotiation process with professional firms, contingencies can be openly discussed and handled. Under the traditional bidding process, unanticipated cost and change orders often become "someone else's fault," creating an adversarial climate. The alleged

fault often lies with either an incomplete Request for Proposal (RFP) detailing scope of service or the design professional not including "all the work" in his or her price.

The QBS process has become widely used by the federal government and by many states and local governments. The process is designed to balance the critical need for affordable professional services with the often unrecognized need to hire qualified professionals capable of successfully completing the school design and construction project.

In reaching a decision, the school board will need to consider and evaluate many factors. QBS enables the school board to evaluate architectural firms according to specific selection criteria established for the project, such as a firm's ability to create effective design solutions to meet program needs, its interest in and commitment to the project, its understanding of project requirements, its communication skills and responsiveness to client concerns, its technical competence and ability to manage projects of similar size and scope. In the recent past, these important and numerous criteria were overshadowed by the need for low professional fees.

The QBS process recognizes the architect as playing a critical role in the design and construction of public school facilities and that the selection of an architect is a very specialized type of procurement. In most instances, QBS includes the following steps (Wisconsin AIA, 1999):

1. The school board as owner develops a preliminary scope of work statement that describes the project and the professional services to be provided by the architectural firm.
2. A schedule of activities is determined that establishes the calendar or timeframe for each step in the selection process (see Chapter 5, "Planning and Programming for a Capital Project").
3. A list of architectural firms is compiled, from which statements of qualifications are requested.

4. Statements of qualifications are received from these firms and evaluated by the school board.

5. A short list of from three to five architectural firms to be interviewed is determined.

6. All architectural firms responding to the request for qualifications are informed of the evaluation results.

7. A tour of the site and/or facility is arranged for the short-listed firms and these architectural firms are informed of the selection criteria and issues to be addressed during a subsequent interview.

8. Interviews are scheduled and conducted with short-listed firms and the architects are ranked in accordance with established selection criteria.

9. All firms interviewed are informed of the selection results.

10. A contract is negotiated with the selected architect. If an agreement cannot be reached with the top-ranked firm, those negotiations are ended and new negotiations begin with the second-ranked firm, and so on until an agreement is reached regarding scope of services, compensation, and other contractual items.

The QBS process arguably provides a proven framework for guiding the project start-up. It encourages improved communication and early understanding of project requirements and owner expectations.

Basic Design Services

The AIA defines five basic services offered by architects in any building type in its B141 Owner/Architect Agreement. These include schematic design, design development, construction documents and specifications, bidding and negotiations, and construction administration.

The design phase of the process including schematic design, design development, and con-

struction documents and specifications can last between six months to a year. The construction phases of the process include bidding and negotiation, and construction administration and can take from eighteen months to two years. As the design progresses through each phase of the facility development process, more detailed and specific information about the technical aspects of the building systems, components, and assemblies need to be addressed (Brubaker, 1998).

At each phase in the design and construction process, school board decisions and approval are required before the next phase can begin. Along with more detailed and specific technical information, each phase requires more detailed estimates of the overall project scope, project budget, and project schedule.

The products during the schematic and design development phases may include sketches, drawings, models, and technical reports that are shared and negotiated with the school and community through public hearings, workshops, and other forms of public relations and community involvement. If the schematic design is based on the educational program, this phase should be uncomplicated, since many of the concerns have been addressed in community forums.

Construction Documents and Specifications

This phase involves the translation of the school design into a set of documents that will eventually become part of a legal contract between the owner and contractor(s). Construction documents include construction drawings and project specifications outlining all building systems in a sixteen-section format established by the Construction Specifications Institute (CSI). (The CSI format is discussed in detail in Chapter 7, "Construction and Construction Management.") Construction documents are legal documents consisting of plans, sections, elevations, details, and schedules that communicate to the contractor, in detail, exactly how all the systems of the school building shall be constructed.

Bidding and Negotiation

The next phase of the school building process is bidding and negotiation. The following description assumes the use of a conventional competitive bidding process. Once the school board approves the construction contract documents, an invitation for bids is publicized to obtain bids from prime construction contractors.

Most states require the school district to accept the lowest responsible and responsive bidder (Bittle, 1996); however, the school district reserves the right to reject all bids. Once low bids are accepted, the school district as owner negotiates an owner/contractor agreement or contract with each prime contractor. If a construction manager is being used, an owner/construction manager agreement is drawn up.

Construction Administration

Following the standard AIA B141 contract, during the construction phase the architect representing the owner in the construction phase acts as construction contract administrator, but the contract and legal relationship are between the school district as owner and each prime contractor.

The construction of the school can last from twelve to eighteen months depending on the project scope, material selections and lead times for shipment to the site, weather, unforeseen subsurface site conditions, and a variety of other factors. In schools especially tied to the school year schedule, project phasing is always an issue that needs to be addressed.

Another factor that can escalate cost and slow up the project are *change orders* to rectify unforeseen conditions or errors and omissions in the original construction documents. Once the need for a change in the scope of work on the project is recognized, the architect prepares a change order that includes drawings and specifications related to that change

and sends the change order to the contractor for pricing. Once the contractor prices the change order, it must be formally accepted by the public school board before any action may be initiated. This entire process can take up to a month, slowing down related work while incurring additional project costs.

Once the architect is satisfied that the project is complete, a certificate of substantial completion is issued to the contractor and the owner can legally occupy the facility. Remaining work must be completed by the contractor in a timely fashion. A punch list of these final items is prepared and final walk-through by the owner, architect, and contractor is scheduled. One year from the date of substantial completion, the architect schedules with the owner a final walk-through of the facility to review the work covered by the one-year contractor warranty.

Community Involvement in Design

As first discussed in Chapter 2, and in later chapters on educational planning, the authors hope it has become clear that community participation during the earliest stages of the design phase can be as critical for stakeholder support as it was in the educational planning process itself (Sanoff, 1994). Participation in the planning and design of schools is more than a way of obtaining support for bond issues and appeasing public and private interests; its benefits in creating exceptional educational architecture cannot be overstated. If the school is the center of community, so should the planning and design of that school be community-centered, open, democratic and de-mystified to the greatest extent possible.

Unfortunately, community involvement in school planning and design is often misused and misunderstood by school administrators and school board members who fear a loss of political control over the planning and design process. In these instances, community involvement can become an exercise in manipulation. However, when properly understood, participation and community involvement can provide a wide range of benefits

(Sanoff, 2002) in addition to community support for bond passage:

1. Full participation in school design allows for the inclusion of the knowledge and expertise of all people affected by design decisions, especially teachers, parents, and students who have different, but equally valid perspectives.

2. Most building projects are complex and require collaborative teamwork, usually among people with different expertise and frames of reference; participation provides a clear framework for collaborative success.

3. Involving future users in the school building design is an effective way of gathering information for the design as well as for influencing design decisions that result in better school buildings.

4. Providing opportunities for teachers, students, and parents to be involved in the initial stages of design recognizes the value of their contribution to the design solution.

5. The act of participating helps teachers increase their awareness and ability to articulate how the school building accommodates their educational objectives and enhances learning.

6. Full collaboration of the school community in design can foster a positive school community spirit that can live on in the occupied building for years to come.

Methods of participation are wide and varied, and their choice must be based on the objectives of participation agreed on by the school building committee and design professional often responsible for planning and organizing the participation process. Most often, community involvement is *passive*, that is, not more than a public forum in which the public can ask questions of the architectural firm's already completed design that was worked out ahead of time with a design review committee or taskforce. However, if there is political will in the district and, expertise on the part of the design professional, par-

ticipation can go well beyond informing the community, to *actively* engaging the community in a process that shares design decision making in the process itself. This process can become messy and confusing, especially for participants and professionals not accustomed to an open decision-making process, so careful planning of the process is critical to its success. The school board, design subcommittee, and design professional need to agree on who will be welcome to participate and to what degree, when and in what manner, and what outcomes are expected from such a process. Certainly, involving representatives from a vocally resistant group can become a balancing act between sharing project control and losing it. Additionally, the advantages of involving teachers and parents must be weighed against their potential dissatisfaction when they perceive their comments are not being taken seriously.

Methods of participation in design must be chosen carefully to ensure the proper management of information that has been gathered. Methods can range from the use of surveys and interviews to community meetings and more complex planning and design techniques such as workshops or day-to week-long design charettes in which various segments of the entire community are in attendance. Sanoff (1994, 2002) provides a number of easy-to-use checklists, rating scales, attitude and observational surveys, design simulation games as well as case study examples for planning and organizing effective participation in the design of a school. (See the Davidson Elementary School case study below for a further description of the methods commonly used in participatory planning and design processes.)

Sharing the results of these data collection exercises and indicating how these exercises have influenced the design of the school are just as important as the initial community involvement itself. Reporting back results can take many forms as well, from the public forums to distributing full copies of preliminary findings for review and comment. Providing multiple opportunities for feedback, through forums, presentations, public media outlets, and mailings, takes into consideration the problems of providing ample forums for participation, as well as engendering some redundancy that may aid in clarifying and "triangulating" key issues of importance to the community as a whole.

APPLICATIONS OF SCHOOL DESIGN PRINCIPLES

This section provides selected educational architecture case studies (including elementary, middle, and high schools) to illustrate how the school design principles in Chapter 2 and those in the research section of this book have been successfully integrated to produce exemplary school designs. Table 6.1 on pages 134–136 provides an overview of the most prominently emphasized school design principles in each of the fourteen case studies that are presented in this chapter. Although there are many other examples of good educational architecture, the authors believe that the case studies included in this chapter best illustrate the innovative application of school design principles in educational architecture practice today.

1. Fearn Elementary School, North Aurora, Illinois

The tradition of school design found in Crow Island (see Chapter 1) lives on, first in the work of the late C. William Brubaker (1998) and in the work of present-day school architects at the Perkins & Will architectural firm. Fearn Elementary School in North Aurora, Illinois, completed in 2001 and designed by Gaylaird Christopher of Perkins & Will, is a successful example of the replication of some of the more important lessons of Crow Island. It is a K–5 grade configuration serving 600 students in 58,000 square feet of space on a 6-acre site (Figures 6.1 and 6.2, page 137). Just as with its predecessor, Crow Island, Fearn's design evolved through intense interaction between Perkins & Will and the district's Design Committee that included the superintendent, school board members, district administrators, Aurora University, faculty from various curriculum areas, the City of North

Aurora, and the Fox Valley Park District. During a series of workshops, committee members took tours of significant public school projects, evaluated various building concepts, and shared their own design ideas. Major design innovations that became part of Fearn's detailed program were a direct result of this collaboration.

Fearn is part of a community campus that includes a middle school and the Fox Valley Park District. In response, the school design provides community access to a multipurpose hall for dining, athletics, and performances. The school's design strengthens the sense of community by the school's internal "village street" linking resource centers, the library office, an art room, and administrative offices (Figure 6.3, page 138). Fearn's partnership with Aurora University reinforces the notion of life-long community learning. Through community partnership and flexible design, students benefit from the school's multiple and innovative resources. With students and faculty from Aurora University using Fearn as an educational laboratory, teaching methods, curriculum, and classroom settings can be tailored to meet changing students' needs. A mobile media center

FIGURE 6.1 Entrance to Fearn Elementary School, North Aurora, Illinois.

Source: Courtesy of Perkins & Will, Architects.

TABLE 6.1   Design Principles Evident in Case Studies

CASES ⇒	CROW ISLAND ELEMENTARY SCHOOL*	1. FEARN ELEMENTARY SCHOOL	2. DAVIDSON ELEMENTARY SCHOOL	3. CRAGMONT ELEMENTARY SCHOOL	4. CROSSWINDS ARTS AND SCIENCE MIDDLE SCHOOL	5. NOBLE HIGH SCHOOL	6. THE SCHOOL FOR ENVIRONMENTAL STUDIES	7. THE GARY AND JERRI-ANN JACOBS HIGH TECH HIGH SCHOOL	8. HARBOR CITY CHARTER-SCHOOL	9. HENRY FORD ACADEMY	10. GRANGER CENTER FOR IMAGINATION AND INQUIRY	11. CANNING VALE HIGH SCHOOL
Principles for Site and Building Organization ⇓												
Plan schools as neighborhood-scaled community learning centers				✔								
Plan for learning to take place directly in the community							✔	✔		✔		
Create Smaller Schools												
Respect contextual compatibility while providing design diversity				✔	✔							
Consider home as a template for school												
Meander circulation while ensuring supervision		✔	✔		✔			✔				✔
Design for safe schools						✔			✔			
Principles for Primary Educational Space												
Cluster learning areas												
Provide space for sharing instructional resources												
Design for a variety of learning groups and spaces												
Keep class sizes small												
Provide resource-rich well-defined activity pockets												

TABLE 6.1   Continued

CASES ⇒	CROW ISLAND ELEMENTARY SCHOOL*	1. FEARN ELEMENTARY SCHOOL	2. DAVIDSON ELEMENTARY SCHOOL	3. CRAGMONT ELEMENTARY SCHOOL	4. CROSSWINDS ARTS AND SCIENCE MIDDLE SCHOOL	5. NOBLE HIGH SCHOOL	6. THE SCHOOL FOR ENVIRONMENTAL STUDIES	7. THE GARY AND JERRI-ANN JACOBS HIGH TECH HIGH SCHOOL	8. HARBOR CITY CHARTER-SCHOOL	9. HENRY FORD ACADEMY	10. GRANGER CENTER FOR IMAGINATION AND INQUIRY	11. CANNING VALE HIGH SCHOOL
Integrate early childhood education into the school	✔		✔									
Provide a home base for every learner												
Regard teachers as professionals												
Provide studios to support project-based learning												
Encourage administrative leadership by decentralizing administrative space												
Principles for Shared School and Community Facilities												
Establish a community forum				✔	✔	✔	✔	✔				✔
Allow for community conferencing space						✔						
Create privacy niches	✔	✔	✔		✔		✔	✔	✔			
Weave together virtual and physical learning spaces					✔	✔	✔	✔	✔			
Community spaces												
Provide for opportunities job training								✔				
Provide a parents information center												
Provide health care service centers												

continued

TABLE 6.1 Continued

CASES ⇒	CROW ISLAND ELEMENTARY SCHOOL*	1. FEARN ELEMENTARY SCHOOL	2. DAVIDSON ELEMENTARY SCHOOL	3. CRAGMONT ELEMENTARY SCHOOL	4. CROSSWINDS ARTS AND SCIENCE MIDDLE SCHOOL	5. NOBLE HIGH SCHOOL	6. THE SCHOOL FOR ENVIRONMENTAL STUDIES	7. THE GARY AND JERRI-ANN JACOBS HIGH TECH HIGH SCHOOL	8. HARBOR CITY CHARTER-SCHOOL	9. HENRY FORD ACADEMY	10. GRANGER CENTER FOR IMAGINATION AND INQUIRY	11. CANNING VALE HIGH SCHOOL
Character of All Spaces												
Design places with respect for scale and developmental need												
Maximize natural and full-spectrum lighting	✔	✔	✔	✔								✔
Design healthy buildings				✔								
Design for appropriate acoustics							✔					
Site Design and Outdoor Learning Spaces												
Allow for transitional spaces between indoor and outdoor spaces	✔	✔	✔									✔
Establish a variety of outdoor learning environments	✔		✔	✔			✔					
Separate children and pedestrians from vehicles and service	✔	✔	✔	✔	✔							

*Note: Crow Island School, included as an exemplary case study of early modern school design, is described in Chapter 1 and is included in this list as a means of comparison.

enhances teachers' ability to meet students' needs by delivering rsources attuned to a specific curriculum, age level, or project to the classroom. The partnership with Aurora University provides an on-site professional development center serving as an accessible teaching laboratory, promoting a rich interaction between educational researchers, university students, and school staff.

The flexibility of the school's mobile media center and wireless computer network not only expanded teachers' educational resources, it also increased the space of each classroom cluster to include dedicated resource and project areas. Classroom clusters were designed to support a variety of curricula and teaching methods including looping (i.e., students of the same grade stay with

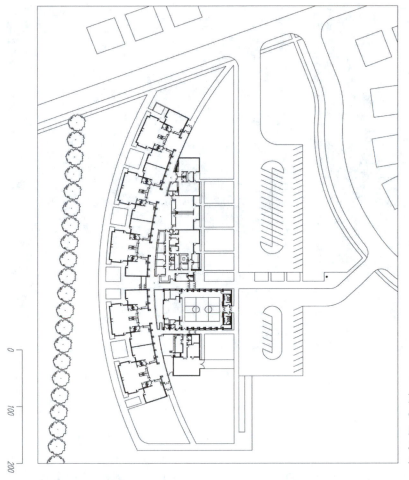

FIGURE 6.2   Site and floor plan of Fearn illustrate classroom space groupings that recall Crow Island.

Source: Courtesy of Perkins & Will, Architects.

the same teacher for two or more years), multi-grade classrooms, and traditional self-contained classrooms. Study resource areas support the need for more intimate learning experiences. Flexible walls help redefine both classrooms and gathering spaces; by closing one wall, the stage converts into a music classroom, or by opening the opposite wall, the classroom becomes a setting for special learning activities and small performances (Figure 6.4, page 138).

By providing each major learning space with direct access to the outside, the building can be easily exited in an emergency. The bay windows and

clerestories throughout the building also provide the generous natural light needed to promote a healthy educational atmosphere.

2. Davidson Elementary School, Davidson, North Carolina

Davidson Elementary School is an exemplary case study of what can be accomplished if an entire community is actively involved in the planning and design process of a school building and the results of that participation are taken seriously (Figures 6.5 and 6.6, page 139). Davidson Elementary School,

FIGURE 6.3   "Village Street" Leading to Class-rooms at Fearn.

Source: Courtesy of Perkins & Will, Architects.

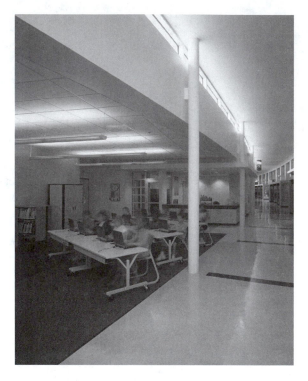

FIGURE 6.4   Flexible Instructional Space off Fearn's "Main Street."

Source: Courtesy of Perkins & Will, Architects.

completed in 1997, was designed by the Adams Group in cooperation with school planner Henry Sanoff to serve 700 grade K–5 students of the Charlotte Mecklenburg Schools community, North Carolina, in an 82,000 square foot facility.

The planning and design process for Davidson was very participatory, utilizing a charette process, community meetings, focused interviews, game simulations, and workshops (Sanoff, 1994, p. 57). The involvement of the community included all students and teachers at the school, school administration representatives, parents and PTA members, Town of Davidson Council and Historic Appearance Commission members. Specific participatory methods were designed to solicit ideas from each group. The teachers and school administration

participated in a design game where they developed alternative site concepts and room arrangements for the proposed school using materials developed by the architect. The students were engaged in developing a wish poem, a series of statements beginning with the phrase "I wish my school _____." These statements were combined with dream drawings the students completed for the image of the new school. The architect used one of these student images to create the final elevations for the school.

The Town of Davidson Council and Historic Appearance Commission participated in the editing of site images presented by the architects of the project shown in the broader neighborhood context; the group was able to communicate desires for the building color, finishes, building massing, and

FIGURE 6.5 The front elevation of Davidson Elementary School was inspired by student drawings completed during the participatory planning process.

Source: Courtesy of Henry Sanoff.

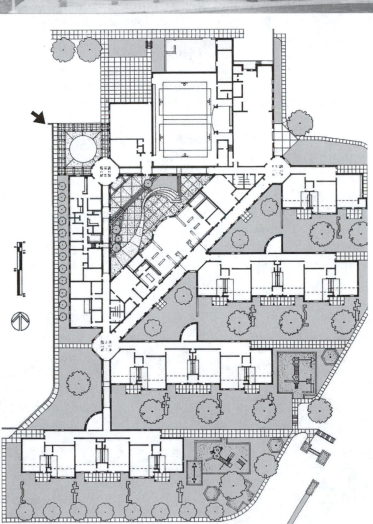

FIGURE 6.6 Plan of Davidson illustrates single-loaded corridor house groups of six classrooms, with each classroom provided direct access to outdoor learning environments.

Source: Courtesy of Henry Sanoff.

site details for the project. The 20-acre site design reserved eleven acres as a natural preserve. This compact utilization of the building site represents a sensitive response to preserving natural resources and animal habitats.

Broader community groups were also involved in the design of the school. Local artists who often contributed their time each week to tutor at the school expressed a desire to have places to exhibit student work as well as art developed by the local community. A gallery space was designed in response to allow for permanent artwork, designed and installed by the students working with a local artist, as well as areas for temporary art display. In addition, the community working through the PTA expressed a desire to have a full-sized gymnasium that could serve as a community center for the public and a recreation area for the school. The gymnasium, not a standard feature of most elementary schools in the region, was planned in exchange for code-required road improvements provided by the Town of Davidson.

The Davidson Elementary School was designed to support learning in a number of ways. The interior classroom design is developed using learning centers arranged as a house group of six classrooms (Figure 6.6). Each classroom allows the teacher to form developmentally appropriate areas for learning activities. Corridors are arranged such that six classrooms are located on a single loaded corridor. By offsetting the center classrooms, the wider corridor is formed, creating the opportunity for a shared learning center. By reducing the traffic circulation pattern associated with each house, the shared areas can be used in unique ways as specified within each teaching group; some of these areas utilize a couch and soft furniture for reading areas, while other shared areas form table and display areas for group activities.

The classroom design allows for flexibility in team teaching and multigrade configurations. By locating K–1 classrooms in each wing, the school plan affords the development of alternative curriculum approaches. The design takes advantage of southern sun exposures to further enhance learning by providing outdoor learning areas adjacent to each classroom for creating art and science projects and other classroom activities.

3. Cragmont Elementary School, Berkeley, California

Cragmont Elementary School in Berkeley, California, completed in 1999 and designed by ELS Architects, is located on a 3.5-acre site that focuses on environmental education using the landscape as a teaching tool (Figure 6.7). What is significant about this school facility, beyond its focus on environ-

FIGURE 6.7 Outdoor Landscape on the Site of Cragmont Elementary School, Berkeley, California.

Source: Courtesy of ELS Architects.

mental education in an urban context, is the impact the surrounding community had in the school's making. The school district had not planned on rebuilding on this site due to seismic and land constraints. However, parents from the surrounding community successfully lobbied for the school to be constructed. Both the program and design of the school were developed in an intensive series of workshops organized by ELS Architects with an active group of parents, teachers, administrators, neighbors, and students. Meetings took place every month through the design and construction process.

The resulting plan was a school building with an explicit focus not only on environmental education but community use as well, going beyond the joint-use opportunities of the library and multipurpose room. Community use is encouraged through a community garden, outdoor classrooms for nature classes, a roof terrace off the media center for public gatherings, and a courtyard functioning as a community square for the neighborhood. Neighborhood festivals are regularly held there. One neighbor commented: "People like to come in and stay a while." Once inside, the school feels like a "high-end conference center," that "entices us to want to stay and talk" (Figure 6.8).

FIGURE 6.8 The media center at Cragmont emphasizes the use of natural light.

Source: Courtesy of ELS Architects.

Additionally, the design emphasized small school size to promote a sense of belonging and community in a very diverse student population. Along with the environmental focus, the school design maximizes daylight for its potential impact on learning as well as for reducing energy consumption. The use of natural materials was a strategy employed to reduce the utilization of renewable resources. Every classroom has an outdoor patio and trellis for small outdoor peer teaching groups.

4. Crosswinds Arts and Science Middle School, Woodbury, Minnesota

Crosswinds Arts and Science Middle School in Woodbury, Minnesota, designed by Cunningham Architects, is a case example of how facilities can be planned and designed to actively support the middle school model. There are many examples across the country of middle school buildings designed, going back to the 1980s, with "house" arrangements, in which a larger student body is broken down into "families" of 100 students who share a "house." Crosswinds Middle School represents the latest thinking along these lines in which the metaphor of house and home is taken farthest: to the principle of educational architecture—"provide a home base for every learner" (Figure 6.9, page 142).

Crosswinds Arts and Science Middle School is the outcome of seven school districts working cooperatively and sharing the facility (Cuningham, 2002). Crosswinds was planned to operate as a year-round school with an arts and science emphasis for 600 students, grades 6–8, from all seven districts. Predesign meetings of educators, parents, and community members focused on developing a vision for the school through a process of defining the learning context, outcomes, process, organization, partnerships, and staff that would make up this learning community. Technology and the environment were other important factors discussed during these predesign meetings. Based on these discussions and the consensus achieved on critical issues, the architects created what they called "filters" to guide participants in all subsequent decisions. One such filter of

FIGURE 6.9   Entrance to Crosswinds Arts and Science Middle School, Woodbury, Minnesota.

Source: Courtesy of Cuningham Group, Architects.

particular importance to the school concerned discussions about how middle school students learn. A key result of discussion on the learning process was the formulation of a learning environment where disciplines would be interconnected in hands-on, project-based learning that includes developing students' presentation and description skills.

There are no classrooms in the traditional sense of the self-contained classroom; in its place are what the school calls "home bases" consisting of individual student workstations with resource areas where small groups can meet, and a larger gathering and performance area (Figure 6.10).

The school was designed for multiage learning houses, with home bases designed for 100 students, each of mixed grade levels (Figure 6.11). Each of the houses features lab and discovery space where students work alone or in small groups exploring subjects. The students then develop language and presentation skills by reporting on their projects to larger groups of students in presentation areas within each house. Spaces were created specifically to suit a hands-on, project-based learning methodology that engages students on multiple levels. The home bases open onto a larger central area, the "heart" of the school, which contains an all-school performance area and social hall. Outdoor "living" labs supplement the labs in each house to take advantage of the school's unique

FIGURE 6.10   Home Bases at Crosswinds.
Source: Courtesy of Cuningham Architects.

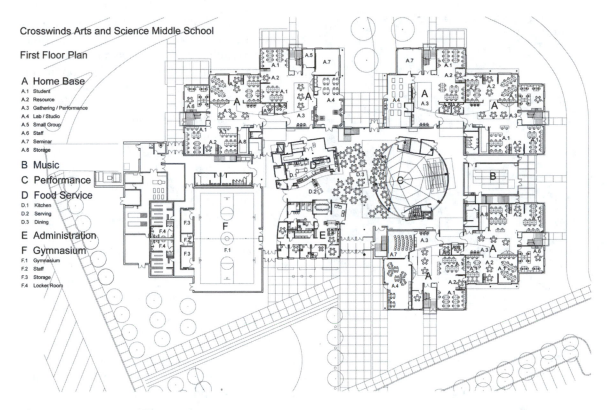

Crosswinds Arts and Science Middle School

First Floor Plan

A Home Base
A.1 Student
A.2 Resource
A.3 Gathering / Performance
A.4 Lab / Studio
A.5 Small Group
A.6 Staff
A.7 Seminar
A.8 Storage

B Music

C Performance

D Food Service
D.1 Kitchen
D.2 Serving
D.3 Dining

E Administration

F Gymnasium
F.1 Gymnasium
F.2 Staff
F.3 Storage
F.4 Locker Room

FIGURE 6.11   Floor Plan of Crosswinds.

Source: Courtesy of Cuningham Group, Architects.

location adjacent to a park and a wetland area (Cuningham Group, 2002, pp. 27–28, 49).

5. Noble High School, North Berwick, Maine

Noble High School, located in North Berwick, Maine, and designed by Harriman Architects, represents a present trend in educational architecture, creating smaller learning environments within a large school building, or the school-within-a-school design approach. It also represents a new trend in high school designs that attempt to break down the traditional departmental disciplinary-focused organizational structures into interdisciplinary teaching teams to support an integrated curriculum (Figure 6.12, page 144).

Noble High School is a member of the Coalition of Essential Schools (CES), a nationwide organization whose members adhere to a set of principles encouraging innovation in teaching. The district uses a project-based, interdisciplinary approach, where teams teaching mathematics, science, English, and social studies work within learning communities of 100 learners (Figure 6.13, page 145). The traditional departmental high school structure does not exist at Noble. In keeping with CES principles, democratic processes, a collaborative environment, and standards-based curricula are central.

When the district leaders began the planning for the new school, they desired that the new school facility be compatible with CES principles. The district also wanted to encourage life-long learning for all ages and to provide much-needed space

FIGURE 6.12   Front Entrance to Noble High School, North Berwick, Maine.

Source: Courtesy of Harriman Architects.

for community programs in a rural area that had no real center. And despite needing space for 1,500 students, the three towns in the district wanted a friendly, small-school ambiance.

For over a year the planning and design process involved faculty, students, administrators, staff, parents, and community members. Architects held meetings with the faculty and conducted interviews, individually with each teacher and with all interdisciplinary teams. Questionnaires were used to gather information on specific needs and general ideas about the design. A student committee developed a survey questionnaire, and student facilitators led discussions in all classes.

Every element in the design of the school was based on determining what was best for students and began with five basic principles. The new facility should (1) abolish anonymity by creating schools within schools; (2) reflect the concept of teacher as coach, student as worker; (3) accommodate a curriculum collaboratively designed, interdisciplinary, and project-based; (4) be a community center that embraces the community, so community functions are integrated and not separated from education functions; and (5) be flexible in design, material, and function.

In keeping with these goals, the design was organized to respond to the need for collaborative learning and to create a smaller, more personal, less anonymous environment. Fifteen identical schools-within-a-school or learning communities were created, with each including a multipurpose room that functions much like a living room, where the family of 100 students and four teachers can meet to present their work. Student lockers are located in this room to reinforce the concept of community.

Each community has rooms of varying sizes and functions and has state-of-the art technology infrastructure, which facilitates the hands-on, project-based curriculum that recognizes the student as worker and teacher as coach. A large classroom can become two when a movable wall is in place. A science lab has movable tables in the middle of the room, with gas and water lines on the sides. A large project room with a sink and a large storage room facilitate student work. Teachers share an office that includes a window looking out onto the multipurpose room.

One of the paradoxes of building smaller-scaled school environments is the countervailing economic drive for a community to build big to accommodate as many functions as possible to meet the needs of a particular community. Noble High School confronted such a problem in its creation. The school is large for a rural community (270,000 square feet); however, the design features arguably make it appear smaller than it actually is, both fitting its surroundings and heritage while providing an ambiance that students and community find inviting. The building consists of a composition of diverse forms in an attempt to reduce its scale. Over half of the building's size is hidden from view on

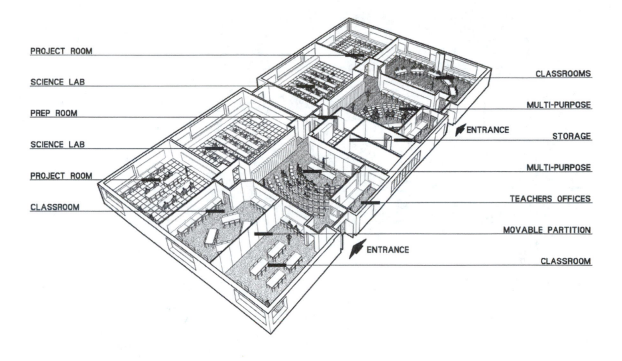

PROJECT ROOM

SCIENCE LAB

PREP ROOM

SCIENCE LAB

PROJECT ROOM

CLASSROOM

CLASSROOMS

MULTI-PURPOSE

ENTRANCE

STORAGE

MULTI-PURPOSE

TEACHERS OFFICES

MOVABLE PARTITION

ENTRANCE

CLASSROOM

Pair of 100-Student Learning Communities

FIGURE 6.13   Student Learning Communities at Noble.

Source: Courtesy of Harriman Architects.

approaching the site. Classroom wings screen parts of the building, the gymnasium wing is pushed back on the site, and large groupings of trees outside were left undisturbed. The use of natural materials such as brick and wood are contextually compatible with the surrounding community and establish a friendly, inviting tone (Figure 6.14, page 146).

The town square entrance lobby provides places to sit, to see, and to be seen, while being sky-lit, bright, and welcoming (Figure 6.15, page 147). Skylights in the cafeteria and large, arched windows throughout the building also bring in light and offer views of the surrounding woods.

Wherever possible, corridors are offset at classroom entrance doors and single-loaded to avoid the institutional look given by traditional long, dou-ble-loaded corridors of most high schools this size. In addition, corridors are wide enough to accom-modate benches along window walls, providing

light-filled areas for informal gatherings or quiet study. Heating units under the windows make the benches comfortable even in winter. In addition to the cafeteria, a small café provides another area for socializing.

The school has an extensive technology in-frastructure, with over 2,000 data outlets to meet current and future needs. This availability has en-abled teachers to take advantage of sophisticated educational software to enhance their curricula, and it is easy for students to avail themselves of the wealth of information and resources online. For students needing specialized help in writing or other tasks, the school has a computerized learn-ing lab. A video equipment studio supports the in-terdisciplinary curriculum. The computer network within the building also provides cost-effective ways for handling administrative tasks. Teachers have individual accounts on the school's computer

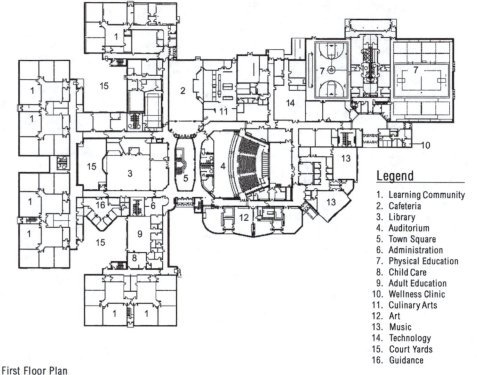

Legend

1. Learning Community
2. Cafeteria
3. Library
4. Auditorium
5. Town Square
6. Administration
7. Physical Education
8. Child Care
9. Adult Education
10. Wellness Clinic
11. Culinary Arts
12. Art
13. Music
14. Technology
15. Court Yards
16. Guidance

First Floor Plan

0 25 50 100 FT

FIGURE 6.14   Plan of First Floor at Noble.

Source: Courtesy of Harriman Architects.

network systems. Student attendance is entered daily over the network, as are report cards and interim reports. Each teacher has a direct phone line with voicemail in his or her room, facilitating contact with other staff as well as parents and other community members. Communications with stakeholders is also enhanced and facilitated through the school website. Teachers can enter homework assignments on the Web, available to both students and parents. In addition, news about school activities and the school calendar are posted online.

Noble High School is also designed to serve the community beyond the school-aged population. A large permanent display case in the town square is set aside for each town in the district, a visible reminder that each town is an owner of the building. The building includes a community health care clinic, and a day care vocational center is located adjacent to the adult education center. A fifty-seat restaurant open to the public provides training for culinary arts students. A performing arts center seating 1,000 is one of the largest and best-equipped theaters in the region. An area within the library is assigned for use by community volunteers to read to early-childhood-aged children. Finally, when not needed for scholastic activities, athletic fields, gymnasiums, and a fitness-training center are all shared with the community.

FIGURE 6.15 **"Town Square" at Noble.**
Source: Courtesy of Harriman Architects.

6. The School for Environmental Studies, Apple Valley, Minnesota

Criticisms of the relevance of the comprehensive school within the context of changes in the global economy are many. However, successful attempts

at school reform have been difficult, and examples of the break-up of the large comprehensive high school are few. Recent attempts have taken the lead from one particularly innovative high school: The School for Environmental Studies (SES). Occupied in 1995, it serves 400 junior and senior students with an interdisciplinary environmental education focus. SES is one of the first schools in the country to plan explicitly for the provision of individual workstations for every student in the school—although this innovation is becoming more common, it is still ahead of its time in providing a true home base for every learner. SES was led first by innovative educational planning at the district level, followed by the innovative facility planning work of Bruce Jilk of Hammel, Green and Abrahamson Architects.

SES, affectionately called the Zoo School by its students and teachers, is an innovative magnet high school that partnered with the Minnesota Zoo, and is located directly on the property of the Minneapolis Zoological Gardens (Figure 6.16). SES also represents a partnership between the Independent School District (ISD) 196, the Minnesota Zoological Gardens, and the City of Apple Valley, Minnesota The school has direct access to a wide variety of animals, and over 500 acres of wetlands and woods. SES integrates language arts, social studies, and environmental sciences using an environmental theme in an

FIGURE 6.16 **School of Environmental Studies, Apple Valley, Minnesota, located on the site of the Minneapolis Zoological Gardens.**
Source: Courtesy of Hammel Green and Abrahamson Architects.

interdisciplinary, collaborative, project-based approach, whereby learners practice becoming community leaders through community-based projects (Wolff, 2002).

The school is organized into four open plan houses of 100 students who are then grouped into ten teams of ten organized in individual desk groupings (or individual learning stations) (Figure 6.17). The main school plan constitutes a modified open plan arrangement with labs and teacher offices providing acoustic separation between houses that include desk pods. These surround flexible open resource areas that can be used for whole-group presentation as well as small-group learning. Each house has a team of four teachers who guide thematic studies to the learners within that house. The learners work with other teachers in elective classes and with community members who are involved in the theme studies courses. The small physical school size of SES offers an open and flexible physical environment supporting a wide variety of personalized learning experiences further supported through

the care and guidance of the staff (Copa, Bodette, & Birkey, 1999, referenced in Wolff, 2002).

Teacher offices are further evidence that teachers are treated like professionals. Teachers within each house share an office with common group space where they can store their materials, plan lessons, and meet informally with their fellow teachers (Figure 6.18). The school day is organized along a block schedule to allow students and teachers more time to explore integrated environmental subjects.

Each house space has a gathering area called a "Centrum" that provides a central, common area that can either accommodate all 100 learners for whole-group instruction, or smaller learner groups for project workspace (Figure 6.19). The Centrum is supported by a decentralized science laboratory, seminar room, and storage spaces for supplies and projects.

The individual work areas are each designed for ten learners on three sides of the perimeter of each house. The design features of the learning station pods include individual workstations with personal, lockable storage, a display space attached

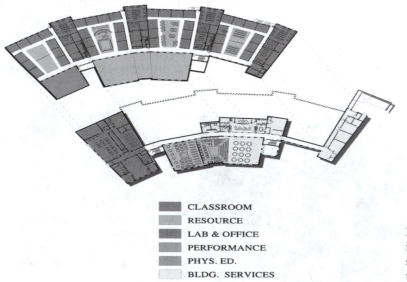

CLASSROOM
RESOURCE
LAB & OFFICE
PERFORMANCE
PHYS. ED.
BLDG. SERVICES

FIGURE 6.17 Floor plan of SES illustrates four houses separated by science labs, seminar rooms, and teacher offices.

Source: Courtesy of Hammel, Green and Abrahamson Architects.

FIGURE 6.18   Shared Teacher Offices at SES.

Source: Photo by Jeffery A. Lackney.

above each desk so each learner can personalize her or his space, and access to a computer. Providing students with individual workspace they control and take ownership of throughout the year is the most tangible evidence that these are actual learner-centered environments (Figure 6.20).

The individual workstation and learning pod innovation make SES unique among school designs in the late twentieth century; however, the concept has been evolving since the late 1950s. C. William Brubaker of Perkins & Will may have been one of the first to conceptualize the individual workstation as early as 1959 in what he first called "space for individual learning," and then "Q-space"—one student's place for an individual quest. This idea evolved in to "turf concept"—five students sharing an office-size home base for individual study, projects, computer work, small group sessions, and meeting with faculty members (Brubaker, 1998, pp. 35–36). It was, however, SES that successfully implemented the idea, which is only now becoming more accepted in school design.

Just as important as the house structure are the more public spaces supporting the houses. The central double-height space, called the "Forum," is a multipurpose area designed for a variety of uses: a commons, cafeteria, gallery, presentation, or conference space. The south wall features floor-to-ceiling windows that provide natural light to the entire school environment while simultaneously providing a view overlooking the pond and

FIGURE 6.19   Student Presentation in the Centrum within the House at SES.

Source: Courstey of Hammel Green and Abrahamson Architects.

FIGURE 6.20   Individual Learning Station within the House at SES.

Source: Courtesy of Hammel, Green and Abrahamson Architects.

woods—an ever-present reminder of the environmental focus of the school. The Forum is not unlike most common spaces in schools, with the difference that this space is physically and visually linked to each house located on the second floor. As a result, the Forum is used as much for whole-group learning activities as it is for eating, informal socializing, and community functions.

7. The Gary and Jerri-Ann Jacobs High Tech High School, San Diego, California

The Gary and Jerri-Ann Jacobs High Tech High School (HTH), occupied in September 2000, was the vision of an industry and educator coalition. A number of high-technology companies, notably Qualcomm, were leaders in the effort driving the vision and raising the necessary capital required for this unique school. The growth of high-technology jobs such as telecommunications, biomedical, biotech, computer software, and electronics manufacturing in the San Diego, California, area has become the catalyst for improving the local economy after the defense manufacturing cuts and recession of the early 1990s. The coalition recognized that while job demand and employment opportunities continue to increase, industries and businesses are facing growing difficulties in finding skilled employees in these areas. They recognized that high school graduates often do not have the basic skills and problem-solving abilities these companies need.

In response to these issues, HTH was envisioned to provide students with rigorous and relevant academic and workplace skills, preparing its graduates for rewarding lives in our increasingly technological society. A small, diverse learning community with a projected 600 students in grades 7–12, this ground-breaking school was founded on three educational design principles: personalization, real-world immersion, and intellectual mission. Each student has a personalized learning plan and an advisor who remains with the student throughout his or her four years at the school. Students pursue their interests through projects and prepare personal digital portfolios to document their achievement. Students engage in real-world projects that enable them to learn while working on problems of interest and concern to adults in the community. In addition, all students complete academic internships in local workplace organizations during their last two years at HTH. Finally, the curriculum is designed to be intellectually engaging and rigorous, providing the foundation for entry and success in higher education. Assessment is performance-based; students create products, solve problems, and present their work to the community for feedback and evaluation.

HTH's facilities are unique among high schools. Designed by David Stephen Design and the Stichler Design Group, HTH represents a noteworthy innovation in public education. Rather than being located in an existing school building, the school is located at the redeveloped Naval Training Center in San Diego. The 43,500 square foot building, which was used by the U.S. Navy as a technical training center, now has fourteen multipurpose seminar rooms, seven labs, four project studios, a centralized commons, and a large, high-ceilinged open area known as the "Great Room" (Figures 6.21 and 6.22). Students have their own workstations for part of the day and move between seminar, lab, and group project workspace. With much more expansive workstation and project space than commonly is found in a school building, the HTH facility allows all students to have their own workstation, and also accommodates classroom, lab, and group project workspace (Figure 6.23). The building includes a nontraditional animation lab, and biochemistry and engineering labs, all connected to an advanced information technology infrastructure that allows the use of laptops, audio and visual systems, and Smartboards.

8. Harbor City Charter School, Duluth, Minnesota

Charter schools often must operate with minimal resources for facilities to house their programs, yet they are fertile ground for fostering creative

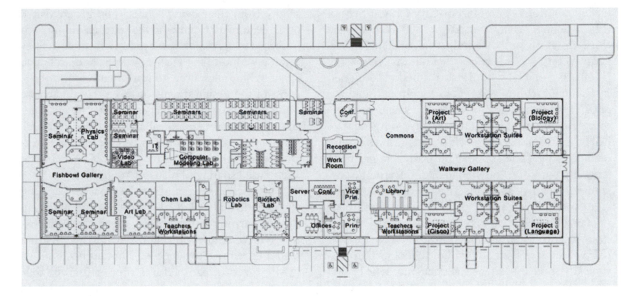

FIGURE 6.21   Floor plan of High Tech High School in San Diego, California, illustrates workstation suites, and laboratory and classroom spaces.

Source: Courtesy of Disney Corp.

FIGURE 6.22   Commons Area off Main Entrance Foyer at HTH.

Source: Photo by Jeffery A. Lackney.

FIGURE 6.23   Workstation Suite at HTH.

Source: Photo by Jeffery A. Lackney.

design solutions. The Harbor City Charter School (High School) that opened in 2002 occupies the third floor of an 1860 industrial building in the central business district of Duluth, Minnesota (Figure 6.24). The school was planned and designed by Randall Fielding and Scalzo Architects (Fielding, 2002). Harbor City provides a small, learner-directed community, encouraging investigative learning and global citizenship, and nurtures a sense of belonging. The school's purpose is to graduate students who are knowledgeable, discerning, passionate, creative, and reflective. A total of 100 seats were available in the fall of 2002, with enrollment of 200. The school expects to expand onto the fourth floor as enrollment grows. The 14,000 square foot third-floor area is small by high school standards—typically about 140 square feet per student or 17,000 total square feet would be utilized. However, the school is located within walking distance of the public library, YMCA, art museum, aquarium, and television station—allowing the school to leverage other facilities for learning.

The process for planning the school was innovative and modeled to some extent on the type of activity expected of students. A handful of teachers with a passion for working with teenagers launched the

FIGURE 6.24 Harbor City Charter School, a Twenty-First Century School Located in an Old Nineteenth-Century Warehouse Duluth, Minnesota.

Source: Courtesy of Randall Fielding.

school from their living rooms. The group visited other exemplary facilities in the state, examining approaches to curriculum and the environment. They hired an educational facility planner and architect, located 200 miles away, to lead the design process. Most of the design discussions were conducted via e-mail and Web-based images. Once schematic design was completed, a local architect was retained. Most of the collaboration between the local architect and design architect was conducted via e-mail and Web-based sharing of plans and details.

Collaboration and project-based learning were identified as key objectives in the planning of this learning environment; these methods foster creative connections and synthesis, skills that students require to succeed. This high school illustrates ten design features supporting collaborative, project-based learning: variable-sized spaces, individual workspace, presentation space, "cave" space for concentrated work, spaces with access to food and beverage, process galleries, studios and labs, collaboration incubators, set-away spaces or niches, display spaces, and access to technology (Figure 6.25).

Each student has a home base made up of a lockable drawer, adjacent coat hook, and an individual workstation shared with one other student. Depending on the time of day and adjacent activities, the workstation can serve as either so-called cave space or a collaboration incubator. Many of the workstations have round conference ends, serving as an informal meeting area. Workstations also include an acoustically absorptive tack board and partial-height enclosure for the display of student work.

The school utilizes a wireless network for general communications, word processing, spreadsheets, and Web research. White boards with a medium-textured surface double as screens for computer projection. At the opposite projection side of each white board, an Ethernet connection with category 5 wiring supports the projection of large graphic, video, or music files. Ethernet connections are also located in the media lab, offices, teacher's room, and library.

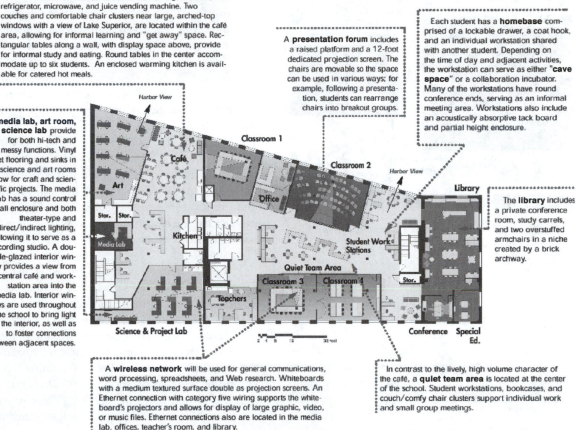

A **cafe** serves as a social team area, with an adjacent sink, refrigerator, microwave, and juice vending machine. Two couches and comfortable chair clusters near large, arched-top windows with a view of Lake Superior, are located within the café area, allowing for informal learning and "get away" space. Rectangular tables along a wall, with display space above, provide for informal study and eating. Round tables in the center accommodate up to six students. An enclosed warming kitchen is available for catered hot meals.

A **presentation forum** includes a raised platform and a 12-foot dedicated projection screen. The chairs are movable so the space can be used in various ways; for example, following a presentation, students can rearrange chairs into breakout groups.

Each student has a **homebase** comprised of a lockable drawer, a coat hook, and an individual workstation shared with another student. Depending on the time of day and adjacent activities, the workstation can serve as either "**cave space**" or a collaboration incubator. Many of the workstations have round conference ends, serving as an informal meeting area. Workstations also include an acoustically absorptive tack board and partial height enclosure.

A **media lab, art room,** and **science lab** provide for both hi-tech and messy functions. Vinyl sheet flooring and sinks in the science and art rooms allow for craft and scientific projects. The media lab has a sound control wall enclosure and both theater-type and direct/indirect lighting, allowing it to serve as a recording studio. A double-glazed interior window provides a view from the central café and workstation area into the media lab. Interior windows are used throughout the school to bring light into the interior, as well as to foster connections between adjacent spaces.

The **library** includes a private conference room, study carrels, and two overstuffed armchairs in a niche created by a brick archway.

A **wireless network** will be used for general communications, word processing, spreadsheets, and Web research. Whiteboards with a medium textured surface double as projection screens. An Ethernet connection with category five wiring supports the whiteboard's projectors and allows for display of large graphic, video, or music files. Ethernet connections also are located in the media lab, offices, teacher's room, and library.

In contrast to the lively, high volume character of the café, a **quiet team area** is located at the center of the school. Student workstations, bookcases, and couch/comfy chair clusters support individual work and small group meetings.

FIGURE 6.25   Annotated Floor Plan of Harbor City.

Source: Courtesy of Randall Fielding.

A café serves as a social team area, with an adjacent sink, refrigerator, microwave, and a juice vending machine. Two couches and one comfortable chair cluster near large, arched windows with a harbor view. These are located within the café area, allowing for informal learning and "get away" space. Rectangular tables along a wall, with display space above, provide for informal study and eating. Round tables in the center accommodate up to six students for eating or project work. An enclosed warming kitchen is available for catered hot meals.

In contrast to the lively, high-volume character of the café, a quiet team area is located at the center of the school. Student workstations, bookcases, and a couch and comfortable chair clusters support individual work and small group meetings (Figure 6.26, page 154). The library includes a private conference room, study carrels, and two overstuffed armchairs in a niche created by a unique brick archway.

A presentation forum includes a raised platform and a 12-foot dedicated projection screen. The chairs are movable, so that the space can be used in various ways. For example, after a presentation students can rearrange into break-out groups around the room.

FIGURE 6.26   The central team area at Harbor City models a real-world workplace.

Source: Courtesy of Randall Fielding.

A media lab, art room, and science lab provide for both high-tech functions and activities likely to result in a mess. Vinyl sheet flooring and sinks in the science and art rooms allow for craft and scientific projects. The media lab has a sound control wall enclosure and both theater type and direct/indirect lighting, allowing it to serve as a recording studio. A double-glazed interior window provides a view from the central café and workstation area into the media lab. Interior windows are used throughout the school to bring light in, as well as to foster connections between adjacent spaces.

9. Henry Ford Academy, Dearborn, Michigan

The Henry Ford Academy in Dearborn, Michigan, designed by Concordia Architects, is a public charter high school with 400 students. The learning environment was developed one grade level at a time over four years, integrating an innovative public educational curriculum with the extensive resources of the existing Henry Ford Museum and Greenfield Village.

The academy demonstrates how the integration of resources can produce more economical and more effective learning environments. The project was built for 20 percent of the cost of a comparable stand-alone Michigan high school. Student retention stands at 98 percent and test scores are four times higher than those of other Detroit public schools.

Built by Henry Ford in honor of his mentor, Thomas Edison, the Henry Ford Museum includes over 1 million museum artifacts located in one 12-acre building. The Greenfield Village complex adds an additional 80-acre outdoor learning environment with more than seventy-five significant buildings representing some of the nation's most noted innovators and their creations. The design provides for the distribution of formal learning activities with access to the entire 80-acre campus (Figure 6.27).

The academy was developed as a collaborative venture that includes the Henry Ford Museum, the Ford Motor Company, and the Wayne County Regional Educational Service Agency. Facilities for each grade level were designed in collaboration with more than 100 students, parents, educators, curators, and museum and school administrators. The result is a facility (see Figure 6.28) serving as both the physical and metaphorical "home base" from which a broad range of student excursions ensue, both within the museum grounds as well as externally through internships with participating adult mentors (Bingler, 2002).

School districts can save money by sharing resources. The cost of the Henry Ford Academy is about one-third of what it would cost to build a more traditional school because the land and building are already there. Plus, there are a million artifacts, including cars, airplanes, trains, sewing machines, computers, and just about every other invention known to man that is being incorporated into the curriculum. Here students are not only learning the "what" of math, science, language arts, and social studies, but also the "why." The Henry Ford Museum donated the site and Ford Motor Company provided the money for renovations and curriculum development. There were no capital costs for the Wayne County educational system.

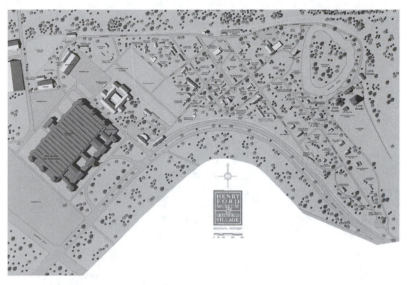

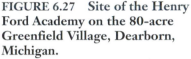

FIGURE 6.27   Site of the Henry Ford Academy on the 80-acre Greenfield Village, Dearborn, Michigan.

Source: Courtesy of Concordia Architects, Inc.

FIGURE 6.28   Students at work at the Henry Ford Academy within the Henry Ford Museum.

Source: Courtesy of Concordia Architects, Inc.

At the Henry Ford Academy in Dearborn, Michigan, every part of every building and every object in the museum's collection is a place to learn about math, science, language arts, and social studies. Added together, there are over 80 acres of buildings and objects with relevant learning content. And yet the Henry Ford Museum is a microcosm of the total environment. In the end, the whole community and the whole city are the real learning environment (Fielding, 1999).

10. The Grainger Center for Imagination and Inquiry, Aurora, Illinois

The Grainger Center for Imagination and Inquiry (Figures 6.29 on page 156 and 6.30 on page 157), a 2,840 square foot facility that supports forty students, was designed by OWP&P, Architects to fit into a traditional existing home economics classroom space within the Illinois Mathematics and Science Academy, Aurora, Illinois, the only residential high school in the state that serves 650 students. Students were engaged in the design through an interactive website where students and teachers envisioned a lab of the future. The Illinois Mathematics and Science Academy is ideally sited near

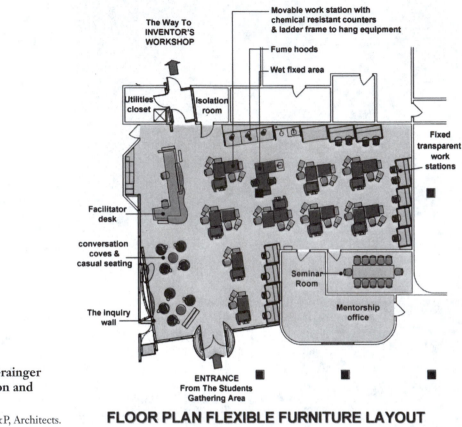

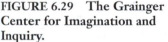

FIGURE 6.29   The Grainger Center for Imagination and Inquiry.

Source: Courtesy of OWP&P, Architects.

FLOOR PLAN FLEXIBLE FURNITURE LAYOUT

the Argon and Fermi Labs and the technology corridor in the state, and students have come to expect the opportunity to work with scientists from these labs on their projects. The program is project-based and student-driven with adult researchers acting as mentors for students. The center is an extension of what has also been referred to as the Tinkerer's Workshop that expands the opportunities for students to "tinker" with their individual plans of inquiry in areas that require technology-assisted research, invention, and experimentation. Projects are initiated in partnership with leading corporate, private, and university research organizations.

The client, Stephanie Pace Marshall, requested from her architect what she called the "infinite flexibility lab." The design team, influ-

enced by MIT's Media Lab, created layers of flexibility with mobile mini-lab stations that can be grouped for collaborative work or arranged for independent work; a secure space to hold experiments for weeks at a time; a student presentation area with pin-up space, a curved bench, and swivel countertop ("science as theatre"); and a "think tank" area with an inquiry wall that includes soft seating. A grid of ceiling trays allows power and data utilities to extend anywhere in the room. Marshall concluded, "If we are truly going to create learning communities for the 21st century, we must look differently at our classrooms, our schools, and our work. We must view them as dynamic, adaptive, self-organizing systems, not only capable but inherently designed to renew

FIGURE 6.30 Interior view of Grainger Center illustrates flexible laboratory space.

Source: Courtesy of OWP&P, Architects.

themselves and to grow and change—not by the rules established from the top, but by relationships created from within" (Marshall, 1996, p. 2).

11. Canning Vale High School, Perth, Australia

In the planning of the 1,200-student Canning Vale High School in Perth (Figures 6.31 and 6.32, page 158), Australia, the Western Australia Department of Education was interested in furthering its educational mission as well as providing good school architecture. Prakash Nair Consultants, of Vitetta, in cooperation with Spowers Architects was asked to lead an educational planning process with the entire school and business community, known as the Project Control Group, in forging a common

set of principles for the design. The following ten project principles were developed based up putting children first:

1. Learning experiences will be designed to nurture mind, body, and spirit.
2. Learning will be personalized for every student.
3. Every student will be supported by an adult mentor and a peer group who will remain with the student throughout his or her school experience.
4. All learning will be authentic with a significant project-based orientation.
5. Every student will have the opportunity to participate in structured workplace learning experiences.
6. The scale and organization of the facility will be broken down so that every student will belong to a small learning community.
7. Flexible spaces will maximize opportunities for various learning styles.
8. The facility will serve as a center of community.
9. All aspects of the facility will have a strong environmental focus.
10. All staff will be trained to function according to these project principles.

Out of these principles an architectural philosophy evolved suggesting the following: The architecture should not be a limiting factor from using space to best meet educational needs, it should be inspirational going beyond function; special attention should be paid to the spaces between buildings since learning happens there as well; and the architecture should allow end users some degree of customization.

In response, the design of the school creates a family unit of no more than sixteen students with each family under the care of one advisor. Families are also intended to encourage and support peer counseling. Scaling up, eight families make one neighborhood (128 students) and five neighborhoods make up the school community (640). Interaction will be encouraged between

FIGURE 6.31   Campus Image of Planned Canning Vale High School, Perth, Australia.

Source: Prakash Nair Consultants, Inc.

neighborhoods, with each neighborhood having its own unique identity. Seamless transitions between indoor and outdoor space were created (Figure 6.31). Meeting places for each neighborhood or *corroborees* (aboriginal term for "gathering places") were provided. Corridors and other circulation space were used to create opportunities for socializing, student display, and large group gatherings. The campus maximizes the use of daylight and natural ventilation, and preserves the natural environment of the site to the maximum extent possible. Finally, a town center is created out of the com-

FIGURE 6.32   At Canning Vale, Meeting Places for Each Neighborhood or *Corroborees*.

Source: Prakash Nair Consultants, Inc.

mons block becoming the "heart" of the school (Figure 6.32).

In developing the design of the facility, a range of idiosyncratic design elements were developed to encourage "un-programmed" learning opportunities, and to create cross-curricular collaboration. For example, the bandstand area contains a permanent multimedia projection backing wall that is open to a "learning street" and cafeteria zone to allow for impromptu performances; the lecture theater is flanked by a climbing wall in the heart of the school; entry points to learning neighborhoods are paired with "making and testing" studios that are not curriculum-specific; and collaboration with a local environmental group has been established to develop "eco-gardens" and a recreated wetland precinct.

The case studies in this section can only begin to demonstrate the variety forms of exemplary educational architecture that ably illustrates how the school design principles (see Chapter 2) have been, and are being, successfully integrated in real projects. New educational architecture that exhibits the direct connection between educational philosophy and architecture and follows the latest research and best practice can now be found globally (http://www.designshare.com; Crosbie, 2001; IPG, 2000; Dudek, 2000; Brubaker, 1998; Sanoff, 2002, 1994).

SUMMARY

School designs based on the outcomes (e.g., program, conceptual drawings) of an effective, multistakeholder planning process are likely to meet or exceed a community's needs and expectations for a school facility for many years to come. Although the specific procedures for design development differ from district to district, there are several steps that commonly occur during the architectural design phase. First, an architecture firm is chosen to prepare all the drawings. Often, this firm is also involved in the planning stage and plays an integral role in programming activities. The American Institute of Architects (AIA) has developed a set of guidelines, the Qualification Based Selection (QBS) process, for choosing an architect based on the firm's qualifications as they relate to a certain job. Basic design services provided by the architectural firm include schematic design, design development, construction documents and specifications, bidding and negotiations, and construction administration.

Although the design process requires the use of a variety of highly skilled professionals, it is also important to involve the outside community in the early stages of design, not just to gain their support for bond issues, but to reap a wide range of benefits, such as a positive community spirit and a better overall school building. Active involvement of community members in the design process can be a time-consuming and complex process, so methods for involving them must be carefully planned and managed.

An examination of school case studies demonstrates how the design trends discussed in Chapter 2 have been incorporated to create learning environments that promote collaboration, independent exploration, appreciation of the natural environment, teacher professionalism, and other desirable outcomes. Evaluations of these schools in the future may provide valuable lessons regarding how these innovative educational facilities affect students, teachers, and the local community.

ACTIVITIES

1. Assuming that the educational facilities plan and program have already been developed using input from a variety of stakeholders, propose a method(s) that you would use to continue to involve them in the early part of the *design* phase.

2. Identify three additional case studies of innovative school facilities. Using a table similar to Table 6.1, identify which of the educational design principles have been incorporated in their designs.

REFERENCES AND BIBLIOGRAPHY

Print Sources

Bingler, S. (Fall 2002). Community-based school planning: If not now, when? *Edutopia:* 4–5.

Bittle, E. H. (Ed.) (1996) *Planning and financing school improvement and construction projects.* Topeka, KS: National Organization of Legal Problems in Education.

Brubaker, C. W. (1998). *Planning and designing schools.* New York: McGraw Hill.

Castaldi, B. (1994). *Educational facilities: Planning, modernization and management.* Boston: Allyn and Bacon.

Cohen, S. (August 1998). School planning: Lessons learned at the Celebration School. *School planning and management.*

Crosbie, M. J. (2001). *Class architecture.* Mulgrave, Victoria, Australia: Image Publishing Group Pty. Ltd.

Crowe, T. (2000). *Crime prevention through environmental design: Applications of architectural design and space management concepts.* National Crime Prevention Institute. Boston: Butterworth-Heinemann.

Cuningham Group (2002). *Schools that fit: Aligning architecture and education.* Minneapolis: Cuningham Group.

Dudek, M. (2000). *Architecture of schools: The new learning environments.* Woburn, MA: Architectural Press.

Earthman, G. I. (2000). *Planning educational facilities for the next century.* Reston, VA: Association of School Business Officials International.

Graves, B. E. (1993). *School ways: The planning and design of America's schools.* New York: McGraw Hill.

Holcomb, J. H. (1995). *A guide to the planning of educational facilities.* New York: University Press of America.

IPG (2000). *Educational spaces: A pictorial view, Vol. 2.* International Spaces Series. Melbourne, Australia: Images Publishing Group Pty. Ltd.

Kowalski, T. J. (1989). *Planning and managing school facilities.* New York: Praeger.

Lackney, J. A. (2000). *Thirty-three educational design principles for schools and community learning centers.* Washington, DC: National Clearinghouse for Educational Facilities (NCEF).

Marshall, S. P. (Summer 1996). Chaos, complexity, and flocking behavior: Metaphors for learning. *Wingspread journal,* 18(3): 13–15.

Sanoff, H. (1994). *School design.* New York: Van Nostrand Reinhold.

Sanoff, H. (2002). *Schools designed with community participation.* Washington, DC: National Clearinghouse for Educational Facilities. Also available at http://www.edfacilities.org.

Internet Sources

Design Share, Inc. http://www.designshare.com.

Fielding, R. (August 1999). An interview with Concordia's Steven Bingler. DesignShare. http://www.designshare.com/Research/Bingler/LearningCommunity1.htm.

Fielding, R. (2002). Harbor City Charter School. http://www.designshare.com.

High Tech High School. http://www.hightechhigh.org.

Metropolitan Regional Career and Technical Center (MET). http://www.metcenter.org/.

Nair, P. (October 2002). 2002 Awards for innovative learning environments. School Construction News & Design Share. http://www.designshare.com/Awards/2002/HonorAwards.asp.

Wisconsin AIA (November 1999). *Quality-based selection owner's manual: A step-by-step process for the selection of architects for public projects.* http://www.aiaw.org/need_an_architect/selecting_an_architect.asp.

Wolff, S. J. (2002). *Design features for project-based learning.* Oregon State University. http://www.designshare.com.

PART IV

SCHOOL CONSTRUCTION AND CAPITAL OUTLAY ACTIVITIES

When the construction phase of the facility development process finally arrives, it is important to be keenly aware of the premises for developing school facilities. Hence, all eight premises may receive some special attention by the school leaders and planners at this time, but the five listed below are most significant, especially, keeping in perspective that available resources are usually less than the demand.

Cost estimates are one of the key concerns since it is recommended that some source for assistance in cost estimation, such as the Tri Service Military Construction Index, be used to assist in estimating. Since cost data are provided early in the construction process, there are cost changes throughout the project that might become a budget concern, especially in very large projects. Computer-assisted estimation procedures are able available to provide an essential guideline to keep cost in line with the budget (see, e.g., http://www.uscost.com and http://www.rsmeans.com). Therefore, it is wise to have a thorough cost estimate (line by line), instead of just adding a certain percentage to a recently completed project similar to the one in question.

Premises for Developing School Facilities

PREMISE	DESCRIPTOR
Premise 4	Goals and objectives are translated into physical places and spaces for teaching and learning.
Premise 5	Planning and design activities are integrated.
Premise 6	Management is systematic: data- and goal-driven.
Premise 7	The demand for resources is greater than those available.
Premise 8	Collaboration and cooperation between the school and community are essential.

Premise 8 is important in construction because a citizen's oversight committee is an essential aspect of monitoring cost and construction (see Myers & Robertson, 2004). All states address the school construction process in some form, and the student of educational architecture and planning may wish to select his or her state to compare its procedures with those reviewed in this chapter and the example in its appendix. California was selected here as an example (see the Appendix in Chapter 7) because of its comprehensive Internet site and the interrelated activities (see, e.g., http://www.schoolconstruction.dgs. ca.gov/index.html). Some states refer to this process as "funding a capital outlay project" (see, e.g., Georgia's procedure at http://www.doe.k12. ga.us/facilities/facilities.asp). Chapter 5 is devoted to the topic of planning a capital project from a broader perspective than the steps and phases as outlined here.

Reviewing the programming activities and phases presented in Chapter 5 will be helpful in un-

derstanding the complexities of school construction. Furthermore, an understanding of the design principles in Chapter 6 is important so you can link the ideas in this chapter to them. One of the very latest steps that must be taken before construction is step Q, prepare final construction documents. Theoretically, like maintenance, construction begins with planning: step A, begin the planning process. This initial activity has been termed "planning to plan." It represents the organizational phase in the long-range planning process, including a timeline and assignment of responsibility (see Chapter 5).

CHAPTER SEVEN

CONSTRUCTION AND CONSTRUCTION MANAGEMENT

Approximately $19.7 billion was expected to be spent on school construction in the United States during the year 2004 (Abramson, 2004). The early years of the twenty-first century experienced costs over $20 billion per year in school construction spending. Construction costs continued to increase throughout the 1990s (U.S. General Accounting Office, 2000). In 1995, for instance, a record $10.3 billion was spent, culminating in school construction spending in the year 2000 exceeding actual 1974 school construction dollars: a year that represented the peak of spending during the post-World War II baby boom (Abramson, 2001). Estimates of the cost to repair and modernize school facilities nationwide continue to grow from $41 billion of need (Education Writers Association, 1989) to the $112 billion estimated by the U.S. General Accounting Office (GAO) in its landmark report (U.S. GAO, 1995), to the National Center for Educational Statistics (NCES) estimate of $127 billion in 1999 (Lewis et al., 2000), to finally the most recent $322 billion estimated by the National Education Association (NEA, 2000). The NCES study, echoing the GAO reports, estimates that over three-quarters of U.S. schools, or 59,400 school buildings, need to expend, on average, more than $2 million per school building to effect repairs and complete renovation or modernizations simply to get their schools in overall good condition. Indeed, even by spending at a record pace of over $20 billion per year, it may take another full decade or more before school facility needs are adequately met.

The United States is in the middle of the fourth wave of school construction. The first major construction period took place during the 1860s and 1880s with the rise of the common school and the Industrial Revolution in the United States following the Civil War, mostly in the Northeast. The second big period of construction occurred from 1900–1920 during the immigration of Europeans to major urban areas across the country, particularly in the Northeast. The modern period of construction commenced right after World War II, between 1950 and 1970. The fourth and latest period began in the late 1980s, leading up to the start of the twenty-first century. At present the United States has over 90,000 school buildings, with close to 10,000 new school buildings being constructed between 1990 and 2000 alone.

Now more than ever, there is a desperate need for school boards, school district administrators, and the public in general to understand the realities of the construction process if the schools districts are to be successful, timely, and cost-effective in their building programs. With the costs of construction continuing to rise, obtaining the desired quality and scope of product on time and on budget is as difficult as ever. The school administrator must understand his or her rights and responsibilities during the construction process, the broad array of construction delivery methods available, procedures of contract administration, and the legal climate of construction.

CONSTRUCTION DELIVERY METHODS

There are a variety of methods available by which a school building can be delivered. School districts need to investigate and understand the advantages and disadvantages of a variety of construction delivery methods available to them. The size and complexity of the project will often determine the most appropriate type of construction delivery method used by the school district (Swartzendurber, 1996). If the project consists of a small number of new buildings and additions and renovations to existing buildings, more conventional approaches may be sufficient. However, if a school district is experiencing rapid growth and expects to be delivering large numbers of buildings over an extended period of time, hiring a full-service construction management firm to oversee the process may better serve the district's needs.

Other less conventional approaches are now being used with greater frequency to deliver large numbers of schools in fast-growing districts under tight schedules and budgets. These methods include design/build and construction management.

Competitive Bidding

Often referred to as design/bid/build, competitive bidding is the construction method most familiar to school district administrators. An architect first completes construction plans and specifications. These plans and specifications are then advertised for bids. Contractors bid the project exactly as it is designed, with the lowest bidder then awarded the work. The advantages of competitive bidding are that it is a familiar delivery method, it is an easy-to-manage process, it is defined in scope and often has a single point of responsibility. In addition, the lowest contractor price is usually accepted. The disadvantages of competitive bidding are that the process requires a longer schedule since tasks are completed one at a time in a linear fashion. In addition, if the lowest bid price is beyond the owner's price, redesign or change orders may be required, further extending the length of time to complete

the project. There is no control over the selection of the contractor or subcontractors used by the contractor since selection is based on the lowest bid and not necessarily on quality.

The conventional approach to project delivery involves the hiring of an architect and/or engineer who through a process partially described in the previous chapter provides detailed construction documents and specifications, which are then competitively bid by multiple prime contractors for general (structural and finish work), mechanical, electrical, and plumbing construction. Each contractor signs a contract with the owner to complete his or her portion of the work. The most common contract between the owner and contractor is Document A101: Standard Form of Agreement Between Owner and Contractor, compiled by the American Institute of Architects (AIA). This contract, along with AIA Document 201: General Conditions of the Contract for Construction, is intended for use on construction projects where the basis for payment is a stipulated sum or fixed price set in advance by either bidding or negotiation (Sweet, 1999).

Construction Management

Another delivery method having grown in popularity in recent years is construction management (CM). A construction management firm has many variations of services that can be offered to the school district. CMs are comprised of architects, engineers, and construction specialists who focus their attention on the owner's schedule and budget. They understand the design process, bidding nuances, and construction operations. Many CM firms are qualified to manage the entire project, predesign, design, construction, and occupancy. There are several forms of CM that have developed in the industry, the most common being CM at-risk.

In CM at-risk, school administrators interview and select a fee-based construction management firm to manage construction before the design is complete. The construction manager and the architect work together to develop and estimate the cost of the proposed design (estimates may also be done by a professional team such as U.S. Cost, Inc.). The construction manager provides the school district with a guaranteed maximum price (GMP) for the entire project. The construction manager then receives proposals from and awards contracts to subcontractors. The final construction price is the sum of the construction manager's fee and the subcontractors' bids. The school district will not pay more than the GMP, and retains any savings realized. The advantages of CM are that the construction firm is selected through an interview based on quality rather than a low bid, and early involvement by the construction manager ensures that the project will be accurately budgeted and reviewed for constructability, enabling fast-track delivery in which construction can begin before the design is complete. In addition, a guaranteed maximum price protects the school district from possible cost overruns. The disadvantage is that the CM fee is not competitively bid. In addition, in order for the budget and schedule to be met, extending the design scope may suffer.

Design/Build

Under the design/build delivery system, the architect and builder (contractor) form a design/build firm hired by the school district to deliver the completed building. A GMP is often provided at the beginning of the project based on criteria prepared by the school district. The architect/builder then develops drawings that fulfill the criteria while maintaining the GMP. Upon completion, the school is either leased or turned over to the school district, depending on the funding source. The advantages of design/build are similar to those for CM in that a single point of accountability for design and construction rests with the design/build firm and the construction can be placed on a fast track, saving time. The disadvantages of design/build are that there is no check and balance between the architect and the builder, and the quality of the project may suffer since the GMP is established before the design is completed.

THE CONSTRUCTION PROCESS

This section will cover the construction process in detail from the perspective of the competitive bidding delivery method since it is the most widely used method in the construction of school buildings in the United States, and in most states, statutory law mandates that public school districts use competitive bidding.

The Construction Project Team

The coordination of construction consists of a communication process between three primary team members of the project team: the owner, the design professional, and the contractor. Each has a general set of responsibilities with regard to the coordination of the project (see Table 7.1 on page 166). The owner bears responsibility for the selection of the project team and in determining when each joins the team.

The Bidding Process

Once the final construction documents and specifications are completed by the architect and engineering consultants and approved by the school board, procedures for bidding by construction contractors can be initiated by the school board with the technical assistance of an attorney. The purpose of competitive bidding is to provide the district with the best competitive price available for the work, while providing an equitable way for all qualified firms to have an equal chance at being selected to provide the necessary services (Earthman, 2000, p. 199).

School board policies normally, but not in every case, cover advertising, opening, pricing, awarding, rejecting and withdrawing bids, as well as bonding and qualifying bidders. Compliance with the public laws pertaining to bidding usually involves a public advertisement in local newspapers and/or trade journals soliciting bids and indicating where the bid documents can be obtained, the deadline for receipt of bids, the location of the bid opening, and how bidders are to submit their pricing. In addition, proof of responsibility from

TABLE 7.1   Roles of Construction Project Team Members

TEAM MEMBER	PROJECT INITIATION	DESIGN PHASE	CONSTRUCTION PHASE	PROJECT COMPLETION
School district (owner/owner representative)	Forming and informing the group. Leading in outlining project requirements for the design professional.	Contributing to decisions in support of design. Participating in design reviews. Communicating changes when necessary.	Providing for qualified inspection and testing as required by contract documents and regulatory agencies. Administering contracts.	Maintaining group coordination and getting the group's attention on follow-up or completion items.
Design professional (architect)	Assisting with project objectives and program requirements. Leading the development process for coordination among team members.	Leading the design effort. Involving the owner and others at appropriate times. Preparing necessary design plans and specifications.	Technical support for required interpretations, changes, shop drawing reviews, or field problems, in a timely way Field observation.	Assisting with follow-up work, completing required manuals and documents, assisting with start-up.
Contractor/ builder	Being an early participant. Contributing to alternative studies and scheduling.*	Assisting in vendor selection and constructability reviews.*	Performing the construction effort. Involving others at appropriate times, such as shop drawings, inspections, tests, etc. Field observation.	Leading the follow-up. Guiding vendor and subcontractor follow-up work.

*Roles to be fulfilled by a construction manager if used.

Source: Adapted from ASCE (1990), Table 4.1.

contractors to adequately perform the necessary work, bids and bid bonds equal to between 5 and 10 percent of the bid, and a bidder evaluation to determine contractor responsibility with respect to finance, skill, past performance, and integrity are usually required of bidders.

The school board should provide predetermined qualification criteria to be used in screening interested bidders (Bittle and Grob, 1996). Prior to "letting" of the construction documents and specifications for bidding, the qualifications of each bidder should be reviewed by the school board with assistance from the design professional. Prequalification can include the type and amount of experience, the number and type of employees, financial security, location of offices, or even the number of minority persons employed by the firm (Earthman, 2000, p. 201). In order to ensure adequate competition, and ideally the best price for the owner, the design professional may contact prequalified bidders and encourage them to submit a bid for consideration.

The official public bid package will include the construction documents and specifications (sometimes called bid documents, contract documents, or "plans and specs") as well as instructions to bidders. Drawings will include architectural plans; elevations; sections and details; civil, structural, electrical, mechanical, plumbing, and telecommunications engineering plans and de-tailed drawings, as well as a technical book of written specifications for the sixteen formal divisions of the Construction Specifications Institute (CSI) (Table 7.2, page 168–172). These are the drawings the contractor will use to estimate the cost of the project. The skill of the construction estimator in interpreting and gathering bids from subcontractors on various subcomponents of the project will determine whether that contractor will have the lowest competitive bid.

The Instructions to Bidders document will often indicate that bids are to be received sealed on or before the scheduled opening of bids. Typically, the instruction to bidders would include requirements for the general contractor to coordinate all work of the mechanical trades including general direction of work at the site, regulation of work progress and scheduling. In addition, the general contractor will be asked to keep records requested by the design professional to monitor the work and keep the owner informed of progress.

Between the time the bid package is let for bids and the scheduled bid opening, there is usually a prebid meeting at which all qualified bidders are invited to ask clarifying questions. If clarifications are required, the architect and/or engineer will produce addendums to the construction documents and specifications as required. These addendums become part of the bid package.

In order to ensure good competition between contractors submitting bids and that the owner receives a responsible bid, a number of guidelines should be followed (WASB, 1987). First, plans and specifications should be prepared in sufficient detail such that it is clear to each bidder what is required for the project. Second, bids should be limited to the contractors with approved prequalifications. Third, the award should go to the "lowest responsible and responsive bidder" unless there is evidence that the previous guidelines have not been followed. Fourth, asking for competitive bids if the intention is to award to a favored contractor is not fair and can be cause for public disputes. Finally, often state statutes require a fixed percentage of participation by minority-owned businesses, local and/or small and disadvantaged businesses as part of the bid (Bittle and Grob, 1996).

The bids once received are opened in public and announced at the predetermined time and place for public scrutiny. The architect advises the school board as to the adequacy of the bids, and based on this advice the board can elect to accept or reject any and all bids. If, for example, the bid was greater than the school district's budget for the project, the board could elect to negotiate with the lowest bidder to lower the bid price offered, or all bids could be rejected and the project could be rebid after some modifications to the scope by the architect. If the cost is significantly below budget, and significantly below all other bids, the board may conclude that the contractor inadvertently left an item out of the bid price and has not provided a "responsive" bid—a bid considered competitive with other bids—and may reject the bid while accepting the next highest bid. In any of these cases, the final recommendation is presented at the next regularly scheduled school board meeting.

Contract Documents

Following board approval of the low bid, the contract document is prepared by the architect in cooperation with the school board attorney. The AIA has developed the Standard Form of Agreement

TABLE 7.2 Construction Specifications Institute's Sixteen Construction Divisions

Division 1: General Requirements	01100 Summary
	01200 Price and Payment Procedures
	01300 Administrative Requirements
	01400 Quality Requirements
	01500 Temporary Facilities and Controls
	01600 Product Requirements
	01700 Execution Requirements
	01800 Facility Operation
	01900 Facility Decommissioning
Division 2: Site Construction	02050 Basic Site Materials and Methods
	02100 Site Remediation
	02200 Site Preparation
	02300 Earthwork
	02400 Tunneling, Boring, and Jacking
	02450 Foundation and Load-Bearing Elements
	02500 Utility Services
	02600 Drainage and Containment
	02700 Bases, Ballasts, Pavements, and Appurtenances
	02800 Site Improvements and Amenities
	02900 Planting
	02950 Site Restoration and Rehabilitation
Division 3: Concrete	03050 Basic Concrete Materials and Methods
	03100 Concrete Forms and Accessories
	03200 Concrete Reinforcement
	03300 Cast-in-Place Concrete
	03400 Precast Concrete
	03500 Cementitious Decks and Underlayment
	03600 Grouts
	03700 Mass Concrete
	03900 Concrete Restoration and Cleaning
Division 4: Masonry	04050 Basic Masonry Materials and Methods
	04200 Masonry Units
	04400 Stone
	04500 Refractories
	04600 Corrosion-Resistant Masonry
	04700 Simulated Masonry
	04800 Masonry Assemblies
	04900 Masonry Restoration and Cleaning
Division 5: Metals	05050 Basic Metal Materials and Methods
	05100 Structural Metal Framing
	05200 Metal Joists
	05300 Metal Deck
	05400 Cold-Formed Metal Framing
	05500 Metal Fabrications

TABLE 7.2   Continued

	05600 Hydraulic Fabrications
	05650 Railroad Track and Accessories
	05700 Ornamental Metal
	05800 Expansion Control
	05900 Metal Restoration and Cleaning
Division 6: Wood and Plastics	06050 Basic Wood and Plastic Materials and Methods
	06100 Rough Carpentry
	06200 Finish Carpentry
	06400 Architectural Woodwork
	06500 Structural Plastics
	06600 Plastic Fabrications
	06900 Wood and Plastic Restoration and Cleaning
Division 7: Thermal and Moisture Protection	07050 Basic Thermal and Moisture Protection Materials and Methods
	07100 Dampproofing and Waterproofing
	07200 Thermal Protection
	07300 Shingles, Roof Tiles, and Roof Coverings
	07400 Roofing and Siding Panels
	07500 Membrane Roofing
	07600 Flashing and Sheet Metal
	07700 Roof Specialties and Accessories
	07800 Fire and Smoke Protection
	07900 Joint Sealers
Division 8: Doors and Windows	08050 Basic Door and Window Materials and Methods
	08100 Metal Doors and Frames
	08200 Wood and Plastic Doors
	08300 Specialty Doors
	08400 Entrances and Storefronts
	08500 Windows
	08600 Skylights
	08700 Hardware
	08800 Glazing
	08900 Glazed Curtain Wall
Division 9: Finishes	09050 Basic Finish Materials and Methods
	09100 Metal Support Assemblies
	09200 Plaster and Gypsum Board
	09300 Tile
	09400 Terrazzo
	09500 Ceilings
	09600 Flooring
	09700 Wall Finishes
	09800 Acoustical Treatment
	09900 Paints and Coatings

(*continued*)

TABLE 7.2   Continued

Division 10: Specialties	10100 Visual Display Boards
	10150 Compartments and Cubicles
	10200 Louvers and Vents
	10240 Grilles and Screens
	10250 Service Walls
	10260 Wall and Corner Guards
	10270 Access Flooring
	10290 Pest Control
	10300 Fireplaces and Stoves
	10340 Manufactured Exterior Specialties
	10350 Flagpoles
	10400 Identification Devices
	10450 Pedestrian Control Devices
	10500 Lockers
	10520 Fire Protection Specialties
	10530 Protective Covers
	10550 Postal Specialties
	10600 Partitions
	10670 Storage Shelving
	10700 Exterior Protection
	10750 Telephone Specialties
	10800 Toilet, Bath, and Laundry Accessories
	10880 Scales
	10900 Wardrobe and Closet Specialties
Division 11: Equipment	11010 Maintenance Equipment
	11020 Security and Vault Equipment
	11030 Teller and Service Equipment
	11040 Ecclesiastical Equipment
	11050 Library Equipment
	11060 Theater and Stage Equipment
	11070 Instrumental Equipment
	11080 Registration Equipment
	11090 Checkroom Equipment
	11100 Mercantile Equipment
	11110 Commercial Laundry and Dry Cleaning Equipment
	11120 Vending Equipment
	11130 Audio-Visual Equipment
	11140 Vehicle Service Equipment
	11150 Parking Control Equipment
	11160 Loading Dock Equipment
	11170 Solid Waste Handling Equipment
	11190 Detention Equipment
	11200 Water Supply and Treatment Equipment
	11280 Hydraulic Gates and Valves
	11300 Fluid Waste Treatment and Disposal Equipment
	11400 Food Service Equipment

TABLE 7.2   Continued

	11450 Residential Equipment
	11460 Unit Kitchens
	11470 Darkroom Equipment
	11480 Athletic, Recreational, and Therapeutic Equipment
	11500 Industrial and Process Equipment
	11600 Laboratory Equipment
	11650 Planetarium Equipment
	11660 Observatory Equipment
	11680 Office Equipment
	11700 Medical Equipment
	11780 Mortuary Equipment
	11850 Navigation Equipment
	11870 Agricultural Equipment
	11900 Exhibit Equipment
Division 12: Furnishings	12050 Fabrics
	12100 Art
	12300 Manufactured Casework
	12400 Furnishings and Accessories
	12500 Furniture
	12600 Multiple Seating
	12700 Systems Furniture
	12800 Interior Plants and Planters
	12900 Furnishings Repair and Restoration
Division 13: Special Construction	13010 Air-Supported Structures
	13020 Building Modules
	13030 Special Purpose Rooms
	13080 Sound, Vibration, and Seismic Control
	13090 Radiation Protection
	13100 Lightning Protection
	13110 Cathodic Protection
	13120 Pre-Engineered Structures
	13150 Swimming Pools
	13160 Aquariums
	13165 Aquatic Park Facilities
	13170 Tubs and Pools
	13175 Ice Rinks
	13185 Kennels and Animal Shelters
	13190 Site-Constructed Incinerators
	13200 Storage Tanks
	13220 Filter Underdrains and Media
	13230 Digester Covers and Appurtenances
	13240 Oxygenation Systems
	13260 Sludge Conditioning Systems
	13280 Hazardous Material Remediation
	13400 Measurement and Control Instrumentation
	13500 Recording Instrumentation

(*continued*)

TABLE 7.2   Continued

	13550 Transportation Control Instrumentation
	13600 Solar and Wind Energy Equipment
	13700 Security Access and Surveillance
	13800 Building Automation and Control
	13850 Detection and Alarm
	13900 Fire Suppression
Division 14: Conveying Systems	14100 Dumbwaiters
	14200 Elevators
	14300 Escalators and Moving Walks
	14400 Lifts
	14500 Material Handling
	14600 Hoists and Cranes
	14700 Turntables
	14800 Scaffolding
	14900 Transportation
Division 15: Mechanical	15050 Basic Mechanical Materials and Methods
	15100 Building Services Piping
	15200 Process Piping
	15300 Fire Protection Piping
	15400 Plumbing Fixtures and Equipment
	15500 Heat-Generation Equipment
	15600 Refrigeration Equipment
	15700 Heating, Ventilating, and Air Conditioning Equipment
	15800 Air Distribution
	15900 HVAC Instrumentation and Controls
	15950 Testing, Adjusting, and Balancing
Division 16: Electrical	16050 Basic Electrical Materials and Methods
	16100 Wiring Methods
	16200 Electrical Power
	16300 Transmission and Distribution
	16400 Low-Voltage Distribution
	16500 Lighting
	16700 Communications
	16800 Sound and Video

Source: Adapted from CSI, Master Spec, http://www.csinet.org.

Between Owner and Contractor (AIA Document A101-1997) as well as the General Conditions of the Contract for Construction (AIA Document A201-1997) specifically for this purpose. If the project must be occupied on a particular date, for instance, the opening of school in September, a construction deadline may be established in the contract. Often, the deadline for substantial completion may come with penalties or incentives to encourage the contractor to complete the project on time. The contractor must in addition provide a schedule for the completion of each phase of the work.

The school board, as a public entity, is required to obtain payment and performance bonds from each contractor to ensure against default of the contract. The performance bond certifies that the contractor will perform the contract as stated. The payment bond certifies that the contractor will make appropriate payments to its material suppliers and subcontractors.

Construction Coordination

The design professional (architect) is the owner's (the school board's) representative or agent on the construction site. The design professional makes periodic visits to the site during construction to verify the progress and quality of the contractor's work. These visits do not in anyway guarantee that the contractor has met all obligations or that the methods of construction are appropriate. The responsibility of the design professional is to advise the owner, the school board, of defects and/or deficiencies that have been observed during the periodic visits to the site and to coordinate the necessary adjustments or corrections as necessary (WASB, 1987, p. 79).

If more exhaustive on-site inspections are deemed necessary, the services of a clerk-of-the-works, or project inspector, may be employed, which would go well beyond the periodic observations made by the design professional. The primary role of the project inspector is observing and reporting, rather than making on-site decisions. The project inspector provides continuous on-site inspection, with reports being made to the design professional and copies sent to the school board. The inspector, without the design professional's approval, should not handle requests for changes. The project inspector does however have the authority to stop construction temporarily when a serious deficiency is discovered and not immediately corrected.

Once the contract is signed, the work is said to commence. Within a short period of time, a pre-construction meeting will be scheduled along with the establishment of weekly or bi-weekly construction project meetings that will be held until the project's completion. Weekly job construction meetings take place with all prime contractor representatives present, along with the design professional, owner, and project inspector.

In addition to the project inspector, periodic code inspection will be conducted by the local building code official at various stages in the construction process. The purpose of building code inspection is to protect the health, safety, and welfare of a state's citizens by checking whether construction practices comply with the requirements of local code. A variety of national building codes have been adopted by states and municipalities that all projects are required to comply with—namely, those of Building Officials and Code Administrators International (BOCA), International Conference of Building Officials (ICBO), and Southern Building Code Congress International (SBCCI). The majority of states around the country have adopted, or are in the process of adopting, a new set of codes integrating the requirements of these long-standing national code organizations. These organizations merged in 2003 under the umbrella of the International Codes Council (ICC), with their centerpiece code called the International Building Code. Many states and municipalities have already adopted the ICC suite of codes with certain exceptions and amendments.

Phasing Construction around School Activities

Major school construction projects can take as little as nine months to as long as two years depending on the complexity of the project. Often, additions, renovations, and alterations to existing school buildings may be conducted during the regular school year. When this happens, extra care must be taken to cover the safety of school occupants, especially children. One way to achieve this is to conduct construction activities during the summer, weekends, or after school hours. Requiring the contractor to work around school activities can increase the cost of the project due to the requirements of scheduling. When it is not possible to work around on-going school activities, it may be best to phase construction. Identifying the phases of construction should be worked out in the design phases of the project with the school board. Project phasing should be planned such that the construction site is not immediately accessible from the occupied areas of the school and construction equipment enters the site far from scheduled educational activities. Noise can also be a problem in such situations and may not be completely avoided. In the event of project phasing, the district should expect that the project will take longer to complete due to the inconvenience of the contractor having to work around school activities. Another strategy is to rent temporary facilities off site so that school activities will not be directly affected by construction activities and noise. Frequently, this is not programmatically, economically, or geographically feasible.

Change Orders

It is rare when a construction project is completed without some changes to the original design intent. Some changes should be expected in any project, on the order of 1 to 2 percent of the total construction cost, with most changes coming early in the process. Unforeseen or hidden site conditions, owner-initiated changes in the educational specifications of spaces, and even errors and omissions in the construction documents are just a few reasons why supplementary drawings, bulletins, and clarifications are required during the construction process. Each deviation from the original construction documents must be supported by a "change order" authorized by the board and recommended by the design professional. Change orders inevitably add to the time and cost of the project and avoiding them whenever possible should be a goal of all parties; however, in some cases this is not possible.

To facilitate construction and avoid interruptions to work every time a change is required, the school board should expect the design professional to make immediate decisions on minor items with the understanding that these decisions will be reported to the board as soon as possible. The design professional should be required to issue bulletins to determine the costs of change orders on major items and to obtain board approval before

going ahead with such a change. Finally, the board should ensure that all change orders are issued in written form indicating the contractor's authority to make changes at specified prices.

Throughout the construction process, the contractor submits payment requests to the design professional for examination and certification. Only on the design professional's recommendation, indicated by the professional's signature on the monthly certificates of payment, should the school board make payments to the contractor.

Substantial Completion

At 95 percent completion of the project, the contractor will submit a certificate of substantial completion to the design professional for approval. Only minor items remain to be completed. The design professional, before signing off, completes a final walk-through of the project, often with the project inspector and school principal, and generates a final punch list for the contractor to complete. Only until the contractor completes the punch list, and the design professional makes the final project inspection, will the certificate of substantial completion be signed requesting the owner to make a final payment to the contractor(s). Often, final payment will be withheld until specific items in the punch list are completed.

Completion of the building officially marks the start of the contractor warranty period, and work provided during this period is required to be in accordance with the warranty agreement made between the contractor and the owner. At this point, the "keys are turned over" to the owner for occupancy.

Building Commissioning

Most buildings never go through a quality assurance process and often perform well below their potential performance level, with problems often surfacing during occupancy that later become additional burdens on the owner. Building commissioning is a systematic process that assures a building performs in accordance with the stated design intent and the owner's operational needs—before occupancy.

Although building commissioning is relatively new to the construction industry, often associated with the testing and balancing of mechanical systems, commissioning as a process has been used successfully by various agencies of the U.S. government for over a century. The goal of commissioning is to ensure the discovery of design and construction flaws before they become operational issues during occupancy. Present-day practice of commissioning is intended to be integrated into project delivery starting in the predesign phase going through the warranty phase and beyond to improve construction coordination, reduce construction and building lifecycle costs, document system basis of design, facilitate installation and operational performance, and adequately prepare the building maintenance staff for their postoccupancy responsibilities. Most recently, the building commissioning process has become an integrative component of the Leadership in Energy and Environmental Design (LEED) system that advocates for continuous commissioning within a sustainable building design framework (USGBC, 2003).

The commissioning authority, the agency responsible for managing the commissioning process, is ideally a third-party commissioning agent, but it can also be either the design team itself, or the owner's in-house commissioning agent. The commissioning authority is responsible for developing, witnessing, and documenting various functional performance tests performed by the contractor throughout the construction process.

Occupancy

Moving in to the new school facility requires the advance planning of a transition team to coordinate the physical transport of furnishings and equipment as well as staff and faculty (Swartzendurber, 1996). Purchasing and scheduling the delivery of furniture systems and office and classroom audio/visual equipment are often the responsibility of the business manager in cooperation with the

principal and transition team. Typically, there is a three- to six-month settling in period in which additional facility problems will emerge that will require attention, from equipment problems and building systems adjustment to new organizational policies. Items that should be addressed by the principal of the new school at this time will include phone lines and number changes, address changes, keying schedules, signage, cleaning schedules, temperature settings, security procedures as well as an open house to celebrate the completion of the project (Swartzendurber, 1996).

One year after occupancy, the architect will conduct a final walk-through with the school administrator to work out any remaining facility issues that have not been resolved. At this point, the architect "closes out" the project.

LIABILITY ISSUES AND DISPUTE RESOLUTION

Few construction projects are completed without some disputes between parties. In some cases, liability claims can surface for several years after the construction is complete. Questions concerning liability may fit into one of three general scenarios (WASB, 1987, p. 83). Errors and commission on the part of the design professional include the unsafe design of the building impacting the health, safety, and welfare of the public. Errors of omission on the part of the design professional include items omitted from the construction documents and specifications, the cost of which the contractor has not included as part of his or her bid. Finally, errors of commission and omission on the part of the contractor include items not in adherence to the requirements in the contract documents, whether such defects or deficiencies are accidental or deliberate.

There are a variety of methods for resolving disputes ranging from court trials, to arbitration, mediation, negotiation, settlement, and partnering. The results of trials and arbitration are a binding decision. In the case of a court trial, the decision is made either by a judge or jury, whereas with arbitration both parties agree to abide by the judgments arrived at by a third party of one's professional peers. Mediation and mock trials represent an alternative dispute resolution option that is not binding. Finally, partnering and negotiated settlements offer immediate and fair results based on compromises that are privately worked out between parties.

SUMMARY

Construction spending for school facilities has increased dramatically over the past several years and the amount needed for new schools, retrofits and additions is staggering. Given the need to improve the stock of school facilities in the United States and the scarcity of resources, it is imperative to ensure that the school construction process is as effective and efficient as possible. There are several different methods of the building delivery process that are used in school construction. The conventional method, competitive bidding (or design/bid/build), entails the design firm's providing detailed construction documents and specifications that are then competitively bid by multiple prime contractors for general (structural and finish work), mechanical, electrical, and plumbing construction. This approach is most familiar to school personnel, is relatively easy to manage, and typically awards a project to the lowest bidder. Because the process is very linear in nature, it may take longer than other approaches. There are other less conventional school delivery methods that appear to be gaining in popularity. Construction management occurs when a school system hires a construction management firm, often to manage an entire project. When a construction manager at-risk process is used, the construction manager works with designers to develop the design and cost estimates and provides school administrators with a guaranteed maximum price. One advantage of this approach is that construction can begin even before the design is complete, reducing the time for facility delivery. In a design/build approach, a single firm (often a partnership between an architectural firm and contractors) is responsible for design and construction,

often streamlining and speeding up the process. A guaranteed maximum price is also prepared. One disadvantage is that there are fewer checks and balances between the designer and contractor when they are part of the same entity.

A detailed description of the competitive bidding process is provided, since it is the building delivery process most commonly used by school districts. Using this method, once the final construction documents and specifications have been prepared, the bid process begins. Contractors are prequalified based on criteria normally provided by the school board. Qualified and interested bidders receive an official bid package containing the plans and specs and other instructions. A prebid meeting allows bidders to ask clarifying questions. Once bids are submitted and opened (in a public setting), the job is awarded to the lowest responsive bidder. Then, contract documents are prepared, which may include a construction deadline. The architect who periodically visits the site to verify progress typically handles construction coordination. A project inspector may be employed to provide more in-depth observation and reporting. Building inspectors also ensure that the project meets code requirements. Summer, when the majority of schools are not in session, is perhaps the busiest time for school construction and renovation projects. If construction activities must occur during regular school hours, construction phasing may be the best way to minimize disruption of classes. Regardless of how smooth the design process goes, there will likely be problems identified during construction that require change orders. Change orders can slow progress, so keeping them to a minimum is an important goal. At 95 percent completion of the project, the contractor will submit a certificate of substantial completion to the design professional for approval. Items that need to be completed (as observed by the architect, principal, inspector, or others) are listed on a "punch list." Once these items have been completed, the architect approves the certificate of substantial completion and the owner will be asked to submit final payment to the contractor. The keys are then turned over to the school system and the building can be occupied. The move in to a new facility requires precise planning activities. Sometimes during the construction process, or even many years after it has been completed, there may be disputes and liability claims. These are handled through trials, arbitration, mediation, and other similar processes.

ACTIVITIES

1. Several approaches to school facility delivery (conventional, construction manager, and design/build) were discussed. Explore these in more depth and discuss the additional advantages and disadvantages of each method.

2. Buildings, in their construction and operation, use an enormous amount of natural resources (e.g., wood, water, metals, energy). One trend in building construction is to recycle the construction waste. Identify and describe at least two case studies in which contractors successfully recycled large quantities of construction waste.

3. Visiting a construction project is an ideal procedure to enhance learning about the various aspects of construction and construction management. Make an "on-site" visit to a school construction project to discuss the process with an architect, engineer, educational planner, school representative, or construction manager. Include questions about the scheduling and sequencing of activities and acquisition of supplies and materials.

4. As a small team project, review the processes and procedures in Chapters 5 through 7. Define major milestones and conceptualize the links between the steps and phases found in these chapters.

REFERENCES AND BIBLIOGRAPHY

Print Sources

Abramson, P. (February 2001). 2001 Construction report. *School Planning and Management, 40:* 27–44.

American Society of Civil Engineers (1990). *Quality in the constructed project: A guide for owners, designers and constructors, Vol. 1.* Manuals and Reports on Engineering Practice No. 73. New York: ASCE.

Bittle, E. H. Grob, E. A. (1996). Fundamentals of competitive bidding. In Bittle, E. H. (ed.). *Planning and financing school improvement and construction projects* (pp. 63–78). Topeka, KS: National Organization on Legal Problems of Education.

Earthman, G. I. (2000). *Planning educational facilities for the next century.* Reston, VA: Association of School Business Officials International.

Education Writers Association (1989). *Wolves at the schoolhouse door: An investigation of the condition of public school buildings.* Washington, DC: Education Writers Association.

Lewis, L., Snow, K., Farris, E., Smerdon, B., Cronen, S., & Kaplan, J. (2000). *Condition of America's public school facilities: 1999.* Washington, DC: NCES 2000-032.

Myers, N., & Robertson, S. (2004). *Creating connections: The CEFPI guide for educational facility planning.* Scottsdale, AZ: Council of Educational Facility Planners, International.

National Education Association (2000). *Modernizing our schools: What will it cost?* Washington, DC: NEA.

Swartzendurber, A. (1996). Planning and constructing school facilities. In Bittle, E. H. (ed.), *Planning and financing school improvement and construction projects* (pp. 17–26). Topeka, KS: National Organization on Legal Problems of Education.

Sweet, J. (1999). *Legal aspects of architecture, engineering and the construction process.* 6th ed. Pacific Grove, CA: Brooks/Cole.

U.S. General Accounting Office (1995). *School facilities: Condition of America's schools.* GAO/HEHS–95–61. Washington, DC: U.S. GAO.

U.S. General Accounting Office (2000). *School facilities: Construction expenditures have grown significantly in recent years.* GAO/HEHS–00–41. Washington, DC: U.S. GAO.

U.S. Green Building Council (February 2003). Building momentum: National trends and prospects for high-performance green buildings. Washington, DC: USGBC.

Wisconsin Association of School Boards, Inc (1987). *To create a school: A design for working relationships.* Winneconne, WI: WASB.

Internet Resources

Abramson, P. (February 2004). 2004 Construction report. *School planning and management.* [http://www.peterli.com/spm/resources/rptsspm.shtm].

American Arbitration Association (ARA). http://www.adr.org/index2.1.jsp.

American Institute of Architects (AIA). http://www.aia.org.

American School Business Officials International (ASBO). http://www.asbointl.org/.

Associated Builders and Contractors. http://www.abc.org.

Associated General Contractors of America. http://www.agc.org.

Building Design and Construction Magazine. http://www.bdcmag.com.

Construction Industry Institute. http://construction-institute.org.

Construction Management Association of America. http://www.cmaa.com.

Construction Resource Council. http://cem.ce.gatech.edu/crc/.

Construction Specifications Institute (CSI). http://www.csinet.org/.

Design Build Institute of America. http://www.dbia.org.

International Code Council (ICC). http://www.iccsafe.org.

National Fire Protection Association (NFPA). http://www.nfpa.org.

School Construction News. http://www.schoolconstructionnews.com.

U.S. Green Building Council (USGBC). http://www.usgbc.org.

GLOSSARY

Advertisement for Bids   Published public notice soliciting bids for a constructed project and included as part of the bidding documents.

Arbitration   A method of settling claims or disputes between parties to a contract, used as an alternative to litigation, whereby an arbitrator selected for his or her knowledge in the field hears the evidence and renders a decision.

Bid Bond   A form of bid security executed by the bidder as principal and by a surety to protect the owner if the low bidder does not accept the award of contract.

Bonus Clause   A provision in the construction contract for payment of a bonus to the constructor for completing the work prior to a stipulated date.

Certificate of Completion   A statement prepared by the design professional on the basis of an inspection stating that the work to the best of his or her knowledge is substantially complete.

Change Order   A written order to the constructor signed by the owner and/or by the owner's representative, issued after execution of a contract, authorizing a change in the work or an adjustment in the contract sum or the contract time.

Codes   Regulations, ordinances, or statutory requirements of, or meant for adoption by, governmental units related to building construction and occupancy, adopted and administered for the protection of the public health, safety, and welfare.

Competitive Bidding   A method, often mandated by law, of selecting constructors for construction projects by price competition between qualified bidders subjected to various rules and procedures.

Punch List   A final list of remaining construction tasks the contractor must complete before the project can be awarded a certificate of substantial completion.

Shop Drawings   New field-coordinated drawings for a project showing actual details, dimensions, materials, assembly methods, and attachments from design drawings.

Substantial Completion   The construction is sufficiently completed in accordance with the contract documents and submission procedures, revised through approved modifications, so that the owner can occupy and utilize the facility for the use for which it was designed.

APPENDIX: CALIFORNIA'S PUBLIC SCHOOL CONSTRUCTION PROCESS

California's public school construction process includes eight phases having interactive Internet links. The general process is reviewed here.

PHASE 1: GETTING STARTED

Increasing enrollments and the trend toward reducing class size have increased the need to build new schools in California. To this extent, the local school district is responsible for the following five activities:

- Analyze enrollment trends.
- Assess its facilities needs.
- Plan for new facilities.
- Provide local financing.
- Carry out its own construction projects.

The process is complex from the start because at least five agencies are involved: The Office of Public School Construction, within the Department of General Services; the School Facilities Planning Division of the California Department of Education; the Department of Toxic Substances Control, within the California Environmental Protection Agency; the Division of the State Architect, within the Department of General Services; and the State Allocation Board. Seven other state agencies operate approximately forty programs that also may become involved under certain conditions. Special Internet links may be found at http://www.schoolconstruction.dgs.ca.gov/index.html.

PHASE 2: FUNDING ELIGIBILITY

Before submitting an application for funding, the school system is required to submit an application for funding eligibility. School districts that are confident they are eligible for funding may apply for funding and eligibility simultaneously. These documents are available on the Internet.

PHASE 3: SITE APPROVAL

When a school district has determined the need for new facilities (phase 1) and its preliminary eligibility for state funding, it is ready to begin the site approval process. Above and beyond the site's adequacy for educational learning environments, the following questions must be answered:

- Will your project disturb 5 or more acres of land?
- Are you building on or near a waste disposal site?
- Are you building within 2 miles of an airport runway?
- Are pesticides used in your vicinity?
- Are you building in an agriculturally protected area?
- Will your project affect historic landmarks or resources?
- Is your school project located in a coastal zone?
- Is your proposed school located in the Delta?
- Does your project disturb a fish or wildlife habitat?
- Will your construction affect the shores or waters of San Francisco Bay or Suisun Marsh?
- Will your school be located near a dam?
- Are you worried about earthquakes or other geologic hazards?
- Is outdoor air quality a problem in your area?
- Are you concerned about lead-related construction or drinking water problems?

179

- Is your school constructing its own water system?
- Do you intend to discharge waters or waste?

PHASE 4: PLAN APPROVAL

Once the site approval process is completed, the school district may proceed with the plan approval process. Before starting, the school is expected to know the basic information for the plan approval process. Internet links provide the following process information:

- What the process involves
- What should already be done
- Who to hire
- Who needs approval
- Who grants approval
- How long the process takes

Additionally, there are a series of questions the applicant needs to ask of the client to expedite the school construction process. If the client answers "yes" to any of the following questions, there is an Internet link explaining what should be done:

- Do you need assistance in preparing educational specifications (program offerings)?
- Would you like to view previously used school designs?
- Do you want ideas on or funding for energy efficiency?
- Are you interested in receiving advice on, and possible funding for, waste management strategies or the use of recycled materials in construction?
- Is construction the result of a declared disaster?
- Will your project disturb 5 or more acres of land?
- Are you building on or near a waste disposal site?
- Are you building within 2 miles of an airport runway?

- Will your construction affect the shores or waters of San Francisco Bay or Suisun Marsh?
- Are you worried about earthquakes or other geologic hazards?
- Is indoor air quality a problem?
- Is your school constructing its own water system?
- Do you intend to discharge waters or waste?

Finally, in addition to answering the above questions, the school system must recognize that plan approval involves:

Producing plans for the district's school construction project

Obtaining School Facilities Planning Division approval of the plans

Obtaining Division of the State Architect approval of the plans

PHASE 5: FUNDING APPLICATION

Funding processes vary from state to state. The California model offers various types of funding depending on the nature of the construction project. State funds may only be used to cover certain project costs. Thus, the planner is advised to read carefully about the funds available to ensure an understanding of available funds and how they may be used. Your district should have already completed the funding eligibility process to verify your eligibility to receive state funds. However, you are not strictly required to confirm eligibility before submitting your funding application. The funding eligibility application may be submitted at the same time as the funding application, if desired.

PHASE 6: CONSTRUCTION

When the school district is ready to begin actual construction, state oversight does not end. Not only must the district account for state money, but it must also continue to meet state building, labor, environmental, and other standards. There are several questions to answer before this phase begins; Internet links provide California school planners with a clear path to follow. Before starting the construction phase, the school should complete site approval, plan approval, and receive funding. Internet links provide the following basic information:

- What the process involves
- What should already be done
- Who to hire
- Compliance With laws and regulations
- Occupational safety and health
- Labor standards enforcement
- Workers' compensation self-insurance
- Apprenticeship standards

The process involves coordinating reviews, inspections, and tests during construction as well as complying with California labor laws and safety regulations before and during construction, and after its completion. This phase is preceded by official approval of the site, plan, and funding. A qualified project inspector approved by the Division of the State Architect (DSA) is hired. The project inspector is also known as the inspector of record, and must pass DSA-administered inspector examinations. Next, various consultants and contractors to complete the construction process are hired, all of whom need to meet certain criteria and be selected in a certain fashion in order to comply with state law. Specifically, if the school system receives state funds, it must use a competitive selection process to obtain all professional services used on the project. It is vital to ensure that the construction contractors and/or subcontractors hired employ an appropriate number of apprentices to meet state apprenticeship standards for public works projects. The school may not award contracts for project construction until the DSA approves all drawings and specifications and provides written approval of the application. Compliance with laws and regulations is monitored. Heavy emphasis is placed on safety and health, and Division of Occupational Safety and Health

(CAL/OSHA) standards are followed throughout the construction process.

Before construction begins, the DSA must approve all drawings and specifications. If the district makes any changes to the drawings or specifications between the time the DSA stamps the drawings and the time the district awards the contract, the architect or engineer of record must initiate an addendum, and the DSA must approve the changes. The district must hire a project inspector (also known as the inspector of record, who must pass DSA-administered inspector examinations), and obtain DSA approval of the inspector.

During construction, the DSA will assign a field engineer to visit the construction site several times to maintain an understanding of the project's progress. The field engineer first visits the site at the beginning of construction, and then every three to four weeks during construction. The field engineer also visits the construction site when problems occur, and upon completion of the project. The DSA has the authority to issue stop work orders if the field engineer finds that the construction is not proceeding in accordance with the approved plans or other serious problems plague the construction itself. A variety of specialized laboratory tests may also be required. These include tests of structural materials incorporated in the project, such as the welding of structural steel members or the compaction of fill soils supporting building foundations. Laboratories performing these tests must be approved by the DSA through the Laboratory Evaluation and Acceptance (LEA) program. The laboratory must send any resulting test reports to the project inspector, the school district's architect/engineer, and the DSA.

The local Division of Transportation Planning office also may inspect and approve work during the construction and completion phases. The state fire marshal enforces fire safety regulations in areas outside incorporated cities and in districts providing their own fire protection services. A school district or the DSA can request a construction inspection.

PHASE 7: PROJECT CLOSURE

The DSA can close projects either by issuing the final certification of construction or by closing the project without certification. The difference is significant. Without certification, the state will not assume liability for the facility. The district's school board members remain liable in any construction-related litigation and should make every effort to complete the certification process.

The final certification of construction certifies that construction complies with requirements of the Field Act, which was enacted in 1933 to:

- Establish "reasonable minimum standards for the design and construction of new school buildings."
- Provide for a rigorous inspection process "to ensure that the work of construction has been performed in accordance with the approved plans and specifications, for the protection of life and property."

The final certification of construction releases the school district's board members from any direct liability connected with construction of the school facility. This certification also indicates project closure and the end of the DSA's responsibilities.

The DSA grants a final certification of construction when:

- All construction is completed and verified.
- All required documentation is received and verified by the DSA.
- The required fee, adjusted for final construction costs (including change orders), is received by the DSA.
- The notice of completion is received by the DSA.

If a project is closed without certification, the school district may pay a nominal fee to have the DSA reopen the project. When the outstanding issues have been resolved, the DSA will issue the final certification of construction and the state will, at that time, assume liability for the facility.

PHASE 8: FOLLOW-UP

Within two years of project completion, the Office of Public School Construction will perform a financial audit of the project expenditures. The Department of Toxic Substances Control may need to monitor long-term operations and maintenance at the school site, if the district was required to prepare a response action for the site.

CONCLUSION

The overview of the public school construction process in California reveals a straightforward process for school construction. Although the authors of this text are not overly excited about reliance on "previously used school designs" as suggested to school boards in the process described above, there are more pluses than minuses in the California model. Adopting prototype schools usually minimizes community involvement in planning and design—a principle that goes against the underlying philosophy of this book. In some cases a prototype school may be better than designs not thoroughly researched for educational efficacy. Nevertheless, the State of California is to be commended for providing a user-friendly Internet site for helping with the enormous job of school construction. Go to http://www.schoolconstruction.dgs.ca.gov/index.html for additional information.

MANAGEMENT, MAINTENANCE, AND OPERATIONS OF SCHOOL BUILDINGS

Part V addresses the way school structures are managed and how best to enhance these vitally important learning tools. It is well known that deferred maintenance has often been the rule rather than the exception for educational facilities, especially during tight budgeting periods. This trend should be reversed to save the investments of taxpayers who have supported the schools in good faith. The three premises for developing school facilities relating most directly to this topic are strong leadership, systematic management, and the demand for resources.

First, strong leadership is essential to keep the management of operations and maintenance from being replaced with seemingly higher priorities in the budgeting cycle. Deferred maintenance results in lost resources in the long run. For example, when a roof leaks in a classroom containing computers, the interior walls and the floors become saturated with water, the damage is usually irreversible to the computers, and eventually the walls and floor coverings begin to grow fungi, such as mold and mildew, that lead to health problems among students and faculty. Deferred roof maintenance is

among the most costly decisions that school leaders make.

The second major premise is that management must be systematic, be supported by relevant and current data, and follow a set of long-range goals. Maintenance must be kept on schedule if the taxpayers are to be given what they are paying for and if the educational program is to reach its full potential. People managing the maintenance and operations component of schools must be aware that the demand for resources is usually greater than their availability. School leaders should not succumb to pressure and continue deferred maintenance.

**Premises for Developing
School Facilities**

PREMISE	DESCRIPTOR
Premise 1	Strong leadership is essential.
Premise 6	Management is systematic: data- and goal-driven.
Premise 7	The demand for resources is greater than those available.

Both the school and community should recognize that the management of school facilities is an insurance policy that protects investments. Facilities management should also be viewed as a vital component of the learning process. Individuals involved in management, and maintenance and operations should be respected, since without them educational operations would suffer substantial losses. Chapter 8 is concerned with some macro levels of management and operations, while Chapter 9 emphasizes some micro aspects of maintenance and operations at the school building level.

CHAPTER EIGHT

MANAGING SCHOOL FACILITIES

While the planning, design, and construction of a school building may take two to three years, the management of that building continues for forty or more years. According to a 2000 report, the mean age of a school building in the United States was forty-two years, with 28 percent of existing school buildings built before 1950 (National Center for Education Statistics, 2000). Many of the building materials, furnishings, and equipment will not last half that long and will require constant upkeep and maintenance and inevitable replacement to postpone building obsolescence. Schools, however, can climb out of the maintenance slump with improved strategies and products if policy makers commit to better buildings in order to enhance the learning environment (Kennedy & Agron, 2004; Strahle, 2004). For example, with proper maintenance, some school buildings in the United States have survived for one hundred years and are, for the most part, functional. Other school buildings reach functional obsolescence in less than thirty years, requiring complete renovation, alteration, and modernization.

The decision to renovate or replace a building is based on a complex mix of factors including the condition and maintenance of building systems and materials, the educational program, and demographic change. As might be expected, the process of managing school facilities over the length of time associated with a building's life is complex and evolving as the educational programs and philosophy contained in those buildings change, educational administration and faculty turn over, generations of students arrive and leave, and societal values ebb and flow. Designing a school building to be flexible to change is one thing; managing that facility to realize the flexibility is quite another.

The management of school facilities has historically received much less attention than facility planning in educational administration literature. Kowalski (1989) argued that this lack of attention has resulted in a "capital renewal crisis" created through years of deferred maintenance at all levels of educational delivery, from schools through universities. This chapter considers the problems, issues, methods, techniques, struggles, and strategies of managing a school facility. The goal is to assist in the improvement of the physical environment to more effectively support the educational process over time.

To illustrate the complexity and scope of the management task, there are a plethora of responsibilities and issues that must be addressed by the facility manager of school buildings. Building systems must be monitored, a variety of services must be procured and maintained, maintenance programs must be planned, and various environmental and organizational issues must be addressed—all within the context of various governmental codes, regulations, and laws. Maintenance and operations of building systems and components include structural, mechanical, ventilation, plumbing, electrical, lighting, energy and power, and telecommunications systems, as well as the maintenance of the school site and grounds, parking surfaces, athletic fields, and the maintenance facilities. The management and operation of various building level services include in-house maintenance and custodial services, food services, transportation services, administrative services, as well as outsourcing services, performance-based contracting, and Web-based procurement systems. Various forms of facility maintenance programs need to be considered, such as deferred, preventive, repair/upkeep, and emergency maintenance. Several environmental quality issues have emerged over the past few decades, such as acoustics, thermal comfort, indoor air quality, water quality and conservation, asbestos, radon, and other hazardous materials. Other issues of concern to a facility manager include organizational behavior issues, such as aspects of classroom management, and safety and security and building vulnerability issues related to discouraging vandalism and acts of violence and terrorism. All these functions must be conducted within a constantly changing set of government mandates, such as energy deregulation, accessibility guidelines, various codes, and other regulations and guidelines at the state and federal levels.

Planning for Obsolescence

Buildings go through a predictable process of obsolescence that is hastened by a combination of functional, economic, technological, and sociocultural factors (Iselin & Lemer, 1993, pp. 20–21). The use of the spaces within the building will change. The costs associated with maintaining various building systems will increase over time as these systems become less efficient and newer systems provide greater efficiencies. Existing building system technologies, instructional technologies, and telecommunication systems will continually fall behind newer technologies. Finally, an entire host of changes in social goals, political agendas, and changes in demographics and type of user will influence the efficiency of the existing facility.

Properly designing and constructing school buildings for the realities of management can often provide cost savings over time that can provide additional funds for educational delivery. Often, many facility management and maintenance concerns are not considered until it is too late. Effective management should, however, begin in the earliest stages of facility planning. Iselin and Lemer (1993), summarize a number of strategies that can be utilized during planning and design to minimize the premature obsolescence of school facilities:

- Conduct facilities programming to address explicitly the possibilities of future functional change.
- Assure that design guidelines and criteria are based on the latest available information and provide for future change in technology and practice.
- Make flexibility an explicit design goal and make appropriate use of design details or integrated building systems that enhance flexibility or adaptability.
- Assure that facilities fit users' needs and gather information for more effective accommodation to users' needs in future facilities.
- Use alternative procurement methods to reduce the time between initial specification and in-service utilization.
- Assure quality in construction to avoid premature deterioration of building components. (pp. 2–3)

Deferred Maintenance in School Facilities

The construction and operation of a school building involve a substantial expenditure of public funds. The investment for construction however represents only a fraction of the cost of operating a school over the life of the building. When life-cycle costs of operating a school are considered (including staff salaries and overhead costs in addition to the maintenance and operations of the facility), the initial cost of the school facility may be less than 10 to 15 percent of the life-cycle costs over a thirty-year period. Life-cycle cost has been defined as "the present value of all anticipated costs to be incurred during a facility's economic life; the sum total of direct, indirect, recurring, nonrecurring, and other related costs incurred or estimated to be incurred in the design, development, production, operation, maintenance, support, and final disposition of a major system over its anticipated useful life span" (Iselin & Lemer, 1993, p. 66). To stay current on the important issues of life-cycle costs of school facilities, we recommend that the reader consult the National Clearinghouse for Educational Facilities (NCEF) at http://www.edfacilities.org and various other Internet sites.

Building life-cycle cost analysis is admittedly difficult for taxpayers and school boards to comprehend when available building funds are very scarce, but the rewards in facility management are potentially enormous. Operational costs for power and fuel, water and sewer, garbage disposal, leases and insurance, building maintenance, and custodial staff are important items in the annual budget, competing yearly for funds identified for educational delivery. An April 2005 survey conducted by *American School & University* magazine reported that school districts nationally allocated 7.7 percent of their net current expenditures (NCE) to maintenance and operations (M&O) (Agron, 2005). (NCE represents the total district expenditures, including teacher salaries, minus the cost of capital outlay, transportation, and debt service.) In a prior publication, Agron noted that the percentage of NCE for M&O has steadily decreased over the past decade (Agron, 2005). Beyond shrinking budgets, other problems maintenance and operations managers must contend with include rising costs of products and services, competition with private sector vendors, and costs associated with new state and federal mandates.

Once a new school building is occupied, a transitional period may be experienced where various building systems might not operate as expected. Various components and equipment of the building may need to be adjusted, rebalanced, or replaced. This is a period often referred to as the building commissioning process, and it can last for a year beyond the substantial completion of the construction process.

As soon as the students, teachers, administrators, and custodial staff begin to occupy the building, the building is said to be operational. From the first day of operation, various components of the building will begin to age, wear, and deteriorate. Some materials will last longer than others. Mechanical systems and equipment may last twenty years, roof systems may last fifteen years, but carpeting and wall surfaces may last only five years. The building aging process, the building life cycle, is natural, universal, and inevitable. For this reason, a well-conceived program of routine maintenance is an integral part of the daily operation of a school building. A preventive maintenance program can save a school district many thousands of dollars in future maintenance by paying attention to the "little things," such as water leaks, lubrication of equipment, erosion of soils adjacent to the building, and repair and replacement of defective temperature controls.

Often, the operational budgets are extremely tight and there may not be available funds for all the required maintenance needed to properly maintain the building on an annual basis. When this situation occurs, various building maintenance items are not completed and the costs associated with those items are deferred to the next fiscal year's budget. Continued deterioration of various building systems and components not repaired may eventually create additional costs, such as when a roof leak left in disrepair may damage interior ceilings, floors, furniture, equipment, and wall surfaces.

Rarely recognized during the budgetary process is the great contribution made by facility managers and custodial staff in maintaining a comfortable and healthful environment in a school building. The impact of deferred maintenance on the educational process is only beginning to be understood and recognized. For instance, research conducted by Edwards (1991) in the District of Columbia public schools indicated that routine maintenance for most facilities becomes more important as a facility ages. Worsening building conditions were correlated with student achievement. As the condition of a school building worsens with age, the greater negative impact that facility would have on student achievement. Conversely, for a school moved from a poor condition category to fair or excellent condition, overall achievement scores increased 5.455 and 10.9 points, respectively. Much more research will need to be completed before we know the full impact of deferred maintenance on educational delivery, but it is clear there is a relationship between the maintenance of a building and student performance, and this finding alone suggests the importance of adequately maintaining our school facilities. The way in which resources, once provided, are used and managed is one aspect of the role of school leaders that is often neglected but where they can make a significant contribution to the life of the institution (OECD, 1989).

At present in the United States as in many other countries, there are numerous examples of the lack of responsive facility management services to maintain and operate, update and modernize existing school buildings in order to adequately meet the needs of teachers and students. For example, abuses in the custodial system of New York City Public Schools have been linked to custodial neglect and the decrepit disrepair of schools in the district (Slater, 1992). In Chicago, a housing court judge resorted to appointing an outside consultant to make much-needed window repairs to a South Side school when the Chicago Board of Education failed to deal with the ten-year-old problem (Ortiz, 1993).

The problem of unresponsive facility management is most often attributed to deferred maintenance policies due to the lack of general operating funds. In most cases, communities draw maintenance and repair funds from state and local funding, which accounts for the majority of their budgets. Larger projects, such as additions or new schools, commonly derive from bond offerings

voters have endorsed. However, due to the shrinking community tax base in many parts of the country and a changing political climate, bond offerings are having more trouble passing, and as a result, resources normally used for maintenance are frequently utilized elsewhere. Reduced funding inevitably leads to reduced, underpaid, and undertrained support staff. A more fundamental problem, however, may be that most facility management services are not functionally integrated with either educational policy-making or budgetary processes. Decisions are not made in ways that focus comprehensively on the problem.

As a result of the growing perception that previous federal, state, and local programs aimed at improving accessibility, and managing hazardous materials such as asbestos abatement, was not addressing the core needs of school facilities, the U.S. Congress passed the Education Infrastructure Act of 1994. As part of this act, the General Administration Office (GAO) conducted a series of national surveys on school infrastructure to obtain a clearer scope of the problem facing the nation's schools.

A year later the GAO published a report (1995) looking at various aspects of the school facility infrastructure, which represented the first assessment of the condition of the nation's school facilities done since in 1965. About two-thirds of U.S schools reported that their school buildings were in overall adequate condition, at most needing only some preventive maintenance or corrective repair. However, about 14 million students attend the remaining one-third of schools reported the need of extensive repair or replacement of one or more building(s), and nearly 60 percent of U.S. schools reported at least one major building feature in need of repair or replacement. Finally, the report indicated that about half of the schools reporting had at least one unsatisfactory environmental condition in their schools, such as poor ventilation, heating or lighting problems, or poor physical security (GAO, 1995). District officials interviewed by the GAO reported that a major factor in the declining physical condition of school infrastructure has been decisions by school districts to defer vital maintenance and repair expenditures from year to year because of the lack of funds.

The GAO report determined that over $118 billion would be necessary to bring U.S. school facilities to a satisfactory condition. A subsequent report by the National Education Association nearly duplicated these earlier estimates. A more recent report sponsored by the U.S. Department of Education and published by the National Center for Educational Statistics, entitled *Condition of America's Public School Facilities: 1999*, indicated that three-quarters of schools in the country are in need of repairs, renovations, and modernizations (National Center for Educational Statistics, 2000). The problem is not going away, but a new national awareness of the need for improved school infrastructure has emerged.

A MODEL FOR FACILITY MANAGEMENT

For many generations of school administrators, caring for a school building was "essentially a chore thought to require little more than common sense and basic custodial skills. Superintendents and principals are now acknowledging that facilities management has taken on greater importance" (Kowalski, 1989, p. 135). Today, this realization has come about from a combination of increased public scrutiny, and more sophisticated and complex building systems requiring skilled operators. Facility managers have witnessed an increase in their responsibilities for providing a safe, secure, comfortable, healthy, accessible, adaptable, efficient, and effective learning environment for students, educators, and parent and community visitors alike.

The conventional notion of building maintenance management primarily emphasizes the physical components of place such as the maintenance of various building systems, and custodial upkeep and cleanliness without specifically addressing the personal and process components of facility management—a "silo" approach to facility management. Building maintenance and operations are seen as a separate departmental function from educational delivery. Most school districts are firmly rooted in the old paradigm of "a storage place for kids" approach to facility management, which has created the current budgetary competition between facilities and education.

Recently, the field of facility management has emerged as a professional discipline in its own right. Facility management can be described as a system of management containing people, process, and place components (Rondeau, Brown, & Lapides, 1995). The personal component (people) includes concerns for human needs and requirements and human factors. The process component recognizes the role of organizational objectives, technology, and organizational change and development. Finally, the place component includes the more traditional concerns of facilities maintenance management such as building systems, environmental quality issues, and the energy consumption of buildings. The International Facility Management Association defines facility management as "the practice of coordinating the physical workplace with the people and work of the organization" (Rondeau, Brown, & Lapides, 1995). The field of facility management integrates the principles of business administration, architecture, and the behavioral and engineering sciences, and in the context of educational theory and practice integrates educational psychology and educational administration as well. This broader—new paradigm—view of facility management integrates and addresses maintenance and upkeep as critical to not only the proper functioning of the organization, but also the management of occupancy and use. Space management in the context of educational institutions would include the responsibility for management, planning, and scheduling of the use of instructional, administrative, and recreational spaces and areas within the school and on school grounds.

The operative term "facilities" in facilities management implies much more than the physical building structure and systems; the term refers to the function or role the building performs in the service of education as a "facilitator of educational delivery" or as a "facilitator of learning." Facilities in its broadest sense includes, in addition to the building, the building grounds and site characteristics, information technologies and telecommunications systems, furnishings and equipment, and a full range of support offerings that include administrative, custodial, food, and transportation services.

Although the facility management function of the organization has been in existence since the evolution of the first workplaces, including the school workplace, only in recent years has it received worldwide recognition. The private sector has come to realize that maintaining a well-managed and highly efficient facility is critical to success. The public sector and school systems are beginning to realize the relationship between facilities and performance in light of the disturbing knowledge about the condition of school infrastructure as reported above. New technologies, environmental consciousness, and health concerns also have had a major impact on the importance of and need for facility professionals in organizations public and private.

Facility professionals must be equipped with a tremendous amount of knowledge and the ability to cope with and solve a multitude of complex problems and challenges. Their numerous job responsibilities can be categorized into the following major functions:

- Facility strategic and tactical planning
- Facility financial forecasting and budgeting
- Real estate procurement, leasing, and disposal
- Procurement of furnishings, equipment, and outside facility services
- Facility construction, renovation, and relocation
- Health, safety, and security
- Environmental issues
- Development of facility policies and procedures
- Quality management, including benchmarking and best practices

- Architecture and engineering planning and design
- Space planning and management
- Building operations, maintenance, and engineering
- Supervision of business services such as reprographics, transportation, and food service
- Telecommunications
- Code compliance

Traditionally, managing a facility was only associated with operations and maintenance duties. Today, a vast array of responsibilities are now associated with the facility management profession, from the control of building systems, to the management of human resources and monitoring cost control measures that serve the organizational goals. With the advent of charter schools and other alternative educational services, facility managers of schools have begun to change their view of facility management from a caretaker/custodial function to a strategic function aimed at impacting educational outcomes. The interest in the impact of facility design and management on student behavior, attitudes, and achievement (Lackney, 1996) and teacher attitudes, and instructional performance (Johnson, 1990) is testament to the strategic role of facility management in the future of school operations.

As the role of facility managers expands, their numbers continue to increase. More colleges and universities are offering course work and degree plans in facility management (e.g., Cornell University, Eastern Michigan University, Michigan State University, University of Southern Colorado).

THE ORGANIZATION OF MAINTENANCE AND OPERATIONS AT THE DISTRICT LEVEL

The locus of control for facility management varies in school systems, depending primarily on the district's size in relation to the number of school buildings, the size of its facilities and enrollments

(Kowalski, 1989). In a small district (2,500 students or less), the superintendent may take a direct and active role where facility management has no formal functional status within the organization. In a moderately sized districts (2,500–10,000 students), a full-time director of buildings and grounds may be employed where facility management becomes a subdivision of a major division, such as business affairs, within the organization that might include separate directors for finance, transportation, and food services. According to Kowalski (1989), this is the most common structure for the facilities management function in schools in the United States. In a large school district (10,000 or more students), a whole department of facilities management with a director with assistant superintendent status may be employed. Many urban districts separate the facilities management function from the facilities planning function as well.

The building maintenance management function, its roles and responsibilities, are most often divided between district and school site. Depending on the size and organizational structure of a school district, different aspects will be divided between these two general levels of organization. Smaller districts will have more decision autonomy, often relying more heavily on site-based management, while larger districts will contain more centralized facility management functions serving the entire district.

The central administration of a school district has a critical role to play in the operation and maintenance of all the school buildings within its jurisdiction. It develops district-wide policies concerning job descriptions, qualifications for hiring, job search and screening procedures, working conditions of the custodial staff, their rate of pay, fringe benefits, and other forms of compensation. It sets work standards and procedures that are implemented by the individual school principals. It develops instructions designed to help the entire custodial staff better preserve and maintain the school buildings they are assigned. Finally, central administration is responsible for providing funds for custodial supplies, cleaning and maintenance equipment, the normal wear and tear of mechanical equipment, and preventive maintenance.

Custodial Services

Determining the size of the custodial workforce is another function of central administration. The central administration of a school district has the basic responsibility of making certain that custodial personnel are not being overworked, while simultaneously being responsible to the taxpayers by keeping the number of personnel to an appropriate minimum. Factors involved in determining the size of the workforce include the number of school facilities, the physical size of each facility, the area of the grounds on which the building is sited, the number, size, and condition of teacher stations throughout each building, the number of students and teachers served in those facilities, and the intensity of use and the age of the facility. All these factors need to be taken into consideration. A detailed formula to determine custodial needs is presented in the next chapter.

Maintenance and Operations Budget

In addition to staffing, the central administration, represented by either a superintendent of buildings and grounds or a director of plant operations in larger school districts, is responsible for providing funds for custodial supplies, cleaning and maintenance equipment, the normal wear and tear of mechanical equipment, and preventive maintenance. As indicated earlier, school districts nationally allocate less than 10 percent of their net current expenditures (NCE) to maintenance and operations. Table 8.1 on page 192 indicates how these national median costs are typically divided among various subcategories as a percentage of the budget and in dollars per square foot of building. To stay current on this topic, the reader is referred to annual surveys conducted by *American School and University* magazine.

TABLE 8.1   Budget for National Median Percentage of Budget and Cost Per Square Foot

MAINTENANCE AND OPERATIONS	PERCENTAGE OF BUDGET(%)
Payroll	51
Energy/utilities	34
Equipment/supplies	9
Outside contract labor	6
Other	1

MAINTENANCE AND OPERATIONS	DOLLARS/SF
CUSTODIAL	**1.33**
Maintenance	0.42
Grounds	0.13
Outside contract labor	0.21
Gas	0.22
Electricity	0.60
Other fuel	0.17
Other utilities	0.20
Maintenance equipment and supplies	0.23
Grounds equipment and supplies	0.06
Other	0.00
TOTAL M&O	3.57
TOTAL NCE*	41.04

*NCE = Net current expenditures including teacher salaries, minus the cost of capital outlay, transportation, and debt service.
Source: Adapted from Agron (2001), pp. 26–28.

In the procurement and use of custodial supplies, the central administration has two central responsibilities: first, to include sufficient funds in the school budget to purchase custodial supplies, and second, an obligation to make certain that the most efficient and least damaging and toxic cleaning agents and maintenance supplies are provided for district buildings. Not only can abrasive powders permanently damage building surfaces, they can be environmentally toxic to occupants as well. Improper use of cleaning agents can be very costly to a school district over time in more ways than one (Castaldi, 1994).

In centralizing the procurement process for custodial and maintenance supplies, care should be taken to insure that the special conditions of individual buildings throughout the district are reflected in the budget. Each building should be considered unique regarding the type and amount of supplies as well as the custodial services required based on their age, size, type of construction, and building systems.

Unlike the practice of establishing reserve or sinking funds for equipment depreciation commonly found in the private sector, school districts rarely have the ability to set aside funds in advance to replace all equipment that is completely worn out through normal use. In fact, in many states, laws forbid the establishment of reserve funds, preventing school districts from carrying forward funds to the next year.

Nevertheless, it is both economically and financially prudent to anticipate the replacement of building systems throughout the life of a school building. Different building systems and components have different life expectancies (see Table 8.2 in the later section "Preventive Maintenance").

Castaldi (1994) suggested that if each piece of equipment were classified in terms of its normal life expectancy, it would be possible to determine its rate of depreciation in dollars per year. The total cost of depreciation of each building system can then be determined each year. This amount of money, representing the total cost of depreciation, could be placed in a reserve fund allowing the school district to replace those systems on a schedule. This practice could apply to building systems, components and equipment such as mechanical systems, lighting and power equipment, but also to motor vehicles, vacuum cleaners, computers, and photocopiers. A tax levy would be required each year to include the proportional amount of money needed

for equipment replacement. Without a system to establish reserve funds for equipment depreciation, school districts will continue to find they are replacing worn crucial equipment on an emergency basis. This existing practice of deferred maintenance is arguably cost-inefficient and a waste of public funds. It will be corrected only when the educational administrators and school building officials make responsible legislators aware of the situation.

The District Maintenance and Operations Program

The generic components of a district maintenance and operations program include a philosophy and mission statement, goals and objectives, policies, a budget, capital improvement plan for renewal and replacement, maintenance programs (upkeep, preventive maintenance, emergency maintenance), in-service staff development and training, program

TABLE 8.2   Average Useful Life of Building Components

MAJOR CONSTRUCTION	USEFUL LIFE (YEARS)
Reinforced concrete with masonry exterior	40–45
Steel frame with masonry exterior	30–45
Wood frame with wood exterior	20–25

BUILDING SYSTEMS	
Roofing systems	15–20
Lighting systems	15–20
Power feed wiring	20–25
Air-conditioning systems	10–15
Heating systems	20–25
Ventilation system fans and exhaust	15
Plumbing systems	15–30
Fire alarm systems	20
Telephone and intercom systems	15
Paving and walks	10–20
Wire fencing	10

Source: Adapted from Maciha (2000).

evaluation, and performance evaluation (Maciha, 2000; Kowalski, 1989). The actual content of the plan depends on the philosophy, available resources, and facility needs of a district. A comprehensive district maintenance program can address policy for a number of management conditions such as management responsibilities that extend from the present (general upkeep and emergency maintenance), to anticipating the future (preventive maintenance) or rectifying the past (deferred maintenance). Included in the program should be clear directives for determining how and when to proceed under these situations—for instance, providing maintenance schedules for specific building equipment in the preventive maintenance plan, or including emergency contacts for power outages and other situations in the emergency management plan. General upkeep or custodial maintenance will be covered in the Chapter 9.

Often, school districts steeped in a cycle of deferred maintenance are caught in a reactive mode, where the majority of maintenance becomes some form of emergency maintenance (work requiring immediate action to restore safe operations). This chapter will focus on what is needed most in school districts to get beyond the cycle of deferred maintenance: anticipating maintenance needs and investing in, and following up on, a comprehensive preventive maintenance program.

FACILITY MAINTENANCE MANAGEMENT

Sometime after fifteen years of continuous use, school facilities often reveal visible signs of wear and experience substantial maintenance deficiencies, especially deterioration in roofing systems and heating and air-conditioning systems. In addition to the normal wear and tear of school buildings, exposure to other factors such as various chemicals, cleaning solvents, airborne particles, radiant energy, and cycles of heat and cold, among others, can reduce the integrity of materials (Maciha, 2000).

Different wear cycles in spaces within the school building are dependent on the material used, the material's maintainability, degree of preventive maintenance performed, and especially the level of abuse inflicted on the building by students. Areas of the school receiving the most intense traffic such as bathrooms, corridors, and entrance foyers will require the most attention.

All building materials and systems have a useful life span, at which point they begin entering what some in the building industry call the "gray life," the stage just before permanent failure or complete building obsolescence. Preventive maintenance can prolong this gray life, but eventually the material and equipment will fail and need to be replaced. Not replacing these components on schedule amounts to deferred maintenance. Table 8.2 illustrates the average life expectancy of various building components.

Forms of Facility Maintenance

In addition to preventive maintenance, Maciha (2000) describes other forms of maintenance typically conducted by facility maintenance personnel. The goal of predictive maintenance, for instance, is to anticipate building failure through the use of technological detection equipment such as vibration analysis, thermography (infrared scanning), and ultrasonic testing. Corrective maintenance refers to the replacement of nonemergency, obsolete, worn, broken, or inoperative building components based on preventive maintenance inspections. Repair maintenance refers to unscheduled repair and/or adjustments of equipment or components. Emergency maintenance, a more specific form of repair maintenance, refers to work that requires immediate action to restore safe operations or services or to remedy problems that could interrupt activities (e.g., repair of a ruptured water line).

Preventive Maintenance. "The forces of nature corrupt much more quickly when human caretakers fail in their diligence to maintain" (Maciha, 2000, p. 1). The goal of preventive maintenance is to maximize the useful life and to prevent the premature failure of building systems and components. The advantages and benefits of putting in place an explicit preventive maintenance program include not only the ability to extend the life and assets of the building and grounds, but also the possibility of identifying code and life safety issues before they become liability problems, reducing energy consumption before the costs of energy depletes operating funds, and maintaining a high level of environmental quality that keeps health issues from arising.

It is essential that school facilities routinely be monitored for compliance with building codes and standards. Fire codes, for example, mandate requirements regarding properly maintained means of egress, rescue and ventilation windows, emergency lighting, and fire alarm systems. The newly established suite of International Building Codes (ICC, 2003) currently being adopted in many states outlines special institutional requirements for smoke compartments, fire sprinkler systems, fire detection systems, refuge areas, smoke barriers, special egress, and other requirements. The Americans with Disabilities Act (ADA) provides accessibility standards for the physical disabled and visually and aurally impaired throughout the building, including entrances, hallways, restrooms, dining areas, and auditoriums, as well as prescribing the heights of drinking fountains, sinks, counters, and toilets. A preventive maintenance program can be used to monitor these and other potential concerns.

Preventive maintenance is the diagnostic tool of facilities management that prevents potential problems from occurring. It consists of planned maintenance procedures intended to ensure that the school operates at its proper efficiency without interruption. Maciha (2000) recommends that preventive maintenance activities be performed at regular intervals to prevent inordinate expenditures at any one time, while prolonging the useful life of each inspected element. In the same publication, *Preventive Maintenance Guidelines for School Facilities*, Maciha also provides a series of comprehensive

preventive maintenance checklists. Table 8.3 on page 196 offers a list of building elements that it is recommended be checked on a biweekly, monthly, semiannual, and annual basis, and thereafter every five years. Methods of preventive maintenance inspection can range from simple visual inspection to performance testing and analysis, from minor adjustments and cleaning to overhauls, and reconditioning to component replacement.

Determining when a particular building component should be maintained is a process of analyzing the financial impact of the failure of that component to perform against the cost of its performance. If the cost of failure exceeds the cost of replacement, then replacement of the component should be scheduled. Examples might include the potential loss of life and assets without proper maintenance of fire alarms, or the cleaning and maintenance of HVAC ductwork to prevent sick building syndrome to ensure healthy indoor air quality, both of which outweigh any expenditure for maintaining the system. From research conducted in the state of California, budgeting for preventive maintenance as a percentage of operating budgets averages 5 percent (Maciha, 2000).

Additional Forms of Facility Maintenance   In addition to preventive maintenance, Maciha (2000) describes other forms of maintenance that can be followed once a comprehensive preventive management program is institutionalized in a school district. These other more technical forms of facility maintenance are beyond the scope of this chapter. The goal of predictive maintenance, for instance, is to anticipate building failure through the use of technological detection equipment such as vibration analysis, thermography (infrared scanning), and ultrasonic testing. Corrective maintenance refers to the replacement of nonemergency, obsolete, worn, broken, or inoperative building components based on preventive maintenance inspections. Repair maintenance refers to unscheduled repair and/or adjustments of equipment or components.

TABLE 8.3   Preventive Maintenance Checklist

SCHEDULE	ITEM
Biweekly	Automatic gates/doors
	Lighting: exterior and interior
	Security systems
	Special requirements
Monthly	Alarm systems
	Fire alarm
	Water flow testing
	Doors and windows
	Gas connections
	Restrooms
	Business offices
	Kitchen and dining areas
	Classrooms
	Library
	Auditorium
	Gymnasium
	Locker rooms
	Swimming pool
	Landscape
	Asphalt
	Signage
	Track and field areas
	Playgrounds
	Tennis courts
	Exterior stairs, decks, and landings
	Maintenance carts
	Nonpower gates
	Special requirements
Semiannually	Fences
	HVAC systems
	Smoke alarms
	Structural members
	Spatial requirements
Annually	Emergency generators
	Backflow devices
	Electrical systems
	Fire extinguishers
	Hot water heaters
	Roofing
	Gutters/roof drains
	Sewer laterals
	Irrigation controllers
	Storm drains
	Special requirements
Every five years	Fire system certification
	Special requirements

Source: Adapted from Maciha (2000).

THE ROLE OF INFORMATION TECHNOLOGY IN FACILITY MANAGEMENT

The revolution in information technology has driven changes in all aspects of education and facilities planning, design, construction, and management. Computer-aided facility management systems (CAFM), computer maintenance management systems (CMMS), and Internet technologies such as Internet Maintenance Management Systems (IMMS) continue to evolve. We cannot begin to cover technology and its influence on schools here, since it is evolving so rapidly. Yet, educational administrators must be aware that information technology is driving integration between many different functions within schools.

Information technology has provided a variety of tools for facility management practices in schools. CAFM, CMMS, and IMMS programs provide interactive databases that inventory building space, furnishings, and equipment. Building automation systems give the facility manager the ability to monitor and control building systems throughout all the buildings in a district from one location. With the advent of Internet technology and telecommunications systems, building systems can be monitored from any location in the district. The Internet has rapidly brought together isolated markets, making it possible for administrators to purchase supplies as well as specialized services. The complete integration of instructional technologies with building system technologies, security systems, and telecommunication systems is just around the corner. What these systems will look like and the impact this integration may have on education and school facilities are not completely known, but what is known is that information technology has yielded a whole host of tools to increase the efficiency and effectiveness of the facility maintenance and management of schools.

Computer-Aided Facility Management (CAFM)

As early as the mid-1980s, computerized facility management systems offered new opportunities for schools to reduce costs and increase the efficiency of operations (Magee, 1988). Computer systems were, in effect, able to represent an automation of all management programs and activities. Computer programs developed in the 1980s provided relational databases that linked building floor plan maps, furnishings and equipment inventories, maintenance work plans and schedules, as well as estimates of replacement costs. More recent CAFM programs incorporate more dynamic elements into the database including the ability to gather data directly through the monitoring of building systems in operation. The typical CAFM program offers an integrated documentation, analysis, and reporting of all planned and unplanned work order processes. The ordering of supplies can be tracked, as well, through the computer. As work activities are completed and documented, data describing completion dates, work hours, materials and supplies ordered, and other expenditures provide a maintenance history for the facility (Magee, 1988, p. 205). The long-term documentation of maintenance practice and costs provides the ability to more accurately identify trends and forecast future maintenance costs. These same functions of computer programs can be extended to equipment and furnishings inventory within the facility.

In only the last few years, IMMS have begun to challenge the CMMS model for maintenance management and the management of facility and work requests, approvals, and assignments. CMMS provides a stand-alone computer system for managing facilities operations that offers an independent, customized solution for a district, but requires support service agreements with computer software companies. IMMS, in contrast, provides 24-7 online service support to school districts a real advantage to districts that do not have the capability to manage their own servers or software. All that is required is access to a Web browser and training in the use of the IMMS system. All employees as well as customers (teachers and administrators) can have access to the system for real-time management of work requests and work orders. IMMS arguably reduces the total cost of ownership by handling back-of-house functions required of CMMS. In addition, IMMS can offer an integrated community of peers in the school maintenance field to exchange best-practice knowledge.

Building Automation Systems

The promise of computerized control of building systems has been around since the 1970s and earlier. The development of energy management systems (EMS) and building automation systems (BAS) that are connected to heating, ventilating, and air-conditioning (HVAC) systems to control and regulate temperatures consistent with occupancy and use has advanced considerably since then. Many existing schools do not possess these systems, but schools being designed and constructed now and in the future will.

Much of the drive for automating systems comes from the realities of energy consumption; it is estimated that K–12 schools spend more than $6 billion a year on energy (Kennedy, 2001). Systems of automating energy consumption are an invaluable tool in reducing the costs of energy. More efficient energy management systems could greatly reduce that number if alternatives such as solar and geothermal power, behavioral changes such as turning off unused lights, or designs that incorporate the use of more daylight to illuminate a school were utilized. This is not a new concept: The energy conservation movement began in the 1970s. However, automating energy management systems has the potential to finally realize the savings promised by these alternatives.

A BAS, also known as a building management control system (BCMS), links microprocessor-controlled building functions including heating, ventilating, and air conditioning (HVAC); lighting; elevators; security devices (cameras, card readers, alarms); and fire alarms, smoke sensors, and other fire-protection devices. In the latest, best-designed intelligent building systems, all the component systems share a common wiring/cabling infrastructure. This infrastructure is often referred to as a backbone (Beaudin, Costa, & Giustino, 1998).

Since the mid-1990s the number of school facilities that use integrated intelligent building systems has grown. More new school buildings are being designed to incorporate structured wiring systems that integrate building automation, energy management, and fire alarm and security functions. The advantages of integrated intelligent building systems include declines in the first costs associated with integrated intelligent systems, long-term savings in energy use and maintenance costs that the systems have produced, and the improved window-based user-friendliness of user interfaces. Centralized control of building systems also allows for control to be portable. A system manager can control from any point in the network, including a laptop anywhere in the district, allowing remote diagnosis of problems as they develop (Beaudin, Costa, & Giustino, 1998).

Role of Internet in Facility Operations

One leading textbook on facility management in business, published in 1995, did not even mention the Internet or the World Wide Web in its definitive statement on trends in facility management (Rondeau, Brown, & Lapides, 1995). The radically rapid and unanticipated change brought about by the Internet and electronic commerce impacting all facets of society, educational delivery, and facility management cannot be overstated. Undoubtedly, many more unanticipated changes can be expected.

The Internet has brought together isolated markets for administrators who are responsible for buying supplies and equipment. Purchasing officials for schools are able to search the Internet and find numerous websites organized specifically for the education market—some are new businesses created online; others are long-standing vendors who have begun to enter e-commerce. Most of these online businesses are in their infancy, but if they perform as promised, they can provide great benefits to budget-conscious schools and universities: More options, better prices, speedier delivery,

TABLE 8.4   Web-Based Procurement Systems

DemandStar.com (http://www.demandstar.com) gives schools the ability to post requests for proposals, invitations to bid, and quotes online. Registered vendors are notified of bid opportunities.

Epylon.com (http://epylon.com) is an e-commerce site for buyers and suppliers in the education and government markets. Provides a catalog of products, supplier and product reviews, online bidding, contract management, and order tracking.

Eschoolmall.com (http://eschoolmall.com) is an online procurement system serving schools and vendors, providing complete electronic procurement, bidding, contract management.

KawamaCommerce.com (http://kawamacommerce.com) provides an electronic purchasing solution for schools, school districts, buying cooperatives, and suppliers endorsed by the American Association of School Administrators and currently doing business with school districts in Florida, Illinois, Missouri, Pennsylvania, and Tennesee.

SchoolDude.com (http://schooldude.com), a members-only Web site, is the online home for school facility, maintenance, and operations professionals. The site connects school facility professionals to each other to solve problems, share best practices, and improve the nation's learning environments. Includes tools for work management, information, and resources as well as online procurement of equipment and school supplies.

Source: Adapted from NCEF at http://www.edfacilities.org/rl/ecommerce.cfm.

and less bureaucracy streamline the process (Kennedy, 2000). At present, bidding and purchasing regulations, which vary from state to state, as well as auditing practices, may prevent districts from taking advantage of all the efficiencies Web-based procurement can offer.

Many companies offer online construction management systems. Some provide software that enables a school or university to set up a website on its computers, while other companies host the website on their own computers. Although it is too soon to state with certainty, construction industry observers believe online management could save billions of dollars. With construction and renovation in the education industry continuing to thrive, using the World Wide Web to manage projects could help schools and universities squeeze more out of their construction budgets.

Those with a stake in education construction projects—architects, contractors, subcontractors, suppliers, and school officials—have had to contend with increasingly complex communication systems, such as voicemail, faxes, and overnight deliveries. A Web-based program provides a highly efficient repository for all the data relevant to the construction process (Kennedy, 2000).

Some websites (see Table 8.4) provide schools and other public agencies with the ability to post requests for proposals, invitations to bid and quotes, event information, and product reviews. Others provide one-stop shopping by aggregating thousands of catalog products online, acting as a resource center for school facility professionals to reach vendors and obtain better prices for equipment and supplies. The entire procurement process can be executed online, from cataloging and requisitioning to paying and reconciling the budget.

OUTSOURCING FACILITY MANAGEMENT SERVICES

Up until now, this chapter has implicitly presented the form and structure of conventional in-house facility management services. However, outsourcing, contracting for various facility management services with outside contractors, has become increasingly popular in many school districts due to the impact of shrinking operational budgets on the facility management function in schools. More school districts also are contracting out maintenance and operations to private firms. Approximately 19 percent of school districts report that they contract out building maintenance and operations services, while 20 percent use privatized grounds services up from the previous year (Agron, 2005).

Outsourcing is a management innovation that emerged in the 1980s to decrease the costs of maintenance and operations on the organization. School district leaders were attracted to outsourcing as a strategy for effectively managing their school support services, such as custodial, grounds, crossing guards, lunchroom and playground monitors, other supervision services, intra-school mail delivery, warehouse operations, mail distribution, print shop, and before- and after-school child care programs.

Some schools began outsourcing their food service as long as fifty years ago. Today, it is a more common practice among smaller (2,500–4,000 students) and mid-sized (4,000–10,000 students) districts. Yet the numbers are growing nationwide among all sizes of school districts. Nationally, 15 percent of districts currently outsource school food service, with an additional 9 percent indicating that their districts expect to rely more heavily on outsourcing in the near future (Haertsch, 1999).

Haertsch argues that the advantages of outsourcing are that it provides a potential strategy for managing facilities to more effectively meet goals for district efficiency as well as meeting higher expectations of students and teachers. Outsourcing also provides a way for school leaders to regain their focus on the core mission of the school. Managed service companies can offer economies of scale not available to smaller school districts. The best managed service firms have experts in marketing and merchandising, facilities planning and design, purchasing and distribution, and training and development. In addition, outsourcing companies can offer employees more opportunities for career growth and professional training than those available through the school district. Service companies have responded more effectively to demand and expectations by offering additional services such as child care and educational programs for before and after school. In addition, it is argued that service companies are better able to respond to student demand for more sophisticated food services like food courts while continuing to deliver nutritional options (Haertsch, 1999).

What should decision makers look for if their district is considering outsourcing? Haertsch (1999) provides a few tips: Look for a company that will be a real partner; examine the firm's track record; learn how they treat their employees; consider community relations; cost is important, but do not make it the number one priority; and finally, challenge the school support services company to customize a program that meets your unique needs.

FACILITY MANAGEMENT AND ORGANIZATIONAL CHANGE

Facility management conventionally emphasizes the maintenance and operations of the school facility. However, there are equally critical organizational issues that dovetail with the management function of the facility professional who, at the school site, is often the principal or assistant principal. The facility itself, as we have discussed in earlier chapters, provides a vehicle or stage effecting not only the educational process, but aspects of school climate and culture as well. Facility managers need to have an understanding of the informal facility management that takes place daily in school buildings.

Invisible to the public eye, for years public schools across the country have had to, as they say, "make the best out of what they have" with their facilities. Many schools have been creative in efforts to maintain and improve the environmental qualities of their schools by informally changing their environment, sometimes in spite of centralized facility maintenance programs put in place by the "main office." As school organizations continue to change, buildings must be eminently manageable in accommodating these changes. Flexible school designs capture only half of the solution. Management strategies should be articulated in which the realities of managing organizational change are emphasized, not just the physical building systems in schools.

The site-based management reform movement provides an opportunity for schools to take control of the management of their facilities. This is an aspect of the role of school leaders that is "often neglected but where they can make a significant contribution to the life of the institution . . . in so far as they lead to greater job satisfaction and better running of the establishment they can be welcomed as contributing to the quality of schooling" (OECD, 1989, p. 122).

Facility management is perceived by educators to be as much their responsibility and the responsibility of students (Bussler, 1998) and the neighboring community, as it is the manifest responsibility of building maintenance professionals serving them. Further, facility management is perceived by educators to influence the quality of their school environment and contribute to the success of their teaching and their students' learning (Lackney, 1996).

Educators feel they, their students, and the community as a whole have, by implication, some measure of responsibility, influence, and control over qualities of the physical environment. In essence, the management of the facility, of the school as a place, is the responsibility of everyone, not just facility managers. The character and spirit of classrooms, corridors, and cafeterias are made and remade every fall and spring with new signs, pictures, and decorations that provide the appropriate mood. Teachers continuously reinvent their classrooms each year, attempting to solve small furniture arrangement problems they could not resolve the year before.

Yet, unfortunately, some teachers lack adequate knowledge about how to effectively utilize, maintain, and manage classroom space to support their instructional efforts. Open instructional areas are perceived as being too distracting and noisy, while some self-contained classrooms are seen as too constraining. In addition, although teachers do not have a strong sense of control over building functionality and crowding/spaciousness, they expect their school administrators to address these issues through educational policy.

There is growing pressure from educators indicating that administrators are addressing few factors beyond basic facility management and maintenance services. Educators insist that school facilities must be managed to support educational program needs as well. Beyond the recognized reduction of classroom size to twenty-five or fewer students, beyond the standard and critical maintenance services of custodians, and beyond constant shuffling of desks and tables by classroom teachers, are more complex problems of facilities that simply do not effectively support the educational programs contained within them.

How can schools collectively address problems of managing open plan instructional areas with all the visual and acoustic distractions accompaning them? How can schools collectively address problems associated with effectively laying out both open space and self-contained classrooms for cooperative learning and other instructional strategies? How will schools interested in increasing the range of community services accommodate these services adequately without adversely affecting their traditional educational program activities? How do schools create smaller learning communities in facilities designed to serve thousands of students? These are questions that require a collaborative effort to integrate the knowledge of educators and school administrators, facility managers, and community organizations and agencies. How can this be accomplished?

First, educators need to become more aware of the potentials and opportunities the physical setting presents to them—they must become environmentally competent "placemakers." Educators, through reflective practice, and in-service and professional development, need to learn more about how to structure physical classroom settings to meet their instructional goals and activities.

Second, facility managers should become more cognizant of the role the physical environment plays in supporting the educational process. Problems of classroom adaptability and building functionality can be solved through a core competency of space planning: a competency well established in other building types such as office facility management. Either Departments of Facilities must take the lead in providing this type of service, or local schools, through their school improvement and site-based management teams, must develop or obtain this competency if they are to solve some of the intractable problems classroom teachers have lived with since educational philosophies first began their rapid change in the 1960s.

MAINTENANCE AND OPERATIONS AT THE SCHOOL SITE

Keeping in mind that job responsibilities for custodians and maintenance professionals vary significantly from district to district, in the year 2000, the amount of square feet maintained by a single custodian averaged little more than 21,000 square feet, while the average square feet maintained by a maintenance worker ranged from 87,000 to 93,000 square feet, and the acreage maintained by a single grounds worker was just over 40 acres (Agron, 2005). Median salaries for custodial, maintenance, and grounds personnel can also vary, but on average custodial salaries in the year 2000 stood at $22,574, while maintenance salaries were at $27,942, and salaries for grounds personnel average $23,100 (Agron, 2000). This area should be studied from the standpoint of improving the quality of service provided. Perhaps job titles should be realigned with function.

Depending on the degree of severity of the maintenance problem, the skill level of the custodian, and the degree of urgency in solving the problem, a maintenance item may become the responsibility of central office maintenance staff or be outsourced

to a private contractor. Areas where this situation might occur could include major repairs of mechanical, electrical, and/or plumbing equipment, roof leaks, painting, finished carpentry, and the replacement of broken windows.

The role of custodian is often equated with that of a janitor, and, as a result, it has come to be thought of in a pejorative manner. The word custodian means to "take custody" and implies much more than maintaining the upkeep of the building. The men and women who maintain the school building provide an important function in service of the educational process. They maintain a physical and ambient environment that is conducive to effective learning, but they also serve a vital social role as a kind of "customer service representative" for teacher concerns, as well as serving as adult role models for students they come in contact with on a daily basis.

Castaldi (1989) outlined a comprehensive list of maintenance and operational responsibilities for custodians; any or all of them may need to be performed, or required, on a daily, weekly, or periodic basis. These responsibilities will be explored in depth in the following chapter.

SUMMARY

The importance of effective school facility management over the life of a building cannot be overstated, although this topic has received much less attention in the educational administration literature than school planning. With an average building age in the United States of more than forty years and building systems and other materials requiring replacement much sooner, school facility managers, custodians, and school principals face many facility-related challenges, particularly since the amount of resources (money, staff, etc.) needed is almost always greater than what is available. The tasks of a school facilities manager are more complex than ensuring that building systems (e.g., structural, mechanical, electrical, plumbing, lighting) are in working order. The responsibilities typically include the management of the school grounds (athletic fields and parking surfaces), food services, outsourcing functions, performance-based contracting, transportation services, safety and security, reducing vandalism, and many others, all within a climate of ever-changing codes and guidelines.

Without fail, school facilities will undergo a process of obsolescence due to aging building systems and materials, and changes in demographics, space needs, technology, and pedagogy. It is important to minimize premature obsolescence by utilizing strategies in the planning stage such as making flexibility a design goal and ensuring quality construction. One of the primary problems plaguing school facilities is the practice of deferred maintenance—putting off scheduled maintenance because the funds are not available. One study indicates that billions of dollars are needed to repair and modernize schools in the United States, and another demonstrates that as many as three-quarters of school facilities need renovations, repairs, or modernization.

Facilities management has emerged as a professional discipline in recent years. Depending on the size of a school district, facilities management may have no formal place in the organization or it may be an entire department with a facilities director at the helm. An increasing number of school districts are turning to the practice of outsourcing school support services such as custodial, grounds, crossing guards, intra-school mail delivery, warehouse operations, print shop, and before- and after-school child care programs. Managed service companies may provide greater economies of scale and better opportunities for employees while meeting the needs of students more appropriately than schools performing these functions on their own.

Useful tools have emerged from the information technology domain to assist school facilities managers with tracking data such as maintenance and repair schedules, costs, inventories of furnishing and equipment, and a complete maintenance history. Building automation systems linking microprocessor-controlled building functions such as heating, ventilating, and air-conditioning; lighting; elevators; security devices; and fire alarms are currently being integrated into most new school designs. They not only provide more data and better controls, but also help reduce operation and maintenance costs. Internet maintenance management systems provide access to information such as work requests and work orders twenty-four hours a day. The Internet also provides a host of other tools, such as Web-based procurement and online construction management systems.

Regardless of the tools and personnel available, the school principal, as the direct operational supervisor of all physical plant personnel assigned to the building, cannot escape duties related to facility management. A team effort is required among principals, facilities managers, custodians, grounds keepers, food service personnel, and others to ensure that school buildings are operated and maintained to provide safe, appropriate learning environments year after year.

ACTIVITIES

1. Write a complete job posting for an available position for a facilities manager who will oversee eighteen schools in a district with a total enrollment of approximately 10,000 students. Be sure to include a job description, as well as qualifications and experience necessary, for the position.

2. Obtain organizational charts for three different types of school districts (e.g., large, small, urban, rural, etc.), within a single state. Identify those persons or divisions primarily responsible for facilities management functions. Describe similarities and differences in the organizational structure of these three school districts and how that might affect the roles of facilities management personnel.

REFERENCES

Agron, J. (April 2001). Dwindling support. 30th Annual school maintenance and operations cost study. *American School and University*, 73(8):24, 26–28, 30, 32. Also available at http://asumag.com.

Agron, J. (April 2005). Challenging times 34th Annual School Maintenance and Operations Cost Study. *American School and University*, 77(8): 45–49.

Beaudin, J. A., Costa, J. G., & Giustino, G. (October 1998). Smart schools. *American School & University*. http://asumag.com/mag/university_smart_schools/index.html.

Bussler, D. (1998). No more principals! No more custodians! *Phi Delta Kappan*, 80(4): 317–318.

Castaldi, B. (1994). *Educational facilities: Planning, modernization, and management*. Boston: Allyn and Bacon.

Edwards, M. M. (May 1991). *Building conditions, parental involvement and student achievement in the D. C. public school system*. Unpublished master's thesis, Georgetown University, Washington; DC.

Haertsch, T. (August 1999). To outsource or not to outsource? *School Planning and Management*, 38(8): 20–30.

International Code Council (2003). *International building code*. Falls Church, VA: ICC.

Iselin, D. G., & Lemer, A. C. (eds.) (1993). *The fourth dimension in buildings: Strategies for minimizing obsolescence*. Washington, DC: National Academy Press.

Johnson, S. M. (1990). *Teachers at work*. New York: HarperCollins.

Kennedy, M. (July 2000). The road to e-commerce. *American School & University*, 72(11): 14–16, 18. Also available at http://asumag.com/ar/university_road_ecommerce/index.htm.

Kennedy, M. (2001). The top ten issues impacting school administrators. *American School & University*, 73(5): 19–22.

Kennedy, M., & Agron, J. (2004). No buildings left behind. *American School & University*, 76(7): 47–51.

Kowalski, T. J. (1989). *Planning and managing school facilities*. New York: Praeger.

Lackney, J. A. (1996). *Quality in school environments: A multiple case study of environmental quality assessment in five elementary schools in the Baltimore City Public Schools from an action research perspective*. UMI Dissertation Services No. 9717142, School of Architecture and Urban Planning, University of Wisconsin-Milwaukee.

Maciha, J. C. (2000). *Preventive maintenance guidelines for school facilities*. Kingston, MA: RS Means.

Magee, G. H. (1988). *Facilities maintenance management*. Kingston, MA: RS Means.

National Center for Educational Statistics (June 2000). *Condition of America's public school facilities: 1999*. Washington, DC: Report NCES 2000-032.

Organization of Economic Cooperation and Development (1989). *Schools and quality: An international report*. Paris: OECD.

Ortiz, L. (December 17, 1993). Judge: We'll fix schools ourselves: Board of education bypassed on repairs. *Chicago Sun-Times*, pp. 1, 20.

Poston, W. K., Stone, M. P., & Muther, C. (1992). *Making schools work: Practical management of support operations*, Vol. 7. F. W. English (series ed.), Guidebooks to Effective Educational Leadership. Newbury Park, CA: Corwin.

Rondeau, E. P., Brown, R. K., & Lapides, P. D. (1995). *Facility management*. New York: John Wiley.

Slater, J. J. (December 16, 1992). Remembrance of things past. *Education Week*, 26. Available at www.edweek.org/ew/articles/1992/2/16/15slater.h12.html.

Strahle, J. (2004). Mending your ways. *American School & University*, 76(7): 47–51.

U.S. General Accounting Office (February 1995). *School facilities: Condition of America's Schools*. Washington, DC: GAO.

CHAPTER NINE

MAINTENANCE AND OPERATIONS OF THE SCHOOL FACILITY

The Role of the Principal

Facility management responsibilities are typically shared between the district and building site. This section introduces the role of principal in facility management. School administrators often have a vision of the ideal place for learning. The vision and reality, however, often do not coincide. The challenge is to make the reality of the school congruent with the ideal vision of the place for learning (Poston, Stone, & Muther, 1992). It is the responsibility of the administrator to set standards for the care and upkeep of facilities and resources. School facilities must be cleaned, protected, preventively maintained, operated, repaired, and environmentally regulated. It is at this level that many administrators begin their efforts to improve the quality of the learning environment.

In a study of the impact of facility management in schools on the educational process, Lackney (1996) asked a principal to describe in her own words how she perceived her role in managing the school facility: "I deal with facility management issues more than I want. I don't want to talk about panic bars, to me that's not exciting, but I know it's in my purview. But, I'd like it to be dealt with and be gone so that our focus can be just on academics. So, I'm not happy when I have to make a case about something we expect to be working and it's not working" (p. 207).

This principal estimated that her attention to facility management issues may have accounted for as much as 10 to 15 percent of her workload.

The school principal is the key person in the school district responsible for the operation and maintenance of the school building to which he or she is assigned. The principal is the direct operational supervisor of all physical plant personnel assigned to the building. In some districts, the custodian has a dual administrative responsibility. The custodian will typically report to the school principal for all functional matters associated with the operation and maintenance of the assigned school building, such as cleaning schedules for instructional space. Simultaneously, the custodian is accountable to central administration for all technical matters related to his or her work responsibilities, such as the procedures for cleaning or the cleaning agents to be used.

In the daily operation of a school building, the principal can reasonably expect that the custodian will have a general knowledge of the principles of heating, ventilating, sanitation, and care of school buildings, as well as the skill to correctly operate the mechanical equipment of the school. In addition, the custodian should have knowledge of the best tools, materials, cleaning agents, and methods for custodial work and the skills to carry out his or her tasks efficiently under a variety of conditions. The principal should expect the custodian to possess a demeanor that makes possible harmonious cooperation with students and with the administrative, educational, and other custodial staff. The principal should also expect the custodian to have a personal philosophy of what good custodial service entails, and an appreciation of cleanliness and the importance of custodial service to both the educational objectives of the school and the protection of school property (Harrison, 1973).

Conversely, the principal is required to know a great deal about the physical environment and its connection to the maintenance of his or her particular school, as well as the policies, procedures, and plans that give structure to maintenance work through the school district. Principals need to have a record of personal information for their custodial staff, including contact information for, the skill sets of, and work assignments of each custodian (Kowalski, 1989).

Since the role of the school principal is vital in the school planning and development process, it is important to compile some special information that he or she should consider, even as the design and construction of the school are being completed. Especially during the construction phase of a new school, the principal should have access to every detail of the building to ensure improved operations once the school is opened. This chapter, although focused on a school that is in operation, should influence the principal working in the planning phase of school development and help him or her to acquire an in-depth understanding of the relationships among maintenance and operations and student outcomes. Maintenance begins in the planning phase of all educational facilities—this fact should ensure the principal's position on the planning team and the monitoring of construction.

While the persistent need for maintenance and operation of the school facility may seem obvious to many seasoned planners and architects, it is important to understand that numerous school principals have spent their entire professional life in school as a student, teacher, or assistant princi-

pal. Most principals have limited awareness of the wide array of complexities surrounding the school's need for custodial care and maintenance. The majority of educational leadership or educational administration training programs do not provide substantial information for the school principal regarding school maintenance and its relationship to the school custodian. Given this problem, the school principal is urged to read about "planning for facilities maintenance" (U.S. Department of Education, National Center for Education Statistics, National Forum on Education Statistics, 2003, pp. 13–23). In addition to this work and the Internet references it contains, the information offered in this chapter should help raise awareness and provide information to assist the principal with this vital component of the school system's maintenance and operations (M&O) program. Emphasis is focused on the physical learning environment as a contributing factor in student outcomes. Where students learn does make a difference in their attitudes, behavior, and cognition.

ORGANIZATION AND MANAGEMENT OF M&O

In most school systems the custodial care and maintenance programs are organized under the assistant superintendent for business services (Johnson, 2000). If the school system is small, there may be a supervisor of school facilities who has direct authority over the head school custodian. In larger school systems there may be a foreman in the line of authority between the supervisor and the head school custodian. Given either organizational structure, the head custodian has responsibility for the other custodians in the school. Johnson (2000) noted that one factor which has not changed throughout the years is the dual responsibility of the custodian. That is, the head custodian reports to the supervisor or foreman and also to the school principal.

> Custodians have distinct responsibilities within a school over which the building principal must exercise control. At the district level, it is impor-

tant that custodial responsibilities be coordinated to provide comparable work schedules, duties, responsibilities, salaries and benefits. The lines of communication within the custodial staff will normally be through the head custodian (or someone with a similar title); through the principal or his/her designee for day to day direction of activities; and through the supervisor of custodial services for the total job responsibilities and expectations on a system-wide basis. (Johnson, 2000, p. 2)

What is obvious in most school district organizational charts is that the school principal does not have direct formal authority over school custodians. This may put him or her in a difficult position if the school is not being maintained satisfactorily. The question is, therefore, should the principal have direct "line" control over the duties of custodians who work in his or her school?

Whether or not the school principal should have responsibility for the management of the custodial program is a function of policy. Those principals who do not have direct responsibility over custodians must somehow work with the school district or a private company delivering custodial services to provide students and teachers alike with a safe, clean, healthy, and comfortable environment. The Association of School Business Officials (1981) has stated, "Custodians have distinct responsibilities within a school over which the building's principal must exercise control. It is equally obvious that all duties of custodians must be controlled at the system level by the supervisor of custodial services or his designee (foreman or similar title)" (p. 1). According to Davis (1973), it is imperative for the principal to understand the lines of authority for supervisory control of custodial personnel. Policies must be established that stipulate the extent of control that the principal has regarding custodial personnel in the school building and on the school grounds. This is important because without clear policy, the principal and custodial staff will be confused about work assignments and routine M&O.

Most principals express the view that it is essential for them to have immediate supervision

authority over custodial employees in their schools. This type of power base, however, can come into conflict with the practice of giving direct authority over custodians to the district-level supervisor of custodial services. An organization operating under this structure appears to always be in a position for miscommunication. Consequently, this may explain why so many schools in the United States are in poor repair. When a problem arises with custodial services concerning productivity, the custodians can easily point to the principal and central office management. Perhaps a more effective organizational structure is the one depicted in Figure 9.1 on page 208.

In reviewing this structure, the assumption must be made that the school facility is part of teaching and student learning. Under traditional educational policy, the school facility, its maintenance, and custodial services appear to be disjoint from teaching and learning. We suggest that custodial services and maintenance, just like the entire school environment, should be considered, part of the educational program because where students learn is an important part of instruction. Those in business and facilities services at the district level might view this as a challenge to their authority. However, we recommend that the school principal have the authority and power to keep the school's physical environment clean, healthy, safe, and beautiful. Custodial activities may then be viewed as an extension of teaching and learning, not business and facilities services—an office and group of people sometimes far, far away from the actual place where students learn. The business management function, given this suggested structure, might focus on the quality of work through audits and the distribution of supplies and equipment. It might also develop and suggest work schedules and manage payroll and benefits. Hence, under our suggested organizational arrangement, business services could assume a role similar to the one it already performs for teachers.

A clean and attractive school does not just happen. High-quality custodial services require planning and scheduling workloads among the

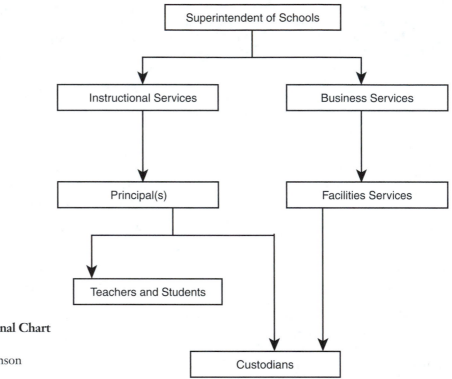

FIGURE 9.1   Organizational Chart for Custodial Services

Source: Modified from Johnson (2003, p. 3).

custodial staff, and an adequate budget administered by business services. Professional contractors may provide custodial services, but whether services are provided from within the school system or by a professional service, the principal must have a working knowledge of operations (see also Chapter 8). In fact, he or she should have general knowledge of school custodial services and be prepared to implement the actions presented in the checklist shown in Table 9.1.

School custodial care and maintenance often rank too low on the list of the school principal's job responsibilities. This may be another reason why so many schools across the United States have high maintenance costs and why so many unkempt and unattractive schools may be found. The list of items a principal should know about or know how to do applies even if the custodial services are contracted out to commercial professional services. If this is

the case, the principal should observe, for example, the demonstration of concern for the welfare and work of the custodian. This activity fosters good human and public relations, and benefits the school by enhancing a positive organizational climate whether services are totally or partially outsourced, or not contracted out at all.

As Black and English (1986) noted, "Next to secretaries, custodians are about the most valuable support people in the school" (p. 226). Sometimes called "janitors or maintenance engineers," they can be observed "sweeping, cleaning, polishing, digging, fixing, spraying, carrying, moving all kinds of objects, dusting, dumping trash cans, brushing, scrubbing, painting, replacing broken this and that, and interacting with the staff and kids" (p. 226). Black and English pointed out that custodians are not lowly workers, but people. The best custodians run their schools as if the entryway to the school

TABLE 9.1   Checklist of Forty Skills: What the School Principal Should Know about School Custodial Services and Be Prepared to Implement

1. Plan and budget for maintenance and cleaning.
2. Break down costs, including personnel, equipment, and supplies.
3. Analyze custodial time/costs by area of the school.
4. Compare time/costs among schools to determine effectiveness and efficiency of operations.
5. Audit work procedures and performance—corners and edges, streaks and residue, dust buildup, and neglect.
6. Audit problem areas—corridors, offices, conference rooms, laboratories, cafeteria, and classrooms.
7. Control consumption of cleaning supplies and materials.
8. Standardize supplies and materials.
9. Implement time standards for various jobs.
10. Keep custodians on custodial tasks.
11. Schedule times for various cleaning jobs—daily, weekly, monthly, and annually.
12. Establish standards for cleanliness of all areas of the school.
13. Develop and implement instructions for various cleaning tasks.
14. Form and explain lines of authority among the custodial staff regarding work for school building personnel.
15. Determine which time of the day or week is best for certain cleaning jobs.
16. Work in harmony with a unionized labor force.
17. Work with persons contracting special custodial services.
18. Help to coordinate in-service training programs for custodians.
19. Supervise the stocking of supplies and equipment.
20. Set up, take down, and store cafeteria tables and bleachers.
21. Implement snow and ice removal procedures.
22. Maintain checklist for receipt of supplies and materials.
23. Conduct safety checks on mechanical equipment and boilers.
24. Conduct fire extinguisher inspections.
25. Stock items for food services.
26. Prepare reports to the district office concerning custodial services.
27. Manage complaints about maintenance and custodial services.
28. Keep inventory of supplies, materials, and equipment.
29. Monitor the care of equipment after use.
30. Provide literature to the custodians concerning housekeeping and maintenance.
31. Review maintenance practices for safety concerns.
32. Arrange demonstrations of products by suppliers.
33. Involve custodians when plans are being made for new construction.
34. Ensure that a healthy and qualified custodial staff is employed.
35. Provide training for workers beginning work in a new building.
36. Provide regular training programs for the custodial staff.
37. Assist the custodian in understanding assignments and responsibilities.
38. Facilitate computerized maintenance management systems.
39. Reward suggestions for the improvement of the delivery of custodial services.
40. Demonstrate concerns for the welfare of and appreciation for the work of the custodial staff.

Source: Modified from Davis (1973, pp. 107–109).

was their own living room, and finding a bit of graffiti in the bathroom is a personal insult.

> Custodians we know who make a difference know the kids and the teachers. They go out of their way to help teachers build and maintain a safe environment for kids. They fix things. Classrooms are always spotless. Spilled paint, grease, ink, paste, and chemicals are gone overnight. Those kinds of custodians are always busy. . . . The key person who works with the custodians is the chief custodian. Chief custodians can make things happen that no one else can. They can be human magicians in a school. They can also block things from happening. They can be whiners and moaners who are never around when you need them. They find a thousand reasons why the room was not set up for the Curriculum Council, why the gum was left on the hardwood floor, why burned out light bulbs are not replaced, why there is no toilet paper in the bathroom stalls, and why the place looks filthy and unkempt. (p. 227)

Black and English also noted that if the chief custodian is not attending to custodial needs, then the principal will not be able to make much else happen in the school. They contend that a rundown school is an advertisement for an ineffective one. "It doesn't matter if anything else is happening, the stain of the mess leaves a bad impression on anyone entering it" (p. 228). They also advise principals to take careful stock of the chief custodian. "If he is incompetent and can't change or won't change, he's got to go. If he is a blocker, a person who always finds a reason why it can't be done, and he can't change or won't change, he's got to go" (p. 228).

It is the job of the school principal to convey the message to the chief custodian that the way the school looks is not only the responsibility of the students and teachers, but also the custodian's responsibility. The school principal who does not recognize that the custodial staff is important "is not going very far in the business. These are the 'little' 'big people' who make the schools effective or ineffective" (Black & English, 1986, p. 228).

Black and English summarized their contentions about custodians and principals in this way:

- The real basics are always custodial.
- The best custodians run your school like it was their own home.
- When a student gets sick in the hall, slops ink on the walls, whom do we call? *The grime busters!*
- The chief custodian is *your chief* or there are too many chiefs in your school.
- Ineffective custodians work for administrative wimps.
- If you can't keep the school clean, chances are you are not able to improve learning in it either; so who needs you? (p. 229)

VARIABLES AFFECTING THE QUALITY OF M&O

Maintenance and operation of the school's environment are logical continuations of planning, design, and construction activities. They may be viewed as the systematic upkeep of schools to ensure safe, secure, clean, healthy, and beautiful places for students to learn. Safety and security are direct functions of design, and proper custodial care and maintenance can also enhance these vital environmental components. People completing well-designed schools have kept safety and security as top priorities in the planning and design phases of development. For example, it is logical that we should start the school facilities development process with confidence that the site is in a safe location. A safe location enhances security and influences exactly how secure the students and educators are, and how they consequently feel about safety and security. We all know the reasons for not locating a school in or near high-density air traffic and ground traffic areas, major air pollution areas, and waste dumps. We should abide by these basic common-sense directives. What may be less obvious is how other aspects of school design influence the safety and security of the students and educators who work there. Key to safety and security are the overcrowding and density of the school population per building and site.

Crowding and School Capacity

Crowding and density are factors in safety and security—more than adequate space per student is an important consideration when focusing on the amount of space needed for learning and instruction. However, these spaces must be maintained and also they should be kept clean. The crowding of too many students into places and spaces designed for learning increases the chances of structural abuse, furniture abuse, mechanical overload, increased behavioral problems, and lower student achievement. Crowding is a direct function of growth and school capacity, while capacity is the result of planning and design. The capacity of a building changes with a significant alteration in the curriculum, even though the physical facilities remain unchanged. Our concepts of school buildings influence estimates of the number of students who may be adequately housed. For example,

> If a school building is looked upon as just a shelter from the weather, many youngsters can be placed within a given space before it is over capacity. On the other hand, if a fundamental purpose is to facilitate the instructional process, the number of pupils who can be placed within a given space without crowding will be different. The school building surrounds the pupils and teachers for a purpose. Crowding interferes with the realization of this purpose. The educational program has an important bearing upon the measurement of the pupil capacity of a building. (Davis, 1973, p. 95)

Sufficiency of space is judged by many variables, and among the most important are curriculum functions and the multicultural composition of the students and teachers. We do not know exactly how much space is needed given these critical variables. Our current standards for the places needed for student learning were established for, and most

often by, white middle-class individuals without information pertaining to territoriality, or the personal and social distance characteristics of other cultures (Tanner, 2000). Crowding and density issues should undergo some rigorous scientific research to ensure that all students are allowed enough personal and social space for learning.

Capacity represents the largest number of students who can be instructed in a school building without curtailing the desired educational program, according to Castaldi (1994). Yet, what we know about capacity should be challenged through research because there are some subjective variables included in original capacity formulae that need to be reconsidered, given the time in and circumstances under which they were developed. Furthermore, whether school capacity is what Castaldi (1994) called the sum of the capacity of the individual spaces multiplied by a student station utilization factor of 0.80 for secondary schools and 0.90 for elementary schools is not known—it has only been assumed that these percentages are correct. At best, they are supported by the idea of *best practices*, and at worst they are damaging to the planning and design of schools. When listening to the best practices argument, we must always question whose best practices and when and where they occurred.

In a substantial effort to address this issue, Conrad and coworkers (Brooks, Conrad, & Griffith, 1980, p. 60), recommended a procedure for approximating school building capacity. According to them, given that the school should be planned and designed in terms of the educational program, capacity ought to include several variables. For example, it should encompass the types of teaching stations, suitability of rooms or spaces, and size of spaces and places. Also the number of student stations, desirable average class size, room and space assignment policies, location of teacher work stations, and the nature of the educational program are extremely important in this calculation. Finally, the length of the class periods, types of schedules (block, e.g.), and areas of specialization should be considered in the formula. Conrad integrated these variables in the following formula:

Formula 9.1 BC = (TS × DS × T × E)/PP

The building capacity (symbolized in Formula 9.1) that can be accommodated in a given subject area is represented by BC. TS is the number of teaching stations in a given subject area, DS the desired class size in a given subject area, T the total effective periods of instruction per week in the schedule of classes, and E the average total school enrollment for one week. These variables are multiplied and divided by the total pupil periods PP of instruction per week in a particular subject area. This formula may be adjusted to various combinations of school organizations (elementary, middle, or high school). If after applying the formula across all subject areas to a given school, the number of students attending is greater than BC, then we may assume that the school is overcrowded and the density is too high. Utilization of technology and the philosophy of teaching also become variables in this complex formula. Technology may require more space, and a school leaning toward a constructivist philosophy may also require more space. *The difficulty of adequately completing all these adjustments makes this formula extremely difficult to apply in middle and high schools.* This formula should be tested in a large research project, because subject areas and the total number of effective periods per week complicate it. Once it is computerized for use in spreadsheet form, the formula may prove more user friendly. Regardless of the complications in capacity formulae, the main objective in making such a comparison is to keep classrooms within an acceptable density level for student learning.

A more straightforward formula was developed by Duncanson (2004), who explored the use of classroom space and suggested steps to create more space in existing classrooms. He also supported Tanner's (2000) contention that 49 square feet of usable space per student in a classroom is ideal. While the arguments for space needs and just

how to determine the capacity of a school are surfacing as research questions in the literature, we may employ some suggested approximations by Hawkins and Lilley (1988). Recognizing the changing needs of school curriculum, Hawkins and Lilley suggested that the use of gross square footage be applied in determining building capacity. Gross square footage is the total amount of space within the exterior walls; therefore, the capacity of a school building may be determined by dividing the total gross square footage (TGS) of the building by the accepted gross square footage per student (AGS):

Formula 9.2 Capacity = TGS/AGS

The burden of proof for researchers then becomes *what is an acceptable gross square footage per student?* Hawkins and Lilly recommended the following:

90 gross square feet per student for elementary schools

120 gross square feet per student for middle schools

145 gross square feet per student for high schools

As noted for all these methods of determining capacity, measurements should be tested with further research. Somewhere within the Conrad model, the 49 square feet of usable classroom space suggested by Tanner, and the Hawkins and Lilly model, we may be able to develop an adequate computerized procedure that will make the notion of capacity more scientific and less difficult to determine.

The expected consequences of an "overcapacity" school are a rapidly deteriorating structure resulting from overuse and the deterioration of student behavior and learning. "The consequences of high-density conditions that involve too many children or too little space are excess levels of stimulation, stress, and arousal; a drain on available resources; considerable interference; reduction in desired privacy levels; and loss of control" (Aiello,

Thompson, & Baum, 1985). If the school is determined to be overcrowded, the school principal and other school leaders should employ the suggestions of Duncanson (2004) to make more space, and organize special arrangements for the increased care of school buildings and mechanical systems, with an emphasis on safety, security, health, and beauty. Beyond the issue of M&O, the principal should also work to educate the community on hazards of high density as discussed by Wohlwill and van Vliet (1985).

Regardless of the program changes or amount of crowding that has occurred, schools and their contents deteriorate over time. But, this is a natural development, which may be prolonged through scheduled care and maintenance. We have all marveled at some well-preserved historic sites, imagining the great care and detail necessary to maintain them for such a long time. Somehow, the type of care given to these special historical sites must become part of the philosophy for school care if we are to achieve our goals for education and operate effectively and efficiently. School care begins with a positive relationship among the students, teachers, school principal, and custodial and maintenance staff.

Levels of Perceptions of Cleanliness

The level of cleanliness maintained in a school influences M&O in the long run. Cleanliness is directly tied to the design and health of the environment as well as the health of the people inhabiting and caring for it. The International Sanitary Supply Association (ISSA at http://www.issa.com/) has set standards for defining "clean," and the Association of Higher Education Facilities Officers (APPA at http://www.appa.org/) has developed classifications for "clean" ranging from spotlessness to neglect. The perceptions of health and cleanliness that the people occupying a space or building have and those responsible for the cleaning and maintenance have may differ—they usually do. There is a sliding scale among people when defining terms such as clean, healthy, safe, secure, and beautiful. We have found that the definition of these important factors of M&O is often left to the principal of the school. The underlying philosophy for M&O should be that "the school can never be too clean, safe, healthy, secure, or beautiful."

The school principal should know that organizations such as the APPA (1998) includes K–12 schools in its membership and provides educational programs, including annual meetings and conferences, an institute for facilities management, and a bimonthly magazine covering the scope of facilities management. This organization provides workshops and printed materials, including topics on energy and utilities, general administration and management, maintenance and operations, and planning, design, and construction.

Particularly of interest to school principals and other administrators are the *Custodial Staffing Guidelines for Educational Facilities* (second edition), a publication offered at the APPA website. It highlights staffing, evaluation, and staff development. Regarding staffing, the organization suggests five levels of custodial services and clarifies the work assignments necessary to maintain a certain level of cleanliness.

Cleanliness at level 1 is "orderly spotless." This is the highest level developed for the corporate suite, a donated building, or a historical focal point. Floors and base moldings shine and/or are bright and clean; colors are fresh. There is no buildup in corners or along walls. All vertical and horizontal surfaces have a freshly cleaned or polished appearance and show no accumulation of dust, dirt, marks, streaks, smudges, or fingerprints. Washroom and shower tile and fixtures gleam and are odor-free. Supplies are adequate. Trash containers and pencil sharpeners are empty, clean, and odor-free.

Level 2 is classified as "ordinary tidiness" and is only slightly lower than the top level. Level 3 is "casual inattention," reflecting the first budget cut or another staffing-related problem, and may be the top level for many schools. This level represents the lowering of normal expectations, and while not totally acceptable, the learning environments have yet to reach an unacceptable level of cleanliness. Floors are swept clean, but upon close observation, dirt and stains, as well as the buildup of dirt, dust, and/or floor finish in corners and along walls, can be seen. Dull spots are found on matted carpet in walking lanes, and streaks and splashes are observed along moldings. Dust, dirt, marks, smudges, and fingerprints are found on all vertical and horizontal surfaces. All lamps and fixtures work and are clean, while trash containers and pencil sharpeners are empty, clean, and odor-free.

The definition of level 4 is "moderate dinginess," with conditions somewhat worse that those described in level 3. For example, less than 5 percent of the lamps are burned out and fixtures are dingy. Trash containers and pencil sharpeners contain old trash and shavings. They are stained and marked, and trash containers smell sour. "Unkempt neglect" describes level 5. The facility is dirty, with cleaning accomplished at an unacceptable level. Floors and carpets are dirty and exhibit visible wear and/or pitting. Colors are faded and dingy, and there is a buildup of dust and dirt, and/or floor finishes in corners and along walls. The base molding is dirty, stained, and streaked. Gum, stains, dirt, dust balls, and trash are evident. There are major accumulations on vertical and horizontal surfaces, and it is obvious that no cleaning is done on these surfaces. Over 5 percent of the lamps are burned out and fixtures are dirty. The trashcans and pencil sharpeners overflow. They are stained and marked, and trash containers smell sour. Unfortunately, many schools in the United States approach the level of cleanliness as described in level 5.

The principal of a school and custodial manager may need help in achieving high cleanliness levels. If this is the case, then professional organizations such as APPA (1998) and the Association of School Business Officials (ASBO) can provide suggestions for staffing levels, materials, training, equipment, and supplies needed to reach an acceptable level. This usually entails providing information about such variables as age of the buildings, square footage, and the number of students using certain spaces on a daily and weekly basis.

Milshtein (1998) presented a case that utilized APPA's techniques. Through his association with the APPA organization, Kerry Leider, Director of Facilities, Duluth Public Schools developed a formula to solve some major custodial problems. The Duluth school principals and custodians faced the primary issue of "how clean is clean" regularly. After receiving a number of requests to assist with custodial problems in the midst of budget cuts, Leider developed a way to measure the impact of losing custodial staff. His formula was based on the question: What is clean? First, the issue of average time required to clean a space acceptably was determined through some internal studies. These were compared to national standards before settling on a specific time for a specific cleaning assignment. Obviously, it was found that different areas require different amounts of time to clean. While the square footage of a space remained an apparent consideration, materials also constituted another variable. For example, a stone hallway took considerably less time to clean adequately than a carpet-covered one. Wall coverings, furniture, and windows were other variables.

The square footage and its materials were documented on a computer-assisted design (CAD) program having blueprints for all the schools. This created a database for individual spaces, including floor and wall coverings, furniture, and other objects that would affect the amount of cleaning time. This procedure yielded exact information on how long it should take to clean one square unit of any specific area in a school. Next, the question of how often to clean was addressed. Frequency of cleaning depended on the nature of the activities taking place within certain spaces and places. Milshtein (1998) noted that a classroom housing preschoolers would obviously need more frequent cleaning than a high school English class. Furthermore, middle and high school corridors, because of constant foot traffic, would need cleaning several times a day, while primary and elementary school hallways would not require as much attention because they are not used as pathways in the upper schools.

Armed with the qualitative and quantitative information described above, the formula determined by Leider was straightforward:

Formula 9.3 (The average time to clean one square foot) × (square footage) × (frequency) = cleaning time

According to Milshtein (1998), a middle school corridor, made of vinyl composition tile, took 0.005 minutes per square foot to clean. With an area of 4,500 square feet, according to this formula, it should take a custodian 22.5 minutes to clean 4,500 square feet (4,500 × 0.005). Furthermore, if this space needed to be cleaned two times a day, the hallway would require 45 minutes (22.5 × 2) of a custodian's time per day. If spaces need to be cleaned every other day, then a multiple of 0.5 should be used. It is important to consider that it takes time for the custodian to assemble supplies and cleaning equipment and attend to other emergency situations such as spills in the hallways. A strict schedule may be unrealistic; therefore, some flexibility should be built into the custodial workload if high cleaning standards are to be achieved.

Custodial Work Schedule and Workload

In most cases, it is the job of the school principal to assign custodians extra tasks, since no school actually runs on a lockstep schedule where custodial services are concerned. When extra tasks are assigned, the schedule begins to slip. Consequently, it is advisable to build in extra time slots in the custodian's master schedule for unexpected emergencies that happen daily in schools. Flexibility like this keeps the partnership between principals and custodians strong (Milshtein, 1998). Creating standards for cleaning and establishing "time to clean" schedules yield positive results for the custodial staff and the schools. With these expectations in place, possible disputes about work-

load and the time required to do a job are eliminated.

Table 9.2 provides a sample cleaning schedule checklist for a school. The frequency of cleaning needed for each space will vary depending on the school type (elementary, middle, or high school) and the other variables discussed in this chapter.

As noted in Table 9.2 on page 216, the custodial staff is confronted with a large number of varied tasks to be scheduled around school activities. The schedules that were reviewed prior to compiling this table recommended that toilets and gymnasiums be cleaned once daily. However, our observations lead us to recommend that activity at least twice daily to minimize odors in the toilets and to remove dirt from the floor of the gymnasium, which might cause hazards and unnecessary wear.

A defensible working schedule is based on what constitutes a proper service schedule for each custodian. Knezevich and Fowlkes (1960) noted that "determining a proper work load is one of the more difficult administrative problems in the operation of the school plant" (p. 235). They enumerated key factors found by Reeves and Ganders (1928, pp. 28–30) to influence the service load of the custodial staff (Table 9.3, page 217). It is interesting that much of this 1928 report is still valid today when developing a service load for custodians.

Work ethics of the school principal and the custodial staff also enter into the productivity equation. The classic formula for estimating custodial staffing needs, as published by Brooks, Conrad, and Griffith (1980, p. 200) and Castaldi (1994, p. 408), was first developed by Baker and Peters (1957).

Baker and Peters (1957, pp. 77–78) outlined a six-step formula for developing a custodial workload. We have made some minor modifications in the format as compared to their original presentation, but the basic formula has not been adjusted.

Step 1. Given one custodian for eight teachers, find the teacher factor:

(Number of teachers)/8 = teacher factor (TF)

TABLE 9.2   Sample Checklist for Frequency of Cleaning

SPACES	TWICE DAILY	DAILY	ALTERNATE DAYS	WEEKLY	MONTHLY	OTHER
Public areas		✔				
Classrooms		✔				
Toilets	✔					
Private offices			✔			
Public offices		✔				
Sidewalks				✔		
Gymnasium	✔					
Showers		✔				
Locker-rooms		✔				
Windows (outside)						✔
Windows (inside)					✔	
White boards		✔				
Major carpet care					✔	
Major hard floor care						✔
Elevators		✔				
Auditoriums						✔
Other						

Source: Modified from Castaldi (1994, pp. 413–419).

Step 2. Given one custodian for every 225 students, find the student factor:

(Number of students)/225 = student factor (SF)

Step 3. Given one custodian for every eleven rooms[*] to be cleaned, find the room factor:

(Number of rooms)/11 = room factor (RC)

Step 4. Given one custodian for every 15,000 square feet of usable architectural area (1,395 square meters) of building area, find the square footage factor:

(Total square footage of the building)/15,000 = square footage factor (SF)

Step 5. Given one custodian for each 2 acres of grounds, of that must be maintained find the grounds factor:

Total acres of upkeep grounds)/2 = grounds factor (GF)

Step 6. Sum the five factors and divide by 5, and add the CK factor to find the number of cleaning custodians needed. Frohreich (1987) suggested an additional factor for this timeless equation. Known as the C and/or K factor, it includes 0.1 for a cafeteria and 0.2 for a kitchen.

[*]Rooms include all classrooms, toilets, storage areas, and offices that are to be cleaned. For gymnasiums and other large rooms, use 1,000 square feet (~93 square meters) of floor space to define one room.

TABLE 9.3   Checklist of Key Factors Influencing Custodial Service Load

- Pupil behavior in the school
- Area or number of rooms in a building
- Age and physical condition of the building
- Location of the building
- Climatic conditions and type of fuel burned
- Type of building construction
- Kind of school organization—elementary, etc.
- Social background of the pupils
- Total enrollment
- Type and variety of classrooms
- Amount and kind of floor area
- Area, size, and location of windows
- Area, kind, and utilization of chalkboards (white boards*)
- Type and arrangements of desks and other furniture
- Size of site and type of playground coverings
- Area and placement of sidewalks
- Type and condition of ventilating (cooling) equipment
- Type and condition of heating equipment
- Amount and type of installation of plumbing
- Type and condition of service systems to facilitate custodial work
- Custodial shops and storerooms
- Cleaning equipment

*The items in parentheses were added to the original list.
Source: Reeves and Ganders (1928, pp. 28–30).

Formula 9.4 (correct to two decimals)
$\{(TF + SF + RC + SF + GF)/5\} + C$
$+ K =$ cleaning custodians needed

There are some possible modifications to this formula that might be made with information from a local study of custodial operations such as those provided by the Association of Higher Education Facilities Officers. For example, the standards for the number of rooms per custodian might vary from seven to twelve, depending on the neatness and values of the principal, teachers, and students. The total number of square feet per custodian might also vary from 14,000 to 20,000, depending on whether the work is performed during the day or evenings, type of cleaning equipment, or when the students are away from school. Kenezevich and Fowlkes (1960), stated that "the number of pupils per custodian range

from 125 to 350. the problem is to justify what are more or less rule-of-thumb designations" (p. 235). The key factors in the formula (8 teachers, 225 students, and 15,000 square feet) have, however, remained constant in the literature since 1957.

The question of "how long a job should take" can be answered by research findings in a local school and compared to standards for the time and frequency of each task. This becomes the basis for a custodial workload. The work schedule for custodians presented in Table 9.4 might serve as a guideline for comparison, but it does not include preparation and clean-up times.

For example, the time required to mop and rinse a 900-square foot classroom is 40 minutes. Additional time is required by the custodian to fill a water bucket, add detergent to it, place the container with the cleaning agent back on the shelf, locate the mop, and carry these materials from the custodial closet to the classroom. The time standard of 40 minutes does not include the time necessary for the custodian to return to the custodial closet, clean the mop(s), dispose of the dirty water, and rinse the buckets. (Castaldi, 1994, p. 415)

Schedule for Custodians.   It is important to schedule custodial activities in such a manner that they do not to interfere with the educational program. A rotating schedule is an issue that hinders effective supervision of custodians by the principal, but can be an effective way to get the school clean. Many school custodians work a late shift. For example, in one school building, one custodian may work from 6:00 a.m. to 2:00 p.m., another from 10:00 a.m. to 5:30 p.m., and four may work from 2:00 p.m. to 11:00 p.m. Because it is impossible for the school principal to stay at school until 11:00 p.m. nightly, the chief custodian may work this late shift and the principal must rely on him or her to supervise the rest of the custodial staff. The lesson here is that trust must be placed in the chief custodian to meet the standards for a clean school.

Harrison (1973) developed a sample daily schedule of work for three custodians that may be applicable to various school buildings (see Table 9.5 on page 220). The assumptions for the sample schedule are no more than *25 teachers*, serving no more than *600 students*, with a maximum of *35 rooms* and *45,000 square feet of usable architectural area*. The site contains *16 acres*: *6 acres* of upkeep grounds and 10 acres used for playing fields and outdoor learning that are not part of the custodial load. A cafeteria and kitchen are also part of this workload. If these data are placed into the workload formula (Formula 9.4) for determining the number of custodians needed, the results are $(3.13 + 2.67 + 3.18 + 3.00 + 3.00)/5 + 0.1 + 0.2 = 3.296$ or 3.3 (custodians). This schedule should serve as a guide for the principal to use in developing a sample custodial schedule. Although all three custodians in the example are working the same eight-hour shift, it

is more likely that at least one will begin work at 2:00 p.m. and end daily work at 11:00 p.m.

The Custodian's Qualifications and Job Description.   Competent and well-trained custodial personnel are the keys to providing top-quality housekeeping and maintenance. The typical job titles suggested by ASBO and reported by Johnson (2000) were head custodian, night foreman, custodian I, custodian II, and relief custodian. If the school system is large, there may be a position of supervisor of custodians having duties and responsibilities pertaining to production improvement, personnel relations, and efficiency.

Supervisor of Custodians.   According to the results of reviews of several public documents and advertisements for custodial positions, the typical job announcement for the supervisor of custodians includes the following.

Responsibilities.   This position reports to the school district administration and principals. The successful applicant will supervise custodians in the cleaning, care, and maintenance of school facilities (classrooms, laboratories, corridors, restrooms, offices, conference rooms, and public areas). He or she will:

- Conduct performance evaluations and inspections.
- Make commendations and recommendations for counseling or reprimand.
- Provide training and instruction; coordinate work assignments.
- Supervise the assignment of keys to other custodial personnel.
- Provide initial responses to calls from teachers and the principal.
- Plan and coordinate the activities of custodial services to support school events.
- Develop department policies and procedures.
- Evaluate the effectiveness of custodial services.
- Recommend methods for improvement/expansion of these services.

TABLE 9.4   Time Normally Required to Complete Selected Custodial Tasks*

TASK REQUIRED	FREQUENCY	TIME
a. Dusting	Daily	5 min per room
b. Sweeping	Daily	12 min per room
c. Damp mopping	As needed	23 min per room
d. Wet mop and rinse	As needed	40 min per room
e. Machine scrubbing	As needed	25 min per room
f. Machine polishing	As needed	15 min per room
g. Wet vacuum pickup	As needed	14 min per room
Servicing classroom	Daily	15 min per room
a. Removing waste paper		
b. Sweeping floor with treated mop		
c. Dusting chalk tray, window sills, etc.		
d. Closing windows and adjusting shades		
e. Adjusting temperature controls		
f. Making note of needed repairs		
Servicing men's lavatory	Daily	35 min per lavatory
Servicing women's lavatory	Daily	38 min per lavatory
Lavatory area		
a. Cleaning lavatory	Daily	1 min per fixture
b. Cleaning toilet bowl and seat	Daily	1 min per fixture
c. Cleaning urinals	Daily	2 min per fixture
d. Cleaning urinal trap	Weekly	2 min per fixture
e. Cleaning wash sink	Daily	2 min per fixture
f. Mopping toilet floors	Daily	2 min per 100 sq ft
Stairways		
a. Damp mopping	Weekly	4 min per flight
b. Sweeping	Twice daily	6 min per flight
Other		
a. Cleaning drinking fountains	Daily	1 min per fixture
b. Dusting fluorescent tubes	Monthly	12 tubes per min
c. Sweeping auditorium	Daily	15 min per 1,000 sq ft
d. Sweeping corridors	Twice daily	8 min per 1,000 sq ft
e. Sweeping gymnasium floor	Daily	5 min per sq ft
f. Washing glass	As needed	1 min per 10 sq ft
g. Buffing and reconditioning plastic-finished floors	As needed	50 min per 1,000 sq ft
h. Machine scrubbing traffic areas		
Light-soil areas	8–24 months	90 min per 1,000 sq ft
Medium-soil areas	Every 6 months	100 min per 1,000 sq ft
Heavy-soil areas	Every 3 months	110 min per 1,000 sq ft
i. Refinishing floors (waxless finish)	As needed	20 min per 1,000 sq ft

*Based on a classroom with an assumed area of 900 square feet.
Source: Castaldi, B. (1994) *Education facilities planning, modernization, and management.* Boston, MA, pp. 416–417. Used with permission of Allyn & Bacon.

TABLE 9.5 Sample Custodial Schedule

TIME	HEAD CUSTODIAN	CUSTODIAN I	CUSTODIAN II
7:00–7:30 a.m.	Raise flag. Open building. Check heating plant. Check fire bells. Check building.		
7:30–8:00 a.m.	Dust all classrooms, principal's and secretary's offices, library, and any other room to be used during the day.	Same	Same
8:00–10:00 a.m.	Sweep sidewalks. Check with office. Install glass if needed. Check heating plant. Make minor repairs.	Wash sweeping mops.	Begin dusting in corridors. Clean some inside hall glass. Sweep stairs and corridors if needed.
10:00–10:30 a.m.	**HIGH SCHOOL** Check all toilet rooms—see that all fixtures are flushed, if needed. Insure proper ventilation. Pick up paper from floor. Replenish towels, paper, and hand soap as needed. **ELEMENTARY SCHOOL** Repeat the same steps as for high school, but completed immediately following the morning recess.	Same	Same
10:30–11:00 a.m.	Check Boiler. Check with office. Walk building to check for needed repairs.	Return to dusting and cleaning in halls.	Same as helper.
11:00–12:00 p.m.	Check toilet rooms. Shake out doormats.	Lunch	Check drinking fountains and wash sinks (clean and replenish soap and towels).
12:00–1:00 p.m.	Lunch	Brush and pick up papers in corridors. Clean sweeping brooms and mops.	Lunch
1:00–1:30 p.m.	All toilet rooms—same as 10:00–10:30 Check all toilet rooms—see that all fixtures are flushed, if needed. Insure proper ventilation. Pick up paper from floor.	Same	Same

TABLE 9.5   Continued

TIME	HEAD CUSTODIAN	CUSTODIAN I	CUSTODIAN II
	Replenish towels, paper, and hand soap as needed.	Same	Same
Time 1:30–2:40 p.m.	Custodian Check drinking fountains and wash sinks. Burn (dispose of) paper and rubbish collected during day. Clean some inside door glass and any writing from walls. (In the high school, complete these steps right after noon recess.)	Helper	Maid
2:40–3:00 p.m.	Ready equipment and materials for afternoon cleaning. Give help. Take a 5-min rest period.	Same	Same
3:00–4:00 p.m.	Sweep all classrooms and halls. Clean all toilets. Mop toilet floors. Carry out trash and paper. Empty pencil sharpeners. Begin checking so entire building is checked prior to day's end. Secure building. Take down flag.	Assign individual classroom no. for same activities.	Same

Source: Adapted from Castaldi (1994).

Qualifications. One to two years of increasingly responsible experience in a supervisory capacity; providing leadership to a large staff involved in facility maintenance activities in a major complex setting; demonstrated knowledge and experience in assigning, scheduling, and evaluating the effectiveness of services; the ability to manage effectively in a bargaining unit environment, and skill in conflict resolution and grievance administration. Experience that demonstrates the ability to form cooperative working relationships; effectively communicates orally and in writing. Demonstrated competence in the use of standard PC software applications. Ability to act independently to resolve problems, meet, deadlines and ensure the continuity of operations; recognize needs and take appropriate actions; understand, interpret, apply, and convey school policies and procedures to others.

Head Custodian. Most school systems have job descriptions for this important staff position. For example, it is common to find qualifications for custodians listed as follows: "Knowledge of and skill in using materials and machinery necessary for cleaning and general repair of buildings." But, we suggest stronger criteria. For example, Wisconsin Department of Employment Relations

(2001) listed the following specific qualifications for a job comparable to ASBO's definition of a head custodian:

1. Knowledge of proper methods, materials, and equipment for a wide range of janitorial work in general, and for cleaning and preserving floors in particular.
2. A trained cleaning eye—habitual alertness is seeing and noting for necessary action unsightly, unsafe, or unsanitary conditions and other indications of needed cleaning or maintenance work wherever they occur.
3. Understanding of the interrelated needs and priorities involved in housekeeping and janitorial activities, cleaning and sanitation, safety, appearance, and the results desired by management.
4. Foresight and judgment to plan, lay out, and organize cleaning tasks, projects, and schedules so as to obtain results economically and efficiently, with the optimum balance of needed and desired results in all areas consistent with available resources.
5. Skill in promoting teamwork and cooperation among subordinates.
6. Flexibility and willingness to learn, adapt to, and apply new and changing methods, requirements, and priorities.
7. Physical ability to climb, bend, stoop, move furniture, and perform sustained physical activity.
8. Reading skill sufficient to understand a variety of written instructions regarding equipment operation and maintenance, safety rules, work standards and schedules, etc.
9. Knowledge of safety considerations and precautions necessary in housekeeping work.
10. Knowledge of the proper operation and care of floor scrubbing and polishing machines, household and industrial dry and wet-dry vacuums, power sweepers, and other mechanical equipment used in assigned housekeeping and related responsibilities.

In addition to specific qualifications such as these, the principal and/or school district administrators interview and check the references of applicants with other characteristics in the forefront. For example, the ideal custodian will also have

- No criminal record
- Excellent health and clean appearance
- Superb work ethic and a sense of responsibility
- An understanding of good sanitation practices
- Comprehend cleaning techniques
- A valid driver's license in the state of employment
- Acceptable language habits
- Good people skills and ability to work cooperatively with others
- Knowledge about school facilities operations
- A willingness to be trained or retrained, if experienced

Above all, the ideal custodian will understand and respect students and teachers. The ideal chief custodian should possess all these characteristics.

One important individual in the custodial force is the person in charge on evening and night custodial duties. Johnson (2000, pp. 12–13) outlined a job description for this individual, as follows.

Night Foreman

Function.   Under the general direction of the head custodian, the night foreman is responsible for the night operation of the physical plant.

Characteristic Duties and Responsibilities.
1. Supervises the night cleaning shift.
2. Performs cleaning duties.
3. Carries out daily and scheduled housekeeping duties as required.
4. Executes security and fire hazard checks and advises the appropriate supervisor as required of emergencies arising during his or her shift.

5. Inspects school daily to ensure that it has been cleaned to meet required standards.
6. Prepares for school rentals and acts as the board's representative to ensure that board interests and policy are safeguarded during these rentals.
7. Handles related duties as required. These may vary in different schools.

Qualifications.
1. Education: high school graduate or equivalent desirable.
2. Two years as a custodian desirable.
3. Supervisory ability.
4. Ability to communicate with persons at all levels in the school community.

Policing or Evening Shift Custodians.   The night foreman or another member of the custodial staff may perform these daily policing activities:

1. Reports to the head custodian for instructions.
2. Checks all classrooms to ensure that they are secure and windows are closed (particularly important in winter to prevent freeze-up conditions).
3. Lowers flag at sunset.
4. Checks areas periodically where rentals are being used, to ensure that all school property is protected.
5. Spot-checks the school, particularly when part-time custodians are being used, to ensure that cleaning measures up to required standards.
6. Inspects mechanical equipment before leaving to ensure that heating and ventilation systems are operating.
7. Ensures that all doors are secure before leaving.

Job descriptions are political and may vary across school systems. The job description for a Custodian I according to the ASBO (1981, p. 17) was as follows.

Function.   Under general supervision, the Custodian I assists in cleaning the physical plant, classrooms, and other areas.

Characteristic Duties and Responsibilities.
1. Performs scheduled housekeeping duties as required.
2. Assumes specific housekeeping duties as required:
   - Vacuuming and cleaning offices
   - Dust-mopping floors
   - Dusting
   - Cleaning washrooms
   - Cleaning board offices and committee rooms
   - Setting up board rooms and committee rooms as required
   - Cleaning spots on tile floors
   - Cleaning glass as required
   - Damp-mopping washrooms
3. Carries out related duties as required.

Qualifications.
1. Eighth grade education desirable
2. Some housekeeping experience

Given the complex nature of much of custodial work today, it is imperative that the school principal and school leaders understand custodial training classes are as important for the custodial staff as in-service classes are for the teachers. Larger school systems will offer training classes periodically and the principal should expect the custodial staff to attend these important sessions. For example, many school systems offer classes on issues such as hazardous chemical orientation, asbestos awareness, and procedures for preventing infectious disease.

STUDENT CARE OF THE LEARNING ENVIRONMENTS

The students attending a school could perform many custodial activities and develop a sense of ownership for their learning environments. This is not as horrible as it sounds if we assume that part of the school curriculum should be to teach values such as cleanliness, orderliness, respect, ownership, and responsibility for property. Such a change in American culture would be positive if we could persuade parents and educators to view student participation in custodial activities as components of the "values curriculum."

One example of students working to maintain and clean their school may be found at the Athens Montessori School, Athens, Georgia, a private school founded on the Montessori and constructivist philosophies. Students attending this outstanding school participate in recycling, cleaning floors, cleaning doors and windows, dusting, washing and drying cleaning cloths, and cleaning all the toilets. The toilets are conveniently located within the learning areas and are exceptionally clean and odor-free. The students perform all the custodial services at this school, and a professional custodial service cleans the school only twice weekly. This is a money-saving management practice as well as a positive learning experience.

The teachers and headmaster at Athens Montessori School find the custodial activities for students to be extremely important in the educational program. Students assume ownership of their own learning according to the Montessori method; they also take ownership of the care of their indoor and outdoor learning environments. When students take on a custodial role in their school, they learn to respect materials and property and care for things—a significant deviation from what we observe in many schools around the world.

Other public and private schools might consider establishing a values curriculum that includes the provision of custodial services by students. This move would question all the equations and formulae now in existence under the assumption that "students do nothing" and require a new approach to custodial services.

THE SCHOOL PRINCIPAL'S ROLE IN SCHOOL MAINTENANCE

According to Maciha (2000), the maintenance of school facilities is challenging, rewarding, and frustrating; above all, a disciplined maintenance program is essential for the long life of the school. "Too often the school leadership cries 'lack of funding' when the root cause is more accurately a lack of maintenance discipline. Maintenance properly addressed is a fraction of the cost of deferred maintenance" (p. 1). Immediate attention to maintenance needs is important and a school system policy of "zero tolerance" for maintenance defects is imperative. The mission of the school maintenance program should be to sustain the physical learning and play environments, ensuring future generations' enjoyment of the educational process in a setting of adequate function and physical appearance (Maciha, 2000).

School maintenance begins while the school is in the planning and design phases. Therefore, maintenance personnel should be involved in the planning and design of the school. It is in the design phase that far-sighted maintenance personnel can have the greatest impact on future maintenance costs in a school. After construction has begun, the likelihood of making changes to improve maintenance decreases. During construction, Maciha (2000) recommended that maintenance personnel should have access to the building site to view items such as conduits and piping that will be concealed once the construction has been completed. It is a sound policy to employ the school principal during the school's planning and design phase so that he or she can make frequent site visits during construction to learn about maintenance features.

Highly organized school systems, according to Kowalski (1989), distinguish between tasks that are to be performed by the school district maintenance staff and those to be performed by the school custodians. If union contracts exist, then there are usually boundaries for work assignments. This places a school principal in the position of finding out exactly what responsibilities school custodians can and cannot perform to address the needs of the school. When these union-controlled jobs are identified, the principal may work to establish differentiated assignments for custodians. For example, one custodian may be responsible for removing trash, maintaining floor surfaces, cleaning toilet floors, and ground maintenance, while another may be responsible for cleaning toilet fixtures, cleaning windows, mirrors, and walls, dusting, inventorying custodial supplies and equipment, and maintaining equipment.

Whether or not union contracts are part of school M&O, the school principal must deal with an elaborate system of policies and procedures concerning various aspects of the maintenance operation. For example, general maintenance; building maintenance; mechanical, electrical, plumbing, appliance, and refrigeration maintenance; and reoccurring maintenance are some of the possible departments that may exist in a large school system. The Spring Branch Independent School District (SBISD), Houston, Texas, is an example of such an elaborate school maintenance organization. Each department has a designated link in the SBISD web page and offers online ordering of services. To illustrate how the maintenance department may be helpful in providing instruction, consider the online guidelines for approved planting of flower gardens for butterflies and hummingbirds. The principal and teachers should regard this effort as a direct tie to the school's curriculum. This particular department also offers policies and procedures for pest management, a planting guide, a shrub guide, and a tree guide—many technicalities that coordinate with the outdoor curriculum.

Regardless of whether the school system is large or small, the school principal should be aware of minor maintenance practices that may be performed by the custodial staff or system maintenance workers. The school principal should also be aware of professional organizations that work with custodians and maintenance personnel, for example, the National School Plant Management Association (http://www.nspma.com) and the International Executive Housekeepers Association (http://www.ieha.org).

The amount of maintenance to be performed by the custodial staff usually varies according to school district policy and size of the school district and their expertise. According to Baker and Peters (1963), custodians should have all the tools necessary to operate in an efficient manner. Because the replacement of damaged school equipment is costly, it is desirable for custodians to perform minor maintenance duties and to take care of all the tools and equipment issued to them. It is highly desirable that the school principal have a working knowledge of general needs related to maintenance and simple strategies for caring for tools and equipment. To this end, Baker and Peters (1963) provided some suggestions for the care of tools:

1. Always hang a hair broom up—never allow it to rest on the bristles.
2. Never use hair brooms in water or on a wet surface.
3. Hang dust mops up.
4. When finished with a scrub machine, clean it, including its brush and electric cord. Never leave the brush on the machine—hang it up.
5. Clean and dry tanks of the vacuum pick-up.
6. It is a good idea to mark all tools in your possession so that they might be easily identified.
7. Each custodian should always carry a putty knife, pliers, and a screwdriver to do minor maintenance and furniture repair. (p. 188)

The ASBO (1981) also offered suggestions for the care of housekeeping equipment. For example, ASBO suggested that dust mops not be used on oily floors; and when soiled, the mop head should be washed and rinsed thoroughly. It should be hung up, with the head not touching the floor, when not in use. Regarding floor machines, ASBO recommended that the machine rest on its wheels instead of the brush; the solution tank and its lines should also be emptied and cleaned before storage. Never leave the brush on the machine when storing it. The mop bucket and wringer should be cleaned after each day's use. Rotating the brush on a push broom helps extend its useful life. Squeegee blades should be dried after each use and stored out of direct sunlight. Vacuums, wet or dry, should be emptied after each use, and the tank should be cleaned with a disinfectant solution on a monthly basis to minimize the growth of algae and bacteria. Wet mops, the sources of many offensive odors in the custodial closet, should be hung to dry or allowed to drip into the sink or drain, not touching the wall or other objects.

School principals and administrators should treat the maintenance of a school building and grounds as continuous and also understand that it is an important part of the school program. Without adequate maintenance, the educational program will eventually begin to diminish. Since the school principal is responsible for all activities within the building, what should he or she expect of the custodial staff? While it would be impossible to list all the minor maintenance jobs the principal might expect custodians to perform, Baker and Peters (1963) have identified a basic list of jobs:

1. Fix loose screws in tables, chairs, doors, etc.
2. Install pencil sharpeners and map rails.
3. Regulate, externally, classroom thermostats (head custodian only).
4. Set up occasional tables and chairs.
5. Replace faucet washers.
6. Adjust drinking fountains.
7. Oil hinges.
8. Make minor repairs to custodial machines.
9. Revarnish tabletops.
10. Water lawns and shrubs.
11. Clean stopped traps and drains.
12. Clean grease traps. (pp. 188–189)

Other related jobs of the custodian might include the servicing of sagging doors and repairing them as needed; and checking exterior locks and repairing or reporting any related problems or failures. It is also important for the custodian to check

doorknobs to ensure that they are turning and that the latches are working properly.

Keys can present problems. It is highly desirable that original key blanks be used when duplicating keys. This ensures a good fit and helps eliminate the breaking of keys in locks. In the interest of safety, the principal and the custodian should keep fire exit doors in good working order by checking latches and servicing them periodically.

Other custodian jobs may include the cleaning of light fixtures regularly and replacement of lamps. The custodian may also perform maintenance on lighting fixtures. For example, globes may need replacing and fixtures may require tightening. Unless trained and licensed in the use of electricity, it is not safe for the school or the custodian to engage in major electrical wiring repair.

Like electrical repairs, school policy varies regarding the extent of plumbing duties custodians may perform. The size of the school and district, influence of unions, and location of the school district influence this activity. However, minor plumbing maintenance is expected in most school systems. For example, flush valve repair is often needed and this activity may require some special training. Custodians are frequently asked to adjust the flow of water at drinking fountains, lavatory sinks, and faucets. This may be accomplished by a regular "flat head" screwdriver or an Allen-head wrench. Some modern plumbing systems even require other special tools furnished by the maker of the plumbing appliances. This is usually a strategy to prevent students from adjusting the flow of water with more common tools. Other plumbing maintenance jobs include faucet washer replacement, toilet seat replacement, and the cleaning of stoppages in traps and toilets. Such tools as plungers, force pumps, and augers are required for these jobs.

FIRE PREVENTION AND PROTECTION

Most fires are caused from improper maintenance. The school principal and custodial staff should be on guard against the buildup of rubbish, the storing of oily cloths used in cleaning, and improper storage of flammables (paint, paint thinner, and gasoline or diesel fuel for lawnmowers). The most effective way to fight a fire is prevention; of all the mechanical devices used in the maintenance of a school, fire alarms are most critical because they deal with human safety. The school principal should be aware of the needed maintenance and repair of fire alarms and ensure that frequent mechanical checks be made on these life-saving devices.

Knowing which fire extinguisher to use in case of fire is vital. First, the custodian, principal, and teachers should know the different classifications for fires. A class A fire involves the burning of wood, trash, paper, plastics, or cloth, for example. A soda–acid extinguisher is appropriate for putting out a fire burning these items, or just forcing water on a class A fire will generally contain and eliminate it. The class B fire involves the burning of oils, paints, grease, gasoline, and other flammable liquids. Foam extinguishers having water and aluminum sulfate to blanket the area are effective against a class B fire. The class C fire involves electrical wiring and may be extinguished with carbon dioxide and dry chemical extinguishers. If an electrical fire erupts, quickly turning off the power source will be beneficial. Hence, the school principal must know where the school's main breaker is located and be able to quickly turn off the power. A class D fire involves the burning of metals, potassium, sodium, aluminum, and magnesium and could possibly occur in a laboratory. A special extinguishing agent such as Metal-X and foam is suggested to fight a class D fire.

Dry chemical extinguishers extinguish a fire by coating it with a thin layer of dust (fine powder made primarily of monoammonium phosphate and pressurized by nitrogen), separating fuel from oxygen in the air. The powder also works to interrupt the chemical reaction of a fire. A fire extinguisher filled with the dry chemical solution is designed for use on class A, B, and C fires, and a standard blue and white label also indicates the types of fires for which the extinguisher is designed. Proper maintenance and service of fire alarms, just as for fire extinguishers, are vital to the safety and security of the school.

Johnson (2000) has provided a chart and maintenance schedule for portable fire extinguishers (p. 85). It includes effectiveness ratings of various fire extinguishers, and the models, discharge range, and suggested service schedule for nine types of fire extinguishers. When checking a fire extinguisher, it is important to inspect the nozzle for operation and obstructions, determine if seal or tamper indicators are in place, read the pressure gauge to determine if the pressure is satisfactory, and ensure that the instructions are legible and face forward.

Some major points for the school principal to consider are that the fire extinguishers are conspicuously located and readily accessible in case of fire. The extinguisher should be set on a shelf, bracket, or hanger, and be approximately 4 feet (1.1 meter) from the floor. It must have an inspection tag attached, showing maintenance or recharge dates and the signature of the person or service agency that performed the service. Defective extinguishers must not be allowed to remain in service.

MECHANICAL CRAFTS AND MAINTENANCE

It is important to recognize the contributions made by the mechanical crafts in the schools. This important unit is responsible for maintaining the air climate in school facilities. It is usually responsible for all the electrical power equipment between the power service and the individual outlets in the classroom. If the clock and bell systems are not working properly, then the school day is disrupted and learning may be diminished. It is vital that clocks and bells be maintained; this is usually the job for centralized staff, but the principal and custodian might also monitor the effectiveness of this service and suggest upgrades as they become affordable and feasible.

KNOWLEDGE OF THE CUSTODIAL WORKSTATION

The school principal should have some basic criteria to evaluate whether or not the custodian has access to an adequate workstation, the custodial closet. It should be located in a place or places central to the duties of the custodian and have storage space for tools, equipment, supplies, and materials. Figure 9.2 illustrates a custodial closet having sliding doors. This design allows for more convenient storage and removal of carts and buffing equipment. It represents a safety feature since the pocket doors do not swing out into the hallway. The utility sink is located in the center of the closet and mops may be hung from the upper shelf directly over the sink. The height of the closet should extend above the normal ceiling height and into the attic area for ventilation. The closet should also serve as an entryway the school's attic area.

PRIORITIES AND CHECKLISTS FOR PREVENTIVE MAINTENANCE

One perspective of maintenance is that "all school maintenance is preventive." However, preventive maintenance (PM) has found a special place in the literature, as evidenced by the work of authors such as Maciha (2000), Castaldi (1994), Kowalski (1989), and Davis (1973). An organized PM program for scheduled routine maintenance tasks is necessary for protecting the public's interest. Also encouraging and allowing the school principal to discover and report maintenance problems as they arise are key. Good communication between the central maintenance administration, the school principal, and school custodians is essential. Principals should have the authority to identify and report maintenance needs that are outside the regularly scheduled routine maintenance procedures. Furthermore, the central administration should provide the school principal with a routine maintenance schedule to keep him or her informed about various activities planned for the school property. Information sharing is important, especially for activities relating to the servicing of alarm systems, clocks, fire extinguishers, other

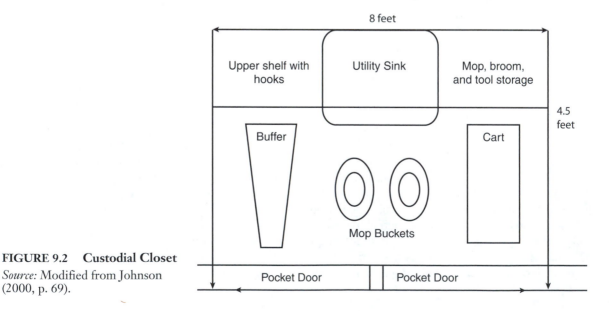

FIGURE 9.2   Custodial Closet
Source: Modified from Johnson (2000, p. 69).

safety equipment, and air filtration systems. One quick way to test information sharing is to ask the school principal when a certain system was serviced. If the principal knows, then the school system is probably following a good communications policy. Furthermore, if the school principal knows where the systems are located and also how to check them, then we may assume that an awareness of the total school environment is encouraged by the central administration. Having a principal with such skills and knowledge is a positive influence on the school and its occupants. A school system allowing communications and participation as described here is ideal.

One major issue that the principal addresses daily is safety and security systems. This includes such items as metal detectors (in some schools), fences, special doors, alarm systems, security officers, dog patrols, monitoring systems, and lighting (or the lack of it). Maciha (2000) has prioritized PM procedures as follows: human safety, overall safety, regulatory requirements, known requirements, equipment life cycle, energy efficiency, and other (p. 18).

Monitoring is the key to preventing deterioration and malfunction. The core of PM includes routine inspections and immediate service or repair. A detailed PM checklist is provided in the work entitled *Preventive Maintenance Guidelines* (Maciha, 2000). Upon purchasing the book, electronic versions of the various checklists may be retrieved from http://www.rsmeans.com/supplement/schfacil.html. Topics include:

Asphalt	Fences
Auditorium	Fire alarm water-flow
Automatic gates/doors	testing
Alarm systems	Fire extinguishers
Back-flow devices	Fire system certification
Business offices	Gas connections
Classrooms	Gutter/roof drains
Doors and windows	Gymnasium
Electrical systems	Hot water heaters
Emergency generators	HVAC systems
Exterior stairs, decks,	Irrigation controllers
and landings	Kitchen and dining areas

Landscape	Security systems
Library	Sewer laterals
Lighting: exterior and	Signage
interior	Smoke alarms
Locker-rooms	Special requirements
Maintenance carts	Storm drains
Nonpower gates	Structural members
Playgrounds	Swimming pool
Restrooms (toilets)	Tennis courts
Roofing	Track and field areas

While it is unlikely that the school principal will have a detailed working knowledge of all these areas, it is important for him or her to understand the need for PM in them. The principal should learn about some of the most important areas, such as safety and security. For example, the school principal ought to know the items on the smoke alarm deficiency checklist. They include batteries, connections, housing, mounting, overall operation, overall condition, and other (Maciha, 2000, p. 154).

Another area of special interest the school principal should have is the classroom. Maciha (2000) details the classroom PM checklist as follows:

Fire Safety
- ❏ Electrical outlet load
- ❏ Positioning of paper/flammable materials away from heat sources
- ❏ Accessible rout
- ❏ Emergency exit visibility

Furniture: desks, chairs, tables, and shelves
- ❏ Surface conditions, including deficiencies such as excess wear, rough areas, or protruding hardware
- ❏ Part conditions
- ❏ Cleanliness
- ❏ Stability
- ❏ Overall condition

Teaching module
- ❏ Task lighting condition
- ❏ Lectern location and condition
- ❏ Overall condition

Blackboard/dry-erase board
- ❏ Mounting condition/stability
- ❏ Overall appearance
- ❏ Cleaning capability
- ❏ Overall condition

Audio/visual equipment
- ❏ Overhead equipment condition and stability
- ❏ Housing condition
- ❏ Electrical service condition
- ❏ Part condition
- ❏ Screen operation and condition
- ❏ Speaker system operation
- ❏ Electrical cord and outlet conditions
- ❏ Overall condition

Computer system/modules
- ❏ Electrical integrity/surge protector conditions
- ❏ Equipment condition
- ❏ Cleanliness
- ❏ Overall operation
- ❏ Workstation and member parts function
- ❏ Overall condition

Partitions
- ❏ Lubrication
- ❏ Stability
- ❏ Overall condition, including deficiencies such as excessive wear, vandalism, improper function, or broken/missing parts

Flooring
- ❏ Service condition, including deficiencies such as excessive wear, vandalism, improper function, or broken/missing parts

Plumbing systems
- ❏ Sink conditions and drainage
- ❏ Overall condition, including deficiencies such as leaks, corrosion, or failure potential

Trash receptacles
- ❏ Location
- ❏ Cleanliness
- ❏ Overall condition

Interclass speaker system operation
Clock function
Closets/storage areas
- ❏ Door/lock operation
- ❏ Appearance, interior/exterior
- ❏ Overall condition for debris and safety hazards

Wall map function and general condition
Panic button/security operation
Fire extinguishers
- ❏ Tag currency
- ❏ Placement in correct proximity to potential hazards per code
- ❏ Housing condition
- ❏ Hose condition
- ❏ Overall condition

Other
It is the job of the principal to take a leadership role in the vital area of PM. Teachers and students should also be made aware of how these vital areas affect the classroom and school.

SUMMARY

Most people seem to understand that school facility maintenance is vital to providing a good education. Maintenance staff members are integral to the creation of a school environment that enhances teaching and learning. The organizational structure of maintenance personnel varies depending on the size of the school district, but typically the head custodian within a single school must report to the school principal as well as a supervisor. The principal, however, does not usually have direct, formal authority over custodial staff. An alternative organizational structure is proposed in this chapter whereby the custodial employees within a school are considered part of the educational program and are under direct supervisory control of it. Business management and facilities services departments would continue to conduct audits, handle the distribution of supplies and equipment, develop work schedules, and manage payroll and benefits (unless these services are contracted out). Regardless of the organizational structure in which maintenance staff work, it is imperative that the school principal be familiar with certain aspects of the physical facility, and the roles and responsibilities of the custodians. But perhaps even more important is the relationships that custodians have with the principal, teachers, and students, which, in turn, affect his or her attitude about keeping the school well maintained.

Other factors, such as crowding and density, perceptions of cleanliness, and the custodial workload, also affect the level of maintenance in a school facility. More research is needed to understand how much space per student is needed given a variety of curricular functions and the multicultural composition of students and teachers within a learning environment. However, crowding has been associated with structural and furniture abuse, mechanical overload, increased behavioral problems, and lower student achievement. Perceptions about "how clean is clean" vary from person to person, so objective, published guidelines may be helpful in resolving discrepancies about this variable. The custodial workload is influenced by a large number of factors, such as student behavior, age and condition of the building, amount and kind of floor area,

and type and condition of mechanical equipment. It is important to develop realistic expectations for custodians. Creating standards for cleaning and establishing "time to clean" schedules may yield positive results for both the custodial staff and the school. With these expectations in place, possible disputes about workload and the time needed to do a job are eliminated. Some schools have eased custodians' workload (and saved money) by having the students perform much of their work instead, including cleaning bathrooms, doors, and windows, and even dusting. The rationale is that students who help keep their school clean develop a sense of ownership while learning about values such as cleanliness, respect, and responsibility for property.

In addition to clearly understanding the responsibilities of custodians, school principals must also be aware of a variety of other important issues, ranging from fire prevention and protection to ensuring that the maintenance staff has a safe and adequate custodial closet. Good communication between the central maintenance administration, school principal, and school custodians is essential. The principal can help identify maintenance needs as he or she walks through the school. Effective school maintenance is a team effort that is vital to providing learning environments that promote desirable educational outcomes.

ACTIVITIES

1. Using an organizational chart for a local school district and comparing it to the one shown in Figure 9.1, present a clear and concise argument (either written or in a verbal presentation) convincing school board representatives to change the organizational structure of the school system so that it is more similar to Figure 9.1.

2. Determine the number of custodians needed for a school with 28 teachers, 550 students, 30 classrooms, 57,000 square feet of assignable area, a cafeteria and kitchen, and 8 acres of upkeep grounds.

3. For an actual school facility, use the workload formula to calculate the number of custodians needed.

Compare that number to the actual number of custodians in the school. Is the actual number adequate? Justify your response based on not only the formula, but also other factors such as whether or not some services are contracted out, the principal's level of satisfaction with custodial services, and other variables affecting custodial requirements.

4. Conduct an inspection of a school facility one morning just as school is about to go into session for the day and rate it as a level 1 through 5 school based on the criteria described in this chapter. Record observations supporting your rating.

5. Select a school (perhaps the school where you work) and determine its capacity by using the following formula:

Formula 9.2 Capacity = TGS/AGS

Is this school under or over capacity?

6. Develop a job description for a relief custodian according to the following format:

Function. The person performing this job may relieve the custodian I or II, head custodian, or night foreman in any school regardless of size. This person also performs other duties as assigned when his or her services at the higher level are not required and may be a retired person or one that is seeking the job of custodian I or II, head custodian, or night foreman.

Salary.

Develop a range.

Characteristic Duties and Responsibilities.

Develop a list.

Desirable Qualifications.

Develop a list.

7. Outline a *job schedule* for the following positions using Table 9.5 as a guide:

   a. Middle school, *custodian I*, hours: 6:30 a.m. to 3:30 p.m.
   b. High school, *head custodian*, hours: 7:00 a.m. to 4:00 p.m

8. **Team Activity.** Brainstorm a list of the activities that might influence the workload of a school's custodial staff.

9. **Team Activity.** Brainstorm a list of the fifteen most important "things that the school principal should know" about school maintenance and operations.

10. Go the your favorite search engine on the Internet or a major library and do a search on such words as *school maintenance*, *school custodians*, or other terms related to the maintenance and operations of a school. Reviewing the results on such a search will enlarge your perspective on this vital and ever-changing part of school operations and make you aware of current information and activities in the field. List at least two sites or references related to topics in this chapter that are not included in the electronic reference list or set of references here.

11. The National Clearing House for Educational facilities provides numerous references for school maintenance and operations. Go to http://www.edfacilities.org/ and conduct a search on *school maintenance*. Conduct a separate search at this website for *school custodians*. List and describe four references that relate to the issue of school maintenance and operations.

12. Find a source such as R. S. Means and develop a maintenance schedule and PM checklist for one selected area of a school.

REFERENCES AND BIBLIOGRAPHY

Print Sources

Aiello, J. R., Thompson, D. E., & Baum, A. (1985). Children, crowding, and control: Effects of environmental stress on social behavior. In Wohlwill, J. F., and van Vliet, W. (eds.), *Habitats for children: The impacts of density*. Hillsdale, NJ: Lawrence Erlbaum, pp. 97–124.

Association of Higher Education Facilities Officers (1998). *Custodial staffing guidelines for educational facilities*. APPA.

Association of School Business Officials (1981). *Custodial methods and procedures manual*. Park Ridge, IL: ASBO.

Baker, J. J., & Peters, J. S. (1957). *School plant operations*. Stanford University: School Planning Laboratory.

Baker, J. J., & Peters, J. S. (1963). *School maintenance and operation*. Danville, IL: The Interstate Printers and Publishers.

Black, J. A., & English, F. W. (1986). *What they don't tell you in school of education about school administration*. Lancaster, PA: Technomic Publishing Co., Inc.

Brooks, K. W., Conrad, M. C., & Griffith, W. (1980). *From program to educational facilities*. Lexington, KY: Center for Professional Development, College of Education, University of Kentucky.

Castaldi, B. (1994). *Educational facilities: planning, modernization, and management.* Boston, MA: Allyn & Bacon.

Davis, J. C. (1973). *The principal's guide to educational facilities: Design, utilization and management.* Columbus, OH: Charles Merrill.

Duncanson, E. (2004). Classroom space. *The educational facility planner,* 38:24–28.

Frohreich, L. E. (1987). *Creating and maintaining educational facilities.* Winneconne, WI: Wisconsin Association of School Boards.

Harrison, O. B. (1973). *Suggested methods for custodians for the routine care of schools.* Nashville, TN: Yearwood and Johnson Architects.

Hawkins, H. L., & Lilley, H. E. (1988). *Guide for school facility appraisal.* Phoenix, AZ: CEFPI, International.

Johnson, D. J. (2000). *Custodial methods and procedures manual.* Reston, VA: ASBO International.

Knezevich, S. J., & Fowlkes, J. G. (1960). *Business management of local school systems.* New York: Harper & Brothers, Publishers.

Kowalski, T. J. (1989). *Planning and managing school facilities.* New York: Praeger.

Lackney, J. A. (1996). *Quality in school environments: A multiple case study of environmental quality assessment in five elementary schools in the Baltimore City Public Schools from an action research perspective.* UMI Dissertation Services No. 9717142, School of Architecture and Urban Planning, University of Wisconsin-Milwaukee.

Maciha, J. C. (2000). *Preventive maintenance guidelines for school facilities.* Kingston, MA: R.S. Means Company, Inc.

Poston, W. K., Stone, M. P., & Muther, C. (1992). *Making schools work: Practical management of support operations,* Vol. 7. English, F. W. (series ed.), Guidebooks to Effective Educational Leadership. Newbury Park, CA: Corwin.

Reeves, C. E., & Ganders, H. S. (1928). *School building management.* New York: Teachers College, Columbia University.

Tanner, C. K. (2000). The classroom: Size versus density. *School business affairs,* 66:21–23.

U.S. Department of Education, National Center for Education Statistics, National Forum on Education Statistics (2003). *Planning guide for maintaining school facilities.* NCES 2003-347, prepared by T. Szuba, R. Young, and the School Facilities Maintenance Task Force, Washington, DC.

Wohlwill, J. F., & van Vliet, W. (1985). *Habitats for children: The impacts of density.* Hillsdale, NJ: Lawrence Erlbaum.

Internet Sources

Association of Higher Education Facilities Officers. http://www.appa.org/.

Association of School Business Officials. http://www.asbointl.org/.

International Executive Housekeepers Association, Inc. http://www.ieha.org/.

International Sanitary Supply Association. http://www.issa.com/.

Milshtein, A. (1998). Setting the cleaning standard. In *School planning and management.* http://www.spmmag.com/articles/misc/cleaning.html.

National Clearinghouse for Educational Facilities. http://www.edfacilities.org/index.html.

National School Plant Management Association. http://www.nspma.com/.

Planning Guide for Maintaining School Facilities. http://www.nces.ed.gov/pubsearch/pubsinfo.asp?pubid=2003347.

Preventive Maintenance Guidelines for School Facilities. http://www.rsmeans.com.

State of Wisconsin, Department of Employment Relations. http://der.state.wi.us/static/class/89103spc.htm.

PART VI

LEGAL AND FINANCIAL ISSUES IN DEVELOPING EDUCATIONAL FACILITIES

When it comes to school law and finance, the most important premise for developing school facilities is strong leadership (premise 1). From knowledge about ADA to bonding for capital improvements, strong leadership by school administrators and planners is essential. Chapter 10 addresses some major legal issues for planning, designing, and maintaining schools, including contract law. Chapter 11, the finance section, describes and explains approaches to management, reaffirming the premise that the demand for resources is always greater than those available (premise 7).

Premises for Developing School Facilities

PREMISE	DESCRIPTOR
Premise 1	Strong leadership is essential.
Premise 6	Management is systematic: data- and goal-driven.
Premise 7	The demand for resources is greater than those available.

CHAPTER TEN

LEGAL ISSUES IN SCHOOL FACILITIES PLANNING, DESIGN, AND CONSTRUCTION

KEVIN JENKINS
University of South Carolina

JOHN DAYTON
University of Georgia

Due to the nature of their professional activities, educators tend to focus primarily on student achievement in academics, behavior, and a variety of other areas. With effective educators, this focus pervades their thinking in all their professional activities, including the design, construction, and maintenance of educational facilities. When undergoing facilities construction or renovation projects, school systems should place primary importance on designing facilities to support the educational goals of the system. Nonetheless, those responsible for educational facilities do not function in utopian worlds in which they may focus on one area of human activity to the exclusion of all others. Rather, as in all professions, certain limitations are placed on educational facility planners. Notable among these limitations is the legal environment of school facility planning. Failing to plan in accordance with local, state, and federal laws, regulations, and ordinances can result in the wasting of significant amounts of money, time, and personnel resources, the scarcity of which is ubiquitous among school systems.

The need to protect scarce resources from being diminished further by preventable legal action makes it important for educational facility planners to be aware of some basic principles of law. Such principles will undoubtedly be a part of any project to build, maintain, or renovate school facilities. This chapter will briefly address some of the common legal issues with which facility planners across the country should be familiar. Such issues include contract law, relevant restraints on government actions, zoning and building codes, compliance with federal statutes, tort law, use of facilities, and equity issues. It is important to note, however, that while some federal laws apply to school facility projects across the United States, most of the laws governing public school facilities are state laws. Although this chapter will provide examples of state laws illustrative of general legal principles, it is impossible in a single chapter to cover all applicable federal laws, and those of fifty states. Consequently, it is essential that school officials work closely with qualified legal counsel for advice regarding their specific situations.

CONTRACTS

Despite the desire of many school systems to continually take on more responsibility regarding the development of children and adolescents, many aspects of school facility construction simply cannot be accomplished efficiently using in-house resources. Likewise, sometimes building maintenance can be performed more efficiently by hiring outside contractors. When such a situation arises, school systems must establish contractual relationships with outside providers of goods and/or services. Paramount to getting the desired benefits from a contract is a clear understanding of the basic elements of contract law. While we shall discuss these in the context of school construction, all contracts share similar basic elements. Therefore, the elements discussed below apply equally to contracts to purchase land, materials, and/or services.

At the heart of a valid contract are an offer and an acceptance of the offer. Additionally, this agreement must be supported by consideration, thus establishing a quid pro quo arrangement whereby something of value is exchanged for something of value, that is, a school system offers a sum of money to a property owner for a designated piece of land, and the owner accepts the system's offer. The title to the land is then exchanged for the agreed on sum of money. Importantly, a unilateral commitment cannot constitute a contract under U.S. law. A contract is not binding if one party, for example, receives a written offer, makes a change to it, signs it, and then returns the amended document to the other party. In other words, there must be a meeting of the minds over the final version of the contract for it to be valid.

When all parties to a contract are pleased with the circumstances, the contract process can be unremarkable. However, when one or more parties are unhappy with the results, or with the process itself, they may choose to pursue litigation to either enforce or rescind the contract. Causes for dissatisfaction with a contract are myriad, and include mistakes, delays, failure to perform, accidents, etc. In order to win a lawsuit for breach of contract, the plaintiff seeking relief must establish one or more of the following: There was a mutual mistake or no "meeting of the minds" in the terms of the contract, the contract constituted an unconscionable bargain, there was a misrepresentation of a material fact, a party to the contract committed fraud, the contract dealt with illegal subject matter, there was undue influence or duress used to gain the contract, a party was legally incapable of entering into the contract, or the contract violated the statute of frauds. The complexities of contract law and the intricacies of the construction process make it necessary that, in this context, contracts must be in writing.

If the plaintiff meets the burden of proof for establishing one of the above defenses to the contract, the plaintiff is then entitled to a remedy. The standard for meeting the burden of proof will generally be a "preponderance of the evidence," which is to say that the plaintiff must show that more evidence supports his position than supports that of the defense. Appropriate remedies may include rescission of the contract, liquidated damages, specific performance, and award of the benefit of the bargain to the plaintiff, or other equitable relief. It should be remembered that the party seeking relief for a breach of contract has a duty to mitigate damages. This simply means the aggrieved party must try to find a way to minimize the damage done by the breach of contract, including seeking cover goods and services to substitute for those not supplied by the contractor.

RESTRAINTS ON GOVERNMENT ACTIONS

Open Meetings

An important principle public school officials must understand is that in their official capacity, they represent the government. The Constitution of the United States, and those of the several states, were carefully crafted to provide for the manner in which government must operate, and to set forth limitations on the use of government power. To further these purposes, many states have enacted statutes that help ensure governmental agencies respect the constitutional limitations on their power, and to ensure that the government treats citizens fairly. When dealing with construction projects that can often cost millions of dollars, corrupt officials may be tempted to use their official position to further their own interests. They may also make mistakes that could potentially be avoided if caught in time by an engaged public. In order to protect the public from such an abuse of power or avoidable mistakes, many states enact "sunshine" or open meeting laws. While the details vary from jurisdiction to jurisdiction, generally the laws define a meeting as a gathering of a quorum of the governing body of a governmental agency at a designated time and place, during which gathering official business is acted on and/or discussed. If a gathering of officials meets those two criteria, it is subject to open records laws. Decisions made or policies adopted at meetings that are not held in compliance with open records laws are usually not binding.

As the purpose of open meetings laws is to ensure the public has the opportunity to stay informed about the workings of government agencies, generally they require that the public be given reasonable notice about the time and place of upcoming meetings. This can usually be accomplished by publishing the notice in the local legal organ, such as the newspaper, along with a sign at the location of the regular meeting place of the agency. Advertisements for meetings should include an agenda of items to be discussed, when possible. To further inform the public, open records laws often permit, if not require, written, verbal, or video transcripts be made of the proceedings. A summary of the proceedings should be made available to the public in sufficient detail to identify issues discussed, testimony given, and positions taken by the various members of the body. Furthermore, a verbatim transcript should be made available to citizens on request.

While the public needs the opportunity to stay informed on the workings of governmental agencies, there are exceptions to this rule. Exceptions typically include proceedings held for investigative purposes mandated by statute such as a grand jury, meetings of law enforcement agencies when the revelation of discussions would compromise investigations or officer safety, and meetings discussing the hiring, firing, and evaluation of specific employees, when such meetings do not involve hearing evidence or arguments. The most notable exception pertinent to the subject at hand is that of meetings discussing the purchase of real estate by the governmental agency. Even in this case, the public should be notified that the meeting will occur, and minutes should be kept to disseminate to the public after the acquisition has taken place, or is no longer under consideration. Failure to comply with open meetings laws may result in judicial injunctions to comply or possible criminal penalties.

Due Process and Eminent Domain

The Fifth and Fourteenth Amendments to the U.S. Constitution state that government may not deprive any person of "life, liberty, or property, without due process of law." The Fifth Amendment further states "nor shall private property be taken for public use without just compensation." All fifty U.S. states have similar provisions in their own constitutions, as well as statutes outlining the conditions under which private property such as land may be taken, and the procedure for doing so. The legal justification for the taking of private property is known as eminent domain, a concept that has a long history in the common law. The Constitution contains no specific justification for eminent domain, but the Supreme Court recognized as early as 1897 in the case of *Bauman v. Ross* that the Fifth Amendment does imply the power of eminent domain, and that it is an "offspring of political necessity."

Despite the availability of eminent domain, the requirement of due process seeks to protect citizens from government abusing its power in this regard, as well as many other contexts. In its most rudimentary form, due process includes two elements: notice and hearing. When government actions may deprive a person or persons of a protected interest, affected parties must be notified of the possible deprivation. Further, they must be given a hearing at which they have the opportunity to argue against the proposed deprivation. Most commonly in the school construction process eminent domain will come into play when a school board uses its power to condemn land for private use, and then acquire the land for the public use of building a school facility. Government may not simply take the land, however. They must pay "just compensation" to the owner of the property, which is determined by fair market value.

Wise school officials must also consider political considerations when condemning land. School board members are politicians by definition, and should consider the possible consequences of causing community disharmony by taking land by force. The law is a system of conflict resolution, preferably one of last resort. If there is no conflict, that is, the school system can reach a deal to purchase land that is, agreeable to both parties, that would likely be a better arrangement for all involved parties. This is provided, however, that the land can be bought for a price which does not expose taxpayers to a waste of money.

Zoning and Building Codes

As applied to both public and private institutions, zoning and building codes serve multiple purposes such as minimizing unnecessary health and safety risks to the occupants of and visitors to the building and attempting to protect the property value of surrounding locations. Additionally, when applied to public institutions like public school systems, zoning and building codes often seek to maximize the efficient use of taxpayer dollars. Typically, state statutes will give authorization for some administrative body such as the state department of education to enact regulations that provide the details of how to carry out general legislative mandates. For instance, Section 20-2-261 of the Official Code of Georgia mandates that "the State Board of Education shall establish common minimum facility requirements which each public school facility must meet . . ." and that those requirements must

include provisions to comply with state laws regarding "fire and physical safety; sanitation and health, including temperature and ventilation; minimum space, size, and configuration for the various components of the instructional program; and construction stability, quality, and suitability for intended uses."

Some jurisdictions, such as the state of California, go into considerable detail in designing building codes for public schools. For example, Title 5 of the California Code of Regulations lists not only minimum standards for educational facilities, but also detailed standards for site selection, procedures for site acquisition for both state-funded and locally funded districts, placement of the buildings on the lot, etc., and gives specific requirements for the size and layout of at least twelve types of classrooms. The California Code of Regulations, Division 1, Chapter 13, goes so far as to mandate the type of lighting and window treatments used in classrooms. While such regulations may seem draconian in nature, they may also serve to ensure some degree of equity in school facilities across the state. Additionally, regulations can help educators focus on designing facilities to support instruction by mandating that facilities be designed with the instructional program in mind. The laws of many states also allow for appeals for exceptions to burdensome requirements when justified by legitimate educational or economic rationale.

COMPLIANCE WITH FEDERAL STATUTES

Section 504 of the Rehabilitation Act

While most building and zoning laws are state laws, there are also federal statutes with which school facilities must comply. With the passage of the Rehabilitation Act of 1973, Congress recognized that persons with disabilities could not participate in many common activities, including those at public schools. In an attempt to remedy this circumstance, Section 504 of the Rehabilitation Act states that "no otherwise qualified individual with a disability . . . shall, solely by reason of his or her disability, be excluded from the participation in, be denied benefits of, or be subjected to discrimination under any program or activity receiving Federal financial assistance."

Virtually all public school systems in the country receive federal funds in some form or other, most from many statutory sources. As recipients of federal funds, public schools are required to provide "reasonable accommodations" in their programs and facilities to allow for the participation of otherwise qualified persons with disabilities. Under 34 C.F.R. Section 104.12, recipients must "make reasonable accommodations to the known physical or mental limitations of an otherwise qualified" handicapped individual, including making facilities "readily accessible to and usable by handicapped persons."

Special concerns surrounding compliance with Section 504 exist regarding public school facilities. Concerning facilities, 34 C.F.R. Section 104.21 states that "a recipient shall operate each program or activity to which this part applies so that the program or activity, when viewed in its entirety, is readily accessible to handicapped persons." Section 104.22 notes that compliance can be achieved through "redesign of equipment, reassignment of classes or other services to accessible buildings, assignment of aids to beneficiaries, home visits, delivery of health, welfare, or other social services at alternate accessible sites, alteration of existing facilities and construction of new facilities" in conformance with the Uniform Federal Accessibility Standards (UFAS). However, Section 104.22 also notes: "This paragraph does not require a recipient to make each of its existing facilities or every part of a facility accessible to and usable by handicapped persons." Complete accommodation in every element of a school's programs and facilities is neither required nor often possible. Instead, Section 504 requires reasonable accommodations for otherwise qualified persons. An accommodation is not reasonable, and therefore not required, if it would result in unreason-

able safety risks, health risks, or costs. Further, an institution is not required to provide a specific accommodation requested by an individual. Rather, an institution is only required to provide a reasonable accommodation, and when more than one reasonable accommodation exists, the institution may choose which reasonable accommodation to provide.

It may not be possible to accommodate every handicapped individual in every part of the facility. This is a special problem in older or historic facilities, where alterations may be impossible, may be cost-prohibitive, or may destroy historic artifacts. However, in new construction or when significant renovations are being made, special rules apply. Concerning the design and construction of new facilities, 34 C.F.R. Section 104.23 states: "Each facility or part of a facility constructed by . . . a recipient shall be designed and constructed in such manner that the facility is readily accessible to and usable by handicapped persons."

The Americans with Disabilities Act

The Americans with Disabilities Act (ADA) of 1990 is considered by many to be the most sweeping antidiscrimination law since the Civil Rights Act of 1964. Although Section 504 protected handicapped persons from discrimination in institutions receiving federal funds, individuals with disabilities remained unprotected in many other important areas of life. Congress passed the ADA to provide protections for individuals with disabilities in employment, public accommodations, telecommunications, and other areas. Many provisions of the ADA are similar to Section 504 provisions, but provide broader coverage. Because passage of the ADA was based on Congress' power to regulate interstate commerce, the law prohibits discrimination against individuals with disabilities in both the public and private sectors, regardless of whether any federal funds are received. Title II of the ADA prohibits discrimination in all state and local government programs, including public schools. Similar to Section 504, Title II of the ADA declares that

No qualified individual with a disability shall, by reason of such disability, be excluded from participation in or be denied the benefits of the services, programs, or activities of a public entity, or be subjected to discrimination by any such entity. 42 U.S.C. Section 12132 (1997)

The ADA prohibits discrimination based on a disability, and requires modifications for accessibility and other reasonable accommodations for individuals with disabilities. Although the law provided significant new protections for individuals with disabilities, especially in the private sector, its impact in public schools was less dramatic. Discrimination against handicapped persons in schools receiving federal funds was already prohibited by Section 504.

Nonetheless, there are some situations in which the ADA impacts the operation of schools, especially in the area of facilities. For example, schools are required to make public accommodations such as athletic stadiums, auditoriums, and other facilities barrier-free for individuals with disabilities attending school events. Further, all new school construction must comply with barrier-free design requirements mandated by the ADA.

Individuals with Disabilities Education Act

For much of the history of public education in America, many children with disabilities were prohibited from attending public schools. Congress changed this with passage of the Education for All Handicapped Children Act of 1975 (Public Law 94-142), most recently reauthorized in 1997 as the Individuals with Disabilities Education Act (IDEA). The IDEA has had the greatest impact on delivery of instructional services to students, but the law also has ramifications on school facilities. Most notably, 34 C.F.R. 300.551(a) mandates that schools offer a continuum of placements for students with disabilities, ranging from placement in the regular classroom to an environment as restrictive as a residential placement. In choosing the

type of classroom appropriate for an individual student, the Individualized Education Plan (IEP) Committee must consider each of the possibilities along the continuum and place the child in the environment it believes is the least restrictive appropriate for that child. Almost every school will have some children living in its attendance zone who need placement in a self-contained special education classroom. Such rooms need to be accessible to disabled individuals, and generally will have restroom facilities either attached, or very close by. Ideally, a phone line should be installed in case of emergency, as some students in self-contained settings have serious health conditions that may require immediate medical attention.

There are thirteen categories of disabilities under which a student may qualify for special education services. These categories may be found at 34 C.F.R. 300.7(c)(1)–(c)(13). A category particularly pertinent to the discussion of school facilities is that of "emotional behavior disorder" (EBD). Students categorized as EBD and placed in a self-contained setting need a classroom equipped with special equipment such as isolation study carrels, and, in some cases, even sound-proof, padded rooms for particularly violent outbursts. It should be noted, however, that padded rooms are often not located in local schools. Rather, they tend to be in psycho-educational facilities to which severely emotionally disturbed children are assigned. Facility planners nonetheless must bear in mind the requirement to provide such services as needed. Larger school systems often have their own such facility, while smaller systems, due to smaller demand and high per pupil cost, often share this type of facility and provide busing to students who need it.

When a student with a disability exhibits behavior that is so disruptive or dangerous his presence in the local school is no longer appropriate, school officials, in accordance with 34 C.F.R. 300.522, may assign the student to an interim alternative educational placement, including an alternative school for a maximum period of 45 days. During this 45-day period, the school must still provide educational services to the student as dictated in the student's IEP. While it is not necessary to provide the full range of services in the IEP while the child is assigned to the alternative school, some must still be provided. Paramount among these provisions would be any concerning the health and safety of the student as discussed above. Consequently, facility planners for school systems should take into account the provision of IEP services when planning alternative school facilities. This may be most efficiently carried out at the system level, however, or even intersystem, in order to share expenses as with the psycho-educational facilities discussed above.

TORT LAW

When parents send their children to a public school, they do so under the assumption that the students will return home safely at the end of the day. Additionally, employees and visitors to the school generally assume they are entering an environment reasonably free of dangerous conditions. School officials are obligated to provide such an environment in which to conduct school. If they fail to do so, and someone is injured due to the negligence of school employees, the school system may be open to a lawsuit. School officials must regularly monitor their facilities for emerging dangers, and use reasonable care in supervising maintenance of their facilities to avoid legal liability. Examples include removing known dangers such as ice on sidewalks, potentially dangerous animals or people, exposed nails, splinters, tree roots and dead branches that could cause injury to children; ensuring parking lot and bus lane safety; and the safe and effective removal of toxic substances. In order to avoid placing themselves and or their school system in legal jeopardy, school officials must take reasonable precautions to protect the safety of all persons who enter the school facilities or grounds.

The area of law relating to monetary or other compensation for injuries is known as tort law. Under tort law doctrine, the injured party may seek compensation for injuries caused by either intentional acts or omissions, or by negligence. Gener-

ally, an act of negligence is committed when an individual acts or fails to act as a reasonable and prudent person would have acted in similar circumstances. Historically, government agencies enjoyed a degree of immunity from being sued by citizens. This immunity descended to our system of laws from the "sovereign immunity" once enjoyed by monarchs. While few in American society still believe that either a king or a government can do no wrong, society does have an interest in protecting the limited budgets of school systems from lawsuits that could divert money from its intended purpose of supporting instruction. On the other hand, it may be untenable for government agents to carelessly or maliciously violate the rights of individuals and then hide behind sovereign immunity statues for protection. In order to balance society's need to protect public resources with society's responsibility to protect the rights of its citizens, many states have enacted legislation allowing school systems to purchase tort liability insurance. This type of legislation is often coupled with the provision that the limit of the insurance is the maximum amount for which a school system may be held liable, and that the school system retains immunity outside of the insurance coverage.

With or without the possibility of being sued, school officials should take care to avoid causing injury to persons through dangerous design or maintenance of school facilities. Taking proper care in these areas should minimize liability on the part of the system and its agents. In order to prevail in a torts lawsuit against school officials, the plaintiff must establish the following four elements: The school official(s) (1) had a duty to the plaintiff under the circumstances; (2) breached that duty through an unreasonable act or omission; (3) the breach of duty caused harm to the plaintiff; and (4) the harm resulted in compensable damages. Just as with contract law, the plaintiff in a torts suit has a duty to mitigate damages. As a defense against a torts suit, school officials may assert assumption of risk, contributory negligence, last clear chance, or comparative negligence on the part of the plaintiff, or immunity on the part of the school system.

Playgrounds

The guiding principle in tort law is that one is obligated to do what a reasonable person would do under the circumstances. With advancement in the field of engineering, what was considered a safe school facility only a few years ago may now be considered a death trap. One could make a strong argument that a reasonable school official would take steps to ensure that school facilities are modernized on a schedule designed to keep up with safety advancements. Play areas may pose a special risk in this area, considering they are perhaps the only place in school in which children are supposed to run, jump, and generally play in an unstructured fashion. Anyone old enough to be reading the first edition of this book may well recall play areas from their childhood that were made of concrete and steel in order to provide durability. By contrast, children have always been made of flesh and bone, and collisions with steel and concrete often resulted in substantial harm to them. Fortunately, today's playgrounds are made of softer materials that, while they may require more frequent maintenance, are also less likely to cause avoidable injury to children. Considering that the standard for liability in torts suits is "what a reasonable person would do," school officials should modernize antiquated playground equipment as soon as possible, and deny children the opportunity to play on it until it is modernized.

Toxics and Environmental Impact

When choosing a site for a future school facility, school officials often do so with budgetary concerns in mind. Consequently, officials may be inclined to buy the cheapest land available. In certain instances, purchases of relatively cheap land may be unwise due the presence of toxic substances from dumps or businesses that may have once occupied the area. Both from a legal and an ethical perspective, responsible parties should carefully review the history of proposed building sites before attempting to purchase them. Cleanup costs, as well as possible liability to exposed parties, may offset any benefit from buying the cheapest land available.

When researching possible building sites, another area of concern is the impact a facility will have on the surrounding environment. Issues such as ground water management and sewage treatment can have a direct effect on the value of adjoining properties, or even parcels of land that are miles away, but down river, or along the prevailing air currents. Additionally, county and/or municipal governments will generally charge an environmental impact fee for new buildings to cover the added drain on the power grid and other public utilities.

In managing pests and weeds in their facilities and on surrounding property, school officials should also consider less toxic means of treating these problems, prior to introducing highly toxic substances into the school environment. To avoid potential liability under tort law, one must always do what a reasonable person would do under the circumstances. To meet this standard, school officials should be aware of emerging trends in pest and weed management, including the increasing use of Integrated Pest Management (IPM). Advocates of IPM encourage schools to reduce children's exposure to potentially harmful pesticides and herbicides by using the least toxic methods of achieving effective pest and weed management. These may include, for example, the use of nontoxic traps, biological controls, appropriate plant selection and alternative landscaping, and the least amount of pesticides and herbicides necessary to achieve effective control of pests and weeds. Further, these pesticides and herbicides should be applied by qualified personnel, and in times, places, and manners designed to minimize children's exposure to these dangerous chemicals, as children are especially vulnerable to environmental toxins. Care should also be taken to assure that pesticides and herbicides are not washed into area streams and rivers, and that these chemicals are properly applied, stored, and disposed of. A carefully designed and implemented plan for using IPM and alternative landscaping in managing school property may significantly reduce the exposure of children and employees to toxins, and may also prove more cost-effective in the long run, by reducing illness and health care costs, and due to long-term savings in labor, supplies, and lower watering costs associated with low-maintenance alternative landscaping.

NONCURRICULAR USE OF PUBLIC SCHOOL FACILITIES

Public school systems often develop policies regarding the use of school facilities by noncurricular groups.* Such policies typically mandate that groups wishing to use school facilities do so outside of school hours, thus reserving exclusive use of the facilities for school purposes during the school day. This restriction is especially true if the group in question includes community members that may have no relationship to the school at all. Other schools allow student groups to meet during nonacademic time during the day, but these meetings usually do not allow persons from outside the school to attend. Policies regarding after-hours use of facilities vary widely, with some systems insisting that only student groups are allowed to use the facilities, while other policies allow for use by groups that have no direct relationship to the school whatsoever. A major concern of opponents of these policies is that some may view the school as endorsing the opinions of outside groups that meet in school facilities. Given the Supreme Court's relatively broad interpretation of the Establishment Clause, it comes as no surprise that proponents of Jefferson's concept of "a wall of separation between church and state" may fear this perception of government sponsorship most when the group using school facilities espouses a religious message.

Considerable disagreement exists about the legality of religious groups using public school facilities. Not only is the battle ongoing, the tenor of the debate is often rancorous. In the case of *Santa Fe v. Doe*, 530 U.S. 290 (2000), which concerned school-sponsored prayer at a school football game, the Court felt it necessary to threaten judicial sanctions due to the fact that some community members were trying to discover the identity of the anonymous plaintiffs who opposed the saying of the prayer at the game. The Court was concerned that these community members would try to take some action against the plaintiffs if they were successful in discovering their identity. Despite the continuing rigor of the debate, the law, for those who choose to follow it, is relatively clear regarding the use of facilities.

The First Amendment to the U.S. Constitution protects individuals from federal government interference with their freedoms of religion, speech, and assembly, among others. Further, the Fourteenth Amendment extends these same restraints to state and local government agencies. In order to protect the First Amendment rights of religious groups to use public school facilities on the same basis as other groups, Congress passed the Equal Access Act of 1984 (Public Law 98-377). Section 802(a) of the act states that "it shall be unlawful for any public secondary school which receives Federal financial assistance and which has a limited open forum to deny equal access or a fair opportunity to, or discriminate against, any students who wish to conduct a meeting within that limited open forum on the basis of the religious, political, philosophical, or other content of the speech at such meetings." The statute goes on in Section 802(b) to define a limited open forum as granting "an offering to or opportunity for one or more non-curriculum related student groups to meet on school premises during non-instructional time."

States have also passed laws dealing with the use of school facilities by non-curriculum-related

---

*A "noncurricular group" is generally recognized as a group that has little or no direct connection to classes taught at the school. For example, the math and foreign language clubs probably would be curriculum-related, while the chess club, recycling club, and boy scouts would likely be considered non-curriculum-related clubs. See *Board of Education v. Mergens*, 496 U.S. 226 (1990).

groups in order to try to clarify who may and who may not use school facilities within a state. It is important to remember, however, that states may not pass laws that restrict or inhibit the exercising of individual rights guaranteed by federal law, either in the U.S. Constitution or federal statutes. School systems in the state of New York were instructed on this principle twice in an eight-year period when they were sued over local school district implementation of a state law. The law in question specified ten purposes for which local school systems could open their facilities to outside vigroups. In 1993 the U.S. Supreme Court heard the case of *Lamb's Chapel v. Center Moriches Union Free School District*, 503 U.S. 385 (1993) in which a local church (Lamb's Chapel) challenged the school system's denial of a request to use school facilities for the purpose of showing a film series by Christian author and radio personality Dr. James Dobson. In a unanimous decision, the Court held that since the school allowed the facilities to be used by other groups speaking on similar topics, it was a violation of the Free Speech Clause of the First Amendment to deny Lamb's Chapel's request, simply because it approached the topics from a religious perspective. The Court noted that restrictions on free speech must be viewpoint-neutral in order to pass constitutional muster. Simply put, once a school system has opened its forum, in this case its facilities, to a class of speech, it must open the forum to all similar speech on a viewpoint-neutral basis. The Lamb's Chapel Court went on to discount the possibility that allowing the use of facilities by a church would constitute an establishment of religion in violation of the First Amendment. Relevant factors the Court considered in dismissing the school system's Establishment Clause defense included the fact that the "film series would not have been shown during school hours, would not have been sponsored by the school, and would have been open to the public" (*Lamb's Chapel*, p. 386).

The second New York case to reach the U.S. Supreme Court on this issue was *Good News Club v. Milford*, 533 U.S. 98 (2001). In the *Good News Club* case, Milford Central School denied the application for use of facilities by a local Christian group, the Good News Club, for the purposes of meeting to sing songs, pray, learn Bible verses, etc. As in *Lamb's Chapel*, the Court ruled in favor of the Christian group, holding that the school system's denial violated the Free Speech Clause of the First Amendment. As it had done in its *Lamb's Chapel* decision, the Court in *Good News Club* rejected the Establishment Clause justification proffered by the school system. Importantly, Milford Central School is an elementary school, and therefore has students most likely to be impressionable. Even with a young student body, the Court did not find any reason to fear coercion or other undue religious influence on the part of the school system that might support an Establishment Clause defense.

Educators should take from these cases the lesson that school facilities are to be open to groups on a viewpoint-neutral basis, regardless of the age of the students attending the school. This does not mean, however, that schools must open their doors to whomever may wish to use them. The Court recognized in both *Lamb's Chapel* and *Good News Club* that the school systems did not have to open their facilities to anyone outside the school. As the Court stated in *Lamb's Chapel*, "There is no question that the district may legally preserve the property under its control, and need not have permitted after-hours use for any of the uses permitted under state law" (*Lamb's Chapel*, p. 385). But, when a school system opens its facilities to any group to speak on a topic, that is, groups promoting the community welfare, it must open them to all like groups on a viewpoint-neutral basis.

FUNDING EQUITY AND FACILITIES

Historically, American public schools have been built at the community level in order to serve the discreet population of an individual community. Funding of public schools, including related facilities, has often also been the responsibility of these communities. Just as the wealth of separate communities varies greatly from county to county, and even within counties and cities, the size and serviceability of school facilities have varied greatly. Disparity in public school facilities is usually the result of funding mechanisms that are based on property tax values, or are otherwise tied to the wealth of the district in which the school is located. Further, such disparity has been the subject of extensive litigation. Although this litigation has a long history, the modern era of funding litigation began with the Supreme Court of California's landmark decision in *Serrano v. Priest* (1971), which resulted in victory for funding equity plaintiffs, and established a model for similar litigation in other states. In the thirty years since *Serrano*, thirty-five states' highest courts have ruled on the merits of constitutional challenges to their states' funding systems, with eighteen courts upholding states' systems of public school funding, and seventeen courts declaring school funding systems unconstitutional (Dayton, 2001).

Funding equity litigation is increasingly focused on variations in the quality of local public school facilities. For example, in defining what constituted an adequate education under the South Carolina Constitution, the Supreme Court of South Carolina stated in *Abbeville v. State* (1999, p. 540):

> We define this minimally adequate education required by our Constitution to include *providing students adequate and safe facilities* in which they have the opportunity to acquire: 1) the ability to read, write, and speak the English language, and knowledge of mathematics and physical science; 2) a fundamental knowledge of economic, social, and political systems, and of history and governmental processes; and 3) academic and vocational skills [emphasis added].

Concerns over inadequate school facilities were significant factors in many state high court declarations that states had failed to meet constitutional mandates concerning public education. Facilities are likely to remain a focal point of future public school funding equity litigation because of the serious inadequacies in many school facilities, and the powerful impact of facilities-related

evidence. Plaintiffs have introduced evidence of deplorable conditions in their state's poorest schools, documenting conditions in facilities ranging from the merely inadequate to the dangerous, including evidence of asbestos, deteriorating floors, lead in drinking water, etc. Plaintiffs have used photographs, building plans, state inspection reports, and other tangible evidence of inequities that may have a stronger evidentiary impact than more traditional testimony concerning abstract statistical comparisons of fiscal equity. This especially holds true since the matter at issue in these cases is the quality of educational opportunity and not mere mathematical equivalence of expenditures. While it is one thing to enter into evidence the fact that some children may have more money than others available for their education, it is quite another to enter into evidence the fact that while some children have state-of-the-art facilities, Olympic-sized swimming pools, and tennis courts, children in poorer schools have "deplorable restroom facilities . . . holes in the floor" and elementary children "playing on *imaginary* playground equipment" (Opinion of the Justices, 1993, p. 121).

SECURITY

Public schools must increasingly consider security concerns in the design and operation of public school facilities. Tort law requires school officials to do what a reasonable person would do under the circumstances, and as technology makes it possible to create a safer and more secure environment for children, reasonable school officials would take advantage of this technology to protect their children. Appropriate use of technology, and a well-planned facility and grounds can significantly enhance the safety and security of students by making it difficult for unauthorized persons to enter without being detected by school officials. Further, school facilities should be designed to aid in preventing students from unauthorized exit from the building, a special concern regarding special education students with disabilities that may increase their risk of injury if unsupervised. Facilities should also be designed to limit unauthorized or accidental access to mechanical and storage areas that might contain dangerous equipment or supplies. Failure to take reasonable precautions in securing personnel, facilities, and supplies could not only result in significant danger or injuries to students or faculty, but also could result in tort liability for negligence.

DEMOGRAPHICS AND DESEGREGATION

Throughout much of American history, children attended schools that accommodated only other students of their race. This phenomenon occurred due to the de jure, or by law, system of racial segregation in many states' public schools. In those sections of the country where there was no legal mandate for segregated schools, the schools were often segregated anyway in accordance with custom. Contributing to this situation, housing patterns in many cities led to de facto segregation, or segregation caused by the private housing choices of individuals. In the years immediately following the Supreme Court's seminal decision in *Brown v. Board of Education* (1954), courts tended not to distinguish between de jure and de facto segregation. Instead, courts ordered desegregation efforts to take place in systems with both types of segregation, and retained the responsibility for monitoring school systems to ensure that their orders were carried out. The costs of complying with desegregation orders, in terms of finances and administrative burdens, were often very high.

Since significant time has elapsed from the era of de jure segregation, courts will no longer issue desegregation orders to remedy de facto segregation. Consequently, as Dayton (1993) recognized, desegregation efforts in the United States are rapidly coming to a close. Most public schools in the United States are no longer under desegregation orders. Absent proof of a new constitutional violation, resegregation due to de facto segregation is not legally actionable. Nonetheless, school officials responsible for planning new school facilities would be wise to consider local social and demographic shifts that may affect the racial composition of new schools, as race is likely to remain a hazardous political issue even in the absence of any judicial intervention.

SUMMARY

School administrators and designers alike must be cognizant of the legal environment in which they operate. This chapter presents an overview of several topics that are pertinent to the planning, design, and construction of school facilities. Whether purchasing land or equipment, or hiring out services (e.g., architectural, cleaning), school systems enter into contractual relationships with a variety of outside parties. For a contract to be valid, there must be both and offer and an acceptance of the offer. When one or more parties are unhappy with the results of a contract, or with the process itself, they may choose to pursue litigation to either enforce or rescind the contract.

In order to protect taxpayers and help ensure that governmental agencies respect the constitutional limitations on their power, most states have enacted open meeting (or "sunshine") laws that provide the public with access to meetings and/or copies of their transcripts. The government does indeed have power that it can exert with respect to school construction. The legal justification for the taking of private property for use by the government (for the purpose of siting a school, e.g.) is known as eminent domain. School officials must become familiar with the statutes outlining the conditions under which land may be taken, and the procedure for doing so if they are considering using their authority in this manner. This is a very unpopular approach to acquiring a school site.

As applied to both public and private institutions, zoning and building codes serve multiple purposes, such as minimizing unnecessary health and safety risks to the occupants and visitors of the building and attempting to protect the property value of surrounding locations. Additionally, when applied to institutions like public school systems, zoning and building codes often seek to maximize the efficient use of taxpayer dollars. In addition to state and local zoning and building codes, there are federal mandates regarding facilities with which schools must comply. For example, Section 504 of the Rehabilitation Act of 1973 states that "no otherwise qualified individual with a disability . . . shall, solely by reason of his or her disability, be excluded from the participation in, be denied benefits of, or be subjected to discrimination under any program or activity receiving Federal financial assistance." Schools must therefore make reasonable accommodations for disabled persons. Further strengthened by the Americans with Disabilities Act (ADA) of 1990, all new school construction must comply with barrier-free design requirements mandated by the ADA. Certain types of facilities and equipment may also be required under the Individuals with Disabilities Education Act (IDEA) of 1997 for students qualifying for special education.

Tort law pertains to cases involving monetary or other compensation for injury. School officials are obligated to provide a safe environment for students, employees, and visitors and they must regularly monitor their facilities for emerging dangers, and use reasonable care in supervising the maintenance of their facilities to avoid legal liability. School playgrounds are areas where injury is perhaps most likely, but the trend towards the use of softer materials, unlike the concrete and steel of the past, and a keen eye toward safety make injuries less likely. Students, school employees, and neighboring properties must also be protected from toxics and other environmental hazards. Strategies such as minimizing the use of herbicides and pesticides on school property should be implemented. Schools must also provide safe, secure places for occupants. Failure to take reasonable precautions in securing personnel, facilities, and supplies could not only result in significant danger or injuries to students or faculty, but also could result in tort liability for negligence.

Schools are increasingly becoming community resource centers that provide space to noncurricular groups, both during and after school hours. While there are many benefits to students and the broader community that may be derived from such arrangements, school officials must understand that if they allow school facilities to be used by outside groups, they must not prohibit certain groups from holding meetings in the facility based on the viewpoint (e.g., religious) of the meeting. Another on-going legal battle faced by educators is related to funding equity, which is increasingly focused on variations in the quality of local public school facilities that often occurs as a result of school funding mechanisms based on the wealth of the community served. In several cases, school funding mechanisms have been declared unconstitutional. School desegregation issues were, in the past, dealt with in the courts. Although court-ordered desegregation efforts (such as busing) in the United States are now coming to a close, officials responsible for planning new school facilities would be wise to consider local social and demographic shifts that may affect the racial composition of new schools.

ACTIVITIES

1. Identify and describe in detail one lawsuit involving a school or school system within the past five years pertaining to tort law. Be sure to include a citation for the source from which it was obtained. Based on the information you acquired, do you agree with the court's decision? Why or why not? You will be asked to share this in class.

2. Integrated Pest Management (IPM) is one strategy presented in this chapter for preventing exposure to hazardous and toxic substances in schools. Identify and describe in detail at least three other types of strategies schools can implement to minimize the risks of hazardous chemicals or harmful biological contaminants.

3. Identify and describe two lawsuits brought against a school system or state regarding the constitutionality of public school funding mechanisms. One case should illustrate the court's upholding of a funding mechanism, but the other ought to be a case in which the funding mechanism was declared unconstitutional.

4. Sometimes, the quality of school construction is less than what was originally expected by the school and community. There are inferior materials, and poor construction techniques that may become a problem. For example, problem areas may include leaking roofs, failure to insulate the buildings properly, inadequate air exchange, and low-quality electrical systems. Search the literature or ask some school leaders if there are any legal cases regarding poor and unsafe school construction in their area. Develop a short report on these issues.

REFERENCES

Abbeville v. State, 515 S.E.2d 535 (S.C. 1999).

Americans with Disabilities Act, 42 U.S.C. § 12101 (2001).

Bauman v. Ross, 167 U.S. 548 (1897).

Brown v. Board of Education, 347 U.S. 483 (1954).

California Code of Regulations (2004).

Code of Federal Regulations (2004).

Dayton, J. (1993). Desegregation: Is the court preparing to say it is finished? *Education Law Reporter*, 84:897.

Dayton, J. (2001). Serrano and its progeny: An analysis of 30 years of school funding litigation. *Education Law Reporter*, 157:447.

Equal Access Act, 20 U.S.C. § 4071 (1984).

Good News Club v. Milford, 533 U.S. 98 (2001).

Individuals with Disabilities Education Act, 20 U.S.C. § 1400 (1997).

Lamb's Chapel v. Center Moriches Union Free School District, 503 U.S. 385 (1993).

Official Code of Georgia (2004).

Opinion of the Justices, 624 So.2d 107 (Ala. 1993).

Rehabilitation Act of 1973, 29 U.S.C. § 794 (1990).

Santa Fe v. Doe, 530 U.S. 290 (2000).

Serrano v. Priest, 487 P.2d 1241 (Cal. 1971).

Uniform Federal Accessibility Standards (UFAS), 41 C.F.R. § 101 (2003).

United States Constitution (2004).

CHAPTER ELEVEN

FINANCING SCHOOL INFRASTRUCTURE PROJECTS

CATHERINE C. SIELKE
The University of Georgia

Other chapters in this book have emphasized the importance of planning for school infrastructure projects. Of vital importance to the planning process is an understanding of financing the projects. Knowledge of debt limitations and allowable financing mechanisms is absolutely necessary. This chapter explores the many options available to school districts to fund school infrastructure projects, providing basic information about local, state, and federal funding available to local school districts, and it presents information that will aid the local school district management in deciding what options to use in funding school infrastructure projects. The reader is strongly advised to consult state laws to learn what is available in his or her local district.

School district administrators and planners need to be aware of the funding mechanisms available to them as they plan for construction and/or renovation of facilities. State laws sometimes severely limit the amount of indebtedness a school district can incur. Some require matching funding or some form of local effort to receive state aid. Some states provide no direct aid to the local district. A few school districts have found themselves in the position of having developed aggressive building plans (or sometimes not so aggressive) building plans (or sometimes not so aggressive) only to discover that the plans cannot be implemented because of fiscal limitations.

This chapter will first present a short historical overview of funding. Next, local funding options will be discussed. The majority of this section will concern the bond issue, since it is still the mainstay or financing capital projects. Subsequently, the chapter will explore state funding options, and conclude with federal funding initiatives.

THE HISTORICAL PERSPECTIVE

Traditionally, the schoolhouse has been the symbol of community spirit and local ownership and control. Like many other public buildings, groups of community members came together in the early years of public schools and donated the materials and time to construct the nation's schools. These schools were usually one-room schoolhouses and were uncomplicated structures. There was no air-conditioning. Heat came from a stove or fireplace that was probably not efficiently situated, and there was no concern about handicapped accessibility.

As enrollments grew and curriculum requirements changed, our nation needed more schools, and the facilities needed to accommodate the demands of new curriculum standards. Local citizens could no longer provide the time and materials needed to construct the needed school facilities, and so the community had to find ways to finance these investments in education. The bond issue became the vehicle to raise the necessary funding while allowing citizens to stretch the repayment over many years.

Today, Americans still face the problem of providing school facilities and other related infrastructure. Enrollments are again growing; many of our nation's schools are in disrepair and/or facing health and safety issues. While many states have come forward with very large sums of money to help finance capital projects, the mainstay of funding these projects is still the school bond issue. Although states have increased their activity in funding capital projects, much of the funding is still provided by the local community, and much state funding is premised on the local passage of a bond issue.

The next section will discuss local funding options available to school districts. The bonding process will be discussed in detail due to its importance in the funding of capital projects.

LOCAL FUNDING OPTIONS

Determining What Is Affordable

Whether the district uses a very large community-based committee or a small central office committee to plan for the district's capital projects, it is absolutely necessary that district officials have a realistic grasp of the financial resources available to the district and what the planned project(s) will cost.

Most school districts are not fiscally able to engage in capital projects using current year revenues. Bond issues are the most common form of borrowing school districts use to fund these capital projects. Most states impose some kind of debt limitation on local school districts. The debt limit is a function of the tax base that will be used to refund the borrowing that occurs. This debt limit is usually expressed as a percent of the taxable property or *assessed valuation* (AV) of the school district.

For example, Michigan law (Michigan School Code, 1996) prohibits school districts from issuing bonds for an amount greater than the 15 percent of the total assessed valuation of the district. In a 1998 study using the restricted range, Sielke showed that assessed valuation ranged from a low of $32.8 million to a high of $1.2 billion. These figures reveal that the district with the low assessed valuation can only go into debt for approximately $4.8 million, which is hardly enough to finance a new elementary school. On the other hand, the district on the high end can go into debt for approximately $179.4 million. Of course, another key factor is enrollment. The Michigan study showed that taxable property wealth per pupil ranged from $49,019 to $242,356. This means that one school district could go into debt approximately $7,353 per pupil, while the other district could go into debt approximately $36,353 per pupil. In other words, even on a per pupil basis, some districts may have almost five times as much capacity per pupil to borrow. These disparities exist in all states where bond issues are used and no equalizing state aid plans exist.

It is important that school district administrators understand these potential limitations as they work with stakeholders to develop plans for school capital projects. Credibility of the district's administration could certainly be called into question if the administration were to lead the stakeholders into developing an extensive and costly capital projects plan only to find out later that the district is prohibited by law and/or that aid is not available to fund the plan.

Debt limits vary widely from state to state. Readers are urged to contact their state department of education to find out their districts' debt limitations.

The Bond Issue

The most common source of funding for school infrastructure projects is the bond issue. All states, with the exception of a few, allow local school districts to bond for school facilities. A few states, such as Alabama, that had dependent school districts place the authority to bond with the governing municipality. In Alaska, Hawaii, and Maryland only the state has the authority to issue state bonds. Even much of the funding that derives from state sources comes from state-issued bonds (see Sielke, 2003). The bond issue has great advantages but it is not without its disadvantages.

Advantages.   Probably the greatest advantage of the bond issue is that it places very large sums of money into the school district at one time. There is no need for the district to save dollars over the years; bond funding is available as soon as the bonds are sold on the bond market. The fact that the money arrives all at one time allows the school district to invest the funds. Since school construction and renovation projects can extend over several years, the interest accrued can be used to further fund the project. School district administrators must be aware, however, of the many rules and regulations involved in the handling of these monies. Some of these issues, such as arbitrage, will be discussed later.

A second advantage of the school bond issue is that the debt is *amortized* so payment is deferred over time. Restrictions vary from state to state as to the length of time the bonds can be repaid. The deferring of payment means that many people will share in the responsibility of paying for the building project. Schools last a long time, and, like homes, it is often thought to be advantageous to spread that debt over a number of years.

For the investor, school bonds (also referred to as municipal bonds) are attractive investments. Although the bonds usually carry lower interest rates than other investment options, interest earned from municipal bonds is exempt from federal income tax. (In some states, interest from municipal bonds is also exempt from state income tax.) In addition, this investment is very secure because the school district has the taxing authority to raise the required amount due. Further, in times of stock market turmoil, the bond market tends to remain very stable.

Disadvantages.   A definite disadvantage to bonding is that, like borrowing for any other need, the borrower (i.e., the school district) pays much more, sometimes two or three times as much, for the capital project due to the interest costs. Another disadvantage identified by Brimley and Garfield (2005) is that bond issues may result in buildings which are larger and more elaborate than necessary. They contend that because the money is more readily available, buildings may become more extravagant than if the building is constructed using existing resources.

A definite disadvantage to bonding is that most states require voter approval. According to Sielke (2003), seven states (Iowa, Mississippi, Nebraska, New Hampshire, North Dakota, Oklahoma, and Oregon) require super-majorities. We must not forget that taxpayer revolt is as American as apple pie (remember the Boston Tea Party). Americans are living in a recent era of taxpayer revolt that began in the 1970s in California and continues to the present day. In today's world of taxpayer revolt, many school districts have trouble getting bond issues passed.

Bond issue data are difficult to come by, as many states do not collect the data systematically. The U.S. General Accounting Office or GAO (2000) reported that nineteen states were able to provide data on bond issues in 1998. According to the report, 455 referenda were placed before the public. Only 54 percent of bond issue initiatives were successful, and these successful referenda provided $9,052 million, which was 54 percent of the amount requested. In other words, only about half of the dollars needed for school infrastructure needs was made available. In fact, the amount of unmet needs may be greater because tax limitations and debt limits may have prohibited some school districts from requesting the full amount needed. So while bond issues remain a major contributor to the construction and renovation of schools, they are victims of the voter protest that has been occurring in America since the 1970s.

Several journals, such as *School Business Affairs* and *The American School Board Journal*, contain articles that relate stories of successful bond issues. The reader may find those articles helpful in planning for a bond issue. The caveat must be given, however, that these stories are anecdotal. Very few research-based studies have been conducted regarding voter behavior in bond issues.

Perhaps the greatest disadvantage to bonding is its link to property values, raising issues of both student and taxpayer equity. Part of the inequity was shown in the Michigan example above when discussing debt limitations. As long as the bond issue is the only funding mechanism available in some states, children who reside in low-wealth districts may never enjoy the same facilities that children in other districts do. At the same time, taxpayers in low-wealth districts will need to put forth greater local effort (pay high millage rates) to provide their children with equitable facilities unless the state intervenes in the funding process. While the courts addressed this issue early on in *Serrano v. Priest* (487 P.2d 1241 (Cal. 1971)), they have been slow to apply the same equity principles to school facilities. Arizona litigation (*Roosevelt Elementary School District No. 66 v. Bishop*, Ariz. 233; 877 P.2d 806, 1994) addressed solely the issue of inequitable school facilities. A more recent Ohio case (*DeRolph v. State*, 766 N.E. 2d 733; Ohio, 1997) had much broader concerns than the Arizona case, but facilities in general and rural school systems' facilities in particular were very much an issue in this lawsuit. In both states, part of the remedy was to create an agency *outside* of the state department of education. These two cases may suggest a trend toward more legal challenges of current school infrastructure funding practices.

Establishing a Credit Rating

Like private individuals and private businesses, school districts must also be concerned about their credit rating. Bonding is borrowing, and a district's credit rating can have a major impact on the interest rate charged for the bond issue and on the marketability of the issue. Investors are more likely to buy bonds from school districts having high credit ratings. Casillas and Hamill (2002) report that there are three nationally recognized credit-rating agencies: Standard and Poor's, Moody's, and Fitch IBCA. The Security and Exchange Commission (SEC) regulates these rating agencies. Casillas and Hamill further report that almost 3,000 school districts in the United States have been rated by Moody's.

Because investors—those people school districts expect to buy their bonds—have neither the time, knowledge, nor expertise to personally investigate a potential investment, they rely on the rating given by one of the rating agencies. The most common rating agencies are Standard and Poor's and Moody's. On the Standard and Poor's scale, bonds are rated from AAA (the best), AA, A through D (the worst). Moody's rate bonds from Aaa (the best) to D (the worst). The bond rating can have a substantial impact on the interest rate the local district will have to pay. A low rating may even discourage buyers from purchasing the bonds at all. Casillas and Hamill (2002) estimate that a $10 million bond issue rated BBB that is amortized over twenty years at 2001 interest rates might cost a district about $465,000 more in interest than a $10 million bond issue rated A.

Districts need to always be concerned about their credit rating. There is little that a district can do in a hurry to "fix" a bad credit record. However, some of the criteria for judging creditworthiness are not within the control of the district. Credit agencies analyze the following factors (Casillas & Hamill, 2002):

- Managerial governance
- Outstanding debt
- Tax base
- Financial trends
- Other issues

Clearly, the district has much less control over the tax base and financial trends than the governance of the district and outstanding debt. Getting a rating for a bond issue usually requires a trip to New York or San Francisco to meet with the credit agencies. Casillas and Hamill (2002, p. 13) list the following essential documents as essential in the review process:

- Audited financials for the previous three years
- A current adopted budget
- A draft offering statement
- Legal resolutions that describe the bonds, legal structure, and source or repayment of the debt service
- Estimated sources and uses of funds
- A financing calendar
- Appropriate statutory or legislative references
- Descriptions of the projects to be financed
- The overall capital improvements program or phased bonding program
- A ratings presentation that includes economic, financial, and statistical information on the district and other entities that may impact the bond issues (city, county)
- District's mission statement
- Organizational and management chart
- Résumés of top district management

As noted in the above process, this is a meeting for which a lot of preparation is involved. The procedure requires that school district management constantly update the information and enforce the highest quality of district fiscal management from budgeting to auditing.

BOND ISSUE DO'S AND DON'TS

Hiring Consultants

The bonding process is very complex. The money spent in hiring financial experts and bond counsel is usually a good investment. The district needs to have consultants working with them whose everyday job is to forecast property value growth, to aid in the preparation of the documents to be used in the credit rating process, to calculate the amount needed to fund the project(s), and to provide the

needed legal assistance in wording the ballot. School district officials are strongly advised to check the credentials of consultants before employing them. Huge sums of money are involved in capital projects and the chances for fraud or just plain incompetence are greater when dealing with these projects than when working with general fund expenditures. (See, e.g., "55 PA Districts Victimized by Alleged Financial Scheme," *Education Week*, November 12, 1997.)

Wording the Ballot

The wording of the bond issue ballot is extremely important. Unlike referenda that request millage increases, the bond issue usually must state the specific amount and the specific purpose for use of the requested funds. Approval of the bond issue gives the school district the right to levy property taxes in the amount needed to meet the annual principal and interest payments. School districts are not allowed to use this funding for other purposes. For example, if a ballot requested funding for a new school, and there is money remaining after the construction is completed, the district may *not* use the excess for general fund expenditures.

Accounting Procedures

The passage of a bond issue necessitates the creation of two new funds—one a capital projects fund and the other a debt service fund. Agencies overseeing the accounting of school district funds, such as the Governmental Accounting Standards Board (GASB), and organizations that work with school business officials (such as the Association of School Business Officials, ASBO) recommend the establishment of self-balancing accounts for each capital project. "Differences in each bond issue's proceeds, interest rate, interest payment dates, maturity dates and in the purposes for which revenue may be used make it desirable to use separate and independent funds for each major capital project" (Everett, Lows, & Johnson, 1996, p. 133).

The capital projects fund is used to record the revenues and the expenditures for the project. The revenues are the proceeds from the bond issue. The expenditures are the payments for the construction, architects, etc. that are part of the project. All revenues placed in this fund must be used for the project(s) that were approved on the bond ballot. Funds that result from the bond issue, taxes levied to repay the debt, state aid earmarked for capital projects, etc. may not be commingled with the monies in any other fund.

The debt service fund is used to repay the principal, interest, and fees associated with the bonds. The revenues recorded in the debt service fund can come from many sources. The most common revenue is the property tax proceeds resulting from a mill levy earmarked exclusively for the purpose of servicing the debt. Other revenues may come from state grants or other sources allowed in a particular state. The expenditures are the payments of principal and interest owed to the bondholders (those who purchased the bonds) and fees associated with the handling of this debt servicing. The payment of principal and interest is set by an amortization schedule.

State laws usually require that money collected for capital projects or for debt service remain within those funds and restrict their use to eliminating the principal and interest.

Budgeting Issues

Budgeting is an essential element of financing school projects. Capital projects extend into multiple fiscal years, so budgeting and cash flow management require a somewhat different perspective than general fund budgeting. For example, all the bond proceeds come to the district at one time. However, the majority of the money may not be expended until well into the second or even third year when the capital project is completed or nearing completion. Therefore, the district needs to look for ways to invest the funds for longer periods of time than might be possible with general fund revenues. Wise investing increases the amount of available funding. On the other hand, the district needs to manage the budget and cash flow so that the funds are available to complete the specific proj-

ects that were promised to voters when they approved the bond issue.

The Internal Revenue Service (IRS) closely monitors school district borrowing. School districts enjoy tax-exempt status. The IRS code does not allow school districts to borrow and profit from it. Because school districts are tax-exempt, they can often borrow money, whether it is for cash flow or for bonding, at lower than usual interest rates. School districts have sometimes borrowed at low rates and then invested the borrowed money in higher (sometimes much higher) interest-bearing instruments. Engaging in this activity is referred to as arbitrage. The IRS can levy penalties and interest on school districts that engage in *arbitrage* and can also revoke their tax-exempt status. However, the IRS usually allows school districts to take advantage of accruing interest from the proceeds of bond issues as long as 85 percent of the proceeds are used for the purpose for which they were issued and are expended within three years of the issue date (Everett, Lows, & Johnson, 1996).

LOCAL OPTION SALES TAXES

At least three Southeastern states—Georgia, Florida, and North Carolina—allow local school systems to levy a special local option sales tax. Georgia and North Carolina allow a one cent tax, and Florida's limit is one half cent. This additional levy requires voter approval. The GAO (2000) reported that in Georgia, the special local option sales tax has been so successful that bond issues are rarely being used to fund school infrastructure needs. Iowa allows a county, not a school district, sales tax for the purposes of capital projects.

There are many advantages to a local option sales tax. One of those advantages is that it offers a school system the ability to raise very large sums of money in a very short period of time. It is virtually a pay-as-you-go method.

A second great advantage is that, unlike the property tax that is used to repay bonds, the tax can be transferred to people who do not live in the school district or even in the state. Everyone who buys something taxed within the school system is supporting that school district's school facility projects.

The local option sales tax is not without its drawbacks and its critics. First of all, states such as Georgia and Florida have county school systems, which are very large. A small school district, such as those existing in the Northeast and Midwest, may not have enough of a commercial base to even think about using a sales tax as a substitute for a bond issue. In fact, rural school districts in Georgia have been vocal in their opposition to the local option sales tax because not only do they not have a base to tax, but they also support a neighboring school system when they go to a large mall area to shop.

Projecting the revenues from a sales tax can be more difficult than projecting the revenues from a property tax levy. Property taxes are relatively inelastic. Property wealth does not fluctuate much (and particularly not negatively) with changes in the economy. In fact, this is why the property tax has been such a wonderful workhorse for education throughout the years—it is incredibly stable and predictable. Sales tax revenues are highly correlated with the upswings and downturns of the economy. Districts relying on the sales tax must carefully plan their projects so as not to find themselves unable to finish projects due to a downturn in revenues. School district administrators must also be attuned to commercial growth in neighboring school districts. All it takes is one new shopping mall to redirect shoppers and sales tax revenue.

SINKING FUNDS

Other local funding options may include the sinking fund. This option allows districts to have a special savings account earmarked for facility needs. Once again, however, this option frequently requires voter approval for the additional millage that will be levied and placed in the fund. Proponents of the sinking fund see it as a way to finance future needs on a cash basis. The sinking fund is usually established for a set number of years (again, controlled by state law) and has the potential to increase in size as the fiscally prudent school district administration wisely invests the revenues in safe, interest-bearing investments.

Critics point to the fact that over the years the needs of the district may change. The board members and administrators who planned and guided the public in setting goals for the district may be gone when the sinking fund has matured and is ready for use. Or else, the needs of the district may have changed tremendously, and the projected needs no longer exist.

Some states, particularly those with very high enrollment growth, are using developer or impact fees to pay for the construction of school buildings to accommodate the children that arrive with new homes. This option is seen as a way to have those who benefit most from the school directly paying some of the costs. Of course, the developer passes on the cost to the home buyer. In some areas of the country, however, the impact fee is being levied by not only school districts but also by city and county governments that must supply water lines, roads, additional police and fire, etc. The compounding of these fees serves to make homes in the community much more expensive to purchase.

LEASE-PURCHASE AGREEMENTS AND CERTIFICATES OF PARTICIPATION

The lease-purchase option for acquiring school facilities has become available to more school districts in recent years. The increase of interest in this option may be due to the need to construct school facilities when districts cannot access the bonding option. Perhaps the debt limit holds the district back from being able to bond for all the required funding, or perhaps the district has been unable to develop a successful bond referendum. The lease-purchase agreement may, depending on state law, eliminate the need for voter approval.

In using the lease-purchase option, the district acquires a building whereby ownership of the title resides with another party. The district will enter into an agreement to pay a determined dollar amount per year, and at the end of the contract, the building will belong to the district and the title will be transferred. The advantage to a lease-purchase agreement is that the need for a facility is satisfied in a short period of time.

There are, however, many disadvantages and risks involved with the lease-purchase process. The first disadvantage is that the lease-purchase option may cost more than more traditional routes. Second, if the building to be leased has not been used for educational purposes, the district may incur additional costs in remodeling and retrofitting the building to meet the curricular and noncurricular needs of the students (this includes technology considerations).

A definite disadvantage, and where the risk factor increases, is that the payments are paid out of current year, general fund revenues. The lease-purchase may, then, place the district in the position of having to raise the local mill levy in order to meet the payments, and this may require a referendum. Taxpayers, who may not be appreciative of these efforts, might decide to vote against an increase in millage and force school district administrators to cut the regular programs and services that students have been receiving. In addition, taxpayers highly disapprove of a decision to bypass voter approval for a bond issue and incur debt that must be paid from current year dollars.

A similar option to the lease-purchase agreement is what is being called "certificates of participation" (CAPs). These more closely compare with tax anticipation notes (TANs). The CAP is actually a loan from an investor, and like any other loan to a school district, it must adhere to all rules and regulations regarding borrowing. The school district receives the money from the CAP and uses it to build the property and/or schoolhouse. The investor holds the title on the property. The school district repays, out of current revenues, the investor for the specified number of years. The premium is often as high as twenty points over the general obligation bond due to the risks involved. (Remember that the general obligation bond gives the

district the right to levy the needed millage to make the payments and these bonds are almost always voter-approved.)

One school district that is using a CAP explained that due to the economic downturn, sales tax receipts had dropped. The district, which is experiencing very rapid growth, had been relying totally on sales tax dollars to fund construction. The district found that it was unable to complete some of the construction that was already under way and could not start any new construction. It is aware of the risks, but believes the community is more unhappy with the number of students that are not housed in regular school buildings than they are with the alternative funding method. The district is obviously hoping that the sales tax revenues will rebound soon.

PAY-AS-YOU GO

The pay-as-you-go method is self-explanatory. The district pays for its capital projects on an annual basis. Some states allow districts to levy special mills for the explicit purpose of these capital projects. The amount generated by these additional mills is, of course, highly dependent on the property wealth of the district. Very wealthy districts may be able to use this annual revenue to meet many of its facility needs, while districts with lower property wealth will only be able to address less expensive capital projects. Depending on the state, these mills may be authorized by the board of education or they may require voter approval.

STATE FUNDING OF CAPITAL PROJECTS

Direct State Aid

While a majority of the funding for school construction and renovation has been generated at the local level, state funding has also been available in certain states. As early as 1898, some states were providing grants for school facility needs as an incentive for consolidation. However, by as late as the 1940s, only twelve states were providing aid for capital outlay and debt service (Thompson & Wood, 2001). By 1994 thirty-five states were providing some type of capital outlay funding (Gold, Smith, & Lawton, 1995). By 1999 that number had increased to forty-one (Sielke et al., 2001; Sielke & Holmes, 2001).

In 2002 eight states (Louisiana, Michigan, Missouri, Nevada, North Dakota, Oklahoma, Oregon, and South Dakota) provided no state funding for school infrastructure projects (Sielke, 2003). In the rest of the forty-two states, funding support ranged from full state funding to minimal amounts of per pupil funding. The increased state involvement in funding school construction results from a number of factors: recent litigation that has expanded equity from programmatic issues to facilities issues, increased enrollments, state mandates that require more classrooms, and large state fund balances.

State interest in funding capital projects is shown by the amount of legislative activity that occurred in the area of school finance. Crampton's (Crampton, 2000, 2001) tracking of state legislative activity revealed that in 1994 only eighteen bills affecting funding for facilities were passed by state legislatures and signed into law. That number increased to seventy bills in 1997 and then dropped to sixty bills in 1998. However, legislative activity peaked in 1999 when ninety-three bills were passed and signed into law.

Two states, Ohio and Arizona, have developed state agencies that are directly funded by their legislatures and are responsible for all school capital projects. The only state to have complete state funding is Hawaii, which is one school system. Arizona funds all school facility projects that are state-approved projects. However, the approval and funding are limited to the state-set standards. Districts planning to build school facilities that exceed state standards are required to seek local funding, usually bond issues, to finance those efforts.

Several states, while improving funding, are requiring approval of projects by the state depart-ment of education. Some states, such as Georgia, offer additional fiscal incentives if districts choose to use state-approved plans, architects, construction managers, etc. While many may question the balance between state and local control on this issue, states view these incentives as ways to improve the ability of low-wealth districts to finance school infrastructure needs.

Flat Grants

Several states offer flat grants on a per pupil basis as part of their facility funding. The flat grant is not considered to be equitable since everyone gets the same amount regardless of need or ability to pay. In several states, the funding for school facility needs is part of the formula calculation for the basic support program.

Equalized Grants

Most states that provide funding for capital project needs use some type of equalized funding. This means that districts having greater fiscal capacity receive less state funding. And concurrently, those having lesser fiscal capacity receive greater funding. When equalized funding is used in the general state aid formulas, almost every district gets funding. When funding capital projects, this is not always the case. While almost all states are providing some funding, very few states have been able to meet all the infrastructure needs. States are much less likely to fund capital projects based on fiscal capacity alone. States are much more likely to use need as the "equalizing" factor. Need is often defined by states as high enrollment growth, health and safety issues, and general disrepair of buildings.

States providing equalized funding usually require school districts to submit planned projects for approval. Those projects are then prioritized at the state level. The legislatively approved funding is then distributed based on the need. The amount each district receives is in inverse relationship with its ability to fund the project on its own.

Some states provide state aid only for debt service, which means that the district has had to have an approved bond issue. Others may provide aid on a match basis, requiring the district to somehow raise even dollars locally to qualify, which again usually means the passage of a bond issue. While there has been a definite improvement over the years in state contributions to the funding of school infrastructure needs, the qualifying requirements may keep some school districts from being able to participate.

Categorical Grants

Some states provide categorical grants, which by definition are funds provided for specific needs or policy goals. Many of the categorical grants that states offer for capital projects are for needs such as meeting the accessibility needs of persons with disabilities, or making "sick" buildings well. Some may be for eliminating portable classrooms in high-growth districts, and others may exist to further the goal of consolidation.

State Loan Authorities

Some states provide loans to school districts that cannot raise the needed funding on their own. Such funding may allow the low-wealth district to complete needed capital projects while borrowing from the state at a very low interest. While these loans are very helpful, it must be remembered that the loan needs to be repaid, and this is often accomplished through the bond issue.

FEDERAL FUNDING

The federal government has a rather large initiative, the Qualified Zone Academy Bond (QZAB), in place to fund the renovation and remodeling of school buildings. The QZAB Program may not be used for new construction. All states are eligible to participate in the program, and funding is for individual schools, not for a school district. The federal funding goes to the state, and each state develops its own procedures for distribution within federal guidelines.

As with most federal programs, there are qualifying factors allowing schools to participate in this funding. First of all, the school needs to be located in an Empowerment Zone or Enterprise Community, or at least 35 percent of its students are eligible for a free or reduced-priced lunch under federal guidelines. The second qualifying factor is that the school district must pass a bond issue for the intended capital project. As discussed above, the passage of a bond issue is sometimes not an easy task.

The QZAB program eliminates the need for the school district to repay the interest associated with bond issues. The district must repay, usually through a property tax levy, the principal amount of the bond issue. Instead of bondholders receiving both a repayment of principal and interest, the federal government allows bondholders a tax credit on their federal income tax.

At this time, there are no data available on the success rate of bond issue referenda when tied to the QZAB program. Obviously, for the school district, the savings can be in the millions of dollars since it must only repay the principal and not the interest. Again, however, the QZAB bonds can be used only for renovation and remodeling and only in qualifying schools.

Other federal programs may be available for certain qualifying school districts. The U.S. Department of Agriculture's Community Facilities Program makes available some funding to rural schools. School district administrators are encouraged to obtain more information about federal aid for school facilities at http://ruralschools.org/news.

START-UP COSTS

This chapter has explored many of the funding options available to local school districts for capital projects. A topic usually ignored is the cost associated with actually opening a new building. The author is personally aware of several schools that remained empty for a year or more because the general funds were not available to hire the staff, purchase the books and supplies, and provide the other items necessary to occupy a school building.

Part of the school district planning associated with capital projects must include the costs of opening a new building. Bond issues and most state funding do not provide funding for the day-to-day operations of school. These funding mechanisms apply to the capital project—the bricks and mortar, so to speak. In opening a new building, the district may need new bus routes and more buses. What about food services? Has that been considered? What about building maintenance and the costs of utilities? Fiscal planning cannot stop at the physical plant level.

SUMMARY

Historically, when students attended simple one-room schoolhouses built by local citizens, often with donated materials, financing school facilities was not much of a challenge. Today, financing these capital projects is one of the most important aspects of school facility planning. The primary responsibility of funding school facilities rests with the local community. The *bond issue* has become the most frequently used vehicle for borrowing needed capital. There are several advantages to using the bond issue to generate revenue. As soon as the bonds are sold, large sums of money are available for school construction at one time. Since school projects usually last over a period of a few years, the interest earned on this money may be used on the project as well (under certain rules and regulations). The debt is also spread out over a number of years. One disadvantage of the bond issue is that due to the interest, the local district will pay much more for the facility than if they were able to pay for a facility outright. And, the bond issue requires voter approval, which is not

always easy to obtain. Most states impose debt limitation on local districts, typically based on the assessed valuation (a percentage of taxable property) of the district, making it difficult for poorer communities to build new schools.

In order to borrow funds through the bond issue, school districts must establish a credit rating and districts must always be concerned about maintaining a high rating. Once a bond is passed, two new funds are created — a capital projects fund (to record revenues and expenditures) and a debt service fund (for repaying principal, interest, and fees). Budgeting can be a complex process of decision making about investment and cash flow issues and must be carefully managed.

The *local option sales tax* is another mechanism for funding school construction projects. Used successfully by some states, when voters approve of this special-purpose sales tax increase (typically, 1/2 to 1 percent), this mechanism may provide large sums of money in a short period of time. But if shoppers are drawn outside a school district to neighboring retail centers, sales tax revenue will fall. Also, rural districts lacking in commercial businesses often oppose the local option sales tax because they are unable to generate much revenue themselves, while supporting neighboring districts when they shop in their stores. This mechanism also makes planning more difficult since it is impossible to predict exactly how much money will be raised.

Sinking funds is a third option available to local districts for raising capital funds for school construction. The sinking fund also requires voter approval in most circumstances. Using this mechanism, a special savings account is set up for a specified number of years (according to state law) for the additional millage levied. Sometimes, districts will impose developer or impact fees to raise funds for school buildings. The difficulty of predicting school facility needs in the year the sinking fund matures is a disadvantage of using this funding mechanism.

The *lease-purchase* is another option for school districts. With this mechanism, the school district may enter into an agreement with a building owner to pay a certain amount each year until the end of the contract, at which time the title is turned over to the school district. Although the lease-purchase agreement may help local districts that are unable to pass a bond issue, this option may cost more than traditional methods. Because funds are paid out of current year general revenue funds, a referendum may need to be passed by voters. If turned down, the school district may need to cut other services to meet its lease obligations, making this a higher-risk mechanism. A similar option is the "certificate of participation" (CAP). With this mechanism a private lender loans money to the school district and holds the title for a specified number of years. During this time the district repays the loan out of current year revenues, also making this a risky funding mechanism.

Finally, with the *pay-as-you-go* option school districts pay for capital investments on an annual basis. This sometimes requires the levying of a special mill, either authorized by the state board of education or requiring voter approval.

Some states provide financial assistance to local school districts through direct assistance, grants, or loans. Grants are typically one of the following: flat grants, based on a per pupil basis; equalized grants by which districts with lesser fiscal capacity receive greater funding; or categorical grants, provided to meet certain policy goals. When states provide low-interest loans, the school district often must pass a bond issue to repay the loan. The federal government has initiated the Qualified Zone Academy Bond (QZAB) initiative to fund school renovations and remodeling. Qualifying school districts must pass a bond issue for school facility projects. By paying back only the principal and not the interest, districts may save millions of dollars. Investors who purchase the bonds are given a tax credit on their federal income tax rather than interest for their investment. School administrators must be knowledgeable about school funding mechanisms available to their districts and understand that capital projects require extensive fiscal planning and quality fiscal management.

ACTIVITIES

1. Contact your state department of education to find out how school facilities are funded.

2. In your state:

   a. What is the debt limit?
   b. Apply the debt limit to your school district's tax base (equalized, assessed). How much debt can your district incur?
   c. How many and what kind of facilities could your district construct given the tax base and the debt limit?
   d. Is this enough to satisfy the district needs?

3. Does your state provide state aid for school facilities? If so, what kind of aid is provided (flat grant, equalized, etc.) and how much?

4. What options other than bonding are being used in your district to fund capital outlay projects?

5. What are the advantages and disadvantages of the options you listed above?

6. Obtain your latest school district financial audit.

   a. Is there a capital projects fund and/or a debt service fund represented in the audit?
   b. What kinds of revenues are accounted for in the capital projects fund? The debt service fund?
   c. What kinds of expenses are accounted for in the capital projects fund? The debt service fund?
   d. Is there an amortization schedule included in the audit?
   e. If there are any notes pertaining to the capital projects fund and/or the debt service fund, read them and summarize their content. What do they tell you about the capital outlay program for your district?

REFERENCES

Brimley, V., Jr., & Garfield, R. R. (2005). *Financing education in a climate of change*, 9th ed. Boston: Allyn & Bacon.

Casillas, R. A., & Hamill, G. M. (2002). How public school districts can improve their bond ratings. *School Business Affairs*, 68:11–15.

Crampton, F. E. (2000). Education finance legislative activity and trends at the state level. *Journal of Education Finance*, 25:597–607.

Crampton, F. E. (2001). Financing education in the twenty-first century: What state legislative trends of the 1990s portend. *Journal of Education Finance*, 27: 479–500.

Everett, R. E., Lows, R. L., & Johnson, D. R. (1996). *Financial and managerial accounting for school administrators*. Reston, VA: Association of School Business Officials International.

Gold, S. D., Smith, D. M., & Lawton, S. B. (1995). *Public school finance programs of the United States and Canada: 1993–1994*. Albany, NY: The Center for the States.

Michigan School Code (1976). Compiled laws as annotated, Part 17, 135 § 380–1351a. Available at http://www.legislature.mi.gov.

Sielke, C. C. (1998). Michigan school facilities, equity issues, and voter response to bond issues following finance reform. *Journal of Education Finance*, 23: 309–322.

Sielke, C. C. (2003). Financing school infrastructure needs: An overview across the 50 states. In Crampton, F., & Thompson, D. (eds.), *Saving America's school infrastructure*. Greenwich, CT: Information Age Publishing, pp. 27–51.

Sielke, C. C., & Holmes, C. T. (2001). *Highlights of the American Education Finance Association's public school finance programs of the United States and Canada, 1998–1999*. Washington DC: American Federation of Teachers. Also available at http://www.ed.sc.edu/aefa/.

Sielke, C. C., Dayton, J., Holmes, C. T., & Jefferson, A. (2001). *Public school finance programs of the United States and Canada: 1998–1999*. Publication no. NCES 2001-309. Washington, DC: U.S. Department of Education, National Center for Education Statistics. Also available at http://www.nces.ed.gov/edfin/statefinance/statefinancing.asp.

Thompson, D. C., & Wood, R. C. (2001). *Money & schools*, 2nd ed. Larchmont, NY: Eye on Education.

U.S. General Accounting Office (2000). *School facilities*. GAO/HEHS-00-41. Washington, DC: GAO.

Additional Suggested Readings

Crampton, F. E., & Thompson, D. C. (eds). (2003). *Saving America's school infrastructure*. Greenwich, CT: Information Age Publishing.

Garner, C. W. (2004). *Education finance for school leaders: Strategic planning and administration*. Upper Saddle River, NJ: Pearson Education.

Odden, A. R., & Picus, L. O. (2004). *School finance: A policy perspective*, 3rd ed. New York: McGraw-Hill.

Ray, J. R., Hack, W. G., & Candoli, J. C. (2001). *School business administration: A planning approach*, 7th ed. Boston: Allyn & Bacon.

U.S. Department of Education, National Center for Education Statistics (2003). *Financial accounting for local and state school systems: 2003 edition*. Core Finance Data Task Force, National Forum on Education Statistics, NCES 2004-318. Available at http://nces.edu.gov/pubsearch.

PART VII

RESEARCH ON THE PHYSICAL ENVIRONMENT

This section presents some examples of research focusing on educational facilities planning and architecture. Regarding the premises for developing school facilities, research presented here enhances premises 2, 4, and 5 by providing defensible information that will give the school planning and design process direction, supporting goals and objectives with facts, and providing data interpretation for management and planning.

Premises for Developing School Facilities

PREMISE	DESCRIPTOR
Premise 2	The school system has a defined direction—a mission and a vision.
Premise 4	The educational program's goals and objectives are translated into physical places.
Premise 5	Planning and design activities are integrated.

Research on school facilities is often overlooked in academic literature, and historically there has been limited or, at best, sporadic interest in the influence of the physical environment on student learning. The major part of research available, however, is limited to doctoral dissertations, a few unpublished documents that may be retrieved electronically, some articles in trade magazines, and an even smaller number of refereed articles. The main concern planners, architects, and decision makers should have is whether the reported research is sound.

Research, like any other commodity, may be classified according to how, where, and by whom it is produced. The purist sees unbiased scientific research as the only acceptable source for making decisions. Such research entails a random sample of subjects, statistical analysis, and inferences from the sample data to the population. There are two kinds of organizations most likely to produce unbiased scientific research—universities and independent contractors, including policy institutes. For the works of these groups to be accepted by the purist, they must be published in refereed journals (including refereed or peer-reviewed electronic journals). Other means of dissemination not as high on the purist's list are theme journals, dissertations, and the Educational Resources Information Center (ERIC). None of these places as a vehicle of dissemination are perfect in supplying totally unbiased results. Although peer-reviewed journals are the choice of elitists, other methods certainly have merit. The dissertation is usually reviewed by several professionals, and with the advent of improved technology, we are now able to retrieve complete dissertations directly from the Internet. Even the people in charge of refereed journals have biases, which can prevent new and sound research from being published. We see these biases in the field of medicine, where acceptable alternative treatments are administered successfully, but go unnoticed in the main journals because of prejudice against alternative medicine. Bias and prejudice are prevalent in educational research too, where school facilities research has not been viewed as important as behavioral research. Table VII.1 reveals a possible classification scheme for research in educational architecture and planning.

The literature that should be unbiased may be found in the refereed materials published in academic journals. Refereed journals require blind review of submissions and accept only a small percentage of submitted papers for publication. Unfortunately, materials on the physical attributes of learning environments as related to student outcomes are scarce because minimal attention has been given to this area in educational studies. In some educational journals, there has been a bias against research conducted on the physical environment. Perhaps this is a result of people not considering the possibility that the physical environment does influence behavior and subsequently learning, perhaps as much as organizational structure, for example. Attention in educational research has been focused in-

stead on social, cultural, behavioral, and program variables not associated with facilities and the outdoor environment's effects on student outcomes. When information is published about the physical environment, it is often published in non-peer-reviewed journals. Such journals may from time to time publish research, but their quality control is usually in the hands of only one person—the editor. Theme journals (journals selecting various themes) may print "best practices" findings. These can be informative; however, caution should be placed on best practices research, since bias as a result of a small sample may override good science.

Doctoral dissertations are refereed by as many as five professionals, depending on the institution, and are most frequently on a sound and unbiased research footing. Caution should be exercised when making statements based on dissertation research, however. It is advisable to ask where the study was completed and who directed it. Research I institutions usually produce sound doctoral research, but even they may allow a substandard piece of research to slip through the system from time to time. A Research I institution, according to the Carnegie Foundation (2001), offers a full range of baccalaureate programs, is committed to graduate education through the doctorate, gives high pri-

TABLE VII.1   Chart of Research Classification and Dissemination

CLASSIFICATION	WHO PERFORMS THE RESEARCH	ORIGINAL PLACE OF DISSEMINATION
Unbiased scientific research	Universities and some independent contractors	Refereed journals, theme journals, dissertations, and ERIC
Opinion research and action research	Universities, independent contractors, and special interest groups	Refereed journals, theme journals, dissertations, ERIC, and nonrefereed trade journals
Best practices, qualitative research, and production research	Universities, independent contractors, special interest groups, and individuals	Refereed journals, theme journals, dissertations, ERIC, nonrefereed trade journals, internet

ority to research, awards fifty or more doctoral degrees per year, and receives annually at least $40 million in federal support (Carnegie Research I Universities, 2001). The term "Research I" have recently been replaced by the term "Doctoral/Research Universities—Extensive."

There is some production (action) research that comes to the forefront as sound because of who made the statement or wrote the article in a popular magazine or journal. For example, Day's (1999) comments on sound and Abramson's (1991) recommendations on square footage are examples of experienced people sharing what they know to be best practices. In addition, the Council of Educational Facilities Planners, International is an organization, that, over the years, has reported sound action research regarding school facilities. The American Association of School Administrators (AASA), American Institute of Architects (AIA), and Association of School Business Officials (ASBO), International all have shown interest in

school facilities research as well. Also, the Association for Supervision and Curriculum Development (ASCD) has offered information on school design (Meek, 1995).

The research methods, procedures, and results presented in this section have been reported in peer-reviewed journals or defended in dissertations produced at a Research I University. The first presentation, Chapter 12, is a compilation of research from several studies and efforts of sustained study since 1997 at the University of Georgia's School Design and Planning Laboratory (2001). Its focus is the elementary school and includes some work completed by Yarborough (2001). The second study, Chapter 13, is a variation on the work by Andersen (1999), focusing on an assessment of middle schools. Chapter 14 examines relationships among school conditions and educational outcomes, revealing a gap in knowledge concerning important links between these types of variables.

REFERENCES

Abramson, P. (1991). Making the grade. *Architectural Review*, 29:91–93.

Andersen, S. (1999). *The relationship between school design variables and scores on the Iowa Test of Basic Skills*. Unpublished doctoral dissertation, University of Georgia, Athens, GA.

Carnegie Foundation for the Advancement of Teaching (2001). http://www.carnegiefoundation.org/Classification/index.htm.

Carnegie Research I Universities (2001). http://www.washington.edu/tools/universities94.html.

Day, C. W. (July 1999). Sounding off. *American School and University*. http://industryclick.com/magazinearticle.asp?magazineid=134&releaseid=3735&magazinearticleid=33067&siteid=17.

Meek, A. (ed.) (1995). *Designing places for learning*. Alexandria, VA: Association of Supervision and Curriculum Development.

University of Georgia's School Design and Planning Laboratory (2001). http://www.coe.uga.edu/sdpl.

Yarborough, K. A. (2001). *The relationship of school design to academic achievement of elementary school children*. Unpublished doctoral dissertation, University of Georgia, Athens, GA.

CHAPTER TWELVE

THE PHYSICAL ENVIRONMENT AND STUDENT ACHIEVEMENT IN ELEMENTARY SCHOOLS[1]

The conventional wisdom of some school leaders is that educational facilities are only "containers" in which learning occurs. Unfortunately, many educational decision makers, teachers, school board members, parents, and architects think that the design of these containers has little to add to the educational process. While contemporary thought about student learning places strong emphasis on the pupil as the center of the learning process, current educational trends also emphasize heuristic curricula having a variety of objects and projects that are essential to the discovery process. With significant emphasis being placed on educational reform and attention given to smaller schools and new construction, it is timely to consider the physical environment as something other than containers (Bingler, 1995).

The physical environment of schools in the United States is in peril as emphasized in a recent study by the National Center for Educational Statistics (NCES, 2000); hence, the study presented in this chapter hypothesizes that the substandard condition of facilities and, in particular, the inappropriateness of much school design may influence student achievement negatively. The NCES reported that about one-fourth of the schools in the United States were in less than adequate condition. Forty-three percent of the schools in the NCES study were rated as unsatisfactory in at least one of the following environmental design areas: lighting, heating, ventilation, indoor air quality, noise control, and security. Schools in small towns and rural areas were more likely to be deficient in these areas than urban and suburban schools ("47 percent compared to 37 percent," p. v). Based on the capacity of such schools, approximately 25 percent were overcrowded and large schools were likely to be more overcrowded than small schools. "Schools with a high minority enrollment (more than 50 percent) were more likely than schools with low minority enrollment (5 percent or less) to be seriously overcrowded" (p. vii).

This NCES landmark study documented numerous physical problems in the schools and focused on common environmental conditions. It excluded other design variables such as movement classifications, large group spaces, architectural layout, daylighting with views, color, scale, and location of the school site, instructional neighborhoods, outdoor learning areas, and instructional laboratories. While the NCES study is of great value in characterizing physical conditions and describing and explaining the schools as containers and mechanical, it did not compare measures of student achievement to components of the physical environment.

We must challenge the notion that educational facilities are only "containers" having little to contribute to the educational process. One assumption of the study presented in this chapter was that it is important for facilities to be viewed as tools that influence learning. Furthermore, this study was conducted under the theory that the physical environment plays an important role in student behavior and learning. Only a few studies have been conducted to analyze the effects of the physical environment on students' learning.

Problem.   There are no valid and reliable measurements indicating if or how much the school's physical environment contributes to or influences the student's cognitive learning. Unfortunately, school environments are frequently built on the whims of architects and unsupported "best practices" or the hearsay evidence of educational planners and decision makers. The issue of best practices often goes unchallenged regarding whose best practices they are, and what, when, where, and how they might influence various educational and cultural settings.

Purpose.   The purpose of this study was to quantify design classifications in the school's physical environment and analyze how they might relate to the academic achievement of students. "Design classifications" as employed in this study refer to a school's structural and movable architectural components and natural, outdoor learning components that are akin to classifications as defined by Alexander, Ishikawa, and Silverstein (1977) in their seminal *A Pattern Language*. Academic achievement was limited to measures of third and fifth grade mean scores, composite scores on the Iowa Test of Basic Skills (ITBS) from a sample of twenty-four schools. The ITBS was only administered to the third and fifth grade students in the population for this study.

Theoretical   Perspective.   The   underlying assumption in this study was that the design classifications of the school's physical environment influence student achievement. Several authors

(Bingler, 1995; Greenman, 1988; McGuffey, 1982; Moore & Lackney (1994); Tanner, 2000; Weinstein, 1979; and Wohlwill & van Vliet, 1985) have debated similar theories. This hypothesis parallels the supposition that schools should be viewed as comprehensive learning environments. The philosophy of teaching and learning and the supporting curriculum representing this philosophy dictate spaces for learning. Furthermore, learning styles of students and teaching styles reflect cultural and community contexts. Philosophy and curriculum should dictate all the structural and movable components of the architectural and natural learning support systems.

BACKGROUND: THE SCHOOL'S PHYSICAL ENVIRONMENT

Sporadic and often inconclusive information exists in the literature concerning the effects that the physical environment has on students. Therefore, the need exists for current, valid, and reliable data to support or refute the theoretical perspective underlying this inquiry. If consistent relationships can be found between school design classifications and student achievement, then architects, school system personnel, and policy makers could employ this information to make scientifically informed decisions regarding school environments. The results could be optimal learning environments. If no relationships are found, then the theoretical perspective is weakened.

In keeping with recommendations from the American Psychological Association (APA, 1995), this chapter avoids an exhaustive discussion of the literature. Readers interested in more detail on the topic of the physical environment and student learning may refer to Chapter 2 and studies reviewed by the School Design and Planning Laboratory.[2] The following sections provide an overview of the school design classifications supporting the theoretical foundation of this particular inquiry.

Movement Classifications

Research on movement classifications, described in this study as links to main entrances, pathways with goals, circulation classifications, density or freedom of movement, personal space, and social distance has been of interest to researchers in the field of environmental psychology and architecture for many years. In the twentieth century Alexander and coworkers (1977) and Sommer (1969) made significant contributions to this field, with Sommer focusing on personal and social distance and Alexander addressing design classifications and their relationships to people, towns, regions, and the global environment.

Regarding personal and social distance, Wohlwill and van Vliet (1985) summarized the effects of high student density. "It appears as though the consequences of high-density conditions that involve either too many children or too little space are: excess levels of stimulation; stress and arousal; a drain on resources available; considerable interference; reductions in desired privacy levels; and loss of control" (pp. 108–109). Works such as this have led to the assertion that a high-density school influences achievement negatively.

The issue of density may be viewed through psychological implications by studying territoriality of place, according to Banghart and Trull (1973). We know that the student is always dependent on the environment for psychological and sociological clues and always interacting with the physical environment. Since the school is a social system within the cultural environment, social distance as it relates to crowding and density is a function of school design and decision making.

Another aspect of density is the lower middle range for social distance for men and women. It is 7 feet (Banghart & Trull, 1973, p. 233). Sommer (1969) completed several studies on small group ecology and found that when people are 3.5 feet apart, they shift their seating positions in favor of "side by side" as opposed to "across" from each other (p. 66). Sommer's finding thus correlates with the 7 feet (2 × 3.5 feet) needed for social distance by men and women as recommended by Banghart and Trull (1973).

According to Castaldi (1994), the architectural design of student circulation space has an obvious influence on the educational function of a school building. Space in a room delivers a silent message to students, where the flow and shift of distance between people is a large part of the communication process (Duncanson, 2003; Hall, 1959). Special attention should be given to circulation classifications that permit student traffic to flow quickly from one part of the building to another. Movement within the school should not consist of a progression of individual experiences, but instead be a conscious and perceptible environmental exchange; complex structures that cause crowding should be avoided. Movement within a school is an important part of learning. A school design should have pathways both inside and outside of the building. Indoor pathways could be color-coded to aid in keeping students oriented to the front, back, and other important locations within the learning environments. Pathways may link structures together and into the natural environment. Pathways free of obtrusions between activity areas and classrooms improve the utilization of learning areas.

Large-Group Meeting Places

According to Colven (1990), there is a growing awareness of the importance of social areas in schools. This goes beyond the traditional requirements of rooms in which pupils and teachers can meet and eat, and stems from the perception that an overall atmosphere needs to be created with which pupils can identify. Furthermore, students need to feel ownership of the spaces and environments in which they study and play. Social space should provide places for quiet contemplation and for formal and informal play. Colven (1990) noted that a variety of places are needed, both inside and outside the school, where children can meet together in groups, sometimes small and sometimes large. Such spaces need the characteristics that provide a welcome, and promote a feeling of belonging.

Needs for large-group meeting places seem to reflect the community and culture in which the school is located (Crumpacker, 1995). In urban, densely populated areas, people like to find a place to get away from others. In a rural area, people view school as a place to meet and gather and are less likely to want places for privacy.

When measuring the personal space required by undergraduate students, Cochran, Hale, and Hissam (1984) discovered the limits of one's "comfort zone." Their study revealed that interpersonal closeness generates less discomfort in open spaces, which indicates the need to include larger spaces and outdoor learning in school designs. Public places in schools are spaces that foster a sense of community or unity and belonging. These spaces should be inviting and comfortable and include ample lighting. Examples of large-group meeting places in schools include media centers, dining areas, places for casual student meetings (commons areas), amphitheaters, and auditoriums.

Architectural Design

Fiske (1995) indicated the need for rethinking all aspects of the structure of schooling, including the design of school buildings and other physical aspects of the learning environment. The organization of space has a profound effect on learning, and students feel better connected to a building that anticipates their needs and respects them as individuals (Herbert, 1998). When children attend a school obviously designed with their needs in mind, they notice it and demonstrate a more natural disposition toward respectful behavior and a willingness to contribute to the classroom community (Herbert, 1998).

The need exists in architectural design for the development of spaces that engage, challenge, and arouse. Brain-compatible learning requires much more interaction with the environment than current facilities allow. Taylor and Vlastos (1975) suggested that educational architecture is a

"three-dimensional textbook." This means that the learning environment is a functional art form, a place of beauty, and a motivational center for learning. Their research indicates that the architecture of learning environments can kindle or subdue learning, aid creativity, or slow mental perception. School buildings are visual objects, and as such they can be stimulating both in terms of their intrinsic design and their use.

An alternative to monolithic buildings, the dominant architectural design of schools found in the United States, is the campus plan or at least well-planned spaces such as those found in Reggio Emilia. Garbarino (1980) stated that when large groups of students are housed in a single facility, they become anonymous. A campus plan design cultivates closer peer and teacher associations. Garbarino (1980) also indicated that large numbers of students in a single facility are harder to control than small groups. Plath (1965) found that, to a large extent, the campus plan design lowered student deviancy.

Architectural design should include a friendly entrance that is age-appropriate and highly visible. The entrance evokes a welcome (Alexander, Ishikawa, & Silverstein, 1977). The school administrative offices are centralized for convenience and connection. Main buildings have an obvious reference point, a feature that heightens the sense of community. The concept of paths with goals translates to places designed to provide focal points when walking to different locations (Alexander, Ishikawa, & Silverstein, 1977). Variation of ceiling heights and intimacy gradients help blend public and private places in schools and give the effect of drawing people into an area.

Daylight and Views

The presence of natural light in classrooms has received attention from several researchers. An extensive research effort was completed in 1999. In a controlled study of over 21,000 students in California, Washington, and Colorado, the Heschong Mahone Group (1999) found that students with the most daylight in their classrooms progressed 20 percent faster on mathematics and 26 percent faster on reading tests over a period of one year than students having less daylight in their classrooms. Similarly, students in classrooms having larger window areas were found to progress 15 percent faster in mathematics and 23 percent faster in reading than students in classrooms having smaller windows. Students occupying classrooms with well-designed skylights, those that diffuse daylight throughout the room and also allow teachers to control the amount of light, also progressed significantly faster than students in classrooms without natural light.

> We also identified another window-related effect, in that students in classrooms where windows could be opened were found to progress 7–8% faster than those with fixed windows. This occurred regardless of whether the classroom also had air conditioning. These effects were all observed with 99% statistical certainty. (Heschong Mahone Group, p. 3)
>
> . . . From this study, we have made a number of important findings: We found a uniformly positive and highly significant correlation between the presence of daylighting and student performance in all three districts. We found that daylighting, provided from skylights, distinct from all the other attributes associated with windows, has a positive effect. We found that this methodology, of using large pre-existing data sets, can be a successful and powerful tool for investigating the effects of the physical environment on human performance. (p. 62)

Research published by Kuller and Lindstern (1992) suggested that windowless classrooms should be avoided for permanent use. They referenced medical doctors who reported a biological need for windows. Rather than being a distraction, which disrupts the learning process, an argument often used by the "conventional wisdom" side, windows provide a necessary relief for students. This relief associated with window gazing is less likely to demand the focused attention used to draw pictures or "doodle" in a notebook. It is much easier for students to refocus their attention back on the teacher when engaged in tasks requiring minimal attention (such as window gazing) rather than those requiring more concentrated attention.

Exposing children to harmful forms of lighting in poorly designed schools is reason enough for us to seriously consider Alexander and coworkers' (1977) notion of "wings of light." "Windows (views) overlooking life" is another positive aspect of design amenable to the translation of the theories of "pattern language" to the school environment. Light is the most important environmental input, after food and water, in controlling bodily functions (Wurtman, 1975). Lights of different colors affect blood pressure, pulse, respiration rates, brain activity, and biorhythms. Full-spectrum light, required to influence the pineal gland's synthesis of melatonin, which in turn helps determine the body's output of the neurotransmitter serotonin, is critical to a child's health and development (Ott, 1973). To help reduce the imbalances caused by inadequate exposure to the near ultraviolet and infrared ends of the spectrum, full-spectrum bulbs that approximate the wavelengths provided by sunshine should replace standard fluorescent and tungsten bulbs (Hughes, 1980). There is ample evidence that people need daylight to regulate "circadian rhythms" (Alexander, Ishikawa, & Silverstein, 1977, p. 527). Poorly lit and windowless classrooms can cause students to experience a daily form of "jet lag." Furthermore, forms of florescent lighting may affect some students and teachers by causing mild seizures.

Not all research, however, favors natural light for learning environments. For example, Romney (1975) studied how windowed and windowless environments affected rote learning tasks, concept learning tasks, and perceptual tasks of sixth grade students. No significant relationship was found to exist between the absence and presence of windows on rote learning, or perceptual tasks.

Color

Color and light complement each other and both are much too complex and interrelated to provide a comprehensive review here. Color refers to the use of color schemes and classifications in the building. The influence of interior coloring on academic achievement has been investigated by several researchers and shown to have an effect on achievement and behavior. Thompson (2003) discussed the use or misuse of color in a learning environment, indicating it plays a major role in student performance. Horton (1972) noted that the repetition of color is boring unless variations and contrasts interrupt it. Rice (1953) conducted a study in three schools in the Baltimore area that were similar in size, age, teacher–pupil ratio, and socioeconomic status. One facility was not painted, another was painted with a traditional white ceiling and green walls, while the third was painted according to a paint manufacturer's specifications and involved bright, warm, or cool colors. Report cards before the schools were painted were compared to report cards after the schools were painted. Kindergarten children in the unpainted school experienced a 3 percent improvement; students in the traditionally painted school had a 7.3 percent improvement; and students in the experimentally painted school showed a 33.9 percent improvement. In grades 3–6, the experimental school experienced a 10.5 percent improvement in language arts, a 12.6 percent improvement in social studies, an 8.5 percent improvement in arithmetic, and a 10.0 percent improvement in art and music. The findings of this empirical study suggested that a carefully planned color scheme appears to influence the achievement of elementary school children. Ketcham (1964) noted that the greatest improvement in social habits, health and safety habits, work habits, language arts, arithmetic, social studies, science, music, and art occurred in the schools painted with combinations of colors.

Color experts agree that reds, oranges, and pinks are warm and stimulating colors, while most blues and greens are considered cool and relaxing. Most grays are thought of as neutral. Tints are "receding" and make the room look larger, while deep tones are "approaching" and make the room look smaller. Different-age children prefer different colors. Young children prefer red, blue, green, violet, orange, and yellow. Although young children prefer bright colors, too many high contrasts should be avoided because they can produce fatigue. Upper elementary classrooms should be painted with the cooler hues of blue and green. Secondary school students require less visual distraction and do well with the cooler hues such as pastel green or aqua. In an auditorium the center of attention is the stage. The stage area should be in contrast to the surrounding side walls, which should be a relaxing color like beige, peach, or pastel green. The gymnasium is a room that produces more body heat; therefore, it should be painted in a cool receding color with little color contrast. The cafeteria should be painted a color that will stimulate the appetite. Such colors include pearl, coral, rose, or pumpkin (Smith, 1980).

Color may be evaluated on a continuum from warm to neutral to light hues and tones. Hue (shade or tone) is a circular dimension of color that is referred to as a scale of perceptions ranging from red through blue. The importance of color and lighting together has been discussed by Castaldi (1994, pp. 263–264), who noted that the color of an object within a room is determined by the color of the object (as seen in daylight) and by the color of light that is illuminating it within the room. Color cannot be considered without also including the effects of light in a learning environment.

Scale

Scale is just one of many vehicles of communication (Ackerman, 1969). The concept of scale suggests that everything is seen according to its relationship with other things (Crowe, 1995). Adherence to scale is necessary to produce user friendly schools. Some design features may shock adults but be student friendly. For example, "You're at the front door (of Crow Island School), and what you notice is that the door handle is too low. Too low for you, just right for children" (Meek & Landfried, 1995, p. 53). Other aspects of scale include windows low enough for children to "see out," handrails at three levels, and classrooms that resemble children's rooms at home. Herbert (1998) reported some reflections from alumni of Crow Island School: "The light switches were at my level and the auditorium had benches, starting with the little ones in front. . . . Everything was within my reach" (p. 70). Building to the scale of children promotes a sense of belonging. For children to feel competent in regard to their personal needs, the environment must be "child-scaled." Water fountains, sink, toilets, doorknobs, and light switches must be easily accessible and effortless for children to use (Weinstein & David, 1987).

Location of the School Site

When new schools are built, numerous variables are taken into consideration. For example, school systems consider the instructional needs of the students they serve, enrollment, and whether to replace an old building or simply remodel it (Graves, 1993). Other technicalities considered when building a new school are zoning, tax base, community growth classifications, socioeconomic problems, ethnic and racial composition, and the transportation of students (Sleeman & Rockwell, 1981). According to Earthman (2000), the rapidly increasing cost of sites in almost every section of the country has made site selection one of the most difficult tasks a school system encounters.

Recently, some school systems have begun to consider the natural surroundings and built environment that surrounds the school, thereby allowing the school's architecture to match its surroundings. This notion has sparked an interest in sustainable design, which is minimizing the harmful effects of the building on the environment (Christopher, 2002), or as explained by Spearnak and Brelig (2004), "the systematic consideration of a project's life cycle impact on environmental and energy resources" (p.17).

Noise pollution of the surrounding area is an important factor of concern. Bronzaft and McCarthy (1975) conducted a study on the effect of train noise and reading ability. Public School 98, a five-story building in Manhattan, was located approximately 220 feet west of an elevated subway track. Between the hours of 9:00 a.m. and 3:00 p.m. each day, eighty trains passed the school. The average noise level of a sixth grade class measured 59 decibels. When a train passed, the average noise level rose to 89 decibels. Classes on the east side of the building were interrupted every 4.5 minutes for an interval of 30 seconds by the noise of the passing trains. The study indicated that the students were hindered in their reading proficiency by elevated levels of noise. Students on the east side of the school building, which is only 220 feet from an elevated subway track, were found to be academically behind their peers on the quiet west side of the building by as much as one year.

A school site should be safe, healthful, attractive, and properly located with respect to students' homes. Sites should be free of air pollution and noxious gases. Sites should be far from sources of noise or danger such as greatly traveled highways, airports, and heavy industry. Aesthetic considerations should be stressed in the selection of a site. Trees, brooks, parks, or golf courses near a school do much to beautify the area surrounding an educational facility. A good site should have several physical characteristics. Its topography should be slightly convex and slightly higher than the area immediately surrounding it. Safety should be given high priority when selecting a school site. Sites should not border a heavily traveled highway, railroad, or high-tension electric wires; and a landscape architect is an essential person needed in site planning. Trees, shrubs, flowerbeds, and the arrangement of walks and drives contribute to the general learning environment of a school building. Both the design of the building and the layout and development of the site are important ingredients in the creation of an atmosphere that is educationally stimulating. The building should blend pleasingly into the terrain, and the structure should accentuate the beauty of the site (Castaldi, 1994). The school should be in harmony with nature and blend in with its surroundings, bringing nature into the learning environments. Site planning should emphasize the consequences of maximizing the north and south exposures and minimizing windows and openings that face in an easterly or westerly direction (Christopher, 2002).

Instructional Neighborhoods

Bete (1998) presented information on Celebration School located in Celebration, Florida, describing an instructional neighborhood as an area that includes large- and small-group areas, spaces for student and teacher planning, wet areas for art, a hearth area, and toilets for the students and teachers. One Celebration School instructional neighborhood includes 6,000 square feet designed for 100 students and 4 teachers and their aids. The instructional neighborhoods at Celebration School also include windows for viewing outside the classroom and for bringing natural light inside. They contain open and closed spaces to maximize flexibility, and permit teachers and students to manage their own time and space.

According to Weinstein (1979), there is considerable evidence that the classroom environment can affect nonachievement behaviors and attitudes. "Soft" classrooms have been associated with better attendance, greater participation, and more positive attitudes toward class, the instructor, and classmates. "Relatively minor design modifications introduced into already functioning classrooms have been shown to produce changes in student's spatial behavior, increased interaction with materials, decreased interruptions, and more substantive questioning" (pp. 598–599).

Although teachers and students feel the need for differentiated learning spaces, research to guide the customization of classrooms is scarce. The traditional "one size fits all" classroom is quickly becoming obsolete as we move toward technology and outdoor learning. Desks are being replaced with workstations and furniture suitable for cooperative

learning. Space is needed to build, store, and display objects. The setting in which students are taught may be uncrowded and in good condition, but are they adequate for the functions that need to be undertaken? Adequacy of learning environment depends not only on square footage, but also on how the square footage is configured and organized with relation to other areas (Duke, 1998).

After conducting extensive research, Moore and Lackney (1995) suggested that the classrooms of tomorrow will be similar to studios. There will be workstations and research space for each student. There will also be an assortment of spaces of various sizes. Common in schools will be central gathering places and presentation arenas. Workspaces for cooperative learning, quiet private areas, and nooks where students can think and work independently will be found in tomorrow's schools. Finally, teachers will have offices where they can do individual testing and counseling, organize individualized study programs, or telephone parents. Schools should be flexible enough to support a variety of changing instructional strategies. Folding partitions, large-group lecture rooms, small-group spaces, and staff offices are a few of the designs that are viewed as necessary.

Because curriculum and instruction are continually changing to meet the needs of the students, so must the classroom space. Building flexibility into the classroom space is vital according to Lang (1996). He suggested that the physical environment should respond and adapt to the needs of both the teacher and the learner. Brubaker (1991) studied classroom space and found that even though there have been changes in technology, classroom space has, in effect, been left unchanged since the 1950s. Colven (1990) indicated that teachers should strive to make spaces for teaching and learning exciting and stimulating. Teachers should be prepared to develop and redevelop these spaces. This underscores the need to design buildings as flexible as possible.

Lomranz and colleagues (1975) studied the amount of personal space children required. Measures of personal space were collected from seventy-four children aged 3, 5, and 7 years. A significant difference at the 0.05 statistical level was discovered between the space needed by the 3-year-old and that required by the 5- and 7-year-old children. The 3-year-olds needed significantly less personal space than the older children. According to Proshansky and Wolfe (1974), privacy has been shown to contribute to a child's growth and development. Although students like to withdraw, they do not like total seclusion.

Outdoor Environments

Outdoor learning environments are becoming more popular as curriculum innovation seeks to involve students in the study of ecology and greener environments. Often overlooked considerations for schools include the design and development of green areas, natural quiet areas, and play areas. The developing interest in outdoor learning brings the design of outdoor rooms into focus (Freeman, 1995).

A significant portion of the reform movement deals with the teaching of values. To this end, it is important to infuse physical settings for children with the sense of being in nature (Prescott, 1987). Natural things have unending diversity, people do not create them, and they offer a feeling of timelessness. Views overlooking life provide quality to the school's learning environment, while allowing spaces for small animals in schools offers students the opportunity to "care for life." Accordingly, caring for living things helps to teach a sense of responsibility and values.

Teaching in natural situations offers a context in which no textbook or computer-based learning environment can compete. For example, if the learning goal is to understand the nature of a pony, why only ask students to read about a pony, draw a pony, or color a pony in a classroom setting? Instead, why not perform these associated classroom activities and also experience the real pony with all its antics and graceful movements in a natural setting? This is better pedagogy because the process integrates abstract and hands-on learning activities (Tanner, 2001).

At best, authors of textbooks and virtual learning packages only pass along second-hand information they obtained from observation and discovery. This is true for discussion groups as well. But, it is the person who sees, discovers, and explores a situation who really gets the most out of it. According to research by Sharp (1973), this is the entire thesis of outdoor education, which is faster, more deeply appreciated, and retained longer.

Why go outside to the world of snow and ice, heat and mosquitoes, auto exhaust, wind, and rain? In his classic work on children's environments, Greenman (1988) noted that the outdoors has weather and life, the vastness of the sky, the universe in the petals of a flower. He also observed that some view the very qualities that make the outdoors different as obstacles or annoying side effects. The openness with its weather is a good reason to stay inside, and landscape and life are things to be eliminated. "A playground, considered the primary, if not the only outdoor setting, performs the same function as a squirrel cage or a prison exercise yard—it is a place for emotional and physical release and a bit of free social interchange" (p. 175). We need more than just a squirrel cage to integrate outdoor learning and academics.

Other experts' warnings preceding Greenman's performance research specified that the notion of the school's educational responsibility taking place only inside the building is outdated (Taylor & Vlastos, 1975). Schools have traditionally been perceived as places that children leave by 3:00 p.m.; the school day is over, and the doors are closed (Dryfoos, 1999). Today, many school systems are providing after-hours, evening, weekend, and summer programs that include outdoor learning activities which involve more than playgrounds.

After consistently studying outdoor learning areas for more than twenty years, Stine (1997) in her extended research has concluded that there are nine basic design elements for developing outside spaces for children. Both elements in each of the nine pairs are needed to meet the needs of children intellectually, socially, cognitively, and physically. The nine elements are:

- *Accessible and inaccessible.* An environment should provide cues about what is accessible and what is not.
- *Active and passive.* This space should have spaces where children can be loud and participate in large muscle activities in conjunction with areas for children to relax and be calm.
- *Challenge/risk and repetition/security.* Children should learn about their competencies and limitations in this area. All children fall along a continuum of low to high physical abilities. This area should allow children to progress along the continuum without frustration.
- *Hard and soft.* This is a space where an environment gives way under the body's touch. It appears "soft." Children need to touch and feel mud, grass, sand, etc. However, for students to use toys with wheels, stack blocks, or colors, a hard surface is required. There should be both hard and soft areas to accommodate children's needs.
- *Natural and built.* To learn about, value, and ultimately protect their world, children need to understand and experience their world in both its natural and built forms. They need to understand the process to appreciate the product.
- *Open and closed.* Open-ended activities let a child become involved with the process of an activity without concern about an end product. There is no particular goal when the activity is finished. These activities allow for discovery and exploration. Closed activities provide the child with feedback, indicating that a product is finished or that an activity is completed. The activities help develop self-esteem.
- *Permanence and change.* Children need landmarks to help them feel safe in knowing that they can negotiate the area and find their way back. Children also need to be a part of chang-

ing their environment. When an environment cannot be rearranged, the students lose out on an opportunity for creativity and problem solving.
- *Public and private.* The environment should have different spaces where children can gather and be with friends and spaces where a child can be alone. Children need to be able to make choices to be in a group or alone.
- *Simple and complex.* When an area has more than one type of material with more than one obvious use and allows for manipulation and change, it is called a complex area. Complex areas encourage children to make choices and decisions. Simple areas have items that have one obvious use only. These simple areas provide structure and direction for the child. (Stine, 1997, pp. 24–40)

Instructional Laboratories

American schools have invested billions of dollars in technology primarily because teachers and policy makers alike see computers as a crucial element in educational reform. Designing flexible environments that facilitate these technical processes is essential (Latham, 1999). This is especially important, if the rapid changes in technology of the recent past continue into the future.

Wenglinsky (1998) found that technology positively impacts student achievement. Achievement gains were higher for the eighth graders who used computers than it was for the fourth graders who used computers. Also, students who had teachers who had received staff training on how to use computers to teach higher-order thinking skills had larger gains than the students of teachers who did not receive any such training. Beyond having the correct technology available, access to the equipment and flexibility are also important keys to instructional success for students and teachers. Technology integration and connectivity will help learners connect with their community and the global community (Agron, 2004).

Other instructional laboratories also exist in schools. Music laboratories require special acoustical treatments and flexibility. Art laboratories have special safety needs (electrical cords dropping from the ceiling, e.g.), special floor coverings that may be cleaned efficiently and effectively, natural light, and sinks and water.

Environmental

Weinstein (1979) stated that experience has convinced most people that noise can interfere with performance of intellectual tasks, yet research has produced inconclusive and often contradictory results on this topic. Acoustics may be a factor in preventing appropriate sound to travel to students. Since Weinstein offered her commentary, more attention has been given to the acoustical environment, and a growing body of performance research confirms that many students cannot hear clearly and comfortably in class. Audiologists add that even students with no hearing impairments may have difficulty hearing what a teacher is saying in a modern classroom as a result of poor acoustical design. Everyone is affected by poor acoustics, but the ones hindered most are those students who are hearing-impaired, learning-disabled, or have limited English proficiency (Day, 1999).

School buildings are filled with many different sounds from many different sources. Classroom acoustics are based on three factors: ambient noise level, reverberation time (RT), and the signal-to-noise ratio (S/N). Ambient noise is background noise. Examples include the hum of the heating system, cars passing by, and other students whispering. Reverberation time (RT) is defined as the interval needed for a sound introduced into an environment to reduce its intensity once the sound is turned off. "Signals" are the desirable sounds and "noise" is the undesirable sound. The association between signals and noise is the S/N ratio (Day, 1999). Schools frequently have hard floors, concrete walls, high ceilings, windows, and chalkboards, all of which cause a long reverberation time (Scott, 1999). Other factors at schools that cause

noise are playgrounds, corridors, ventilation systems, scraping of chairs, doors slamming, peoples' voices, and passing traffic (Day, 1999).

Signals are what people desire to hear; noise interferes with this desire. The signal should be stronger in intensity than the interfering noise. In a classroom with an above-average acoustic design, students with no hearing impairments understood 71 percent of what the teacher said. However, students with hearing impairments only understood 48 percent of what was said by the teacher (Day, 1999). Cohen and Lezak (1977) concluded that human energy and efficiency decline due to unwanted noise.

Woodhead (1964) conducted tests concerning noise with eighty-four young men enlisted in the Royal Navy with normal hearing. The subjects were allotted 10 seconds to remember a six-digit number. A four-digit number then appeared on the screen, which they had to subtract from the original six-digit number. Some of the subjects heard bursts of noise during the memorization of the six-digit number and some did not. Some of the subjects heard bursts of noise during the calculations and some did not. When the bursts of noise occurred during memorization of the six-digit number, more errors tended to be made in the calculations.

Thermal environment or climate control is another environmental factor that has been the topic of several studies. The comfort index strongly influences the physiological state of the student and the teacher. A comfortable temperature of 72 degrees Fahrenheit requires a relative humidity of 60 percent. As the temperature of the air rises, the humidity should decrease to maintain comfort level (Castaldi, 1994).

Herrington (1952) found that workers who performed minimal physical exertion produced the least errors at 79 degrees Fahrenheit. As temperatures rose to 97 degrees Fahrenheit, errors increased from twelve per hour to ninety per hour. He also noted that women who control thermostats would set them an average of 3 to 4 degrees higher than men. Also, younger children prefer a temperature of about 5 degrees cooler than an older adult.

In a survey conducted by McDonald (1960), teachers were asked what effect air conditioning had on their attitudes, work classifications, and classroom conditions. Of the teachers surveyed, 28 percent reported improved grades, 38 percent reported a willingness to do more work, and 85 percent reported that their students showed a greater ability to concentrate when functioning within an air-conditioned environment.

McCardle (1966) conducted a study involving forty matched pairs of sixth graders. His study showed that pupils in a thermally controlled room committed significantly fewer errors on conceptual learning tasks and needed less time to complete assigned tasks than those in the room with no thermal controls. Curtis and Stuart (1964) showed that the gain of student achievement in climate-controlled facilities was superior to those in non-climate-controlled schools. Their study involved 5,000 pupils in three different grade levels at four different schools and spanned two academic years.

Chan (1980) found that students in schools that were air-conditioned scored significantly higher, at the 0.05 level on the vocabulary section of the ITBS, than students in non-air-conditioned buildings. Chan's study showed a consistent pattern of higher achievement for students in the air-conditioned schools.

Much attention has been given to roof systems, yet studies regarding the relationship of the roof system to learning do not exist. Bennett (1990) wrote that George Washington was plagued with roof leaks at Mount Vernon that caused him to write, "that there could have been little attention or judgment exercised heretofore in covering it is a fact that cannot admit doubt; for he must have been a miserable artisan or a very great rascal indeed" (p. 14). Like Mount Vernon, schools are often plagued with leaks that cause mold, mildew, and rot. In return, the air quality of such schools is compromised (Liska, 1988). Given these facts, it was also hypothesized that a leaking roof can disrupt student learning.

With the increase in concern for health conditions such as asthma and parental concerns about the links between indoor air quality and health, research in this area is likely to increase. Litigation has also been a driving force that has emphasized the need for more information. It is not uncommon to hear teachers complain about the quality of air inside their schools, particularly those in portable classrooms where ventilation is often inadequate. Increasingly, school personnel are seeking out resources such as the Tools for Schools package available through the Environmental Protection Agency (EPA) to help them identify and solve common problems that contribute to poor indoor air quality in their facilities (Bosch, 2003).

METHOD

Instrumentation

Using the eleven sets of design classifications presented in the above section as a foundation, we developed an instrument including a ten-point Likert scale per item. The purpose of the instrument was to provide a systematic method for assessing physical learning environments. Each question focused on a particular aspect of school design and allowed the rater to record the degree (or percentage) that the item was present in the school's setting. This instrument represents an accumulation of works determining actual design items and their validity and reliability estimates. Contributions were made to the development of the scale by Andersen (1999), Ayers (1999), Tanner (1999), and Yarborough (2001). The test–retest reliability of the instrument was found to be 0.82 (Tanner, 1999). The complete instrument used in this study is located in the chapter appendix.

Each item on the instrument may be scored from 0 to 10, where 0 or a blank indicates that the item is not present. A value of from 1 to 10 may be given to a design item in the physical setting, depending on its quality and functionality. Scores for each subsection are assumed to be additive. The instrument may be used for evaluating existing schools (post occupancy evaluation). More important, its contents and findings resulting from its application may be employed to influence new school design.

Reliability of the Instrument

Following the data collection, a reliability analysis was conducted to refine the subscales. An item to scale analysis (Cronbach's alpha) was performed to determine the relationship between an individual item and the remainder of each subscale. A Cronbach's alpha is the number of items times the average covariance between items, divided by the average variance. This result is divided by 1 plus the number of items minus 1 times the average covariance divided by the average variance of all the items (Norusis, 1990).

This statistic is interpreted as a reliability coefficient or index of stability. There are various acceptable levels of reliability according to Garrett and Woodworth (1958). At this point in the study, it became important to know if the reliability coefficient for each subscale was satisfactory; according to these authors, the size of the reliability coefficient that is needed depends on the nature of the instrument and the purpose for which it was designed. Garrett and Woodworth (1958) noted that a reliability coefficient no higher than 0.50 or 0.60 is acceptable, if the instrument is designed to make a diagnosis (separating or classifying people or objects, e.g.). Since this study focused on identifying and classifying design classifications, a reliability of 0.50 was established as a criterion for each subscale. If through the process of eliminating design items in the subcategories, the 0.50 could *not* be obtained for a subscale, it was eliminated from the data set to maintain acceptable reliability. The seventy-eight items contained in the instrument were derived from the literature and research on school design and planning, as discussed in the background section above. Table 12.1 reveals the reliability coefficients for each of the nine subscales. Two subscales did not meet the criteria of 0.50 and were eliminated from this study. It is important to note that the elimination of these two

subscales does not mean that these items are not valid or valueless for future studies; in fact, they should be included in assessment, as well as the addition of new design pattern areas as we study the impact of the built environment on student outcomes.

Data Collection

A total of twenty-five rural elementary schools (k–6) were included in the sample, which was located in the west-central geographic region of the state of Georgia. The study region included six contiguous counties. Because of identical design classifications in two schools, the data set was reduced to twenty-four schools. These schools served approximately 11,500 students.

School design information was observed during site visits requiring approximately 2 hours each. The purpose of each visit was to complete a guided tour of the educational facilities and outdoor learning environments. The comprehensive tour was necessary to accurately complete the design assessment instrument for each facility. Only one researcher trained in school design and assessment conducted each site visit. That same researcher completed the instrument for each facility within one hour of concluding the visit and before beginning assessment of another school. All the site visits were completed before the ITBS data were obtained from the Georgia Public Education Report Card for Parents, since having no knowledge of student performance reduced the chance of biasing the rater.

Upon the completion of all twenty-four site visits, other data were collected by school from the Georgia Department of Education for the following variables: achievement data (average composite third and fifth grade ITBS scores per school), number of students representing various ethnic groups, the average length of teaching experience of teachers and their levels of training, the number of gifted students, and a proxy for socioeconomic status (percentage of students receiving a free or reduced-cost school lunch, SES). These data served as control variables (covariates) in making estimates of ITBS scores based on scores recorded on the assessment instrument.

TABLE 12.1   Reliability Analysis for the Subscales

CATEGORY	CRONBACH'S ALPHA	SPEARMAN–BROWN EQUAL LENGTH	SPEARMAN–BROWN UNEQUAL LENGTH
Movement classifications ($n = 17$)	0.63	0.76	0.76
Large-group meeting places ($n = 3$)	0.70	0.63	0.65
Architectural design ($n = 6$)	0.70	0.65	0.65
Daylighting and views ($n = 5$)	0.82	0.87	0.87
Color schemes ($n = 6$)	0.79	0.81	0.81
Scale* ($n = 7$)	0.49	0.50	0.50
Location ($n = 3$)	0.74	0.68	0.69
Instructional neighborhoods ($n = 16$)	0.54	0.79	0.79
Outside learning areas ($n = 6$)	0.87	0.86	0.86
Instructional laboratories ($n = 6$)	0.74	0.74	0.75
Environmental* ($n = 3$)	0.19	0.20	0.17

*These subscales were eliminated from the study because their reliability coefficients were less than 0.50.

Research Question and Assumptions

The primary question for this study was: Does the school's physical environment influence cognitive learning in elementary schools? In order to arrive at a scientific answer to this question, backward regression, analysis of covariance, multiple regression analysis, and reduced regression models were employed in predicting student achievement (the dependent variable) with the well-defined design variables (independent variables) representing the physical environment. Under the hypothesis that places and spaces where students learn make a difference in what and how much they learn, several assumptions guided the study: (1) The school's physical environment may be classified according to sets of design classifications that are measurable in terms of the degree of relative function and quality. (2) Validity and reliability can be established for an instrument that measures the functionality, quality, and amount of a certain pattern's existence in a given school setting. (3) Individuals who are familiar with the design classifications included in an assessment scale can accomplish evaluation of school learning environments. (4) The ITBS is a valid and reliable measure of cognitive learning. (5) Regression analysis is an appropriate statistical technique to determine relationships between academic achievement and the physical environment, thereby estimating the effect size of the influence of the physical environment on student achievement. Although the effect size does not ensure causality, repeated studies yielding similar effects can approach this elusive relationship.

RESULTS

Third Grade

The analysis began with the backward elimination regression procedure to improve the prediction and reduce the variance of the estimator. Since each school was the unit of analysis, the students' mean ITBS scores were employed as the dependent variable, and all the variables not associated with the design classifications were designated as the predictor variables ($\alpha = 0.05$). The objective of this step was to determine the best possible prediction equation for the composite ITBS scores by using the independent variables not related to the physical environment. These variables included ethnicity (percentage of black, multiracial, American Indian, Asian, Hispanic, and white students), socioeconomic status (SES), average teaching experience of the teaching staff per school, percentage of gifted students in the school, and the level of certification held by teachers (T4, T5, T6, and T7) in each school.

Given the school mean ITBS scores and the above variables, the backward elimination procedure yielded variables that would not add significantly to the prediction equation. The results of the analyses are given in Table 12.2. All predictor variables but multiracial, black, and socioeconomic status were eliminated ($F = 12.03, p < 0.01$). The F statistic indicated that the relationship was linear and significant. The multiple correlation among the composite third grade ITBS scores and these three independent variables was 0.80, while the R^2 was 0.64341. Therefore, 64.341 percent of its variability in third grade ITBS scores was attributed to ethnicity and socioeconomic status.

TABLE 12.2　Backward Elimination to Isolate the Best Predictors of Third Grade Composite ITBS Scores

MODEL SUMMARY

MODEL	R	R SQUARE	ADJUSTED R SQUARE	STD. ERROR OF THE ESTIMATE	CHANGE STATISTICS				
					R SQUARE CHANGE	F CHANGE	DF1	DF2	SIG. F CHANGE
1	0.802	0.643	0.590	8.54782	0.643	12.029	3	20	0.000

a. Predictors: (Constant), MULTIRAC, FREELUNC, BLACK

ANOVA

MODEL		SUM OF SQUARES	DF	MEAN SQUARE	F	SIG.
1	Regression	2,636.654	3	878.885	12.029	0.000
	Residual	1,461.304	20	73.065		
	Total	4,097.958	23			

a. Predictors: (Constant), MULTIRAC, FREELUNC, BLACK
b. Dependent variable: TCOMPOSI

COEFFICIENTS

MODEL		UNSTANDARDIZED COEFFICIENTS		STANDARDIZED COEFFICIENTS		
		B	STD. ERROR	BETA	t	SIG.
1	(Constant)	83.574	5.994		13.942	0.000
	FREELUNC	−0.721	0.125	−1.031	−5.755	0.000
	BLACK	5.835E-02	0.022	0.632	2.663	0.015
	MULTIRAC	−0.909	0.295	−0.679	−3.083	0.006

a. Dependent variable: TCOMPOSI

Next in the process of analysis, the amount of variability in ITBS scores was investigated to determine how student academic achievement might be influenced individually by each set of design classifications. The statistical technique used in this step was regression reduction, with the purpose of isolating each contribution of the subsets. For example, the full regression for the design pattern "movement" is shown in Table 12.3. The multiple correlation was significantly different from 0 ($R = 0.81443$, $R^2 = 0.66330$, $F = 9.3576$, $p = 0.002$). Subsequently, each full and reduced regression was compared for the remaining eight design classifications—removing movement and replacing it with "large group meeting places," removing large group meeting places and replacing it with "architectural design," etc. Independently, each variance related to the design classifications

TABLE 12.3   Full Regression for the Design Pattern "Movement," Third Grade

MODEL SUMMARY

MODEL	R	R SQUARE	ADJUSTED R SQUARE	STD. ERROR OF THE ESTIMATE	R SQUARE CHANGE	F CHANGE	DF1	DF2	SIG. F CHANGE
					CHANGE STATISTICS				
1	0.814	0.663	0.592	8.52172	0.663	9.358	4	19	0.000

a. Predictors: (Constant), MOVEMENT, FREELUNC, MULTIRAC, BLACK

ANOVA

MODEL		SUM OF SQUARES	DF	MEAN SQUARE	F	SIG.
1	Regression	2,718.185	4	679.546	9.358	0.000
	Residual	1,379.774	19	72.620		
	Total	4,097.958	23			

a. Predictors: (Constant), MOVEMENT, FREELUNC, MULTIRAC, BLACK
b. Dependent variable: TCOMPOSI

COEFFICIENTS

MODEL		UNSTANDARDIZED COEFFICIENTS B	STD. ERROR	STANDARDIZED COEFFICIENTS BETA	t	SIG.
1	(Constant)	54.293	28.273		1.920	0.070
	BLACK	4.508E-02	0.025	0.488	1.790	0.089
	MULTIRAC	−0.857	0.298	−0.641	−2.877	0.010
	FREELUNC	−0.640	0.147	−0.915	−4.362	0.000
	MOVEMENT	0.196	0.185	0.184	1.060	0.303

a. Dependent variable: TCOMPOSI

was summed to provide a total. The results of these calculations are exhibited in Table 12.4. The accumulation in variance across the nine design classifications accounted for 8.675 percent of the variance in third grade ITBS scores; the change in the F value for each independent variance was significant ($\alpha \leq 0.05$).

To test the significance of the total R^2 change, the two models used in the analysis were compared. The reduced regression model may be found in Table 12.2. The complete regression model (Table 12.5) indicates the F change of 2.372, with the significant F change = 0.082. Therefore, the multiple correlation was not significantly different from 0 ($\alpha = 0.05$).

A possible policy question arising from this finding becomes: Regarding the set of school design variables, is the sum of the independent effects (8.675 percent) of the variance in the ITBS scores of benefit to the students? In the complete regression (including all the variables simultaneously) the amount of variance accounted for was 0.721 ($\alpha = 0.082$). This was not statistically significant ($\alpha = 0.05$) for third grade ITBS composite scores.

Fifth Grade

The procedure employed in the third grade analysis was also utilized to develop the prediction equation for fifth grade ITBS scores. Table 12.6 on page 284

TABLE 12.4   Contributions to Variance in Third Grade Composite ITBS Scores Made by School Design Variables

CRITERION VARIABLE (RANK OF DIFFERENCE)	MULTIPLE CORRELATION		REGRESSION R SQUARE	DIFFERENCE (EFFECT)	F CHANGE*
Movement (1)	Full	0.81	0.66330	0.01989	9.358
	Reduced	0.80	0.64341		
Large-group meeting places (2)	Full	0.81	0.66080	0.01739	8.571
	Reduced	0.80	0.64341		
Architectural design (7)	Full	0.80	0.64503	0.00162	8.575
	Reduced	0.80	0.64341		
Daylighting and views (3)	Full	0.81	0.65934	0.01593	9.069
	Reduced	0.80	0.64341		
Color (8)	Full	0.81	0.65041	0.0070	8.837
	Reduced	0.80	0.64341		
Location (9)	Full	0.80	0.64358	0.00017	8.577
	Reduced	0.80	0.64341		
Instructional neighborhoods (4)	Full	0.81	0.65605	0.01264	9.060
	Reduced	0.80	0.64341		
Outside learning areas (6)	Full	0.80	0.64661	0.00320	8.691
	Reduced	0.80	0.64341		
Instructional laboratories (5)	Full	0.81	0.65232	0.00891	8.912
	Reduced	0.80	0.64341		
Grand total				Σ **8.675%**	

*F Change was significant for all design variables ($\alpha \leq 0.05$).

TABLE 12.5   Complete Regression for the Third Grade Scores

MODEL SUMMARY

| MODEL | R | R SQUARE | ADJUSTED R SQUARE | STD. ERROR OF THE ESTIMATE | CHANGE STATISTICS | | | | |
					R SQUARE CHANGE	F CHANGE	DF1	DF2	SIG. F CHANGE
2	0.849	0.721	0.417	10.19058	0.721	2.372	12	11	0.082

a. Predictors: (Constant), INSTRUCTION LABS, OUTSIDE, BLACK, MEETING, COLOR, INSTRUCT, LOCATION, FREE LUNCH, MOVEMENT, MULTIRACIAL, DAYLIGHT, DESIGN

ANOVA

MODEL		SUM OF SQUARES	DF	MEAN SQUARE	F	SIG.
2	Regression	2,955.632	12	246.303	2.372	0.082
	Residual	1,142.326	11	103.848		
	Total	4,097.958	23			

a. Predictors: (Constant), INSTRUCTION LABS, OUTSIDE, BLACK, MEETING, COLOR, INSTRUCT, LOCATION, FREE LUNCH, MOVEMENT, MULTIRACIAL, DAYLIGHT, DESIGN
b. Dependent variable: TOTAL COMPOSITE

indicates that the SES proxy accounted for 74.511 percent of the variance in fifth grade composite ITBS scores ($F = 64.31108$, $p < 0.01$). This served as the reduced regression for the remainder of the analysis of the fifth grade information.

The proportion of variance in the fifth grade ITBS scores accounted for by SES was compared independently to each subscale representing specified design classifications. The full regression for "movement" is presented in Table 12.7 on page 285. This procedure, conducted for all nine sets of design classifications, yielded the findings in Table 12.8 on page 286. Considered independently, design classifications accounted for 12.254 percent of the variance in fifth grade composite ITBS scores.

A summary of the reduced regression in Table 12.6 on page 284 and the full regression (all variables entered simultaneously) reveals a difference

in the R^2 values of $(0.859 - 0.745) = 0.114$ (Table 12.9, page 287). Therefore, when considered as a group, the design variables and the proxy for SES produced a multiple correlation of 0.927, $F_{10,13} = 7.934$, $p = 0.000$. Collectively, the full regression produced an $R = 0.927$, which was significantly different from 0. Independently, the summation of the difference between the full and reduced regressions was 0.12254 (Table 12.8), while as a group it was 0.114. The difference between the two percentages of variance is a result of the degrees of freedom in the two approaches. For example, in the complete regression, the degrees of freedom were 10 and 13 (Table 12.9), while the incremental values for degrees of freedom were 2 and 21 (Table 12.7). The policy question is: Do these variances add enough variance to be practically significant? It is important to note that as a group, the amount of variance in fifth grade ITBS composite scores was 0.859.

TABLE 12.6   Backward Elimination to Isolate the Best Predictors of Fifth Grade Composite ITBS Scores

MODEL SUMMARY

| MODEL | R | R SQUARE | ADJUSTED R SQUARE | STD. ERROR OF THE ESTIMATE | CHANGE STATISTICS | | | | |
					R SQUARE CHANGE	F CHANGE	DF1	DF2	SIG. F CHANGE
1	0.863	0.745	0.734	6.31953	0.745	64.311	1	22	0.000

a. Predictors: (Constant), FREE LUNCH

ANOVA

MODEL		SUM OF SQUARES	DF	MEAN SQUARE	F	SIG.
1	Regression	2,568.356	1	2,568.356	64.311	0.000
	Residual	878.602	22	39.936		
	Total	3,446.958	23			

a. Predictors: (Constant), FREE LUNCH
b. Dependent variable: FIFTH COMPOSITE

COEFFICIENTS

MODEL		UNSTANDARDIZED COEFFICIENTS B	STD. ERROR	STANDARDIZED COEFFICIENTS BETA	t	SIG.
1	(Constant)	81.088	3.933		20.617	0.000
	Free lunch	−0.553	0.069	−0.863	−8.019	0.000

a. Dependent variable: FIFTH COMPOSITE

This leaves $(1.00 - 0.859) = 0.141$ of the variance in ITBS scores for variables such as curriculum impact, teaching style, and other extraneous variables like philosophy of teaching, discipline, aesthetics, and organization climate.

A comparison of the findings for the two grade levels appears in Table 12.10 on page 288. The overall rank may be viewed as the importance of the design pattern in this study; notwithstanding, scale and environmental components were excluded because of unacceptable reliability coef-ficients. Large-group meeting places such as the auditorium, amphitheater, media center, commons spaces, and dining areas related significantly to achievement, although they were ranked 7 and 8, respectively. Instructional neighborhoods were more important for fifth grade students, while movement classifications and circulation ranked higher for third grade students. Daylighting and views and instructional laboratories ranked above average, while color was more important for fifth grade students. Outside learning areas

TABLE 12.7   Full Regression for the Design Pattern "Movement," Fifth Grade

MODEL SUMMARY

				STD. ERROR	CHANGE STATISTICS				
MODEL	R	R SQUARE	ADJUSTED R SQUARE	OF THE ESTIMATE	R SQUARE CHANGE	F CHANGE	DF1	DF2	SIG. F CHANGE
1	0.867	0.751	0.727	6.39077	0.751	31.699	2	21	0.000

a. Predictors: (Constant), MOVEMENT, FREE LUNCH

ANOVA

MODEL		SUM OF SQUARES	DF	MEAN SQUARE	F	SIG.
1	Regression	2,589.277	2	1,294.639	31.699	0.000
	Residual	857.681	21	40.842		
	Total	3,446.958	23			

a. Predictors: (Constant), MOVEMENT, FREE LUNCH
b. Dependent variable: FIFTH COMPOSITE

COEFFICIENTS

MODEL		UNSTANDARDIZED COEFFICIENTS B	STD. ERROR	STANDARDIZED COEFFICIENTS BETA	t	SIG.
1	(Constant)	69.238	17.029		4.066	0.001
	FREE LUNCH	−0.538	0.073	−0.839	−7.363	0.000
	MOVEMENT	7.979E-02	0.111	0.082	0.716	0.482

a. Dependent variable: FIFTH COMPOSITE

and location appeared to be less important. Architectural design occupied the middle rank. There were differences in rank on all items, implying that needs for fifth and third grade students are significantly different. The results of Spearman's rho (−0.109) revealed an alpha level of 0.781, further substantiating that there is no relationship between the two grade levels when the effects of design classifications are compared to student outcomes.

CONCLUSIONS AND DISCUSSION

This study was initiated with the uncertainty that any significant relationships between school design classifications and student achievement could be found. However, a uniformly positive and highly significant multiple correlation between school design classifications and student performance was found for the fifth grade students' ITBS scores. Further analysis with the F test led to the

TABLE 12.8   Independent Contributions to Variance in Fifth Grade Composite ITBS Scores Made by School Design Variables

CRITERION VARIABLE (RANK OF DIFFERENCE)	MULTIPLE CORRELATION		REGRESSION R SQUARE*	DIFFERENCE EFFECT	F CHANGE*
Movement (5)	Full	0.87	0.75118	0.00607	31.699
	Reduced	0.86	0.74511		
Large-group meeting places (9)	Full	0.86	0.74477	−0.00034	30.707
	Reduced	0.86	0.74511		
Architectural design (3.5)	Full	0.87	0.76038	0.01527	33.429
	Reduced	0.86	0.74511		
Daylighting and views (6)	Full	0.87	0.74822	0.00311	31.143
	Reduced	0.86	0.74511		
Color (3.5)	Full	0.87	0.76038	0.01527	33.183
	Reduced	0.86	0.74511		
Location (7)	Full	0.86	0.74557	0.00046	30.769
	Reduced	0.86	0.74511		
Instructional neighborhoods (1)	Full	0.90	0.80853	0.06342	44.338
	Reduced	0.86	0.74511		
Outside learning areas (8)	Full	0.87	0.76533	0.00202	34.244
	Reduced	0.86	0.74511		
Instructional laboratories (2)	Full	0.87	0.76237	0.01726	33.686
	Reduced	0.86	0.74511		
Grand total				Σ **12.254 %**	

*F statistic was significant for all entries ($\alpha \leq 0.05$).

conclusion that the effect sizes were significant. This finding led to the hypothesis that distinct from all other attributes associated with student achievement, school design classifications had an effect on student learning among fifth grade students in the twenty-four schools.

Since the data revealed an alpha level of 0.082 for the third grade level, the design classifications did not produce a significant effect on student outcomes. This might have been a result of test results, implying that third grade test scores are less reliable than fifth grade scores. Both grade levels were present in each of the twenty-four schools.

There are uncertainties that remain. This type of observational study cannot determine a causal relationship, only an association between the presence of certain design classifications and student achievement. The school design classifications isolated in this study seem to be good predictors of student academic performance, but there are other possible variables that might be involved in this association. The most obvious one is that teaching ability might be better in some schools than others. The training and experience measures did not measure teaching ability, although they might have approximated it. The fact that the scale and environmental variables were eliminated in the reliability analysis does not necessarily detract from their importance. They should be included in replication studies where variability may be more appropriate for analysis than was the case in this study.

TABLE 12.9 Summary of the Full Regression for the Fifth Grade Scores

FULL REGRESSION MODEL SUMMARY

MODEL	R	R SQUARE	ADJUSTED R SQUARE	STD. ERROR OF THE ESTIMATE	CHANGE STATISTICS				
					R SQUARE CHANGE	F CHANGE	DF1	DF2	SIG. F CHANGE
1	0.927	0.859	0.751	6.10974	0.859	7.934	10	13	0.000

a. Predictors: (Constant), INSTRUCTION LABS, OUTSIDE, COLOR, MEETING, FREE LUNCH, MOVEMENT, IN-STRUCT, LOCATION, DAYLIGHT, DESIGN

ANOVA

MODEL		SUM OF SQUARES	DF	MEAN SQUARE	F	SIG.
1	Regression	2,961.682	10	296.168	7.934	0.000
	Residual	485.277	13	37.329		
	Total	3,446.958	23			

a. Predictors: (Constant), INSTRUCTION LABS, OUTSIDE, COLOR, MEETING, FREE LUNCH, MOVEMENT, IN-STRUCT, LOCATION, DAYLIGHT, DESIGN
b. Dependent variable: FIFTH COMPOSITE

Because the instrument in this study was in its developmental stages, more rigorous tests of validity and reliability should be conducted. Factor analysis might be used to test the appropriateness of items grouped in each of the subscales. Discriminant analysis (inner-scale correlation) may also be employed to verify the independence of the individual subscales. For example, the relative low reliability of the instructional neighborhoods subscale may be a result of too many items of a different nature in one subscale (i.e., item 61 measures atmosphere instead of space).

IMPLICATIONS

What implications do these findings have for teachers, educational decision makers and planners, architects, school boards, and educational policy makers? It is important to note that there were no negative relationships between school design factors in the instrument and academic achievement. Implications are that the way these twenty-four schools were designed does make a difference in student achievement. While we should be cautious in generalizing these findings, measures of the school's physical environment do correlate significantly with academic achievement in this sample of twenty-four schools.

One implication for teachers is that arrangements allowing for more freedom of movement and circulation classifications within classrooms can be a positive influence on student learning. This parallels findings by Kritchevsky and Prescott (1969) who studied organization of space and found that as the quality of the space increased, student performance also increased. Zifferblatt (1972) obtained similar results, attributing improved behavior to physical arrangements permitting spatial freedom. The question remains as to whether there was a correlation between teaching ability and the

TABLE 12.10 **Ranks of Design Classifications According to Their Individual Contributions to the Variance in Test Scores**

DESIGN PATTERN	OVERALL RANK	THIRD GRADE RANK	FIFTH GRADE RANK
Instructional neighborhoods	1	4	1
Movement	2	1	5
Instructional laboratories	3	5	2
Daylighting and views	4	3	6
Architectural design	5	7	3.5
Color	6	8	3.5
Large-group meeting places	7	2	9
Outside learning areas, large	8	6	8
Location	9	9	7

teacher's assignment to certain spaces having specific design classifications. For example, in the study of daylight and student learning, a concern arose regarding teachers with more seniority or training or experience being assigned to classrooms with more daylight and windows. " It might be a function of teachers in day lit classrooms being more motivated or alert or responsive to students" (Heschong Mahone Group, 1999, p. 58).

Teachers are rarely exposed to information or literature in their formal training that ties the physical environment to student achievement. Even in schools where windows are available to allow natural light into the classroom, it is not uncommon to find blinds pulled or other obstructions that prevent views to the outside and daylight from entering. "Students in classrooms with the most daylighting were found to have 7% to 18% higher scores than those with the least" (Heschong Mahone Group, 1999, p. 3). The implication from this finding is that teachers, teacher educators, and people developing curriculum for teacher training should consider daylight and views as important dimensions of student learning. Speculation regarding the design classifications in this study and other design classifications not included should spark an interest in further research in this neglected area of educational research.

Implications for educational decision makers, school boards, and planners are that in designing and planning new schools or remodeling older schools, the importance of design as defined in this study is straightforward. First, design classifications having large-group meeting places, instructional neighborhoods, ample circulation classifications, natural light and views, appropriate color, and outdoor learning areas are extremely important. For example, the contention regarding movement was supported in the literature reviewed for this study. Weinstein (1979) reported findings parallel to this study. Regarding crowding and density (movement and circulation classifications), she stated that "the evidence is sufficient to suggest a number of undesirable reactions, such as dissatisfaction, nervousness, less social interaction, and increased aggression" (p. 588). Design scores on movement classifications such as ample egress and excellent circulation classifications correlated positively with student achievement in this study. Planners and decision makers should strongly consider the effects of the physical environment on student learning when working on capital outlay projects.

School architects who have relied on best practices and old designs may utilize the information found in this study to bring architecture in line with current teaching and learning philosophy. In addition to overall design, the architect should ensure that the school entrance is friendly, that the school has a point of reference, that paths with goals are plentiful, and that teacher workrooms are close to classrooms. Furthermore, hallways should be adequate to display student work, intimacy gradients should be plentiful, and ceiling heights should vary to allow for individual visual comfort and intimacy within the school. These design classifications correlated positively with student achievement in this study.

All areas of school design discussed in this study have implications for the educational policy process. In particular, movement classifications should be of interest to educational policy makers given the debates over smaller class size and smaller schools. In reporting on a study on class size versus density, Tanner (2000) stated that

> these findings have strong implications for government policy. If smaller is better, then fewer students per existing classroom is the answer. We cannot simply put smaller classes in smaller places by dividing the spaces we already have. Such action would compound the density problem by having more students in less space. (p. 22).

Wohlwill and van Vliet (1985) who noted that high-density conditions influence student performance in a negative manner have summarized the effects of high density. Space needs are receiving attention across the United States as the concept of "smaller is better" gains popularity among professional educators and policy makers. If the findings in this study can be consistently replicated, then a strong case may be made for the design classifications presented here to become an integral part of policy on the building and modification of educational environments.

This study tested the theory that the design classifications of the school's physical environment influence student achievement. A significant relationship between the physical environment and student achievement was found, adding credibility to the theory. If these findings can consistently be replicated, then the underlying theory in this study can be substantiated. This theory suggests that schools should be viewed as comprehensive learning environments and the physical environment should be dictated by teaching and learning theory. School architecture should not dictate learning and teaching styles. Quite the opposite, teaching and learning styles should dictate school architecture.

SUMMARY

Schools in the United States are suffering from poor building conditions such as inadequate ventilation, poor indoor air quality, noise, bad lighting, uncomfortable thermal conditions, and overcrowding. There is a wealth of research data to suggest that physical facility conditions affect educational outcomes such as academic achievement and behavior, but such data are sporadic and often inconclusive. This chapter presents a study that examined the relationship between eleven design classifications and mean student test scores (Iowa Test of Basic Skills or ITBS) for third and fifth grade students in a sample of twenty-four elementary schools in west-central Georgia. The underlying assumption in this study, supported by the literature, was that the design classifications of the school's physical environment influence student achievement. The design classifications include movement classifications (e.g., circulation classifications, density or freedom of movement, personal space); large group meeting places; architectural design (e.g., welcoming front entry, centralized administration); daylight and views; color; scale; location of the school site; instructional neighborhoods; outdoor environments; istructional laboratories (e.g., technology integration, music and art labs); and environmental (e.g., thermal conditions, noise) classifications. These eleven design classifications were the basis for the development of a 78-item instrument to provide a systematic method for assessing physical learning environments (using a ten-point Likert scale per item) in elementary schools. School design information was collected during site visits by one trained researcher. Upon completion of the site visits, the following data were obtained for each school: achievement data (average composite third and fifth grade ITBS scores per school), number of students representing various ethnic groups, the average length of teaching experience of teachers and their levels of training, the number of gifted students, and a proxy for socioeconomic status (percentage of students receiving a free or reduced-cost school lunch). These data served as control variables (covariates) in making estimates of ITBS scores based on scores recorded on the assessment instrument.

The sum of the independent effects of the variance in ITBS scores for third grade students was equal to 8.675 percent. Considered independently, design classifications accounted for 12.254 per-cent of the variance in fifth grade composite ITBS scores. A ranking of the importance of the design pattern in this study (excluding scale and environmental components that had unacceptable reliability coefficients) implies that the needs of fifth and third grade students are significantly different. A uniformly positive and highly significant multiple correlation between school design classifications and student performance was found for the fifth grade students' ITBS scores. Further analysis with the F test led to the conclusion that the effect sizes were significant.

Since the data revealed an alpha level of 0.082 for the third grade level, the design classifications did not produce a significant effect on student outcomes. This type of observational study cannot determine a causal relationship, only an association between the presence of certain design classifications and student achievement. The school design classifications isolated in this study seem to be good predictors of student academic performance, but there are other possible variables (such as teaching ability) that might be involved in this association.

The results of this study imply that physical characteristics of the learning environment do affect academic achievement and that teachers may want to allow for more freedom of movement and circulation classifications within classrooms. It is important for educational decision makers, school boards, and planners to consider the design classifications of having large-group meeting places, instructional neighborhoods, ample circulation classifications, natural light and views, appropriate color, and outdoor learning areas when designing and planning new schools or remodeling older ones. School architects should ensure that the school entrance is friendly, that the school has a point of reference, that paths with goals are plentiful, and that teacher workrooms are close to classrooms. Furthermore, hallways should be adequate to display student work, intimacy gradients should be plentiful, and ceiling heights should vary to allow for individual visual comfort and intimacy within the school.

ACTIVITIES

1. Arrange a visit to an elementary school in teams of three or four persons. Each person will independently rate the school using the Design Appraisal Scale for Elementary Schools located in the appendix. Do not discuss the scoring until after each of you has completed the design instrument for the school. When completed, write a description of your experience (one write-up per group) using the Design Appraisal Scale and discuss the similarities and differences in your responses. You may even want to calculate your inter-rater reliability. What measures could be taken to improve the reliability of the tool if your group was responsible for rating a large number of schools for a study similar to the one described in this chapter?

2. Collect and compile data for five elementary schools (including the one you visited for activity 1, if applicable) in your state for the following:

achievement data (select from the test scores available), number of students representing various ethnic groups, the average length of teaching experience of teachers and their levels of training, the number of gifted students, and the percentage of students receiving a free or reduced-cost school lunch (or some other proxy of socioeconomic status). If this information is not readily available, select similar data that might serve as controls. Prepare this information in a table or spreadsheet. What other available data might be useful in a study similar to the one presented in Chapter 12?

3. Chapter 12 included a review of some basic literature pertaining to each of the eleven design classifications included in the study, but the review was intentionally not exhaustive, since many of the ideas were covered in other parts of this text. Select one of the eleven design classifica-

tions and update the review of literature that evaluates how that design classification may affect educational outcomes. Be cautious about placing too much emphasis on "best practices" research.

4. Develop some possible "new" areas of design classifications that might be added to the survey instrument, emphasizing the face validity and content validity of each item. [Face validity is concerned with how a measure or procedure appears and whether it is a reasonable way to gain the information the researchers are attempting to obtain. Unlike content validity, face validity does not depend on established theories for support (Fink, 1995).] [Content validity is a representative sample of the content or substance of the new design classification and helps answer the question: Is the content representative of the universe the characteristic being measured?]

REFERENCES

Ackerman, J. S. (1969). Listening to architecture. *Harvard Educational Review: Architecture and Education*, 39:4–10.

Agron, J. (2004). Schools of tomorrow. *American School and University*, 76(5):16–27.

Alexander, C., Ishikawa, S., & Silverstein, M. (1977). *A pattern language*. New York: Oxford University Press.

American Psychological Association (1995). *Publication manual of the American Psychological Association*, 4th ed. Washington, DC: APA.

Andersen, S. (1999). *The relationship between school design variables and scores on the Iowa Test of Basic Skills*. Unpublished doctoral dissertation, University of Georgia, Athens, GA.

Ayers, P. D. (1999). *Exploring the relationship between high school facilities and achievement of high school students in Georgia*. Unpublished doctoral dissertation, University of Georgia, Athens, GA.

Banghart, F. W., & Trull, A., Jr. (1973). *Educational planning*. New York: Macmillan.

Bennett, D. T. (1990). *The relationships among roof problems and roof types on public school buildings in Georgia*. Unpublished doctoral dissertation, University of Georgia, Athens, GA.

Bete, T. (1998). The school of the future. *School Planning and Management* 37:70–73.

Bingler, S. (1995). Place as a form of knowledge. In Meek, A. (ed.), *Designing places for learning*. Alexandria, VA: Association for Supervision and Curriculum Development, pp. 23–30.

Bosch, S. J. (2003). *Identifying relevant variables for understanding how school facilities affect educational outcomes*. Unpublished doctoral dissertation, Georgia Institute of Technology, Atlanta, GA.

Bronzaft, A. L., & McCarthy, D. P. (1975). The effects of elevated train noise on reading ability. *Environment and Behavior*, 7:517–527.

Brubaker, C. W. (1991). Lessons in high school planning and design. *School Business Affairs*, 57(1):6–10.

Castaldi, B. (1994). *Educational facilities: Planning, modernization and management*, 4th ed. Boston, MA: Allyn & Bacon.

Chan, T. C. (1980). *Physical environment and middle grade achievement*. ERIC Document Reproduction Service, No. ED 198645.

Christopher, G. (2002). Design for sustainable learning. *Educational Facility Planner*, 37(2):15–17.

Cochran, C.D., Hale, D., & Hissam, C. (1984). Personal space requirements in indoor versus outdoor locations. *Journal of Psychology*, 117:121–123.

Cohen, S., & Lezak, A. (1977). Noise and inattentiveness to social cues. *Environment and Behavior*, 9: 559–572.

Colven, R. (1990). *The quality of the physical environment of the school and the quality of education. Conclusions of a seminar.* ERIC Document Reproduction Service, No. ED 324791.

Crowe, N. (1995). *Nature and the idea of the man-made world.* Cambridge, MA: MIT Press.

Crumpacker, S. S. (1995). Using cultural information to create schools that work. In Meek, A. (ed.), *Designing places for learning.* Alexandria, VA: Association for Supervision and Curriculum Development, pp. 31–42.

Curtis, H. A., & Stuart, F. (1964). *A digest of climate controlled and non-climate controlled schools—An evaluative study conducted in Pinellas County Florida.* ERIC Document Reproduction Service, No. ED 001128.

Day, C. W. (July, 1999). Sounding off. *American School and University.* http://industryclick.com/magazinearticle.asp?magazineid=134&releaseid=3735&magazinearticleid=33067&siteid=17.

Dryfoos, J. G. (1999). The role of the school in out-of-school time. *The Future of Children,* 9:117–134.

Duke, D. L. (1998). Does it matter where our children learn? ERIC Document Reproduction Service, No. ED 418578.

Duncanson, E. (2003). Classroom space: Right for adults but wrong for kids. *Educational Facility Planner,* 38(1):24–28.

Earthman, G. I. (2000). *Planning educational facilities for the next century.* Reston, VA: Association of School Business Officials, International.

Fink, A. (ed.) (1995). *How to measure survey reliability and validity, vol.* 7. Thousand Oaks, CA: Sage.

Fiske, E. B. (1995). Systematic school reform: Implications for architecture. In Meek, A. (ed.), *Designing places for learning.* Alexandria, VA: Association of Supervision and Curriculum Development, pp. 1–10.

Freeman, C. (1995). Planning and play: Creating greener environments. *Children's Environments,* 12:381–388.

Gabarino, J. (1980). Some thoughts about school size and its effects on adolescent development. *Journal of Youth and Adolescence,* 9:19–31.

Garrett, H. E., & Woodworth, R. S. (1958). *Statistics in psychology and education.* New York: David McKay Company.

Gentry, K. J. (2000). *The relationship between school size and academic achievement in Georgia's public high schools.* Unpublished doctoral dissertation, University of Georgia, Athens, GA.

Georgia Department of Education (1999). *School report cards.* http://www.doe.k12.ga.us.

Graves, B. E. (1993). *School ways: The planning and design of America's schools.* New York McGraw-Hill.

Greenman, J. (1988). *Caring spaces, learning places: Children's environments that work.* Redmond, WA: Exchange Press, Inc.

Hall, E. (1959). *The silent language.* New York: Anchor Books.

Herbert, E. A. (1998). Design matters: How school environment affects children. *Educational Leadership,* 56:69–70.

Herrington, L. P. (1952). Effects of thermal environment on human action. *American School and University,* 24:367–376.

Heschong Mahone Group (1999). *Daylighting in schools.* Fair Oaks, CA: Heschong Mahone Group.

Horton, C. G. (1972). *Humanization of the learning environment.* ERIC Document Reproduction Service, No. ED 066929.

Hughes, P. C. (1980). The use of light and color in health. In Hastings, A. C., Fadiman, J., & Gordon, J. S. (eds.), *Health for the whole person: The complete guide to holistic medicine.* Boulder, CO.: Westview Press, pp. 71–83.

Ketcham, J. (1964). These colors fit your school décor. *Nations Schools,* 74:61–80.

Kritchevsky, S., & Prescott, E. (1969). *Planning environments for young children: Physical space.* Washington, DC : National Association for the Education of Young Children.

Kuller, R., & Lindsten, C. (1992). Health and behavior of children in classrooms with and without windows. *Journal of Environmental Psychology,* 12:305–317.

Lang, D. (1996). *Essential criteria for an ideal learning environment.* Center for Environment, Education and Design Studies. http://www.newhorizons.org/article_dalelang.html.

Latham, A. S. (1999). Computers and achievement. *Educational Leadership,* 56:87–88.

Liska, R. W. (1988). *The development of a systematic process for enhancing the awareness of the potential for indoor air pollution in schools.* Unpublished doctoral dissertation, University of Georgia, Athens, GA.

Lomranz, J., Shapira, A., Choresh, N., & Gilat, Y. (1975). Children's personal space as a function of age and sex. *Developmental Psychology,* 11:541–545.

McCardle, R. W. (1966). *Thermal environment and learning.* Unpublished doctoral dissertation, University of Iowa, Des Moines, IA.

McDonald, E. G. (1960). Effect of school environment on teacher and student performance. *Air Conditioning, Heating and Ventilating,* 57:78–79.

McGuffey, C. W. (1982). Facilities. In Wallberg, H. J. (ed.), *Improving educational standards and productivity.* Berkeley, CA: McCutchan Publishing, pp. 237–258.

Meek, A., & Landfried, S. (1995). Crow Island School: 54 years young. In Meek, A. (ed.), *Designing places for learning.* Alexandria, VA: Association of Supervision and Curriculum Development, pp. 51–59.

Moore, G. T., & Lackney, J. A. (1994). *Educational facilities for the twenty-first century: research analysis and design patterns.* Report R94-1, School of Architecture and Urban Planning, University of Wisconsin-Milwaukee, Center for Architecture and Urban Planning Research.

Also available from ERIC Document Reproduction Service, No. EA 026223.

Moore, G. T., & Lackney, J. A. (1995). Design classifications for American schools: Responding to the reform movement. In Meek, A. (ed.), *Designing places for learning*. Alexandria, VA: Association of Supervision and Curriculum Development, pp. 11–22.

National Center for Education Statistics (2000). *Condition of America's public school facilities: 1999*. NCES 2000-032. Washington, DC: U.S. Department of Education.

Norusis, N. J. (1990). *SPSS base system user's guide*. Chicago, IL: SPSS, Inc.

Ott, J. (1973). *Health and light*. New York: Simon & Schuster.

Plath, K. R. (1965). *Schools within schools: A study of high school organization*. New York: Bureau of Publications, Teachers College, Columbia University.

Prescott, E. (1987). Environment as an organizer in child-care settings. In Weinstein, C. S., & David, T. G. (eds.), *Spaces for children: The built environment and child development*. New York: Plenum Press, pp. 73–88.

Proshansky, E., & Wolfe, M. (1974). The physical setting and open education. *School Review*, 82:557–574.

Rice, A. J. (1953). What research knows about color in the classroom. *Nation's Schools*, 52:1–8.

Romney, B. M. (1975). *The effects of windowless classrooms on the cognitive and affective behavior of elementary school students*. ERIC Document Reproduction Service, No. ED 008565.

Scott, E. (1999). Sound decisions improve learning. *American School and University*. http://www.asumag.com/magazine/Archives/1199acoustics.html.

Sharp, L. B. (1973). What is outdoor education? In Hammerman, D. R., & Hammerman, W. M. (eds.), *Outdoor education*. Minneapolis, MN: Burgess Publishing Company, pp. 2–6.

Sleeman, P. J., & Rockwell, D. M. (1981). *Designing learning environments*. New York: Longman.

Smith, N. R. (1980). Color selection—a key element in learning. *CEFP Journal*, 18:6–7.

Sommer, R. (1969). *Personal space*. Englewood Cliffs, NJ: Prentice-Hall.

Spearnak, M., & Brelig, G. (2004). Pathway to sustainable schools. *Educational Facility Planner*, 38(3):16–19.

Stine, S. (1997). *Landscapes for learning*. New York: John Wiley & Sons.

Swift, D. O. (2000). *Effects of student population density on academic achievement in Georgia elementary schools*. Unpublished doctoral dissertation, University of Georgia, Athens, GA.

Tanner, C. K. (November, 1999). *A school design assessment scale*. Paper presented at the annual conference of the Council of Educational facility Planners, International, Baltimore, MD.

Tanner, C. K. (2000). The influence of school architecture on academic achievement. *Journal of Educational Administration*, 38:309–330.

Tanner, C. K. (2001). Into the woods, wetlands, and prairies. *Educational Leadership*, 58:64–66.

Taylor, A. P., & Vlastos, G. (1975). *School zone: Learning environments for children*. New York: Van Nostrand Reinhold.

Thompson, S. (2003). Color in education. *School Planning and Management*, 42(12):30–32.

Weinstein, C. S. (1979). The physical environment of the school: A review of the research. *Review of Educational Research*, 49:577–610.

Weinstein, C. S., & David, T. G. (eds.). (1987). *Spaces for children: The built environment and child development*. New York: Plenum Press.

Wenglinsky, H. (1998). *Does it compute? The relationship between educational technology and student achievement in mathematics*. ERIC Document Reproduction Service, No. ED 425191.

Wohlwill, J. F., & van Vliet, W. (1985). *Habitats for children: The impacts of density*. Hillsdale, NJ: Lawrence Erlbaum Associates.

Woodhead, M. (1964). The effect of bursts of noise on an arithmetic task. *American Journal of Psychology*, 77:627–633.

Wurtman, R. J. (1975). The effects of light on the human body. *Scientific American*, 233:68–77.

Yarborough, K. A. (2001). *The relationship of school design to academic achievement of elementary school children*. Unpublished doctoral dissertation, University of Georgia, Athens, GA.

Zifferblatt, S. M. (1972). Architecture and human behavior: Toward increased understanding of a functional relationship. *Educational Technology*, 12:54–57.

NOTES

1. The data set for this study was collected by Dr. Kathleen Yarborough, part of which she used in her dissertation. Special thanks are owed to her for her efficient work. Dr. Yarborough is an experienced elementary school teacher and administrator. She also holds a certificate in school design and planning (SDP). Different analyses were employed in the study reported in this chapter as compared to her 2001 study. The research was funded by a grant from the College of Education, the University of Georgia. No

human subjects were used in the study presented in this chapter. The unit of analysis was the schools' mean test scores and design scores. The ITBS scores are publicly available information.

2. Students in the School Design and Planning Laboratory (SDPL) (http://www.coe.uga.edu/sdpl) at the University of Georgia have completed 18 dissertations on school facilities and their relationships to student learning. Numerous references pertaining to design classifications and student achievement are found in the early works by Andersen (1999), Ayers (1999), Gentry (2000), Swift (2000), and Yarborough (2001). Other dissertations on school planning and design that followed the five cited in this chapter include:

Carrie Ann Colvin Booher (2001). *Design standards for elementary, middle/junior high, and high school counseling facilities.* Unpublished doctoral dissertation, University of Georgia, Athens, GA.

Cathy Lynn Folden (2002). *Perspectives of middle school principals regarding floor covering and a comparison of student performance with sound intensity levels.* Unpublished doctoral dissertation, University of Georgia, Athens, GA.

Kathleen Smith Hlavaty (2002). *Design preferences of media specialists for elementary school media centers in the state of Georgia.* Unpublished doctoral dissertation, University of Georgia, Athens, GA.

Patricia Ann Langford (2002). *Perceptions of elementary school principals regarding floor covering and a comparison of elementary school students' performance with sound intensity levels.* Unpublished doctoral dissertation, University of Georgia, Athens, GA.

Amy Melissa Garner Smith (2002). *A measurement of acoustics, density, academic achievement and teachers' perceptions in portable classrooms and in-building classrooms.*

Unpublished doctoral dissertation, University of Georgia, Athens, GA.

Sue Ellen Snow (2002). *Teachers' perceptions and use of classroom space.* Unpublished doctoral dissertation, University of Georgia, Athens, GA.

Joy Rice Tolbert (2002). *A study of factors affecting high school safety and security.* Unpublished doctoral dissertation, University of Georgia, Athens, GA.

Roy Franklin Morris, Jr. (2003). *The relationships among school facility characteristics, student achievement, and job satisfaction levels among teachers.* Unpublished doctoral dissertation, University of Georgia, Athens, GA.

Rex Milford Wallace (2003). *Design standards for a high school museum resource center.* Unpublished doctoral dissertation, University of Georgia, Athens, GA.

Christopher A. McMichael (2004). *Perspectives of school planners, architects, and professional educators regarding elementary school facility design characteristics.* Unpublished doctoral dissertation, University of Georgia, Athens, GA.

David Calvin Phillips (2004). *A comparison of historic and modern school facilities in rural northeast Georgia according to Henry Barnard's* Principles of School Architecture. Unpublished doctoral dissertation, University of Georgia, Athens, GA.

Susan Rogers Simpson (2004). *Health clinic environments in Georgia elementary schools.* Unpublished doctoral dissertation, University of Georgia, Athens, GA.

Jennifer Landrum Hadden (2005). *Educational facility design features in Georgia schools.* Unpublished doctoral dissertation, University of Georgia, Athens, GA.

Special gratitude is extended to these former doctoral students in SDPL for providing consistent efforts in the study of the physical environments.

APPENDIX: DESIGN APPRAISAL SCALE FOR ELEMENTARY SCHOOLS

■ ■ ■ ■ ■ ▬▬▬▬▬▬▬▬▬▬▬▬▬▬▬▬▬▬▬▬▬▬▬▬▬▬▬▬▬▬▬▬

Instructions.   Please score design classifications on the scale 1 to 10 as defined in each section. If the school does not have a specific feature, then the score is 0 for that item. Place each score on the fill-in to the left of individual items. Design includes the way the schoolhouse is made, how it is arranged, and how the outside areas near the school complement the curriculum. The scale measures the degree to which each item is present in the learning environment. The following sample scale suggests that the design classification under consideration received a high assigned score (95):

WEAKER <---+----I----+----I----+----I----+----I----I-●-> **STRONGER**
0 1 2 3 4 5 6 7 8 9 10

MOVEMENT CLASSIFICATIONS

The school's design may be judged in regard to its ability to enable students and teachers to enter and move freely within and around a facility.

_____ **1.** Promenade—Outside walkways linking main areas; ideally placing major activity centers at the extremes.

AMBIGUOUS <---+----I----+----I----+----I----+----I----> **DISTINCT**
0 1 2 3 4 5 6 7 8 9 10

_____ **2.** Pathways—Clear and comfortable pathways allow freedom of movement and orientation among structures. These play a vital role in the way people interact with buildings. This pattern defines the overall philosophy of the layout.

AMBIGUOUS <---+----I----+----I----+----I----+----I----I----> **CLEAR**
0 1 2 3 4 5 6 7 8 9 10

Circulation Classifications—Indoor spaces for circulation (especially classroom spaces). The passages should be broad and well-lit, allowing for freedom of movement.

_____ **3.** Within learning environments.

POOR <---+----I----+----I----+----I----+----I----> **EXCELLENT**
0 1 2 3 4 5 6 7 8 9 10

_____ **4.** Hallways—Passageways allowing students personal space when moving within the school (ample spaces = noncrowded).

MEAGER SPACE <----+----+----+----+----+----+----+----+----> **AMPLE SPACE**
                   0 1 2 3 4 5 6 7 8 9 10

_____ **5.** Supervisable circulation classifications (percentage of supervisable circulation classifications: 0 = 0%, 1 = 10%, . . ., 10 = 100%).

_____ **6.** Egress—Many exits from the building. The best situations allow students to exit (to the outside) directly from their classrooms.

NONE <----+----+----+----+----+----+----+----+----> **AMPLE**
         0 1 2 3 4 5 6 7 8 9 10

_____ **7.** Classrooms—Exterior doors lead to a courtyard or garden area.

LACKING <----+----+----+----+----+----+----+----+----> **EXTENSIVE**
            0 1 2 3 4 5 6 7 8 9 10

*Spaces for physically challenged students (MC-multicultural).

LIMITED <----+----+----+----+----+----+----+----+----> **UNLIMITED**
            0 1 2 3 4 5 6 7 8 9 10

_____ **8.** (a) Access to classrooms.

_____ **9.** (b) Access to hallways.

_____ **10.** (c) Access to lunchroom.

_____ **11.** (d) Access to gymnasium.

_____ **12.** (e) Access to school buildings.

_____ **13.** (f) Access to toilets.

_____ **14.** (g) Access to drinking fountains.

_____ **15.** (h) Access to computer stations.

_____ **16.** (i) Access to school grounds.

_____ **17.** (j) Access to living center (teaching center).

LARGE-GROUP MEETING PLACES

Public Areas—Spaces fostering a sense of community (unity and belonging). Inviting and comfortable settings including ample lighting.

POOR <----+----|----|----|----|----|----|----|----|----|-----> EXCELLENT
         0   1 2 3 4 5 6 7 8 9 10

_____ **18.** (a) Auditorium.

_____ **19.** (b) Amphitheater.

_____ **20.** (c) Media Center.

ARCHITECTURAL DESIGN

_____ **21.** Entrance Area—A friendly space connecting the outside world to the inside world. This age-appropriate space should be inviting and highly visible to students and visitors. It should evoke a "welcome" feeling.

NOT WELCOMING <----+----|----|----|----|----|----|----|----|----|-----> WELCOMING
             0   1 2 3 4 5 6 7 8 9 10

_____ **22.** Administration Centralized—The main administrative offices are grouped together in a centralized area allowing for connection and convenience (assistant principals may be located elsewhere in the school). If there are schools within a school or a campus plan, the person in charge should be readily accessible, at least for the safety and security of the children. (Accessibility)

POOR <----+----|----|----|----|----|----|----|----|----|-----> EXCELLENT
         0   1 2 3 4 5 6 7 8 9 10

_____ **23.** Reference—Main building has an obvious point of reference among the school's buildings in which paths and buildings connect. This design feature heightens the sense of community. An example might be a clock tower at the front entrance.

OBSCURE <----+----|----|----|----|----|----|----|----|----|-----> OBVIOUS
           0   1 2 3 4 5 6 7 8 9 10

_____ **24.** Paths with Goals—Places designed to provide focal points when walking to particular locations (e.g., displays of students, work, meaningful posters, benches, or plants).

NONEXISTENT <---+----|----+---+----+----+----+----+----|----|----> **PLENTIFUL**
$$0 \quad 1 \quad 2 \quad 3 \quad 4 \quad 5 \quad 6 \quad 7 \quad 8 \quad 9 \quad 10$$

_____ **25.** Intimacy Gradients—A sequence from larger to smaller, public to private spaces. This gives the effect of drawing people into the area. Usually found in main entrances, but may be used throughout the learning environment.

NONEXISTENT <---+----|----+----+----+----+----+----+----+----|----> **PLENTIFUL**
$$0 \quad 1 \quad 2 \quad 3 \quad 4 \quad 5 \quad 6 \quad 7 \quad 8 \quad 9 \quad 10$$

_____ **26.** Hallways—Adequate/inadequate for displaying student work.

INADEQUATE <---+----|----+---+----+----+----+----+----|----|----> **ADEQUATE**
$$0 \quad 1 \quad 2 \quad 3 \quad 4 \quad 5 \quad 6 \quad 7 \quad 8 \quad 9 \quad 10$$

DAYLIGHTING AND VIEWS

Windows—Spaces bringing natural light into the learning environment. Windows may have some form of glare control, but should be in use (when glare is not a problem) and free of painted obstructions and other devices restricting views. Windows should invite the outdoors inside.

_____ **27.** (a) Views overlooking life.

NONE <---+----|----+----+----+----+----+----+----|----|----> **NUMEROUS**
$$0 \quad 1 \quad 2 \quad 3 \quad 4 \quad 5 \quad 6 \quad 7 \quad 8 \quad 9 \quad 10$$

_____ **28.** (b) Unrestricted views (when glare/curtains is/are not a problem).

SPARSE <---+----|----+----+----+----+----+----+----|----|----> **AMPLE**
$$0 \quad 1 \quad 2 \quad 3 \quad 4 \quad 5 \quad 6 \quad 7 \quad 8 \quad 9 \quad 10$$

_____ **29.** (c) Adequacy of natural light (includes skylights and borrowed light, natural and reflected light).

NO MIXTURE <---+----|----+----+----+----+----+----|----|----> **AMPLE MIXTURE**
OF LIGHTING $$0 \quad 1 \quad 2 \quad 3 \quad 4 \quad 5 \quad 6 \quad 7 \quad 8 \quad 9 \quad 10$$

_____ **30.** Living Views—Views of indoor and outdoor spaces (gardens, animals, fountains, mountains, people, etc.). These allow minds and eyes to take a break.

INADEQUATE <---+----|----|----|----|----|----|----|----|-----> ADEQUATE

0 1 2 3 4 5 6 7 8 9 10

_____ **31.** Natural Light/Full Spectrum—Artificial light plus natural light from the outside, preferably on two sides of every room.

NO MIXTURE OF <---+----|----|----|----|----|----|----|----|-----> AMPLE
LIGHTING   0 1 2 3 4 5 6 7 8 9 10 MIXTURE

COLOR SCHEMES

[Tone = quality: hue = a scale of perceptions ranging (circular) from red to yellow to green to blue to red]

_____ **32.** (a) Classroom.

NEUTRAL

WARM HUE <---+----|----|----|----|----|----|----|----|-----> LIGHT HUE WITH
            0 1 2 3 4 5 6 7 8 9 10 STRONGER COLOR
                                              FOR FRONT WALL

_____ **33.** (b) Hallways.

NEUTRAL

DARK HUE <---+----|----|----|----|----|----|----|----|-----> LIGHT HUE WITH
            0 1 2 3 4 5 6 7 8 9 10 BRIGHT ENDS

_____ **34.** (c) Lunchroom.

NEUTRAL

DARK HUE <---+----|----|----|----|----|----|----|----|-----> LIGHT HUE WITH
            0 1 2 3 4 5 6 7 8 9 10 BRIGHT COLOR ACCENTS

_____ **35.** (d) Gymnasium.

NEUTRAL

DARK TONES <---+----|----|----|----|----|----|----|----|-----> LIGHT TONES WITH
              0 1 2 3 4 5 6 7 8 9 10 BRIGHT COLOR
                                                ACCENTS

_____ **36.** Background Detail—Spaces of colorful displays on walls and doors (e.g., light switches, wall outlets, louvers, and surface raceways) that might go unnoticed by adults.

INHIBITS LEARNING <----+----|----|----|----|----|----|----|----|----|----> **PROMOTES LEARNING**
0 1 2 3 4 5 6 7 8 9 10

_____ **37.** Visual Stimulation—Walls and finishes that effectively display color and vivid classifications.

INHIBITS <----+----|----|----|----|----|----|----|----|----|----> **PROMOTES**
LEARNING 0 1 2 3 4 5 6 7 8 9 10 **LEARNING**

STUDENT'S SCALE

A place designed and built to the scale of children (e.g., door handles or handrails are low enough for children to reach to accommodate their heights).

_____ **38.** (a) Light switches.

TOO HIGH/LOW <----+----|----|----|----|----|----|----|----|----|----> **APPROPRIATE HEIGHT**
0 1 2 3 4 5 6 7 8 9 10

_____ **39.** (b) Door handles.

TOO HIGH/LOW <----+----|----|----|----|----|----|----|----|----|----> **APPROPRIATE HEIGHT**
0 1 2 3 4 5 6 7 8 9 10

_____ **40.** (c) Handrails.

TOO HIGH/LOW <----+----|----|----|----|----|----|----|----|----|----> **APPROPRIATE HEIGHT**
0 1 2 3 4 5 6 7 8 9 10

_____ **41.** (d) Shortened steps.

UNSUITABLE <----+----|----|----|----|----|----|----|----|----|----> **SUITABLE**
0 1 2 3 4 5 6 7 8 9 10

_____ **42.** (e) Water fountains.

TOO HIGH/LOW <----+----|----+----|----+----|----+----|----+-----> APPROPRIATE HEIGHT
                  0   1   2   3   4   5   6   7   8   9 10

_____ **43.** (f) Views (doors/windows that allow the student to easily see the outside).

TOO HIGH/LOW <----+----|----+----|----+----|----+----|----+-----> APPROPRIATE HEIGHT
                  0   1   2   3   4   5   6   7   8   9 10

_____ **44.** (g) Percentage of developmentally appropriate playground equipment (0 = 0%, 1 = 10%, . . ., 10 = 100%).

LOCATION OF THE SCHOOL

_____ **45.** Safe Location—The site and learning environments are free of excessive nonpedestrian traffic and noise. Natural or built barriers may protect these areas.

NOT SAFE <----+----|----+----|----+----|----+----|----+-----> VERY SAFE
              0   1   2   3   4   5   6   7   8   9 10

_____ **46.** Context—The school and grounds are compatible with the surroundings and are sufficient to facilitate the curriculum and programs.

NOT COMPATIBLE <----+----|----+----|----+----|----+----|----+-----> COMPATIBLE
                    0   1   2   3   4   5   6   7   8   9 10

_____ **47.** Harmony—The school is "in harmony with nature." It blends with the surroundings and brings nature into the learning environment.

DOES NOT BLEND <----+----|----+----|----+----|----+----|----+-----> BLENDS
                    0   1   2   3   4   5   6   7   8   9 10

INSTRUCTIONAL NEIGHBORHOODS

Places [wing(s) of the building] including teacher planning spaces, flex zones (places for multiple use), small- and large-group areas, wet areas for science and art, hearth areas, and restrooms. The hearth area is a place used for reading and quiet time.

_____ **48.** (a) Teacher planning areas.

INADEQUATE <---+---|---+---|---+---|---+---|---+---|----> **ADEQUATE**
            0 1 2 3 4 5 6 7 8 9 10

_____ **49.** (b) Flex zones.

POOR <---+---|---+---|---+---|---+---|---+---|----> **EXCELLENT**
       0 1 2 3 4 5 6 7 8 9 10

_____ **50.** (c) Small-group areas.

INADEQUATE <---+---|---+---|---+---|---+---|---+---|----> **ADEQUATE**
            0 1 2 3 4 5 6 7 8 9 10

_____ **51.** (d) Large-group areas.

INADEQUATE <---+---|---+---|---+---|---+---|---+---|----> **ADEQUATE**
            0 1 2 3 4 5 6 7 8 9 10

_____ **52.** (e) Wet areas for science.

INADEQUATE <---+---|---+---|---+---|---+---|---+---|----> **ADEQUATE**
            0 1 2 3 4 5 6 7 8 9 10

_____ **53.** (f) Wet areas for art.

INADEQUATE <---+---|---+---|---+---|---+---|---+---|----> **ADEQUATE**
            0 1 2 3 4 5 6 7 8 9 10

_____ **54.** (g) Hearth areas.

POOR <---+---|---+---|---+---|---+---|---+---|----> **EXCELLENT**
       0 1 2 3 4 5 6 7 8 9 10

_____ **55.** (h) Activity Pockets—Spaces designed for small-group work.

NONEXISTENT <---+---|---+---|---+---|---+---|---+---|----> **PLENTIFUL**
             0 1 2 3 4 5 6 7 8 9 10

_____ **56.** (i) Toilets in classrooms (percentage of toilets in classrooms: $0 = 0\%$, $1 = 10\%, \ldots, 10 = 100\%$).

_____ **57.** (j) Storage—Secured spaces for teachers and students to store their personal belongings, tools, and supplies.

NONE <---+----+----+----+----+----+----+----+----+----> AMPLE
     0   1   2   3   4   5   6   7   8   9   10

_____ **58.** (k) Classroom Walls—Walls are adequate/inadequate for displaying students' work.

INADEQUATE <---+----+----+----+----+----+----+----+----+----> ADEQUATE
           0   1   2   3   4   5   6   7   8   9   10

Quiet Areas—Solitary places where students may go to pause and refresh themselves in a quiet, supervisable setting.

_____ **59.** Inside Places.

INADEQUATE <---+----+----+----+----+----+----+----+----+----> ADEQUATE
           0   1   2   3   4   5   6   7   8   9   10

Private Spaces for Children—Social, supervisable places where a small group of children may go to be alone (i.e., reading areas, quiet places, reflection areas, listening areas, etc.).

_____ **60.** Inside Places.

INADEQUATE <---+----+----+----+----+----+----+----+----+----> ADEQUATE
           0   1   2   3   4   5   6   7   8   9   10

_____ **61.** Excitement—Classrooms create an atmosphere of excitement for learning.

INHIBITS <---+----+----+----+----+----+----+----+----+----> PROMOTES
LEARNING 0   1   2   3   4   5   6   7   8   9   10 LEARNING

_____ **62.** Technology—Computers are placed within the learning environment in a manner that complements teaching and learning. Computers appear as an integral part of the curriculum.

INHIBITS <---+----+----+----+----+----+----+----+----+----> PROMOTES
         0   1   2   3   4   5   6   7   8   9   10

_____ **63.** Space—General personal distance per student in classrooms and work areas.

CLOSE (4'–7') <---+----I----I----I----I----I----I----I----I----> **FAR (7'–12')**
0 1 2 3 4 5 6 7 8 9 10

OUTSIDE LEARNING AREAS

_____**64.** Outside Places.

INADEQUATE <---+----I----I----I----I----I----I----I----I----> **ADEQUATE**
0 1 2 3 4 5 6 7 8 9 10

_____ **65.** The campus contains soft areas for the students to work (clusters of spaces for group work, including benches, tables, gardens, trees, and designated areas).

INADEQUATE <---+----I----I----I----I----I----I----I----I----> **ADEQUATE**
0 1 2 3 4 5 6 7 8 9 10

_____ **66.** Outdoor Rooms—Defined spaces outdoors, enough like a classroom, but with the added beauties of nature.

LACKING <---+----I----I----I----I----I----I----I----I----> **EXTENSIVE**
0 1 2 3 4 5 6 7 8 9 10

_____ **67.** Outdoor Spaces—Places that are defined; may be surrounded by wings of buildings, trees, hedges, fences, fields, arcades, or walkways.

NONEXISTENT <---+----I----I----I----I----I----I----I----I----> **PLENTIFUL**
0 1 2 3 4 5 6 7 8 9 10

_____ **68.** Green Areas—Outside spaces, close to the school building, where trees, grass, or gardens may be seen (but no cars or roads).

NONEXISTENT <---+----I----I----I----I----I----I----I----I----> **PLENTIFUL**
0 1 2 3 4 5 6 7 8 9 10

_____ **69.** Animal Life—Places in a school or on the school grounds for animals to live (includes butterfly houses, bird houses, trees, etc.). Caring for animals helps teach students a sense of responsibility and respect (values).

LACKING <---+----|----+----|----|----+----|----+----|----> **PLENTIFUL**
         0   1   2   3   4   5   6   7   8   9 10

INSTRUCTIONAL LABORATORIES

Technology for Students—Spaces with computers, compact disks, programs, learning packages, Internet connections, television, and video.

_____ **70.** Computer laboratories are arranged in a _____ manner.

RIGID <---+----|----+----|----+----|----+----|----+----|----> **FLEXIBLE**
       0   1   2   3   4   5   6   7   8   9 10

*Music (MC)—Quality of designated spaces for music.

_____ **71.** (a) Instruction.

INHIBITS <---+----|----+----|----+----|----+----|----+----|----> **PROMOTES**
LEARNING 0   1   2   3   4   5   6   7   8   9 10 **LEARNING**

_____ **72.** (b) Performance.

ADEQUATE <---+----|----+----|----+----|----+----|----+----|----> **INADEQUATE**
          0   1   2   3   4   5   6   7   8   9 10

*Art (MC)—Quality of designated spaces for art.

_____ **73.** (a) Instruction.

INHIBITS <---+----|----+----|----+----|----+----|----+----|----> **PROMOTES**
LEARNING 0   1   2   3   4   5   6   7   8   9 10 **LEARNING**

_____ **74.** (b) Display (international photo gallery).

ADEQUATE <---+----|----+----|----+----|----+----|----+----|----> **INADEQUATE**
          0   1   2   3   4   5   6   7   8   9 10

_____ **75.** (c) Display (students' display areas).

ADEQUATE <---+----|----+----|----+----|----+----|----+----|----> **INADEQUATE**
          0   1   2   3   4   5   6   7   8   9 10

ENVIRONMENTAL

_____ **76.** Acoustics—Control of internal and external noises levels.

POOR <---+----|---+----|---+----|---+----|---+----|-----> **EXCELLENT**
           0   1   2   3   4   5   6   7   8   9 10

_____ **77.** Climate Control—A system to maintain a comfortable temperature in the classroom learning environment.

CENTRALLY   **INDIVIDUALLY**
CONTROLLED <---+----|---+----|---+----|---+----|---+----|-----> **CONTROLLED**
               0   1   2   3   4   5   6   7   8   9 10

_____ **78.** Roof System—A leaking roof can disrupt student learning.

LEAKY <---+----|---+----|---+----|---+----|---+----|-----> **NO EVIDENCE OF LEAKS**
          0   1   2   3   4   5   6   7   8   9 10

*These items may be used to study multicultural variables.

CHAPTER THIRTEEN

CLASSIFICATIONS OF MIDDLE SCHOOL DESIGN

Toward a Pattern Language

C. KENNETH TANNER

SCOTT A. ANDERSEN
Long Meadow Public School District, MA

American educational facilities have evolved from simply sheltering teachers and students to serving an extremely diverse set of needs. According to Taylor, Aldrich, and Vlastos (1988), the facilities and learning environment "can be designed, engineered, and provisioned to serve as an additional learning tool," and consequently they help shape us. For many years, little attention has been given to the physical environment of education. Education primarily consisted of books and people—teachers and students. School buildings were incidental to the learning process. Wherever the Athenian teacher could hold a discussion with a group of students, that marked the spot of the school facility. Education was basic in those days. Frequently, the school was nothing more that a teacher and a small group of students meeting on the open stairs of an ancient temple (Castaldi, 1994).

Just like changes since ancient times, emerging educational issues today will influence the architectural design of future facilities. The school of the future will be serving more people with a wider range of levels and ages, and for longer periods of time during the day, night, and year (Davis & Loveless, 1981). One norm is the middle school.

This reform in education has changed the way many districts address the unique needs of the middle school student. The middle school movement has been one of the largest and most comprehensive efforts in educational reform in the past thirty years.

Because, as Berliner and Biddle (1995, p. 3) declared, "Good-hearted Americans have come to believe that the public schools of their nation are in a crisis state," public schools have been subjected to various reform efforts in recent years. Recent reform movements have increased the expectations of student achievement and higher standards. Higher standards most often entail test scores for students, stricter guidelines for teacher certification, student discipline, and attendance. This trend has also filtered through to the international level.

Reforms in middle schools throughout the United States are in response to increasing educational standards and raising test scores (George, 1994). They include teaming teachers and students in an arrangement similar to the school-within-a-school concept, the use of flexible block of time schedules, core knowledge curriculum, and exploratory courses. These efforts are designed to increase achievement, accountability, and to ease the transition from elementary school to middle school and then from middle school to high school.

Evidence of the effects that school design elements have on student performance is unheard of in major reform efforts. Many students today are learning about topics that were never even identified or understood at the time that the facilities were designed. For instance, many students today use computers in the classroom and in computer labs. Many of these activities occur in older schools that were built before the advent of the personal computer. With computers, students have access to software that manages information with great ease. Students then, in turn, use presentation software like hypermedia, Internet web pages, and desktop publishing to disseminate information to their fellow classmates, teachers, and the world. With all these changes, it is difficult to arrive at standards for our educational facilities, including design and construction, that are held to the same increasingly higher expectations as other parts of the educational system. In fact, a report entitled *Wolves at the Schoolhouse Door* highlighted the questionable state of our nation's public school infrastructure (Education Writers Association, 1989). Furthermore, in 1995 the U.S. General Accounting Office estimated that it would cost $112 billion to bring our school facilities up to basic safety and health standards. This figure did not even take into account design needs to improve student learning or new school construction. By 2000 this figure had risen sharply. "For schools that indicated the need to spend money to bring the school into good overall condition (n = 903 U.S. Schools), the total amount needed by all schools was estimated to be approximately $127 billion. The average dollar amount for schools needing to spend money was about $2.2 million per school" (National Center for Educational Statistics, 2000, p. 16).

THE PROBLEM

Bradley (1996) noted that people close to the field of education and furthest from the field of architecture are more concerned with providing basic operational necessities than other considerations. In contrast, those furthest from the field of education and closest to the field of architecture are less concerned with providing basic operational necessities and more concerned with applying architecture in creative ways to address issues in education. These goals need not be in opposition to one another.

Furthermore, in order for students to achieve their maximum potential, all aspects of the educational experience need to exist in harmony. An assumption underlying this study was that school facilities are a key part of the educational experience. In fact, the ecological environment of the school (the objective, perceptual context of student behavior; the real-life settings within which students behave) provided a framework for the independent variables (Baker, 1968). The ecological environment, in this study, is defined in terms of school design characteristics. *The research question was: How do school design characteristics relate to middle school students' academic achievement scores?*

Achievement scores were one representative measurement of student outcomes. The assumption was made that if design characteristics could be found to relate significantly to student achievement, then a theory for middle school design might be developed. Such theory would be a means to bring architecture and education closer together and also prescribe a way to allow the educational program to dictate school facilities—not vice versa. Student achievement was represented by scores students earned on the Iowa Test of Basic Skills (ITBS).

THE UNIQUE CHARACTER OF MIDDLE SCHOOL STUDENTS

The place to begin any discussion about physical environments is with the students whom the facilities will serve. The physical and psychological needs of middle school students are becoming better understood as unique. One Carnegie report described the middle grade school, the junior high, the intermediate, and the middle school as society's potentially most powerful force to recapture millions of youth who are adrift (Carnegie Council, 1989). Researchers for the National Association of Secondary School Principals (1993) have written that middle-level students are unlike any other age group, and even more important, the students are more unlike each other than any other age group. Middle school students are in constant motion and continually changing (Carr & Stevenson, 1993). The students are kinetic and learn by doing, which can be accomplished sitting or standing, quietly or noisily, inside or outside. Middle school students are in transformation from childhood to adulthood. Their emotional, physical, psychological, and mental boundaries are stretched daily. The middle school student is involved in and aware of an interactive environment (Wohlwill & van Vliet, 1985). These pre-adults face a myriad of disturbances ranging from emotional, physical, and social, and these disturbances are unique and frenzied. With all this kinetic energy congregated in one mass, how can the middle school physical environment enhance and/or impede middle school programs? Are there specific design elements that support the middle school concept.

Middle School Facility Design

Changes can be expected in a middle school's programs during the life of the facility. Enrollments change and new types of instructional programs will be implemented. Middle school facilities must be designed to be able to meet the changing needs rather than hinder the present and future changes in education (Aughtry, 1995). As curriculum and instruction are adapted to meet changing student needs so must the classroom space. Building flexibility into the classroom space is important, especially since the physical environment should be responsive to individual teacher and student needs (Morriseau, 1972).

School facilities are significantly important in implementing the middle school program; as

Alexander and George (1993) stated, "The middle school building must be organized in a way which permits the development of close personal relationships with teachers and a sense of community which leads students away from the protective atmosphere of the elementary school" (p. 408). The floor plan layout correlates positively to a generally well-defined educational program. Instructional space should be adaptable to cooperative teaching by virtue of direct accessibility to adjacent classrooms, central group activity space, and teacher planning areas.

Spaces of varying sizes are provided for large- and small-group instruction and for different degrees of privacy. Areas are provided throughout for individual learning. Integration of various subdivisions of the building, each designed to accommodate a specific program function, creates an interesting spatial variety that should, in a natural and efficient way, stimulate learning on both an individual and group level (Alexander & George, 1981).

The effective middle school concept should embrace flexible architectural arrangements that maximize learning for the student (Aughtry, 1995). Wiles and Bondi (1986) identified thirteen specific areas to consider in the design of a new middle school. These areas included (1) basic instructional area; (2) science area; (3) team planning area; (4) corridors/halls; (5) restrooms; (6) media center; (7) special classrooms; (8) gymnasium/gymtorium; (9) cafeteria/cafetorium; (10) auditorium/multipurpose or assembly area; (11) guidance area; (12) administrative area; (13) commons/mall or courtyard areas. These design elements may fit into three major categories: environmental, cosmetic, and other, as outlined in the survey used to evaluate design characteristics in this study.

Environmental Attributes

The environmental design characteristics investigated in this research project included an assessment of the various trends in educational architecture presented in Chapters 2 and 12. For example, light may be viewed as a significant environmental input for learning, while proper sound control should be treated as one of the most pervasive contributors to academic achievement in the school environment. Thermal control is deemed necessary for maximizing student achievement in indoor learning environments.

Another important factor to be considered in student achievement is the amount of usable space devoted to classrooms. It was hypothesized that a low-density school influences achievement positively. Proper environmental scale has an impact on student outcomes, since it promotes a sense of belonging. Flexible spaces, ventilation, indoor air quality, and physical security were assumed to be vital, while less clutter and clean buildings are considered variables that contribute to improved achievement.

Even the color of classrooms and other parts of the physical environment has been shown to have an effect on student performance, achievement, and behavior. Overall, the aesthetics and maintenance of a building can impact student achievement. According to *Design Issues*, the newsletter for the Thomas Jefferson Center for Educational Design (1998), "a good learning environment is one in which the quality of desired learning experiences dictates the quality of the setting and not vice versa" (p. 4).

When considering the planning of educational facilities, it is important to remember that schools and classrooms are expected to last fifty years, so they should not be designed only for today's students. It is essential to anticipate the changes in educational practice as well as the future demands on the schools (Millet & Croteau, 1998). Some of the results of planning should be the development of green areas, natural and quiet areas, and play areas. In this vein, providing places for animals in the learning environment can provide an opportunity to teach responsibility, values, and respect for life and other behavioral concepts.

Although tomorrow's students must be technologically literate, technology must not be considered as an end in itself to education. Technology is an important tool in the learning process and can be utilized in various ways (Millet & Croteau, 1998). The schools of tomorrow will need to be designed with the hardware of technology, including wiring, transmission stations, other methods of transmission (no wiring), and workstations. As we move forward in the twenty-first century, there is evidence that PC transmitting cards may replace wiring. Designing environments that facilitate new processes seems clear. One of the best approaches to anticipating change in technology is to review the developments of the past ten years and extrapolate the expected rate of change.

Schools must do more than provide a place for a town meeting or a joint library. Communities of learners of a variety of ages with multiple learning goals will be seeking space for round-the-clock activities or accessibility. Flexibility of space will be a key as communities change (Millet & Croteau, 1998). School facilities can house a nature museum, a fine arts theater, a natatorium, a mock courtroom, and a range of programs that require special facilities.

The campus plan correlates to such design factors as neighborhood access. It may also address design aspects relative to the ethnic, religious, and cultural background of the students, the economic mix of parents, and the educational profile of the community. Attention could be given to these areas in the design of the school (Bingler, 1995; Crumpacker, 1995).

Learning Spaces

Proshansky and Fabian (1987) reported studies that support places for privacy in schools. For example, the open classroom is an extension of the home and neighborhood. It encourages spatial freedom where children can explore, work with manipulatives, and participate in innovative activities. The classroom constitutes a small community or a "family" in a "house." In order to achieve the small community effect, the design of the open classroom includes suites, each with classrooms, lounge space, office space for teachers, lockers, private bathrooms, window seats, terraces, hallway display cases, and small seminar rooms (Genevro, 1992). The learning space must also include places for indoor and outdoor play activities since it is through these activities that middle school students acquire and refine social, cognitive, and physical skills (Gaunt, 1980).

In a study of general environmental preference, children preferred variety and balance among the environmental elements in the learning scenario. These elements include forest, rock, and sky (Bernaldez et al., 1987).

When considering space needs for middle schools, many aspects of Alexander's (1977) characteristic language theory should be reviewed. For example, special attention should be given to circulation characteristics. In particular, this involves avoiding complex structures that cause crowding and force students to become disoriented. Movement within a school is an important part of the process of learning. School design needs pathways to the outside and also indoor pathways and streets (hallways). Indoor pathways may be color-coded to assist in keeping students oriented toward the front, back, and other important locations within the learning environments. Pathways may tie the structures together and into the natural environment.

Procedural Attributes

Throughout this text, an awareness of procedure and involvement of the community have been given special attention. Alexander (1979) emphasized that at the core of architecture, building, and planning is an age-old process by which physical environments are organized, planned, and designed from our own perspectives. These perspectives are partially influenced by our own memories of what establishments such as schools are and what they should be. Additionally, Alexander and coworkers (1977) offered a theory on quality that may be extended to educational environments. For example, quality in school design is

generated, not made, by the ordinary actions of people.

Sanoff (1994) has discussed participatory design, where the school's stakeholders—the student, the parent, the teachers, the administrators, and the architect—are all key players in the educational change process. Sanoff (2000) also placed strong emphasis on the participation of the total community in design and planning.

Taylor, Aldrich, and Vlastos (1988) have introduced what they call the "rethinking of the educational setting" (p. 2). They provided a categorization of the educational settings that students, teachers, and administrators can utilize to aid in school design and also identified four premises on which achieving well-ordered learning rests:

- People are considered an integral part of, not apart from, the environment.
- The architectural environment can affect behavior.
- The environment can be designed, engineered, and equipped to function as a learning tool.
- The learning environment can be evaluated as a learning tool.

The categorizations offered by Taylor and colleagues (1988) include eleven zones of the educational setting that guided the development of the instrument in this study: entry, work, storage system, display and mini-museum, living things, research area and library, soft, graphic arts, teacher, technology, and indoor–outdoor relationships. This set was modified in this study.

Instrumentation

From the review of literature emphasized in Chapters 2 and 12 of this text, thirty-eight independent variables were formulated as descriptors of the ecological environment for middle schools (design classifications). A similar design scale for elementary schools (Tanner, 2000) having detailed justification for the inclusive items was reviewed in Chapter 12. Variables were grouped into eleven zones similar to those proposed by Taylor, Aldrich, and Vlastos (1988). Even though some variables could possibly have been placed in several of the components of the design scale discussed below, they were placed in their area of dominance.

The following section presents the independent variables used in this study. Each variable is followed by a semantic differential used to judge its relevance to a particular school or ecological environment. These scales may need to be refined and expanded to include components for the assessment of high school designs.

COMPONENTS OF THE DESIGN ASSESSMENT SCALE FOR MIDDLE SCHOOLS

Each item is described and followed by its evaluation scale. For example, the linkage of outside areas is classified as the "promenade." It is evaluated on a ten-point Likert scale from "Not Linked" (1) to "Linked" (10). The direction of the scale is set so that the higher score implies a better classification of the design characteristic. Some variables such as item number 4 could be argued from a philosophical basis, indicating that "Not Centralized" is better than "Centralized." Such items obviously require more study to validate their importance to improved student outcomes.

Zone 1: Entry/Movement

1. *Promenade*. The main outside activity areas are clearly linked. This ideally places major activity centers at the extremes. (Not Linked < > Linked)
2. *Entrance area*. A friendly space connecting the outside world to the inside world. This age-appropriate space should be inviting and highly visible to students and visitors. It should evoke a welcome feeling. (Not Welcoming < > Welcoming)

3. *Public areas*. Spaces that foster a *sense of community* (unity and belonging) were identified as public areas (auditorium, amphitheater, media center, commons, and dining room). Inviting and comfortable settings include ample lighting. (No Sense of Community < > Strong Sense of Community)
4. *Administration centralized*. Administrative offices are grouped together in a centralized area allowing for connection and convenience. The person in charge should be readily accessible (location of assistant principals offices are less important in this context). (Not Centralized < > Centralized)
5. *Accessibility to adjacent classrooms*. The ease by which classes can come together in large group settings or share resources is a significant design feature. This could be accomplished through the use of interconnecting doors or collapsible walls. (Restricted < > Unrestricted)
6. *Reference*. The main building is an obvious point of reference among the school's buildings in which paths and buildings connect. This design feature heightens the sense of community and helps to keep a child oriented. (Obscure < > Obvious)
7. *Pathways*. Clearly defined areas that allow freedom of movement among structures, including covered walkways, that are partly inside and partly outside are essential to good school design. These play a vital role in the way people interact with buildings. Pathways may also connect buildings one to another so that a person can walk under the cover of arcades. Pathways, inside and outside, help to keep children oriented and minimize crowding. (Ambiguous < > Clear)
8. *Adjacent to community areas*. The school is adjacent to community areas such as parks, playgrounds, and recreation complexes. (No Areas Adjacent < > Numerous Areas Adjacent)
9. *Circulation classifications*. Ample spaces that allow students to circulate in and between

rooms should be part of the design. The passages should be broad and well-lit, allowing for freedom of movement. This characteristic is also related to crowding. (Poor < > Excellent)

10. *Hallways*. Passageways that allow students personal space when moving within the school are necessary. This variable is akin to pathways. (Meager Space < > Ample Space)

Zone 2: Work

11. *Scale*. The school and its facilities are designed to the scale of the middle school student, for example, light switches, chairs, restrooms. (Unsuitable < > Suitable)

12. *Instructional neighborhoods within schools*. These areas include a teacher planning area, flex zones, small- and large-group areas, wet areas for science and art, a hearth area, and restrooms (toilets). The hearth area is also a place used for reading and quiet time. It is amenable to technology. (Inadequate < > Adequate)

13. *Multifunctionality of the facility*. Multifunctionality reflects how versatile the facility is in relation to the different tasks it can accomplish. (Rigid < > Versatile)

14. *Physical education areas*. P.E. or play areas are special places where students are given the opportunity to be together, exercise, build muscles, and test new skills in supervised settings. Releasing energy is an important activity observed in these areas. (Uniformity < > Variety)

15. *Activity pockets*. Spaces should be designed for small-group work. (Inadequate < > Adequate)

16. *Safe place*. The indoor and outdoor environments guarantee students and teachers security and comfort. Supervisable circulation classifications, security systems, safe grounds and equipment, and toilets in classrooms are important safety factors. (Safety in Question < > No Safety Concerns)

Zone 3: Storage Systems

17. *Storage*. Spaces for teachers and students to store their personal belongings, tools, and supplies are necessary for sound school design. (None < > Ample)

18. *Personal artifacts*. Places for the display of items of a personal nature that relate to each student improve school design. (None < > Ample)

Zone 4: Display and Mini-Museums

19. *Classroom walls*. Walls are conducive for displaying students' work. (Inadequate < > Adequate)

20. *Hallway display*. Hallways (walls and alcoves) are suitable for displaying student work. (Inadequate < > Adequate)

Zone 5: Living Things

21. *Windows*. These should give the best possible views overlooking life and bring natural light into the school building. (None < > Numerous)

22. *Natural light/full spectrum*. Artificial light plus natural light from the outside, preferably on two sides of every room, is ideal. Natural light influences student behavior and attitudes. (No Mixture of Lighting < > Ample Mixture)

23. *Green areas*. Educationally sound school design includes places outside, close to the school building, where trees, grass, or gardens may be seen, but no cars or roads are in view. (Nonexistent < > Plentiful)

24. *Living views*. Views of indoor and outdoor spaces (gardens, animals, fountains, mountains, people, etc.) improve school design. Views allow minds and eyes to take a break. Views should not be blocked by curtains, blinds, or other obstructions. (Inadequate < > Adequate)

Zones 6: Soft Areas

25. *Quiet areas.* Quiet areas are spaces where students may go to pause and refresh themselves in a tranquil and supervised setting. (Inadequate < > Adequate)
26. *Private spaces for students.* Supervised private places (inside or outside) where children may go to be alone (i.e., reading area, listening area) are essential. (Inadequate < > Adequate)

Zone 7: Teacher Spaces

27. *Workrooms.* Workrooms are near classrooms. (Far from Classrooms < > Close to Classrooms)

Zone 8: Technology

28. *Technology for students*: Special spaces with computers, compact discs, software, Internet connections, television, and video are important for learning activities. (No Access < > Easy Access)
29. *Technology for teachers.* Computers, multimedia, and Internet connections are easily accessible. Teachers have access to technology outside the media center for use in research and planning lessons. (No Access < > Easy Access)
30. *Communications.* Phones in classrooms, intercom, faxes, e-mail, and Internet are necessary for educationally sound design. (Inadequate < > Adequate)

Zone 9: Indoor–Outdoor Relationships

31. *Outdoor rooms.* A partly enclosed space outdoors, like a room but with the added beauties of nature, defines an outdoor room. This is a room with a sense of freedom. (Lacking < > Extensive)
32. *Egress.* Doors allow easy access to the outside environment and learning areas. This is

also a safety feature allowing for quick evacuation. (Lacking < > Extensive)

Zone 10: Environmental

33. *Acoustics.* Internal and external noise is controlled through design. (Poor < > Excellent)
34. *Climate control.* A system of climate control maintains a comfortable temperature in the classroom learning environment. (Poor < > Excellent)
35. *Roof system.* A leaking roof can disrupt student learning. (Leaky < > No Leaks)

Zone 11: Aesthetics

36. *Paint.* The quality and color of the paint in the halls and classrooms influence behavior. The walls and finishes should be visually stimulating. (Low Quality < > High Quality)
37. *Variation of ceiling heights.* A variation of heights allows for individual comfort and intimacy within the school. (No Variance < > Varying)
38. *Overall impression.* A student friendly and teacher friendly learning environment provides a positive impression. This involves aspects of all positive or negative design classifications. (Negative < > Positive)

Scoring and Reliability

All of the above design characteristics were scored according to the semantic descriptors following each set of statements (each score ranges from 10 = 100% to 1 = 10% for each variable/characteristic). If no evidence of the variable was found, that item was rated accordingly and received 0 percent. For example, a score of 9 on characteristic number 38 indicates a score of 90 percent, meaning that the overall impression is positive. On the other hand, a leaky roof throughout the school should receive 0 percent on characteristic 35 (item 80).

The School Design Assessment Scale was tested for content validity by educators and architects (Tanner, 1999). Fifteen educators experienced and trained in school planning and design participated in a pilot study in the summer of 1999. The test–retest reliability coefficient was found to be 0.82 (Tanner, 1999).

Procedures

The population of this study consisted of fifty middle schools located in fourteen contiguous counties in central Georgia. The counties were chosen because of geographic location and contiguity. Information on the schools and their ITBS scores were obtained from the *Georgia Public Education Report Card 1997–1998* (1998), published by the Georgia Department of Education.

The initial phase was the selection of a sample based on composite ITBS scores. Before selecting a sample, an analysis of covariance was completed on the population of schools by using socioeconomic (SES) variables (the percentage of students receiving a free lunch, race percentages, and teacher experience) as predictors of composite percentile ITBS scores. This was done to eliminate sampling bias. The composite percentile ITBS scores served as the dependent variable.

Four of the independent variables entered into the regression equation. They were teacher experience, percentage of white students, percentage of black students, and percentage of students receiving a free lunch. An R^2 of 0.908 indicated that 90.8 percent of the variability in composite scores was accounted for by the four variables. The regression procedure assigned predicted composite scores (Table 13.1). This statistically removed the bias from independent variables.

The regression equation also assigned predicted composite scores that remove the bias of those independent variables. Table 13.1 on page 316 shows the independent variables and the dependent variable along with the predicted composite scores for the entire population. Upon the removal of any statistical bias from the population of schools, their predicted composite ITBS scores ranked them from high to low. The top eleven and bottom eleven

schools were then selected for use in the sample. A t-test between the two extremes confirmed a significant difference. As expected, the top eleven predicted composite scores were significantly higher than the bottom group [mean (top 11) = 78.91; mean (bottom 11) = 40.28], $t(10) = 52.105$, $p < 0.01$].

The reasoning for the bipolar sample was that if significant correlations between design scores and a wide range of high and low ITBS scores were obtained, then a sound basis for a prediction instrument could be established. Significant extremes might also add credibility to the results.

The second phase of the study involved performing site visits to each of the selected schools. Each school in the sample was visited and evaluated according to the thirty-eight items on the design scale. Application involved a thorough walk-through of the school facilities and its grounds. The walk-throughs required between 90 and 120 minutes for completion. Immediately upon finishing the walk-through, the instrument was scored.

Each item for each school was judged according to the appropriate semantic descriptor as found in the instrument. The final phase of the study involved the analysis of data on information obtained from the site appraisals.

Analysis and Findings

Following the data collection phase, a Pearson's correlation analysis (Table 13.2, page 317) was completed for the thirty-eight design classifications ($n = 22$ schools) and the composite ITBS scores. The alpha level was set at 0.05 to minimize the type I error. This minimized rejecting the null hypothesis when it was true. However, this level also increased the chances of accepting the null hypothesis when it was false.

Data refinement, the next step in the research process, involved the goal of finding design variables that were statistically significant predictors of ITBS scores. The guiding question was: Is the R^2 significantly different from 0? On the basis of the adjusted R^2 (0.99) found in Table 13.3 on page 318, it was

TABLE 13.1 Profile of Sample Schools

SCHOOL	ENROLLMENT	BLACK	WHITE	% FREE LUNCH	TEACHER EXP.	COMPOSITE ITBS	PREDICTED COMPOSITE
A	1,747	3.1	85.3	5.2	13.66	82	85.51
B	1,398	6.3	79.9	1.4	10.93	82	82.37
C	1,385	4.5	85.8	0.9	8.64	82	82.24
D	1,266	1.4	91.6	1.1	15	85	81.10
E	787	7.6	86.8	1.9	14.65	78	80.59
F	931	9.2	81.7	5.6	12.86	84	78.76
G	1,002	4	93.1	1.3	13.03	84	77.72
H	845	14.7	68.3	10.9	13.77	75	76.97
I	896	4.7	88.8	3.2	11.93	78	74.97
J	1,185	13.5	75.8	10	13.12	74	74.42
K	1,767	3.5	94.2	3.6	11.51	69	73.38
Top 11							
Mean	1,200.82	6.59	84.66	4.10	12.65	79.36	78.91
P	497	75.3	23.9	82.7	13.02	32	32.40
Q	762	80.4	19	77.4	12.22	39	34.28
R	565	94.3	4.8	78.1	14.38	38	35.45
S	661	75	20.9	73.4	11.15	43	36.32
T	967	62.6	36.7	73.5	12.2	24	36.48
U	949	67.7	24	66.1	9.75	37	37.53
V	1,096	45.3	34.9	56.7	9.93	44	44.06
W	793	63.9	34.6	58	12.13	38	44.63
X	760	45.7	52.6	55.1	13.38	48	46.81
Y	272	41.2	54.7	51.8	11.76	54	47.55
Z	953	30.7	61.7	37.1	8.56	44	47.55
Bottom 11							
Mean	752.27	62.01	33.44	64.54	11.68	40.09	40.28
Entire Sample							
Mean	976.55	34.30	59.05	34.32	12.16	59.73	59.60

concluded that twenty-seven out of thirty-eight design variables identified above account for nearly all the remaining variance in the composite ITBS scores in this sample (eleven were eliminated because they did not correlate significantly with the ITBS scores). This is an extremely high multiple correlation—a result of having accounted for most of the variance of the other variables by applying the analysis of covariance on the population of schools. The SES variables, ethnicity percentages, and teacher experience were covaried, allowing only the design variables as predictors of composite percentile ITBS scores.

Next, through the backward elimination process, fourteen predictor variables were found (significance level for retaining a variable = 0.05). The backward solution starts out with the squared multiple correlations of all independent variables with the dependent variable. The independent variables are deleted from the regression equation one at a time. This makes it possible to observe which variable adds the least R^2 when entered last. When the deletion of any one variable produces a meaningful or significant loss to R^2, the analysis is terminated (Pedhazur, 1982, p. 158). The adjusted

TABLE 13.2   **Significant Correlations between Design Scores and ITBS Scores ($n = 22$)**

(#) VARIABLE (DESIGN CHARACTERISTIC)	CORRELATION COEFFICIENT	ALPHA LEVEL
(2) Entrance area	0.42	$p \leq 0.05$
(3) Public areas	0.68	$p \leq 0.01$
(4) Administrative offices centralized	0.51	$p \leq 0.05$
(9) Circulation classifications	0.50	$p \leq 0.05$
(12) Instructional neighborhoods	0.74	$p \leq 0.01$
(13) Multifunctionality	0.48	$p \leq 0.05$
(14) Play areas	0.66	$p \leq 0.01$
(15) Activity pockets	0.53	$p \leq 0.05$
(16) Safe place	0.44	$p \leq 0.05$
(18) Personal artifacts	0.47	$p \leq 0.05$
(19) Classroom walls	0.44	$p \leq 0.05$
(20) Hallway display	0.47	$p \leq 0.05$
(21) Windows	0.61	$p \leq 0.01$
(22) Natural light/full spectrum	0.59	$p \leq 0.01$
(23) Green areas	0.50	$p \leq 0.05$
(24) Living views	0.52	$p \leq 0.05$
(25) Quiet areas	0.48	$p \leq 0.05$
(26) Private spaces	0.71	$p \leq 0.01$
(28) Technology for students	0.51	$p \leq 0.05$
(29) Technology for teachers	0.61	$p \leq 0.01$
(30) Communications	0.64	$p \leq 0.01$
(31) Outdoor rooms	0.65	$p \leq 0.01$
(32) Egress	0.64	$p \leq 0.01$
(34) Climate control	0.72	$p \leq 0.01$
(35) Roof system	0.55	$p \leq 0.01$
(36) Paint quality	0.55	$p \leq 0.01$
(38) Overall impression	0.82	$p \leq 0.01$

R^2 of 0.99 was significantly different from zero ($F = 2{,}534.29$, $p < 0.01$) and indicated a strong prediction equation as presented in Table 13.4.

While this is an unusually high R^2 in educational research, it may be explained by the interrelationships among the thirty-eight variables and, as previously mentioned, the effect of the covariants. Such relationships are reasons to describe and explain school design variables in terms of a characteristics or a pattern language much like Alexander, Ishikawa, and Silverstein (1977) did in

their classic work. School architecture is a representation of social and economic values. It is a cultural statement.

Supposition

Perhaps this initial work in assessing middle school design will lead to a "pattern language" for successful middle schools (defined here in terms of academic achievement). A design language for the successful middle school is a network. There is no

TABLE 13.3   Linear Regression of the Twenty-Seven Predictor Variables

Multiple R	0.99997
R square	0.99995
Adjusted R square	0.99944
Standard error	0.50000

ANALYSIS OF VARIANCE

	DF	SUM OF SQUARES	MEAN SQUARE
Regression	19	9,375.86364	493.46651
Residual	2	0.50000	0.25000
$F = 1,973.86603$	Significant $F = 0.0005$		

"one design characteristic" that perfectly captures the successful middle school. Presently, any evolving theory must be restricted to the findings in the prediction equation (Table 13.4). The successful middle school in this study was defined as one with high ITBS scores, although there are many other factors that define success, especially on the affective and behavioral levels.

In moving toward a pattern language theory for middle schools in the United States, we want to emphasize the language that primarily gives shape to groups of buildings, individual buildings, and individual classrooms. "A building cannot be a human building unless it is a complex of still smaller buildings or smaller parts which manifest its own internal social facts" (Alexander, Ishikawa, & Silverstein 1977, p. 469).

TOWARD A PATTERN LANGUAGE THEORY

Since this theory is limited to schools having an academic emphasis,[1] the pattern language for middle schools similar to those in this sample may be stated as follows.

The academically successful middle school has a friendly entrance area connecting the outside world to the inside world. This space is inviting and highly visible to students and visitors. It evokes a "welcome" feeling. Public areas of the middle school (auditorium, amphitheater, media center, commons, and dining room) foster a sense of community—a sense of unity and belonging. Students and parents can easily find the administrative offices because they are grouped together in an area allowing for connection and convenience (administration centralized). Circulation classifications within the classrooms and among the learning environments are clearly defined, well-lit, and allow for freedom of movement.

Various learning tasks can be easily accomplished in the academically successful middle school because its design is not rigid. This school is multifunctional. Physical education areas offer students a variety of special places to develop and test new skills and release energy. Small-group work may be accomplished in adequate and supervisable activity pockets within classrooms and outdoor learning areas. The indoor and outdoor environments guarantee students and teachers secure, comfortable safe places to teach and learn.

---

[1]Dr. Scott Andersen granted special permission to use selected parts of his dissertation in this chapter.

TABLE 13.4   The Prediction Equation

Multiple R	0.99990
R square	0.99980
Adjusted R square	0.99941
Standard error	0.51402

ANALYSIS OF VARIANCE

	DF	SUM OF SQUARES	MEAN SQUARE
Regression	14	9,374.51409	669.60815
Residual	7	1.84954	0.26422
$F = 2{,}534.27592$	Significant $F = 0.0001$		

VARIABLES IN THE EQUATION

VARIABLE	B	SE B	BETA	T	SIG. T
Entrance areas (2)	−3.915250	.079110	−.798872	−49.491	.0000
Public areas (3)	.841311	.024521	.498302	34.310	.0000
Administration offices centralized (4)	4.401660	.111536	.709794	39.464	.0000
Circulation classification (9)	4.220504	.154198	.670097	27.371	.0000
Multifunctionality (13)	−2.293052	.206878	−.178144	−11.084	.0000
Play areas (14)	.846677	.047495	.230142	17.827	.0000
Activity pockets (15)	20.003795	.377193	.919660	53.033	.0000
Safe place (16)	−1.091458	.045910	−.513557	−23.774	.0000
Classroom walls (19)	7.896192	.321817	.488036	24.536	.0000
Green areas (23)	−2.442343	.149512	−.299791	−16.335	.0000
Quiet areas (25)	−4.247516	.205526	−.587320	−20.667	.0000
Egress (32)	7.832694	.122501	.884088	63.940	.0000
Roof system (35)	−2.200407	.253019	−.189876	−8.697	.0001
Overall Impression (38)	−2.730469	.216083	−.337789	−12.636	.0000
(Constant)	−24.587382	1.270738		−19.349	.0000

VARIABLES NOT IN THE EQUATION

VARIABLE	BETA IN	PARTIAL	MIN TOLER	T	SIG. T
Instructional neighborhoods (12)	.044471	.627364	.029165	1.973	.0959
Personal artifacts (18)	−.018657	−.529697	.025092	−1.530	.1770
Hallway display (20)	.016293	.215860	.023016	.542	.6077
Windows (21)	.029714	.482995	.021142	1.351	.2254
Natural light (22)	.026033	.588829	.022238	1.784	.1246
Living A. views (24)	.013200	.257703	.017571	.653	.5378
Private spaces (26)	.009921	.217091	.031147	.545	.6056
Technology for students (28)	.010125	.127005	.012628	.314	.7644

(continued)

TABLE 13.4 Continued

VARIABLE	BETA IN	PARTIAL	MIN TOLER	T	SIG. T
Technology for teachers (29)	−.020110	−.359992	.018794	−.945	.3811
Communications (30)	−.032181	−.513557	.024828	−1.466	.1930
Outdoor rooms (31)	−.015916	−.366350	.034319	−.964	.3721
Climate control (34)	−.048435	−.583527	.021292	−1.760	.1289
Paint quality (36)	−.049179	−.518135	.006560	−1.484	.1884

Bathrooms (toilets) are located inside the classrooms, the circulation classifications are supervisable, and security systems are ample. Classroom walls are conducive to displaying students' work.

Outside spaces of the successful academic middle school include green areas where views of trees, grass, and gardens are plentiful from classrooms and other areas of the school. Supervisable quiet areas are found where students may pause and refresh themselves in a quiet inside or outside setting. There are extensive exit doors to the outside environment and learning areas (egress). The roof system does not leak and interfere with teaching and learning and the overall functioning of the school.

Involving all aspects of school design, the overall impression of the successful academic middle school is that "learning environments are student and teacher friendly." The successful academic middle school is a superior facility and gives a positive impression with respect to the design variables addressed in the study.

Developing a pattern language theory for school design is a bold undertaking given the flexibility found in school plans common in the United States. It is our belief, however, that such a taxonomy will evolve to guide school planning and design. We hope this study encourages more research on the ecological environment of schools, since it is our contention that school architecture is a significant variable in student learning and must be treated as such.

NEED FOR FURTHER STUDY

The need to include affective and behavioral variables in research pertaining to the ideal middle school is acknowledged. Furthermore, it should be extended to all grade level classifications as well as review the impact of No Child Left Behind Act—a job that makes this area of research *a new frontier in educational research*. We strongly suggest a series of research studies that simultaneously deals with the affective, behavioral, and cognitive dimensions of learning. Hence, we will then have not only a pattern language for the academically successful middle school, but also a language that describes the successful educational environment in behavioral and affective terms.[2]

SUMMARY

Middle school students transitioning from childhood to adulthood experience a myriad of physical, social, and psychological changes. Educational reforms intended to help these students succeed both academically and personally often rely on the physical school environment to support them. These efforts include teaming teachers and stu-

[2]Parts of this article appeared in a 2001 issue of *Educational Planning* (vol. 13, no. 3).

dents in an arrangement similar to the school-within-a-school concept, the use of flexible block of time schedules, core knowledge curriculum, and exploratory courses. It is important that the middle school facility provide areas for both group activities and individual study, and the building should enhance a sense of community while providing students with opportunities for a personalized experience. Perhaps the most important consideration is making the building flexible enough to adapt to the changing needs of students and teachers, as well as innovations in the educational program.

This chapter provides an example of research conducted in middle schools to identify relationships between thirty-eight independent descriptor variables and student achievement, as measured by composite percentile scores on the Iowa Test of Basic Skills (ITBS). From an original sample of fifty schools, the top eleven and bottom eleven schools, based on ITBS scores, were selected for assessment using the Design Assessment Scale for Middle Schools (see the example in Chapter 12). The walk-through assessment of the school facility and grounds required between 90 and 120 minutes to complete. Immediately upon finishing the walk-through, the instrument was scored using a ten-point Likert scale for each of the design variables (which were grouped into eleven categories). Analysis of the data showed that twenty-seven of the thirty-eight design variables were significantly correlated with ITBS scores. Through backward elimination, fourteen predictor variables were identified. Based on the data, an academically successful middle school may be described as being multifunctional with a flexible design. Physical activity areas offer a variety of areas to test new skills and release energy. Both indoor and outdoor areas are safe and comfortable, security systems are ample, and circulation spaces are supervisable. Bathrooms are located inside classrooms. On the outside of the successful middle school, there are views of nature including green areas and gardens, and there are extensive exit doors to access the outdoors. Supervisable, quiet areas exist indoors and outdoors for private reflection. The roof system does not leak and the overall impression of the school is positive. While more research is needed, particularly to evaluate affective and behavioral outcomes, this study provides designers and school planners with information to improve middle school designs.

ACTIVITIES

1. This chapter presents a brief discussion of the unique character of middle school students. Based on your own review of available literature, write up a justification of why you might choose to investigate how school facility variables affect this specific group of students.

2. Identify an example of a middle school that closely fits the description (resulting from this study) of an academically successful middle school. Describe those design features and how they support the middle school program.

3. In teams of three or four persons, discuss your own middle school (or junior high) experience, either as a student, teacher, or administrator.

   a. Did the facility support the educational program? How or how not?

   b. Would you describe this school as one that should be academically successful based on the fourteen predictors identified in this study? (See Table 13.4.) For example, did the school feel safe? Were there views of nature? Were there supervisable private areas?

4. Select a middle school for a walk-through evaluation of the learning spaces. In small teams of three or four individuals, rate the school according to the Design Assessment Scale and then compare each team's ratings. Discuss the differences and similarities of each team's score per section of the Design Assessment Scale for middle schools.

REFERENCES

Alexander, C., Ishikawa, S., & Silverstein, M. (1977). *A characteristic language*. New York: Oxford University Press.

Alexander, C. (1979). *The timeless way of building*. New York: Oxford University Press.

Alexander, W. M., & George, P. S. (1993). *The exemplary middle school*, 2nd edition. New York: Harcourt Brace College Publishers.

Aughtry, G. M. (1995). A study of design features in fifteen selected North Carolina middle schools. *Dissertations abstracts international*, 57(02A), 0519. University Microfilms No. AAI 9616183.

Baker, R. G. (1968). *Ecological psychology*. Stanford, CA: Stanford University Press.

Berliner, D. C., & Biddle, B. J. (1995). *The manufactured crisis: Myths, fraud, and attack on America's public schools*. New York: Addison Wesley Longman.

Bernaldez, F. G., Gallardo, D., & Abello, R. P. (1987). Children's landscape preferences: From rejection to attraction. *Journal of Environmental Psychology*, 7:169–176.

Bingler, S. (1990). Place as a form of knowledge. In Meek, A. (ed.), *Designing places for learning*. Alexandria, VA: Association for Supervision and Curriculum Development, pp. 23–30.

Bradley, W. S. (1996). *Perceptions about the role of architecture in education*. Unpublished doctoral dissertation, the University of Virginia, Charlottesville, VA.

Carnegie Council (1989). *Turning points: Preparing American youth for the 21st century*. Washington, DC: Carnegie Council on Adolescent Development.

Carr, J., & Stevenson, C. (eds.) (1993). *Integrated studies in the middle grades: Dancing through walls*. New York: Teachers College Press.

Castaldi, B. (1994). Educational facilities: Planning, modernization and management, 4th ed. Boston: Allyn & Bacon.

Crumpacker, S. S. (1995). Using cultural information to create schools that work. In Meek, A. (ed.), *Designing places for learning*. Alexandria, VA: Association for Supervision and Curriculum Development, pp. 31–42.

Davis, J., & Loveless, E. E. (1981). *The adminstrator and educational facilities*. New York: University Press of America.

Education Writers Association. (1989). *Wolves at the schoolhouse door: An investigation of the condition of public school buildings*. Washington, DC: AASA.

Gaunt, L. (1980). Can children play at home? In Wilkinson, P. F. (ed.), *Innovation in play environments*. London: Croom Helm, pp. 36–51.

Genevro, R. (ed.). (1993). *New schools for New York: Plans and precedents for small schools*. New York: Princeton Architectural Press.

George, P. S. (1994). *New evidence for the middle school*. Columbus, OH: National Middle School Association.

Georgia Public Education Report Card 1997–1998 (1998). http://www.doe.k12.ga.us.

Millet, E., & Croteau, J. (1998). Restructuring educational facilities. Center for Environment Education and Design Studies. http://www.newhorizons.org/restruct.htm.

Morriseau, J. J. (1972). *Design and planning: The new schools*. New York: Van Nostrand Reinhold.

National Association of Secondary School Principals (1993). *Achieving excellence through the middle level curriculum*. Reston, VA: NASSP.

National Center for Education Statistics. (2000). *Condition of America's public school facilities: 1999* (NCES 2000–032). Washington, DC: U.S. Department of Education.

Pedhazur, E. J. (1982). *Multiple regression in behavioral research*, 2nd ed. New York: Holt, Rinehart, and Winston.

Proshansky, H. M., & Fabian, A. K. (1987). The development of identity in the child. In Weinstein, C. S., & David, T. G. (eds.), *Spaces for children: The built environment and child development*. New York: Plenum Press, pp. 21–40.

Sanoff, H. (1994). *School design*. New York: Van Nostrand Reinhold.

Sanoff, H. (2000). *Community participation methods in design and planning*. New York: John Wiley & Sons.

Tanner, C. K. (November, 1999). *A school design assessment scale*. Paper presented at the annual conference of the Council of Educational Facility Planners, International, Baltimore, MD.

Tanner, C. K. (2000). The influence of school architecture on academic achievement. *Journal of Educational Administration*, 38:309–330.

Taylor, A., Aldrich, Robert A., & Vlastos, G. (1988). Architecture can teach. *In Context*, 18. http://www.context.org/ICLIB/IC18/Taylor.htm.

Thomas Jefferson Center for Educational Design (1998). *Design Issues*, 3:1–3.

Wohlwill, J. F., & van Vliet, W. (1985). Habitats for children: The impacts of density. Hillsdale, NJ: Lawrence Erlbaum Associates, Publishers.

Wiles, J., & Bondi, J. (1986). *The essential middle school*. Gainesville, FL: Wiles, Bondi, and Associates, Inc.

CHAPTER FOURTEEN

RESEARCH PRIORITIES
How Facilities Affect Educational Outcomes

SHEILA J. BOSCH
Georgia Institute of Technology

Our lack of understanding of school facility effects on students and teachers is gaining national attention as a serious problem. In 2001 President George W. Bush's No Child Left Behind Act was passed. The goals of this legislation were to increase accountability for states, school districts, and individual schools through standardized testing; to provide parents and students attending low-performance schools with more school choices; to improve flexibility for state and local governments in spending federal education dollars; and to emphasize reading proficiency, particularly in younger students. The act includes amendments from the Healthy and High Performance Schools Act, sponsored by Senator Hillary Clinton of New York, that recognizes the need for research to assess the health and learning impacts of environmentally unhealthy schools on students and teachers. The Secretary of Education has been authorized to conduct various studies, including one that examines the "characteristics of those public elementary and secondary school buildings that contribute to unhealthy school environments" (personal communication, October 2, 2002). The study described in this chapter supports the goals of the Department of Education.

The findings of this research project most directly support researchers who study *school facility effects* (hereafter referred to as SFE) on educational outcomes, but may indirectly support school decision makers, including educators, school designers, architects, and building managers, by focusing future research efforts on acquiring knowledge that is relevant to them. This study is an important step in improving our understanding of the links between physical school variables and measures of student, school, or school district success, ultimately contributing to the development of higher-quality schools and smarter, more well-rounded students. Figure 14.1 on page 324 illustrates how research to better understand school facility effects benefits students.

RESEARCH PROBLEM

For researchers to contribute to the development of better schools, *it is important to understand how school facilities affect students and other building occupants*. Researchers from various fields (e.g., education, environment-behavior) and subspecialties (e.g., indoor air quality, lighting design) have

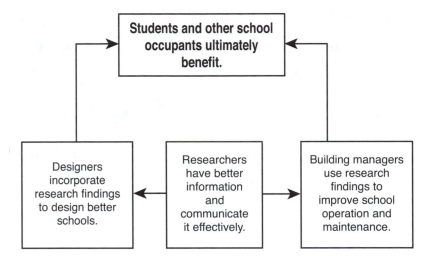

FIGURE 14.1 Students benefit from facility research.

provided evidence that the physical environment in school facilities, such as lighting, acoustics, and overall condition, affects various types of educational outcomes such as academic achievement and behavior. Yet, in spite of past research efforts, it is still not common practice to incorporate research findings into the design and operation of school facilities. There are three primary obstacles to the utilization of research, according to Knott and Wildavsky (1980). These include a lack of knowledge; decision maker's unawareness of the knowledge that does exist; and/or decision makers awareness of the knowledge that exists but their refusal to adopt it. Within each of these broad categories, there is likely a large number of factors affecting why research regarding school facilities to date has not significantly affected the way schools are designed and operated, such as the availability of funding, poor communication between researchers and practitioners, organizational barriers to implementing innovative facility designs, etc. There is an entire body of literature dedicated to "research utilization" or "knowledge utilization," and a discussion of that domain is outside the scope of this study. This study investigated one aspect of research utilization—whether or not there is a lack of knowledge in the field. There are many ques-

tions surrounding school facility effects that remain unanswered. For example, how do school facilities enhance or detract from the learning process? What are the mediating factors? How do school facilities affect student behavior? What are the causal relationships among correlated variables? Although studies exist that have examined the effects of overall building conditions, building age, finishes, lighting, noise, humidity, class size, and other factors on educational outcomes, the results are scattered; many studies have not been published beyond a master's thesis or doctoral dissertation, and few studies have been replicated.

While there is still much to learn about school facility effects on students, teachers, and other school occupants, *a formally stated set of research priorities for understanding these relationships does not exist.* It is important to identify research priorities for the field because there are likely thousands of physical variables and educational outcomes that could be studied. Without a formal set of research priorities, researchers will continue to make progress in this area, but a set of priorities may help move the field in a fruitful direction more quickly *and* with the buy-in needed to secure funding to conduct relevant research. Funding for research is limited, and selecting priorities will help focus available funding dollars to deliver the most "bang for the buck." It is important that research priorities address the needs of practitioners. Lackney (1996, p. 25) suggested that environment-behavior research regarding school environments has not led to improvements in environmental quality because "it has not, in many cases, addressed problems, concerns, issues and questions of relevance to educational practitioners," due partly to the differences in interests and goals of researchers and practitioners. For this study, a multimethod approach was used to solicit information from educators and researchers familiar with school facility effects literature to develop a set of research priorities to guide future research.

METHODOLOGY

This study addressed only K–12 schools because these facilities are designed for intentional teaching and learning, house a large number of occupants, and young people spend an enormous amount of time inside them. The specific questions addressed in this study included:

1. What physical variables and education outcomes have been studied in the SFE literature?
2. What are the most important educational outcomes (i.e., measures of student, school, or school district success), as perceived by educators (specifically principals, teachers, and guidance counselors)?
3. Are there important educational outcomes (as perceived by educators) that have been overlooked in past evaluations?
4. What are the most important physical variables that affect student outcomes, as perceived by those who are experienced in conducting SFE research?
5. Are there important physical variables (as perceived by SFE researchers) that have been overlooked in past studies?
6. If the data indicate that there is a gap in existing knowledge about links between physical school facilities and educational

outcomes, what research priorities will focus efforts on the most plausible links?

A four-phased approach (Figure 14.2, page 326) was executed to address these questions: an analysis of the literature; the use of concept mapping techniques to identify measures of student, school, and school district success that are important to educators; a Delphi method for identifying the most important physical variables (and hypotheses to describe plausible relationships with educational outcomes); and an analysis of the data to identify knowledge gaps and to develop research priorities.

Phase I: Literature Analysis

Published studies examining the effects of physical school conditions on students and teachers were derived from the literature in the domains of psychology, environment-behavior, physiology, and others. Four types of data sources were utilized: peer-reviewed journal articles; books; doctoral dissertations; and some non-peer-reviewed articles or reports. The sources were identified through several means. The purpose of the literature analysis was three-fold: (1) to identify educational outcomes to seed the brainstorming exercise in phase II; (2) to identify physical variables that are plausibly related to educational outcomes to seed the brainstorming list used in phase III; and (3) to identify gaps in current knowledge. Correlational or causal studies and review articles that could readily be obtained were included in the analysis. Only studies that were conducted in school facilities were evaluated, excluding related studies in which researchers have evaluated the effects of specific types of physical variables on human behavior or performance in other settings. The studies included in this literature analysis evaluated the types of physical variables that have been observed in recent literature reviews (Schneider, 2002a; Young et al., 2003), guidance documents that are used for creating high-performance schools (Bosch & Pearce, 2003), and the National Clearinghouse for

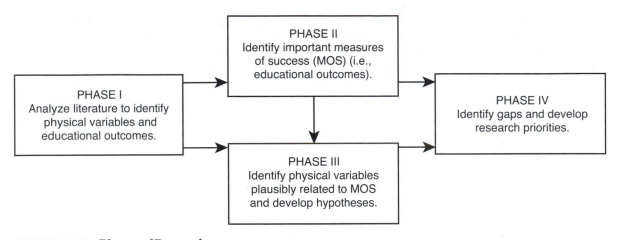

FIGURE 14.2   Phases of Research.

Educational Facilities' *Impact of Facilities on Learning* resource list. The task focused more on acquiring all identified studies regarding ambient conditions (e.g., overall building condition, thermal comfort, indoor air quality), but there was no attempt to accumulate a comprehensive set of studies that examined class size, school size, or open versus traditional plans. There is a large body of research in each of these three areas and a complete review of that literature was outside the scope of this study. Further, an analysis of the selected sample of literature is appropriate for achieving the purposes of this research.

Phase II: Identifying Measures of Success Using a Concept Mapping Methodology

The purpose of phase II was for educators (teachers, counselors, principals, and assistant principals) to identify educational outcomes (i.e., measures of student, school, or school district success) that they believe are important to monitor or otherwise track. If past and future research does not address the educational outcomes that educators perceive as important, the impact of SFE studies will be reduced. For this study, a convenient, yet purposive sampling strategy was used to select participants. Anticipat-

ing the difficulties associated with gathering busy educators from a variety of schools and districts into one place for this study, a cohort of eighteen doctoral students pursuing their doctorate in education in school improvement at the State University of West Georgia was invited to participate.

Concept mapping, the method selected for phase II, is defined as "a type of structured conceptualization which can be used by groups to develop a conceptual framework which can guide evaluation or planning" (Trochim, 1989). Using this approach, ideas expressed in the form of statements, such as "teacher retention" or "mathematicsematics achievement," are generated by participants, and the relationships among these ideas are represented using multidimensional scaling and cluster analysis, resulting in a relational map showing the relative similarities/dissimilarities of those ideas. The map represents the group-level data generated when participants sort these ideas into categories that make sense to them and rate them according to their relative importance. Typically, the group will interpret the maps and decide how they will be used (Trochim, 1989). The process engages participants using an inductive approach, beginning with specific brainstormed ideas and resulting in the development of broader, more general concepts or categories. Because concept mapping is a structured process with a well-defined be-

TABLE 14.1 Concept Mapping Process Overview

Prepare the project.	The facilitator (i.e., the researcher) will: ■ Identify the specific focus of the study (i.e., What will participants be asked to do in order to gather desired data?) and generate the focus statement—the phrase that prompts the brainstorming activity. ■ Develop rating focus statement—a statement and rating scale that guides participants when rating the relative importance of the concepts or ideas that are generated. ■ Identify participants, make initial contact, develop a schedule for completion, and prepare software (if it will be used).
Generate ideas (brainstorming).	■ Participants generate ideas related to the focus statement.
Structure ideas (sort and rate).	■ Participants sort the ideas into piles that make sense to them and rate each idea (typically using a Likert-type scale) regarding its importance, as described by the rating focus statement.
Compute maps.	■ Computer software is typically used to generate a point map, cluster map, point rating map, and/or cluster rating map (described below). ■ Facilitator selects number of clusters to be used.
Interpret maps.	■ Participant group reaches consensus regarding the labels (or titles) for the clusters.
Utilize maps.	■ Participants work with the facilitator to determine how the maps will be used. Examples include examining priorities, developing a structure for a computer database, or creating a strategic plan. For this study, it is the facilitator (i.e., researcher) rather than the participants who used the concept maps. The *data* contained in the point rating map and cluster maps, rather than the maps themselves, were used in latter phases of this research.

ginning and end, the outcome may be achieved in a predetermined timeframe. The tasks for participants are simple to complete, and the results are visual and easily understood (Concept Systems Incorporated, 2002). The steps for concept mapping are described in Table 14.1.

Concept mapping is most often used for planning and evaluation processes. In evaluation, it may be used to express concepts related to measures or outcomes that are believed to be relevant. An advantage to using this approach is that many different types of concepts can be generated and then sorted into categories—like sorting a pile of apples, oranges, and pears into their own separate baskets. The sorting process is quite simple. Table 14.2 on page 328 lists the rules for sorting.

The primary outcome of the concept mapping process is visual representation of the work of participants. There are four types of maps that may be created using the concept mapping method (and software). These include the point map, the cluster map, the point rating map, and the cluster rating map. The point map is created using the data generated by the participants and represents how often statements were grouped into the same piles or categories. The computer generates a binary

TABLE 14.2   Rules for Sorting Statements

Group the statements in terms of how similar in meaning they are to one another. You will be creating a main topic name for each group you create. Do not group the statements according to how important they are, how high a priority they have, etc. Another part of the process will ask you to rank the importance of each group.

1. There is no right or wrong way to group the statement. You will probably find that you could group the statements in several sensible ways. Pick the arrangement that feels best to you.
2. You cannot put one statement into two piles at the same time. Each statement must be put into only one pile.
3. People differ on how many piles they wind up with. In most cases, anywhere from ten to twenty piles usually works out well.
4. A statement may be segregated alone as its own pile if you think it is unrelated to the other statements or it stands alone as a unique idea, but you cannot have one pile for each statement.
5. Make sure that *every* statement is put somewhere. Do not leave any statements out. Do *not* create any piles that are "miscellaneous" or "junk" piles. If you have statements left over that you cannot place, put each statement in its own pile.

symmetric similarity matrix for each individual to identify which statements were sorted together. This consists of a table with as many rows and columns as there are statements (e.g., 100 × 100). In each cell, a 0 is placed where the two statements were not grouped together, and a 1 indicates that they were sorted into the same pile. From this, a group similarity matrix is computed using the combined data. A point map is then computed using multidimensional scaling analysis. Each point represents a statement, and the locations of the points on the map represent their similarities (i.e., the closer the points on the map, the more often they were grouped together) (Trochim, 1989). The outcome is a point map in which each point or dot represents a statement, and the nearness of each point to other points on the map represents how often the statements were grouped together by the participants.

The cluster map uses the same data that are input for generating the point map. However, the cluster map shows boundary lines around those points that cluster together based on the data. If software is used, the computer can generate a cluster map for any number of clusters. Cluster analysis is used to group statements on the map into clusters that presumably reflect similar concepts. The Trochim concept mapping process utilizes the X-Y multidimensional scaling coordinate values as input to the cluster analysis in order to achieve clusters that group statements according to their location on the point map (Concept Systems Incorporated, 2002). The final cluster map is a visual picture of polygons that represent the selected number of clusters. Each cluster contains a set of statements that have been grouped together.

The point rating map and cluster rating map combine the participant data regarding how to group statements with their Likert-type ratings. These maps illustrate the average importance ratings assigned by the group. The taller the point or cluster shape, the higher the importance assigned. A point rating map looks similar to the point map, except the height of the points represents the average group rating for each item. The cluster rating map looks similar to the cluster map, except the thickness of the polygons represents the average cluster rating (average rating of all statements in each cluster).

For this particular study, the focus statement to which educators were asked to respond was, "One measure of student, school, or school district success (or lack of success) is _____." Participants were asked to brainstorm terms to complete this sentence. The combined list was used in the sorting exercise. The rating statement with which they rated the importance of each term was "How important do you believe it is to monitor or otherwise track this measure of student, school, or school district success?" Their responses were based on a four-point Likert scale (1 = unimportant, 4 = important).

Phase III: Identifying Physical Factors Plausibly Related to Measures of Success

The purpose of phase III was to solicit the expert judgments of researchers in the SFE field (i.e., those who have studied how school facilities affect educational outcomes) to identify variables that plausibly affect student outcomes identified by educators during phase II. Although current and past literature sources provide a rich set of physical variables, some of which have been shown to affect outcomes such as achievement, this study addressed the question of whether or not there are other physical factors that have not been studied (or only minimally) which should become part of a set of research priorities for the field. Therefore, it was important that this study utilize a methodology resulting in a more inclusive generation of variables and some level of consensus regarding this complex problem. A second goal of phase III was to identify specific hypotheses that SFE researchers perceive to be important to study in the near term and that address the links between physical variables and educational outcomes (i.e., measures of success) which educators perceive as important.

The Delphi technique (originally used in forecasting) was chosen to achieve the purpose of phase III primarily because there is no need for the face-to-face contact of participants, unlike nominal group technique or other group methods that require physical proximity (Delbecq, Van de Ven, & Gustafson, 1975). There are several reasons why Delphi is an appropriate method to use for group communication. Among the several listed in Linstone

and Turoff (1975), three apply to this particular research: (1) The problem can benefit through subjective and collective judgment; (2) a meeting or meetings of the experts is not feasible due to time and cost restraints; and (3) preservation of heterogeneity rather than the dominance of particularly strong voices is desired. One goal of this study was to begin on a broad scale and then narrow the focus based on individual responses to questionnaires, with heterogeneity maintained, particularly in the earlier surveys. The Delphi method typically involves a series of questionnaires given to a group of experts to gain knowledge, opinions, or judgments (Moore, 1987). Through the Delphi process, individual responses to each survey are shared through the development of each successive survey, but individual responses usually remain anonymous. Delphi techniques may be used in different types of applications, such as identifying goals, identifying group values, gathering information, educating respondents, or as in the case of this research, establishing priorities. Figure 14.3 on page 330 graphically illustrates the approach used in phase III.

In phase III, a group of SFE researchers was asked to identify the physical variables that are most plausibly related to measures of student, school, and school district success, to rate the importance of those physical variables, and to form hypotheses for future research. This group is more familiar with findings from past research, and areas of weakness in the existing body of literature, and is typically more up to date on current studies. Therefore, SFE researchers are the ideal group to target in this phase of the study. Also, by asking them to consider measures of student, school, or school district success that were rated highly by educators, they were able to develop hypotheses that will be relevant for educators.

Phase IV: Identify Gaps and Develop Research Priorities

The purpose of this phase is to compare the information gathered in the three interrelated studies of this dissertation research (the literature analysis; the

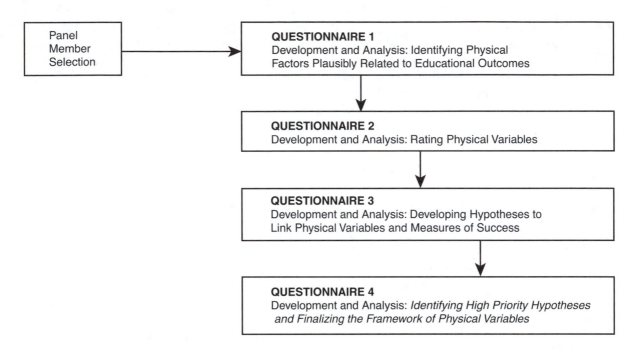

FIGURE 14.3 **The Delphi Process for the Study.**

identification of measures of student, school, and school district success; and the identification of physical variables likely to affect those measures of success) to identify knowledge gaps and to present a set of research priorities to guide future research, based on identified high-priority hypotheses. Phases I through III were designed to provide the information necessary to develop research priorities that will, in the long term, accomplish the following:

■ Guide future research in the field by building on the knowledge acquired from the literature, educators, and SFE researchers.
■ Ensure that research supports the values of educators.
■ Improve the likelihood that money spent on school construction and renovation will create better learning environments.

The selection of research priorities was based entirely on the high-priority hypotheses developed by the SFE researchers in phase III. To investigate whether or not there is a lack of knowledge in the field, a comparison of the findings from the literature analysis, the concept mapping exercises, and the Delphi study were conducted. The following tasks were performed:

1. Identify which of the *educational outcome variables* rated highly (≥ 3.2) by the educators were also identified in the literature and which were not.
2. Identify which of the *physical variables* rated highly (≥ 3.2) by the Delphi panel were also identified in the literature and which were not.

The method of analysis simply involved reviewing the variable ratings by the educators and Delphi panel members, and determining whether or not those variables were identified in the literature reviewed.

FINDINGS

The methodologies applied in this study were successfully used to solicit knowledge and perceptions from various groups of key stakeholders to gain some level of consensus regarding high-priority research topics. The literature analysis provided important physical and outcome variables to seed the brainstorming lists used in following phases of the research. Concept mapping allowed a group of seventeen educators to identify, sort, rate, and categorize a large number of outcome variables (i.e., measures of student, school, or district success) into clusters of those variables to guide future discussions. The Delphi method involved a group of seventeen SFE researchers to identify a list of physical variables that are plausibly linked to educational outcomes, to rate their importance, to develop hypotheses that should be tested, and to select the most important hypotheses that should become research priorities for the field. The overall approach used may successfully be applied in replication studies of this sort, or used in other fields of environment-behavior research. Specific findings from each phase are described.

Phase I: Literature Analysis

The literature analysis has presented evidence that characteristics of the physical school environment do affect student and teacher health, behavior, attitudes, achievement, and other outcomes. However, for each type of physical variable (or set of multiple variables), there is still a great deal that is not understood about *how* the physical environment contributes to or hinders specific outcomes. In fact, only one of the studies reviewed (Evans & Maxwell, 1997) identified a partial mediator to explain *how* aircraft noise affected reading skills (by interfering with speech perception rather than sound perception). This is no surprise, however, based on the fact that there is still so much information lacking even about what physical variables (separately or combined) affect which outcomes. Another consideration about the studies reviewed is that they vary in their scientific rigor. In many cases, the sample size

is very small and almost none of them attempt to show causality, for various reasons. There are many inherent difficulties in showing causality when there are numerous variables that are outside the control of the investigator. The majority of the studies reviewed focus on the outcome measure of academic achievement (particularly mathematics and reading) measured using several different types of standardized tests. Other outcomes that have received the most attention include attitudes (student and teacher) and behavior. Therefore, while there may be convincing evidence of the links between a particular physical variable and a specific outcome (e.g., daylighting and academic achievement), little to no research is available regarding the effects of that particular physical variable on other types of outcome measures (e.g., mood).

Phase II: Identifying Measures of Success Using a Concept Mapping Methodology

The participants, beginning with a list of outcome measures provided to them from the literature analysis, brainstormed (via e-mail) a final list of over a hundred measures of student, school, or school district success. During one class period, they individually sorted each of those items, using computer software, into clusters that made sense to them. And, they rated each measure of success regarding the importance of monitoring or tracking it. Afterwards, the facilitator (researcher in this case) analyzed the data using the mapping component of the software and determined that fifteen clusters was an appropriate number. During a second class meeting, the group developed names for each of these clusters. Table 14.3 on page 332 lists those cluster names and their average importance rating. Figure 14.4 on page 333 is the final cluster rating map developed by participants.

These fifteen clusters contain the entire list of over 100 individual items. Of those items, thirty-six were rated at 3.2 or higher. The top ten included reading skills; attendance; staff development; mathematics achievement; parental involvement;

TABLE 14.3 **Average Cluster Ratings by Educators**

CLUSTER NAME	AVG. IMPORTANCE RATING (1–4 SCALE)
Achievement data	3.25
Parental involvement	3.13
School factors (e.g., attendance, school size, before- and after-school programs)	3.12
Facilities	3.12
Community (e.g., community, involvement, public relations)	3.12
Collaboration	3.09
Staff training, experience, and expertise	3.08
Postsecondary concerns (e.g., student satisfaction with postsecondary preparation, college-related variables)	3.06
School climate (e.g., student friendly environment, student self-concept)	3.01
Student behavior	2.91
Student attitude	2.81
Academics/placement (e.g., retentions, advanced placement enrollment)	2.77
Teacher attitude and behavior	2.66
Support services (e.g., availability of materials and other resources, teacher/administrator mental health concerns)	2.63
Health	1.49

academic growth; student performance; student achievement; language acquisition; and teacher/administrator retention. It is obvious in looking at these data that some of the items are similar. Before the group was asked to sort and rate the items, there was a discussion to clarify some terms, but in a discussion following the exercise, participants stated that it would have been better to have con-ducted the brainstorming exercise in person rather than by e-mail, but unfortunately such was not possible in this case. The outcomes from phase II of the research included:

A list of measures of student, school, and school district success, as generated by educators

Clusters (or categories) containing these measures

Average ratings for each measure of success and cluster to indicate how important educators feel it is to monitor or otherwise track those measures

Concept mapping provided an effective means for asking educators to identify, rate, and cluster measures of student, school, or school district success in a timely manner. The data were readily used in phase III of this study.

Phase III: Identifying Physical Factors Plausibly Related to Measures of Success

Phase III, using the Delphi process, involved a series of four questionnaires to which researchers responded. The purpose of Questionnaire 1 was to identify a list of physical factors in schools that may affect educational outcomes. Delphi panel members were provided with a list of several items derived from the literature to seed this brainstorming exercise. Seventeen panel members (100 percent) responded to Questionnaire 1. The final list of physical factors recommended as plausibly affecting educational outcomes included 114 items.

The purpose of Questionnaire 2 was for the Delphi panel members to rate the importance of the physical variables they identified in Questionnaire 1. Prior to the development of Questionnaire 2, the resulting list of physical variables was sorted into a hierarchical structure called the *Framework for Physical Factors Plausibly Related to Measures of Success*, hereafter referred to as the Framework. The

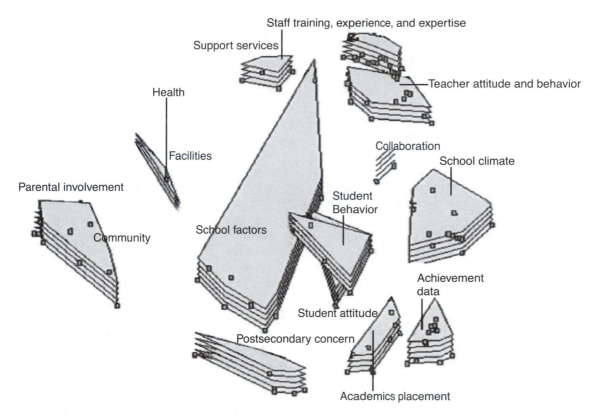

FIGURE 14.4   Final Cluster Rating Map.

purpose of this Framework was two-fold: first, to provide an organizational structure to simplify the rating task of Questionnaire 2, and second, to develop a structure for describing the final set of research priorities. Each panel member was asked to complete two types of tasks, in the following order for Questionnaire 2.

Task I.   Rate each physical item according to its importance.

1 = Not important.

2 = Somewhat important: Plausibly affects educational outcomes, but little to no research-based evidence exists.

3 = Important: Some evidence suggests it affects educational outcomes, but we still do not understand those effects well.

4 = Very important: Strong evidence exists, but we still do not understand those effects well.

Task II.   Relatively rate the elements within each physical factor category by distributing 100 points among those elements to indicate relative importance.

Sixteen (94 percent) panel members responded to Questionnaire 2. There were thirty-eight physical variables that were rated at 3.2 or higher. For the purpose of this study, a rating of 3.2 was used as a cut-off to identify the highest rated items, both for physical items in phase III and measures of success in phase II (although somewhat arbitrary, it was used consistently).

The purpose of Questionnaire 3 was to have the Delphi panel members develop hypotheses to represent plausible relationships between the physical factors (identified by the Delphi panel) and measures of success (identified by educators in phase II). The panel members were first asked to rate their own level of knowledge and experience for each physical item, using the following scale:

1 = Not experienced enough to suggest links to educational outcomes

2

3 = Familiar with this area at a general level

4

5 = Active researcher in this area

When writing hypotheses, the Delphi panel members were asked to focus on those physical factors that they, as a group, rated as important (with an average importance rating of 3.2 or higher) and with which they rated themselves a 3, 4, or 5. However, they could write hypotheses for any of the physical items. Similarly, they were asked to focus on those measures of success with an average group importance rating of 3.2 or higher (as rated by the group of educators). The panel members were encouraged to include mediators and moderators in their hypotheses, where applicable. *Mediators* are those variables that interpret or explain relationships between independent and dependent variables, whereas *moderators* are variables that interact with independent variables to influence the outcome (Evans & Maxwell, 1997). For example, daylighting may induce a more positive mood, thereby improving test scores. In this case, a more positive mood is a mediator variable. If the effect is more prominent among those of lower socioeconomic status (SES), then SES is a moderator. The return rate for Questionnaire 3 was lower than desired, as only ten out of seventeen were returned (59 per-

cent). This questionnaire required more time to complete than the other two questionnaires and at least two researchers reported that it took several hours to complete. Panel members submitted a total of 107 hypotheses. Some of the hypotheses received were not written in the form of a testable hypothesis. The Delphi panel members acknowledged the need to study not just the correlations between specific independent and dependent variables, but also the mediators that explain those relationships. There were several types of mediators that were most prevalent among the hypotheses. Most notable were student behavior, and student and teacher attitudes. Other mediators that appeared in several of the hypotheses were social interaction/social development, and health-related issues. The dependent variables that were most often included in the hypotheses were achievement (by far the most common), satisfaction (students, teachers, and parents), and other teacher/administrator variables (e.g., professional development, absenteeism). The researchers did consider outcome variables that are important to educators.

Once the Delphi panel members had developed a set of 107 hypotheses, too many to include within a set of research priorities, they were then asked (in Questionnaire 4) to narrow this set by selecting those that are most important. The purpose of Questionnaire 4 was two-fold: (1) to narrow the list of hypotheses to a more manageable size in order to identify those that are the top priority for the Delphi panel (part A) and (2) to finalize the Framework (part B). Some of the 107 hypotheses were redundant or did not clearly state relationships between variables; therefore, several hypotheses were omitted from the original list. This shortened list of ninety-eight hypotheses was used in Questionnaire 4. As a result of Questionnaire 4, the list of ninety-eight hypotheses was narrowed to just eleven top-priority hypotheses and the Framework was modified to address researcher comments. To narrow the list of hypotheses, each panel member selected the top ten hypotheses that they believed should be part of a research agenda (to be studied first). The number of hypotheses for which there was agreement (selected by three or more Delphi panel members) is only eleven. Two hypotheses were combined based on their similarity, leaving ten hypotheses grouped as nine research priorities in phase IV.

Phase IV: Identify Gaps and Develop Research Priorities

A comparison of the educational outcomes that educators perceived to be important versus those that were included in the literature reviewed in Chapters 3, 12, and 13 provides several important (as perceived by educators) measures of student, school, and school district success that have not been addressed in previous SFE research. Additionally, there are physical variables that experienced researchers perceive to be plausibly related to those measures of success that have been overlooked in the literature. The gap analysis supports the argument that there are important gaps in current knowledge on this topic

The recommended research priorities (Table 14.4, page 336) identified in phase IV are based on the agreed upon hypotheses developed by the Delphi panel.

The utility of these research priorities may be expanded if they can be used to create a model of the important relationships between physical variables in a school and desired outcomes. Moore and Lackney (1994, p. 15) proposed a mediational-interactional model of environmental factors affecting educational outcomes. In this model, independent factors were categorized under the headings of "physical environment" or "social environment." Mediating factors were "behavioral," "attitudinal," or "physiological." The educational outcomes were categorized as "achievement outcomes" or "pro-social outcomes." It was not possible to fit the research priorities developed in this dissertation into their model exactly. A model for the research priorities has been proposed in Figure 14.5 on page 337 based on the recommended hypotheses proposed by the Delphi panel. This model has been strongly influenced by the Moore and Lackney (1994) model.

DISCUSSION

The literature analysis provided variables that were used in the following two phases of this research and made gaps in current understanding apparent. The concept mapping method was appropriate for accomplishing the goals of phase II. However, the final concept map itself proved to be less useful than the data it contained. Although the cluster rating map identified fifteen groupings of measures of student, school, or school district success and their relative importance, it was the statements contained within these clusters that proved to be most useful in this study. What is evident from the cluster ratings, however, is that although educators do believe that academic achievement (rating = 3.25) is the most important type of variable to track, other categories of variables, such as parental and community involvement, school factors (e.g., attendance, average class size, and student transience), and facility resources, are nearly just as important. During discussions, educators expressed dissatisfaction with the way academic achievement is currently measured using only standardized tests. The focus of student and school evaluation, including that specified in the No Child Left Behind Act, continues to be on academic achievement as measured by standardized tests

Regarding facilities, it is important to note that the educators added two facility-related variables (without any prompting) to the brainstorm list (including well maintained and up-to-date resources; clean and well maintained building and grounds) and rated both of them above 3.0. *More than one educator commented that information about school facilities is entirely absent from most teacher and administrator preparation courses, although it is needed.*

In phase III, Delphi panel members were asked to rate each of the 114 physical variables they had identified. Thirty-eight of these variables received a group average rating of 3.2 or higher (out of four possible points). Of those, twelve (32 percent) relate to ambient environmental conditions associated with lighting, thermal conditions, acoustics,

TABLE 14.4   Top Research Priorities

RESEARCH PRIORITIES	HYPOTHESES
Effects of Student Team Workstations	The provision of spaces where students can work in teams will increase opportunities to use a variety of pedagogical techniques, resulting in the students-feeling more socially connected and a greater satisfaction among teachers, students, and parents as compared to schools where students do not have spaces where they can work in teams.
Effects of Faculty Collaborative Spaces	Hypothesis 1: Teachers in schools with faculty collaborative spaces will feel more supported by their peers and administrators, experience greater satisfaction, and participate to a greater degree in professional development than teachers in schools without faculty collaborative spaces. Hypothesis 2: When compared with students in schools without faculty collaborative spaces, students in schools with them will have better attitudes toward school, feel more socially supported, and experience improved academic achievement; transience will be reduced; and parents will be more satisfied.
Effects of Quiet, Reflective Space	The provision of quiet, reflective space for students and teachers will result in improved student and teacher satisfaction, reduced off-task behavior, and improved student social development and affective performance when compared with the results for students and teachers in schools without private spaces for their use.
Effects of Circulation Spaces with Niches, Seating Areas, and Natural Light	The provision of circulation spaces with niches, seating areas, and natural light provides opportunities for informal interaction among students and teachers, resulting in an improved social climate that will lead to a more student friendly environment, a greater sense of school connectedness, improved student academic growth, improved student attendance, affective performance, and greater teacher retention when compared to school buildings without this type of circulation spaces.
Effects of Overutilization of a School Building	When school buildings are overutilized, student attendance and student achievement will be lower than in school buildings that are not overutilized.
Effects of Adaptable Seating	Students in classrooms with seating that can be adapted to suit a variety of pedagogical teaching strategies will experience reduced off-task behavior and increased academic achievement when compared with students in more static classrooms.
Effects of School Integration into Local Community	When a school is well integrated into the community, students will feel more valued by the school and will experience greater social development, improved job opportunities, reduced transience, and greater satisfaction. Parents will also be more satisfied as compared to the parents of students in schools that are not well integrated into the community.
Effects of Day-lit Classrooms	The provision of predominantly day-lit classrooms is correlated with higher student academic achievement, lower absentee rates, fewer student suspensions, and improved teacher satisfaction when compared with predominantly artificially lit classrooms.
Effects of Level of Maintenance and Building Quality	Students in buildings that are well maintained and of good quality will perform higher on measures of achievement, create fewer disciplinary problems, and have higher attendance rates than students in poorly maintained buildings and of poor quality.

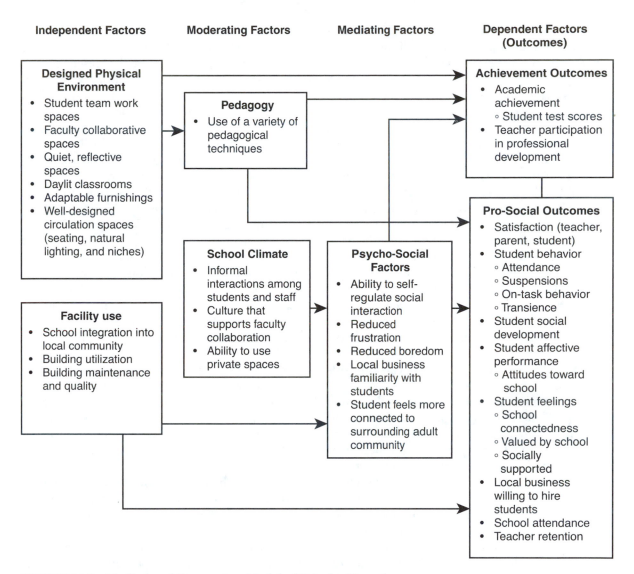

FIGURE 14.5   Mediational-Interaction Model of Priority Hypotheses.

and indoor air quality. The Delphi panel recognized the importance of ambient conditions and their effects on school building occupants. However, only one of the final priority hypotheses includes ambient conditions (daylighting), suggesting that the panel members feel as though enough is known about how ambient conditions affect educational outcomes, or that school decision makers are already aware of the need to provide adequate ambient conditions. Or, perhaps the method used in phase III encouraged researchers to think beyond the traditional types of SFE relationships regarding the effects of lighting, temperature, or acoustics (even if they are not yet well understood) and recommend that future work focus on a broader set of issues. Ambient conditions may be outside the areas of expertise of the Delphi panel members, or they may consider their effects to be a bit mundane when compared with socio-spatial factors that focus on programmatic issues (such as spaces to support pedagogy that encourages collaboration and social interaction) which may interest them more. This is not to suggest that the work of those, such as building technologists, who study the effects of ambient conditions on building occupants is not important. After all, ambient conditions have been shown to affect educational outcomes, and there are still many unanswered questions about how or why these effects occur, particularly with respect to the physiological or psychophysical mechanisms involved. The Delphi panel members recognized a need for research to investigate how physical spaces designed to encourage social interaction and collaboration affect students and teachers, a topic with very little coverage in the current SFE literature.

One limitation of this study is that by asking the respondents to consider physical variables and outcome variables identified as important, it may have encouraged them to generate hypotheses that are more appropriate for univariate interactional types of research rather than transactional. However, by including mediating and moderating variables, the respondents did generate some rather complex hypotheses, such as "A combination of individual student workspace, spaces for students to personalize and lockable personal storage will create a sense of ownership in students that may lead to better attitudes toward school and motivation to learn that will positively influence their performance, greater student attendance and overall success in school, socially and academically." Testing this type of hypothesis would require a multivariate analysis that examined the effects of mediating variables.

The high-priority hypotheses seem to reflect some common trends in school design and include variables that may be considered "hot topics." For example, there has been excitement regarding daylighting in the past few years because of the findings of the study by the Heschong Mahone Group (1999), and daylighting appears on the recommended list of research priorities. It is not surprising that the perceptions of the Delphi panel members seem to be affected by issues of the day (such as collaboration and flexibility, e.g.). However, it is surprising that a hypothesis regarding indoor air quality did not appear in the final list of priority hypotheses, since there has been much attention given to this issue and the U.S. Environmental Protection Agency (EPA) has developed a widely distributed indoor air quality Toolkit for schools to help them identify and correct common indoor air quality problems. There may be some bias toward topics that the SFE researchers personally want to pursue in the future, although they did clearly consider outcome measures that are important to educators. The Delphi method used in this study encouraged participants to think beyond traditional lines of research, such as how thermal conditions are associated with the performance of some type of task. The absence of these types of topics in the final set of research priorities does not diminish their importance, but SFE researchers are ready to pursue a broader set of issues.

While there is still much work to be done to further refine the hypotheses, generate buy-in from a larger audience of SFE researchers and school decision makers, secure funding, and design appropriate studies to investigate these hypotheses, this project has provided an important basis for guiding future research. This study has taken one step in the direction toward a collaborative research approach, one in which all parties equally participate in defining research problems and developing research strategies (Nyden & Wiewel, 1992). Further exploration may indicate that collaboration between SFE researchers and educators will provide the kinds of data that will interest school decision makers and perhaps increase their utilization of research findings in the future to design and operate better schools.

FUTURE RESEARCH NEEDS

The very next step is for researchers to begin tackling the questions presented in the set of research priorities defined in Table 14.4. A very interesting follow-up to this study would involve using the data regarding important physical variables (developed by researchers) and asking educators to rate how important they believe each one is with respect to the measures of success they identified as important. Past studies (Lackney, 1996; Schneider, 2002b) have evaluated educator perceptions about what physical factors affect outcomes related to teaching and learning. There does seem to be a disconnect between the research priorities developed by the Delphi panel and educators' perceived problems with school buildings, such as inadequate science labs and inappropriate room sizes, indoor air quality, and electrical outlets (Schneider 2002b).

A follow-up study to replicate the concept mapping exercise with additional groups of educators would be useful for confirming that the measures of success identified as important to this study group are also important to the broader groups of educators that they represent. Similarly, replication of the Delphi process with another group of SFE researchers, including several outside of the United States, could validate whether the top-rated research priorities apply to a larger population. There is another approach that could also be explored. First, these research priorities, although based on responses from both educators and SFE researchers, should become the starting point for discussion and revision by researchers to increase buy-in. A formal research agenda published by the CEFPI would likely have quite an impact on guiding future research. A series of workshops is envisioned. Beginning with researchers (perhaps in conjunction with a future CEFPI conference), a working group could come to a consensus about the top-priority research questions and suggest methods for addressing them. Further, a plan of action for identifying operationalized definitions for physical and outcome variables is an important next step that could perhaps be tackled in a second work-

shop. Without some agreement on ways to operationalize the variables, researchers will continue to use a myriad of measures that cannot easily be compared using meta-analysis.

Several of the high-priority hypotheses identified in this study include a complex set of relationships between physical variables and educational outcomes, moving SFE research away from a traditional univariate approach, one that links specific physical variables with specific educational outcomes, toward the application of a more ecological approach that considers many variables at the same time and their effects on one another. Further study of these hypotheses will require not only operationalization of the variables, but also new or modified methods to study them. Although these hypotheses will move the SFE field into new directions by focusing attention on complex, multivariate relationships, they will be difficult to study. Yet, it is important to do so. For example, a study that examined whether or not the provision of student team work spaces was associated with students' sense of being socially connected, as well as student, teacher, and parental satisfaction, could be misleading without examining whether or not there was actually increased use of a variety of pedagogical techniques (a mediator) in schools that provide these work spaces. An important next step is for researchers to begin developing appropriate methods for addressing these complex types of relationships. It will be important for researchers to examine nontraditional (i.e., noncorrelational) methods, such as case studies, to evaluate effective schools and identify similar patterns among them.

Finally, another useful extension of this research would be to apply this same methodology in another environment-behavior field, such as the effects of "green" buildings on occupants, to identify high-priority relationships among variables and to develop a set of research priorities. If shown to be effective, this methodology will become a valuable contribution to the environment-behavior field and possibly others.

If the research priorities identified in this study are further refined and pursued, progress will result in understanding the relationships between schools facilities and educational outcomes. Knowledge that is relevant to researchers and practitioners alike may bring about a state of data availability that will supply school designers, decision makers, building managers, and other stakeholders with important tools to help them ensure that schools provide the best environments for learning.

In addition to pursuing a formalized research agenda and investigating important relationships between schools and their effects on occupants, there are two other broad areas of research that may encourage decision makers to utilize research findings to improve school facilities (if given appropriate funding to do so). These include (1) improving communications among researchers and designers/building managers and (2) identifying methods for utilizing postoccupancy evaluation (POE) data collected by practitioners in research.

SUMMARY

Although there have been studies over the past thirty or forty years to examine relationships between school conditions and educational outcomes, this study has shown that there is a remaining gap in knowledge concerning important links between these types of variables. The methodologies used in the past were sometimes not scientifically rigorous, and there have been few replication studies conducted. Even though it is known that the physical environment does affect, to some degree, outcomes such as behavior, attitudes, and achievement, researchers are not yet able to accurately predict the outcomes, nor do they understand the causal mechanisms linking the environment and those outcomes in most cases. Currently, researchers from a wide variety of fields (e.g., architecture, education, building technology) conduct research within their own interest areas. Although there are organizations, such as the Council of Educational Facility Planners, International (CEFPI) and the National Clearinghouse for Educational Facilities, that provide research information regarding school facilities, there is no specific set of

recommended research priorities guiding current and future research to ensure that it is relevant to practitioners.

In phase I of this study, a review of SFE literature (with a primary emphasis on ambient conditions) showed that although previous research has investigated correlations between physical school variables and educational outcomes, little is known about causal mechanisms—only one study reviewed and tested the role of mediating variables. There is a great deal of variety among the methodologies utilized, and sample sizes varied from as few as eight students to tens of thousands. The majority of previous studies focused on relationships between physical conditions and academic achievement, typically measured using standardized test scores. Attitudes and behavior were other outcomes more commonly studied. Prior to this study, it was unclear whether or not previous research focused on educational outcomes that are the most important to those in education. This was addressed in phase II.

A concept mapping methodology was utilized in phase II to solicit feedback from a group of seventeen experienced educators. The educators were asked to brainstorm a list of measures of student, school, or school district success, beginning with a list of items identified in the literature analysis in phase I. Then, they sorted their final list of more than 100 items into categories that made sense to them, and they rated each item in terms of how important it is to monitor or otherwise track. The result was a concept map of fifteen clusters that included these items. The educators rated the "academic achievement" cluster as the most important type of variable to track, but other clusters such as "parental involvement," "school factors," "community involvement," and "collaboration" fell close behind. An evaluation of their ratings for individual items revealed that they rated thirty-six of them as important (using a 3.2 rating out of 4 as a cut-off). The top rated items were reading skills, attendance, staff development, mathematic semantics achievement, parental involvement, and academic growth. Although SFE researchers have examined a host of outcome variables in the past, there seems to be quite a large number of variables that are important to educators which have received very little attention in previous research. Some of these include parental involvement (as an outcome rather than an independent variable); teacher/administrator retention; teacher/administrator participation in professional development; teacher mentoring; community business satisfaction with student employees and graduates; student transience rate; general and special education cohesiveness (i.e., how well the special and regular education programs work together); multiple retentions; and community support.

Once outcomes that are important to educators were identified in phase II, SFE researchers were asked to identify physical variables plausibly linked to those outcomes and to develop hypotheses to guide future research. These tasks were accomplished in phase III using a Delphi technique. Through a series of four questionnaires, a group of seventeen experienced researchers were asked to brainstorm a list of physical variables plausibly related to educational outcomes, rate the importance of those items, develop hypotheses that included top-rated physical variables and top-rated outcome variables (i.e., measures of success rated by educators), and then select from their list of hypotheses those that most need to be studied in the near term. The Delphi panel members generated a list of 114 physical variables and rated thirty-eight of them as important (3.2 or higher out of 4). Like the educators, the researchers on the Delphi panel also identified some high-priority variables that have received very little attention in the SFE domain to date. These include a child's perceived safety; telephones in classrooms; indoor air quality (a recognized research need, but very few studies have been conducted); views to the outside (nonschool studies are available); faculty collaborative spaces; conference spaces; accessible phone, copier, fax (for students,

not just teachers); fluidity of seating and work surfaces to meet changing needs; informal learning spaces; adult-student spatial integration; student display spaces and studios; and acoustic privacy from other groups (when students work in teams). More than 30 percent of the important physical variables were related to ambient environmental conditions (e.g., lighting, thermal conditions, acoustics) and several others were related to facility maintenance (e.g., building condition). An unanticipated outcome was that this list of important physical variables included a much broader set of variables than those that have been previously studied. Several of the physical variables are design elements intended to promote collaboration and social interaction, reflecting a current trend in school design (as well as office design) to create spaces designed for teams to work together or meet informally. There is currently little information about whether or not such spaces actually improve social development, student affective performance, behavior, or academic achievement. Several of these types of physical variables became part of the priority hypotheses developed by the Delphi panel.

The high-priority hypotheses developed by the Delphi panel reflect the fact that SFE researchers are no longer interested primarily in ambient conditions, as only one of them addressed this type of variable (daylighting). These hypotheses, although they address some physical conditions already studied to some extent in the past (daylighting, building maintenance, and utilization of the school facility), largely take future research in a new direction focused on adaptability, collaboration, and social interaction. Also, several of these hypotheses recommended a need to investigate the effects of these physical conditions on a variety of outcomes (not limited to achievement and behavior) and include probable mediators and moderators.

ACTIVITIES

1. Describe, in detail, a method you might use (other than the concept mapping approach described in this chapter) to identify a broad range of educational outcomes that are important to

educators. Develop the tool (e.g., questionnaire, interview protocol, etc.) that you would use. Describe your respondents and how you would involve them with the method you have selected.

How many respondents will you try to include? How will you analyze the data you collect?

2. Refine the hypotheses found in Table 14.4 to include one stem per sentence (or descriptor). That is, include only one idea per descriptor. This will produce several more subhypotheses. Utilize these subhypotheses to evaluate a physical environment by using a scale such as the Likert-type scale found in Chapters 12 and 13.

3. Determine the reliability of your "new scales" (instrument) by applying Cronbach's alpha for subscales, and test-retest or split-half to estimate the reliability for the entire questionnaire.

4. Compare the ratings of the selected school environments according to the subhypotheses (through application of your questionnaire) with measures of student outcomes that may be retrieved from the *school system level.*

REFERENCES

Bosch, S. J., & Pearce, A. R. (2003). Sustainability in public facilities: An analysis of guidance documents. *Journal of Performance of Constructed Facilities,* 17(1):9–18.

Bosch, S. J. (2003). *Identifying relevant variables for understanding how school facilities affect educational outcomes.* Unpublished doctoral dissertation, Georgia Institue of Technology.

Concept Systems Incorporated (2002). *Concept systems knowledge base.* http://www.conceptsystems.com/kb/cshelp.htm.

Delbecq, A. L., Van de Ven, A. H., & Gustafson, D. H. (1975). *Group techniques for program planning: A guide to nominal group and Delphi processes.* Glenview, IL: Scott, Foresman and Company.

Evans, G. W., & Maxwell, L. (1997). Chronic noise exposure and reading deficits: The mediating effects of language acquisition. *Environment and Behavior,* 29(5):638–657.

Heschong Mahone Group (1999). *Daylighting in schools: An investigation into the relationship between daylighting and human performance.* Fair Oaks, CA: The Pacific Gas and Electric Company for the California Board for Energy Efficiency Third Party Program. Also available at http://www.h-m-g.com.

Knott, J., & Wildavsky, A. (1980). If dissemination is the solution, what is the problem? *Knowledge: Creation, Diffusion, Utilization,* 1(4):537–578.

Lackney, J. A. (1996). *Quality in school environments: A multiple case study of the diagnosis, design and management of environmental quality in five elementary schools in the Baltimore City Public Schools from an action research per-*

spective. Unpublished doctoral dissertation, University of Wisconsin-Milwaukee, WI.

Linstone, H. A., & Turoff, M. (1975). *The Delphi method: Techniques and applications.* Boston: Addison-Wesley. Also available in updated form at http://www.is.njit.edu/pubs/delphibook.

Moore, C. M. (1987). *Group techniques for idea building.* Newbury Park, CA: Sage.

Moore, G. T., & Lackney, J. A. (1994). *Educational facilities for the twenty-first century: Research analysis and design patterns.* Milwaukee, WI: University of Wisconsin-Milwaukee, Center for Architecture and Urban Planning Research.

Nyden, P., & Wiewel, W. (Winter 1992). Collaborative research: Harnessing the tensions between researcher and practitioner. *The American Sociologist.* 4:43–55.

Schneider, M. (2002a). *Do school facilities affect academic outcomes?* Washington, DC: National Clearinghouse for Educational Facilities.

Schneider, M. (2002b). *Facilities and teaching: Teachers in Chicago and Washington DC assess how well school buildings support teaching.* Stony Brook, NY: State University of New York.

Trochim, W. M. K. (1989). An introduction to concept mapping for planning and evaluation. *Evaluation and Program Planning,* 12:1–16.

Young, E., Green, H., Roehrich-Patrick, L., Joseph, L., & Gibson, T. (2003). *Do K-12 school facilities affect education outcomes?* Nashville, TN: The Tennessee Advisory Commission on Intergovernmental Relations.

APPENDIX: FRAMEWORK OF PHYSICAL VARIABLES PLAUSIBLY RELATED TO EDUCATIONAL OUTCOMES*

FACTOR	ELEMENT	ITEM
FUNCTIONALITY	*Building Legibility*	Signage
		Relationship and visibility of spaces within building (i.e., how spaces for different types of activities are interconnected)
		Color and lighting
		Floor plan layout
		Scale of building elements relative to one another
		Interior materials
		Exterior materials
	Spatial Features	"Schools within a school": learning "houses" with clear, identifiable spaces if large school
		Learning environment geometric shape (e.g., fat-L, square, rectangular, changeable)
		Academic grade configuration (the manner in which grade levels are organized into a single school, e.g., k–3, k–5, 9–12, etc.)
		Informal gathering spaces
		A building of niches (allows many small groups to claim space and meet in regular locations)
		A town square (large area, all pass through) Centralized versus decentralized offices
		Location of noisy classes, similar classes (e.g., distribute or cluster science classrooms), etc. relative to one another
	Resource Spaces	Library or multiple spaces from where information can be retrieved
		Music rooms
		Creativity studios—art, sound, graphic
		Science laboratories
		Physical education facilities
		Spaces to conceive, design, build, test, and evaluate projects

(continued)

*This Framework is *not* intended to be an all-inclusive list of physical variables that may affect educational outcomes, nor one for which there is consensus among all the participants. However, it may serve as a springboard for future discussion among SFE researchers.

Appendix   Continued

FACTOR	ELEMENT	ITEM
		Presentation space—small and large
		Food service areas (location and accessibility)
		Outdoor learning spaces (natural, man-made)— availability and their location
		Conference and meeting spaces
		Professional spaces for teachers (including work rooms, lounges, offices, professional library)
	Size	Size of school grounds
		School building size (e.g., building square footage)
		Learning environment size (e.g., classroom square footage)
		Size and shape of circulation spaces
		Storage for teaching/learning supplies
	Adaptability	Site—the grounds that surround a school building (refers to having a site that accommodates diverse activities and changing needs)
		School building or buildings (refers to the ability to add on or renovate to meet changing needs/long-range planning)
		Learning environment (e.g., movable walls, portable equipment, etc.)
		Furnishings (seating that is comfortable and accommodating; diverse work surfaces—heights, sizes, and shapes)
		Task lighting (movable)
	Density (Crowdedness)	Overutilization of school building
SOCIABILITY	*Personalization*	Infusion of community culture into the fabric of the building
		Incorporation of student work into the school building
		Facility needs to "fit" the community in design and scale and should have an identifiable and recognizable "front door"
		Space to keep personal items (e.g., coats, boots)
		Lockable, personalized storage
		Student accessible files (students create and maintain an individual learning plan, portfolio of learning evidence)
		Individual workspace (student-"owned," allows a quiet home base, control of the modes of work)
		Spaces for students to personalize
	Privacy	Spaces for quiet reflection (however created—furnishings, walls, doors, etc.) for both students and faculty

Appendix   Continued

FACTOR	ELEMENT	ITEM
	Collaboration and Social Interaction	Access to group work area (allows team members to work on projects as mood and/or opportunity strikes)
		Team workstations/shared spaces
		Spaces to accommodate different-size groups
		Visible presentation area—present acquired knowledge, skills, and abilities
		Spaces for display of ideas, processes, projects, and products
		Spaces for production: design, testing, and evaluation, and application of products (student-developed—even products to sell)
		Commons areas appropriate for age group
		Informal learning spaces where students, teachers, and staff can further learn beyond the confines of the "classroom"
		Space supporting multidisciplinary activities
		Faculty collaborative space
		Interior windows for viewing of instructional areas
COMFORT, HEALTH, AND SAFETY	*Acoustical Comfort*	Interior noise (e.g., ambient, inside the learning environment)
		External noise (e.g., aircraft, highway)
		Acoustic privacy from other groups
		Individual control over acoustical conditions (e.g., closing of door and window)
	Visual Comfort	Daylighting (e.g., windows, clerestories, skylights)
		Electric lighting (general, task)
		Visual conditions (glare, contrast between print and paper, etc.)
		Views to the outside
		Individual control over visual conditions (e.g., illumination level)
	Thermal Comfort	Air-conditioning for cooling (e.g., presence, type)
		Heating
		Relative humidity
		Individual control over thermal conditions (e.g., ventilation, temperature)
	Indoor Air Quality	Adequate ventilation
		Presence or absence of pollutants indoors (e.g., mold, VOCs, etc.)

(continued)

Appendix   Continued

FACTOR	ELEMENT	ITEM
	Safety and Security	Sight lines within building
		Child's perceived safety
		Telephones in classroom (serve as a back-up security device)
		Site safety (visible entries, site lighting, alarms, etc.)
		Presence of school safety officers with easy access and visibility
		Presence of community, business, and parent partners and volunteers throughout the building to add extra sets of adult eyes and create that sense of "safe presence"
		Secure storage of collective projects in process
AESTHETICS AND APPEARANCE	*Sensory Stimulation*	Floor coverings
		Wall coverings or treatments
		Colors
		Ability to use music to stimulate thinking, reflection, or action
		Alternatives to the intercom system—ability to make announcements without "jarring" everyone's senses
	Maintenance	Cleanliness (upkeep, sanitary conditions)
		Quality of learning environment conditions (appearance of furniture, walls, etc.; deteriorating plaster; water stains; paint condition)
		Age of the school building
		Building improvements/modernization
RESOURCES	*Community Resources*	Visitors easily accommodated (parking, access, work areas)
		Proximity of school building to community
		Space for community and business representatives, volunteers, and parents within the school
		Learning spaces within the community—shared spaces such as libraries, physical fitness centers, and museums
		Small business incubator space
	Technology Resources (Students and Staff)	Computers and Internet access (data ports, electric outlets, wireless technology, etc.)
		Accessible phone, copiers, fax—especially important if students are working with business and community partners in producing "real-world" solutions
		School building as a teaching tool (e.g., observed power generation from solar panel)

Appendix   Continued

FACTOR	ELEMENT	ITEM
	Human Resources (Within the School)	Spatial integration of teachers, counselors, and students for access to intellectual and career advice (advice is obtained without special trips through unwelcoming main administrative territory)

MODELS, EXAMPLES, AND APPLICATIONS

In Part VIII we describe and explain some tools for school planning that complement the design process, which is supported by all eight premises for developing school facilities. Chapter 5 included the expression of a need to forecast student population, a vital component for planning a capital project, acknowledging that the demand for resources is greater than those available. Planning a capital project also requires collaboration and cooperation between the school and community.

Three detailed aspects of planning are addressed in Chapters 15, 16, and 17. Chapter 15 explains how to conduct a student population analysis in a spreadsheet format, complemented by the premise that management is systematic and data-driven. An example of planning and design is provided in Chapter 16—strategic planning, where the set of activities draws on all eight premises shown in the table below. There are other good procedures for planning, but we selected the ten-step model for strategic planning because of its applicability. Finally, defining space needs is presented in detail in Chapter 17. A very critical design issue is determining space needs, while a closely related critical planning issue is determining accurate and reliable student population forecasts.

Premises for Developing School Facilities

PREMISE	DESCRIPTOR
Premise 1	Strong leadership is essential.
Premise 2	The school system has a defined direction—a mission and a vision.
Premise 3	Long-range goals and objectives are established.
Premise 4	The educational program's goals and objectives are translated into physical places.
Premise 5	Planning and design activities are integrated.
Premise 6	Management is systematic; data, and goal driven.
Premise 7	The demand for resources is greater than those available.
Premise 8	The school and community should work cooperatively and in a collaborative manner.

CHAPTER FIFTEEN

STUDENT POPULATION FORECASTING

It is highly important for the reader to understand that the contents of this chapter are based on the experiences of many individuals, dating back to activities preceding the survey movement. Perhaps the most important item for the reader to know regarding the application of the models is that *"students 'flow'" through the system (kindergarten to grade 1, grade 1 to grade 2, etc.).* This is a fact that supports the basic functioning of the forecasting models presented in this chapter. Readers who are mathematically or quantitatively challenged might have to labor extremely hard to deal with details presented here. Consequently, they may wish to work with others in developing student population forecasts.

All components of the chapter are linked through some form of quantitative analysis. Planners and demographers may wish to modify their own models for forecasting after reviewing the procedures in this chapter. Clearly, forecasting student population is very risky, and no individual to date has ever been 100 percent accurate in this volatile area of planning. Consider the disclaimer that the models presented here will only help approximate future student population changes.

BACKGROUND

In reviewing the history of school facilities planning, various procedures for estimating student population were discovered. Early attempts to forecast student population were discussed by Englehardt (1925), who concluded that accurate census data and forecasting techniques were not available. By the 1940s and during the survey movement, extrapolations were made on the basis of average change over time. They were most frequently completed according to straight-line estimates based on the average percentage of student population change over the past three to five years. The "child census" was also utilized to determine probable student enrollments. For example, during the summer months it was the job of the school principal to update the school census by visiting homes in the community to develop an estimate of the next school year's enrollment. These records were maintained as a basis for planning for student population growth or decline. During this era, varying versions of the cohort survival ratio began to be introduced as the basis for student population forecasting. A problem arose with this method because various people applied and interpreted it differently. Some planners used the average ratios by grade level and subsequently forecasted a straight line based on average change. Others linked the average ratio between resident live births and grade 1 to district resident live births. This average became a fixed ratio multiplied by resident live births (usually for a forecast of five years).

The progression of calculating the student population forecast went from all division and multiplication operations being completed by hand to the use of the electric calculator (early 1960s). Up until the advent of more widespread use of the computer in the late 1960s, the job of forecasting with the survival ratio technique was one of great difficulty. The time to complete a forecast for a school district was enormous. Furthermore, there were many locations within the mathematical matrix to make errors that would result in an unreliable forecast, assuming that all the basic data were correct. There were at least 156 different calculations needed to develop a five-year forecast for the total school district (K–12). A school system having two elementary schools, one middle school, and one high school required approximately 441 distinct mathematical calculations by hand or calculator (including the total and separate estimates). Depending on the number of schools and their grade level composition, the job of forecasting could take from several days to several weeks prior to computer applications with punched cards.

More recently, electronic databases using spreadsheets have replaced the traditional methods (electric calculators and punched cards) of forecasting student population. Often, the forecasting models have been based on various beliefs and experiences of the people in charge of forecasting. In some school systems, a local "guru" estimated student population. In this case, a guru was a person very close to the community who was able to intuitively forecast student population. These people were usually found in small school districts where little population change was expected. The day of the guru is close to an end.

Arguing the efficacy of forecasting models here is of little value, since most of them have positive aspects amenable to a particular population at any given time. Models based on linear regression do well in areas where trends are steady, but they do not account for unexpected population shifts or fluctuating birthrate trends. Multivariate models are usually more accurate than the x and y graphs in a standard linear model, but their limitation is linearity. Consequently, a model (modified from the survival ratio technique) utilizing resident live births, current net enrollments, and adjustments for demographic trends is presented in this text, taking into consideration the trends over the past five years and changes in the student population as well as rates of resident live births (RLBs).

Several assumptions support this model. One primary assumption is that the future enrollment trends follow the school district's RLB and migration trends. "In migration" as well as "out migration" and death rates are accounted for in the basic data set. This feature is difficult to explain, since it is straightforward and one may be expecting a more complicated data set that is labor-intensive and expensive to generate; however, the best explanation of how these variables are included is that they are "bundled" into the data set. One particular confounding variable in forecasting is accounting for special education enrollment trends. This has been a problem because definitions of exactly who is a special education student change as education policy changes. Another problem arises when school policy allows for the grade-level retention of students. Retained students repeat a grade level and therefore a retention ratio greater than 1 may be created (students overaccumulate in one grade). To account for these problems more accurately, the suggested solution is to conduct frequent forecasts. This is not a major task today with electronic databases, spreadsheets, and geographic information systems, as compared to the past when calculating the rates of change and forecasts was extremely time-consuming.

In addition to the basic research unit at the school system level, each school principal should be equipped to forecast the student population, at least with the spreadsheet programs presented in this text. Building level principals are closer to the student attendance area than any other person in school administration. Furthermore, the spreadsheets of the forecasting models presented in this section can be understood with serious study (special knowledge of Excel is extremely helpful), since they parallel the track that students take from grade level to grade level by year. Once proper data entry has been accomplished, it becomes a simple task to develop a student population forecast with any of these models.

Some larger school systems are turning to Geographic Information Systems (GIS) for analyzing and presenting data that assist in master planning. As more competition is experienced in this growing field, we expect the costs of GIS software and data entry to decline. Presently, one major problem is the intensity required for data input, since the current location of the student is vital to the GIS. This aspect is labor-intensive, but integrated information systems (including the student's geographic location, age, grade level, academic or vocational track, etc.) are expected to emerge through technology improvements, therefore minimizing the labor required for data entry in the current GIS technology.

Another current problem is finding people with adequate expertise to operate software and interpret databases using geospatial information. Educational planners will need to acquire expertise in this new technology and be able to link it to known forecasting models to verify trends generated by GIS. The algorithms incorporated into some GIS technology may need verification. For example, including only three years of base data (net enrollment data) weakens the overall forecast. A comparison of current GIS data with the output of the models shown in this chapter (five years of base data) is a positive step in finding the true enrollment and refining forecasted enrollment trends.

GIS output may replace student locator maps (spot maps), and integrate data into a forecasting model to show various scenarios regarding school attendance boundaries, transportation routes, and student and total population density patterns. GIS provides the foundation for organizing and collecting data, represents student density visually in the form of maps and zones, enhances scenarios ("what if" analysis), and aids in planning for change in student demographics. Regardless of the GIS technology employed, there will continue to be a need to verify student population forecasts. In many geographic areas, the cost and time required to operate GIS may not be justified; therefore, it remains important for planners to be able to forecast student enrollment with methods independent of GIS technology, which currently might produce more

information than the cost could reasonably justify. In order to stay up-to-date with this emerging technology, we recommend that planners and architects attend conferences and track GIS developments on their favorite Internet search engines by typing in the keyword "GIS." One promising worldwide source for data analysis is the Environmental Systems Research Institute, which was founded in 1969.

Notwithstanding the emerging GIS technology, the models presented here are intended to serve as possible verification techniques for schools having employed the GIS technology and also assist master planning in places employing more traditional methods of forecasting. These examples are coded for Microsoft Excel spreadsheets, but any spreadsheet program may be applied once the basic formulas are understood. The sample data sets (included in electronic form at www.ablongman.com/edleadership) presented here were taken from existing school systems, bringing more of a challenge to planning than if the data were manufactured to make certain points about the various idiosyncrasies of the models. The following steps reveal *how to* forecast student population with an electronic spreadsheet. This adapted procedure was programmed according to a modified grade progression ratio model (Tanner, 1971; Tanner & Holmes, 1985).

Student population forecasting requires careful study of demographic trends. After completing the steps outlined below, the planner may make adjustments in the base forecast according to the findings in the demographic analysis. One primary set of information may be found in the population pyramid provided by the U.S. Census Bureau. Density plots by ZIP code and census block are also vital to ensure a more reliable forecast. Finding plans for housing developments and determining how many students per household may be expected are essential steps in achieving more accurate student population forecasts.

Long-range student population forecasts are not frequently recognized as important by state education agencies in the United States. The temporary classroom (often "trailers") market thrives on state and local educational policies that forbid the allocation of government funds for school construction, until the student population has overcrowded the schools. Few geographic areas in the United States are able to plan for public school classrooms and build them before overcrowding occurs. Consequently, this policy may be harmful to learning, since "trailers" frequently have inferior acoustics and poor air circulation systems that make a background noise in excess of 35 decibels, which disturbs teaching and learning. The effects of noise on cognition are closely related to specific types of noise, such as chronic noise or continuous exposure to noise (Evans & Maxwell, 1997).

In addition to being unsafe in severe weather, these temporary classrooms are classified as "slum architecture." One can only speculate as to the damage done to the students' affective dimension of learning when exposed to these temporary classrooms.

The policy limitations may eventually be overcome as the general population begins to discover that effective and efficient planning for new schools, well in advance of a student population explosion or decline, can be achieved. With the various models and databases that exist, as well as those that are emerging, the general public and governmental decision makers should place more confidence in forecasting in the future than has occurred in the past. The validity and accuracy of the procedures discussed in the following sections should improve the perceptions of student population forecasting currently held by some policy makers.

ESTIMATING STUDENT ENROLLMENT: THE MODIFIED GRADE PROGRESSION RATIO MODEL

While it is not the intention of the authors to complicate enrollment forecasting beyond comprehension, it is important for the reader to understand that the process is highly technical and does not allow one to engage in cursory reading with the expectation of a comprehensive understanding. One basic premise of the model is that ratios may be calculated on the

basis of how students "flow" through the school system by grade level and school year. The first phase of the forecasting model below assumes that the recent trends will continue into the future. This is a start toward making a reliable forecast, but there are factors such as change in demographics that must be factored into the final forecast. The number of old and new houses and types of housing generate valuable information needed to adjust the results of the first phase of the model. Age of the female population and birthrates are important variables, and the primary emphasis should be on housing and who inhabits the houses. The size of lots on which the new houses are built is an important bit of information for the planner, and we may expect large lots to correlate with fewer students and small lots to parallel larger student populations. Apartments and "trailer" courts correlate positively with larger numbers of students. These factors notwithstanding, the age of homes comes to bear on the school's student population. Housing cycles must be studied as part of the accompanying demographic analysis. During a housing cycle, the school age population usually undergoes a change. Younger couples usually occupy new homes in the "mid to lower ranges of cost" in their first five years of marriage. Sometimes, more than one family may occupy a new home. During the second phase, which lasts about fifteen years, the birthrates are lower, bringing a decline in elementary school enrollments, but an increase in middle and high school enrollments. In the third phase, the older inhabitants are often replaced by families of lower socioeconomic status, which usually have larger numbers of school-age students. Too often, these communities become slums and blight sets in. Hence, it is vital to consider housing cycles as a major factor in student population forecasting. These topics are covered extensively in Tanner (1971).

Step 1. Obtain Resident Live Births for the County Where the School District Is Located

In some states, the Bureau of Vital Statistics provides this set of data, while in others it may be housed in other departments; nonetheless, it is important to understand that a resident live birth is coupled directly to the address of the mother. The birth of a child by a woman residing in one county, but giving birth to a child in a hospital located in another county, will be recorded as follows: a resident live birth in the county of residence and a live birth in the county where the hospital is located. This distinction is important, since in many areas not having hospitals for child delivery, it may be possible to mix live births and resident live births in the same data set. Mixing these two types of data will obviously yield unreliable results in a forecast.

Another possible problem area arises with the reporting of resident live births by calendar year as compared to the school year. Schools operate on a split year (2006–2007, 2007–2008, etc.), while vital statistics are reported on an annual basis. This distinction is important since overlap occurs in the number of resident live births and number of children entering the program five years later (kindergarten, e.g.). This problem is minimized through averaging over five or more years, not three years as is seen in some existing models, and should pose little concern for the ratio of RLBs to the number of students entering the school system. A child born in 2010 should enter prekindergarten in 2014, kindergarten in 2015, and first grade in 2016. If the birth date of the child were after a set date, say, October 1 in some states, then this child would actually enter prekindergarten in 2015, kindergarten, for example, in 2016, and first grade in 2017. On the average, however, over a five-year period this overlap should not influence the final forecast negatively. This "curve smoothing" function supports the premise that using a five-year data set is superior to three years or less. The limitation to this assumption is that the future RLBs may not be the same ratio (births to child-bearing population) as it was for the historical data set.

Since we are reviewing how to set up a five-year forecast, *the most recent ten consecutive years of resident live births are needed* for the forecasting model. If more than one school district exists in a

county and the school boundaries have not changed over the past five years, there is no problem with utilizing the recent net enrollments and the ten years of resident live births for forecasting enrollments for each school or school system. If boundary changes have taken place, then the net enrollment should be pro-rated (approximated) from the time of the changed boundary lines. The latter problem can be difficult to solve and may require "best estimates" or geospatial technologies such as GIS to redefine the new data set and boundary lines.

In the model (Table 15.1) the resident live births are entered in row 5 (columns D–H and S–W). That is, five years of resident live births match the net enrollment numbers in columns D–H, and the most recent five years match the prediction matrix in columns S–W (Part C in Table 15.1). The appropriate year of the resident live birth is listed in row 4, columns D–H and S–W. *It is vitally important that the resident live birth be matched appropriately with the year that the student is expected to enter the school system.* We have elected to use actual years instead of mathematical symbols to keep this important part of the model simple. Ten years of RLBs are necessary for a five-year forecast.

An issue in selecting the most recent ten years of resident live births is linked directly to verification of recent reports of resident live births. When requesting the past ten years of resident live births, the most recent year is usually not verified; hence, that data set may not be totally accurate to forecast five years of enrollment. Consequently, it is often necessary to estimate this final year because the unverified data set is lower than the actual count. We suggest that this estimate should correlate to the fertility rates of the female population in the county where the school is located. In lower socioeconomic communities, the rate will usually be higher. Furthermore, smaller homes on small lots in low socioeconomic neighborhoods correlate positively with higher birthrates than larger homes on larger lots. Government assisted housing also correlates positively with higher

TABLE 15.1   Student Population Forecasting Model—Total System

PART A: NET ENROLLMENT AND RESIDENT LIVE BIRTHS—TOTAL SYSTEM

1	C	D	E	F	G	H
2	School Year >	2001–02	2002–03	2003–04	2004–05	2005–06
3	4 YR K RLBs >	2771	2617	2690	2561	2512
4	Year of Birth for K >	1996	1997	1998	1999	2000
5	Resident Live Births >	2697	2771	2617	2690	2561
6	4 YR K	125	144	149	146	117
7	Kindergarten	1560	1515	1504	1467	1423
8	Grade 1	1686	1661	1619	1549	1543
9	Grade 2	1597	1559	1545	1533	1463
10	Grade 3	1531	1531	1491	1501	1471
11	Grade 4	1495	1468	1502	1431	1448
12	Grade 5	1528	1463	1424	1445	1399
13	Total Elementary >	9522	9341	9234	9072	8864
14	Total ES EXED >	1045	1079	1083	1122	1152
15	Grade 6	1494	1440	1433	1384	1391
16	Grade 7	1408	1433	1409	1375	1374
17	Grade 8	1386	1369	1403	1437	1336
18	Total Middle School >	4305	4256	4260	4216	4118
19	Total MS EXED >	628	570	618	644	666
20	Grade 9	1698	1721	1693	1738	1797
21	Grade 10	1423	1474	1497	1405	1411
22	Grade 11	1266	1216	1223	1247	1294
23	Grade 12	1133	1128	1084	1110	1127
24	Total High School	5520	5539	5497	5500	5629
25	Total HS EXED >	670	677	696	703	697
26						
27	Grand Total >	21690	21462	21388	21257	21126
28						
29		5 yrs. ago	4 yrs. ago	3 yrs. ago	Last year	Present

PART B: AVERAGE RATE OF STUDENT FLOW BETWEEN GRADES—TOTAL SYSTEM (BASED ON FORMULAE IN PART D OF THE APPENDIX)

I		J	K	L	M	N	O
2							
3							
4							
5							AVERAGES
6	Pre K	0.045	0.055	0.055	0.057	0.0466	0.05182213
7	K	0.578	0.547	0.575	0.545	0.5556	0.56017077

(*continued*)

TABLE 15.1   Continued

PART B: AVERAGE RATE OF STUDENT FLOW BETWEEN GRADES—TOTAL SYSTEM (BASED ON FORMULAE IN PART D OF THE APPENDIX

I		J	K	L	M	N	O
8	Grade 1		0.616	0.584	0.592	0.5736	0.59141004
9	Grade 2		0.925	0.93	0.947	0.9445	0.93654936
10	Grade 3		0.959	0.956	0.972	0.9596	0.96153307
11	Grade 4		0.959	0.981	0.96	0.9647	0.96608933
12	Grade 5		0.979	0.97	0.962	0.9776	0.9720778
13							
	Total ES EXED						
14		0.11	0.116	0.117	0.124	0.13	0.11923664
15	Grade 6		0.942	0.979	0.972	0.9626	0.96411061
16	Grade 7		0.959	0.978	0.96	0.9928	0.97248557
17	Grade 8		0.972	0.979	1.02	0.9716	0.98571866
18							
	Total MS EXED						
19		0.146	0.134	0.145	0.153	0.1617	0.14787126
20	Grade 9		1.242	1.237	1.239	1.2505	1.24191695
21	Grade 10		0.868	0.87	0.83	0.8119	0.84491592
22	Grade 11		0.855	0.83	0.833	0.921	0.85956088
23	Grade 12		0.891	0.891	0.908	0.9038	0.89845398
24							
	Total HS EXED						
25		0.121	0.122	0.127	0.128	0.1238	0.12437136
26							

PART C: FIVE-YEAR STUDENT POPULATION FORECAST—TOTAL SYSTEM (BASED ON FORMULAE IN PART E OF THE APPENDIX)

P–Q	R (Part C)	S	T	U	V	W
	School Year >	2006–07	2007–08	2008–09	2009–10	2010–11
	4 YR K RLBs >	2592	2564	2583	2574	2564
	Year of Birth >	2001	2002	2003	2004	2005
	Resident Live Births >	2512	2592	2564	2583	2574
	4 YR K	134	133	134	133	133
	Kindergarten	1407	1452	1436	1447	1442
	Grade 1	1515	1486	1533	1516	1528
	Grade 2	1445	1418	1391	1436	1420
	Grade 3	1407	1390	1364	1338	1380
	Grade 4	1421	1359	1342	1318	1292
	Grade 5	1408	1381	1321	1305	1281
	Total REG K–5 >	8737	8619	8522	8493	8476

TABLE 15.1   Continued

PART C: FIVE-YEAR STUDENT POPULATION FORECAST—TOTAL SYSTEM (BASED ON FORMULAE IN PART E OF THE APPENDIX)

P–Q	R (Part C)	S	T	U	V	W
	Total E S EXED >	1135	1120	1108	1104	1102
	Grade 6	1349	1357	1332	1274	1258
	Grade 7	1353	1312	1320	1295	1239
	Grade 8	1354	1333	1293	1301	1277
	Total REG M S >	4056	4002	3945	3870	3773
	Total M S EXED >	656	647	638	626	610
	Grade 9	1659	1682	1656	1606	1616
	Grade 10	1518	1402	1421	1399	1357
	Grade 11	1213	1305	1205	1222	1203
	Grade 12	1163	1090	1173	1083	1098
	Total REG H S >	5553	5479	5455	5309	5272
	Total H S EXED	691	681	678	660	656
	Grand Totals					
	School Year >	2000–2001	2001–2002	2002–2003	2003–2004	2004–2005
	Elementary Schools	9872	9739	9629	9597	9578
	Middle Schools	4712	4649	4582	4496	4384
	High Schools	6244	6160	6133	5969	5928
	School System	20827	20549	20345	20062	19890

resident live births. Even the religious background of the people in the school system's service area should be given serious consideration when estimating birthrates. The positive aspect of this estimate, assuming only a five-year forecast, is that only a very small portion of the forecast is influenced by the most recent year of resident live births. If the forecast is to be ten or more years, then special attention should be paid to estimating resident live births because any forecast beyond five years will be an estimate based on an estimate—a risky situation at best. Such a task requires a highly skilled demographer, and paying for this service may not always be worth the difference in obtaining a "best guess" estimate from a local "guru" or a well-trained demographer. To eliminate an outright guess, the 10th year of RLBs may be estimated with a regression line, using the previous nine years as data points. The positive

side to estimating the 10th year of resident live births in a five-year forecast is that the estimate influences only the 4 YR K in the model shown in Part C of Table 15.1.

Step 2. Determine the Net Enrollment by Grade Level for the Past Five Years

Entering net enrollment and resident live births properly in the spreadsheet is second only in importance to obtaining reliable data. Net enrollment data are entered into the matrix, rows 6–25, columns D–H for the entire school system as shown in Table 15.1, Part A. The resident live births are entered as follows: row 3, columns D–H and S–W contain the resident live births for prekindergarten for 4-year-old children [identified as 4 YR K RLBs in the model], while row 5, columns D–H and S–W contain the resident live births for ten years used to develop ratios for kindergarten enrollment. This set of resident live births may also be employed to develop the ratios for the first grade (see Table 15.1, Part B) [note that the data in row 3 are identical to the data in row 5. However, it has been moved one column to the left (see the actual spreadsheet formulae for clarification) to match the prekindergarten (4 YR K RLBs >)]. In the calendar year 1996 a total of 2,697 resident live births were recorded in the county of this school system. These data match the kindergarten enrollment in the model. In 1997 a total of 2,771 resident live births were recorded, and this set matches the data for the four-year kindergarten in row 6.

In summary, data to satisfy the model are matched as follows: Data in row 3 are applied to the data in row 6, while the data found in row 5 correspond to the data shown in rows 7 and 8, respectively. The reasoning here is that better ratios for prekindergarten, kindergarten, and grade 1 may be determined in this analysis, as compared to the traditional method of relating resident live births to prekindergarten, prekindergarten to kindergarten, and then kindergarten ratios to grade 1. Our experience reveals that accuracy can be sacrificed if this approach is not followed in modeling.

Research conducted by the authors has shown a better or more reliable forecast does not necessarily result by using more than five years of information, but drops when less than five years is used as a baseline data set. The models require net enrollment by grade level for five consecutive years. Net enrollment may be defined as the maximum number of students that might attend school on any given day. When conducting studies in the fall or winter seasons in the United States for various schools, we request net enrollment as it existed on October 15 of each school year in order to maintain consistency across the data sample. If the study is being completed in the springtime or summertime, then we usually request enrollment data for March 15 over the past five years. As noted above, if boundary changes have taken place during the

past five years, then the data set should be pro-rated according to the enrollment generated by the most current attendance boundary.

Step 3. Enter the Data Sets in the Model

Enrollment data are coded into a spreadsheet as shown (rows 7–25, columns D–H in Table 15.1, Part A). The symbol EXED refers to the enrollment of special education students. This enrollment data set may best be utilized as a percentage of the total for each classification (elementary, middle, and high school). The entire matrix includes thirty-two rows and utilizes columns C–W. Columns A and B were reserved for the school system name and other relevant information. Column C reveals the descriptors of the data per row. For example, the school year (in row 2) matches the school system enrollment data found in rows 6–25, columns D–H. All the data in Part A may be entered manually (grand totals are calculated automatically, row 27).

Rows 2–5 in columns D–H contain vital information that must be aligned properly with the enrollment data in rows 6–25. For example, in the school year 2001–2002, there were 125 students enrolled in the kindergarten for 4-year-old students (4 YR K), while there were 1,560 students attending kindergarten in the school system. This small number (125 prekindergarten students) is indicative of a limited enrollment as a result of school policy for only a few prekindergarten students and is usually tied directly to limited funding for these programs at the state level (this number will vary as a result of school policy on prekindergarten). Special attention should be given to rows 3 and 5 because the same data are shown, although these data are shifted to the left when keying in the year of birth. For example, in Part A, note that in 1997 there were 2,771 RLBs (resident live births). These appear above 1996 in school year 2001–2002 as 4 YR K RLBs. The logic here is that by shifting data in row 5 to the left by one cell (row 3), it may be simpler for the data coder, since it is important to view the data logically before making the forecast. Rates are established between RLBs for prekindergarten (4 YR K), kindergarten, and grade 1 as follows: For the 4 YR K, the data in row 6 are divided by the data in row 3 by year, and for kindergarten, the data in row 7 are divided by the data in row 5.

Regarding data input, the double arrows shown in Part A indicate the duplicated data used for calculating the ratios between 4 YR K and kindergarten, while the brackets link the numbers in each row used to determine ratios (e.g., see Part B where 125/2,771 = 0.045, 1,045/9,522 = 0.11, etc.). Slanted arrows point to the direction of student flow and also reveal how the ratios are determined (e.g., see Part B where 1,661/2,697 = 0.616 and 1,559/1,686 = 0.925).

Students born in 1997 (2,771—row 5, column E) entered kindergarten in the school year 2002–2003, while some of this same group (125) entered the four-year program in 2001–2002. This establishes the rate of 125/2,771 = 0.045 as found in Part B (row 6, column J). The other reason for employing the 1997 RLBs is to establish the ratio between RLBs and kindergarten; for example, 1,515/2,771 = 0.547 (row 7, column K).

Other ratios in Part B are determined according to the student flow through the school system on a grade-by-year basis. The 0.616 (row 8, column K) is the rate between 1,661 and 2,697 (the 1996 RLBs and the 2002–2003 enrollment for grade 1). The complexities of the model may best be understood by going directly to the Excel program available online and clicking on areas that may not be clear to the reader.

Averages found in Part B are completed by row. They are then applied to (multiplied by) the appropriate data found in Part C.

The data in rows 3, 4, and 5 in Part C pertain to resident live births. For example, it is vitally important to ensure that the school year is aligned with the appropriate 4 YR K RLBs. In the 2006–2007 school year, the number of resident live births is shown as 2,592 (row 3, cell S)—these students were born in 2002. The 2,592 resident live births

(for 2002) also are used to calculate the rates for kindergarten in column T and grade 1 in column U. By referring to Table 15.1 or clicking on each cell in the electronic version of this model, the calculations will become apparent to the reader. With more sophisticated programming, the model may be tied to automated updating of input data as net enrollment changes.

The remainder of the spreadsheet is the analysis and forecast based on the formulae as shown in Parts D and E below. Once the data are coded, the program automatically calculates the forecast.

All the averages calculated in Part B (shown in column O) are applied to the data set as shown in Part E (see the appendix at chapter's end), with the one exception being special education (coded as EXED). Since policy changed frequently for the school system in this example, the ratio of special education students to the other students (column N) was utilized to be reflective of the most current policy. This ratio may be the best estimate of current policy regarding special education classifications.

The ratio in column J, row 6 was determined as follows: (D6/D3 = 125/2,771 = 0.045). This is the ratio of resident live births in 1997 to prekindergarten enrollment in 2001–2002. The average rate of resident live births to entry in the four-year kindergarten program (prekindergarten) was 0.05182213, or about 5 percent. This low percentage may be interpreted according to school policy. In the case of the school system represented by this data set, the prekindergarten program was just beginning. There were other competing preschool programs in this community offered by churches and private schools. The ratio in row 8, column K was determined as follows: E8/D5 = 1,661/2,697 = 0.615869... = 0.616. Here, approximately 61.6 percent of the resident live births, as well as migration and death rates, accounted for in the enrollment data, for this school district enrolled in the first grade. Therefore, the averages found in Part B (Table 15.1) include more than just the ratios between resident live births and enrollment. The model is more than a series of averages, given the definition of the net enrollment and all the dynamics that are included in it.

Three questions will help one to understand exactly how the forecast unfolds in Part C:

1. How is the kindergarten forecast for the 2006–2007 school year determined?

   $O7 \times S5 = 0.56017077 \times 2,512 = 1,407$

2. How is the third grade forecast for the 2006–2007 school year determined?

   $O10 \times H9 = 0.96153307 \times 1,463 = 1,407$

3. How is the fourth grade forecast for the 2009–2010 school year determined?

   $O11 \times U10 = 0.966608933 \times 1,364 = 1,318$

These questions assist in the understanding of exactly how students move through the system; therefore, the model depicts this flow and converts averages and enrollments into an initial forecast, which may be adjusted with information from a demographic analysis. In some cases, there may appear to be rounding error of approximately one student per grade level forecast. This may be adjusted in the Excel program to minimize the error range resulting from rounding.

Step 4. (Optional) Develop a 10-Year Student Population Forecast

Developing a ten-year forecast requires a comprehensive demographic analysis and extensive testing of models and validation of data sets. Some documents available from various sources will probably reveal contradictory information; hence, it is the duty and responsibility of the planner to validate the information supporting his or her forecast. One way to start the process of completing a ten-year forecast is to extend an additional five years of resident live births. This involves the estimation of resident live births, a process extremely difficult to validate. Therefore, it is risky, but not impossible to begin the development of a forecast ten or more years, assuming a defensible set of resident live births can be developed beyond the required first five years of the forecast.

Proceeding to a ten-year forecast and beyond requires an undertaking based on thorough demographic analysis, especially the fertility rates of women in the childbearing population (generally ages 14–40). Fertility rates vary by culture, religion, race, and also geographic location. It is necessary to develop a population pyramid, with special attention to the number of women entering and leaving various age groups. In or out migration rates and death rates must also enter the data set. A demographic analysis to determine expected enrollment beyond five years can be costly because of the time needed to calculate various rates to complete an estimate. Simply computing a regression line for each year has a great probability of yielding an unreliable forecast. When making a long-range forecast, it is advisable for the planner to validate the data sets and the resulting forecast for a period of approximately three consecutive years for the purpose of adjusting the models and validating trends. This concept implies that school districts should calculate student populations on a continuous basis, or if an outside consultant is employed to complete a student population forecast, he or she should work with the school system at least three years to ensure the best forecast possible. A one-time forecast is frequently inadequate for sound planning.

ESTIMATING THE ENROLLMENT FOR VARIOUS LEVELS

One Elementary School

Regarding the above model, the procedures and formulae for the entire school system also apply when making a forecast for one elementary school within a larger district having several elementary schools. System data are replaced by school building-level data. The resident live births used for the entire system forecast remain the same.

One Middle School in a Large School System

In estimating enrollment for a single middle school in a system having two or more middle schools, all the system aggregate net enrollments for elementary schools are utilized as a basis for the forecast. The middle school's actual net enrollment for the past five years is entered into rows 15–19 (as shown in Table 15.1). Note that the symbol EXED refers to the enrollment of special education students. The electronic version of the Middle School Model is available at www.ablongman.com/edleadership.

One High School

In estimating enrollment for a single high school in a system having two or more high schools, all system data are utilized for prior grade levels (see, e.g., Table 15.1). Only the net enrollment for the high school, over the past five years, is entered.

Summary of Steps for the Electronic Spreadsheet

These steps assume familiarity with the electronic spreadsheet version of the model as presented in the above sections. They are straightforward and linear in nature:

- First, obtain the most recent ten years of resident live births.
- Acquire the most recent five years of net enrollment from the school system to be studied. This is by grade level and by school.
- Match RLB data with appropriate year of net enrollment (birth year with prekindergarten, kindergarten, and grade 1).
- Enter the data set according to years "matched" with enrollment. The model now will generate the five-year forecast.
- The results are ready for various adjustments according to the results of a thorough demographic analysis.

ADJUSTING THE STUDENT POPULATION FORECAST: A CASE STUDY OF SUNNY RIVER COUNTY

This section is part of a comprehensive study conducted for a county school system in 2004 by the Facilities Research and Planning Group (FRPG) and the School Design and Planning Laboratory (SDPL). The school system is located between two major cities, on a major highway linking the two cities, approximately 85 miles apart. It is slowly transitioning from rural to rural-suburban. All the data shown here are classified as public information. While the names of the school district and its schools have been changed, the analysis and conclusions are examples of a typical student population study recommended for master planning.

Resident live birth trends and basic assumptions about the forecasting models outlined in the previous section of this chapter help establish the basis for enrollment forecasting in the models employed below. Assumptions regarding the models will be reemphasized at appropriate places in the remainder of the case study. Table 15.2 on page 362 shows the trends in total population and resident live births for Sunny River County Schools. Overall, a steady increase is expected in total population with a slower increase in resident live births. Note that the birth rates per 1,000 of the total population are declining, on the five-year average.

In Table 15.3 on page 363, the student population enrollment data collected in October for the past five years (from 1999–2000 to 2003–2004) reveal a small decline in the elementary school population. In the middle schools there was a slight increase, while an 8.3 percent increase was experienced in the high school. The enrollment of the school system has increased by 3.3 percent since 1999–2000. FTE, as found in the following tables, represents Full Time Equivalent (sometimes referred to as net enrollment) students, and for the purpose of this case study indicates the maximum number of students that might attend school on any given day—a basic assumption employed in master planning for school facilities.

TABLE 15.2 Total Population of Sunny River County Compared to Resident Live Births

YEAR *	POPULATION	LIVE BIRTHS	BIRTHS/1,000
1990	17,113	301	17.60
1991	17,389	289	16.60
1992	17,665	311	17.67
1993	17,941	291	16.25
1994	18,217	292	16.04
1995	18,807	238	12.65
1996	19,397	252	13.05
1997	19,987	244	12.26
1998	20,577	305	14.80
1999	21,167	297	14.07
2000	21,757	296	13.64
2001	22,347	280	12.55
2002	22,952	262	11.44
2003	23,574	320	13.61
2004	24,213	295	12.19

*Estimates by FRPG & SDPL (total population is expected to average about 2.7 percent increase per year).
Source: U.S. Census and Division of Public Health.

Many of the variations found in Table 15.3 are a result of in migration, dropouts, some retention, and students who are attending private school, parochial school, and receiving home schooling. One of the better estimates of the actual number of students available to attend schools in Sunny River County is determined by the Factor of Potential™ (Table 15.4). This factor, an invention of the Facilities Research and Planning Group (FRPG), is determined by comparing school data and base census data. *When the factor is negative, the most likely explanation is that students moved into the area after the U.S. Census was completed.* Overall, the Factor of Potential Enrollments™ is 17 percent for grades K–12. Hence, 17 percent of the available students in the K–12 age group (5–17 years of age) *did not* attend public schools in Sunny River County in 2000. For grades 10–12, we note a factor of 30 percent indicating that there were 30 percent more students available for high school than actually enrolled. These factors include students attending private schools, those attending public schools in other areas, and students that dropped out of Sunny River County Public Schools.

FORECASTS BY YEAR AND GRADE LEVEL

Table 15.5 on page 364 reveals the basic scenario, assuming that future years will approximate recent trends in economics, population growth, and school curriculum. This forecast reveals an overall system increase of 5 percent through the school year 2008–2009. Fluctuations are expected in the school population over this time period, with increases in the student population resulting from occupancy of new housing instead of resident live births. Given the database of Full Time Equivalents and resident live births, the system forecast may be determined as in Table 15.5. In the prekindergarten through the grade 5 category, a 7.4 percent increase is expected within five years (144 students). Grades 3–5 can anticipate enrollment increases of 16 percent by 2008 (see Table 15.5).

Possible Adjustments Based on the Factor of Potential™

What would the student population be if Sunny River County Schools were serving all the students who are eligible to attend its school? While this scenario is less likely than the "business as usual" forecast in Table 15.5, it is important for us to see the maximum potential when completing a master plan for schools. Hence, *the Factor of Potential must be considered as one variable in adjusting the basic forecast.* The Factor of Potential (see Table 15.4) as an aspect in the overall analysis of student population is applied in Table 15.6 on page 365 in order to view the lost opportunities brought on by dropouts, home schools, and private and parochial schools. There are several ways to analyze the information in Table 15.5 by applying the factors found in Table 15.4. To introduce a limited amount of information for discussion, we have kept the analysis to three areas, the elementary school, middle school,

TABLE 15.3   October FTE Counts for Sunny River County Schools (1999–2000 to 2003–2004)

SCHOOL YEAR*	1999–2000	2000–2001	2001–2002	2002–2003	2003–2004
Pre-k + pre-school	190	182	154	181	186
Kindergarten	261	261	272	233	251
Grade 1	265	257	267	278	264
Grade 2	290	267	269	268	298
Grade 3	277	290	277	267	278
Grade 4	283	278	289	292	280
Grade 5	303	285	284	296	299
Total elementary	**1,869**	**1,820**	**1,812**	**1,815**	**1,856**
Grade 6	288	314	281	282	312
Grade 7	284	280	303	283	315
Grade 8	288	281	293	303	286
Total middle school	**860**	**875**	**877**	**868**	**913**
Grade 9	363	349	346	335	371
Grade 10	249	276	289	271	303
Grade 11	186	213	255	229	207
Grade 12	220	176	180	203	222
Total high school	**1,018**	**1,014**	**1,070**	**1,038**	**1,103**
Grand total	**3,747**	**3,709**	**3,759**	**3,721**	**3,872**
*Guide for school year dates	4 yrs. ago	3 yrs. ago	2 yrs. ago	Last year	Present

and high school factors, independently. For example, in the 2004–2005 school year, the opportunity for improvement included approximately 702 additional students (264 + 113 + 325 = 702; see Table 15.6 on page 365). This finding is based on the assumption that the public schools will actually serve *all* students in Sunny River County. While such an ideal scenario is possible for the public schools of Sunny River County, the opportunity for at least some of this potential to be reached exists through improving school programs and school facilities. The physical environment is a powerful factor in attracting students and parents, and is often overlooked in planning for new schools. For example, according to discussions with experienced planners, a new elementary

TABLE 15.4   Factors of Potential™ Enrollments for Sunny River County

GRADE LEVEL CATEGORY	2000 FTE	2000 CENSUS	DIFFERENCE (CENSUS—FTE)	FACTORS OF POTENTIAL (%)
k–4	1,353	1,601	248	15
5–9	1,509	1,717	208	12
10–12	665	953	288	30
k–12	3,527	4,271	744	17

TABLE 15.5   The Sunny River County School System Forecast (2004–2008)

PART A: FORECAST BY SCHOOL, GRADE LEVEL, AND YEAR
Johnson Primary School

SCHOOL YEAR	2004–2005	2005–2006	2006–2007	2007–2008	2008–2009
Pre-k + pre-school	200	189	177	216	199
Kindergarten	288	287	271	254	310
Grade 1	319	311	310	293	274
Grade 2	273	330	321	320	303
Total pre-k–2	**1,079**	**1,116**	**1,079**	**1,083**	**1,086**

Johnson Elementary School

SCHOOL YEAR >	2004–2005	2005–2006	2006–2007	2007–2008	2008–2009
Grade 3	303	277	335	326	325
Grade 4	285	311	284	344	335
Grade 5	285	291	317	290	350
Total Grades 3–5	**874**	**879**	**936**	**960**	**1,011**

Sunny River County Middle

SCHOOL YEAR	2004–2005	2005–2006	2006–2007	2007–2008	2008–2009
Grade 6	304	290	296	322	295
Grade 7	317	309	295	300	327
Grade 8	319	320	312	298	304
Total REG MS	**940**	**920**	**903**	**921**	**926**

Holloway High School

SCHOOL YEAR	2004–2005	2005–2006	2006–2007	2007–2008	2008–2009
Grade 9	344	383	385	376	359
Grade 10	304	282	314	316	308
Grade 11	253	253	235	262	263
Grade 12	184	225	225	209	233
Total REG HS	**1,085**	**1,143**	**1,160**	**1,162**	**1,162**

System Totals

SCHOOL YEAR	2004–2005	2005–2006	2006–2007	2007–2008	2008–2009
Elementary schools	1,953	1,995	2,015	2,043	2,097
Middle school	940	920	903	921	926
High school	1,085	1,143	1,160	1,162	1,162
School system—total	**3,977**	**4,058**	**4,078**	**4,126**	**4,185**

TABLE 15.5   Continued

PART B: SUMMARY OF EXPECTED CHANGE IN STUDENT POPULATION THROUGH 2008

GRADE LEVELS	PERCENT CHANGE FROM 2004–2008 (5 YEARS) (%)
PK–2	1
Grades 3–5	16
PK–Grade 5	7
Grades 6–8	−1
Grades 9–12	7
Total	**5**

school building may attract from 5 to 10 percent more students than an older school. Therefore, the differences in enrollment estimates between Tables 15.5 and 15.6 reveal an interesting area for decision making by the governing school board.

Exactly how much of the opportunity for improvement or OFI (the difference between the original forecast and the added FOP) can the school system capture? This factor is based on program improvements, social and economic conditions, and remodeled or new schools. Therefore, the OFI becomes a "what if" scenario that is studied for each school system. Note that the data set in Table 15.6 suggests a possible annual adjustment in enrollment of over 700 students per year. Decision makers must translate these opportunities into cost and

benefits and work accordingly to achieve a greater share of the OFI factor.

Possible Adjustments in the Forecast as a Result of an Expected Increase in Density

In the following section, we have detailed the three census tracts of Sunny River School District and their percentage changes over the past ten years, plus the forecast for 2005. The tract with the highest percentage change is Tract 503, with a 3.98 percent increase. This tract is located in the southern part of the county. An accompanying population density map (Figure 15.1, page 366) reveals the most likely areas where growth will occur.

TABLE 15.6   Factors of Potential™ (FOP) and Opportunity for Improvement™ (OFI)

SCHOOL YEAR	2004–2005	2005–2006	2006–2007	2007–2008	2008–2009
Elementary schools—FOP	2,217	2,264	2,287	2,319	2,380
OFI	264	269	272	276	283
Middle schools—FOP	1,052	1,030	1,011	1,031	1,037
OFI	113	110	108	110	111
High school—FOP	1,410	1,486	1,507	1,511	1,511
OFI	325	343	348	349	349
Total OFI	**702**	**723**	**728**	**735**	**743**

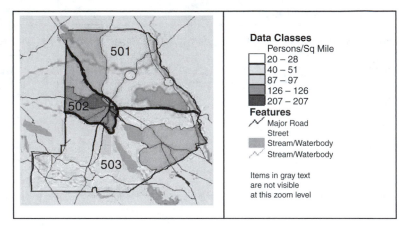

FIGURE 15.1   Density Map by Census Tract of Sunny River School District

Utilizing the census tract information in Table 15.7, the enrollment may be adjusted for any given year. The school enrolment for 2008–2008 is adjusted in Table 15.9 on page 368 according to the information in Table 15.8. For example, the estimated enrollment (original forecast or OF) is multiplied by the density index (DI) times the percentage growth (PG) factor [OF × DI × (1 + PG) = adjusted forecast]. The assumption is made that the 2005 estimated percentage growth is approximately the same for five years forward. The estimated school enrollment for Census Tract 501 is 2,097 × 0.35 × (1 + 0.0334) = 759 for the elementary schools. With the adjustments outlined here, enrollments in the elementary schools were adjusted upward by 946 − 926 = 20 students. This is the equivalent to one new classroom and an additional teacher, which may be a significant increase in many school systems.

A Guiding Factor for All Adjustments

Common knowledge among planners is the importance of the traditional population pyramid. This is one important database in estimating resident live births and other trends according to age classification. For example, a decline in the percentages of females, in the 15–40 years of age categories, from two consecutive census counts, may be an indicator of a decline in birthrates. This factor, however, might be investigated in more detail with respect to fertility rates by ethnic group. Such a comprehensive analysis, while labor-intensive, will improve the accuracy in the modified grade progression ratio model (the base model). Figure 15.2 on page 368 reveals a population pyramid for Sunny River County. The difference in the number of males and females is of interest in the 15–40 age groups, where the female population is lower.

The pyramid data become more meaningful for planning when a comparison is made (see Table 15.10 on page 369). For example, the number of females in 1990 was 3,339, while in 2000 the number had risen to 3,676. However, the percentage of females as compared to the total population declined in this age group. Related data are presented in the earlier Table 15.2. An increasing population and decrease in the number of live births per 1,000 of the total population are indicators that a more detailed analysis of the fertility rates by ethnic group may be necessary.

FINDINGS AND CONCLUSIONS FOR SUNNY RIVER SCHOOLS

Excluding any adjustments based on factors presented above, the Sunny River County Schools are expected to increase in student population by

TABLE 15.7   Expected Population by Census Tract

TRACT/BLOCK GROUP	1990 TOTAL POPULATION	2000 TOTAL POPULATION	2005 POPULATION PROJECTION	STRAIGHT-LINE AVERAGE ANNUAL INCREASE (%)
Tract 501	**6,006**	**8,013**	**9,352**	**3.34**
Block Group 1, Census Tract 501, Sunny River County	1,822	2,445	2,863	3.42
Block Group 2, Census Tract 501, Sunny River County	2,098	3,149	3,938	5.01
Block Group 3, Census Tract 501, Sunny River County	2,086	2,419	2,612	1.60
Tract 502	**5,002**	**5,212**	**5,321**	**0.42**
Block Group 1, Census Tract 502, Sunny River County	1,537	1,353	1,272	−1.20
Block Group 2, Census Tract 502, Sunny River County	934	1,477	1,906	5.81
Block Group 3, Census Tract 502, Sunny River County	2,531	2,382	2,312	−0.59
Tract 503	**6,105**	**8,532**	**10,228**	**3.98**
Block Group 1, Census Tract 503, Sunny River County	2,432	3,291	3,872	3.53
Block Group 2, Census Tract 503, Sunny River County	849	976	1,049	1.50
Block Group 3, Census Tract 503, Sunny River County	2,824	4,265	5,353	5.10
Sunny River County	**17,113**	**21,757**	**24,901**	**2.89**

5 percent over the next five years. This assumes no significant changes in housing, population, and resident live births. The elementary schools are expected to increase by 7 percent, and the middle schools will decrease by 1 percent, but the high schools will expand by 7 percent. These data may

TABLE 15.8   Density Index and Expected Increase in Each Census Tract

CENSUS TRACT	AVERAGE DENSITY	DENSITY INDEX	PERCENT GROWTH
501	112	0.35	3.34
502	143	0.44	0.42
503	68	0.21	3.98
Total	**323**	**1.00**	

TABLE 15.9   Adjustments in Estimates (Table 15.5) for 2008–2008 School Year

	ORIGINAL FORECAST	TRACT 501	TRACT 502	TRACT 503	ADJUSTED FORECAST OF × DI × (1 + PG)
Density index		0.35	0.44	0.21	
Percent growth		3.34%	0.42	3.98	
Elementary schools	2,097	759	927	458	2,144
Middle school	926	335	409	202	946
High school	1,162	408	513	254	1,175
School system—total	**4,185**				**4,265**

change as the population density changes in the northern and southern parts of the county.

More drastic changes could be experienced if a new school were constructed or if significant renovations occurred in any given school. The factor of potential for any given grade structure will yield the most likely maximum number of students.

All these data should assist decision makers in developing the master plans for Sunny River County schools. It should be emphasized that schools having 400 students have been shown to provide better student outcomes than large imper-

sonal schools. The literature is abundant on the "smaller is better" topic.

ACCURACY OF THE BASE MODEL

While the process presented in this chapter is extremely detailed, it represents a micro view of a data set that actually generates results for the macro level of planning. No planning or forecasting model is without error. In experiments conducted over several years by the authors, the error range for the grade progression ratio model is as follows:

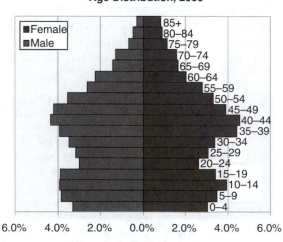

FIGURE 15.2   Population Pyramid for Sunny River County (2000)

TABLE 15.10   Female Age Distribution in Sunny River County (1990 and 2000)

AGE RANGE	1990 (NO.)	1990 (%)	2000 (NO.)	2000 (%)
0–4	592	3.5	660	3.0
5–9	637	3.7	762	3.5
10–14	618	3.6	860	4.0
15–19	647	3.8	741	3.4
20–24	538	3.1	572	2.6
25–29	665	3.9	667	3.1
30–34	752	4.4	735	3.4
35–39	737	4.3	961	4.4
40–44	604	3.5	989	4.5
45–49	538	3.1	849	3.9
50–54	413	2.4	719	3.3
55–59	378	2.2	612	2.8
60–64	370	2.2	444	2.0
65–69	341	2.0	364	1.7
70–74	302	1.8	346	1.6
75–79	256	1.5	249	1.1
80–84	173	1.0	200	0.9
85+	168	1.0	182	0.8

increases or decreases in population, we recommend annual updates to minimize prediction error. Once this model is tested in a particular school system, adjustments may be made according to demographics, housing occupancy permits, and other confounding variables in student population. Adjustments are incorporated after the forecast is made only if they are founded on fact, sound planning data, and "good judgment." Because of advances in technology and data analysis, it is advised that at least two forecasts be made per year—one with October data and the other with April data for public schools in the United States.

SUMMARY

A review of some of the history of student population forecasting with ties to the "survey movement" and the basic steps needed to complete a forecast has been provided in Chapter 15. No attempt was made to discuss other models for student population forecasting because they are complex and beyond the scope of this text. This includes Bayesian statistics (Tanner, 1971).

Examples were presented to help clarify the complex process of forecasting. GIS technology, population pyramids, and other appropriate methods for adjusting forecasts were included. A case study was provided to reveal how population density maps and the Factor for Potential could be applied in adjusting the results of the base models.

year 1, 1 percent; year 2, 1.5 percent; year 3, 2 percent; year 4, 2.5 percent; and year 5, 3 percent. These percentages are for rather stable populations, but are generally reduced by 1/2 with adjustments based on demographic data such as that found in the above sections. In areas having sharp

ACTIVITIES

1. In Figure 15.1, a complete school system data set reveals how information must be entered into the forecasting model. Select a school district and collect the net enrollments per grade level for the past five years and enter it into the model. Also, collect and enter the most recent ten consecutive years of resident live births for the school district (county, city, or another appropriate geographic area). Complete a five-year forecast for the school system by using Model I (total SYS). Go to www.ablongman.com/edleadership for Excel programs designed to solve this problem.

2. Given the various number of elementary, middle, and high schools in the district selected for activity 1, continue the student population forecast according to Model II (A or B), Model III, and Model IV. Go to http://www.ablongman.com/edleadership for Excel programs designed to solve these problems.

3. Using the same school system data set, develop a factor for potential and adjust the forecasts accordingly. Follow the discussion in the section above entitled "Possible Adjustments Based on the Factor of Potential." The spreadsheet program Sunny River (SYS) 5 Year will help facilitate this exercise.

REFERENCES

Engelhardt, F. (1925). *Forecasting student population*. New York: Columbia University.

Evans, G. W., & Maxwell, L. (1997). Chronic noise exposure and reading deficits: The mediating effects of language acquisition. *Environment and Behavior*, 29(5):638–656.

Tanner, C. K. (1971). *Designs for educational planning*. Lexington, MA: Heath Lexington Books.

Tanner, C. K., & Holmes, C. T. (1985). *Microcomputer applications in educational planning and decision making*. New York: Teachers College Press.

APPENDIX: FORMULAE FOR THE BASE MODEL

BASE MODEL: THE MODIFIED GRADE PROGRESSION MODEL

Part A: *Net Enrollment and Resident Live Births—Total System*

1	C School Year >	D	E	F	G	H
2		2001–02	2002–03	2003–04	2004–05	2005–06
3	Births for 4 YR K >					
4	Year of Birth for K >					
5	Resident Live Births >					
6	4 YR K					
7	Kindergarten					
8	Grade 1					
9	Grade 2					
10	Grade 3					
11	Grade 4					
12	Grade 5					
13	Total Elementary >					
14	Total ES EXED >					
15	Grade 6					
16	Grade 7					
17	Grade 8					
18	Total Middle School >					
19	Total MS EXED >					
20	Grade 9					
21	Grade 10					
22	Grade 11					
23	Grade 12					
24	Total High School					
25	Total HS EXED >					
26						
27	Grand Total >					
28						
29		5 yrs. ago	4 yrs. ago	3 yrs. ago	Last year	Present

(continued)

Appendix: Continued

*Part D: Average Rate of Student Flow by Grade (Formulae for **Part B**)—Total System*

I 1 J (PART D)	K	L	M	N	O
2					
3					
4					
5					AVERAGES
6 =D6/D3	=E6/E3	=F6/F3	=G6/G3	=H6/H3	=SUM(J6:N6)/5
7 =D7/D5	=E7/E5	=F7/F5	=G7/G5	=H7/H5	=SUM(J7:N7)/5
8	=E8/D5	=F8/E5	=G8/F5	=H8/G5	=SUM(K8:N8)/4
9	=E9/D8	=F9/E8	=G9/F8	=H9/G8	=SUM(K9:N9)/4
10	=E10/D9	=F10/E9	=G10/F9	=H10/G9	=SUM(K10:N10)/4
11	=E11/D10	=F11/E10	=G11/F10	=H11/G10	=SUM(K11:N11)/4
12	=E12/D11	=F12/E11	=G12/F11	=H12/G11	=SUM(K12:N12)/4
13					
14 =D14/D13	=E14/E13	=F14/F13	=G14/G13	=H14/H13	=SUM(J14:N14)/5
15	=E15/D12	=F15/E12	=G15/F12	=H15/G12	=SUM(K15:N15)/4
16	=E16/D15	=F16/E15	=G16/F15	=H16/G15	=SUM(K16:N16)/4
17	=E17/D16	=F17/E16	=G17/F16	=H17/G16	=SUM(K17:N17)/4
18					
19 =D19/D18	=E19/E18	=F19/F18	=G19/G18	=H19/H18	=SUM(J19:N19)/5
20	=E20/D17	=F20/E17	=G20/F17	=H20/G17	=SUM(K20:N20)/4
21	=E21/D20	=F21/E20	=G21/F20	=H21/G20	=SUM(K21:N21)/4
22	=E22/D21	=F22/E21	=G22/F21	=H22/G21	=SUM(K22:N22)/4
23	=E23/D22	=F23/E22	=G23/F22	=H23/G22	=SUM(K23:N23)/4
24					
25 =D25/D24	=E25/E24	=F25/F24	=G25/G24	=H25/H24	=SUM(J25:N25)/5
26					

*Part E: The Forecast (Formulae for **Part C**)—Total System*

R (PART E)	S	T	U	V	W
School Year >	2006–07	2007–08	2008–09	2009–10	2010–11
4 YR K RLBs >	2592	2564	2583	2574	2564
Year of Birth >	2001	2002	2003	2004	2005
Resident Live Births >	2512	2592	2564	2583	2574
4 YR K	=O6*S3	=O6*T3	=O6*U3	=O6*V3	=O6*W3
Kindergarten	=O7*S5	=O7*T5	=O7*U5	=O7*V5	=O7*W5
Grade 1	=O8*H5	=O8*S5	=O8*T5	=O8*U5	=O8*V5
Grade 2	=O9*H8	=O9*S8	=O9*T8	=O9*U8	=O9*V8
Grade 3	=O10*H9	=O10*S9	=O10*T9	=O10*U9	=O10*V9
Grade 4	=O11*H10	=O11*S10	=O11*T10	=O11*U10	=O11*V10
Grade 5	=O12*H11	=O12*S11	=O12*T11	=O12*U11	=O12*V11
Total REG K–5 >	=SUM(S6:S12)	=SUM(T6:T12)	=SUM(U6:U12)	=SUM(V6:V12)	=SUM(W6:W12)

Appendix: Continued

*Part E: The Forecast (Formulae for **Part C**)—Total System*

R (PART E)	S	T	U	V	W
Total E S EXED >	=N14*S13	=N14*T13	=N14*U13	=N14*V13	=N14*W13
Grade 6	=O15*H12	=O15*S12	=O15*T12	=O15*U12	=O15*V12
Grade 7	=O16*H15	=O16*S15	=O16*T15	=O16*U15	=O16*V15
Grade 8	=O17*H16	=O17*S16	=O17*T16	=O17*U16	=O17*V16
Total REG M S >	=SUM(S15:S17)	=SUM(T15:T17)	=SUM(U15:U17)	=SUM(V15:V17)	=SUM(W15:W17)
Total M S EXED >	=N19*S18	=N19*T18	=N19*U18	=N19*V18	=N19*W18
Grade 9	=O20*H17	=O20*S17	=O20*T17	=O20*U17	=O20*V17
Grade 10	=O21*H20	=O21*S20	=O21*T20	=O21*U20	=O21*V20
Grade 11	=O22*H21	=O22*S21	=O22*T21	=O22*U21	=O22*V21
Grade 12	=O23*H22	=O23*S22	=O23*T22	=O23*U22	=O23*V22
Total REG H S >	=SUM(S20:S23)	=SUM(T20:T23)	=SUM(U20:U23)	=SUM(V20:V23)	=SUM(W20:W23)
Total H S EXED	=O25*S24	=O25*T24	=O25*U24	=O25*V24	=O25*W24
Grand Totals					
School Year >	2000–2001	2001–2002	2002–2003	2003–2004	2004–2005
Elementary Schools	=SUM(S13:S14)	=SUM(T13:T14)	=SUM(U13:U14)	=SUM(V13:V14)	=SUM(W13:W14)
Middle Schools	=SUM(S18:S19)	=SUM(T18:T19)	=SUM(U18:U19)	=SUM(V18:V19)	=SUM(W18:W19)
High Schools	=SUM(S24:S25)	=SUM(T24:T25)	=SUM(U24:U25)	=SUM(V24:V25)	=SUM(W24:W25)
School System	=SUM(S28:S30)	=SUM(T28:T30)	=SUM(U28:U30)	=SUM(V28:V30)	=SUM(W28:W30)

CHAPTER SIXTEEN

A STRATEGIC PLANNING ACTIVITY FOR PLANNING AND DESIGNING EDUCATIONAL FACILITIES

We have presented background information on the theory and principles of planning and designing schools as critical areas of knowledge in Part II, and reviewed the classical method of facilities planning (the school survey process). Hinging on many activities in the traditional survey process, the concept of strategic planning emerges from premise 2 (*the school system has a defined direction*—a mission and a vision) and premise 8 (by involving stakeholders, *the school and community should work cooperatively*), thus ensuring that schools are designed and built to enhance teaching and learning and serve as centers of the community. The development of a mission, philosophy, values, goals, and objectives is an activity characterizing the early stages of school facilities planning, but exactly how they become an integral part of the process may take many paths. The path we will explore in this application chapter is strategic planning—a complete process of deciding on a particular program or activity within the total organization (planning and designing a school), what it should be, and how to best reach the objective of constructing an age-appropriate facility that supports the educational program. One goal of strategic planning is to influence change in school design that matches and facilitates the curriculum.

To this end, this chapter involves a modified case study approach in applied strategic planning (SP). SP, as presented here, is a team process (as defined in premise 8) involving a cross section of key individuals in the school and the community. Its focus here is to assist people in the development of educational specifications and appropriate school designs. In the case below, we have altered the usual strategic planning process leading to the development of a mission, goals, and objectives focused primarily on educational specifications and the design of physical learning environments. Goals are set within the framework of a vision and mission. The results of SP show people how to reach their goals by following linear steps. SP facilitates group decision making and moves the school and the community toward achievable design outcomes. This is accomplished through interactive processes by asking questions such as "Where are we," "Where should we be," and "How do we achieve our goals?"

SP is by no means the only way to achieve participation in school design and planning. Sanoff (2000) devoted an entire book to the subject of participation in design and planning, one of which is strategic planning. Other methods discussed by

Sanoff include the charrette, a process for rapidly finalizing planning and design projects; community action planning; participatory action research; participation games; and various combinations of these, including brainstorming. Myers and Robertson (2004) offer various approaches to participatory planning in *The CEFPI Guide for Educational Facility Planning*. Many of their examples consistently focus on organization, involving stakeholders and employing effective communications methods.

Two aims of this chapter are to create a context for an instructional setting and provide a set of guidelines for an actual SP project in a practical setting. One driving force in parallel to the notion of strategic planning is the national design principles, especially design principle 3 that states "the learning environment should result from a planning/design process involving all stakeholders" (U.S. Department of Education, 2000, p. 7). Interwoven in the process is an opportunity for people to acquire knowledge concerning strategic planning theories, ideas, and methods. The activities and suggested materials should enhance one's skills in developing, carrying out, and evaluating strategic planning procedures for designing and planning educational learning environments. Another goal is to introduce tactics for managing meetings, a critical factor in strategic planning.

ASSUMPTIONS, ADVANTAGES, AND LIMITATIONS OF STRATEGIC PLANNING

The basic assumption underlying SP is that the school system is healthy and ready to solve the problem of building a new school or modifying an existing school. If there is significant discord among key school and community leaders and within the school system, strategic planning may not be the best way to plan. One advantage is that it involves representatives from all parts of the school and community. Once time and money are invested in the process, people usually unite to support the resulting plan because they have "bought

into the process." Collective decision making, with interaction among people involved in the process, is often superior to other methods of decision making. The disadvantage of SP is that it is time-consuming (a minimum of six months of intensive meetings at least twice per month for school facilities planning and design). Because of the time constrains, we recommend an experienced, outside facilitator to oversee the leadership team, one having no vested interest in the outcomes is strongly recommended. For example, it may not always be a wise choice to hire a planner and an architect from the same firm because it is possible for the planner to lead the SP team to a school design that the architect already has on file or in mind. There are many independent planners and independent architects representing different firms who are willing to work together when the appropriate time comes to plan and design schools. Obviously, there are planning and architectural firms that work together often and well, while there are planning and architectural firms working independently of each other who also make superior teams. The advantages and disadvantages of these various combinations is beyond the scope of this text; however, those interested in such a discussion may refer to Castaldi (1994) and follow his arguments for school surveys within or outside the organization (Chapter 3).

PROBLEM-BASED ACTIVITIES

Managing Meetings

Before beginning the SP process it is wise to learn how to effectively manage meetings. One way to achieve this is by studying the classic work of Doyle and Straus (1993). This valuable resource book entitled *How to Make Meetings Work* takes the reader beyond the school facilities planning and design process. Its suggestions apply to interactive meetings for any purpose. For example, it is wise to know why meetings go wrong and be equipped to remedy this problem. This work also focuses on group memory—a vital key to planning.

It is important to find win–win solutions for groups trying to design and plan educational facilities. The "Lost on the Moon" exercise is a team-building exercise included in *How to Make Meetings Work*. One outcome from the exercise is that students and community planning teams will learn that, in most cases, a group decision is superior to an individual decision. The book suggests key team members such as the facilitator and the recorder (of the group memory) and explains the role of each group member. Even the design of the meeting room is discussed—a feature that often enhances meetings. There are other exercises that may accompany this problem-based learning activity, such as showing films on team building and participating in "ropes" courses. The essential lessons to be learned from this work are creating a team atmosphere and learning how to manage meetings before starting any SP activity.

Once the meeting management issue is addressed, we may turn to the activities that will result in a strategic plan. Our method relies heavily on the work of Clay, Lake, and Tremain (1989) and other resources found in this chapter's reference section. The activities show how to develop a strategic plan for school facilities (hypothetically or in a practical setting). The hypothetical setting is a growing rural school system that is becoming a suburban school district (a situation that applies to many communities in the United States). The focus may be planning and designing an elementary school, a middle school, high school, vocational school, or perhaps a community college. The method may accommodate other aspects of planning by slightly changing some of the parameters. The middle school exercise is employed here because it is often a neglected area in the literature.

DEVELOPING A STRATEGIC PLAN—A PROBLEM-BASED FORMAT

This problem-based learning activity is focused on the fictitious schools of Hilldale, located in Hilldale County, United States. Hilldale County presently serves 3,000 students in prekindergarten (PK)–12. There are four separate school sites. During the next ten years the student population is forecasted to reach 5,000. Currently, Hillview (600 students) and Wood Creek (600 students) are the PK–5 elementary schools; Daleview (1,000 students) serves grades 6–8; and Hilldale County High School (800 students) includes grades 9–12. The elementary schools are in good physical condition. The greatest need is to construct one or two new middle schools within the next five years. (Here one might substitute the problem, identifying it instead as a need for a new elementary school, a high school, a vocational school, or a community college. For example, this problem might be framed as a need for a single school, assuming that all the other schools were in excellent condition and that the only need is a new technical college in the area to accommodate students that need job skills, a new high school because of the need to keep the high schools small, or a new elementary school to keep the enrollment below 500 students and minimize school bus transportation time, etc.)

The funding for these schools may come from the Special Purpose Local Option Sales Tax (SPLOST); it may also derive from state and local monies earned for school construction (Or, to fit the exercise to a state that does not have SPLOST, the funding might exist through bonds—a bond referendum.)

A solution to the problem may take several paths. Within the next ten to twelve years, because of the condition of the school (name the school here), one or two new schools (name the schools here) will also be needed. Thus, this exercise may be modified to approximate a planning problem that you might experience.

Approximately 25 percent of Hilldale's student population participates in the "free lunch" program. The dropout rate is approximately 18 percent. Forty-six percent of the workforce takes Interstate 220 West to the state university (see the map), and manufacturing and industrial sites to work in various kinds of jobs—secretarial, electronics, computer technology, skilled labor, custodial, and maintenance. Approximately 5 percent of the adult workers are professors who have escaped the urban environment of the university community in the adjacent county.

Lumber and wood businesses in the Hilldale County employ 510 people to process trees and make furniture and small items for sale at the local chain store and other stores across the nation. This national chain store is also part of a strip mall that is developing along I-220 near the Thunder Highway interchange. The number of jobs in Hilldale County is slowly increasing, but unemployment is also slowly increasing. Most farm labor is equally divided between the county's two wine plantations and eight corporate chicken ranches. While independent farming is small-scale, there are mobile homes on some of the old farm sites, providing rent income for landowners. This may prove to ignite socioeconomic problems if new zoning laws are not enacted to control the proliferation of mobile homes on farmland and forests. Some independent farmers employ seasonal labor to harvest vegetables and fruit. Next year two new fast-food restaurants and a motel will be built at the intersection of I-220 and Thunder Highway. This will add approximately forty minimum wage and five management jobs to the local economy.

The people of Hilldale County support the school system, especially the sports teams, but they have been slow to employ good educational leadership that will inspire a vision for a state-of-the-art educational program. The school and community are in transition, although many of the school board members cling to the past practices of thinking that school facilities of the 1970s can support a twenty-first-century curriculum. The school system has traditionally depended on the state for most of its school construction funds; however, the SPLOST is slowly changing this mind-set, since Hilldale County has a growing sales tax income. Generally, teachers and administrators stand in good favor with the community. The school board appoints the school superintendent. The overall state ranking of Hilldale County Schools is near average on academic issues, while there are tracts of students in advanced

placement classes who are in the top 5 percent of students in the state.

Hilldale Schools have the typical problems and opportunities associated with any school system in transition. But, the most pressing one is to *build new middle school* facilities that will support a relevant curriculum and learning environments. The present middle school is dilapidated. (Here one may select any other type of school planning and design project and state a reason for the need to plan for it.)

The middle school population consists of 1,000 students (expected to increase to 1,200 within ten years), with 65 percent of the growth on the west side of the mountains and equal amounts expected north and south of I-220 (see Figure 16.1). How many middle schools should be constructed? Where should they (it) be located? What educational specifications should be adopted for the new middle schools? What design will accommodate the program? These are questions for the strategic planning team to answer.

In order to find some solutions to the hypothetical problems described above, we will turn to a ten-step model refined from the works of Clay, Lake, and Tremain (1989). The activities are sequenced in linear form and the estimated times for completion of activities are added as a guide for students assigned these activities as part of a class project or time estimates if the model is applied to a "real" strategic planning process. As a student working on the Hilldale exercise, try to assume the frame of mind of people living in this area as you experience the activities. The people are usually upwardly mobile and have a strong work ethic. They want a sound education for their children but are not always willing to pay for it through property taxation. Many have strong religious ties and the majority of the society is highly moral. The culture might not differ greatly from rural cultures on the verge of becoming suburban in many states in the United States. These communities, like Hilldale County, are also gradually becoming multicultural. In a classroom setting for this exercise, it is best for each class member to assume various

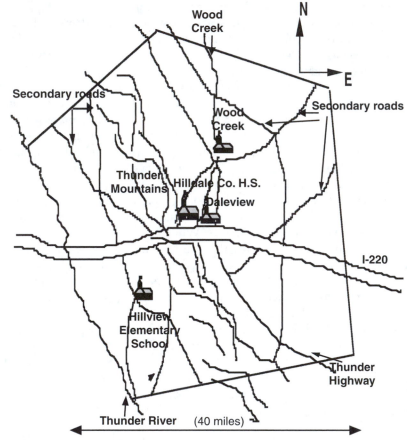

FIGURE 16.1   Map of Hilldale County

roles (parent, student, businessperson, teacher, school administrator, special interest group member, paid consultant, community leader, facilities director, contractor, school board member, school superintendent, and architect).

A MODEL FOR STRATEGIC PLANNING

The steps presented here may be applied to the simulated Hilldale study presented above, or to a practical SP situation. They are straightforward; however, step 5 involves work that may include activities in the school survey. We recommend that the assignments for steps 5 and 8 be given early in the SP process. Collecting data and synthesizing it

for the planning team can be very time-consuming. In a practical setting the environmental scan may be performed by an outside consulting firm. If the survey or environmental scan is done by local people, at least one experienced planner must be in charge to ensure that all the data are collected and analyzed according to the needs of the SP teams.

Step 1. Select Members and Organize the SP Teams

Allow one month for a school system to formulate the SP teams. If the exercise is performed in a class on strategic planning, then a small portion of one class meeting is sufficient in an instructional setting.

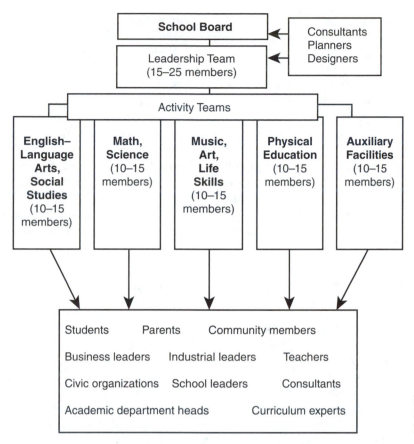

FIGURE 16.2   **Organization of Strategic Planning Teams Planning a New School**

Usually, a *leadership team* of approximately fifteen to twenty-five members who are committed to SP and also represent a cross section of "stakeholders" is ideal to complete planning, programming, and concept design. For example, for the leadership team we recommend the inclusion of an "outside the school system" facilitator, two or three members of each *activity team* as shown in Figure 16.2, and a professional planner and designer. The SP leadership team must be composed of members who are energetic, dependable, knowledgeable, and compatible. Ideally, the facilitator of the activity teams is also a member of the leadership team. Typically, the school system's educational planner has the job of identifying, inviting, and selecting people to participate in the SP process. Often, builders and sub-

contractors are not seen as stakeholders, but representatives from this vital component of the community should be included (these individuals may not necessarily compete for the final building project, but should be represented to add balance to the various ideas that will be discussed). It is important to select membership on leadership and activity planning teams very carefully because these individuals will be working together for a long time. *Activity teams* should include no more than fifteen individuals and at least two members who also work on the leadership team. For example, when planning and designing a new school, teams such as mathematics, science, English, etc., according to subject area, may be formulated to focus on strategic goals, objectives, plans, and design. The suggested sequence of monthly meetings for a practical setting is straightforward: The leadership team and the activity teams meet together, first, for orientation (step 2). Thereafter, all activity teams meet prior to the meeting of the leadership team. In essence, once the teams hold their first meeting, the flow of information from the bottom up helps to shape the strategic plan that includes, vision, mission, goals, strategies, educational specifications, and concept design. When using this set of SP activities in an instructional setting it is suggested that only the role of the leadership team be followed.

The importance of having a good cross section of the school and community in selecting the teams cannot be overemphasized. Civic clubs and volunteer organizations are key places to start looking for members. Ask the key people in the community who can be counted on to do work for the good of the public schools. This is the same approach to be used in selecting representatives from the schools that will sit on the subject and program area committees (activity teams). Beware of people who volunteer without being nominated. These individuals may bring problems of communication and hidden agendas later on in the process. Although some differences in opinion are to be expected, an inflexible or singularly focus person can wreck a SP team.

Since taxpayer money may be used to plan, design, and build a new school, or modify an existing structure, there must be several ways to generate positive publicity for the project. Newspaper advertisements and other media coverage are highly desirable. It is important to keep a positive tone in the process and the meetings. If a planning grant has been received, it is important to let the public know that those people involved in the SP process and receiving compensation are being funded from resources other than local taxpayer money. It is highly unlikely that SP can be accomplished without funds for the facilitator and some of the experts (landscape architect, planner, architect, engineer, etc.) needed to ensure a sound product. The organization of the SP teams as outlined in Figure 16.2 is highly desirable.

It is a good public relations tactic to develop an Internet site devoted to this specific SP process prior to having the orientation meeting. A website can serve as a place for the media to retrieve information as it describes the SP process to the public through radio, newspaper, and television. The website can also be used as a communications tool to announce meeting dates and times. After each activity has been completed and approved by the governing board, it may be useful to post it on the Internet so the leadership team and activity members and the public may view the results. Even allowing a chat room and bulletin board for the community to use in discussing planning and design issues may prove to be worthwhile.

Step 2. Orient Team Members

A one-day orientation meeting is needed for a school SP project. Usually, 180+ minutes is adequate for the Hilldale case study when used as an instructional tool. The main focus of the orientation meeting is team building, so it is important that the environment be warm and friendly. Both the leadership team and activity teams should attend this meeting. Every team member should feel included and important. The objective is to get the teams committed to the planning process and ready for the challenges ahead.

An orientation meeting for elementary school SP teams might include no more than 50 to 60 people, while a middle school SP orientation meeting could include from 65 to 100 members. High school SP teams might require as many as 200 individuals. Some suggested activities related to orientation are:

- Prior to holding the orientation meeting, ask the team's members to read *How to Make Meetings Work* by Doyle and Straus.
- Have the first meeting place set up according to Doyle and Straus's recommendations. Provide snacks and soft drinks. In fact, these should be a part of every meeting.
- Discuss, in some detail, the role of the facilitator, the recorder, and the team members.

- Show a film on team building.
- Engage in team-building exercises.
- Define strategic planning (SP).
- Discuss the advantages and limitations of SP.
- Discuss the educational program and physical learning environments. If no program planning has been done, then expect to double the planning time from six months to one year. At best it will require six months to plan a program, including determining space needs, and six months to go from program to concept design. (Concept design specifies space relationships and dimensions. It is a step beyond the traditional "bubble diagrams" of the 1960s.)
- Discuss educational specifications and how they reflect the school's program.
- Try to ensure that everyone goes away from the first meeting having developed a connection to his or her teams. Providing the group with a notebook outlining the general set of steps in SP is helpful. Compiling a list with the leadership and activity committees' member names, their e-mail addresses, the project's website address, and fax and telephone numbers will also be helpful in facilitating the process.
- Use nametags and allow people time to interact and discuss their concerns.

Each of the remaining steps will employ a component entitled "preparing for the 'next' step." This is a preview of what is to come and describes and explains the necessary activities that need to be accomplished. These may be communicated through the Internet site established especially for the SP process and through the media, depending on how much community coverage of the project is desired.

Preparing for Step 3.   The following suggestions may enhance understanding of the process to be followed in SP, and the suggestions may increase the understanding of values driving the school's philosophy. Each step should include the communications component discussed in step 2, since the school administrators should be informed.

There may be confidential information and some public information that must be kept separated; for example, the consulting fee paid to the facilitator and consulting team might not become public information immediately (although it must be released eventually). Many laypeople do understand the importance of employing competent outside assistance in complex planning processes tied to school facilities. A sound rule of thumb in deciding payment for the facilitator is to multiply the cost of the school facilities project by approximately 0.015 for the estimated cost of a complete package that includes plans, concept design, and educational specifications. This includes the expenses incurred by the SP team. The following items should also be addressed when preparing for the next step:

- In addition to the Internet site, provide a multimedia release to the community. Be sure to include names of the leadership and activity teams and the purpose and objectives of their activities to help ensure that every local individual is made aware of his or her importance. Not all community or team members will have access to the Internet, so the utilization of traditional media outlets is also valuable.
- Give all team members a copy of the school district's philosophy, goals, mission, and values and beliefs' statements. Planning activities to recreate these may or may not be necessary in this SP effort, yet they may be modified to reflect the fact that the school system is planning a new school. It is often difficult to find the physical environment mentioned in traditional philosophy statements. This is because this area has been overlooked as a vital part of student learning.
- Prepare a progress report for the school superintendent and governing board (keep the CEO, other administrators, and school board informed). Once the report has been approved or accepted by the school board, it

may be posted on the SP website and released to the media.

- Develop a detailed agenda with team members (dates and times, etc.). In addition to keeping a hard copy and its inclusion in a notebook, the agenda may be posted on the Internet. This agenda may change. It is simple to change the dates on the website, but in time-constrained situations it may be necessary to inform the group through a telephone or fax "tree" (e.g., each team member calls or faxes two other members when vital information is to be distributed quickly).
- Be cognizant of various holidays for various religious groups in planning dates and deadlines.
- Be aware of multicultural differences in the committee and the population being served by this strategic planning activity.
- Develop and distribute ground rules on such issues as the facilitator, recorder, team member responsibilities, and dates and times. These ideas will be enhanced by information found in Doyle and Straus (1993).
- Secure samples of some educational specifications to use as examples later in the project. There are several examples available on the Internet. Going to an Internet search engine and typing in "educational specifications" will yield some useful guidelines for this activity. Also search libraries for examples. Examples of strategic planning activities are available for review in libraries and on the Internet. Some school districts are willing to share educational specifications as well.
- Do not try to reinvent the wheel.

Step 3. Determine Values about Learning Environments

First, the activity team meets. Next, one to three members of the activity team will repeat this activity with the leadership team. This will require two one-half day meetings for application in a school setting to specify values regarding learning environments (at least one-half day for the activity team and one-half day for the leadership team). Allow 180+ minutes for the Hilldale case study in an instructional setting. It should be clear that in an instructional setting, only one team is expected to operate.

Work Assignment.   Define "values" that influence the school's learning environment. This may be accomplished by consensus. The SP team comes to consensus around a definition of values, and decides what values are important for school environments. Given the philosophy statement, will a wide variety of learning environments be needed, or will traditional facilities be acceptable? It is recommended that participants give some thought to these questions: What are the environmental implications if learners are spending one-third of their day at the computer, one-third of the day talking or interacting with others, and one-third of the day making something? This represents a philosophy of learning proposed by Shank (Fielding, 1999).

Gaining Consensus.   Initially, according to Clay, Lake, and Tremain (1998), in the SP process it is important for the team to decide how it will make decisions. If members decide to make decisions by consensus, then every decision must be worked and reworked until everyone can "live with it and abide by it." Consensus means enough agreement has been reached so that team members will not act against subsequent decisions. It creates a situation of "everyone is winning" by ensuring that everyone can live with or support a decision before the group moves to the next issue. Operating by consensus ensures that all members will be "in agreement, at least to a degree, and on board" with any decision or action. If anyone says, "No, I can't live with that," the process must not go forward, but address the conflict immediately. Hence, the team must stop and address this disagreement. Perhaps the item needs to be reexamined by identifying the points of disagreement.

Consensus is different from the majority rule system, where there are "winners" and "losers." The suggested "Lost on the Moon" exercises in Doyle and Straus (1993) should make this section easier for the team because people have learned more about each other.

a. Write the team's definition of values for viewing on poster paper.
b. Develop the school district's philosophy statement regarding educational learning environments. This may be an extension of the philosophy statement found in the most recent program evaluation. Modify your system's philosophy or browse the Internet for other outstanding examples. In a real-time situation, the philosophy may be retrieved, and usually modified, from the local school system.

SAMPLE PHILOSOPHY STATEMENT

The philosophy of the _____ School District is one of total commitment to educational excellence. The teaching and learning philosophy is progressive and requires nontraditional physical environments to help fulfill this viewpoint. The Board continually seeks curriculum and staff improvement based on reliable research, sound principles of child development, and proven teaching practices. The Board believes that it is the duty of the school organization to serve the community by providing a comprehensive educational program complemented by appropriate physical environments, and it pledges that each school will offer students the opportunity for maximum growth potential in a climate of mutual trust and respect.

The Board also recognizes that home and community have tremendous influence, and the development of students' moral conduct, self-esteem, and academic achievement is a shared responsibility. With parental support, a positive school experience should guarantee that each student receives a quality education and is prepared to meet the future as a well-adjusted, productive member of society. The Board has defined its vision of what a quality education should encompass by adopting a set of goals established by a committee of school personnel and community members. By constantly working toward these goals, it will be ensured that each student has every opportunity to acquire academic knowledge, life skills, and principles of good citizenship and democratic ideals. The Board of Trustees dedicates the efforts and resources of the _____ School District to fulfilling these important commitments to its students and community.

c. Discuss the district philosophy and values and beliefs.

Consider the district values and philosophy in light of the definition developed in the first step. Do existing values and philosophy statements cover everything the team has defined as "values" associated with learning spaces? This helps to ensure that the values and beliefs correspond to the philosophy statement.

d. Brainstorm a list of values currently operating within the _____ school system.

Brainstorming is a common technique used in gaining consensus and affords the opportunity to use the recorder (group memory). One important constraint in brainstorming is not to discuss or criticize any value proposed by others. Setting a time limit of fifteen to twenty minutes should allow a multitude of ideas from which to finalize appropriate values. The brainstorming approach can be a significant technique to encourage participation from all team members in a free-flowing, idea-generating synergistic manner. It is important to set constraints on the amount of time to be devoted to each brainstorming activity. For example, simply state, "We are going to brainstorm for twenty minutes on the topic of *values currently operating within our school system.*"

We strongly suggest the use of team memory through a recorder. A recorder is a team member who agrees to remain neutral while capturing the essence of everyone's ideas and writing them down for later review by the team. No discussion, evaluation, or criticism of any idea is ever allowed. The recorder may say something such as "I don't understand that last idea or please clarify," but that is the extent of his or her input. It is difficult for the recorder to stay focused on the ideas and not interject his or her opinion. Everyone should also be clear on the topic of discussion. For example, "We are going to spend only fifteen minutes brainstorming the topic of how the school environment influences student learning." Stay focused. The facilitator leading the brainstorming session must enforce the rules and stop anyone who begins to evaluate and/or discuss another's suggestion. Like the recorder, the facilitator is not allowed to add ideas while the team is brainstorming. After the session is over, the facilitator and recorder may add their ideas.

e. Clarify and discuss values.

f. Write down ten or more value and belief statements for review by the team. Remember that these should be slanted toward the curriculum and physical learning environment. Some sample value and belief statements are listed below:

We support parallel block scheduling, because PBS will:

- Reduce the student–teacher ratio for mathematics and reading instruction.
- Ensure an equitable distribution of teachers' time to children in different groups
- Guarantee that students do not lose direct instructional time or exposure to higher-level curricular content to attend "pull-out" programs.
- Allow students to spend at least half the school day in heterogeneous groups.

We support good school design that will:

- Require at least 72 square feet (6.70 square meters) of windows for natural light in every classroom as a necessity.
- Include flexible learning spaces to meet changing curriculum and student needs.
- Employ low density.
- Help ensure small schools as a way to minimize discipline problems.
- Enhance student safety and security.
- Maximize student activities.

- Include single-story learning environments with windows overlooking the surrounding world and doors opening into garden areas.
- Incorporate well-planned and well-designed outdoor learning environments.
- Make use of cyber learning areas, including a foodcourt (containing Internet ports or wireless connections).

Preparing for Step 4. Prepare a progress report for the school superintendent and governing board. Distribute information on how to develop a mission statement. Give team members a typed copy of the values and beliefs statements about educational specifications and school design (step 3). Provide sample mission statements for participants.

Step 4. Develop a Mission Statement

This step is devoted to developing a mission statement to support educational specifications and school design that facilitate the proposed curriculum. Given that the values and beliefs are clearly specified, approximately three hours should be sufficient time for the activity teams to establish a mission statement and for the leadership team to do the same. In an instructional setting 90+ minutes should be sufficient.

The mission is a "belief" statement around which the school and community can organize their energies and efforts—what we believe about how the educational learning environments should facilitate the curriculum. It forms the foundation for the remaining SP activities and supports a shared vision for the entire organization. It is a description of why the physical learning environments in the school district exist. Detailed objectives and implementation strategies are built on the foundation of basic purposes and mission. The mission is the benchmark statement against which all planning steps can be tested for relevance. We will follow the planning model of Clay, Lake, and Tremain (1989) that indicates, "The mission should be developed before the goals and objectives." This approach hinges on the fact that the future of our school facilities in the district is determined to a large degree on what we believe, our values, and the identity (design principles) that distinguishes them from other school facilities in neighboring districts. Basic "identities" such as minimum safety requirements, for example, are going to be dictated from sources outside the SP teams' assignment because they are legally binding. The mission statement supporting educational specifications and school design is an honest expression of a school district's basic identity or beliefs about its educational program, design, and architecture. Consequently, the development of a mission statement comes between the clarification of beliefs and values and the steps involved in surveying or scanning the environment (school and community) in which the district exists. Finally, the mission statement helps to guide the educational specifications in the direction deemed appropriate by the SP teams. If plans are aimed in the wrong direction, the last thing needed is to get there more effectively. Assuming that this school system needs a new school designed to meet current and future demands, the following guidelines are suggested:

- Carefully review the value and belief statements previously developed. This is not the focus activity of the process, but can serve as a launching pad to the development of a mission statement.
- Invite each person to respond, independently, to the questions below:
  a. What is the basic purpose for the physical learning environment?
  b. Who are the clients of the physical learning environment?
  c. What are the major activities to be performed in the learning spaces?
  d. What are the various types of learning spaces that will be needed?
  e. What educational specifications and design features will best enhance student learning?

Compare your responses as the team reaches consensus on the answers to the questions (the use of a facilitator is strongly recommended for this activity). Place the team's answers on poster paper for viewing. Following this activity, each individual should now draft an outline for a mission statement supporting educational specifications and school design. For example, "Given our beliefs that the school environment definitely influences student outcomes, the purposes of educational specifications are to provide a comprehensive description of the spaces needed to facilitate the school program. To best fulfill these purposes, we are committed to translating the educational specifications into a school design that facilitates the teaching and learning philosophies of our school district." We recommend that the mission statement contain no more than 100 words.

It may be helpful for the team to use individual responses to the four questions above and draft a mission statement. It is important to put various drafts up for viewing. Take the mission statement to a more specific level than a general mission statement, while keeping if brief.

Examples of general mission statements that may help in formulating a mission statement for this problem-based activity follow (also search the Internet for others):

The mission of _____ Public Schools, in partnership with the community, is to provide age-appropriate educational environments that match sound design principles, enabling all students to reach their highest potential.

It is the mission of the _____ High School to provide and maintain a superior physical learning environment that complements the curriculum and helps students develop to their fullest extent—mentally, socially, emotionally, and physically—so that they can take their places in our society as well-adjusted contributing members.

The _____ School District is a community of caring individuals committed to providing an educationally and architecturally superior physical learning environment for all students, and equipping them with the skills, knowledge, and attitudes to be self-directed, lifelong learners and tolerant, productive human beings.

Preparing for Step 5. Arrange a progress report for the school superintendent and governing board. Allow the school board to accept the mission statement supporting educational specifications and the school design. This is critical. Without their acceptance or approval, the strategic plan is of little value. It is important to send all team members a completed mission statement and provide them with an explanation of external and internal scanning, and also define "surprise-free" scenarios.

Step 5. Scan the External and Internal Environments

This is a comprehensive step in school planning, taking on many characteristics of the traditional "school survey," but also adding a futuristic dimension. These data must be assumed in an instructional setting (classroom setting where students are working on a problem such as the Hilldale simulation), or at least students should be allowed a minimum of one month to accumulate a limited amount of support data for historical, population, demographic, organizational, cultural, political, economic, program, and funding trends. The suggested minimum time in an instructional setting is approximately two meetings of 180+ minutes. However, in an actual SP setting, one to two full days of planning will be necessary, assuming assignments were made in the beginning of the process or that an outside consulting firm has completed the scanning process. The data collection and analysis in a thorough study may require from nine to twelve months.

The focus for the SP team in this step is to use the results of the environmental scans to develop appropriate educational specifications. One of the best solutions to this complicated process in the school setting is to commission a student population forecast, demographic analysis slanted toward how trends might influence the school population and the school program, study of space needs based on program needs and student population trends (step 8), and review of research and literature on school design as it relates to teaching and learning. Finally, the results of this step should

help determine the financial arrangements necessary to support school planning, design, and construction. A minimum of six months is needed to assemble this information. Activities such as described here should be completed before the SP team begins step 5 in order to better evaluate the overall environment's impact on the school.

Another suggested activity for the SP team, an activity complementary to the environmental scan, is to tour some interesting schools and meet people who design and plan schools. The SP team leader may also locate some current websites for virtual tours to enrich this activity. For the virtual tour you may review Internet sites that have headings such as school design and planning, educational architecture, educational design, and school facilities planning.

Assuming that the environmental scanning component was set in motion early on as an assignment to the SP team, or commissioned to an independent research team, review demographics of the area to determine the social, political, and economic forces that influence the schools. Next, it becomes a SP activity to brainstorm the trends and issues found in the environmental scan regarding the relationship of the physical environment and student learning, and to classify these trends as Strengths, Weaknesses, Opportunities, or Threats (SWOTs) (Kaufman, Herman, & Watters, 1996). State the implications for each and categorize trends according to whether they are school- or community-related.

Given the school's program, student population forecast, demographic analysis, and financial information presented as a result of the environmental scans, the SP teams' next job is to develop "surprise-free" scenario statements (step 6) as suggested by Clay and coworkers (1989). With the trends and issues serving as a guide, the SP team develops a list of assumptions about what the school should be accomplishing within ten to twenty years. This activity is based on what has been learned during the external and internal scans. No organization exists in a vacuum. Outside events and organizations always influence schools. In looking outside the school district, the SP teams will be identifying impacts that may not be obvious to people inside the school system. You, as a participant in the SP process, may view changes to your school as threats or opportunities. Also imagine the ideal school (elementary, middle, high school, or vocational college). Consider the trends in economics and education that will influence education locally, regionally, nationally, and internationally. Look for trends that will make the school district significantly different from its past or present.

The following categories are examples of what one might expect to find as the outcome of the internal scan: possible internal trouble spots in the school organization, politicians' agendas for education, and local politics concerning the schools. For example, there may be political pressure to develop prototype schools as a ploy for saving taxpayer money. Such suggestions need to be challenged with value engineering to ensure the efficient use of tax money. They may also be challenged on the basis that each community is unique; therefore, its schools should also be unique in program, specifications, design, and architecture.

Planners must always be cognizant of the average age of the population, changing family structures, immigration, at-risk students, and the impact of local housing and job market on types and numbers of families within the school district. The student population may increase sharply, or it may decline as a result of job opportunities for adults in the community. Economically, local job positions in the service/information economy may change. For example, the environmental scanning activity may uncover plans to open a new "high tech" company within five years with an expected workforce of 350 people. A new hotel and restaurant may open and provide forty low-paying jobs. A local manufacturing plant may be expected to close; therefore, 250 jobs will be terminated, presenting a challenge for some small school districts. Expect trends such as these.

We must also be aware of lifestyle changes that the Internet, space exploration, computers, VCRs, Internet radio, DVDs, and genetic engineering may bring to a community. Changes such as these will influence job markets and school programs in the future. For example, the demand to communicate through the Internet and e-mail may triple within two years and perhaps the use of "T" connections will not be needed because students and teachers will use wireless computers. What school designs will best meet challenges such as these?

Societal values are in constant change; therefore, consider the role of the family, rise/decline of religion, television violence, school violence, terrorism, drugs, and gang warfare's influence on people and their lifestyles. School violence may continue to increase; therefore, what aspects of school design will help eliminate some radical acts of school violence? Terrorism may increase, thus bringing a challenge to planners and designers. Think of these examples as possible findings in a needs assessment and use them to enhance the results of the environmental scans. Such factual and expected trends are to be used in formulating the scenarios for decision making.

Team Activity. Brainstorm the Trends and Issues Found in the Environmental Scans. Display ideas about these issues for team viewing (see Table 16.1 on page 388). What about expected curriculum changes? Will there be changes in the local community (race, religion, and diversity)? Will terrorism become a greater threat to student safety and security? Determine the threats and opportunities to the schools through selection and analysis of relevant political, demographic, economic, technological, social, design, and educational trends and issues. Discuss and classify these trends as SWOTs. State the implications for each. Categorize trends according to school and community. This format or an alternative approach may be used to enhance the scenarios. Trends should be categorized according to school and community as noted in Table 16.1.

Preparing for Step 6. Prepare a progress report for the school superintendent and governing board, and provide all team members with a completed list of the major trends and issues categorized according to SWOTs and by school and community. Send team members an explanation of

TABLE 16.1 Chart for Environmental Scanning

MAJOR ITEMS FOUND IN ENVIRONMENTAL SCANS	STRENGTHS	WEAKNESSES	OPPORTUNITIES	THREATS
Trends—school				
Trends—community				
Issues—school				
Issues—community				
Frequency				

a "surprise-free scenario." A surprise-free scenario is not a "best-case" or "worse-case" scenario. It is based on facts and trends found in the environmental scans. For example, this futuristic technique depends on the opinions of experts who have analyzed data and forecasted trends. This is a major reason why the environmental scans are vital to the SP process. One surprise-free scenario may be that the use of technology in schools will continue to rise over the next fifteen years as we move from the information age to the knowledge age. A surprise-free scenario is much like enrollment projections, since they are the "best guesses" for the future based on professional knowledge, data, and past experiences (Clay, Lake, & Tremain, 1989).

Step 6. Construct Surprise-Free Scenario Statements

With the trends and issues from the environmental scans categorized by school and community and SWOTs serving as a guide, develop a list of assumptions about what the school should look like in five to ten, to twenty years, based on what has been learned during the external and internal scans. One three- to four-hour meeting should be sufficient to generate the scenarios.

Developing a Surprise-Free Scenario. It is impossible to predict the future accurately, but it is necessary to at least make some assumptions about the future. This type of thinking supports what Clay and colleagues (1989) refer to as a "surprise-free" scenario.

With the results of the internal and external environmental scans as a guide, the SP team can now make a reasonable guess about the future. By making certain assumptions, instead of making plans for worst-case or best-case scenarios, the SP team is urged to develop surprise-free scenarios.

Surprise-free scenario statements are direct spin-offs of the internal and external scans. They are assumptions about the future based on past trends, current data, and the best estimates of experts. The examples below are provided to inspire ideas for developing surprise-free scenario statements.

Sample Surprise-Free Scenario Statements

SCHOOL

The school of the future will be a (small, large) school.

The teaching and learning philosophy will be (perennialism, _____, essentialism).

The curriculum will be delivered through (modular scheduling, parallel block scheduling, or _____).

A comprehensive educational program (will, will not) be offered through the school. X percent of the high school freshmen will graduate.

There (will, will not) be a significant change in education in terms of governance and curriculum.

The school's physical environment (will, will not) have an abundance of views (vistas) overlooking the surrounding world.

The school's design will be (monolithic, a campus plan, or _____).

Natural light (will, will not) be plentiful in every classroom.

The school (will, will not) be technology-driven.

(Internet ports and/or wireless capability) will be included in all learning areas, including the cafeteria.

School design patterns (will, will not) change.

Aesthetics (will, will not) replace slum school architecture.

Each classroom (will, will not) have a door leading to an outside learning environment.

The school (will, will not) make available well-planned and well-maintained outdoor learning environments.

Each student (will, will not) be provided with ample space for learning.

COMMUNITY

Families of students will be primarily (blue, white) collar workers.

The majority of parents (both parents) (will, will not) hold jobs outside the home.

The majority of students served by the school (will, will not) attend four-year colleges.

School violence (will, will not) continue.

Terrorism (will, will not) be an issue in this community.

The school population, within ten years, will (increase, decrease) by _____ percent.

Ethnicity (will, will not) be a major social factor in the community.

The school population five years from now (will, will not) be diverse.

The community (will, will not) value education.

Funding for school facilities (will, will not) be a priority of the community.

Religious values of the community (will, will not) be significant influences on students.

Racialism (will, will not) be prevalent among students and parents.

The economy (will, will not) be robust.

Note that all the work done in step 6 is to be used in step 7. Keep a concise group memory.

Preparing for Step 7.   Complete and distribute a progress report for the school superintendent and governing board, and provide all team members with a completed list of surprise-free scenario statements. Send team members an explanation of "creating a vision."

Step 7. Create a Vision of the Program and Facilities

Develop a joint vision of the ideal school of the future as a basis for constructing strategic educational specifications (view these as goals) and suggesting a concept design. This activity will require about one-half day in a real-time situation or 90+ minutes for an instructional activity.

Creating a Vision.   When the SP team has thoroughly studied the educational environment, it is ready to embark on the most pleasant and most exciting step of the SP process—creating a vision of the ideal school of the future. The purpose of this activity is to move the team to a more creative mode. With this vision serving as a guide, the team will then be able to determine strategic goals as educational specifications for the new school and design a school that complements the educational program.

Up to this point, we have focused on five to ten years into the future. Now we want to leap ten to twenty years into the future and focus on the individual school we are planning and designing. This is done to allow the SP team to break free of the present and "imagine the ideal school of the future." Once the team reaches a shared vision of the school of the future, the stage is set for developing strategic goals in the form of educational specifications that will guide the design of the school which we are creating. The point is to have an ideal goal to work toward and then work in the "real world" to decide what must be done immediately to reach the long-range goals. Skeptics may try to lead the SP team backward and get bogged down in rules and regulations, so it is important that the previous activities have been carried out. At this point, the facilitator must be extremely cautious not to allow negative thinking to dominate the planning process. The importance of creating a vision may have been stated best by DeJong (Butterfield, 1999) when he noted that "the number one problem I see in working with communities is helping them to create a vision of what they want their schools to become. Once they have that kind of shared vision, they're willing to support it."

To envision the future, you might ask, what will the culture, the society, and the students be like fifteen years from now? What will be the philosophy of teaching and learning? What lessons will teachers teach? What administrative jobs will be performed and what will administrators do? What courses will the curriculum contain? What will the school buildings (learning environments) be like? Will there be buildings at all? The sky is the limit. You are not being asked to predict the school of the future. You are being asked to envision the school of the future, without constraints that currently exist.

Discuss what the ideal school's physical environment will include in the future. Take into consideration the roles of students, parents, teachers, principals, and community members. Envision the culture, which may be diverse, and society of the future.

Record your ideas in short sentences or phrases. Each individual should complete the following statement: "I envision a school which (or where) _____." Include each of the items in the surprise-free scenarios. Be prepared to eliminate and consolidate overlapping ideas.

Discuss ideas the team generated about the future. Do they seem realistic for the community? The state? If they are not realistic now, then might they be realistic twenty years into the future?

Now develop a scenario-based vision statement from ideas discussed in the preceding steps.

SAMPLE VISION STATEMENT

Within fifteen to twenty years, the schools in this district will have strong academic programs and also programs that develop productive, caring citizens. There will be specific programs to reach these goals. The schools will be smaller, aesthetic, and well designed, and the curriculum will be delivered through (modular scheduling, parallel block scheduling, or _____), based on the constructivist philosophy of teaching and learning. Only 5 percent of the high school freshmen will not graduate. Yet, there (will, will not) be a significant change in education in terms of governance. The schools will have an abundance of appropriate physical designs to help teach values. Natural light will be plentiful in every classroom to enhance student and teacher attitudes. School design patterns will change, and there will also be a special emphasis on student safety and security. Outdoor learning activities will increase as the curriculum becomes integrated, and each classroom will have a door leading to a well-planned and well-maintained outside learning environment. Educational technology will be available to every student and will enhance, rather than dominate the school programs.

However, the basics for learning will still be the foundation of the curriculum. There will be far greater emphasis on how to learn. "Just in time" learning and problem-based learning will replace the traditional core subjects where lecturing and testing were the guiding principles. For example, an integrated curriculum will replace the lockstep English, science, and mathematics classes. School days will be shorter, while the school year will be extended. There will be many school days set aside for students' work in the community as part of their educational program.

The Internet and other multimedia will play a vital role in the lives of students and their families. We will move from the information age to the knowledge age. This will give new meaning to the terms "global village" and "global studies."

Preparing for Step 8. Prepare a progress report for the school superintendent and governing board, and give examples of educational specifications to the SP team. Also encourage team members to begin searching the Internet for examples of educational specifications and school designs, since the design is now in view. At this point, the SP team should know the number of students to be served and the expected program of study (such a study could be completed by some of the SP members, but might best be commissioned to an independent team early in the SP process). This information should correspond to and be influenced by the results of the environmental scans. The types of scheduling to be used in the school must be known before steps 8 and 9 unfold. The SP team must be encouraged to think about the future, and to plan a school for three years from now as well as for twenty to thirty years from now.

Step 8. Develop the Educational Specifications

This is a time-consuming step for the activity teams involving the development of educational specifications based on the surprise-free scenarios and vision for the new school (or a component such as language arts if used as a class exercise). The concept design may also be completed parallel to the specifications or immediately following this activity, since almost nothing in the "real world" is accomplished in a linear manner. Two meetings requiring approximately 180+ minutes are needed in an instructional setting, while as many as three (or more) one-half day meetings spread out over one month may be required in a noninstructional setting, if a subcommittee or consultant develops the detailed documents. One purpose of the educational specifications is to guide the concept design of the school (see also the appendix to this chapter).

Context. Allow the context to be framed as indicated in the two suggestions below:

- Decide how many schools you plan to build.
- Determine class size. This relates the scheduling and type of program. In parallel, block scheduling smaller classes for academic subjects is possible.

Develop Philosophy Statements. Review values and beliefs and vision statements. Now compile a statement of philosophy about each program area (English, language arts, mathematics, history, art, music, auxiliary facilities, etc.). This activity represents the main transition from the overall philosophy developed by the leadership team to the philosophies for program areas constructed by the activity teams. If the above steps have been followed, this transition should flow and the "big picture" should unfold for both the leadership team and the activity teams.

Complete Strategic Design Goals. To accomplish this task, the team will need to review the values, the mission statement, the results of the internal and external scans, and the vision of an ideal school. This may be expedited through media presentations or traditional flip-chart versions of the above items. Each team member may view these before attempting to write the strategic goals.

Some examples of goals related to educational specifications are:

- To build a safe, comfortable, and aesthetically pleasing school having a campus plan design that will serve no more than 500 students
- To provide a program that will accommodate more than one teaching and learning philosophy
- To deliver the curriculum according to parallel block scheduling
- To select furniture that is comfortable, flexible, and amenable to the teaching and learning philosophies
- To provide ample usable space (at least 49 square feet) for each student and teacher within each classroom
- To specify the use of technology in instruction and research.
- To ensure space for student services
- To ensure spaces for community use and service
- To set forth specifications to ensure safety and security for students, teachers, and administrators
- To allow for flexibility and versatility
- To accommodate a multicultural student body and diversity

The rationale for these sample goals for educational specifications should be based on the philosophy, values, surprise-free scenarios, and environmental scans provided in the previous steps.

After viewing the work completed to this point, select subject areas for the strategic goals, focusing on the educational specifications for each curriculum area. For example, one topic area might be communications, with the goal of improving communications by acquiring skills in reading, viewing, listening, and speaking.

After writing down each set of goals, it is recommended that these questions be answered to perform a reality check: Does the goal correspond to the philosophy and mission statements? Does it address one of the needs, problems, or opportunities identified through the environmental scans and scenarios? Can it be accomplished? Is it something worth doing?

It is now time to examine the goals in relation to each other. Does one goal conflict with or prevent the realization of another goal? If so, it must be dropped, or a compromise must be found. Can all goals be reasonably accomplished within the given timeframe? At this point in the "real world," it is advisable to get district personnel (other than those on the SP teams) involved in reviewing and modifying the goals. They might actually review the documents developed from the "Team Memory" and identify topic areas or help prioritize the goals. The final step in goal writing is to put the goals into standard form. The team might decide to write the goals as a unit or delegate goals per topic area to members. Standard form includes using the rationale as illustrated earlier.

Formulate Educational Specifications.   Now it is time to develop educational specifications. The comprehensiveness of the educational specifications will vary depending on the mission, philosophy, and goals defined in the SP process. The suggestions found in Table 16.2 should help set the tone for creativity in this very complex and time-consuming task.

Preparing for Step 9.   The usual information-sharing activities are followed. It is now time to supply technology and materials to take the proposed school's specifications to concept design drawings. *This latter step assumes that a site has been selected for the new school.* Site selection is a process that may parallel the SP activity and take several months.

TABLE 16.2   Outlining and Completing the Educational Specifications (See the Appendix)

- Specify courses (outline the total program per content area, e.g., language arts, science, social studies, etc.)
  a. Number of courses
  b. Components of courses (reading, composition, etc.)
  c. Types? Electives (pull-outs)? Will the schedule allow students to be pulled out of regular classes or electives?
  d. Teacher activities (planning, conferences, communications, etc.)
  e. Student activities
  f. Grouping (size)
  g. Curriculum trends
- Specify space needs
- Project enrollment for required courses
- Estimate class size?
  a. Projected enrollment for electives
  b. Group sizes
  c. Number of sections
  d. Number of periods
  e. Number of teacher stations
- Determine square footage (see the department of education guidelines from your state or use the suggested square footage in this book)
  a. Teaching stations
  b. Teacher work-conference areas
  c. Storage
  d. Student–teacher conference areas
- List Equipment Needs
- List Furniture Needs
- Determine Storage Needs
- Sketch Space Relationships
  a. Within the instructional areas
  b. To surrounding areas
- Define special considerations for expansion and unique programs, student, teacher, and community activities
- Outline specifications for the school site
- Develop educational specifications for the school site
  a. Bus turning radiusb
  b. Parking
  c. Other

Step 9. Go from Educational Specifications to School Design

Sketch the floor plans and several three-dimensional views of the school (see Chapter 5). This will be helpful to the architect in completing the final drawings. Remember one job of the SP team has been that of an educational architect describing and explaining the program and program needs to a noneducator. Therefore, one must assume that the architect will learn the intent for teaching and learning from the collective membership of the SP teams. Educational specifications help to communicate teaching and learning strategies to develop the concept design sketches. The concept design gives the architect a clear perception of what the

SP teams want. This process should minimize misunderstanding about what was intended for the school facility. This activity may require approximately three meetings in a real-time setting or approximately two meetings of 180+ minutes each in an instructional setting.

Activities.   Outline each program area (select only one if the SP process is being used as an instructional activity). Translate strategic educational specifications into concept design. Sketching the concept drawings based on the educational specifications is the objective of step 9. Like the educational specifications, the concept drawings and sketches must follow the surprise-free scenarios and the philosophy and values defined in the strategic plan. Hence, they are direct outgrowths of the overall values, philosophy, vision, the environmental scan, and the surprise-free scenarios. The concept design should be reasonable and achievable, and should correlate to the specifications the SP teams have developed in previous steps. Define and sketch space relationships per area (administrative, instructional, student services, media center, special education, gifted students program, music, art, auditorium, physical education, athletics, technology, nutrition, outdoor learning environments, etc.). We recommend that the concept design process include sketches of the actual spaces, instead of just the traditional bubble diagrams. These concept sketches will show relationships within the instructional areas, among instructional areas, and relationships to surrounding areas. The concept sketch will reveal the overall relationships for all spaces. It is important to develop the sketches to scale to ensure proper placement on the school site. All these items become components of the strategic plan for the school or schools being planned and designed. This is a delicate activity requiring at least one team member who can sketch plans. There are computer programs now available for laypeople that will assist in developing scaled drawings.

To accomplish this task, transpose each strategic design goal (step 8) into sketches. This is not a traditional activity in school facilities planning, since historically it was most likely given to an architect. With the development of inexpensive computer-assisted design (CAD) programs, it is highly likely that one or two SP team members will be able to assemble adequate scaled drawings and three-dimensional renderings that will give a clear view of what the educational spaces should be when translated. The concept drawings or sketches will allow the SP team to provide a test of their specifications and design goals before the architect actually begins the preliminary drawings. Once this idea is tried, it is hypothesized that architects will favor the process. This activity can also become a surprise-free experience for the strategic planning team.

Preparing for Step 10.   Prepare a progress report for the school superintendent and governing board. Get ready to provide all team members with a completed SP document (twenty to thirty pages plus design drawings and educational specifications). This is a compilation of the preceding steps. It should contain, but is not limited, to the following areas:

I. A slide show to emphasize highlights of the strategic plan
II. The report might include the following:
   Title
   List of team members
   Executive summary
   Explanation of the planning process and how the team members were selected
   Introduction
   Statements of values and beliefs (step 3)
   Mission and philosophy statements (step 4)
   Summary of the environmental scans (step 5)
   Surprise-free scenarios (step 6)
   Vision statement (step 7)
   Summary of educational specifications (step 8) (A complete set of specifications should be published in a separate volume.)
   Concept design drawings and sketches (step 9)

Step 10. Present the Strategic Plan and Concept Design of the School Program

Make this an electronic presentation in color with accompanying handouts for each person in attendance. Be specific and do not use too many words per slide. Color illustrations are also helpful. Allow 45+ minutes for the instructional version and for the real-time SP activity. Emphasize that a complete set of educational specifications is available in a larger volume. Show floor plans and digital three-dimensional images of the proposed school.

Present your strategic plan to the governing board. Celebrate!

A celebration is always a good gesture, especially if the project was a success. Even if the project was a failure, a celebration is in order because people have invested time and money into the effort. The next step is to employ an architect and complete the school according to policy and procedures set forth by the owner of the school.

With board approval of the SP, educational specifications, and concept design, it in now time to review the results and allow educators to say what they want without being coached. Finally, this is an excellent time to hire the architect to complete the capital project.

SUMMARY

The applied process of strategic planning (SP) for a new or renovated school facility, as described in this chapter, allows multiple stakeholders to work collectively to ensure that the resulting facility supports their mission, philosophy, values, goals, and objectives. However, the process is time-consuming, requiring at least six months with two or more intensive working sessions per month. During this time, a ten-step SP process may be followed that results in the development of educational specifications and a concept design. A trained and experienced facilitator overseeing the work of the leadership team is essential for moving the process along smoothly.

The first step is to carefully select team members. The leadership team is comprised of approximately fifteen to twenty-five members, including representatives from each activity team, the facilitator, and a professional planner. Activity teams, with no more than fifteen members, are typically assigned to work on specific subject areas (e.g., mathematics, language arts) and report to the leadership team. Once appropriate team members have been selected, it is important for *all* team members to come together for an orientation meeting (step 2) intended to promote team building and increase commitment to the planning process. During the third step the activity teams, then the leadership team, define "values" that will influence what they want in a school's learning environment. Next, the group must develop a mission statement, usually by consensus, regarding how the educational learning environments should facilitate the curriculum. The mission statement forms the foundation for the remaining SP activities. During the fifth step, the team members review the results of the internal and external environmental scans (usually contracted out or conducted by stakeholders earlier in the process). School and community trends (e.g., political, demographic, economic) and other issues identified during the environmental scan are discussed and may be organized according to Strengths, Weaknesses, Opportunities, and Threats (SWOTs) in preparation for the development of surprise-free scenario statements in the following step. These statements are assumptions about the future based on past trends, current data, and the best estimates of experts. Once these have been developed, the team will create a scenario-based vision statement for the program and activities. To develop educational specifications, the next step in the process, the team must develop philosophy statements for each program area (e.g., English, mathematics), write strategic goals, determine class sizes, and specify needs for each space, including furniture, storage, equipment, and special considerations. In the ninth step, the team will translate the educational specifications into a concept design using sketches and drawings. The final step in the SP process is to present the strategic plan and concept design to the school board. Once approved, the architect may be hired to turn the concept design into a reality.

ACTIVITIES

It is strongly recommended that students engage in the instructional exercise outlined in this chapter. However, if time does not permit it, the following activities are suggested.

1. Review educational specifications for your state. Are public schools required to meet these specifications or do they serve as a guide only? Suppose you are on a team that is developing educational specifications for an elementary school supporting a constructivist philosophy. Identify any specifications that would either encourage or discourage a constructivist approach. How might they support or hinder constructivist goals?

2. If you were the school planner responsible for identifying members of the strategic planning team for a new middle school, whom might you invite to participate? You need not include individual names, but titles (e.g., one student from each grade level served, chamber of commerce representative). Prepare your lists individually outside of class and you will be given time in class to discuss these in small groups to formulate a consensus-based list of potential participants.

3. Develop a detailed agenda for the first orientation meeting you will hold with strategic planning team members (from leadership and activity teams). What activity(ies) will you conduct to encourage team building and commitment to the planning process by team members?

REFERENCES AND BIBLIOGRAPHY

Print Sources

Barry, B. B. (1986). *Strategic planning workbook for nonprofit organizations*. St. Paul, MN: Amherst H. Wilder Foundation.

Burkhart, P. J., & Reuss, S. (1993). *Successful strategic planning*. Newbury Park, CA: Sage.

Castaldi, B. (1994). *Educational facilities planning: Planning, modernization, and management*. Boston: Allyn & Bacon.

Clay, K, Lake, S., & Tremain, K. (1989). *How to build a strategic plan*. San Carlos, CA: Ventures for Public Awareness.

Doyle, M., & Straus, D. (1993). *How to make meetings work*. New York: Berkeley Books.

Greenman, J. (1988). *Caring spaces, learning places: Children's environments that work*. Redmond, WA: Exchange Press.

Hawkins, H. L., & Lilley, H. E. (1998). *Guide for school facility appraisal*. Scottsdale, AZ: Council of Educational Facility Planners, International. Also available at http://www.cefpi.com.

Kaufman, R., Herman, J., & Watters, K. (1996). *Educational planning*. Lancaster, PA: Technomic.

MacKenzie, D. G. (1989). *Planning educational facilities*. New York: University Press of America.

Myers, N., & Robertson, S. (2004). *The CEFPI guide for educational facility planning*. Scottsdale, AZ: Council of Educational Facility Planners, International.

Sanoff, H. (2000). *Community participation methods in design and planning*. New York: John Wiley & Sons.

Tanner, C. K. (2001). Classroom size and number of students per classroom. *Educational Facility Planner*, 36(2):11–12.

U.S. Department of Education. (2000). *Schools as centers of community: A citizens' guide for planning and design*. Washington, DC: U.S. Department of Education.

Internet Sources

Architecture can teach. http://www.context.org/ICLIB/IC18/Taylor.htm.

Butterfield, E. (1999). The future of the classroom: Q & A with William DeJong. http://www.designshare.com/Research/DeJong/DeJong1.htm.

Children's environments. http://web.gc.cuny.edu/che/cergfr.htm.

Clearing House. http://www.edfacilities.org/index.html.

Creative problem solving strategies for the 21st century. http://www.designshare.com/Research/Pesanelli/pesanelli_1.htm.

The death of the classroom. http://www.designshare.com/Research/Schank/Schank1.html.

A design assessment scale for elementary schools. http://www.designshare.com/Research/TannerES/DASE.htm.

The design-down process. http://www.cefpi.com/search.html.

DesignShare. http://www.designshare.com/Research/ResearchIndex.htm.

Educational Design Institute. http://www.edi.msstate.edu.

Educational specifications. http://www.coe.uga.edu/sdpl/edspecifications/edspecs101.html; http://ospiwsrv.ospi.wednet.edu/schoolbldg/sfmchap6.htm; http://www.nsba.org/sbot/toolkit/EdSpecs.html.

Fielding, R. (1999). The death of the classroom, learning cycles and Roger Shank. http://www.designshare.com/Research/Schank/Schank1.html.

The factory model is out. http://www.djc.com/special/design95/10002598.htm.

Information age design process. http://www.designshare.com/Research/EdDesignsGroup/Rosen1.htm.

National center for the 21st Century Schoolhouse. http://schoolhouse.sdsu.edu.

Research. http://www.coe.uga.edu/sdpl/research.html.

School Design and Planning Laboratory. http://www.coe.uga.edu/sdpl/sdpl.html.

School Design Research. http://www4.ncsu.edu/%7Esanoff/schooldesign/cd.html.

School Design Research Studio, University of Wisconsin. http://schoolstudio.engr.wisc.edu/index.html.

School Planning and Management. http://www.spmmag.com/articles/facilities.html.

Schools for the 21st century. http://www.context.org/ICLIB/IC18/McClure.htm.

GLOSSARY

Environmental Scanning A comprehensive, data-driven, review of the school and community demographics, operations, and trends that influence education. This may be the school survey discussed in Chapter 4.

Educational Specifications A detailed description of the specific physical characteristics of the school's learning environments—including furniture and color schemes.

Mission A concise statement of beliefs that represents school and community values. The mission, as used in this chapter, indicates the basic purpose of the school system regarding physical learning environments.

Stakeholders People who have a vested interest in the results of the strategic plan.

Strategic Goals Somewhat less specific than an objective, a strategic goal identifies a target area and describes how it may be reached. A goal statement also provides a rationale.

Strategic Objectives A specific futuristic statement that indicates what the issue is, who will accomplish the tasks to fulfill the objective, how the tasks will be performed, and specifically when the tasks will be completed.

Strategic Planning A process of involving people in cooperatively developing a vision, goals, mission, and expected outcomes.

Surprise-Free Scenario A "common sense" statement based on obvious facts. This is a reasonable guess about the future.

Vision Statement Based on school and community beliefs and values, this statement captures the essence of the physical characteristics of the ideal school of the future.

APPENDIX: EDUCATIONAL SPECIFICATIONS

GUIDELINES FOR DEVELOPING EDUCATIONAL SPECIFICATIONS

The following suggestions are modified from an outline originally distributed by the School Planning Laboratory, University of Tennessee, 1978. Recommendations should serve as tentative guidelines for collecting and recording data necessary in writing educational specifications. Read this information carefully prior to attempting to develop the written material.

The purpose of educational specifications, is to serve as a guide to all concerned with designing and developing physical facilities to suitably house an effective educational program. It is also expected that the SP teams will examine alternative solutions to problem areas and in so doing will experience professional growth in their areas of competence. When developing educational specifications, the data should be carefully scrutinized by all members of the assigned team. Care must be taken to avoid allowing individual prejudices and/or traditions to dictate decisions, as final plans should represent the best information and objective thinking of the entire committee.

There are no exact prescribed categories suitable for all educational specifications; however, there are a number of areas that are usually considered important for an adequate description of the program and identification of suitable spaces to house the desired program. It is requested that you utilize the following outline insofar as possible in your writing.

Introduction. Statements regarding the proposed subject area.

I. The Program

Educational Objectives. Objectives (goals) of the subject area should be presented so that they are relatively complete and easily understood.

Discernible Trends. Attention should be given to new ideas or innovations that are taking place within the particular subject area being developed. This usually includes trends in curricular offerings, course content, activities within the classroom, organizational schemes, and the like.

Activities. Specific activities to be conducted in the new facility should be identified as they affect the location and size of the proposed teaching space. These factors will have a substantial bearing on the type and amount of space required.

Enrollments. Enrollment projections should not only consider immediate needs, but also should indicate long-range needs as accurately as possible.

II. Physical Requirements

Space Requirements. The size of teaching spaces is dictated by several factors. Among the more important ones are enrollment data, proposed activities, and furniture and equipment necessary to implement the proposed educational program. Space requirements should be expressed in terms of square feet for each teaching space. Describe dimensions, specify building materials, and emphasize color to give guidance to the architect. Workspaces and conference rooms to be located near teaching areas should be identified.

Description of Spaces.   Each space should be described in some detail. Recommendations should be based on utility, flexibility, comfort, and safety. Only those items of furniture and equipment to be utilized in the immediate future should be specified. Special consideration should be given to the utilization of portable equipment to permit maximum flexibility and ease in future changes.

Specific information regarding type and desired location of needed storage facilities should be considered. Quite often storage space will involve permanent storage facilities (cabinets on casters).

Other Special Requirements.   This includes physical features and facilities not normally included in teaching spaces. For example, sub-requirements may be found in vocational shops, laboratories, gymnasiums, auditoriums, and music areas. Special education needs must be completely met.

Desired Space Relationships.   Some teaching spaces should be located in proximity to one another: Careful consideration should be given to developing functional relationships between instructional spaces, and with all other segments of the school plant.

CHAPTER SEVENTEEN

SIZE AND SPACE
Facts and Guidelines for Planning, Site Selection, and Design

There are some facts and guidelines in the following sections that will be helpful in the process of school planning and design. The tables will be especially helpful for working through the strategic planning case in Chapter 16 and also in school and community planning activities.

SCHOOL SIZE

When considering school size, we must keep several variables in view as guiding principles, but the most important one is density (the ratio of students to usable square feet). The suggested limits for school enrollment found in Table 17.1 may be considered as guidelines, given the program activities needed in each school. Based on our personal research, the allowable school size for a prekindergarten through the sixth grade (PK–6) is 500 students, although we recognize that from 600–650 students can be manageable. The latter number does not correlate well with the "smaller is better" movement, however. Although some planners have suggested that "a school within a school" is the ideal way to achieve the goal of "smaller is better," we do not recommend it because a large school usually has less community involvement since it serves students living long distances away from the school. Logistically, the students attending a large school

are drawn from communities outside the immediate area in which the school facility is located. Many students attending a large school and living in other communities may also travel long distances and spend as many as two hours per day in school buses. These are only two of the prices that students and parents pay for children attending a large school.

The unwritten and often unspoken justification for a large high school (1,000–1,500+ students) is sports teams. It is generally thought that better sports teams can be assembled from large schools than from small schools. This is often the hidden, yet driving force behind larger schools, although the political or stated explanation is often economy of scale and quality-based. The argument is put forth that it is cheaper to build a large school than a small school. Furthermore, it has been argued that a better curriculum can be delivered in a large school, especially in the sciences, mathematics, and foreign language areas. These arguments must be challenged in the age where technology is capable of delivering a comprehensive curriculum to small, isolated schools through multimedia and especially the Internet. Unfortunately, as long as team sports are valued higher than educational achievement in a society, the "smaller is better" argument will struggle against the demand for winning sports teams drawn from large and often overcrowded schools.

TABLE 17.1   School Size: Generally Accepted Net Enrollment Ranges

SCHOOL	ALLOWABLE	MAXIMUM
Elementary (PK–6)	100–500	600–650
Middle (6-8)	150–600	700–1,000
High school (9-12)	200–700	800–1,500
Vocational (2-year)	250–800	900+
Community (Jr.) Community College	300–900	1,000+

Sources: Adapted from Castaldi (1994, p. 139), Tanner (2001, p. 12).

SPACE NEEDS

Perhaps the most important element in the design process is space. Quantity and quality of space provide the basis for the educational program. Having enough space to accommodate the curriculum and its supporting activities is vital; however without a high-quality layout of the school, even large spaces can be of little value. In this section we focus on the suggested quantity of space needed to perform the educational functions.

Exactly how many square feet a student needs in a learning area is to be considered according to the intended function of the classroom; however, what we know about student population density as it relates to student performance has brought new light to this issue (Tanner, 2001). One of the most frequently asked questions when planning a school is "What size should the various classrooms be?" This is a very difficult question to answer because of the many philosophical, social, educational, spatial, and cultural variables that enter the complex equation. There is a more basic problem, too. When we review research on school environments and the achievement of students, it is not difficult to conclude that the major problem may not necessarily be classroom size, but classroom density. Density in schools relates to what Sommer called "small group ecology" (Sommer, 1969). How many students should we place within a specific learning space?

Planners and architects assume that an important factor in building schools is the number of square feet per student. The issues of size and specifications have been addressed in the classic works of Hawkins and Lilley (1998) and Castaldi (1994). In addition to the minimum basic square footage, we should design large media centers, dining halls, and courtyards that can serve as important meeting places for students and teachers and help establish identities for schools. The word "large" is subjective and must be defined in terms of social space needs. Special areas such as science rooms, art rooms, and shops also require more space than the equation revealed in Table 17.2 on page 402. Most important, the curriculum and activities that facilitate it should be the primary dictators of space needs for a classroom.

Because the issues of space, density, and small group ecology are complex, the data presented in Table 17.2 should be applied only as guidelines for traditional classroom activities such as lecture and small-group activities, with computer terminals most likely arranged along the walls of the classroom. In addition, evidence is pointing to natural light and outdoor learning areas adjacent to classrooms as positive factors in learning. These classrooms should have views overlooking the surroundings and an exit door to the outside learning environments.

It is prudent to include ample egress in schools in view of random acts of school violence (the students and teachers need to be able to get out of harm's way quickly). Since overall cost is always a concern in school construction, it is interesting to note that one door per classroom leading to outside areas is usually less expensive than the installation and maintenance of sprinkler systems. The code requiring sprinklers in classrooms or exit doors in classrooms without sprinklers, by default, can be a positive bearing on school design. Egress and circulation patterns are akin to the density issue. People need to exit the school quickly in times of an emergency, and an exit door per classroom in a school having double-loading corridors is an excellent design feature that may also be used as an exit to an outdoor classroom. This outdoor classroom

TABLE 17.2   Suggested Standards for Classroom Size

NUMBER OF STUDENTS PLUS 1 TEACHER	ELEMENTARY SCHOOL, SQUARE FEET (m)	SECONDARY SCHOOL, SQUARE FEET (m)
10	539 (50.13)	704 (65.47)
11	564 (52.45)	768 (71.42)
12	637 (59.24)	832 (77.38)
13	686 (63.80)	896 (83.33)
14	735 (68.36)	960 (89.28)
15	784 (72.91)	1,024 (95.23)
16	833 (77.47)	1,088 (101.18)
17	882 (82.03)	1,152 (107.14)
18	931 (86.58)	1,216 (113.09)
19	980 (91.14)	1,280 (119.04)
20	1,029 (95.70)	1,344 (124.99)

Source: Adapted from Tanner (2001).

may be near the building and off a patio that serves as a landing. Such an area may function as a reading area and an observatory for bird watching, and the viewing of insects, flower gardens, and vegetable gardens.

In addition to egress and circulation patterns, the concept of social distance has become of interest to those that argue the school size and density issue. What does research say about space needs and the dynamics of small groups in traditional American classrooms? Abramson (1991) found higher achievement in schools with adequate space, and further noted that if those larger spaces were used for instructional purposes, the achievement was even greater. A high-density school influences achievement negatively. The effects of high density were summarized by Wohlwill and van Vliet (1985). "It appears as though the consequences of high density conditions that involve either too many children or too little space are: excess levels of stimulation; stress and arousal; a drain on resources available; considerable interference; reductions in desired privacy levels; and loss of control" (pp. 108–109). High density or not enough space also means more repairs and maintenance than normal (National Center for Educational Statistics, 2000). The lesson is clear. Students need ample space because crowding (high density) causes problems in behavior and increases the cost of maintenance.

If we conclude that students need ample space and that crowding is bad for learning, then we need to focus on developing bigger spaces for learning activities. The ideal solution may be smaller schools having larger areas for learning. This issue must also be viewed through the psychological implications from the study of territoriality of place according to Banghart and Trull (1973). We know that the student is always dependent on the environment for psychological and sociological clues. The student is always interacting with the physical environment. Since the school is a social system within the cultural environment, we should consider social distance as a means of calculating the minimum size of a classroom.

The lower middle range for social distance for men and women is 7 feet (Banghart & Trull, 1973, p. 233). Sommer (1969) completed several studies on small group ecology and found that when people are at 3.5 feet apart, they shift their seating positions (p. 66). This distance (2 × 3.5 feet) correlates with the 7 feet needed for social distance for men and women as recommended by Banghart and Trull (1973).

Using this norm of social distance, Table 17.2 was developed as a guide to solve the problem of high density. The square footage is presented as the actual number of square feet or meters needed by the student within the bounds of the indoor classroom (these are not gross or architectural square feet). The calculations for elementary school students were determined according to social distance research findings by using the factor of 49 square feet per person (the lower middle range). Larger students, according to the social distance concept, require 64 square feet (the upper limit of the middle range for social distance). Table 17.2 also reveals the suggested standard according to social distance research for upper school students (Tanner, 2001). These distances may vary from culture to culture, and much research is needed in this vital area.

If "smaller is better," then it is timely to consider the issue of social distance as a major factor in planning physical learning spaces. Consequently, we can adjust the size of classrooms accordingly to deal with the density problem. Either we build classrooms larger to accommodate the standard twenty-five students per classroom, or we take what is currently the accepted size and place from fifteen to eighteen students in existing classroom structures. Consider the average size of the elementary school classroom in the United States, which is approximately 900 square feet. If state policy allows twenty students per teacher, then with social distance as a guide, we expect to find a classroom having 1,029 square feet (instead of 900). This calculation reveals a deficit of 129 square feet by this generous standard of twenty students per classroom.

Regrettably, the data presented here come in conflict with educational policy in many states. The accepted number of students per classroom is closer to twenty-five or thirty in most schools, especially in schools outside the United States. Therefore, the classrooms are too small and the result is high density. From Table 17.2 we can conclude that no more than seventeen students per average classroom is the correct class size for elementary schools in the United States that have approximately 900 usable square feet. This straightforward research-based calculation has been supported by independent research of Achilles, Finn, and Bain (1998). According to social distance theory, the average class size for secondary schools should be 1,024 square feet and accommodate approximately fourteen to fifteen students.

Regarding appropriate space for a multicultural student population, we do not have valid information to suggest specifics; therefore, we must revisit the standards and specifications used as of 2001, while using the data in Table 17.2 as a guide to justify more space per student. Some traditional guidelines not necessarily based on the multicultural issue may be found in Castaldi (1994, pp. 266–368), Hawkins and Lilley (1998), and state minimum standards as set forth in each of the fifty U.S. states. Deplorably, minimum standards most often become maximum standards, and the last resort for advice on ideal school square footage should be minimum standards of the state that may be more interested in economy than learning. Table 17.3 reveals the general classroom square footage where social distance and territoriality have been factored into the space needs equation. Each of these should also include an additional 200 square feet for storage.

TABLE 17.3 Suggested Actual Classroom Square Footage per Twenty Students plus One Teacher

SCHOOL	BASIC	IDEAL
Elementary (PK–K)	1,029	1,350
Elementary (1-5)	950	1,029
Middle (6-8)	960	1,300
High school (9-12)	970	1,344
Vocational (2-year) Community (Jr.)	970	1,350
College	970	1,350

Source: Adapted from Tanner (2001).

The Child Care Center

The primary concern in designing the child care center is safety. School site safety implies that no vehicles should be permitted in or near the children's play areas. Vegetation that may be poisonous (poke berries, e.g.) must be eradicated from the places where children play. Outdoor electrical outlets must also be installed with child safety as the first concern. Any object that will tip over easily, inside or outside, must be stabilized. Inside the facility, all safety hazards should be viewed through the eyes of the child, not the adult. Sharp objects and furniture with sharp edges are not allowed. Everything must be child-proof. The same warning applies to the playground and playground equipment.

The child care center should be a healthful and invigorating environment, easily maintained, and kept spotlessly clean. The selection of all equipment and play items should be made on the basis of whether or not they can be washed and cleaned after use. Because children are capable of incidental learning, the physical environment should stimulate learning. "For example, the metal cover over room thermostats can be replaced with a clear plastic cover so that children can see the inner workings of this control device" (Castaldi, 1994, p. 346). Many other aspects of the building can become learning laboratories; and as Taylor and Vlastos (1975) have pointed out, architectural systems can teach: A school design can be a three-dimensional textbook.

Some of the basic resources in planning for child care facilities have been produced by Greenman (1998), who noted, "Child care centers are complex organizations and engender complex relationships" (p.7). One of Greenman's basic beliefs is that we must work to deinstitutionalize institutions for young children and transform child care centers into a new kind of family center. "These are essential directions to take" (Greenman, 1998, p. 13). The information in Table17.4 is based on suggestions made by Greenman in his classic 1988 book and by Olds (2001). Greenman stated that "after studying state licensing guidelines and the varied recommendations of other organizations and experts, the Children's Environment Project

TABLE 17.4 Space Needs for Child Care and Prekindergarten Facilities

SPACE CLASSIFICATION	SUGGESTED SQUARE FEET PER CHILD
Activity space	49
Support space	38
Adult space	24
Mechanical and corridors	29
Total facility	**140**
Outdoor play area	100
Overall site size (parking, drop off area, loading doc, etc.)	300
Total outside area	**400**

Sources: Greenman (1988), Olds (2001), Tanner (2001).

made the following recommendations as a guideline for adequate space "square feet per child" (1988, p. 100). The activity space in Table 17.4 has been modified upward according to the social distance theory (Tanner, 2001).

The child care center must be organized according to the age level of the child. Olds (2001) recommended that the infant classification include children from birth to eighteen months; the toddler group should range from eighteen to thirty-six months; preschool ages should range from three to five years; and the school-age students should have an age range of five to ten years.

Specifying the appropriate size of the school building for child care is a subject of concern in the literature. No more than seventy-five students should occupy one single building, according to Olds (2001). She suggested that small centers might have the advantages of a less institutional atmosphere, a view that Greenman vigorously supported. One child care building housing from thirty-five to forty students has been suggested as the ideal (Olds, 2001). Combining this information with data presented earlier in this chapter, the ratio of children to square feet and size of site is shown in Table 17.5. Square footage is the single most important design-related factor affecting the quality

TABLE 17.5   The Ratio of Students to Square Feet and Site Size for Child Care Facilities

NUMBER OF CHILDREN	SUGGESTED TOTAL SQUARE FEET PER BUILDING	SIZE OF THE SITE (ACRES)
15	2,100	1.10
20	2,800	1.50
25	3,500	1.90
30	4,200	2.30
35	4,900	2.65
40	5,600	3.00

Source: Translated from Table 17.4.

of the program, the welfare of children, staff, and the budget (Olds, 2001).

Olds (2001) recommended a cluster plan to accommodate young children, and suggested that each cluster accommodate no more than forty students. She defined this design as the residential core model, having three multiage clusters organized around an administrative and school-age area under one roof. "Each cluster consists of an infant, a toddler, and a preschool room surrounding a living room, dining area, and kitchen—its residential core" (p. 62). To date, it appears that Castaldi, Greenman, and Olds have made the most significant contributions to the planning and design phases of child care centers through their writings and research.

Elementary School

The calculation of the capacity of the elementary school organized in accordance with the self-contained classroom is usually straightforward to compute. The first decision is class size. We have recommended, based on research regarding personal space needs, no more than twenty students per classroom with approximately 49 square feet of usable classroom space within the classroom per student and one teacher (at least 200 additional square feet of storage space is also recommended per classroom). If teacher assistants are used, then the usable space should be expanded accordingly.

Castaldi (1994) recommended 1,100 square feet for kindergarten and 850 square feet for the remaining grades. Further, he suggested that the acceptable class size of the elementary school (k–6) range between twenty to twenty-five students in kindergarten (52.38 to 42.31 square feet per person, assuming only one adult in each classroom); and twenty-two to twenty-seven in grades 1–6 (36.95 to 30.36 square feet per student, assuming only one adult teacher). Although this is more generous than the norms among states, we do not agree with this recommendation in light of what we know about student behavior. Further research from the field of environmental psychology is needed.

When estimating the space needs for schools, the architectural area and volume of the structures must be considered. The architectural area of the building is the sum of all the areas of the floor spaces of headroom height measured from the exterior walls or the centerline of walls that separate two buildings, while the architectural volume or cubage of the building is the sum of the products of architectural areas and the height from the underside of the lowest floor to the average height of the surface of the finished roof above the various parts of the building (Brooks, Conrad, & Griffith, 1980).

Until new information emerges through refereed research, we recommend the following formula for approximating the architectural area of an elementary school building:

Architectural area for the elementary school
= 1.35 × [(49 Square Feet × (number of students + teachers + teaching assistants) + (1.35 × usable areas of other spaces)]

The factor of 1.35 accounts for the additional areas for hallways, stairways, thickness of the walls, bathrooms, etc. Other spaces refer to such areas as administration, guidance, auditorium, media center, music, art, special education, food services, storage, health services, community meeting rooms, and physical education. The factor may vary, depending on the materials and design of the structures.

Table 17.6 on page 406 reveals the suggested space needs for an elementary school. Note that there are some significant differences when compared to the usual recommended areas and square footages. For example, every classroom has toilets. The compromise here could be that every two adjacent classrooms may share one toilet (one for girls and one for boys). The reasoning behind this suggestion is safety. The elimination of ganged toilets reduces the possibility of misbehavior and also brings dignity to the student. The classrooms are larger and located near the teachers' places of work. Larger classrooms assume small- and large-group areas as well as spaces for technology. The library space has been reduced and given to the student within the classroom. Given the smaller library, the classroom should have Internet connections and computers. There is speculation among planners that the media center will also be within the classroom complex, eliminating the media center as experienced during the twentieth century. Depending on the design, a self-directed learning environment may have a large group-gathering place for four classrooms, shared teacher planning spaces, and technology areas. Therefore, the space needs outlined in Table 17.5 may vary as design solutions are generated.

TABLE 17.6 Space Needs in the Elementary School

SPACE CLASSIFICATION	NO. NEEDED	CLASS SIZE	RECOMMENDED (MAXIMUM) USABLE AREA (SQUARE FEET)
Kindergarten	1 per 15–20 students	20	1,030–1,350
Storage	1 per room		250–300
Toilets	2 per room		55–60
Classrooms	1 per 20 students	20	950–1,050
Teachers' office	1 per 2 teachers		150–250
Atrium			800–1,200
Commons	indoor/outdoor		950–1,350
School resource officer office			100–150
Library	1 per 350 students		900–1,050
Storage			350–600
Office			150–250
Work room/lounge	1 per school		600–750
Special classrooms	1 per 200 students	10–15	950–1,050
Storage	1 per room		150–250
Auditorium	a. 1 separate unit, capacity: 50% enrollment		15–20 sq ft per 50% enrollment
	b. Combined with cafeteria		
	c. Multipurpose room in small school		
Stage			700–900
Cafeteria	a. Combined with auditorium		10–15 per diner
	b. 1 housing 35% enrollment		1,575–3,500
Kitchen	1 per cafeteria		750–850
Food storage	1 per cafeteria		250–350
Serving area	2 per cafeteria		500–600
Receiving room	1 per kitchen		175–225
Physical education	1 unit per 350 students		2,500–3,000
Storage	1 per unit		450–500

407

TABLE 17.6   Continued

SPACE CLASSIFICATION	NO. NEEDED	CLASS SIZE	RECOMMENDED (MAXIMUM) USABLE AREA (SQUARE FEET)
Principal's office			250–300
Toilet/shower			45–65
Principal's conference room			150–175
Principal's secretary			175–225
School secretary			375–400
Reception area			275–325
Copy/mail room			275–325
Supply/storage			200–250
Assistant principal's office	1 per 350 students		100–250
Records/vault			80–100
PTA/community			
Office			150–200
Toilet			45–55
Counselor's office	1 per 250 students		125–175
Waiting/reception	1 per school		300–400
Toilet			45–55
Conference/testing room	1 per 250 students		250–300
Health services			
Nurse's station			125–175
Cot/clinic	3 units (100–105 sq ft each)		300–315
Toilet			45–55
Custodial Office/workshop	1 per school		550–600
Closets	2 per 350 students		65–70
Storage/maintenance outdoors	1 per school		450–500
Central storage	1 per 350 students		350–600

Source: Castaldi (1994, p. 272). Used by permission of Allyn & Bacon.

Secondary Schools

Moving from the planning of spaces for child care centers and elementary schools to designing appropriate spaces for secondary schools takes a giant leap because programs are more diverse and scheduling is more complex. In the lower schools we expect to find one teacher occupying the same space for an entire school day and teaching the same group of students for the entire school year, but in the upper levels certain subjects may be taught for only one or two periods per day and for only one semester per year, thus freeing this space for other classes and activities. The situation becomes even more complex when moving from the traditional scheduling (changing classes every forty-five minutes, e.g.) to parallel block scheduling, extended day, or some other form of scheduling. In addition to the state-mandated core courses, it is vital that the school and community decide on courses that fit the culture of the community. For example, in addition to the basics, a high school in a rural area might emphasize agriculture and ecology; a suburban school might emphasize the arts and ecology, while an urban school could emphasize industrial arts and ecology as extensions of the school curriculum. With the diversity we expect to find across cultures, it is evident that one prototype secondary school cannot meet all the curriculum needs in a single state or county in the United States.

TRANSLATING THE EDUCATIONAL PROGRAM INTO SPACE NEEDS

It cannot be overemphasized that the total educational program must be completely worked out by the school and community staff and approved by the school board before the difficult job of estimating space needs is initiated. It is the job of the planning and program design team to establish the number of periods per week that each course will be offered to an estimated number of students. Thus, the forecast of the expected student population is of vital importance. One guiding parameter is the forecast of net enrollment per year, which serves as a pool from which to extrapolate the percentages of students that will enroll in the various course offerings. Another parameter is the type of schedule the school plans to follow.

We will limit our discussion to two approaches for estimating space needs, given that the expected enrollment trends have been recorded (see "Student Population Forecasting" in Chapter 15). An elaborate method of estimating space needs was published by Brooks, Conrad, and Griffith (1980, pp 226–240). This work, initially attributed to Conrad, included the determination of a program index. A program index may be calculated for each space required to house a given program, and has been shown to be a useful tool in determining the operating capacity of an existing building for either an ongoing or modified program or for determining space needs when planning new or modified buildings. The program index includes the following factors:

1. The complete contents of the educational program
2. Policies pertaining to the educational program
   a. Suggested average class size
   b. Room assignment procedures
   c. Length and number of class periods per week or schedule cycle
   d. Specialization needed for certain rooms
   e. Schedule (traditional, block, etc.)
3. The impossibility of utilizing 100 percent of the space

With these factors serving as guidelines, what information do we need to estimate space needs in secondary schools? The following basic list is suggested:

1. Student population forecast for five to ten years—(net enrollment)
2. The school program defined in terms of regularly scheduled course offerings and learning activities
3. Percentage of students expected to be in each course per semester (or quarter)
4. Ideal class size

Once the program index is determined for each course, the number of teaching stations is estimated. A teaching station is any space designed for use by one teacher for the purpose of conducting a regularly scheduled class or learning activity. In determining the teaching station requirements for a new or modified school building, the capacity of the school is divided by each of the program indexes (round up if the decimal is greater than 0.50 and round down if it is less than 0.50). The final step in the Conrad method is to translate the teaching stations into square feet.

Another method for determining space needs was developed by Castaldi (1994, p. 295). He focused on estimating teaching station needs according to the percentage of utilization that is desired. However, one must consider that 100 percent utilization of space is highly unlikely. The factor of 1.25 in the Castaldi method allows for 25 percent scheduling difficulties and 1.20 allows for 20 percent scheduling difficulties and variations in class size. Once a utilization factor has been selected, the ratio of the *number of students who wish to take the course* (see item number 3 above) (NS) is divided by the *established class size* (ECS). This ratio is then multiplied by the ratio of the *number of periods per week that a student attends class* (NPSAC) divided by the *number of periods in a week* (NPW). The formula for estimating the *number of teaching stations for a course* (NTSC) where there is an allowance for 20 percent scheduling difficulties and variations in size is

$$NTSC = 1.20[(NS/ECS)\,(NPSAC/NPW)]$$

If the expected number of students to be enrolled in English II five years into the future is 500, and the class meets four times per week, how many rooms (teaching stations) need to be planned, given that the desired class size is eighteen and there are thirty-five periods per week? Applying the formula, we note the answer is 3.81 teaching stations or 4 rooms (rounding up when the answer is above 0.50, and rounding down when the calculated number is less than 0.50). This allows for 20 percent of variance in scheduling:

$$NTSC = 1.20[(500/18)(4/35)] = 3.81$$

This formula's application must be repeated for each course in the school program; therefore, we recommend that the planner develop an electronic spreadsheet for the formula to expedite the planning process.

One feasible way to determine the size of an instructional space is to simply make a list of all the activities expected to occur within it, including the furniture and equipment needs, and number of students participating. This is best accomplished by developing a scaled drawing of the room including furniture and equipment, allowing approximately 64 square feet per person. Therefore, instead of four classrooms in the above example, we may utilize the NTSC of 3.81. Multiply NTSC $\times$ (18 +1) $\times$ 64, and the result is 4,632.96 square feet. Dividing this by 4, the approximate usable space needed for each teaching station for English II is 1,158 square feet. When this space is scaled into a design, it is possible to check to determine if the total area included in a teaching station is adequate. Simply take the sum of the combination of activities conducted simultaneously by placing the furniture and equipment in the arrangement that will use the most space and still be functional. Next, review this arrangement to find out if it is functional. Table 17.7 on page 410 provides an outline for determining space needs for a secondary school expected to accommodate no more than 550 students. The usable area needed is calculated by taking the product of the teaching station needs per class (NTSC), the class size plus one teacher, and the square feet needed for each student. For example, English-language arts needs a usable area of 7,174.40 square feet. Since we have 5.9 teaching stations, the approximate usable area for each classroom would be (7,174.40/6) = 1,196 square feet per classroom having eighteen students and one teacher. Each area should have a minimum of 200 additional square feet for storage. Although we have shown through research that 64 square feet is the ideal amount of space for students in a regular classroom, there are no definitive research reports showing the square footage requirements for an industrial arts shop class, for example. There is a vital need to conduct research on space needs for students of different ages and of various ethnic backgrounds who are engaged in the various program components outlined in Table 17.7. The numbers shown here are only our best estimates.

In addition to the translation of program requirements into instructional space needs, the size of the auxiliary spaces in the school must also be determined. These spaces are outlined in Table 17.8 on page 411.

The information in Tables 17.7 and 17.8 provides approximations for space needs, and will vary with the design of the school. Hence, the value of a good design that saves space is not to be underestimated. Creative architects and planners can provide appropriate spaces for the educational program by developing good space relationships among the various learning areas and auxiliary facilities. We face a challenge: More research on space needs to be conducted, because it is the most important design variable that a planner and architect must consider.

TABLE 17.7   Estimation of Space Needs for a Secondary School (450–550 students)

PROGRAM NAME	NTSC	CLASS SIZE + 1	SQUARE FEET PER PERSON	USABLE AREA (SQUARE FEET)
ACADEMIC				
English-language arts	5.9	19	64	7,174.40
Mathematics	3.8	19	64	4,620.80
Science	3.7	19	75	5,272.50
Social studies	4.6	21	64	6,182.40
Foreign language	0.9	16	64	921.6
Business education				
Computer skills	2.3	19	75	3,277.50
Other business	1.4	21	64	1,881.60
Life skills	2.2	19	75	3,135.00
Art	0.9	19	74	1,265.40
Industrial arts				
Shop	1.9	19	80	2,888.00
CAD	0.8	13	75	780.00
TRADES AND INDUSTRIES—MACHINE	1.3	13	80	1,352.00
Automotive	0.8	13	120	1,248.00
Related	1.5	19	64	1,824.00
Physical education	3.8	21	125	9,975.00
Music	1.5	21	64	2,016.00
Study	1.6	31	64	3,174.40
AUXILIARY FACILITIES		(See Table 17.8)		

Source: Castaldi (1994, pp. 297–298). Used by permission of Allyn & Bacon.

SCHOOL SITES

Site selection and development are significant activities included in school planning and design, and may influence the architectural features of the facilities, especially in wooded, rough, or mountainous terrains. School sites requiring minimal disturbance of the trees, wild flowers, shrubs, and landscape are preferable to the leveled land areas where nature is destroyed. The latter case is usually more prevalent when leaders do not understand the relationship between the physical environment and teaching and learning. If site is considered as a function unrelated to the school program, its potential contribution to teaching and learning may not be given much priority during the planning and design phases. For example, the school may be well planned for a certain educational program that cannot effectively translate to a level site, stripped of its natural characteristics. It will be difficult for the school program to advocate sound ecological practices on a school site that has been stripped of its natural vegetation and character. There is an element of deception in a schoolhouse located on a stripped site whose program advocates ecological and sustainable systems.

Steps in Site Selection

To get a glimpse of just how complicated site selection may be, consider the stakeholders. First determine the type of school to be planned (elementary,

TABLE 17.8   Auxiliary Spaces

SPACE CLASSIFICATION	NO. NEEDED/ DESCRIPTION	CLASS SIZE	RECOMMENDED USABLE AREA (SQUARE FEET)
Library	per 350 students		1,000–1,350
Storage			350–600
Office			150–250
Teachers' office	1 per 2 teachers		150–250
Atrium			950–1,350
Commons	Indoor/outdoor		1,050–1,450
School resource officer office			100–150
Work room/lounge	1 per school		600–750
Special classrooms	1 per 200 students	10–15	950–1,050
Storage	1 per room		150–250
Physical education/sports			
Coaches' offices	1 per sport		100–150
Conference room			200–250
Lockers/showers/toilets			
Boys			1,100–1450
Girls			1,250–1650
Auditorium	a. 1 separate unit, capacity: 50% enrollments		20–25 sq ft per 50% enrollment
	b. Combined with cafeteria		
	c. Multipurpose room in small school		
Stage			800–1,000
Cafeteria	a. Combined with auditorium		15–25 per diner
	b. 1 housing 35% enrollment		1,675–4,500
Kitchen	1 per cafeteria		750–850
Food storage	1 per cafeteria		600–750
Receiving room	1 per kitchen		175–225
Principal's office			250–300
Toilet/shower			45–65
Principal's conference room			150–175
Principal's secretary			175–225
School secretary			375–400
Reception area			275–325
Copy/mail room			275–325
Supply/storage			200–250
Assistant principal's office	1 per 350 students		100–250
Records/vault			80–100
PTA/community			
Office			150–200
Toilet			45–55
Counselor's office	1 per 250 students		135–200
Waiting/reception	1 per school		400–500

(continued)

TABLE 17.8   Continued

SPACE CLASSIFICATION	NO. NEEDED/ DESCRIPTION	CLASS SIZE	RECOMMENDED USABLE AREA (SQUARE FEET)
Toilet			45–55
Conference/testing room	1 per 250 students		250–300
Health services			
Nurse's Station			150–200
Cot/clinic	3 units (100–105 sq ft each)		350–400
Toilet			45–55
Custodial office/workshop	1 per school		550–600
Closets	2 per 350 students		65–70
Storage/maintenance outdoors	1 per school		450–500
Central storage	1 per 350 students		450–700

Source: Castaldi (1994, pp. 295–305). Used by permission of Allyn & Bacon.

middle school, etc.). Next, the planners, the community, educators, and administrators must know the number of students to be served in a given geographic area. Ideally, it would be helpful to know the type of program the school may offer, but this will occur rarely because of the complexity and timing of program development. With the enrollment forecast (ten to fifteen years) in hand, the team may now involve the architect, a landscape architect, urban and regional planners, environmental experts, engineers, and legal counsel to begin the process of searching for a site. This activity usually precedes the design phase.

Having program needs and educational specifications would be very helpful for the site selection team. Although desirable, this is usually beyond normal expectations in site selection. At least the site selection team should know the size of the student population to be served before deciding where the site should be, its size, and the characteristics that it should possess. The following checklist is suggested in site selection:

1. *Decide how many students the new school should serve.*
2. *Estimate space needs with knowledge of the expected number of teaching stations needed.*
3. *Formulate the site selection team.*
4. *Determine site requirements based on the number of students to be served and possibly the program to be delivered (a rough set of educational specifications and design drawings might be available).*
5. *Locate potential sites that will accommodate the student population and the school program, possibly having the program and design information available.*
6. *Evaluate potential sites in light of item 5 above and local, state, and federal regulations, with a special emphasis on safety and ecological concerns.*
7. *Narrow the number of sites based on the above criteria.*
8. *Test and inspect the sites.*
9. *Recommend a site assuming all the above concerns have been met.*
10. *Receive state approval to purchase the site, including Environmental Protection Agency (EPA) approval.*
11. *Purchase the site, given the approval of the governing agencies.*

Membership on the site selection team should be diverse; however, one key person is the landscape architect. Inclusion of the landscape architect is imperative because there is mounting interest among parents and other community members in preserving natural resources, not to mention satisfying the EPA. Such issues as drainage, topography, and soil characteristics are common, but a thorough site analysis, including adherence to the required local, state, and federal mandates, is vital to the success of the school project.

Criteria for Site Selection

The criteria for site selection include specifications for size. Earthman (2000) noted that site selection and acquisition are among the most difficult tasks in the school planning and design process. As communities have grown in total population, increased in commercial activities, and developed industrially, land availability has decreased. There is variation among states regarding size requirements, and usually urban school districts may ask for waivers to purchase smaller plots because the availability of land for school construction is limited. Our generally accepted guidelines appear in Table 17.9.

Another essential criterion for site selection is utilities. Electricity and telephone wire services are essential to the operation of a school, although wireless phones now make the telephone wire less important and this criterion may be mini-mized in the future. As schools move toward on-site power generation, electricity demands from off-site sources will be reduced. However, the need for public water and sewage services is vital be-cause of the cost of installing private filtration systems. Private systems sometimes raise environmental concerns and may only be approved in locations that cannot be served by public sewage systems. But other on-site systems to treat waste-water, such as "living machines" that use a variety of plants and other natural organisms to treat waste-water, have been used successfully in schools to generate clean water for reuse in landscaping, toilets, and other nonpotable applications. These types of alternative, more sustainable systems provide environmental benefits and can be used to teach students about ecological processes.

Without question, safety and security should be the top priority in school site selection. A Phase I Environmental Site Assessment is usually required for school sites. Furthermore, any hazard listed below located within 3 miles of the proposed school site should require a risk/hazard analysis according to the Georgia Department of Education (1999, p. 5):

1. Electrical transmission lines rated 115KV or higher;
2. Oil or petroleum products transmission lines and storage facilities;
3. Hazardous chemical pipelines;
4. Natural gas transmission and distribution lines larger than 10 inches in diameter with a pressure of 200 psi or more;
5. Propane storage facilities;
6. Railroads;

TABLE 17.9   Generally Accepted Standards for the Size of School Sites

SCHOOL	BASIC NO. OF ACRES	ADDITIONAL ACRES PER 100 STUDENTS
Elementary (PK–6)	7–10	1
Middle (6-8)	12–20	1
High school (9-12)	17–30	1
Vocational (2-year)	22–35	2
Community (Jr.) College	30+	2

7. Major highways;
8. Airport approach and departure paths;
9. Industrial/manufacturing facilities;
   a. Using or storing hazardous substances;
   b. Emitting hazardous air pollutants;
   c. 1990 "Clean Air Act Amendment"—Risk Management Plan Sec. 1129.
10. Lakes, rivers, dams, reservoirs, or other bodies of water;
11. Potential flooding because the proposed site is located within the 100-year flood plain or dam breach zone;
12. Nuclear waste storage facilities;
13. Munitions or explosives storage or manufacturing.

A registered, licensed, professional engineer may conduct a risk/hazard analysis. Such an analysis should include:

1. The identification of the hazard
2. An evaluation of each hazard
3. Options for mitigating each identified hazard
4. A statement from the engineer based on his or her professional judgment and the findings of the risk/hazard analysis regarding the suitability of the site for a school

The Phase I Environmental Site Assessment involves the evaluation of whether historic, current, or proposed activities on the site have the potential to cause contamination or if possible contamination originating from off-site sources is likely to have had an impact on the property. The following is an overview of the purpose and scope of work of a Phase I Environmental Site Assessment:

1. Review past and current land use for indications of the manufacture, generation, use, storage, and/or disposal of hazardous substances at the site.
2. Evaluate the potential for site soil and/or groundwater contamination resulting from past and present site land-use activities and, to the extent possible, adjacent off-site operations.
3. Conduct an evaluation of the site and neighborhood to evaluate surface conditions and look for indications of environmental hazards.
4. Review records of governmental agencies such as county services agencies, local health service agencies, local air quality management districts, regional water quality control board, state health services, and the U.S. EPA to gather information pertaining to the storage, handling, or disposal of hazardous materials at the site and in the immediate vicinity.
5. Recommend further assessments, if necessary, to evaluate whether contamination, environmental hazards, or special resource value concerns may exist at the locations identified.

Costs associated with implementing risk reduction measures must be considered before making the final decision regarding a proposed site. For example, any proposed site adjacent to an airport, or final approach or departure pattern of aircraft should be evaluated carefully. This issue relates to safety and protection from interfering noise levels. Some states require that schools be located a reasonable distance from lakes, streams, or bodies of water that might be considered unsafe to children. This regulation, while well-meaning, serves to restrict the science and environmental curriculum and robs students of an aesthetic site. There are numerous examples of schools located on lakes and rivers that have no problem with hazards caused by the proximity of the school to the water.

Other contextual and environmental factors relate to the school's location. The school site should possess physically desirable characteristics and be located such that surrounding areas have characteristics conducive to the educational process. Schools should be insulated from industrial and commercial sites. They should be in harmony with nature and blend into the community. The site should be easily accessible to the community and supportive of efficient transportation (walking, school bus, and automobile).

The cost of the site is always of major concern and must be considered among the other environmental and location criteria. Earthman (2000) has presented a comprehensive set of site selection criteria of value to the site selection team. He details how to select the team, how to commission the team, and elaborates on aspects of data collection and analysis (pp. 145–155). Often, a certified land appraiser may assist the school system in determining whether the cost of the site is reasonable, given comparative information in the area of the site.

In general, the following question must be answered: Will the proposed site support the educational program? Other considerations include whether the site is near parks, museums, and a public library, and if the school blends with the site and vice versa (architect Frank Lloyd Wright's concept of "organic architecture").

THE SITE SELECTION TEAM

Site analysis, in harmony with state and EPA laws and approval, involves the assessment of the site's better features along with the problems that it presents. Site analysis by the landscape architect is more desirable prior to building construction, when buildings can be designed to take advantage of the site's best features. One example is that proper building orientation can be accomplished, thereby taking advantage of passive solar heating in the winter, while minimizing exposure to the sun's rays in the summer months. Planning for minimum glass exposure on the north side permits the designer to focus on plantings for future insulation values rather than just for protection from the north wind in winter. As Hannebaum (1994) noted, it is unfortunate that the landscape architect is often involved after the buildings have been constructed, when the site problems then become building problems.

Hannebaum (1994) recommended a site analysis, including scaled measurements recorded while the designer is on the site. This rough diagram may be later transferred to a scaled drawing of the site and buildings for a more proportionate view. Some basic activities Hannebaum (pp. 23–26) suggested which might apply to the school site are:

- Obtain a plot plan for the building site from city or county offices to help discover easements, building setbacks, parking strips, and other legal requirements.
- Measure site dimensions and locate property stakes to determine boundaries.
- Locate the proposed placement of the school and measure from one corner of the building to two property lines to determine the position of the building. Repeat this activity at another corner to situate the angle of the building.
- Measure and record proposed building features such as windows, doors, and major traffic patterns (people and vehicles).
- Locate all water and utility sources.
- Measure to locate and assess the value and condition of existing plants on the site.
- Locate and assess the value of other natural features of the site, including rock, ledges, boulders, interesting terrain fluctuations, wet areas, etc.
- Take photographs.
- Note the direction of the prevailing winter and summer winds.
- Study the site's terrain and plan for a topographical survey if more accurate study is necessary.
- Note all good off-property views worth retaining. Measure the distance of each view by viewing the horizon along the property lines. Note objectionable views and prepare for developing screens with various plants.
- Move off the property and look at it from all directions, making notes and measurements in preparation for screening others' views into the property.
- Note the need to screen out noise, dust, glare from parked or moving automobiles, or other possible nuisances.

- Make notes about existing macroclimate and microclimate.
- Check the soil for depth, rock content, hazardous subsoil (possibly the site was a former landfill), etc. Probe the soil and take samples for a soil analysis, if needed.

Resources the selection team may use in evaluating sites include the planning commission's comprehensive land-use plan of the geographic area served by the local government. This information reveals zoning patterns, a vital piece of data for site selection. Aerial maps developed by the U.S. Department of the Interior provide an inclusive perspective of an area and may be useful in finding vacant tracts of land. The state transportation or highway department develops current maps of roads that are important in locating school sites. Sanborn maps maintained in urban areas by city planning departments reveal specific dimensions of structures on the school site and show adjacent structures that might complement the school site. The topographical maps, major tools used by landscape architects, show the terrain and its elevations and physical features. The state highway department is usually a good source of topographic maps (Earthman, 2000). There are several commercial services that provide resources linked to Geographic Information Systems (GIS) networks that can facilitate this task (go to an Internet search engine and type in "GIS"). To assist in site selection, one can simply Google for information.

The value of the landscape architect is more than just to preserve some trees or plants and place shrubs and grass around the school—it includes the safety and comfort of the students. This factor may be easily forgotten in the haste to level a site and get on with the building project. The landscape architect analyzes the site and the needs of the people who will use the site. He or she identifies problems to be solved during the landscape design process and the site preparation and construction phases. The landscape architect may be involved in designing outdoor circulation patterns, driveways, parking systems, athletic fields, outdoor classrooms

and learning environments, while planning land contour for making the best use of the land.

Assuming that educational specifications and basic design drawings exist, the architect in cooperation with the landscape architect can project the site characteristics that best accommodate the building. When evaluating various sites, the architect can produce preliminary sketches indicating how buildings should be located to provide a view of desirable and undesirable site features, and how to orient the building to maximize the use of natural lighting, utilize solar gain during the heating season, and minimize solar gain during the cooling season.

Along with the landscape architect, the civil engineer may develop boundary and contour maps to assist the architect in placing the building in its most ideal position. These maps are especially important when the site is irregular.

Early in the site selection process, an engineer must test the site to determine whether or not it will support its planned construction and uses. Drilling to determine the location of underground rock, springs, or caves that might impede construction and require costly remedies is essential. In schools needing their own septic systems, a test for the percolation of water is essential.

The strategic step to site selection is convening a team having expertise and experience in site selection. In addition to following guidelines and regulations of the state and the EPA, the school planner and designer, landscape architect, architect, engineers, appraiser, and school superintendent are vital in selecting an appropriate site. Site selection is a team effort not necessarily exempt from the political arena, making it an activity full of twists and turns.

SUMMARY

There is a wealth of literature that identifies the benefits to students attending smaller schools, although proponents of large schools often cite reduced costs, a broader curriculum, and a greater number of extracurricular activities as reasons to build big. School facility planners must consider that smaller schools (ideally, 100–500 students in elementary schools, 150–600 in middle schools, and 200–700 in high schools) are more desirable if outcomes such as extracurricular participation and students' sense of belonging are goals for the new facility. Regardless of the size of the school, density is an important issue to consider. Creating appropriate density involves more than simply ensuring a certain number of square feet per person. It is necessary to design spaces that allow the comfortable and functional use of spaces to support pedagogy and the variety of activities that may occur in those spaces. Larger spaces, such as dining halls and courtyards, should serve as important meeting places for teachers and students and help establish a school identity. Social distance requirements and territoriality in humans help dictate how much space students need in their learning environments. This chapter provides square footage recommendations for a variety of spaces in child care facilities, elementary schools, and secondary schools. It is best to have a fairly good estimate of the number of students who will be served and the size of the school facility when selecting a site on which to build.

Site selection for a new school facility is a complex and extremely important process. Not only does it need to adequately support the school facility, it must also be safe and provide other amenities (e.g., play areas, walking trails, views, athletic fields) consistent with the educational program. The basic process for site selection, after the number of students and space needs have been estimated, includes form a site selection team, determine site requirements, locate potential sites, evaluate sites, narrow the number of potential sites, test and inspect sites, recommend a site, obtain approval of the site, and purchase it. The availability of suitable land for school construction continues to decrease, particularly in urban areas. The availability of utilities is also an important consideration, although the use of wireless telephones and decentralized processes for power generation (e.g., wind and solar) and wastewater treatment will minimize the need for public utilities in the future. For a selected site, a phase I environmental site assessment is usually conducted to evaluate whether historic, current, or proposed activities on the site have the potential of causing contamination or if possible contamination originating from off-site sources is likely to have had an impact on the property. When selecting a site, the primary question to answer is, "Will the proposed site support the educational program," but site costs and contextual factors are important variables affecting whether a site is suitable. Due to the complexity of site selection, it is vital to form a committed and competent team of professionals and other stakeholders to recommend a site. Team members should include a landscape architect, the architect (if known), civil engineers, an appraiser, the school superintendent, and others who can assist in overcoming the obstacles associated with selecting and developing a school site.

ACTIVITIES

1. Identify the approximate current enrollment for three area elementary schools, three middle schools, and three high schools. Select a variety of rural, suburban, and urban schools. How do enrollments compare with those suggested in Table 17.1?

2. Suppose you are searching for a site on which to build an urban high school in a nearby large city. Identify two potential sites (by address) and specifically describe the process you followed to identify these sites. Do not forget about the possibility of choosing a site that was previously built on.

3. Describe the steps that you must follow in your state/county to obtain approval of a site on which to build a school (in more detail than is presented in this chapter).

REFERENCES

Abramson, P. (1991). Making the grade. *Architectural Review*, 29(4):91–93.

Achilles, C. M., Finn, J. D., & Bain, H. P. (1998). Using class size to reduce the equity gap. *Educational Leadership*, 55(4):40–43.

Banghart, F. W., & Trull, Albert, Jr. (1973). *Educational planning*. New York: Macmillan.

Brooks, K. W., Conrad, M. C., & Griffith, W. (1980). *From program to educational facilities*. Lexington, KY: Center for Professional Development.

Castaldi, B. (1994). *Educational facilities planning: Planning, modernization, and management*. Boston: Allyn & Bacon.

Earthman, G. I. (2000). *Planning educational facilities for the next century*. Reston, VA: Association of School Business Officials, International.

Georgia Department of Education (1999). *A guide to school site selection*. Atlanta, GA: Facilities Services Unit.

Greenman, J. (1988). *Caring spaces, learning places: Children's environments that work*. Redmond, WA: Exchange Press, Inc.

Greenman, J. (1998). *Places for childhoods: Making quality happen in the real world*. Redmond, WA: Exchange Press, Inc.

Hannebaum, L. G. (1994). *Landscape design: A practical approach*. Englewood Cliffs, NJ: Prentice-Hall.

Hawkins, H. L., & Lilley, H. E. (1998). *Guide for school facility appraisal*. Phoenix, AZ: Council of Educational Facility Planners, International. Also available at http://www.cefpi.com.

Heschong Mahone Group (2000). *Daylighting in schools*. Fair Oaks, CA: Heschong Mahone Group.

National Center for Educational Statistics (2000). *Condition of America's public school facilities: 1999*. NCES 2000-032. Washington, DC: U.S. Department of Education, Office of Educational Research.

Olds, A. R. (2001). *Child care design guide*. New York: McGraw-Hill.

Sommer, R. (1969). *Personal space*. Englewood Cliffs, NJ: Prentice-Hall.

Tanner, C. K. (2001). Classroom size and number of students per classroom. *Educational Facility Planner*, 36(2):11–12.

Taylor, A. P., & Vlastos, G. (1975). *School zone: Learning environments for children*. New York: Van Nostrand Reinhold.

Wohlwill, J. F., & van Vliet, W. (1985). *Habitats for children: The impacts of density*. Hillsdale, NJ: Lawrence Erlbaum Associates.

NAME INDEX

SUBJECT INDEX

Note: Page references for figures are followed by an *f* and page references for tables are followed by a *t*.